The Consumer in American Society

Personal and Family Finance

The Consumer in American Society

Personal and Family Finance

Arch W. Troelstrup

Professor of Family Economics
Stephens College

Fourth Edition

McGRAW-HILL BOOK COMPANY

New York St. Louis San Francisco Düsseldorf London
Mexico Panama Sydney Toronto

The Consumer in American Society

Personal and Family Finance

Copyright © 1970 by McGraw-Hill, Inc. All rights reserved.
Formerly published under the title of *Consumer Problems
and Personal Finance* Copyright © 1957, 1965 by McGraw-
Hill, Inc. All rights reserved.
Copyright 1952 by McGraw-Hill, Inc. All rights reserved.
Printed in the United States of America. No part of this
publication may be reproduced, stored in a retrieval system, or transmitted, in any form or by any means, electronic, mechanical, photocopying, recording, or otherwise,
without the prior written permission of the publisher.
Library of Congress Catalog Card Number 73-104740
65207
1234567890 HDBP 79876543210

Sponsoring Editor: B. G. Dandison, Jr.
Editor: Hiag Akmakjian
Designer: Paula Tuerk
Drawings: Graphic and Industrial Design
Cartoons: Tomi Ungerer
Editing Supervisor: Susan Davis
Production Supervisor: Peter D. Guilmette
This book was set in Musica by University Graphics, Inc.,
printed on permanent paper by Halliday Lithograph Cor-
poration, and bound by The Book Press, Inc.

To

Ann and Our Four Children,
Bill, Glenn, John, and Susan Lee,
whose patience has been tested
through four editions.

by Bess Myerson Grant

Future historians may refer to the 1960s as the decade of the consumer. Consumerism, they may say, gained a foothold next to motherhood and the American flag. Consumer protection laws and measures were enacted by Congress and the states. President Johnson appointed a special assistant for Consumer Affairs, and New York City created a municipal department to protect the consumer.

And yet, I predict that even in the 1970s, 1980s, and 1990s, the best protector of his own interests will still be what Professor Troelstrup calls an alert, informed, and responsible consumer. His book is a valuable contribution toward the making of such a consumer. It is a book with a difference—a guide for the consumer written by a man with a conscience. Too often in the past books on consumer education have been noncommittal and antiseptic, almost pathetically eager to be inoffensive. I am glad to say that Professor Troelstrup has taken the first steps to liberate consumer education from its era of impotence.

The old consumer education dealt with comparisons of different types of cloth and instructions for a balanced diet. This book does not ignore what to eat and what to wear, but it goes far beyond exhortations for prudence and thrift. Professor Troelstrup shows how purchasing decisions have psychological components and begins to tell what people are really buying when they make choices in the stores.

Detailed coverage is provided for the consumer movement, in the United States and around the world, and the progress of government regulation from its first halting interference with the powerful trusts to today's intermediate state of regulation. Much of this material is difficult to find elsewhere, as the cause of consumer protection has not as yet suffered from excessive attention or historical analysis.

My own belief is that, in this volume, Professor Troelstrup has set a standard for texts on consumer education and moved the entire field some distance forward. He does this by careful and detailed study of the problems consumers face in meeting their economic and social needs with limited resources. The role of advertising and fashion is frankly discussed. Yet the book is not a polemic. Nor is it an indiscriminate attack on American economic institutions or patterns of conduct. On the contrary, it is a prudent examination of our customs, with recommendations for survival and prosperity within the system.

Professor Troelstrup is no revolutionary, but in his quiet and methodical way, he takes the student over a vast terrain of problems which will affect his standard of living.

We live in a time of change, both in the material style of our lives and in our values. This book is dedicated to no particular system, except that of common sense and rational discussion of issues and exploration of alternatives before deciding on a course of conduct. In the long run, that will be its strength, because as ideologies and styles may vary, the standard of thoughtful exploration and free inquiry will prevail.

The field of consumer protection saw great changes in recent years. The pioneering work of Ralph Nader stimulated a flow of federal and state legislation in the late 1960s. Truth in packaging, truth in lending, wholesome meat, highway safety, all were subjects for congressional action. Many of these bills appear to be the forerunners of further action in their fields, as government increasingly recognizes its responsibility to help to achieve balance between the relative strength of the amateur buyer and the professional seller.

I especially appreciate Professor Troelstrup's determined effort to be fair and reasonable, and yet not to hesitate to describe conditions as he sees them, nor to quote authorities who make points sharply. He is not afraid to question established notions of buying behavior. The extensive references supplied at the end of each chapter will provide serious students with valuable additional material.

In a field of pablum, this book provides solid fare. I am pleased to introduce it to students and readers and to recommend it to browsers and shoppers.

For over 27 years the author has been teaching consumer problems and personal finance to American undergraduate and graduate students. This text is the product of continuous evaluation of the immediate and foreseeable future needs of college students as consumers and citizens. Some four hundred college graduates have contributed to the course and to the text by volunteering after marriage to describe in detail their most important consumer problems in actual family situations.

In addition to the contributions of undergraduates and some four hundred married couples who had been out of college from 4 to 15 years, the author has had the benefit of the advice of a committee of Stephens College instructors who represent a cross section of related disciplines—child study, clothing, foods and nutrition, health, economics, marriage and family, household economics, personal appearance, consumer economics, and psychology. This committee met in two-hour sessions, twice monthly for one year, to analyze the contents, methods, and working relationships of their special fields in order to enrich the course in consumer problems and personal finance.

The cordial reception which college professors, businessmen, and particularly college students and homemakers have accorded the first, second, and third editions is evidence of the need for such a book. But in a dynamic society such as ours, both a book and its author should grow. It is my hope that this fourth edition represents growth. Much has happened in the area of consumer problems and personal finance since the third edition was published in 1965.

In one decade, the 1960s, we have moved from the "let the consumer beware" toward "let the seller beware" and "let the consumer be informed." Not until the continuing concern for the quality of living generated by Rachel Carson's *Silent Spring*, Ralph Nader's *Unsafe At Any Speed*, and the thalidomide tragedy did the consumer revolution begin to turn. Some consumer leaders believe that what really turned it was General Motors' heavy-handed attempt to destroy its chief critic, Ralph Nader. This episode drove home to the people the dimensions of the great imbalance between industry and the society it was supposed to serve. In 1965, the year the third edition of *Consumer Problems and Personal Finance* was published, the federal government finally decided that a systematic assault on the imbalance was necessary.

Since 1965, the federal government has enacted legislation to protect the consumer against everything from dangerous automobile tires to poisonous toys. In rising crescendo there poured from Congress an unparalleled flow of consumer protection legislation, including federal standards on intrastate meat, deceptive credit, deceptive packaging, radiation hazards, natural gas lines, flammable fabrics, and a dozen more. At the same time, Congress launched deep legislative probes into many other areas, from auto insurance to misleading product warranties, accuracy of weights and measures, and marketing and pricing policies, to mention a few.

These and other dramatic changes and problems are presented and evaluated in this fourth edition. *Consumer Problems and Personal Finance* has been completely rewritten. Chapter 11, Family Transportation, is new. Chapter 15, Expenditures and Taxes for Government Services, is new in the sense that the details for filling in a federal tax form are omitted in the text because the U.S. Treasury Department distributes free an excellent teaching kit on how to complete tax forms. The emphasis in this edition is on how the federal income tax measures up to the criteria of productivity, equity, simplicity and economic usefulness, administration, and economic impact. Proposed tax reforms are reviewed, including state and local taxes.

Chapters 16, 17, and 18, on consumer protection through private industry, the federal government, and state and local governments, have been completely rewritten because of the rapid growth of laws and governmental agencies and because of the appearance of many new state and local consumer organizations. Jan van Veen, Executive Director of the International Organization of Consumers Unions, gave generously of his time and knowledge in revising Chapter 19. Most of the Questions for Discussion, Activity Problems, and Suggested Readings are new.

Two new features are included in the fourth edition: Appendix A, A Summary of Ways to Save Money from Marriage to Retirement, and Appendix B, Federal Consumer Agencies and Aids in Washington, D.C.

The author is indebted to many college teachers and other well-informed persons for helpful comments with respect to this edition. The responsibility, however, for final content, errors, and omissions that may have crept into the book is his.

The author has also become even more firmly convinced that the original idea of writing a college textbook on personal and family consumer problems and personal finance that deals with life as a whole rather than in its separate parts is psychologically sound. Such a book appeals to undergraduates and adults who want principles, ideas, and information that are relevant to their needs as consumers and consumer citizens.

I am deeply indebted to Margaret Kingsley, who typed the manuscript in its final form, and to the editor Hiag Akmakjian, whose interest and fruitful ideas led to a good working relationship.

In preparing the manuscript for publication the author's job has been lightened immensely by the help of Ann, his wife, expert and wise in publication matters, proofreader, and helpful critic.

Arch W. Troelstrup

Contents

The Consumer in American Society

Personal and Family Finance

chapter 1

THE CONSUMER
IN OUR SOCIETY

Consumption is the sole end and purpose of all production; and the interest of the producer ought to be attended to only so far as it may be necessary for promoting that of the consumer.

Adam Smith

What are the major challenges that face Americans in their role as consumers? First, consumers need to know their part in the economy. They should know what makes our economy "tick." Consumers should understand that fraud, deceit, and other undesirable practices persist in the economy because of their own lack of organized resistance as well as ineffective protection on all government levels. They need to realize the importance of substituting rationality for emotion in the marketplace.

Second, consumers need to be aware of the increasing efforts of business to deceive and misinform the consumer. The business of making and selling is highly organized and calls to its aid at every step complex and expert skills. The business of buying is conducted by the smallest unit, the individual or the family. The capacity of sales personnel to aid the consumer has deteriorated. Furthermore, the trend toward automatic services, self-service, discount stores, catalog buying, and persuasive advertising has increased the chances of buying uninformedly. The manufacturer and distributor speak with a well-organized and powerful voice in national affairs. The interest of the consumer is often overlooked because he is voiceless.

Third, consumers need to understand their function in the economy. Is their job to spend in order to keep the economy going? Is it to do the bidding of profit-seeking persuaders? Or is their job that of guiding and controlling the production of goods and services with which to satisfy their wants? In other words, what is the function of the consumer?

THE PURPOSE OF AN ECONOMY

The purpose of an economy is to produce goods and services, large in quantity, high in quality, reasonable in price for maximum satisfaction in consumer use. Every economic system, be it capitalist, Communist, or Socialist, faces three questions: What shall we produce? How much shall we produce? For whom shall we produce?

Different economic systems solve these problems differently. Today, most economic systems are "mixed" in the way they set up their goals and manage their resources. They are neither purely private enterprise nor purely Socialist. And most economic systems are changing constantly.

Business enterprise in the United States is largely private, and its rationale is that consumer demands determine what is produced. Business tries to produce the goods and services that consumers want. And business tries to do so at the lowest possible cost. In most cases, business also seeks to influence consumer demands through advertising and other selling devices. Business will use labor, land, and machinery to produce the goods and services consumers demand. Businesses, in turn, pay out income to workers, landowners, and other suppliers of productive services. These incomes make it possible for consumers, in turn, to buy the goods and services in the marketplace.

Markets are the places where prices rise and fall in response to changing demands and supplies, and they provide the links that mesh together consumers and businesses. Individuals and businesses save part of their income and invest those savings in new productive facilities.

The rationale of our economy also assumes that individual freedom of choice is central to our economic way of life. But individual freedom of choice is limited by laws and by social and moral pressures, for the protection of the individual and society. Thus, markets and prices are the chief regulator of the allocation of scarce resources. But the government sets the ground rules under which competition takes place and sometimes participates actively in the processes of production and distribution. Thus we have a "mixed" economy.

WHO IS THE CONSUMER?

Anyone who spends money buying goods and services is a consumer. We all spend money for goods and services. Therefore, we are all consumers.

At the end of 1968, there were over 200 million consumers in the United States. This number will increase at the annual rate of about 3 million. By 1980, there will be over 235 million consumers in America.

Today there are about 60 million households. By 1980 there will probably be 75 million. Three out of four of these new families will live in urban centers. Non-city dwellers will be in a declining minority, thus eroding even further the image of America as a rural, small-town culture.

By the end of the 1970s, Americans will have close to 24 million children under 5 years of age and 40 million children between the ages 5 and 14. High school youths, ages 15 to 19, will have increased several million and there will be about 40 percent more people between 20 and 35 years of age. The under-25s will constitute almost half the population in the early 1970s.

The number of Americans in the age bracket 35 to 55 will increase only slightly in the 1970s. Finally, there will be more consumers over 55 years of age than there were in that bracket in 1969.

Less apparent, but no less significant, the percentage of males within the nation's huge job force has been decreasing from about 67 percent in 1961 to about 61 percent currently. The female invasion of the job market has been led, not by ambitious young single girls, but by housewives. The National Industrial Conference Board reports that more than 15 million wives now work— more than twice as many as in the early post-World War II era; about 35 percent of all wives earn a pay check today, up from only 20 percent right after World War II. And, interestingly, over half of all college-educated women in America keep on working after marriage.

Income Differences among Consumers

The total number of consumers includes children, teen-agers, young marrieds, middle-agers, and old-age persons. For each of these groups there are different incomes and interests. In 1966, the median family income was $7,436, compared to $5,727 in 1956—if allowance is made for the changing value of the dollar due to inflation. The median income for the "typical" group of families, with both husband and wife present, was $7,838 in 1966. Fourteen percent of the 1966 families had under $3,000 annual income; approximately 41 percent of families with heads 65 years of age or over received under $3,000 annual income in 1966; and 41 percent of families with heads between ages 45 and 54, 38 percent of those between 35 and 45, 33 percent of those between 55 and 64, and 25 percent of those between 25 and 34 received $10,000 or more in family income.

The National Industrial Conference Board has come up with these predictions for the mid-1970s:

1. More than two out of five young families (with family head under 25) will have incomes over $7,000.
2. In the 25-34 bracket, two out of five will go over the $10,000 mark.
3. In the 35-44 bracket, almost one out of four familes will be in the $15,000-plus category.
4. About half the families in the 45-64 bracket will have over $10,000 annually.
5. As for those over 65, one out of five can count on a $10,000 yearly income or more.

Teen-agers

For many sellers, the teen-age market is important. Lester Rand, head of New York's Youth Research Institute, estimates that there are 25 million youths in the United States between 13 and 19 with more than $18 billion in earnings, gifts, allowances, and family "loans" to spend pretty much as they wish. According to a market study by Scholastic Magazines, Inc., 17 percent of the teen-agers owned their own TV sets, 18 percent owned tape recorders, 21 percent outboard motors, 42 percent electric razors, 68 percent cameras, and 87 percent watches. By 1970, Rand estimates that teen-agers will number over 30 million with disposable incomes totaling $30 billion.

In many cases, the teen-agers' spending far outweighs their numerical strength. Teen-age boys, for example, are only about 12 percent of the male population but buy more than 40 percent of all sportswear sold, while teen-age girls now purchase nearly a third of the nation's cosmetics output. Beyond their own purchases, they influence at least $35 billion of adults' spending, says Rand.

While most of the teen-agers are not in the market for homes and appliances, they soon will be. Over 40 percent of all brides are teen-agers; more wives have their first child in their nineteenth year than in any other, and one out of every six teen-age wives has two or more children. As consumers, many of these young marrieds believe in "go get tomorrow today." Advertisers are not unmindful of these teen-agers. For example, the senior editor of Seventeen, "America's Teenage Magazine," recently put it:

Catch a teen-age girl and put her in your pocket now and you'll keep her forever. Now's the time to sew her up—before the rice is in her hair, before the stork is on the roof, before the wolf is at the door. Set her textured stockings on the path to your product now—and she'll come back blindfolded. . . .

Market consultant Bernice Fitz-Gibbon said to 1,500 leading merchants meeting in New York, "If you haven't struck the shimmering, glimmering teen-age lode, there must be something wrong with you."

What Makes the Economy Tick?

Why are these consumer income figures important? Because the spending and saving of money, directly and indirectly, of our 200 million consumers today are what make our economy tick. In 1967 and 1968, as in recent past years, consumer expenditures constituted about two-thirds of total expenditures in our economy. On January 1, 1969, for example, consumers collectively had over $715 billion in annual personal income and were spending over $500 billion annually. If family incomes increase, as they usually do for most consumers, their expenditures are likely to increase. If spending increases, the economy will grow. In fact, consumers are so important to a healthy economy that periodic reviews to ascertain the attitudes and buying intentions of consumers are made by the University of Michigan Survey Research Center and made public. Business, government, and consumers in general use these data for planning production, capital expenditures, and investing.

Consumers still have money (savings) left after all of their expenditures. The savings in recent years have been at a rate of 5 percent of total disposable income (amount left after deducting personal taxes). At the end of 1968, however, personal savings for the year amounted to $40.0 billion, a 7.1 percent of disposable personal income. This was the highest rate in the last 14 years. This money is invested mostly in ways which help to lay the foundation for future business expansion. This is what we mean when we say that consumer spending and saving are what make our economy tick.

THE CONSUMER INTEREST—THE REAL ISSUE

The concept of consumer sovereignty still persists after nearly a century of experience. According to this theory, the role of the consumer is to guide the economy to the production of goods and services that he wants. In short, the consumer expresses his wishes by casting dollar votes. In this way, the consumer is supposed to determine what shall be produced.

Consumer Sovereignty

Playing umpire is not a new role for the consumer. In theory, consumer sovereignty—consumer freedom of choice—is indeed the keystone of our economic system. It is from this assumption that the free competition, private enterprise system derives social justification for its division of rewards for effort. Withdraw consumer sovereignty from this concept, and free competition resembles a kind of economic jungle warfare. We are now fairly far along in the process of withdrawing true consumer sovereignty from the marketplace. The question is: Can we bring back into the marketplace a rational umpire—the consumer?

Consumer Economic Power

Dr. Robert D. Schooler, professor of marketing at the University of Missouri, states that the "reduction in consumer power is almost complete"; that the "maldistribution of power and the consequent abuse of the consumer are totally violative of the principles and rationale of a market economy"; that consumers and government are preoccupied with "consumer interest at the point of sale, with matters of packaging, advertising, and retail pricing methodology. While these are legitimate issues, they are secondary; if the consumer interest is to be served the issue of progress-sharing must take priority and the consumers' case against producers must be prosecuted vigorously."[1] In other words, consumers have lost their collective power in the marketplace. The road back is for consumers to act collectively in the marketplace.

Price and output are set in this market by supply and demand or by market power (monopoly), and the consumer can take it or leave it. The solution, according to some economists, is for consumers to organize effectively as a power group such as the founders of the Consumers' League relied upon in the 1890s and later. The only power the league had was the collective effort of every buyer to refuse to buy. The league founders were wealthy socialites in large urban centers who were primarily interested in poor working conditions in retail stores. The league made fairly successful use of consumer collective power in correcting some of the poor working conditions in retail stores. Perhaps this early illustration of the fairly effective use of consumer collective power offers some insight into the more complicated problems in our modern marketing system. The league defined its goals and pursued the means to accomplish these goals. For example, the league set up standards of fair practices for retailers, and later for manufacturers. It then publicized the firms which met these standards, and league members were asked to buy only at these stores. The league also adopted a label to identify goods made under approved conditions. Shoppers were alerted to look for this seal of approval.

Ultimately, the league urged legislation to require all firms to observe minimum standards for wages, hours, and working conditions. While the ultimate appeal was to law, the league tried to arouse public opinion. The league's pol-

---

[1]"The Consumer Interest—The Real Issue," *Journal of Consumer Affairs,* Summer, 1967.

icy expressed the value judgment that all consumers had a "moral duty" to carry out the goals of the national Consumers' League.

Today, however, consumer exploitation has replaced labor exploitation. Almost all consumer organizations agree that the consumer does not have the collective power to make effective changes in the marketplace. The newly created Consumer Federation of America with headquarters in Washington, D.C., could be the nucleus of a modern national consumer action group. Theoretically, collective consumer power is possible. But is it likely to come about under present and foreseeable conditions? In other words, is "consumer sovereignty," the collective power of all consumers, likely to come about even after great effort on the part of all consumer organizations working together for national consumer goals?

THE MODERN MARKET ECONOMY

The Consumers' League did not direct all of its economic power to getting remedial legislation. But the fact remains that it did effect legislation just as modern consumer organizations attempt to do. The league also used preferential buying and the boycott. These are weapons used today by Negro and other minority groups, by recent action of housewives boycotting retail food stores, and by affluent families reading *Consumers Union Reports* and following their recommendations for preferential buying and for government action. The real question is not whether the force of collective consumer demand is as great as it ever was. It is potentially as great today as in the decades of the league's activities. The realistic problem today is that the modern market economy, as described in economic texts, can rely upon what Adam Smith called the "invisible hand" to regulate it properly *only* if certain conditions exist. Dr. James Morgan, professor of economics at the University of Michigan, recently described these conditions:

> First, there must be enough competition among sellers, and among employers of labour, to assure no monopolistic restrictions of price or output, though sometimes countervailing power may help when two large units of labour and management clash.
>
> Second, there must be a *reasonably fair* distribution of income available for families to spend, so that individual market demands reflect real social needs and priorities.
>
> Third, there must be a proper and sufficient development of the public sector—the provision of goods and services by community or national action—where they cannot be provided by individual initiative. I refer, of course, to such things as parks, roads, clean water, and fresh air.
>
> Fourth, there must be informed and intelligent consumers, with the understanding necessary to implement their desires effectively in the market place. This requires a proper mix of consumer education, consumer information, and consumer protection from fraud and harmful products.
>
> Among all these requirements, the consumer interest threads, but in the first three of the four—preservation of competition, the equity in distribution of income, and

Figure 1-1   The Power of the Consumer Illustrated by the Recent Nationwide Boycotting of Grapes Grown in California. The boycott was in support of the organizing attempts of Mexican, Filipino, and other migratory workers in their fight to raise their wages to more than subsistence (or lower) levels. The boycott was so effective in the year 1968 alone (12 percent decline in profits for the large grape-growing combines) that supermarkets experienced a drop in sales of even those grapes coming from South America, because for a while consumers in some stores stopped buying *all* grapes unless they were sure of their origin—hence the above sign displayed in a New York supermarket. (Photograph by Mary Ann Schatz.)

the proper provision of public goods and services—the consumer can act only as a voter and our help is restricted to informing him as to his interests. Even in the fourth, where voluntary consumer organisations must focus, a major responsibility for general consumer education belongs in the school systems, and the major responsibility for protecting the consumer from fraud and dangerous products belongs to the Government.

Granting these limitations in our marketplace, how long do consumers have to wait for effective collective consumer power? Is effective collective consumer power possible today? It is hard to conceive of a time when consumers in a large, populous country like the United States can effectively balance the power of producers, corporations, labor, and government. Today we have in fact an industrial autocracy, an autocracy in which power rests with a managerial class believing basically in non-price competition. In regard to corporate power, there is also a real abuse most serious to the consumer welfare—the abuse of the power to price. Control of price is a different thing from effective competition among many producers.[2]

The Power to Price

Today there are only four automobile firms; four companies produce 85 percent of all the breakfast cereals sold in the United States. There are less than 20 sugar refiners. Only four companies produce about 75 percent of all tires and tubes. About 50 large corporations produce a quarter of total manufacturing output. The market does not determine price and quality or output for these companies. Each of these, and other large producers, can and does control the prices at which it sells. In short, competition has given way to monopoly and oligopoly and to markets controlled by big business.

Since, in many if not most markets, power to price is exercised by comparatively few companies, producers and sellers do not have to follow the ideal controls of supply and demand. They do not even have to cater to consumers' desires unless they choose to do so. Instead, a few powerful companies can pretty well dictate to consumers because they control not only output and prices of consumer goods they sell, but their markets as well. These companies can and do manipulate consumer demand so that buyers will buy what these manufacturers produce. Through the power of massive material advertising, packaging, design of products, and other appeals, these firms are usually able to divert consumers from another brand to their brand, and often from what people need to what they are persuaded to want. This control and abuse of the power to price are most serious to the cause of consumer welfare, and any marketing practice that renders rational choice more difficult is a subversion of the American economy.

Most people in this country believe in private enterprise. But in order for private enterprise to work at its best and fairest, we must also have free competition. And here is the rub. The expression "free enterprise" has become a meaningless political slogan used interchangeably with "free competition." Many businessmen believe in free enterprise but do not believe in free competition. Yet is is impossible to have one without the other. If business desired free enterprise without free competition, it would have socialism at the top—companies reaping all the benefits of private enterprise without having the risk of free competition. Anyone who follows the activities of the Antitrust Division of the Department of Justice knows that many firms do not like competition, or the operation of the free market, and seek to replace it with a closed system that assures them profits and gives the consumer no real choice between com-

[2]Robert F. Lanziloth, "Why Corporations Find It Necessary to Administer Prices," *Challenge,* January, 1960, pp. 45-49.

petitors. Those who pursue this policy really want two contradictory things—freedom to make profit without interference, and also protection for themselves from the nuisance of free competition. This is a paradox of free enterprise. And it hurts the consumer because it makes free choice in the marketplace meaningless.

Labor and Producers

Labor and producers together often exact higher wages and higher profits through the application of power. Higher wages and higher profits won by workers and producers in the competition of the marketplace are acceptable and expected in normal, competitive markets. The use or application of power is something else. One authority, Dr. Edward S. Mason,[3] argues that because of changes in the size and structure of business and labor organizations, the American economy has been transformed from an economic democracy to an industrial autocracy in which power rests with the managerial class unrestrained by real competition as written in the economics textbooks. Our whole economic life, goes the argument, is shot through with wage and price controls by private control, not government control. Big business controls prices and labor controls wages. It is difficult to accept such controls by private institutions if we believe in competition and if we believe that the goal of our economic system is consumption.

Government

Our form of government lends itself to pressures exercised by organized groups. At times government has played the role of accessory to the exercise of monopoly power against the consumer. At other times it has become a party to the negotiation of inflationary wage increases. Government has also provided laws and programs to protect the consumer interest. Most of the federal consumer legislation came as a result of scandals in the marketplace. Federal meat inspection, for example, was required only after the shocking conditions in the country's meatpacking plants were so starkly revealed by Upton Sinclair in *The Jungle*. Deaths and horrible injuries attributable to drugs brought about enactment of the first federal drug act in 1906 and later amendments in 1938 and, following the thalidomide catastrophe, in 1962. Several pages could be filled with a recitation of specific situations which finally gave rise to each of the federal consumer-related laws. Governmental policy as it relates to the consumer is, unfortunately, random, being responsive to narrowly defined needs rather than to a comprehensive effort to assess the situation and develop

[3] "The Apologetics of Managerialism," in Perry Bliss (ed.), *Marketing and Behavioral Sciences,* Allyn and Bacon, Boston, 1963.

appropriate corrective programs. This aimless policy is also reflected in the absence of any effective administrative apparatus in the federal government designed to view the consumer as a whole. This is true despite the recently created Consumers' Advisory Council, the Committee on Consumer Interests, and a Special Assistant for Consumer Affairs. This conglomeration of councils, committees, and the special assistant to the President that represent the consumer at the highest possible federal government levels resembles the disorganized assortment of activities that are carried out by about thirty-five principal departments and agencies. These groups have been hurriedly assembled to meet vaguely felt needs. The job of even the Committee on Consumer Interests and the Consumer Advisory Council is not to implement, but rather to advise. The point at which one ends and the other begins is not clear, like so much governmental activity in the consumer area. Perhaps in due time there may be created a consumer agency to implement and coordinate the many federal consumer programs.

THE DIFFICULT ROLE OF CONSUMERS

Reflection and observation indicate that too many consumers are unprepared for the role of sovereignty in our present complex economy. They are easily manipulated and are ignorant concerning the ways of the ever-changing marketplace. For example, how many consumers ever consider these questions?

1. Are present-day prices competitive?
2. Does present-day competition resemble competition 50 years ago?
3. To what extent are the prices of consumer goods a measure of the actual cost of producing and distributing them?
4. Do I know what goods and services are best in terms of my own welfare?
5. Do I buy only the goods and services that are beneficial?
6. Am I able to judge quality?
7. To what extent can I check quantity measurements of my purchases?

Economists assume that consumers are rational. Psychologists and sociologists, however, insist that we are social men rather than economic men. Our motivations include a desire for status, for conformity, for prestige, and for power, to mention only a few.

Economists also assume that consumers buy only for individual or family consumption, whereas there is much institutional buying today. There is also considerable public buying by the military and by schools, parks, highways, and many other public bodies.

Another serious defect in the assumption that the consumer is king lies in the fact that income is unevenly distributed. Consumers with many dollars can cast many votes. Others have to be satisfied with casting fewer dollar votes. Obviously, such a system gives some consumers more influence than others.

The Inarticulate Consumer versus Pressure Groups

Another reason the consumer is not king in our mid-twentieth-century economy is that consumption is a function common to all and peculiar to none. We are all consumers, but we are first a worker, a manager, a producer, a government clerk, a teacher, a doctor, a farmer, a lawyer. In such roles, each person's interest is direct, and he is willing to promote his direct interest through group action, through organized effort, or through political appeals to governing bodies. In his role as a consumer, his interests are indirect and consequently are neglected. Nobody is willing to organize effort, to obtain political support, to rally his fellow consumers solely in behalf of consumer interests. It becomes apparent, then, that in our present-day democratic society, where government responds to pressure groups, inarticulate consumers are largely at the mercy of more effectively organized groups.

Interest groups are organized primarily to improve the relative position of their members. They are never organized to improve the position of all the members in society. While groups attempt to present their own special interests as being identical with the interests of the general public, it frequently results that their behavior indicates a pathetic ignorance of the general welfare. Everybody is for the consumer until more direct interests conflict. Then nobody is for the consumer, and consumer interests are neglected.

As long as the marketplace was an adequate regulator and coordinator of economic activity, admittedly in the distant past, there was less need for government to act as protector of consumer interests against exploitation by producer interests. But as industrialization developed, with its urbanization, consumers' dependence on sources of supplies beyond their own control has continued to increase rapidly. This increasing consumer dependence, in turn, has been responsible for partial public realization that the material health of each individual is becoming inseparably bound to the economic health of the entire community.

Other significant economic changes that require revision of the consumer sovereignty assumption have taken place in the economy in the last 25 years. One important change has been the growth of giant corporations to a dominant position in our economy.

Another significant change has been the tremendous expenditures by the military for national security—expenditures of such magnitude that a sudden drastic curtailment would most likely cause a recession.

Corporate farming and labor unions have had increasing influence in our economy. Corporation farming is encroaching on family-type farming. Consumers pay an annual multi-billion dollar subsidy for farming. When big business and giant unions reach an impasse, as in the 1959-1960 steel strike, the economy suffers and consumers usually pay higher prices.

Another change has been the tremendous power of radio and television in stimulating sales. Actually, the price competition of a simpler economy has been replaced by the non-price competition of giant corporations monopolizing the choice listening hours on radio and TV.

These changes can be in the consumer interest. In England, for example, the BBC television reports the results of independent testing of consumer goods, giving brand names and comparative prices.

What Choice Does the Consumer Have?

Some economists would argue that the consumer choice remains the same regardless whether we have an ideal competitive-model market or a market powered by price controls. In both kinds of markets, these economists would say that the consumer is a price-taker. If the consumer does not like the price or the product, he can take it or leave it. This conclusion must assume that the real difficulties are not in price and other controls by power groups like business, labor, and government, but in ourselves as careless and uninformed buyers. Can enough buyers be taught to care? Can any consumer group organize the economic power of consumers to balance the present power groups? Perhaps the consumer weapons of boycotting and preferential buying can be applied here and there at different times. But the history of the use of these two weapons is not reassuring in the United States. Public involvement in consumer action in a large country like ours is possible but not likely except in very unusual situations like the recent housewives' strike against food prices. Such collective movements unfortunately are short-lived and therefore ineffective, on the whole. So, if the best method, collective consumer power, is not successful, consumers will have no alternative except to direct their energy toward real but secondary issues of adequate market information and supporting effective legislation so as to make free choice in the marketplace meaningful.

CONSUMER PRIORITIES IN THE NEXT DECADE

In the United States, consumption means more than merely acquiring the food, clothing, shelter, and other things we need to stay alive. It also means acquiring those things which will enrich life for the individual. We need, therefore, to be clear on the difference between a consumption-directed economy and a consumer-directed economy.

In a consumption-directed economy, almost anything would be permissible. Deceptive and false advertising would be permitted as long as it encouraged people to buy. Planned obsolescence as a means of increasing consumption would be the rule rather than the exception. Disregard for such public problems as poverty, the shrinkage of our natural resources, air and water pollution, and problems faced by the elderly and the low-income minority groups would be tolerated as long as the employment and gross national product statistics (economic growth) appeared favorable. All that is important is that there be many things to buy and that they be bought. Such a system contains the seeds of its own economic and moral destruction. Where people are encouraged to emphasize the materialistic way of life, without regard to skill, craftsmanship, and quality, satisfaction is more likely to give way to emptiness and joy to be replaced by excitement—a kind of excitement based on the sating of appetites dreamed up by copywriters. This excitement often turns into frustration when the promise of a mediocre product or service is not fulfilled.

In a consumer-directed economy, the individual is treated as something else than a "buying machine"—a robot created to consume the good, bad, and indifferent products and services of our economic system. Rather, he is treated as an individual where natural inclination is toward self-improvement and the improvement of his environment. For this to happen, we need to emphasize and educate for the pursuit of high standards in goods and services and of a better environment.

The Quality of American Life

Almost everywhere we turn, quality is becoming an issue: the quality of the air we breathe, the water we drink, the meat we buy, the repair services we need, and the TV and radio programs that stream endlessly into our homes. And beyond these are the quality of our urban centers and the quality of our relations with one another.

Why are we concerned about fraud, with lack of real choice, with the absence of meaningful competition, with poor housing, and with overpriced medical services? Why do we worry about consumer credit and collection practices, and why do we want truth-in-lending? Certainly to cure specific evils, but more fundamentally to help to make us as consumers meaningful participants in our economy and our government and to bring to our life a quality to match the quantity.

The world over, the "American way of life" stands for abundance and quantity. We can be proud of the abundance, though not in the way that we have excluded a sizable segment of our people from it. We face the difficult task of dealing with racism and poverty. We also face the challenge to develop in every facet of our lives, and especially in those who touch us as producers and consumers, as sellers and buyers, ever higher standards. In other words, we are called out not to build bigger junkyards and worse ghettos; not to turn out shoddier products; not to reduce the quality of repair services; not to set new records in obsolescence in consumer products or in the speed with which we waste our natural resources. We are called to seek higher standards, to do the best in what we produce, and to act as responsible consumers in the marketplace. This is not a remote ideal but an urgent necessity. Some of the recent consumer legislation, especially since 1962—the year when President John F. Kennedy proclaimed the consumers' four-pronged rights—the right to safety, the right to be informed, the right to choose, and the right to be heard—symbolized consumerism. They became the basis for important new consumer legislation.

Focus on Consumers

The Kennedy consumer "rights" proclamation became the basis for enactment of several important new consumer laws and of amendments to other laws already on the books—Fair Packaging and Labeling Act, Consumer Credit Protection Act, Wholesome Meat Act, Fire Safety Act, Hazardous Products Commission Act, and Flammable Fabrics Act, to mention a few. More consumer protection legislation is in the works concerning areas such as fraud and deception in sales, a major study of automobile insurance, protection against hazardous radiation from television sets and other electronic equipment, closing the gaps in poultry inspection, the sale of unwholesome fish, prevention of death and accidents on our waterways, warranties and guarantees, improving honesty and fairness in repair work and servicing, pipeline safety, electric power reliability, land sales frauds, mutual fund reform, appointment of a lawyer to represent the consumer interest in the Department of Justice, the safety of natural gas lines, cigarette labeling and advertising, truth-in-trading stamps, full disclosure of costs when buying a home, advertising claims for dietary, vitamin, and mineral products, dishonest lumber grades, grade standards for more food products, and permitting the National Bureau of Standards to publish the results of their testing of consumer products. And there will be more consumer legislation in the years to come.

If It Is Good for the Public, It Is Good for Business

Business, in general, has discovered over the years that good consumer protection laws are in the interest of ethical, competitive business. E. B. Weiss, a veteran marketing and advertising executive, illustrates this point of view:[4]

> Each industry affected by proposed legislation has tended, on balance, to oppose uncompromisingly each new legislative proposal on behalf of consumerism. The food industry fought truth-in-packaging bills for five years. Truth-in-credit legislation was opposed by the credit industry for seven years. . . . In short, after six years of tuning up, Washington is literally racing toward additional legislation, regulation, and organization. State governments are doing the same thing, and so are many city governments. But industry's attitude tends to remain a mixture of confrontation, lamentation, and pious posturing. The marketing fraternity, especially, is almost united in its opposition. Marketing conventions resound with wails of anguish, of frustration, of bewilderment.

Mr. Weiss then predicted that continued opposition to consumer legisla-

[4] In an article he wrote in the *Harvard Business Review* for July-August, 1968.

tion will lead "to quasi-utility status for marketing. . . . Marketing will be regulated by law far more than it has ever been before. Most marketing leaders have only themselves to blame if they do not like this prospect."

This is a strong indictment of the general opposition of business and marketing men to consumer legislation, from a respected marketing and advertising executive. Mr. Weiss is receiving some support for his views from some leaders of business. Mr. Thomas J. Watson, Jr., International Business Machines board chairman, for example, said, "If we businessmen insist that free enterprise permits us to be indifferent to those things on which people put high value, then the people will quite naturally assume that free enterprise has too much freedom."[5]

There are many evidences of new interest in consumer issues. In addition to the general support by the people for better consumer protection of goods and services, as indicated in all of the recent legislation, the Opinion Research Corporation in 1968 reported on home interviews at all income levels, and discovered that:

1. Seven out of 10 Americans feel that present federal legislation is inadequate to protect their health and safety;
2. Fifty-five percent feel that further laws are needed to help consumers get full value for their money;
3. Thirty-four percent would like to see packaging and labeling of grocery products further investigated; and
4. Sixty-two percent favor a proposed law requiring doctors to prescribe by generic rather than brand names.[6]

Consumer Issues and Areas for Attention

What are the issues and problems consumers are likely to be concerned with in the years ahead? Dr. Gordon E. Bivens, economist and professor in the School of Home Economics at the University of Missouri, prepared a paper in which he discusses some issues arising from urbanization, mobility, youthful spenders, rising consumer incomes, increasing complexity of consumer goods and services, depersonalization of the market, and increasing interdependence of nations. Dr. Bivens said that the consumer issues needing attention in the future are these:[7]

1. Need to rethink the ethics of consumption. An estimated three-fourths of the U.S. population will soon be living in urban areas. In such a highly urbanized society, consumption must take place in a setting of closeness to others. People both as individuals and as a society will need to give increasing consideration to ways of reducing noise, fumes, litter, and other by-products of their consumption activities that impinge on their neighbors.

[5] Thomas J. Watson, Jr., *A Business and Its Beliefs,* McGraw-Hill Book Company, New York, 1963, pp. 88-90.
[6] Reported by the National Association of Manufacturers and reprinted in *Dollars and Decisions,* Extension Service, University of Vermont, Burlington, 1968.
[7] *Family Economics Review,* June, 1968, pp. 9-12.

2. Need to cope with increasingly complex market. The function of consumers as buying agents for households will become even more generalized than it is now, as the number and variety of goods and services on the market increase and the income consumers have to buy goods rises. Consumers will have to make decisions about so many items they cannot possibly have specialized information about all of them. At the same time, the selling side of the market situation undoubtedly will become more specialized—in advertising, selling, and promotional techniques.

3. Need to clarify values. As their buying functions become more complex, consumers will need to be honest with themselves and think through carefully the values and goals that guide their decisions. Otherwise, they may be too easily influenced in their buying by sales pressures.

4. Need to consider giving. Consumers are going to face important decisions about how much and what types of giving they want to support. The question will be how much of their private consumption they are willing to give up to contribute to peace at home and abroad. This will involve gifts for domestic relief and developing nations, both by public means (taxation) and private giving.

5. Need to consider public versus private consumption. Consumers will have to give more thought to which goods and services should be privately acquired and used and which provided by public means. Such decisions must be guided by considerations of how these can be provided at the lowest real cost, and what the longtime needs of society will be. An example is the need for setting aside public lands for play areas and parks, resulting from the increased urbanization. In any event, consumers will have to be concerned with public as well as private decisions. This means they will need to use their right to vote, so that the people most likely to act in accordance with their views are elected.

6. Need to relate present to future decisions. As goods become more complex and require more specialized service for repair and even maintenance, consumers must recognize more than ever before that their decisions today will affect those of the future. For example, deciding to buy an automatic washing machine this year commits one to future expense for repairs and maintenance if the washer is to be used and enjoyed. This precommitment of spending, then, restricts choices in other areas of future spending.

7. Relation to consumers in other countries. As countries become more interdependent, U.S. consumers will need to be concerned about such matters as (1) the effect of tariffs on potentials for growth in other countries as well as on prices at home, (2) standardization of sizes and terms used for consumer goods in international commerce, and (3) the effect of the quality of consumer goods we send abroad on international relations.

8. Need to appraise resource use and cost. The rates at which the various consumer resources—money, time, energy, skill, and interests—can be substituted for each other will have to be constantly reevaluated as incomes rise, goods on the market change, and opportunities to learn expand. For example, because of rapidly changing conditions, consumers will need constantly to reevaluate the relative importance of saving time in buying and saving money by searching the market.

As part of their appraisal of resource use, consumers may need to sharpen their figuring of costs of owning goods by counting as part of this cost what they could have earned in interest if they had saved or invested an amount equal to the purchase price. This type of calculation will be especially important in their decision to buy or to rent—houses and major durable equipment, for example. The option to lease, as an alternate to ownership, is likely to become important for more and more goods.

9. Need to know legal rights. In the years ahead consumers will be involved in more and increasingly complex contractual arrangements. They will need to be aware of their legal rights and responsibilities, and know when to consult legal experts.

10. Need to make likes and dislikes known. As markets become more impersonal and direct communication between consumer and decision-making personnel in the market becomes more limited, consumers may need to initiate—through group action or other means—ways to make their likes and dislikes constructively known. Although such communication is finally worked out through the market, it is only with a good bit of lag and then not perfectly.

This list of ten consumer issues, which will need attention in the coming years, aptly sums up the responsibilities of consumers in years to come.

The Consumers' Magna Charta

On March 15, 1962, President John F. Kennedy proclaimed, as has been noted previously, a "declaration of rights" for consumers in a free society. This historic message to Congress was devoted entirely to a "Consumers' Protection and Interest Program." In this first consumer message to Congress the President listed the following consumer rights:

1. The right to safety—to be protected against the marketing of goods that are hazardous to health or life.
2. The right to be informed—to be protected against fraudulent, deceitful, or grossly misleading information, advertising, labeling, and other practices, and to be given the facts needed to make informed choices.
3. The right to choose—to be assured, wherever possible, access to a variety of products and services at competitive prices. And in those industries in which competition is not workable and government regulation is substituted, there should be assurance of satisfactory quality and service at fair prices.
4. The right to be heard—to be assured that consumer interests will receive full and sympathetic consideration in the formulation of government policy and fair and expeditious treatment in its administrative tribunals.

On February 5, 1964, President Johnson sent another historic message to Congress in which he reiterated the four consumer rights proclaimed by President Kennedy. On March 21, 1966, President Johnson transmitted a message to Congress requesting effective laws on lending charges and packaging practices. Congress passed legislation on these matters in 1967 and 1968.

On February 6, 1968, President Johnson presented the fourth of these messages on the American consumer, enumerating the steps taken to achieve present progress and setting forth a new program for 1968. President Johnson said that this was not a partisan program or a business program or a labor program. It was, he said, a "program for all of us—all 200 million Americans."

Consumer Responsibility

How do you react to questionable methods and devices for selling the nation's abundant productivity? Are deceit, fraud, dishonesty, illusions, planned obsolescence, and plain cheating the only ways to utilize this abundant productivity? Is there no place for good standards, fairness, and honesty when exchanging dollars for goods and services? And, finally, do you agree with some marketing experts who say that the best way to utilize our abundant production is to "make consumption our way of life, that we should convert buying and use of goods into rituals, that we seek our spiritual satisfactions, or ego-satisfactions, in consumption"? In short, these marketing experts say that "the way to end glut is to produce gluttons." What do *you* think?

Faced with these multiple issues, what can consumers do about it? In the first place, a consumer can become an alert, informed, and responsible person. Anyone can spend money. A responsible person, however, should know his role and function in the economy. In this way he can influence what is to be produced.

A second consumer responsibility is to exercise independence of judgment and action. Then he is not likely to yield to commercial selling pressures, to conspicuous consumption, to group pressures, and to the lure of excessive credit. This suggests that the mature consumer has a continuing need for consumer information and education.

A third consumer responsibility is to recognize the dangers inherent in needless waste of limited natural and human resources. Many of these resources are irreplaceable.

The consumer also has a responsibility to buy products and services that are produced most efficiently. Such efficiency, however, ought not to be at the expense of exploitation of people on the basis of sex, age, color, or national origin.

The responsible consumer should be honest in his dealings, just as he expects industry, merchants, and repairmen to be honest. He has the responsibility, for example, not to abuse the privilege of trying out merchandise.

He should also take the time to write protest letters to irresponsible industries, merchants, and repairmen. How else will irresponsible businessmen and servicemen know that you are aware of their deceitful and dishonest dealings? Lacking support of informed and responsible consumers, the fair-minded businessmen find it difficult to withstand dishonest and unethical competitors. Consumer awareness of deceit and fraud will help industry help itself. The consumer who knows how he is being filched from by dishonest merchants can exercise his sovereignty (his buying decision) by rewarding the honest and more efficient producer with his business.

Sometimes the collective effort of consumers brings about a change. The American consumers who protested against car design in the late 1950s showed their preference for smaller automobiles by purchasing such cars made in other countries. Likewise, consumer protest has led to the creation of new and different ways of distribution of goods and services—for example, discount stores, consumer cooperatives, and credit unions.

The overall responsibility was stated by President Johnson in a speech delivered at the University of Michigan. He said:

> For half a century, we called upon unbounded invention and untiring industry to create an order of plenty for all our people. The challenge in the next half century is whether we have the wisdom to use the wealth to enrich and elevate our National life, and to advance the quality of our American civilization.

chapter **2**

CONSUMER DECISION MAKING

The greatest gift is the power to estimate correctly the value of things.

de la Rochefoucauld

The real challenge of this chapter on consumer decision making or choice rests on the consumer's desire, ability, and willingness to get the maximum satisfactions from the spending of his money, time, and energy.

GOALS AND CHOICE

Choice is a fundamental problem for all human beings, and it is also a complex problem—complex because we are living in an "embarrassment-of-riches" age. There are new products, new kinds of entertainment, new services coming along constantly. Shop windows, newspapers, magazines, radio, television, movies, and travel influence us to want more and more. Consumers are literally overwhelmed by a variety of goods and services. Choice making is therefore more difficult than in the make-what-you-need economy of pioneer times.

The choices we make, consciously and subconsciously, determine to a large extent the character of our lives. In other words, our choices determine what we get out of life. It goes without saying, however, that setting up goals of family spending is not enough. We need the ability to work them out. Nevertheless, if we can decide on major goals, we are doing something that many people seem unable to accomplish. The biggest determinant of what we *get* out of life is what we *want* out of life. It follows, then, that intelligent choice is the first important step in wise consumption.

One of the major aims of consumer education should be to teach consumers how to spend their money, time, and energy to bring expressed wants into harmony with considered needs. And all this should be done within the limits of the income of each family.

The average person needs little food, shelter, clothing, and recreation. But many are not satisfied with supplying only these needs. They want a great many things they do not need, often more intensely than what is needed. A man may commit suicide if he is jilted by the lady he loves. Some parents risk all they have for the sake of sending a son or daughter to a university. So often, however, the things prized the most are the things needed the least. Why? Perhaps it is because people do not consciously and deeply consider what they want most out of life and how best to get it.

If consumers will probe through the surface reasons for wanting certain things, they may get down to the real reasons and thus make more intelligent choices and so get the fullest satisfaction out of supplying their important wants.

THE DECISION-MAKING PROCESS

The key to decision making is alternatives—to help us, as consumers, to learn how to evaluate alternative courses of action so that we may arrive at a better decision—a decision which will lead to results more satisfying than those made without the benefit of considering the alternatives. Most of us do not choose a product at random the first time it is purchased. We usually go through a process of careful selection called "decision making." Many products are purchased periodically and habitually. Products involving a relatively large outlay are more likely to be purchased after going through rather careful selection. Usually we are not concerned with decision making until we are interested in buying a particular product. Having decided on the objective or use of the particular product desired, we may go through two or more of the following phases:

1. Searching for the best product for our purpose among the several commodities on the market.
2. Determining relevant alternatives by making general evaluation of the products available.
3. Appraising relevant alternatives seriously by securing important facts about the product.
4. Making a final decision.

The final decision may or may not lead to a purchase. We may decide not to buy if the net satisfaction derived is not large enough to offset the cost. In this case we may seek other alternatives or delay the purchase.

Decision making, however, is not a simple process. There are many external and internal forces acting upon the individual and the family.

The Individual and Decision Making [1]

In making a decision, an individual is influenced by a number of basic forces. There are, also, subcategories too numerous to mention here.

Physical needs is a broad category which includes food, housing, clothing, and other items. Protein needs, for example, can be met with relatively low-cost foods such as variety meats and skim milk. On the other hand, they can be satisfied with more expensive exotic cheeses and steaks.

Social needs, another broad category, are important to many people for reasons other than attainment of physical pleasure. Some of the obvious social needs affecting decision making are achievement (highest satisfaction), affiliation (location of home in best neighborhood), prestige (keeping up with the Joneses), and exhibition (four-car garage).

There are many other social forces that play a role in consumer decision making, such as passively submitting to external forces, impulse, yielding to the influence of someone whom one admires, and purchasing to avoid humiliation.

Values and individual attitudes are other factors which account for differences in spending patterns. For example, some individuals place a higher value on savings than on spending. They value financial security higher than things.

[1] For details, see James N. Morgan, "Household Decision-Making," a paper presented at the University of Michigan; Calvin S. Hall and Gardner Lindzey, *Theories of Personality,* John Wiley and Sons, Inc., New York, 1957.

A person's choice of alternatives is also influenced by day-to-day happenings. For example, there may be changes in income or prices, and there may be new information which may influence a decision.

Risk and uncertainty may also be influential in decision making. For example, the decision with regard to introducing a completely new food to the family presents an uncertainty situation.

These forces are interrelated and complex. Typically, one is influenced by a number of these forces simultaneously.

The Family and Decision Making

Family-made decisions are far more complex than those made by the individual because they involve participation of family members. The same forces mentioned above may be involved, but the forces will have a varying impact on each participating family member. If tastes and preferences are relatively similar, no conflicts are apt to arise. But if there are differences in tastes and preferences, a decision can become involved and complex. [2]

WHO MAKES THE DECISION?

Let us examine some of the evidence on how consumers—particularly women—buy. Women not only purchase most of the goods consumed by American families but also have a large voice in determining what is bought.

Someone has said, "Never underestimate the power of a woman." At any rate, that seems to be the moral of a marketing survey by Paul D. Converse and Merle Crawford, of the University of Illinois, which is depicted in Figure 2-1, Family Buying: Who Does It? Who Influences It? The study shows that women buy about 55 percent of all the consumer goods for the family; men buy 30 percent; husbands and wives shopping together buy 11 percent; and children buy 4 percent. These percentages represent actual purchases.

Women are even more important when it comes to determining what is to be purchased. Women, according to the same survey, have 57 percent of the influence in determining what is to be bought; men have about 35 percent and children, 8 percent.

The influences within families were marked. Converse found that women buy 88 percent of their own clothing, but that men have 16 percent and children 3 percent of the influence on its purchase. Women buy only about 4 percent of men's suits and overcoats, but they influence 27 percent of the purchases. Wives also have about 27 percent influence in buying the family car, although they actually purchase only 6 percent of the cars sold.

The changes in family purchasing habits shown in Figure 2-1 were brought out in the same survey.

[2] Morgan, op. cit., p. 25.

What to Buy?

Mom, Pop, and the kids exert this
influence on buying decisions, but . . .

Who Buys It?

Here's who actually makes the purchases
across the retail store counter

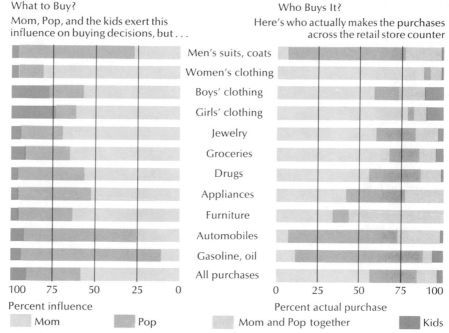

| 100 | 75 | 50 | 25 | 0 | | 0 | 25 | 50 | 75 | 100 |

Percent influence

Percent actual purchase

Mom   Pop   Mom and Pop together   Kids

Figure 2-1   Family Buying: Who Does It? Who Influences It? Source: By permission of *Business Week,* **Jan. 7, 1950, p. 30; data from** *Current Economic Comment,* **Bureau of Economic and Business Research, University of Illinois, November, 1949, pp. 38–50.**

1.   Men are apparently making more of the family purchases, women somewhat less, children slightly more, and there seemed to be more shopping together of husband and wife.

2.   Men nowadays are doing more of the shopping for women's clothes, women's toilet articles, draperies, and kitchenware, although women still make most of their own purchases.

3.   Men are buying more of the furniture than ever before.

4.   There has been an increase in joint shopping, especially for groceries, women's clothing, kitchenware, draperies, hardware, gas and oil, and drugs.

While the old contention that women did about 80 to 85 percent of the family purchasing may not stand up against present-day marketing surveys, the fact remains that they still play the major role in family purchases, as well as in influencing what is purchased. This being true, any progress made in teaching women how to get greater satisfaction and results from the spending of the family income will no doubt be appreciated by them as well as by their families.

The University of Oregon in 1957 reported a study by Theodore B. Johannis, Jr., of 1,027 high school students and their parents in Tampa, Florida. The significant findings are shown in Table 2-1.

TABLE 2-1   PERCENT OF FATHERS, MOTHERS, AND TEEN-AGE SONS AND DAUGH-
TERS PARTICIPATING IN SELECTED FAMILY ECONOMIC ACTIVITY (N = 1,027 NON-
BROKEN WHITE FAMILIES)

ACTIVITY	A SHARED ACTIVITY	FATHER	MOTHER	TEEN-AGE SON	TEEN-AGE DAUGHTER
1. Selects large household equipment	61.9	68.7	90.2	5.0	6.8
2. Shops for furniture and furnishings	61.3	62.3	93.5	4.6	13.7
3. Shops for groceries	55.1	42.5	84.1	32.0	37.4
4. Plans family's savings	47.2	68.8	73.2	3.0	2.1
5. Shops for family's clothes	46.4	29.3	95.6	30.1	44.3
6. Shops for family's new car	46.4	91.3	46.5	10.8	15.0
7. Provides children's spending money	45.7	77.3	56.1	21.4	4.6
8. Pays bills	39.7	76.8	58.2	7.4	7.6
9. Earns money for family	38.3	97.9	32.8	15.7	2.2
Range:					
High	61.9	97.9	95.6	32.0	44.3
Low	38.3	29.3	32.8	3.0	2.1

SOURCE: *The Coordinator,* September, 1957, pp. 15-16.

The fathers were found to be playing their traditional role of family provider in 98 percent of the homes. Two mothers out of five had jobs outside the home. Mothers were the central figures in family purchasing agent roles in all but one of the five items studied. This one exception was the car, for which nearly twice as many fathers as mothers shopped.

Shopping for furniture, household furnishings, and large household equipment was shared actively in six out of ten families. The central figure in the financial operation was the mother. Shopping for food was a shared activity with mother playing the central role. About an equal proportion of fathers and mothers planned the savings program.

In general, the participation by members of the family in economic activities followed along fairly recent traditional lines. Teen-agers, on the whole, were not given a real chance to learn to be intelligent consumers. The data indicate that the sharing process in the family economic field has not moved as far along as had been believed.

CONSUMER BUYING HABITS

A habit is any activity repeatedly performed in the same manner without much conscious attention to how it will be done each time. If habits are long-established, they tend to become customs. Many daily actions, such as dressing and eating, tend to become habits. While there are several kinds of habits, here we are primarily concerned with the buying habits of modern Americans.

People are creatures of habit. More human activity is habitual than deliberate. This may be due to the fact that change requires work. Of course, there are people, probably a minority, who enjoy tackling new problems and modifying habits. However, firmly established habits are not easy to change. Custom, too, tends to impose barriers to progress that are difficult to modify.

Buying, spending, and using habits are receiving a great deal of attention because of producers' efforts to meet consumer demands. The Consumer Testing Institute estimates that seven out of ten customers are habit buyers. The following summary of various studies reveals some consumer buying habits.

1. 69.8 percent of bakery goods purchases were bought on impulse.
2. 57.2 percent of supermarket shoppers shopped only one supermarket; 36.2 percent shopped in two or more; and 15.5 percent shopped at an independent market also.
3. 42.4 percent of the families studied made only one shopping trip a week to supermarkets; 19.9 percent made two trips a week; and 13.7 percent marketed six times a week.
4. Approximately 50 percent of supermarket customers do not use a shopping list, compared to only about 15 percent in the early years of the supermarkets. Over one-third of all purchases were impulse purchases. Eight out of ten customers do some impulse buying.
5. There is a steady trend toward the more convenient one-stop, self-service retail units.
6. Buying at department stores has increased less rapidly than total retail sales. A larger percentage of upstairs customers are shopping the basement departments. Many department stores stage special campaigns for male customers, since they are taking a more active role in the purchasing activities of their families.
7. Within a few days after receiving the pay check, most of the money is spent. People tend to pay the first bills that come and let the others wait.
8. Charge account customers purchase three times as much as cash customers.
9. There is a tendency to buy on "easy terms" (installment buying) without considering the total cost of the merchandise.
10. People tend to spend five dimes more readily than 50 cents. This accounts for listing the price of an article on the basis of several small prices for each of the parts of a single piece of merchandise.
11. There are a large number of consumers who do their shopping after buying. Customer abuse of the return goods privilege is a buying habit acquired only by a small percentage of customers. These irresponsible consumers, however, account for millions of dollars of loss to retail merchants. This loss, as a rule, is added to the cost of goods.
12. Goods well bought are often used improperly, to the disadvantage of the consumers. For example, failure to read and follow instructions for mechanical goods is said to account for about 40 percent of all service calls.

Thus, habits dominate large areas of consumer conduct. It should be remembered, however, that habits are not necessarily associated with poor consumership. A good habit can economize on time and energy. Good habits can actually raise one's standard of living just as poor habits can lower it. The challenge to consumers is in the direction of desiring to learn good buying habits.

Characteristics of Male and Female Shoppers

Generalizations about the characteristics of male and female shoppers are a little dangerous. However, considerable evidence of a fairly reliable nature has appeared with regard to shopping characteristics of men and women. Here are a few observations of women as shoppers.

1.   Women, more than men, are influenced by their senses. A faint but pleasant smell, for example, is likely to help them make a decision in favor of certain merchandise.
2.   Women are sensitive to appearance and to failure to cater to their comfort and convenience.
3.   Women are inclined to believe that high price means high quality.
4.   Women tend to be submissive, especially if the sales technique shows a delicate touch of erotic dominance, usually in the form of male admiration of her choice of goods or her personality.
5.   Women prefer to be led into decision making.
6.   Women want good living now.
7.   Women like to have things that are different from those of their friends and neighbors.
8.   Women tend to follow closely the buying habits of the social group above them.
9.   Women find it hard to resist a "bargain."
10.   Women are better than men in comparing store prices and qualities.

The following are characteristics of men shoppers.

1.   Men are less strongly influenced by brand names and personal emotional reactions to store salespersons.
2.   Men tend to avoid store sales. They cannot or will not stand the rush and the crowds.
3.   Men are likely to be satisfied by shopping one store.
4.   Men are more influenced by friendships and fair dealings.
5.   Men tend to make quicker decisions and to return far less merchandise.
6.   Men make larger individual purchases and they expect fewer special concessions.
7.   Men customers are more loyal to a store but also are likely to be more quickly alienated by "sharp" practices.

What is the significance of such a list of characteristics of men and women as shoppers? It matters not so much whether you agree or disagree with the above generalizations. What does matter, however, if you want to get better satisfactions as a shopper, is that you analyze your own personality in terms of what makes you buy something. Such an analysis is a complex process. Yet business is spending huge sums of money on motivational research in the hope of learning more about consumer behavior.

Motivational research has reached a stage in growth that has forced economists to take a new and critical look at it. As a matter of fact, these broader studies in consumer behavior add to the theories of the conventional economist the facts offered by sociologists, psychologists, psychiatrists, and anthropologists. These studies are of importance because they are greatly influencing consumers on what to buy. Since the retailer wants to sell more goods and services, it is largely up to the consumer to learn how to plan and buy as rationally as possible.

Understanding and Predicting Family Expenditures

Income has been a favorite resource used by economists to explain consumer expenditures.[3] Not only do economists differ in interpretation of the impact of family resources on decision making, but their data do not help much in predicting or understanding individual or family purchasing behavior with respect to a particular product. Furthermore, these data reflect the end product or final choice of decision making. In a study at the University of Michigan, Katona found great variations existed in the way in which 1,000 different consumers went about buying the same type of commodity—durable goods such as TV sets, refrigerators, automatic washing machines, and kitchen stoves:[4]

1. Forty-six percent of them disregarded price.
2. Thirty-one percent were careful about brand.
3. Chief sources of information were friends and relatives.
4. Forty-seven percent shopped more than one store.
5. Thirty-five percent sought other facts than brand and price.
6. Those who preplanned their purchases tended to seek reliable information.
7. College-educated people sought reliable information in *Consumers Union Reports* and *Consumers' Research Bulletin* and shopped around.
8. The older the head of the family and the higher the income, the less the care in arriving at a decision.
9. Repeat buying of the same brand was infrequent.

It would appear, then, that family resources are a factor influencing family decision making. Family resources, however, provide only a partial explanation of expenditure behavior. It is also necessary to consider family characteristics (noneconomic) such as family life cycle, occupation, level of education, residence, race, and religion. A considerable amount of data is available which illustrates the relationship between family characteristics and expenditures. One illustration may suffice. Food expenditures change as families move from the "newly married couple without children" stage to the period when they have children, to the time when the children are not on the family payroll, and finally to the retirement period. The change is likely to

[3] Warren J. Bilkey, *Vector Analysis of Consumer Behavior,* University of Connecticut, Storrs, Conn., 1954; James S. Duesenberry, *Income, Saving and the Theory of Consumer Behavior,* Harvard University Press, Cambridge, Mass., 1949; Milton A. Friedman, *Theory of the Consumption Function,* Princeton University Press, Princeton, N.J., 1957; Ruby Turner Norris, *The Theory of Consumer's Demand,* Yale University Press, New Haven, Conn., 1941; and George Katona, *Psychological Analysis of Economic Behavior,* McGraw-Hill Book Company, New York, 1951.

[4] George Katona, "A Study of Purchase Decisions: Part I," in Lincoln H. Clark, ed., *Consumer Behavior: The Dynamics of Consumer Reaction,* Consumer Behavior Series, New York University Press, New York, 1955, vol. 1, pp. 30-36.

be attributable to changes in the family's income and their physical, social, and psychological needs.

While there are many internal and external factors influencing decision making (and much is still unknown), the American consumer apparently is no composite creature possessed of a single set of buying habits. He fits no single mold. He is not uniquely an apartment dweller, a suburbanite, a rural person, a ghetto dweller, or a trailer resident. He has no one level of buying competence. His purchasing habits reflect his position in the life cycle, his education, and his occupation and income as well as his nationality and cultural background. Indeed, he reacts with a highly variable degree of response to the numerous influences which surround him.

Considering the pitfalls American consumers may encounter, as well as their lack of adequate information, there is an alert contingent of buyers at one end of the buying spectrum—a group that purchases after considerable deliberation, particularly in the area of durable goods in which quality characteristics are important. At the other end of the spectrum is an equally substantial group being victimized by high-pressure selling and advertising and possessed of little discernment, a group which does not understand the new forces of hidden persuasion.

Between these extremes are the great mass of American consumers exercising varying degrees of intelligence in product purchasing. So it would seem that the Survey Research Center findings concerning durable goods afford some evidence that the American consumer is not a standardized creature in his buying deportment. As a matter of fact, we seem to be developing an ever-widening gulf between the discerning consumer and the backward consumer— the latter being a victim of his own ignorance and of manipulation by others.

Much of the problem of wisdom in consumer choice lies in little-explored territory. David Riesman, a sociologist, contends that the typical American middle-class family has, by social conditioning, set for itself a goal of acquiring a "standardized package of goods and services" containing such items as furniture, radio, TV, refrigerator, and standard brands of food and clothing. In his view this group is trained to spend up to and beyond their income and gradually accumulate the full basic package. How wise this basic spending pattern is remains open to question. There is undoubtedly much truth in William Whyte's somewhat cynical comment that the "consumer is trying to tune in on his fellow consumers to find out what is right, while they, equally baffled, are tuning in on him—and the producer is tuning in on them." This, in part at least, is the process of consumer choice, and we go round and round and come out in debt.

The task of becoming an intelligent consumer has become ever more difficult because of the nature of the American market, the spectacular development of new products, the persuasive influence of advertising, and the lack of quality information at the point of sale available to the consumer.

ADVERTISING AND DECISION MAKING

Adequate information as a basis of purchase decisions is essential to the consumer; it is also important for effective functioning of our economic system. Advertising provides information, and, at times, social pressure, to behave in a certain fashion.

Purpose of Advertising

The purpose of advertising is to stimulate the sale of goods and services. It is a way of reaching many people via TV, radio, newspapers, direct mail, posters, placards, circulars, and other means. Perhaps the chief function of advertising today is that of a salesman. It can reach many millions of people more efficiently than can personal selling. The emphasis, therefore, is on preselling the consumer on a particular brand of service. And for this, and other advertising, consumers pay about $17 billion annually.

The justification for advertising, then, is to efficiently market products and services; to bring new and better products economically to the consumer; to contribute to a growing economy by expanding the consumption of goods and the circulation of capital; and to build a better way of life in an increasingly affluent and sophisticated society. There is no quarrel with these objectives. The basic quarrel with advertising is that this medium is misused and, under certain circumstances, the cost of advertising is excessive.

Advertising Expenditures.   How much do advertisers spend? The current estimate is $17 billion annually. Advertisers claim that the typical consumer is exposed to 1,600 advertisements daily. The ads range from a local room to rent to the $245 million spent by Procter and Gamble. The top 125 advertisers spent over $4 billion in 1965. The biggest advertisers, in this order, were Procter and Gamble, General Motors, General Foods, Ford, and Bristol-Myers. Advertising expenditures, as a percentage of sales, were 27.6 for Bristol-Myers, 10.9 for Procter and Gamble, 8.7 for General Foods, 1.0 for Ford, and 0.8 for General Motors.[5] Of the top 125 advertisers, 26 were food and soft drink producers, 16 drug and cosmetic firms, 9 brewers and distillers, and 8 tobacco manufacturers.

In a typical year advertisers spent about 30 percent of their advertising dollar for newspaper ads, 16 percent for television, 15 percent for direct mail, 8 percent for magazines, and 6 percent for radio. These media account for nearly 75 percent of all advertising expenditures in the United States.

When huge sums—$17 billion—are spent annually on one aspect of sales efforts, we need to ask: "Does advertising provide the answer to the consumer's need for important information about a product? Does advertising increase productivity? Does advertising aim to reduce costs or maximize profits? Does advertising increase competition and, thus, benefit the consumer?

[5] According to *Advertising Age*, Aug. 29, 1966.

"Advertising's Credibility Gap."   In a recent report E. B. Weiss, formerly an advertising executive, editor of *Printer's Ink,* and in 1967 director of special merchandising for Doyle Dane Bernbach, Inc., concludes:[6]

> There is ample cause to be concerned by the adverse image of advertising. . . . Who can dispute that the main causes for the criticisms lie not in Washington, not among rabble-rousers, but in the dull, boring commercials the public is forced to listen to; to bad taste of much advertising such as some of the proprietary drug commercials the public is forced to digest with dinner, and in the excessive buffoonery, unbelievability, bad taste, boorishness and boredom that characterizes so much of advertising today. There is also the over-commercialization of television with network commercials, station breaks, program promotion, etc., all tumbling over each other.
>
> A good part of the criticism directed against advertising is justified. An increasingly sophisticated public will become less tolerant of advertising's abuses. . . . It is entirely probable that in the decade of the 70's, advertising will come under more and more intelligent criticism than ever before in its history. This means that advertising must close its credibility gap . . . government will correct what advertising neglects to improve.

How can advertising try on a halo for size when a slacks ad shows the boss's wife with her foot on a young man's ankle (under the slacks) while her husband dozes at the table; a swinger takes off his shirt for a final "permanent press test," while, superimposed on the ad, an apparently naked girl waits expectantly; a man is urged to "come on strong . . . go all the way" with a name-brand sports coat while a reclining girl with bared knee holds out her hand?

Since the problems of half-truths and pseudo-truths are also present in modern advertising, is it true that:

> . . . a "woman in Distinction foundations is so beautiful that all other women want to kill her"?
> . . . if "a woman gives in to her divine restlessness and paints up her eyelids with The Look, her eyes will become jungle green . . . glittery gold . . . flirty eyes, tiger eyes"?
> . . . a " new ingredient in Max Factor Toiletries separates the men from the boys"?

Perhaps we have a new kind of truth emerging—pseudo-truth—which may be defined as a false statement made as if it were true but not intended to be believed. No proof is offered for pseudo-truth. Its proof is that it sells merchandise; if it does not, it is false. Is the function of language giving way to a misguiding function? If so, this is tragic to people who care about the quality and price of things. One wonders if *Esquire* Magazine had a point in its January, 1961 issue when it stated in reference to advertising that the "only thing we have to fear is truth."

MODERN MARKETING

Marketing research is the arm of marketing that finds out things and lays the basis for marketing strategy. It is concerned with the facts of what people

---

[6] E. B. Weiss, *A Critique of Consumerism,* Doyle Dane Bernbach, Inc., New York, 1967, chap. 4.

buy, when they buy, where they buy, and why they buy. To get answers to this question asking, American business spends over $200 million a year. A big company like Procter and Gamble will spend $4 million a year in its own research and spend another $2 million on outside advice. A. C. Nielsen, of Chicago, the biggest marketing company today, has an annual $45 million business exclusive of its much publicized broadcast measurement services.

To represent about fifty of the nation's largest food manufacturers, Nielsen uses a sample of about 1,600 stores, including most of the national chains. Teams of Nielsen field men are constantly in a selected store counting packages on the shelves and in storage rooms, examining invoices, and noting special displays, cents-off deals, and shelf prices. Almost every two months these reports go out to their clients. If a client wants a report on one item, such as cold cereal, he pays about $50,000; a report on hot cereals will cost another $50,000.

Nielsen confines his counting to retail stores. Other marketing research organizations set up consumer panels and keep tab on when they buy and how much. The cost for this service is also high.

Marketing research people concentrate on facts of who buys how much of what. But to know which way consumers will jump next, you need to know why they make their decisions. That's where the motivation researchers rush in with their bagful of clinical tricks with fancy names.

MOTIVATION RESEARCH: "ENGINEERING CONSUMER CONSENT"

The greatest commotion in advertising circles has centered on a probing technique called "motivation research." This "depth approach" to consumers involves the use of psychiatry and the social sciences to get inside the consumer's subconscious to discover the "psychological hook" that will stimulate him to buy a certain product.

Interestingly enough, the man who is quoted more frequently than any other on consumer motivation is Thorstein Veblen, whose basic concept in *The Theory of the Leisure Class* is the desire of people for *conspicuous consumption*. Conspicuous consumption has its roots in man's desire to conform outwardly to the consumption practices of his neighbors or to surpass them. Veblen gives most attention to pecuniary emulation, the desire to equal or excel one's neighbors in relatively costly ways by showing that one can afford expensive things.

Veblen's basic motivation is still used by some consumers, but according to marketing experts, there are at least 600 different motives for being willing to buy. Therefore, motivation as practiced in advertising and selling today is complex and has advanced far beyond the conspicuous consumption stage.

Probing Present-day Consumer Motives

With over 600 identifiable motives for being willing to buy, admen have had a field day in exploring the possibilities for influencing and learning more about the behavior of the consumer. Batten, Barton, Durstine & Osborn, Inc., set up a division called the National Panel of Consumer Opinion. Several thousand housewives on this panel can earn merchandise premiums by answering questions about products and about their daily buying habits. Dr. George Gallup, long a researcher for advertisers, set up a "sample bank" of people that he called "Mirror of America" and began probing the consumer to discover what triggers the sale of a product.

Most of the leading advertising agencies now have psychologists and psychiatrists on their payrolls. Meanwhile, several dozen motivation research firms have sprung up. The most famous is the Institute for Motivational Research, Inc., at Croton-on-Hudson, New York. Several hundred people in the area constitute Dr. Ernest Dichter's "psycho-panel." They have been depth-probed and card-indexed as to their hidden anxieties, hostilities, and so on. If he wants to know how much impact a sales message has on hypochondriacs, for example, he has a group of bona fide hypochondriacs on call. Rival corporations are raiding each other's customers with selling campaigns mapped out by these doctors of psychology.

Among the more common techniques used to lure consumers are playing on anxiety feelings; selling sexual reassurance; creating a personal image in the product (playful gasoline for playful people); encouraging impulse buying; reminding consumers that a product can fill hidden needs (security, self-esteem); selling a status symbol; offering ways, via the product, to channel aggressive feelings; conditioning the young; making consumers style-conscious and then switching styles.

Questionable Probing Techniques.   A few of the techniques used to probe consumer motives are largely borrowed from psychiatric clinics and sociological laboratories: social-layer analysis, lie detectors, projective picture and word-association tests, psychoanalysis (minus the couch), and hypnosis. When other motives are discovered, the mind experts bait the hooks that hopefully will lure the consumer.

Motivational researchers have performed constructive services for good products. The successful job that Dr. Dichter performed on prunes is a case in point. The lowly prune just wasn't selling. Why? Dr. Dichter's probers discovered that the prune, in our society, had a host of unfortunate connotations—"dried-up old maids," "witches," "constipation," "boardinghouses." So the fruit has been "rediscovered" as the "California wonder fruit," and advertising pictures the prune in colorful, gay, zestful settings. The prune industry has shown a healthy revival of a good product.

The probers, however, are also using techniques that give cause for concern. These techniques are planned to catch the consumer when his conscious guard is down. An example is the inserting of "flash" sales messages in TV and movie film. The film flash is so fast that bits of film are not "seen" by the conscious eye. In 1956, the London Sunday Times stated that advertisers had produced a notable increase in ice cream consumption at a cinema in New Jersey during experiments in this subliminal advertising. The use of this technique raises an ethical question, especially if hidden appeals are used for political purposes.

A large advertising agency explored the subconscious minds of sample humans to find out how to prepare messages that would have a great impact on people of high anxiety, hostility, passiveness, and body consciousness.

To learn how to sell cake mixes more effectively, another agency has experimented with a psychiatric study of women's menstrual cycle and the emotional states that go with each stage.

Efforts are made to manipulate children. One agency made a study of the psyche of straight-haired little girls to discover how to persuade them and their mothers that little girls might feel doomed to ugliness and unhappiness if they did not have lovely, curly hair. The agency, of course, was promoting the sale of home permanents.

A final example of questionable appropriateness in the use of motivational research is the effort to exploit the consumer's deepest sexual sensitivities. The Institute for Motivational Research counseled motorboat builders that men could be appealed to on the basis that power boats express the feeling of power in "almost a sexual way."

Responsibility for Constructive Advertising Techniques

Advertising, in general, is constructive and indispensable in the economy. But some of the agencies are becoming too powerful, and some need to be more responsible in the use of the newer techniques. Many thoughtful people are raising questions like these:

1.   Should advertising invade the privacy of the mind?
2.   Should advertising provoke anxieties in people, since some are especially sensitive?
3.   Should advertising promote waste in the areas of limited resources?
4.   Should advertising push consumers toward conformity and passivity?
5.   Should advertising encourage consumers to be irrational in their buying?

Motivational research in promoting the selling of consumer goods and services is here to stay. It can perform a useful service to consumers, but quackery and irresponsibility in the field need control. Said Dr. Wallace H. W. Wulfeck, of the Advertising Research Foundation's committee on motivational research: "Not more than twenty of the 120 firms offering this kind of service are really qualified to do it."[7]

A significant point of view on the scientific engineering of consent was expressed by the editor of *Printer's Ink,* an advertising trade journal. He said in part:

Are scientists getting ahead of advertising's ability to use their findings wisely? . . . As few and tentative as are the studies in the field of psychological research, they

[7] Harry Henderson, "Why You Buy," *Pageant,* January, 1956, p. 9.

point the way to a more skillful manipulation of the human mind. The results can be as dangerous as they are significant. . . . The very real possibility that the techniques of social research and psychology will be used by those ill-fitted to use them presents to advertising one of the greatest challenges in its long history.[8]

Advertising and Competition

On June 2, 1966, Donald F. Turner, head of the Antitrust Division of the Justice Department, spoke to the Federal Bar Association. He suggested that excessive outlays on advertising may well have an important impact on the degree of market power which is exercised in many industries, and that it may defeat the objectives of our antitrust laws. He went on to say that there is a real danger that new firms may not be able to compete with firms having large advertising budgets. This would stifle competition in the marketplace and hurt both small businesses and consumers. The consumer is at a disadvantage in a noncompetitive market because the price tends to be higher. Even if the price is not higher than those of similar products produced by a few small manufacturers, the tendency of purchasers is to choose the well-known (advertised) brand over one which is unknown. Since there are few quality standards on most consumer goods in the United States, choosing the better-known brand is his best way to cope with the problem of uncertainty. Moreover, where the firms in an industry are few in number, the large firms with huge advertising budgets achieve extensive monopoly rewards. Mr. Turner cited several studies to support his central thesis.

Studies seem to show that increased efficiencies do not necessarily occur when large firms acquire smaller competitors. Dr. Joe S. Bain, professor of economics at the University of Southern California, found that the largest companies in eight out of ten industries producing highly advertised goods could operate just as efficiently if they were substantially smaller. His findings were corroborated recently by John M. Blair, chief economist for the Senate Antitrust and Monopoly Subcommittee. Figure 2-2, Economic Concentration,[9] shows, for example, that the big-four breakfast cereal makers (Kellogg, General Mills, General Foods, and Quaker Oats) had a 79 percent share in 1947. By 1963 they had increased their share to 86 percent. These companies spent about $27 million on network television in 1963. The story repeats itself in the other highly advertised items in this study. The conclusion drawn in the study is that the ability to afford network television "tends to give the big companies a larger share of the market and force small companies, which cannot afford network advertising costs, to merge with them."

The point is that in most firms which command large advertising budgets and have a national market for their products, volume is such that the minimum level of production costs has long since been reached. When advertising costs of a company, or for a given product, reach a level of 20 to 40 per-

[8] Reported in *Consumer Reports,* June, 1957, p. 301.

[9] Senate Subcommittee Hearings, part V, 1966, on "Economic Concentration."

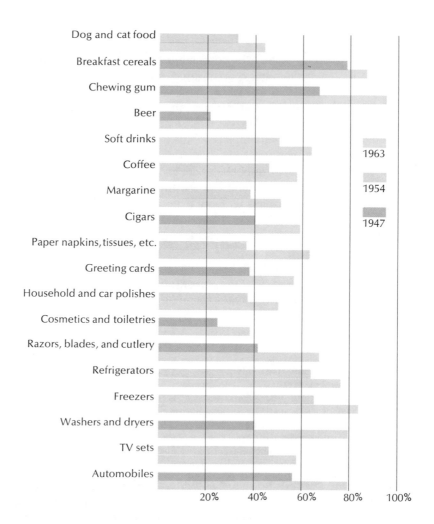

Figure 2-2   **Economic Concentration.**

cent of sales, it is unrealistic to accept the argument that costs and prices are being reduced. Rarely is the most heavily advertised product of a given type the least expensive one on the market. The aim of a company is not to minimize costs but to maximize profits. The argument that mass advertising reduces prices, as the president of Procter and Gamble stated, [10] is true only if the industry is one whose costs of production per unit decline as production increases. The validity of this argument as a whole has not been established. What we do know is that advertising, as practiced by large companies, is becoming a powerful substitute for price competition. The important question, then, is, What are the appropriate ways of dealing with the abuses of advertising?

[10] In *Advertising Age,* Nov. 14, 1960.

Solutions?

First, it is well to recall that the consumer's basic quarrel with today's advertising is that the medium has been misused, that it has often led more to consumer bewilderment than to enlightenment. What are the appropriate ways of dealing with the abuses of advertising? In working toward a program of self-regulation it is important to keep in mind that the right of the advertiser is not to secure non-price competition; it is not the right to keep important facts about a product from the consumer by either omission or misrepresentation; it is not the right to monopolize public channels of communication; it is not the right to turn markets into a jungle or to shriek stupidities and distortions; it is not the right to make claims for more than is scientifically known about what can be expected from any drug; it is not the right to destroy competition in the marketplace through mergers; and it is not the right to be unethical just because it is "legal."

Presently we have advertising bounded on one side by clients some of whom want to sell any way they can. On another side are consumers, who are increasingly critical and unbelieving. On yet another side is government, increasingly concerned and impatient.

Is Self-regulation the Answer?   E. B. Weiss, a spokesman for advertising, stated recently that

> Advertising must close its credibility gap—and not through propaganda, but through more responsible leadership. . . . This business of advertising needs intelligent, critical analysis—needs it seriously . . . from within its own ranks. . . . Its cancerous growths simply must be eradicated. Unfortunately, to date this has not happened through pressures generated from within advertising. The common habit of the advertising fraternity is to defend advertising, right or wrong. . . . Unfortunately, what advertising has been getting is a new school of irresponsible thinking that is strident, controversial, abusive, insulting, flip and undignified.[11]

Pretty strong criticism from a responsible, well-known advertising and merchandising executive. It would seem, then, that not much can be expected from advertising people because they have developed a functional blindness to their own defects. The American Association of Advertising Agencies' excellent study on "Consumer Judgment of Advertising" found that 53 percent of consumers agreed that advertisements did not present a true picture of the product advertised. The study also found that a large percentage of consumers were just plain unhappy about the total amount of advertising on television and radio. What has the industry done to improve this situation? Two years have elapsed, and despite efforts by advertising leaders like John Crichton and others, little interest has been generated because "they won't see their problems." Does this mean that Congress will have to do the job for them in the form of truth-in-advertising legislation?

A Truth-in-advertising Law.   Advertising has generally been under attack in terms of its "truthfulness" and omission of "important facts" about a prod-

11*Op. cit.,* pp. 24 - 27.

uct. Today critics are raising serious questions about advertising's influence over the structure of our economy, its social responsibilities, its ethics, its morality, and its esthetics. Years ago railroads, banks, public utilities, and stock exchanges were the targets of public criticism. The end results were the ICC, the Federal Reserve Board, the SEC, and other congressional legislation. It is possible that advertising may not be able to clean up its own problems and, thus, will invite congressional action.

Action by the Courts.   On April 11, 1967, the U.S. Supreme Court struck a blow in the cause of the consumer. It did so by concurring, 7 to 0, with a Federal Trade Commission finding that the nation's largest advertiser, Procter and Gamble, violated the antitrust laws in 1957 when it acquired the Clorox Chemical Company. The FTC was largely persuaded, in annulling the merger, by the very large television advertising power gained for Clorox household bleach as a result of the merger. Television, the FTC said, can be a monopoly tool in the hands of a very large advertiser, who can get special discounts and other privileges not available to a small advertiser. FTC proved to the Court that through television commercials and promotion, P & G spent over $5,400,000 in 1957 to promote the name "Clorox," which sold at a higher price generally than competitive products despite the fact that the product was no better than rival products; that bigness was not needed to efficiently sell this product because the processes were not subject to a patent or a trade secret; and that rivals priced their product below Clorox and made a good profit; that the only difference in sales statistics (Clorox had 48.8 percent of total sales and its nearest rival, Purex, had 15.7 percent) was not product differentiation but the ability to preempt commercial time on television networks on a national scale.

One crucial test of a merger's legality, then, may be whether economies of much advertising will be passed along to the consumer in the form of lower prices. The federal government may now have the weapon it needs to reverse the trend toward unwarranted economic concentration in consumer goods industries achieved through the use of unfair advantages available only to big advertisers. Vigorous use of the weapon could bring about a deemphasis of advertising as a substitute for price competition to the benefit of the consumer and of private enterprise.

Comparative Testing of Brands.   In the proposals of Donald F. Turner, mentioned earlier, he suggests the use of federal funds to support the work done by independent, nonprofit consumer goods testing organizations like Consumers Union. Comparative testing of consumer products is very expensive and the small Consumers Union's budget of $6.5 million would be woefully inadequate. It would be a great challenge to the advertising industry to have the facts about comparative products widely distributed. It could mean that our so-called competitive system to which we give lip service might really become competitive. Moreover, more information on more consumer products can have a substantial effect on improving the consumer's standard of living.

[12] *Consumer Reports,* July, 1967, p. 360.

Caveat Venditor.   The best element of business supports the principle that honesty should govern competitive enterprises, and that the rule *caveat emptor* (let the buyer beware) should not prevail in the marketplace. *Caveat venditor* (let the seller beware) is a more recent principle which might be extended to the advertising agency promoting a client's product. In 1965, for the first time, an advertising agency was held responsible for what it said about a client's product. [13] The product was Regimen, a popular reducing pill, on which $10 million was spent for promotion between 1957 and 1961. The Federal District Court imposed a $50,000 fine and an 18-month jail sentence on Regimen's promoter for deceiving the public, and a $53,000 fine on Drug Research Corporation, the promoter's company. The advertising agency was found guilty of using the mails and television to defraud, and was fined $50,000. The agency argued that it wrote the advertising but had nothing to do with the truth of the claims made for the product. The court ruled otherwise.

If the court decision is upheld, it may help advertising agencies to resolve some of the issues which they refuse to face up to. There is no good reason why every advertisement should not be a warranty to the purchaser concerning the price and the quality of a product with the burden of proof laid squarely upon the seller—that all the claims made for the product represent a full disclosure of the merits or demerits of the product in its intended use. Advertising should not be poised on the slippery edge of irrelevance or misrepresentation.

Free Choice.   Free choice is the core of democracy in our economic system. But free choice depends upon a fair exchange of knowledge—knowledge of price, knowledge of quality, knowledge of quantity, and knowledge of the limitations of a product for which we exchange a fixed and standard value of our incomes in dollars and cents. Uninformed choice is not free. Advertisers so often say that when a consumer buys a product, it is a vote of confidence in the agency and in the company. But one cannot boast of a vote of confidence when the voter has been denied the knowledge necessary to rational choice.

What is likely to happen? Nobody really knows. But there is some leadership in the advertising fraternity that understands the nature of the problems. Earlier we quoted E. B. Weiss saying that "advertising must close its credibility gap and not by propaganda, but through more responsible leadership. . . . Maybe it is high time for the manufacturer to beware, rather than the shopper to beware."

Another advertising executive, Leo Greenland, said: "The objective of consumerism is to protect the consumer, to make sure that he knows what he is buying. . . . As a consumer, I'm glad. As an advertising man, I'm glad. Consumerism will provide a new challenge for the creation of exciting advertising that views products from the consumer's side." [14]

[13] *Changing Times,* October, 1965.
[14] *Advertising Age,* Feb. 19, 1968.

QUESTIONS FOR DISCUSSION

1.   While the wife apparently still does most of the purchasing for the family and makes even more of the decisions on what should be bought, how do you account for the increase in husband and wife shopping together?

2.   Comment on the following statements.
   a.   "High price means high quality."
   b.   "Women prefer to be led into decisions."
   c.   "Women make more impulsive purchases than men."
   d.   "Men are generally satisfied in shopping at one store."

3.   In what ways are our choices determined by what we want out of life?

4.   What are the ingredients of an adequate standard of living according to your desires?

5.   What part does consumer choice play in our daily living?

6.   How is consumer choice restricted?

7.   Is intelligent choice making always based on reasoned judgment?

8.   Perhaps you have recently purchased a hat, sweater, suit, dress, radio, or something else of sufficient value and price to require careful consideration. Why did you buy it? Make a serious effort to get down to your basic motives. Be honest. Avoid rationalization except as it may have been a factor in the purchase.

9.   Why is it difficult to analyze motives for choices and purchases?

10.   Is it necessarily wrong to spend money to win social recognition and to feel more adequate or superior?

11.   "People are creatures of habit." In what respect do you regard yourself as a habit buyer?

12.   Are consumer buying habits good or bad?

13.   In what respect do you agree or disagree with the foregoing analyses of men and women as shoppers?

14.   Business is spending millions of dollars on motivational research to influence you to buy more goods and services. As a consumer, should you try to build a defense against this psychological barrage? If so, what can you do?

15.   Why do consumers feel that they are not the "final arbiters" when they spend their money?

16.   Explain the statement: "There is an ever-increasing informational gap between producers and consumers."

17.   Are there any dangers in the ways that the human mind is influenced by some advertisers?

ACTIVITY PROBLEMS

1.   Make a study of the real underlying motives that determined your purchase of certain merchandise, services, or pleasures. For each purchase, give the reasons that come to mind first. Then consider possible hidden or subcon-

scious motives. Would you spend your money again for the same item, service, or fun?

2. Examine several advertisements in popular magazines. Identify and classify the kinds of sales appeal in the advertisements. How effective are these appeals?

3. After reading Thorstein Veblen's theory about "conspicuous display" in *The Theory of the Leisure Class,* can you find illustrations in present-day consumption? Are there new motives for consumption today?

4. Trace the history of a particular fashion. Who created this fashion? Were consumers ready for it? Did it need sales promotion? Was there any noticeable consumer resistance? How long did the fashion last? Who was most satisfied with this particular fashion article? Was there an economic waste?

5. William James said that "man is a bundle of habits." Some of these habits may be good and others bad. How would you try to change a bad habit? How would you strengthen a good habit? Reflect on the habits that influence choices in the market.

6. Is your behavior as a consumer consistent with your philosophy? This is really a tough question. It involves probing questions like these: "What do you want out of life?" "Have your choices been consistent with your goals?" "Are your goals consistent with your moral principles?"

7. What is meant by "the good life"? What is meant by "plain living" and by "high thinking"?

8. How have beliefs changed through the years (early man, Greeks, Romans, Ascetics, Epicureans, Puritans, and so on)?

SUGGESTED READINGS

Bishop, Jr., James, and Henry W. Hubbard: *Let the Seller Beware,* The National Press, Washington, D.C., 1969.

Greenland, Leo: "Consumerism," *Advertising Age,* Feb. 19, 1968.

Katona, George: *The Powerful Consumer,* McGraw-Hill Book Company, New York, 1960, chap. 9.

Magnuson, Senator Warren G., and Jean Carper: *The Dark Side of the Marketplace,* Prentice-Hall, Inc., Englewood Cliffs, N.J., 1968.

Maynes, E. Scott: "The Payoff for Intelligent Consumer Decision-Making," *Journal of Home Economics,* February, 1969.

Metzen, Edward: "Advertising as a Source of Information," in *Freedom of Information in the Marketplace,* School of Journalism, University of Missouri, Columbia, Mo., 1967, pp. 83-90.

Myers, James H., and W. H. Reynolds: *Consumer Behavior and Marketing Management,* Houghton Mifflin Co., Boston, 1967.

Troelstrup, Arch W.: "The Consumer Interest and Our Competitive System," in *Freedom of Information in the Market-Place,* School of Journalism, University of Missouri, Columbia, Mo., 1967, pp. 77-82.

chapter 3
MONEY AND
MARITAL HAPPINESS

Spending money may be America's favorite sport, but marriage is our favorite institution. Ninety percent of our population marries. Why do so many marry? Ask the average married couple, and they will probably answer, "We love each other." Just as simple as that.

Most of these couples believed that they could have a happy and successful marriage. But love alone is not enough, apparently. More and more marriages end in divorce. Prior to World War II, there was one divorce to every five marriages in this country. In 1945, there was about one divorce to every 3.0 marriages. Currently the ratio is 1 to 4. And we ask, "Why?" What happens to all these marriages that begin with such high hope?

CHANGING TIMES AND CUSTOMS

Customs are changing so fast that each generation lives in a world of its own, known only in part to the one that precedes it or the one that follows. Home as grandmother knew it does not exist. It can never return. We have a kind of family life that is quite different from grandmother's family. Of course, we cannot and should not cut ourselves off from our roots. There are certain basic family needs that can be served well by the application of grandmother's philosophy. But the differences between the generations are great. We need, desperately, to understand these differences and then do something about them to help young couples to "live happily ever after."

In 1890, about 65 percent of American families lived in the rural areas. In 1965, 67 percent were living in metropolitan centers.[1] Grandmother never went far from home. She was almost constantly under neighborly surveillance. City young people are free from external and neighborly controls within 10 minutes from the time they leave the house or apartment. They are on their own. Their standards, on the whole, come from within themselves. At first, these standards are usually set by the home. Soon young people find that many of the home standards are in conflict with other standards. What was "right" at one time becomes relative to the time, the place, and the people. And this experience is likely to be confusing.

Challenging Choices

In 1870, there were only about 338 vocations. Today, as a result of industrialization, there are from 30,000 to 35,000 vocations. A son no longer has to follow in his father's footsteps. A daughter can have a career in the business and professional world. She can work or not, as she pleases. She does not need to marry for her "board and keep."

The automobile, too, has changed our recreational experiences tremendously. Cars and good roads have revolutionized personal activities. The choices are numerous and confusing. The problems of wise choice about where to go, what to do, how much to spend, and what to be are always present. From this

[1] *Finance Facts,* 1968 Yearbook, National Consumer Finance Association, Washington, D.C., 1968.

array of new experiences, and many not mentioned here, you must select those that are to be your way of life. The choices made now will be, in large measure, the blueprint for marriage later.

We use money and spend it as our parents and grandparents probably never dreamed of using and spending it. We live in a money world. We depend on money for food, clothing, shelter, recreation, and education. We even depend on money alone to take care of us when we are old, rather than the family farm or a family business.

We run much of our lives on a cash basis, and therefore feel the pressures of money. And money troubles may be a cause of worry. Money can set up a host of problems. Sometimes there are tragic disagreements in a family about how money is to be used. And at times money may become a symbol of other disagreements and problems. If a member of a family hungers for an argument, he can always argue about money. Can it be that we are confused about the right values and goals for a happy family life?

THE CONFUSED AMERICAN FAMILY

Why are American families the richest in the world and yet so often in debt and unhappy? First, we should be careful to avoid false and antisocial answers to the question of why American families are increasingly getting into debt. We need to consider the possibility that the real answer may be that many families are very confused about what standard of living they ought to have. Second, we should recognize that this confusion is not only the fault of the borrower. The confusion is probably the result of tremendous changes taking place in our society. The third idea is that American society is certainly going to keep on changing. And with change, we are likely to witness the rise of new standards and morals about borrowing and saving money. And some of us are going to disagree with the new standards.

It may be alarming to read about the $99.2 billion short-term consumer credit debt in 1967. Some people believe that most consumers are so deeply in debt that they cannot possibly get out. In fact, they have been saying that for decades. Yet somehow most debtors manage to liquidate their debts.

There must be a limit to debts, but the basic problem may not be whether or not the debts will be liquidated. They continue to be liquidated right along. The real problem is: "Why has it become so common for families to have such worries and guilt feelings about their debts?" The answers to this question are important because they are related to money and marital conflicts.

Many of us are familiar with the guilty suspicion that our neighbors are having less difficulty in paying their bills than we are having. Actually, this may not be true. In a study A. C. Spectorsky made of residents in the wealthier suburbs of New York City, where men were earning from $12,000 to $30,000 a year, he found that the average family was spending about 40 percent more than its annual income. He also found that every Tom or Harry in the community believed that he was the only man who had to borrow $500 to buy a hi-fi set, while his neighbor, Dick, could afford to go to Bermuda. Dick felt guilty about owing $500 for his "fly now, pay later" Bermuda vacation when his neighbor, Tom, could afford an expensive hi-fi set.

Tom and Dick illustrate a lot of boring statistics. Most families know that it has become quite common among American families, except the poorest and the richest, to owe enough money to feel anxious and guilty.

Individual worries are not the only problems resulting from the high consumer debt. Some economists mention it as a factor in the instability of our economy. And some sociologists have mentioned it as a factor in social disorganization. Psychiatrists mention it as a factor in the climbing rate of mental illness.

Willingness to Incur Debts

So the fact that relatively well-off families are becoming more and more willing to incur debts is an important change in our society. One of the consequences of this change, especially for "young marrieds" and "growing families," is that this system is promoting debt as a way of life. In other words, more families want more immediate possessions than they can afford on a cash basis, and consumer credit is made to order for them.

Why has an increasingly large number of families changed from paying cash to assuming debts? There are many answers, but most of them appear to be unsatisfactory.

The first theory is found in most consumer-economics textbooks and in the Federal Reserve Board's excellent six-volume study of consumer credit. This answer says that people always have wanted more things than they could afford at a given time and that consumer credit was a natural evolution of merchandising methods to satisfy these wants. People used to buy laundry service from a man who owned a laundry, and transportation from a man who owned a livery stable, but nowadays they buy their own washer-dryer, their own automobile, and their own TV set. They can do this because they can get credit to buy these and many other expensive possessions immediately.

All this is true, but it is not the complete answer. People have always wanted more than they had, but Noah could not have paid for the Ark on the installment plan because such plans did not exist then. Credit is so much a natural evolution of distribution methods that you cannot help but wonder why it almost never existed until the twentieth century.

Part of the answer is simple. Throughout most of history, borrowing and lending at interest had been considered immoral and had been strictly taboo. The lender was usually considered a parasite and often a criminal. The borrower was usually considered improvident and even a sinner.

What Happened to Traditional Morals?

What changed such morals? Can it be that more people use more credit nowadays because they are economically more rational? The danger of this answer or theory is that it assumes the borrower is not confused by moral traditions and is acting by some kind of new, sensible standard. But the credit manager who assumes that every loan applicant knows what he is doing is asking for trouble.

The other two kinds of inadequate theory offer an answer to what happened to traditional morals, which is that people are becoming more immoral. There are the "naïve moralists" who blame high debt levels on immoral individuals, and the "sophisticated moralists" who blame it on a bad system that forces people into debt. The naïve moralists are people like John Keats, who said that immoral people are imitating the government's philosophy of deficit spending, and that we are becoming a nation of immature people who like to open Christmas presents the week before Thanksgiving. Or they are men like William Whyte, the sociologist, who says borrowers are immoral because of a contagious social-psychological neurosis called "budgetism"; or Eugene Barnes, a psychologist who believes that people have no "credit conscience."

But how can these explanations explain enough, especially when we consider that year after year the same percentage of different income classes have personal debts? About one-third of factory-worker families are in debt; about one-half of white-collar workers are in debt even though their average income is higher than that of the self-employed. It seems a strange thing when the same percentage of individuals decides to be "immoral" as concerns debt year after year in the different groups of our society. It is a little like criminals. Criminals have been considered immoral, and society has generally worked on them as individuals to mend their ways. But when society realized that slums turn out high percentages of criminals, a study of the effects of their environment began. We still don't know all that causes criminals, but at least society no longer believes that they are merely immoral individuals.

Involvement of the Social System

In much the same way that slums help produce criminals, white-collar jobs help produce debtors. More white-collar workers have debts than self-employed people, whether the income of the self-employed is higher, lower, or the same. It would seem, therefore, that the social system is involved in some way.

The sophisticated moralists recognize this fact. The naïve moralists still insist that borrowers are basically immoral, but they blame the system for making them that way. John McPartland, the novelist, blames the "easy credit system" for tempting him. A. C. Spectorsky, the sociologist who conducted the study in the wealthy New York City suburbs, blames the "status" system. John

Kenneth Galbraith, the economist, blames the whole economic system for just plain overselling of consumer goods.

All these suggestions are part of an adequate explanation. Perhaps they explain too much. The systems they mention do exert constant pressure. But they do not explain why, year after year, one-third of blue-collar workers do not have debts, nor do two-thirds of the self-employed, nor one-half of the white-collar workers.

Besides, history shows that it is best to be suspicious of every generation that says that the younger generation is becoming more and more immoral. As often as not it has turned out that the morals were changing, and that often the new morals were better for their times.

We have to remember that before social morals were established, it was all right for a man to knock any other man over the head and drag away his property and his woman. Most husbands are grateful for the change in morals since that time.

Basic personal morals like the Ten Commandments remain generally unchanged. But specific little morals, in areas like economic and political behavior, change with the times. Economic behavior that produced the Robber Barons of two generations ago and was admired, or at least accepted, at the time would now be immoral and illegal.

Are Credit Users Immoral?

It seems that when a set of morals becomes obsolete, and when there is no workable set of standards to replace the old ones, people become confused and begin experimenting until a suitable set of new morals is developed and accepted. Perhaps the rapid expansion of consumer credit represents that kind of experimenting, caused by that kind of confusion.

Let's consider the confusion that might make the former morals regarding thrift and debt become obsolete. In our early economy, capital had to be created largely by thrifty acts of individuals. Therefore, the virtue attributed to thrift, along with the moral taboo on using credit for consumer goods, was essential in causing a rapid rate of economic growth.

Thrift also had important motives for the individual. Before 1900, success came along usually with the "expansible possession"—that is, a little farm or a little shop or business that required only constant thrift to gain enough capital to become a big estate or a big factory or business.

But things have changed for the economic system and the individual. It appears at present that the economic system can form capital more easily than it can maintain purchasing power. And the individual does not as often find success with the expansible possession. Instead, he pins his hopes on the forward-looking job. To make the most of a job or position, thrift is not of much help. What is needed is a standard of living that will show that the family appreciate and want better things—even if they have to borrow to buy them.

So it seems that for both the economic system and the individual times have changed, and it makes more sense to attach moral virtue to spending than to thrift.

This is by no means a full explanation of the eagerness for credit. Perhaps social change could have removed the moral restrictions on credit without its resulting in a $317.8 billion total debt if American families were not so eager to borrow. Perhaps this eagerness may be the result, not of confusion about changing morals, but of confusion about standards of living.

Desire for Change in Standard of Living

Your *level* of living is based on the amount of money you spend. Your *standard* of living is the way you want to live. One man's standard may require a shack by the seashore, one good suit, and regular meals. Another man's standard may require a trilevel home, two cars, and a yardman.

Where do these standards come from? Through most of human history, they simply became a part of a people during the process of their growing up in families. Chances are that most of us came from a middle-class family. Chances are that a majority had grandfathers or even fathers who were farmers, immigrants, or factory workers with less education than their children. The point is that each generation could not live according to the standards of the preceding generation because each grew up in a different environment. And millions of American families have been experiencing this environmental change.

In a situation where every generation is living in a different kind of world from the preceding one, of what use are many of the living standards of grandfathers or even fathers? Each generation has to experiment with new standards. We are generally guided by our own ambitions and by the standards of friends— the Joneses, who have debts we don't know about. Or maybe we are guided by the mass media—TV, motion pictures, magazines. If, under these circumstances, the average American family were not confused about an approximate standard of living, you would have something really difficult to explain.

The growth of consumer credit, then, may not be so much a matter of immorality as a consequence of confusion, and this confusion may be rooted in actual moral social change, not in bad psychology.

Near the beginning of this century, credit institutions and others helped make it respectable for people to admit that they needed to borrow in emergencies. At midcentury, it was standard practice for young married couples to place heavy mortgages on their future earnings in order to start out with a standard packet of durable goods when they needed them most. This packet might now include a stove, refrigerator, washing machine, dishwasher, a car, a television set, and a record player. By the end of the century, who knows? A family-size airplane, clothes that you toss into the ashcan after a few weeks' use—well, you guess!

The trend will likely be more use of "buy now, pay later," until we move out of the form of credit that has induced ownership and move into a system of less ownership but more continuous renting of needed goods and services. If this happens, credit will have a different meaning.

And perhaps we ought to do our part to eliminate the obsolete feelings of worry and guilt that keep people from talking about their use of credit. Too many people are like the man who went to the psychiatrist because he worried all the time. The doctor asked how he lived, and he listed numerous expensive habits. The doctor said, "This is wonderful, why worry?" The client said he was making only $5,000 a year. The psychiatrist answered, "My friend, you're not sick. You're simply overextended and overconfused."

Education Neglects Our Needs

Most families perform their functions well when they have learned how. Grandmother's family, for example, taught children the kind of responsibilities they needed in their time. It was really an apprenticeship. And apparently they did a pretty good job as long as the family functions remained the same. But when the family functions changed, this system broke down. Something else was obviously needed.

The modern family has a real job in building personalities capable of adequately meeting the complexities of modern life. Understanding a child today is quite different and considerably more complicated or involved than it was years ago. Apprenticeship will no longer do the trick. Customs change too rapidly. We need families that can grow in their ability to live together happily and successfully. Divorce and separation statistics and other evidence of marital discord indicate that something is out of gear somewhere.

Money and Quality of Family Life

The individuals entering into marriage bring attitudes, impressions, and expectations created throughout years of separate existence in a money society. They also use money in a variety of ways. Personal habits of spending are often used in instances of discordant marital relationships as a point of attack by the partner, or are viewed as an attack. For example, a husband may be dominating with regard to his wife, rigidly holding her to a tight budget. He may come from a home in which the father was the authoritative, thrifty provider, as responsible for the financial management of his home as for his business. On the other hand, this controlled disbursement of money may be a measure of the husband's recollections about a hungry youth in a period of economic depression and insecurity. To certain neurotic husbands, money may be an unconscious symbol of masculinity and power. The wife's retaliation, irrespective of the factors underlying his actions, may take several forms. She may spend money wastefully as an expression of hostility toward him, or even at an unconscious level to maintain a dominant role in her own right. She may handle the situation simply by making no effort to operate within the budget he has prescribed. To his practice of limiting her funds as a way of keeping his mate in a dependent relation to him, the wife may respond by setting limits of her own. She may deny his basic psychological needs—expressed, perhaps, through gambling, or excessive use of money for alcohol—in charges of inadequate support and by refusal to feed him properly.

Considerable tension may be aroused because of the wife's working for pay outside the home. Problems on this score are minimal if there are common goals understood and accepted by both partners. Many money problems grow out of environmental economic situations. There may be, for example, an unexpected loss of a job, or a reduction in income. Or the nature of the husband's work may involve considerable traveling. But if the partners have achieved a satisfactory joint ego ideal, and if they are reasonably well-integrated personalities, they are likely to make the necessary adjustments to situations.

In the remainder of the chapter we cannot hope to thoroughly explore marital adjustment with respect to a factor so important as the use of money. We shall only summarize a few studies on the use of money and point out the importance of seeking a practical, workable plan for meeting this inescapable aspect of marriage.

WHAT MONEY DOES TO MARRIAGE

Marriage experts, in general, agree that some conflict is inevitable. Some conflict is open quarreling. Then there may be what William Graham Sumner termed "antagonistic cooperation." This kind of conflict may be more subtle. Some couples learn to live with such problems. It would seem, then, that the attitude taken toward a disagreement is significant in working out a satisfactory solution.

Conflict in Marriage

What causes marital conflict? Marriage counselors are not absolutely certain about the basic causes of conflict. As tensions develop in a family, any incident may spark the disagreement. The incident may not actually be the real cause for the conflict. Thus what seems to be the cause may not be so at all. An analysis of the major causes of conflict as reported by married couples may give us some tips for successful marriage.

The *Ladies' Home Journal* asked representative American women the question: "What things have you noticed husbands and wives quarrel about most frequently?" The reasons were given in this order: money, jealousy, rearing of children, little things, drinking, and in-laws.

TABLE 3-1   EFFECTIVENESS OF COLLEGE EDUCATION

	PERCENTAGE OF HUSBANDS WHO FREQUENTLY DISAGREED	PERCENTAGE OF WIVES WHO FREQUENTLY DISAGREED
Management of income	17	19
Religion	10	7
Politics	11	14
Relatives	16	20
Entertainment of relatives	7	9
Choice of friends	10	9
Ideals of conduct	9	10
Philosophy of life	12	12
Recreations	16	14
Entertainment of friends	7	9

SOURCE: C. Robert Pace, *They Went to College,* The University of Minnesota Press, Minneapolis, 1941, p. 82. Reprinted with permission.

Clifford Adams, Penn State psychologist, reported the testimony from 1,000 married couples.[2] He selected the replies from 100 of the most unhappy marriages. The following reasons for marriage conflict are in the order of their frequency: lack of companionship, lack of money, sex, in-laws, housework, children, social life, personal traits, lack of affection, and religious differences.

Judson T. Landis, professor of sociology at the University of California, received information from 409 couples, married an average of 20 years, who were parents or friends of students taking the marriage course at Michigan State College.[3] This group was above average in income and education. Most of the husbands and wives agreed that it had taken longer to achieve sex adjustment than adjustment in any other area. The second most difficult adjustment was in reaching an agreement on how to spend the family income. For some of them, it took an average of 7 years to end disagreement. About 10 percent were still quarreling over money problems. Other causes of conflict included quarreling over social and recreational activities, in-laws, religion and mutual friends.

Effectiveness of College Education on Marital Conflict.   C. Robert Pace reported on a study of 951 former University of Minnesota students between the ages of 25 and 34. Half were men, half were women; half had graduated, and half had left college after 1 to 3 years. The questionnaire aimed to probe the effectiveness of a modern college education. The results, shown in Table 3-1, Effectiveness of College Education, throw light on the inadequacy of family relations education.

Disagreements occurred most frequently over the management of money.

[2] *Ladies' Home Journal,* January, 1949, p. 26. Reprinted with special permission. Copyright 1949. The Curtis Publishing Company.

[3] Associated Press report, May 29, 1948.

This is an interesting sidelight, because money management is the most frequent cause of conflict among couples in the upper third or fourth of the nation's families according to economic status. Pace says that "bringing together evidence from all parts of the study relating to income management leads to the generalization that, although many of the young adults expressed a desire for more information about ways to economize, many were also engaging in uneconomical practices."

A brief analysis of the discrepancies and inconsistencies between attitudes and practices among this group is most revealing. In spite of relatively high incomes, most of them were dissatisfied with their incomes. While they said that they had good food, were well dressed, comfortable, and happy on their present incomes, nevertheless 35 percent of them found it difficult to keep out of debt. Over 40 percent expressed the need for money management information, yet less than half had a family spending plan. Furthermore, their marketing habits were needlessly expensive. About one-fourth had medical indebtedness, yet less than one-fifth of these took advantage of health insurance plans. With such discrepancies between feelings and practices, it is not difficult to understand why income mismanagement was a frequent source of conflict between these husbands and wives.

The case studies of about 100 college graduates from coast to coast (78 of whom were married) by the Merrill-Palmer School in Detroit throws further light on the nature of marital conflicts. Table 3-2, Percentage of Problems of 78 Married Women, shows that the chief issue for marital difficulties was the conflict over finances. More specifically, these conflicts were over (1) how

TABLE 3-2 PERCENTAGE OF PROBLEMS OF 78 MARRIED WOMEN

TYPE OF PROBLEM	PERCENT OF CASES
Personality	98
Financial	97
Health	96
Husband-wife	89
Relations with associates	88
Recreational	84
Housekeeping	82
Relations with relatives	80
Parent-child	78
Crisis	74
In-law	60
Sex	56
Religion	52
Vocation	34
Education	20

SOURCE: Reproduced from Robert G. Foster and Pauline Park Wilson, *Women after College*. Copyright 1942 by Columbia University Press, p. 27.

the money was to be spent, and (2) who was to make the decision. Most of the women had taken a course in economics in college. Yet there seemed to be little or no carryover from such a course into the everyday problems of money management. When the counselors mentioned budgeting, nearly all the women resisted the idea as a device of Satan designed to restrict their spending habits. Nor did the size of income alter the general complaint that they could not make ends meet.

These women had almost entirely ignored the evident need to be prepared to meet certain inevitabilities in their lives—to be intelligent, effective, conscientious consumers. Most of them had prepared for a job, but neither college nor home had prepared them for the time when they would give up a job and manage a home.

It is strange that, although many college women expect to marry and have a home and children, few really prepare for this important function. Fewer yet do any mature thinking on combining homemaking and a career. Too many do not look on homemaking as a career for which they have to fit themselves. This fact goes a long way toward solving many of the problems that puzzle social economists and moralists. For it is at the bottom of much of the discontent that permeates many homes.

Problem of Human Relations

Money management may be the primary cause for marital discord. Behind the problems of money management, however, and all the other so-called "big" causes are the hard-to-analyze human behavior relationships. Whether the area of conflict concerns money or sex, characteristic and basic behavior patterns are revealed in subtle and, at times, unconscious ways. Along with each outward act go certain feelings and attitudes that are impossible or difficult to see.

In some cases, two persons will react differently to the same general problem. For example, a certain husband battled continuously with his wife over her "extravagant spending." Another husband's reaction to his wife's extravagant spending was: "I'll just prove to her that I can make more money than she can spend." The attitude toward the same general situation was quite different. Open conflict resulted in the one case, and an acceptance of the situation in the other.

It would seem logical to conclude that we need to discover the personality traits that lead married people to quarrel over money, sex, or any of the other "big" causes of family disagreements.

Psychologists tell us that the relationship between husband and wife is loaded with disguised impulses. And sometimes the least important part is what we see. Yet what we see and hear are extremely important, because they may be the advance signs—a symptom of what cannot be seen. A timely recognition of the symptom may give the clue that will lead to the solving of the difficulty.

Income versus Success and Happiness

In New York, a well-dressed woman called on a personal finance advisor at her bank. She said that, despite her husband's income of $18,000 a year, they had no money for fun. A Hollywood actor with an income of $100,000 a year went bankrupt. He had only $3,000 in assets to meet liabilities of $50,000.

The assumption of certain economists that most personal problems would be solved if the income of each couple could be raised sufficiently is not borne out by some studies of marital adjustment. In the case studies of 78 married women, the Merrill-Palmer School clinicians found that regardless of their incomes—whether they had $3,000, $5,000, or $10,000—they felt that it was insufficient.[4] In fact, as income increased in arithmetical ratio, personal problems seemed to increase in geometric ratio.

Somewhat in contrast, Cottrell's study of 526 couples found that families on moderate income seemed to have made better adjustments than when incomes were either high or low.[5] Hamilton, in studying 200 persons—50 husbands with incomes over $5,000, and another 50 husbands whose incomes were less—found happiness approximately equally distributed.[6] Terman found little relationship between happiness and income.[7]

Robert C. Williamson reported that economic variables are more important in marital adjustment than has been generally observed in previous investigations.[8] A total of 210 couples, representing a cross section of the Los Angeles white population, were interviewed in their homes by two interviewers. The husband and the wife were interviewed separately with a questionnaire that contained personal background and social and economic items, as well as a marital-adjustment test. On the scores secured in the adjustment test, the sample was divided into happily and unhappily married groups. The happy group totaled 86 men and 85 women; the unhappy group, 66 men and 62 women. There was an intermediate small group that could be considered neither happy nor unhappy. Some of the important economic variables in marital adjustment were these:

1.   Lower incomes (below $436 a month) prevailed among the unhappy group. Conversely, higher incomes were found among happy husbands and wives.
2.   Both the men and the women in the poor residential area were maritally less happy than those in the better areas.

[4] Robert G. Foster and Pauline Park Wilson, *Women after College*, Columbia University Press, New York, 1942, p. 51.

[5] Ernest W. Burgess and Leonard S. Cottrell, *Predicting Success or Failure in Marriage*, Prentice-Hall, Inc., Englewood Cliffs, N.J., 1939, pp. 152-153.

[6] G. V. Hamilton, *A Research in Marriage*, Albert & Charles Boni, Inc., New York, 1929, p. 97.

[7] Lewis M. Terman, *Psychological Factors in Marital Happiness*, McGraw-Hill Book Company, New York, 1938, pp. 169-171.

[8] Robert C. Williamson, "Economic Factors in Marital Adjustment," *Marriage and Family Living*, November, 1952.

3.   It was found that for both partners there was a higher percentage of happy marriages among those having savings of at least $600.

4.   The husbands who had no debts, or less than $300 in debts, were significantly happier than those who had $300 or more in debts.

5.   The highest proportion of happy husbands and a still higher proportion of happy wives were among the highest security ratings (insurance, savings, debts, and type and regularity of employment).

6.   There was no significant difference between the happy and unhappy groups in the matter of keeping budgeting records.

7.   There was a significant difference favoring successful adjustment among those who did not overspend more than two months per year.

8.   There was a significantly higher percentage of maladjustment among those who admitted having to borrow three or more times during the past 5 years than among those who borrowed less or not at all.

H. Ashley Weeks[9] and William J. Goode[10] in separate studies found an inverse relationship between economic level and divorce rate—the higher the economic level, the lower the rate, and vice versa. Even more important than the quantity of the money are the couple's attitude toward it and the use to which it is put.

University of Pennsylvania researchers[11] interviewed 300 couples to determine why and how often they quarreled. Two hundred were chosen from families that had at one time sought family counseling help. The others were from a group of couples who considered their marriages sufficiently successful to compete in a nationwide contest for "representative families" from each state. The husbands and wives were given a list of possible points of disagreement and asked to indicate, independently of each other, what they fought about and how often. The 300 couples rated their problems in order, going from points of most conflict to those of least conflict. Fights over "finances" headed the list as the most common occasion for conflict.

When the answers of the two groups—the 200 and the 100—were tabulated separately, it was found that the couples who had had marital trouble ranked the problems in almost the same order as those who had considered themselves happily married. The difference was not in the nature of issues but in the extent of disagreement. Ironically, the one thing husbands and wives in both groups tended to agree on was which issues they disagreed about.

Economic Factors in Marital Adjustment

Frances Lomas Feldman, who directed the research of the Money Management Project of the Welfare Planning Council of the Los Angeles Region, made these interesting observations of the feelings of people about money.

[9]"Differential Divorce Rates by Occupations," *Social Forces*, March, 1943, pp. 334-337.

[10]"Economic Factors and Marital Adjustment," *American Sociological Review*, December, 1951, pp. 802-812.

[11]Reported in *Changing Times*, October, 1966, pp. 21-22.

The world we live in is characterized by continual change. There are technological advances, increasing population with shifting urbanization and explosive suburbanization movements, economic depressions and recessions, wars, and changing fashions and standards of living. One pivotal factor, however, remains constantly important: money. But never before in the history of western civilization has the word "money" meant so much to so many. Money is the medium of exchange, a means for distributing the vast and increasing outpouring of the goods and services of our economic system. Money is a symbol of status and achievement, often the measure for human values and dignity. This is truly the age of the economic man.

Economists have tended to view money as having an objective reality, a life of its own, isolated from the emotional and intellectual life of the human beings whom it was designed to serve. They have applied complicated mechanistic concepts, frequently expressed in elaborate mathematical formulas, to describe objectively the flow and use of money. Recently, however, there has been a mounting awareness and emphasis on the importance of the so-called subjective aspects of money, on the unique significance of psychosocial influences. There is increasing cognizance that an essential ingredient in skillful working with people is the understanding of the objective and subjective influences which affect, and are the effect of, money—the understanding of the dynamics of the interactions in the socioeconomic and cultural climate in which the individual grows and develops.

The universality of money as a causative or symptomatic component in a strikingly high proportion of the problems and preoccupations of human beings in our culture is evidenced almost daily in the headlined stories in the public press. One reads about the distraught husband who kills his wife because of "arguments over finances," about the parent who solves his inability to provide for his children by ending their lives or by armed robbery. One reads about the divorce suit in which "stinginess" is offered as one justification for the action, or about the divorced wife petitioning for increased child support from the ex-spouse who has remarried and has another family to support.

The ironic humor of the many current cartoons with a money theme provides another barometer of the feelings of people in our society about money. [12]

Financial columnist Sylvia Porter in 1962 quoted top jurists as saying: "Quarreling about money is a major reason for America's unprecedented divorce rate. It is difficult to overestimate the vicious part financial trouble is playing in destroying the American home."

There are other, unexpected areas where failure to manage money properly can produce dire results. More and more personnel officers are asking applicants direct questions about how they handle their family income.

Couples seeking to adopt children through reputable agencies also must account for the disposition of their income. One case worker said: "Young couples—both employed and with joint incomes of from $12,000 to $14,000—come in here and tell us they have assets of no more than $200 or $300. Before we will even consider their application, we ask them to demonstrate to us that they can change their values. We give them a year to do it."

From these studies and surveys it is evident that economic variables are more important in marital adjustment than has been generally recognized. The chain of cause and effect, however, is very complex in marital adjust-

[12] *Journal of Home Economics,* December, 1957, p. 267.

ment. The relationship that exists, for example, between savings and a happy marriage may be due in part to education or high intelligence. Or the negative relationship of loss of income to marital happiness may be a reflection of some other factor, such as illness. All this adds up to the fact that economic factors have never received sufficient attention in the studies of marital relations.

Attitudes toward Spending Money

Happy working partnerships of husband and wife are not common. They are difficult to achieve, largely because of the complicated attitudes of both husband and wife toward money and work. Contemporary society is regrettably money-conscious. Too often a husband is judged, not by how fine a father he is, but by how good a provider he is.

If money stands for success and perhaps authority, the manipulation of the family income and spending takes on emotional relationships. These relations may be handled satisfactorily or disastrously, depending on the attitudes of husband and wife. A husband might ask his wife to come to him for every little expenditure. He may be led to feel that he is not a good provider. This feeling can easily creep into ordinary discussions. Can we afford a new car? Can we go away for the summer? Each of these questions may be interpreted as an attack on the husband's ability to provide adequate income. On the other hand, such things need not be turned in the direction of conflict if the attitude itself is proper.

Money matters, however, cannot always be handled rationally. Psychological attitudes toward spending money are as real as the money itself. One family may agree, for example, to spend one-fourth of their income on clothes. "And why not?" they say. "We get more fun out of planning and wearing new clothes than we do in seeing a dozen shows. We live within our income, and we like it this way." This attitude apparently is right for them. On the other hand, such disproportionate spending of money on clothes could be a focal point for a serious quarrel in another family.

"Living Up to the Joneses."   Spending more money than your neighbors is not necessarily dangerous to family happiness. But "living up to the Joneses" is potential dynamite, because such a mental attitude leads to the strain of living beyond one's means. When John found that his promising insurance business could not provide for everything that Jane and he wanted, he gave it up to enter his father-in-law's business. Soon John became so resentful over his lack of vocational independence and his wife's extravagance that divorce was the result. John returned to his first love, insurance, and later married a girl whose charge accounts were in harmony with their income.

Helen, a society girl, married Dick, whose wholesale vinegar business went bankrupt two years after their marriage. Helen's friends were sure she was headed for divorce. Instead, Helen mastered typing and shorthand and pitched in as her husband's secretary. Several years later, their business was flourishing. A woman who marries with the expectation of mink is likely to prove an unhappy partner if she finds herself wrapped in rabbit—unless she does something about her attitude.

Foster and Wilson, in reporting on the case studies at the Merrill-Palmer School, concluded that the economic position of her associates may accentuate many of the individual's attitudes about her own position.[13] They report that among a few of the women of the study who belonged to the same sorority there were wide differences in income. One woman, who had the lowest family income and was unable to dress and entertain as elaborately as the others, accepted the situation, participated actively in the group, and took life in her stride. In this same set was a woman whose income was several times as great. But she constantly complained about her clothes, her home, and so on. She felt that her income was insufficient.

Attitudes toward housekeeping problems are important, too. Dislike for household tasks, lack of skill, and difficulties with household help are usually the foremost problems in this area.[14] These dislikes and difficulties are important because they are related to family happiness and success. Some women manage these tasks well and are able to use artistic and creative ability in many of the household duties. The new household aids might help to solve some of these problems. But modern appliances will not of themselves alter attitudes toward household duties.

Too High a Financial Goal.   There is the danger, too, of setting the money goal too high. The young husband who is determined to make a million dollars before he reaches the ripe old age of 35 years is a menace to himself and his family. Edward was such a person.[15] Most of his friends and business associates thought he was a hard worker and never knew a day of worry in his life. He worked long and hard and seemed to thrive on it. Soon he had the highest salary in his office. Still he was not satisfied. A little success spurred him on to greater effort. He began to spend money lavishly, bought a large house, and put money in risky investments. He became so excited that he neither slept nor ate well.

Then Edward began to change. He lost his feeling of self-confidence. He was no longer so sure of his business judgment. He often stayed away from his office. He told his wife that he would soon lose his job and began to blame himself for ruining his family.

Most psychologists would call Edward's difficulty a "manic-depressive" illness. Manic-depressives become so when they are not attaining the goals they have set for themselves. Most of them are ambitious. They are overly

[13] Foster and Wilson, *op. cit.,* p. 51.

[14] *Ibid.,* pp. 48-50.

[15] George Thorman, *Toward Mental Health,* Public Affairs Committee, New York, 1946, pp. 7-9.

anxious to achieve financial and social success. When they fall short, conflict results. Psychologists say that this kind of worry or moodiness is dangerous. Many of these people are potential suicides. Too high a financial goal is no solution to family happiness and success.

Money Is Not Everything. Money is not only dollars and cents. It is a symbol of personal attitudes toward marriage and life. The first essential is to acquire financial attitudes that will harmonize with what you and your family want out of life. It is not the amount of money but the way it is spent that counts.

Some families have a savings complex. The attitude of excessive savings in proportion to income can lead to unhappiness. Generally, each spouse blames the other for spending too much money. These people usually do not realize that they are living so completely in the future that they cannot find happiness in their day-to-day living. Perhaps this spending complex is related to what some psychologists refer to as "compulsive spending," which is merely an attempt to answer some other need.

THE WORKING WIFE AND MOTHER

Working wives and mothers have brought problems to our economy and to their families as well as higher standards of living to their homes.

Married Women in the Labor Force

Of the slightly more than 200 million total population in the United States, about 81 million (40 percent) are in the labor force. Currently, married women, husband present, make up one-fifth of the labor force in contrast to 11 percent in 1947. Over one-third (37 percent) of all wives—16 years old and over—were part of that force in 1967 in contrast to one in five in 1947. (See Figure 3-1.)

Education and Jobs. Wives with higher levels of education are more likely to be employed than others, according to a study of women college graduates in June, 1967, by the Women's Bureau of the U.S. Department of Labor. Among wives 18 years old or older, 50 percent with a college education and 40 percent with high school training were working in March, 1967, compared to only 19 percent of those with less than five years of schooling. Undoubtedly educated women have many more jobs open to them. Also, those who have invested time and money in education may feel a need and responsibility to use the knowledge and skill they have acquired.

Age and Jobs. Wives are more likely to work outside the home after they have completed their families than while they are in the prime childbearing years and have youngsters to care for. In March, 1967, wives from 35 to 44 and from 45 to 54 years old had higher labor force participation rates

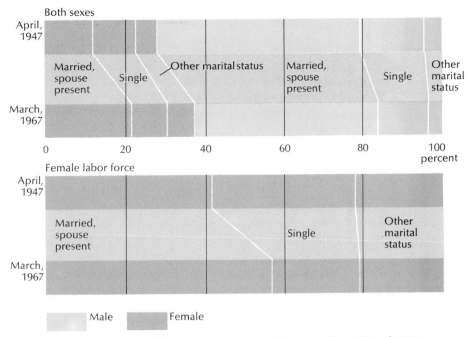

Figure 3-1   Change in Composition of Labor Force by Marital Status and Sex, 1947 and 1967.

than other age groups—43 and 45 percent, respectively. Although the labor force participation rate of younger wives (from 25 to 34 years) was somewhat lower, it had increased more since 1960. The rate for this younger group rose from 28 to 35 percent—7 percentage points—while that of wives aged 45 to 54 rose from 41 to 45 percent—4 points. This recent increase in the number of younger married women workers has reversed the long-time upward trend in the median age of working wives. The median reached a high of 41.7 years in 1964, then fell off gradually to 41.3 years in 1967.

Among wives under 35 years old, about 65 percent with no children under 18 worked in March, 1967, compared with 49 percent with children aged 6 to 17 and 26 percent with children under 6 years. Mothers of preschool children were more likely to work if there were older children or other female relatives present in the home. The data indicate that the more children a woman has, the shorter her work life outside the home. A first child reduces her average work life expectancy by about 10 years. Each additional child further reduces it by 2 or 3 years.

Income and Jobs.   Although wives mention economic reasons more often than any other when asked why they are working, the wives whose husbands have the lowest incomes are not the ones with the highest labor force rates. About 40 percent of the wives whose husbands had incomes of $3,000 to $7,000 were in the labor force in March, 1967, compared with 33 percent

TABLE 3-3   SOME THINGS THE LADIES TOLD US

AMONG WORKING WIVES GROUPED BY . . .	Percent of Total	THIS MANY ARE WORKING FULL TIME	THIS MANY HIRE DOMESTIC HELP	AND THIS MANY GIVE AS THEIR REASON FOR WORKING . . .				
				Pay off Debt	Better Living	Saving for Home	Children's Education	Escape Boredom
Age								
18 to 24	9%	80%	2%	24%	34%	28%	6%	8%
25 to 34	20	66	11	35	30	15	10	8
35 to 44	29	69	26	18	28	11	26	18
45 to 54	25	73	18	17	40	7	31	10
55 to 64	12	76	30	7	35	11	20	14
Over 65	2	62	35	14	32	5	19	11
Children								
None	20%	83%	14%	14%	40%	20%	9%	14%
Preschool	16	56	12	40	30	17	15	12
Elementary	29	63	23	33	33	10	25	12
Junior High	19	63	26	23	29	8	37	12
Senior High	23	72	21	18	36	7	38	12
College	20	77	22	15	29	6	47	13
Family Income								
Under $5,000	9%	69%	13%	24%	42%	13%	13%	4%
$5,000 to $8,000	27	68	8	35	31	14	21	6
$8,000 to $10,000	23	69	15	14	38	11	20	13
$10,000 to $15,000	22	78	33	15	29	9	30	18
Over $15,000	10	78	43	7	21	9	17	28

of those with husbands at lower or higher income levels. The age of the wife and of her children made a difference here, too. For example, among wives 16 to 34 years old whose husbands' incomes were $5,000 to $7,000, 71 percent with no children under 18 worked, 52 percent with youngsters aged 6 to 17, and 31 percent with children under 6.[16]

Why Married Women Work

As mentioned earlier, wives work mainly for economic reasons, or so they say. A recent study of about 600 randomly chosen working wives in 35 states were given a list of nine reasons for working and asked to number them in order of importance.[17] Eighty-eight percent of the women listed a financial consideration first. The three reasons most frequently mentioned were: to provide better living for the family; to provide for the children's education; and to get out of debt. Table 3-3 is an interesting breakdown of this survey.

It is interesting to note that the nonfinancial reason for working—getting away from the boredom of housekeeping—was ranked first by only 8 percent of the wives. This is in contrast to a University of Michigan Survey Research Center study during which 1,925 girls (ages 11 to 19) were asked about their future plans. Although 94 percent said they hoped to marry, only 3 percent wanted to be housewives.

Although 88 percent listed a financial reason first, a Bureau of Labor study in 1964 reported only 49 percent of the wives in 1963 worked mainly for economic reasons.[18]

A careful study of the *Changing Times* table will be rewarding in many ways. For example, the reasons for going to work varied by age, income group, and family situation; of the wives working between the ages of 18 and 24, 16 percent were working to help their husbands finish their education; working wives with preschool children or with no children are more likely to be saving for a home; and, as children get older, the emphasis shifts to education funds.

Like her pioneer forebears, today's housewife and mother is seeking the best the world has to offer for her family and herself. But there is still the question of how much net income a working wife can earn.

What Is a Wife Worth?

How much income does it take for a family to maintain an adequate but modest standard of living? There are many answers to this question, so each

[16] U.S. Department of Labor, Bureau of Labor Statistics, *Monthly Labor Review,* February, 1968, and April, 1968; *Special Labor Force Reports,* nos. 13, 50, and 94.

[17] Conducted by *Changing Times* magazine and the Bureau of Laundry and Dry Cleaning Standards and reported in *Changing Times,* July, 1965, pp. 7-10.

[18] *Monthly Labor Review,* September, 1965, pp. 1077-1082.

family will need to come up with their own figure. The Bureau of Labor Statistics of the U.S. Department of Labor reported in a study completed in late 1967 that the annual cost of a moderate living standard for a family of four, son age 13 and daughter age 8, in an urban community averaged $9,191 in the autumn of 1966. The variation in cost ranged from $8,028 in Austin, Texas, to $11,190 in Honolulu. The point of the above statistics is that it would be well for the family to study its own financial situation carefully before making a decision about a wife going to work. There are no simple answers to the question of a wife working. The answer that is right for you should be arrived at after the husband and wife have thought about it and talked over the following questions:

What is the net income of the wife after deducting job-related and extra expenses and taxes?

Are the emotional as well as the material needs of the children being met?

Is there a woman in the household—a grandmother, an aunt, or an older sister—who can provide the children with the type of guidance which few servants can give?

Does the husband feel that the wife is competing with him?

Does the husband feel he is being deprived of his role as provider for the family?

The husband needs a wife, a companion in fun, and a social hostess. Can the working woman handle these responsibilities in addition to her job? If not, the marriage is in for trouble.

Is the husband willing and able to help the wife with household chores when they both come home from work?

Does the fact that both husband and wife work give them more in common?

Can the husband and wife arrange to take their vacations together?

Does the wife's employer know of her home responsibilities, and is he willing to make allowances for them?

Is there agreement between husband and wife about what is done with the money the wife earns?

Let's go back to the economic question: Can a wife afford to work? Expenses directly related to the working wife's job—taxes, getting to and from work, and extra clothing—were estimated at between $900 and $1,000 a year, according to a recent study in Ohio by the U.S. Department of Agriculture. [19] Gross earnings of 744 working wives averaged $2,900. The wife's net income, after taking out her job-related and extra expenses, amounted to about three-fifths of her gross earnings. This was so when the household consisted of adults and older children. In a household with preschool children, net income was about half of gross earnings. This was for 1964. Cost of living and taxes seem to go up every year, although wages go up, too. The big irritation is that every dollar she earns goes on top of her husband's pay for

[19] "Job Related Expenditures of Gainfully Employed Wives in Ohio," *Home Economics Research Report*, no. 27.

tax purposes. This means that it will be taxed in a higher bracket than his. The more the husband earns, the stiffer the tax bite on her income.

In low-income families it helps considerably for the wife to work. A $5,000-a-year man, married, with no children, pays over $800 in taxes. If his wife earned $325 a month in 1968, her taxes ran over $800 a year.

She will encounter other charges—transportation, lunches away from home, more and dressier clothes, laundry and more drycleaning, beauty treatments, and so on. These may come to $18 to $25 a week, or about $900 to $1,000 a year. Overall, the net increase in the family income is around $2,000. If her husband earns $15,000, taxes will take about one-third of her $3,900. The net increase for the family will be about $1,800. That's less than half her earnings, and it increases the family net by about 14 percent. If this information is discouraging, you might look at the hidden benefits.

Some Hidden Benefits of a Working Wife.   There are some hidden benefits for the working wife that do not show up in the pay check. The Social Security benefits, after working a year and a half, have very substantial money value. And most workers get substantial fringe benefits in the form of insurance—medical and hospitalization—and pension funds. Women employed in stores usually get discount privileges and perhaps bargain-sale opportunities. Finally, by knowing how to handle a job, a wife is acquiring economic security that would be valuable in the event of premature death of her husband.

But when all the dollars-and-cents benefits are taken into account, the fact remains that the vast majority of some 16 million working wives get anything but a glamorous financial deal. Even where the net addition to the family income made by wives is modest, many of them report that it makes the difference between "getting by" comfortably and having a nerve-jangling shortage of family income.

Two Can Live as Cheaply as Two.   The persistent question that this chapter raises and attempts to settle is: "Will our pocketbook be ready when our hearts are ready for marriage?" The answer must depend largely on the young couple who are thinking of marriage. Some couples achieve a successful and happy marriage on a surprisingly low income during the first years. Such couples have an abundance of courage and faith and perhaps other sustaining forces.

This is no argument for a premature marriage. A couple very much in love is in the disquieting position of thinking via the heart. It is so easy to conclude that two can live as cheaply as one. It is wiser to figure that two can live as cheaply as *two*. We have pointed out that studies show that financial conflicts are the most-mentioned cause or symptom of marital unhappiness. While money in itself does not bring happiness, the absence of money can bring much unhappiness.

QUESTIONS FOR DISCUSSION

1. How would you explain the statement that "education neglects our needs"?
2. How can one overcome the discrepancy and inconsistency between attitudes and practices in money management?
3. Would an increase in income solve the problems of marital discontent for a family that constantly quarrels over money management?
4. Is it possible to be a success in making money but a dismal failure in spending it?
5. Can you conceive of the problems that may arise when a wife earns more money than her husband?
6. How can you know when a wife should be a part-time or a full-time working woman outside the home?
7. What are some of the important factors to consider when raising the question: "How much income do we need to marry?"

ACTIVITY PROBLEMS

1. Many studies show that management of family income is often a major reason for disagreement and marital discord. Perhaps you know two or three families who feel that disagreements over family financing are largely responsible for unpleasant family relations. Further investigations may reveal discrepancies and inconsistencies between attitudes and practices. For example, you might check on uneconomical practices such as (a) use of charge accounts, (b) meals at restaurants, (c) poor buying habits, (d) expensive recreation, and so on. If serious uneconomical practices seem to prevail among these families, what could be done to lessen such tensions?
2. Using the ideas in this chapter with regard to marital problems when both husband and wife work outside the home, prepare appropriate questions for interviewing married couples who have had or are now having this experience. A summary of these experiences could be the basis for a lively class discussion.
3. Should marriage be subsidized by parents? Invite married couples who have had such experience to discuss this issue with the class.
4. Ask ten students: "How much money do you need to get married?" Summarize the answers. What are your reactions to their answers?
5. What are lifetime income prospects for a boy or girl who does not finish high school? How many high school graduates go to college? How many complete college? What do we know about employment opportunities of the future based on current trends in employment and technology? What kinds of education and training will be needed in the future? Is a person's education ever finished?

SUGGESTED READINGS

Atwood, William, George B. Leonard, and Robert J. Moskin: *The Decline of the American Male,* Random House, Inc., New York, 1958.

Bergler, Edmund: *Money and Emotional Conflicts,* Pageant Books, Inc., New York, 1959.

Bernays, Doris F.: *A Wife Is Many Women,* Crown Publishers, Inc., New York, 1956.

Cotton, Dorothy W.: *The Case for the Working Mother,* Stein and Day, New York, 1965.

Freidan, Betty: "Woman: The Fourth Dimension," *Ladies' Home Journal,* June, 1964, p. 48.

Lobsenz, Norman M., and Clark W. Blackburn: "Hidden Meanings of Money," *Ladies' Home Journal,* July, 1968.

"So Mom Wants to Get a Paying Job," *Changing Times,* January, 1969.

"The Working Wife and Mother," *Changing Times,* July, 1965, p. 7.

chapter 4

MONEY AND DEMOCRACY IN HOME MANAGEMENT

All happy families are alike. All unhappy families are different, each in its own way.

Tolstoy, *Anna Karenina*

Money is not only dollars and cents. It is a symbol of personal attitudes toward marriage and life. It is in the early years of family life that the first tests of the quality of the partnership are made. The kind of relationship which the husband and wife establish, the nature of its strengths, and the depths of its weaknesses will largely determine the quality of the family relationships which will follow. Marital harmony has many qualities. Marital discord takes many shapes. If they are not understood and alleviated or resolved in the beginning, before the children arrive and complicate it, the family structure is placed in jeopardy.

THE QUALITY OF FAMILY RELATIONSHIPS

Marriage, parenthood, and all relationships within the family are affected by the inescapable psycho-socioeconomic demands of the money world. Individual attitudes are developed within the framework of each one's own immediate family as he grows from infancy through childhood and adolescence and is graduated into an adult world with adult responsibilities. The child's experiences during his growing-up years, the economic and social position of his family, the neighborhood environment (ghetto, urban, suburban, town, or farm), the attitudes and feelings of the family about money and social position, income and standard of living, and the way money is handled with the child inevitably will color the formulation of his own complex attitudes.

For example, children are particularly sensitive to parental anxieties about money and home surroundings. They sense the tension which is created when the father loses his job or brings home a smaller pay check. They quickly become aware of dissension centered around money matters. Their own feelings are aroused when parents quarrel over the management of money. In fact, an aura of awe and mystery surrounds money; it has importance for the parents and involves the children's own feelings of happiness and unhappiness, security and insecurity.

MONEY

Money does more than buy the goods and services that we use every day. We live in a money world. Money influences us in our relationships with members of our family as well as with others around us. It affects our standard of living, our goals, and our emotions. It takes considerable experience to establish sound money values and to develop desirable relationships with all members of the family. In fact, close students of family relationships are beginning to see a correlation between distorted parental attitudes toward money and family unhappiness. Indulgent parents often deprive their children of the knowledge and experience that will help them to have the proper attitude toward money throughout their lives.

No one is born with ability to handle money intelligently. If children are to grow up as happy, independent, economically competent adults, they must learn to use money wisely, just as they learn to read, write, spell, and figure.

Normal and Neurotic Attitudes toward Money

Psychologists and psychiatrists say that almost everyone has some form of money neurosis. A surprisingly large number of people act peculiarly in matters concerning money. Dr. Edmund Bergler, a psychiatrist, in his book *Money and Emotional Conflicts* presents a behavior chart that helps the layman understand normal and abnormal attitudes toward money.

A case in point is that of a young husband with a wife and three small children who patronized the merchandisers of debt until he found himself in a psychologist's office. After considerable discussion of his attitudes toward money, he snorted: "Nonsense! There's nothing emotional about my money worries. I'm trying to pay off a mortgage, a washing machine, an automobile, and a fur coat. I'm not neurotic—I'm just broke!"

Under questioning, however, he revealed that he bought the expensive house to "knock the eyes out" of his patronizing in-laws, the mink coat so his wife could go to parties with his boss's wife, and the car, a European sports model,

ATTITUDES TOWARD MONEY

Normally, money is a means to an end, that end the acquiring of things one desires.

Neurotically, money is an end per se.

Normally, one does not allow himself to be taken advantage of in money matters and will do his best to avoid it.

Neurotically, the fear of being taken advantage of in money matters is greatly out of proportion to the threat itself.

Normally, one tries to make money as best he can and as much as he can, but in the process will not sacrifice either health, love, hobbies, recreation, or contentment to this end.

Neurotically, money becomes the center of life; everything else—love, health, hobbies, recreation, and contentment—is subordinated to the urge to possess it.

Normally, money has no infantile strings attached to it.

Neurotically, money is a blind for existing and repressed infantile conflicts.

Normally, the spending of money is taken for granted; it needs no surgical operation to put a dollar into circulation.

Neurotically, the possession and hoarding of money becomes the predominant motif.

Normally, unjustified demands for money are warded off (out of necessity) in a matter-of-fact way.

Neurotically, demands or requests for money generate fury, excitement, and indignation.

Normally, the phrase "I cannot afford it" is a simple statement of an objective fact.

Neurotically, the phrase "I cannot afford it" represents a defensive triumph.

"just for fun." Clearly this highly emotional mixture of childish self-indul-
gence, antagonism, and snobbery (all common symptoms of a neurotic) was
responsible for his agonizing money problems.

It is human to want to live a cut or two above one's means. It is probably
all right to attempt it, especially during those years when family needs seem
to grow faster than pay checks. We know the future can stand some mortgag-
ing, but we may certainly question the emotional stability of the many thousands of irresponsible borrowers and spenders who have an adequate income
but are outraged at the idea of being forced to live within it. Their homes are
crammed with new furnishings and gadgets, yet they are not satisfied. Once
the new acquisitions have been exhibited to admiring or envious neighbors,
the proud owners lose much of their interest. It is the spending itself that gives
these people a thrill.

At the other end of the scale are the people who find a miserable kind of
happiness by living—and usually insisting that their families live—far below
their real means. These people go in for endless shopping for bargains. They
haggle over prices. They boast that they never buy anything on time. Every
penny is accounted for. In such a family, the child who mislays a quarter is
in for real trouble. In such a family, the money neurotic usually wears the pants.

It is obvious that both types, the penny pincher and his more wildly spending counterpart who cannot meet his bills, are tortured by inner anxiety. Both
unfairly blight the lives of their mates and children.

The Emotional Power of Money

Marriage counselors have taken a new look at money problems in marriage.
They have found that it is no more possible to be objective about money than
about love. If a husband and wife are constantly arguing about their spending,
the source of the problem lies in their attitudes, not in their arithmetic. Dollars
are important, but studies tend to show that marital happiness is less likely
to be affected by the size of the weekly check than by the difference in opinions
on how to spend it. Strangely enough, many married couples know little about
each other's point of view when it comes to money and are often confused
about their own attitudes. If you doubt this, ask a wife or a husband to guess
how much the family spent on clothing in the last 6 months! Ask what each
of them would do with a $500 legacy.

Almost invariably there is a breakdown in communications in a family because of the tremendous emotional power that money exercises over people's
lives. To one person, money means love; to another, power; to another, a
weapon to fight with; to yet another, protection from life's cruelties; and to
others, comforts.

Emotional money disorders, like so many other disorders, grow out of the
experiences of early childhood. When a little child is given a toy, which has

cost money, he recognizes this as a gesture of love. Is it any wonder, then, that after several such experiences a child reasons that money (the receiving of things that cost money) means love? The child very early translates money and material things into symbols of love. Some parents try to get rid of their guilt feelings toward a child by material overindulgence. This is especially true in many white-collar and middle-income families where both parents work, particularly where the mother is working to buy nice things for the home. Feelings that the child is somehow being deprived often cause overgiving, even to a very young child.

Because of their personality structures, parents sometimes are unable to meet a child's emotional needs or to handle child-training problems constructively. Money then may become a substitute for love or an instrument for manipulation and control or a weapon for punishment. The use of money as a bargaining agent to secure a child's cooperation in doing his fair share of the family tasks is a poor substitute for helping him to achieve a sense of his importance, both as a contributing and as a receiving member of the family.

Bribing a child with money to put forth more effort in his schoolwork or to practice his music lesson sets up a false stimulus for achievement. It emphasizes the reward rather than the personal development and the increased satisfaction that come from accomplishment. Likewise, depriving a child of money to force him to atone for a misdeed or for an injury to another is also unwise, since the payment of money cannot in fact compensate for such actions and may actually lead him to believe that any kind of conduct is acceptable as long as he can pay his way out of consequences.

The Real Relation of Money to Life

The inappropriate use of money or its substitution for the basic elements in the parent-child relationship obscures the child's view of the value of money. The real relationship of money to life becomes clouded, and this creates a handicap for him when he grows up. And all of us know grownups whose money attitudes are still those of a child of 5. A woman who clings to the notion of equating love and money cannot tolerate a budget that threatens to deprive her of things—clothes and accessories—that to her mean love. Unfortunately, such a person has no idea that this belief—money or things equals love—and not her limited income may be the real cause of her budget trouble. If necessary, she will manufacture a dozen other reasons for her money difficulty.

Not long ago Dr. William Kaufman, a Boston psychiatrist, told the American Association for the Advancement of Science that "money sickness is the most common psychosomatic illness of our times." He said that the trouble does not necessarily come from how much money you have or don't have. It comes from the particular "meaning" you have come to place on money, and how you spend it. And he said it could come from the feeling that you need more money when actually you do not need it. He, too, believes that the attitude toward money you have as an adult begins in childhood. Most of us have experienced childhood disappointments when our parents were unable to provide all the things we desired. Dr. Kaufman said the manner in which a child resolves his early conflicts about money will determine some of his basic personality and behavior patterns. He goes on to say parental bribing, substitution of handouts for real love, or overcriticism of a child's use of money may establish habits that, if uncorrected, may set the stage for a money-sickness candidate in later life.

Analyzing Attitudes toward Money

Actually, how many ordinary people do you know who are well balanced in their attitude toward money? Do you know an embarrassingly stingy tipper? A couple always in debt? People who insist on telling how much they paid for everything? A family trying to keep up with other families in the neighborhood? People trying to live up to the standard of living of their neighbors and friends? Persons who find peace of mind through entrapment? People who are using installment credit without figuring total costs? You will probably discover that the percentage of level heads and the amount of good judgment based on known family goal values is frighteningly low!

Reports of many psychiatrists show that about 75 percent of their patients are suffering from some degree of abnormality in their attitudes toward money. This does not mean that you need to consult a psychiatrist about your attitude. Why not determine for yourself whether your attitude toward money is healthy and useful or damaging and potentially dangerous to a happy family life?

DEMOCRACY IN HOME MANAGEMENT

Fiction writers, sociologists, anthropologists, educational philosophers, psychologists, and others have recognized the importance of the home in promoting the democratic way of life. Jan Struther, for example, has written:

> Democracy begins at home, and it begins very early in the morning—not at breakfast, but when the first reluctant eye is opened by the first devilish trill of the alarm clock and when everybody thinks that everybody else takes much too long in the bath. The home, and not a college of political science, is the place to learn democracy—but it's no good for us grownups to try to teach it to our children unless we teach it to ourselves as well—and oh my! we've certainly got a lot to learn. . . .[1]

Sait and Nimkoff, sociologists, expressed themselves as follows:

> Consideration for others and willingness to cooperate are fundamental social attitudes. They are best secured through an orderly home routine, designed in such a way that,

[1]"Democracy Begins at Home," *Adult Education Journal,* vol. 1, no. 3 (July, 1942), p. 118.

as early as possible, the child begins to help himself and to engage in communal tasks. . . .[2]

Science has established two facts meaningful for human welfare; first, the foundation of the structure of human personality is laid down in early childhood; and second, the chief engineer in charge of this construction is The Family.[3]

Margaret Mead, the well-known anthropologist, recognized the importance of the democratic family when she wrote: "Unless we democratize family life it is idle to talk of democracy."[4]

Democracy Begins at Home

What is democratic living? To answer this question is not easy. Definitions are tricky and inadequate, especially when they deal with an idea or a way of life. Fundamentally, democratic living means sharing—sharing of rights and responsibilities, duties and decisions based on beliefs. This definition is almost meaningless unless considered in relation to ordinary daily family experiences.

When turning the spotlight on daily family experiences, keep in mind that there is no one "right" way, no simple pattern. Democracy as a way of life may be expressed quite differently in different families. What is important is that the spirit of democracy—of cooperative sharing, of consideration for the rights of each in the family—is expressed through whatever is done. The following family rules, although incomplete and no doubt debatable, will help your family to lead a democratic life.

1. Assign well-defined chores to each person.
2. Talk over with the children decisions that affect the entire family.
3. Give the children a reasonable amount of privacy.
4. Avoid favoritism.
5. Encourage the children to invite their friends into the home.
6. Encourage the children to help select their own clothing.
7. Have fun with your children.
8. Consider the family tastes when planning meals.
9. Allow the children freedom to be themselves.
10. Give fixed allowances to the children to cover ordinary expenses.

The child who learns democracy in his family circle will be better able to practice it as a member of his gang, as a student, and as a citizen. University of Chicago social scientists found that children from democratic homes were better equipped for the give-and-take of daily life. They seemed to get along

[2] Una B. Sait, *New Horizons for the Family,* The Macmillan Company, New York, 1938, p. 687.

[3] M. F. Nimkoff, *The Family,* Houghton Mifflin Company, Boston, 1934, p. ix.

[4] "The Comparative Study of Culture and the Purposive Cultivation of Democratic Values," *Science, Philosophy and Religion,* Conference on Science, Philosophy and Religion and Their Relation to the Democratic Way of Life, New York, 1942, p. 63.

better with their playmates and with teachers, church workers, and Scout leaders. They also rated higher in such traits as loyalty, honesty, moral courage,
friendliness, and responsibility.

They were preferred by adults as after-school employees. They even tended
to earn higher grades in school—perhaps because they were able to work to
the full extent of their abilities.

There seems to be little doubt that the foundations of democracy are laid
in the home. There, better than anywhere else, children can learn to do their
share of the work and to make their share of the decisions, to respect each other's differences, to sacrifice together, and to have fun together. There they can
learn to recognize the rights of others and to reject the idea of special privilege—even for themselves.

Evidence of Sharing in Homes.   There are insufficient data on the evidence
of the democratic way of life in the homes of this country. It seems probable,
by the definitions given above, that only a modest percentage of American
homes practice democracy as a way of life. Mary S. Lyle, in her study of 120
homes in a small town and surrounding area in Iowa, came to the following
conclusions.[5]

1.   In 75 per cent of the homes the husband shared the financial management with
his wife, but children had a voice in management in only about 17 per cent of the
families.
2.   Planning for the use of the total family income by all the family members mature
enough to understand the situation was rather rare.
3.   Slightly over 40 per cent of the 147 high school students reported that they "had
no choice in the duties they did or how they were to be done." Only slightly over 18
per cent of the students "exercised some volition in what they did."
4.   Over 53 per cent of the students claimed "home duties as a subject of some disagreement."
5.   Recreational activities were shared by several family members in the majority
of these homes but 30 per cent of these families did not share recreation.
6.   Some families seemed to plan together for family projects and seemed to have
a common understanding of the family goals, but the evidence was too meager to
proclaim this as characteristic of the group.
7.   The pattern of these families tended toward autocracy rather than democracy.

This picture, if general among American families, is serious in terms of maximum development of all the members of the family. This is especially true if
we agree that first among the values looked for in home life is the quality of
family relationships that permits full development of the personalities that
make up the family.

Achieving Personality Fulfillment.   Studies show that families in which psychological relationships are sound can absorb severe strains in crises. These
same studies reveal that the kind of personality each individual has is chiefly
determined by the kind of family in which he grew up. When children are
young, they need secure environment. They need to be loved generously and

[5] Mary S. Lyle, *Adult Education for Democracy in Family Life,* The Iowa State University Press, Ames, Iowa, 1944, pp. 65-69. Reprinted with permission.

spontaneously. Children who experience rigid controls usually build up resentments that often are carried into adult life. Children need parents who can help them to build confidence in themselves and to feel that they have an important role to play in the family.

Children learn to be considerate of others and willing to cooperate for the family good when they are given increasing responsibility in family affairs. Even young children can help plan (1) how some of the family income is to be spent, (2) how leisure time is to be used, and (3) how, when, and by whom family chores are to be done. They, too, can contribute to discussions on how grievances and difficulties can best be handled.

This does not mean that parents should abdicate. Children cannot always have their way. But the chance to express themselves fully, to weigh ideas of others in the family, is important in development of personality. Procedures need to be planned for giving children more and more responsible independence, because eventually they must assume complete responsibility for their own actions. Many children have never had to think about the problems a family has to face. Someone else did all their thinking.

If family problems are shared according to age and ability, all members become aware of the realities of living. Thus they discover that family life consists of more than sweetness and love.

Division of Work in the Family.   No one can prescribe exactly how work should be divided for every family. The family chores differ according to the financial status of the family and according to whether they live in the city or in the country, in a house or in an apartment. These differences must be recognized in family conferences about sharing activities and work.

Children's contributions to household tasks can be of considerable importance. In the pioneer family, the children were expected to assist with the homework as early as age and ability permitted. There never was a question about this matter in those days. Today there is much the same situation on the farms, according to Mary Lyle's study of democracy in family life. Her study of rural and small-town families in Iowa revealed that "in the majority of the farm families who had children, the children were cooperating in the daily tasks."[6]

The situation was different in the town families, for in "only 38.6 per cent of the homes with children were these children participating in the common tasks." This was not because the children of town families were too young to participate, for there were only three town families whose children were under the age of 6, as compared to 17 farm families with children younger than 6. On the farms, nearly "100 per cent of the children over six years of age shared the everyday tasks while in the town less than 50 per cent of the children over six years had this privilege."

Furthermore, many of them participated unwillingly in home tasks. Home duties expected of the children ranked fourth among 16 subjects of possible

[6] *Ibid.*, p. 63.

disagreement with their parents. Mary Lyle concluded that "it may well be that the autocratic procedure followed by the parents was in a measure responsible for some of the conflict."[7]

Life in city apartments presents some problems when it comes to work in and around the home. There, almost all activities must relate of necessity to the household. Outside jobs are not available as a rule. The distinctions between the sexes in regard to household work become less marked than on farms or in small towns. Still, here as in rural homes, there are floors to be waxed, windows to be cleaned, some painting that can be done, and perhaps furniture to be repaired. These tasks are in addition to cleaning, preparing meals, bedmaking, dishwashing, and caring for babies and pets.

It is easier today, in contrast to pioneer days, for the family to neglect to plan work experience for their children. With fewer children per family, parents become more child-conscious and perhaps overprotective. It is so easy to decide: "I had to work too hard in my home when I was a child. I'm going to see that my child does not have to work so hard." While some parents, no doubt, had to work too hard at home, that fact does not justify taking the extreme opposite point of view. In a home dominated by that kind of philosophy, how are the children going to become mature and responsible persons? One cannot suddenly become mature through intellectualizing about the problem. Work experience is needed in the home, in an atmosphere where parents and children live, plan, and work cooperatively.

The chief reasons for having children work in and around the home are to give them a feeling of usefulness and importance in relation to their family and to society and to develop worthy attitudes and skills that will build family solidarity and happiness. Their help also reduces the time and energy spent by father and mother in home tasks.

DEMOCRATIC CONCEPTION OF THE FAMILY

There was a time when many families lived under the rule of a parent dictator or tyrant. In such homes, the parents were the source of all wisdom and control. In some of these homes, this control was stern and serious; in others, it took the form of benevolent despotism. In the latter type of family life, the parent may be a kindly person who believes that he is doing everything possible for the welfare of his family. He may, in fact, be completely self-sacrificing.

This kind of patriarchal or matriarchal family is gradually being replaced by the democratic family, which emphasizes the importance of the dignity and responsibility of the individual.

The democratic family (1) recognizes that human relations should be characterized by respect for each person in the family, (2) recognizes sharing ac-

[7] *Ibid.,* p. 68.

cording to age and ability in policy making as well as in the effort to achieve jointly determined goals, and (3) believes in intelligent discussion as to the means of successfully solving conflicts and settling family problems.

Both children and adults can assist in deciding (1) how to divide work, (2) who is to do it, (3) how to use family income for the maximum happiness of all, (4) how to participate in community activities, (5) how to use the vacation period, and (6) how to solve many problems of family life. Through sharing in the planning, all can feel the responsibility for carrying the plans through successfully.

The democratic process of sharing does not mean that there is no control and no direction. On the contrary, there are regulations; there is direction. The basic change is in the means to the end—the process. The rules and regulations are developed by those whom they directly affect.

Children, and everyone else, resent controls if they cannot see sense and purpose in them. Rules discussed and made by the group are more easily adhered to by the individuals who discussed and made them. If the regulations do not work out as planned or wished, each member of the group knows that they can be restudied and changed. Uncooperative action becomes the concern of all the members. As a result, disapproval by the group is often more effective than discipline by one member of the family.

There are always times in a family when adult control must swing into action. Safety of a child, for example, demands mature control when the child is too young to understand the consequences of dangerous actions. Gradually, as the child matures, he can take on more and more personal responsibility for his own and the family's safety.

The Family Council

The so-called family council is one effective way in which to carry out the democratic idea in family life. Each family will have to decide on the kind of council suited to its members.

Whether a family session is formal or informal is of no great importance. There are times when informal sessions may be more appropriate—for such decisions as concerning holiday outings, preferred foods, clothes, play equipment, hours, and so on.

With added experience, an older child can have a part in the more difficult decisions. In time, the area of choice may be expanded until each child is able to make or help make major decisions.

When there is joint planning, suggestions made by the children should be accepted with an open mind. Even an impossible idea needs to be handled so that the child will continue to feel free to say what he thinks and know that his idea will be heard and treated fairly. He must be taught, however, to accept other points of view and in the end, possibly, negative group voting.

Discipline should not be handled in a family meeting. Cross-examinations of such matters as who daubed paint on the neighbor's garage or why the lawn wasn't mowed are best handled outside the family council. In fact, family councils often help to prevent such problems.

What are some of the ways of making a family council work successfully?

1. At first, plan a meeting to take care of something simple and perhaps pleasurable, in which all can have a part—a picnic.
2. Select a time for the session when the whole family is naturally together.
3. Listen to each person's ideas respectfully—even silly ideas.
4. See that everyone has a chance to air his opinions.
5. Get all the important facts.
6. Compromise when necessary.
7. Try different solutions in dividing the common family chores until satisfactory agreements are worked out.
8. Be sure that the entire group makes the decisions.
9. Praise growth in responsibility and cooperation with others.

The Role of the Expert

The democratic family accepts the principle of the "role of the expert." There are certain decisions that the expert, usually mother or dad, must make without benefit of the children's advice. The distinction between sharing policy making and heeding expert advice should be clarified with the children as soon as they can grasp the idea. A family vote on a policy-making matter is one thing, and the advice of the expert to carry it out is another thing.[8]

Parents should not use the false technique of allowing the family a voice in certain matters and then arranging a final outcome different from the family decision. Likewise, parents should not stack the cards so that in reality no choice is possible. Other tricks are used by some parents in family conferences, but such actions are deceitful. They will affect the children's attitudes toward their parents and will lead to distrust and misunderstanding of the democratic process as a means of developing a successful and happy family.

CHILDREN AND MONEY

The younger generation is "going to the dogs." A great philosopher said: "Our youth now love luxury. They have bad manners, contempt for authority. They show disrespect for elders and love chatter in place of exercise. Children are now tyrants, not the servants of their households. They no longer rise when elders enter the room. They contradict their parents, chatter before company, gobble up their food, and tyrannize their teachers."

[8] See James S. Plant, "Democracy Turns to the Family," *Journal of Home Economics,* January, 1942, p. 4.

If Socrates had not written this statement in the fifth century B.C., it would be considered a present-day comment. There are, of course, some differences in the 1970s. Most children are urbanites. Nearly half of them live in suburbs surrounding a large city. There are fewer opportunities for parents to teach their children certain kinds of responsibilities. Homes are filled with laborsaving devices. As the children grow older, many mothers are reluctant to trouble them with the few chores that remain around the house. Instead, the drive is all for the children being "successful," and it is difficult for some parents to recognize how proficiency in bedmaking will contribute to their children's success in life. Many children won't mow the lawn or wash the car without pay.

The affluent child—and there is many a one—hears a good deal of talk at home about shortages of money, but usually these conversations make little sense to him. If parents are short of money, how come they have a second or third car? How come parents can go to Florida for two weeks to escape winter? Why talk about saving money when there is always more where the last supply came from? Can money really be short when a child can usually squeeze more cash or more presents out of his parents through tricks of the trade?

Money Training for Children

Money affects everybody. In our homes, money determines our standard of living. More than that, money determines our outlook on life. Money also determines the relations of members of the family and, to a large extent, our relations to the community.

Said a regretful parent: "I wish somebody had given me the chance to have some sound and happy first impressions of money. I must have thought that money grew on trees by all the trouble I've had making it behave in my grownup years." The regret of this parent could have been prevented if his parents had realized that we learn how to handle money just as we master any other skill.

We are not born with "money sense." It takes time and experience on the part of parents to help children learn how to handle money for maximum use and happiness. The attitude of parents toward money, therefore, is of primary importance.

Children generally become conscious of money very early in life. Their attitudes toward money are shaped by much the same forces as their attitudes toward anything else—family, friends, school, hobbies, and many other forces. Advertising on radio and television and in newspapers, magazines, and movies leaves impressions of considerable weight. Then, too, children face some of the same problems that adults must face when managing money. Their wants are greater than their ability to purchase. They are tempted to buy things because friends have done so. Children, too, can become selfish or generous, conservative or impulsive, about spending money. They can easily mistake money as a "goal" in itself rather than as a means to good living.

In a certain sense, money training cannot be set apart from a child's general upbringing. Child-guidance and family-finance experts generally agree that money problems really stem from the more basic emotional and social problems of growing up. The two are easily confused. For example, a child needing social acceptance within his group may place the blame for his frustration on the lack of money. Therefore, parents need to be aware of the needs and drives, the pains and pangs, of their growing children. By identifying the underlying difficulties, they eliminate much needless bickering, and money training can be relatively free of emotional entanglements.

The Teen-age Consumer

Lester Rand, head of the Youth Research Institute of New York, estimates that there are 25 million youths in the United States between the ages of 13 and 19 with more than $18 billion to spend as they see fit. By 1970, according to Rand, teen-agers will number about 30 million with disposable incomes of some $30 billion. According to Alice M. Stewart, extension specialist in consumer education at Cornell University, four out of ten high school boys and two out of ten girls have their own credit cards.[9] For good or bad, credit cards for teen-agers are a reality added to the educational responsibilities of parents. This is disquieting to many parents, because many plans do not require the consent and signature of parents.

Time was when a boy's chief possessions were his bike and baseball glove and bat, and a girl's party wardrobe consisted of a fancy dress with costume jewelry. What parents once considered luxury items, children now regard as necessities. Teen-agers are surrounded with a great array of expensive items— 13 million cameras, 10 million phonographs and hi-fi sets, 1 million TV sets, plus cars and sports equipment. No one knows accurately how much parents spend on them or to what extent the youngsters act as hidden persuaders. A *Seventeen* magazine survey, reported in the *New York Times Magazine,* June 5, 1966, estimates that teen-agers influence "at least $35 billion of adults' cash outflow." Is it just possible that many teen-agers will achieve individuality not through achievement and job satisfaction but through consumption? Are they relentless consumers, "hooked" on a passion to possess the things which give them satisfaction—this *is* me? If the answer is "Yes," both parents and youth can expect merchandisers to spend millions of dollars to exploit the youth market. In a well-documented book, *Teen-age Tyranny,* Fred and Grace Hechinger express fear that society is opening up "vast opportunities for commercial

[9] *Consumer Close-ups,* May 29, 1967, p. 4.

exploitation and thereby sets off a chain reaction which constantly strengthens teen-age tyranny."

Commercial Exploitation of Teen-age Consumers

One of the significant business trends of this midcentury is the effort to woo the teen-age market. A few years ago Charles and Bonnie Remsburg wrote: "Aided by a growing stable of researchers, promotion artists, public relations experts, merchandising consultants, ad agency psychologists and others who specialize in converting quirks of the teen-age psyche into cash receipts, our economy is mounting the biggest youth-kick ever."[10]

Apparently no area of retailing is omitted. Now there is a *Teen-agers' Guide to the Stock Market* which tells youth that they can now play the stock market and "enjoy a great experience" by learning how to sell short and reminds them that at stockholders' meetings they "frequently serve free luncheons."

Dr. Norma Werner, a psychologist who researched youth for the Leo Burnett advertising agency, points out that the main goal of a girl is marriage, and therefore she is interested in learning how to achieve the "body beautiful." This pressure makes girls "tremendously insecure about glamour." The Montgomery Ward Company, for about $10, offers a teen-age girl a six weeks' course in which she receives personal "charm counseling" from professional models.

The Ford Motor Company has been sending race drivers, mechanics, and car stylists to teen-age hot-rod and auto-customizing shows, where they offer "inside tips" on souping-up cars, motor vehicles being the one item with which teen-age boys are likely to be intensely involved emotionally. When one consultant informed these boys that the family car could be given added power by installing a certain camshaft, Ford parts departments were sold out of the units within three months.

Many other appeals are made that are calculated to overcome teen-age embarrassment that inhibits 9- and 10-year-olds from spending money for bras; that employ youth panels to invent entirely new items for adolescents; that discover products and services which rebel against adult standards and yet remain within the framework of acceptability. For example, Dr. Irving White, founder of Creative Research Associates in Chicago, discovered most teen-agers would not go for goof-balls until a pill came out that had all the ingredients of milk, flavored like liquor, and called a "goof-ball." "Man, that would fly!"

Where does it all end? It doesn't. We already have shopping centers for teen-agers, complete with teen-age banks (California); a hospital has a special teen-age wing that offers unlimited snacks, jam sessions, and wheelchair races (Portland, Oregon); a doctor in Boston has launched a medical specialty, ephe-

---

[10] In the *New York Times Magazine*, June 5, 1966.

briatrics—the treatment of teen-age ills. And more commercial exploitation of youth is on the drawing boards.

The big question is: Where and how can teen-agers learn how to use and control the use of money wisely and to their satisfaction? Some believe the place is in the home; some say, the public schools; others believe it should be taught in both places. Even if we have not decided where it should be done, we can substantiate the need for it.

The Teen-age Consumer in the Ghetto

Even though the affluent families are getting more company, the fact remains that 29.7 million Americans, or about 15 percent of the population, including over 7 million families, are living in poverty.[11] The Social Security Administration and the Council of Economic Advisers place the poverty line at an after-tax income of $3,100 for a family of four and $1,540 for a single individual.

Studies of teen-agers, as consumers, who live in the ghetto in urban centers, are rare indeed. The information and insights on the ghetto teen-ager, as a consumer, is taken from a series of conversations with teen-agers in various sections of Los Angeles—Watts (black), southeast (Mexican), and nearby Venice (Hippie Center). About forty of these youngsters were transported to a ranch some hundred miles from Los Angeles in order to get an away-from-home environment which might serve as a means of stimulating a free flow of ideas. The conversations were conducted by young men experienced in the ghetto sections. The study provides some hopeful insights into ghetto teen-age expenditures. The conversations also show how most of them are completely alienated from and hostile to the present system.

Some Typical Remarks. [12]   One young Mexican said: "First of all, if this country continues to let poverty and racial injustice and prejudice exist, we won't have a country and we won't have to worry about what youths want."

And a black youth adds: "Everyone wants something nice. You work for a good car, then the cops come and ask where you got it. White people have good things. They don't stop them. Some say what the hell."

And a Mexican responds: "This is the attitude. You are Mexican. You are inferior. If you want to succeed, be like an Anglo. If you want to be a Mexican, forget about succeeding. Teachers say, 'If you can't dance to my music get out.'"

Another boy said: "As far as consumer goods go, I really don't feel it a part of my life because it doesn't relate to me . . . . People just don't talk about it."

Many other insights are revealed in this study. They said that "prices are higher in our stores"; "there are no clothing stores in Watts"; buses are "too

[11] Committee of Government Operations, *House Report* no. 1851, Aug. 7, 1968, p. 3.

[12] An unpublished report, *Los Angeles Teenager as a Consumer,* by Arthur Carstens, director of the study supported in part by a grant from Consumers Union.

expensive"; "very few own cars" because the "police will take it away"; the "personal touch is important, like a flower painted on the pants' leg"; a "car is just wheels, not a status symbol"; "the opinion of the peer group determines what a teen-ager buys."

It appears that their first problem is to exist—just exist. They want a good education, good jobs, and a nice home with all the consumer goods that the affluent class possess. But, how? When? They also want to be respected and treated like white people. The feelings of many of the youth in Watts were stated by a black youth:

WHAT I WANT

I feel I want my people to be free. People think that Negro people are nothing but trouble makers, riot starters, and uneducated people. But they are not all of that. When people are being dogged around by police, and when they are aware that they do not have jobs, have run down homes, poor schools and not too many of them have a lot to eat, they feel like "so what, they hate us, we hate them." And this always leads to riots and race problems, but the way I see it the answer to this is:

1. Give my people more and better jobs
2. Give my people and their kids better schools
3. Let my people live where they want to
4. Give them better playgrounds to play in

These are only a few things that will help keep the riots down. These are not much to ask. The white people have these, and I do not know how come my people can't have them. Is it asking too much or is it because we are black? We must know this. We must try to live together, work together and try to solve the race problem together and stop these riots. Let us stop all of this. Let us make America and our city the greatest in the world. So this is why I want to see my people free.

It is clear, from this study, that teen-agers in the ghetto of Los Angeles, and probably in ghettos elsewhere, are more sensitive to the need for basic changes—better education, better jobs, open housing and decent housing, respect and fair treatment—than to the need for more and better consumer goods. A higher standard of living, they argue, will be a by-product of the basic needs mentioned above. This conclusion may not be as valid if applied to the parents of the teen-agers. The Caplovitz study of the consumer behavior of low-income families in New York City, for example, indicates a keen interest and active participation in consumer durable goods. One wonders whether these two studies do not tell the deep, disturbing differences in attitudes of parents and their teen-agers.

"The Consumer Behavior of Low-income Families"[13]

This study by David Caplovitz, a sociologist at Columbia University, concentrated on consumer behavior of low-income, recent migrants to New York City—

[13] David Caplovitz, *The Consumer Behavior of Low-income Families,* Bureau of Applied Social Research, Columbia University, New York, 1961.

blacks from the South, Puerto Ricans, and whites—living in four low-income public housing projects. A summary of the findings is:

1.   Most low-income families are consumers of high-cost durables.
2.   Most families depend upon high-cost credit when making these purchases. This restricts most purchases to their neighborhood stores and to door-to-door peddlers, who for the most part work for the small neighborhood stores. Their credit debts may not be larger than those of families of comparable income elsewhere, but they are much more likely to have less savings. About one-third of these families have such large debts in relation to assets that they border on insolvency.
3.   These families are vulnerable to exploitation by unscrupulous merchants because of poor education and language difficulties, and because many are recent migrants and tend to be naïve shoppers, vulnerable to the lure of "easy credit." About one-third of them suffer at the hands of unscrupulous merchants and door-to-door peddlers. Most of them who encounter severe consumer difficulties are not apt to know where to go for professional help, and consequently they respond with helpless resignation to their consumer problems. Furthermore, nonwhites are charged more for credit, so that blacks and Puerto Ricans are penalized in the marketplace.

Any Solutions?   These, in brief, are the major findings in the study. The question inevitably arises about what can be done to help these families with their consumer problems. More specifically, what can be done to change their consumer practices? What can be done to protect the consumers through control of the suppliers? To change buying patterns of low-income consumers is usually difficult. Underlying much of the problem confronting low-income consumers is the fact that their consumption goals tend to outstrip their means for realizing them. Can they save money for their major durable goods? Unless society can offer alternative sources for credit, these families are not apt to change their shopping habits, say some investigators.

This disparity of consumption goals and limited resources has its origins in the "revolution of expectations" in an affluent society. The very success of American people in raising their standard of living lies behind the runaway aspirations of low-income consumers. Goals that at one time did not seem possible—exposure to constant radio and TV advertising emphasizing better living—now appear to be obtainable. So we find that aspirations for material possessions are easily learned; earnings increase more slowly and consumer sophistication takes time to be acquired.

Besides education in better planning and buying habits, low-income consumers need legislation and law enforcement designed to protect the consumer from unscrupulous merchants and from himself—that is, from his own propensity to get into trouble as a consumer.

What has all of this to do with money and democracy in home management? We said earlier in this chapter that youngsters are particularly sensitive to parental anxieties about money and home surroundings. They sense the tensions between parents, and often they are the victims of such tensions. Admittedly, low-income families have more than a normal amount of tensions. It is a wonder that family dissension and discord have been kept down to an "almost tolerable" level. The ugly fact is that there is both an indirect and a direct relationship between family discord and disintegration and low income and low consumer sophistication.

Income and Savings of Teen-agers.   The average income of junior and senior high school students in the spring of 1962 was $6.77 a week, according to a nationwide survey. Senior high school boys averaged $11.67 a week and girls $7.24, while junior high school boys averaged $4.29 and girls $3.88 a week.

Over half the students reported at least two sources of income. Some 49 percent received a regular allowance, 48 percent earned money from part-time jobs away from home, 33 percent received odd amounts from parents, and 18 percent earned funds by doing special tasks at home.

The average amount saved was $4.78. Of those who had received money during the week before the survey, 72 percent had saved some part, according to the study. Over two-thirds mentioned that they kept saved money at home; about two-thirds saved in a bank or savings and loan association; 15 percent bought United States savings bonds; 8 percent belonged to a Christmas or vacation club plan; and 7 percent bought insurance.

But are young people wise consumers? Are they good managers of money? What are their values and goals? Do they know their legal rights as consumers? And, finally, who is largely responsible for teaching them the basic begin-

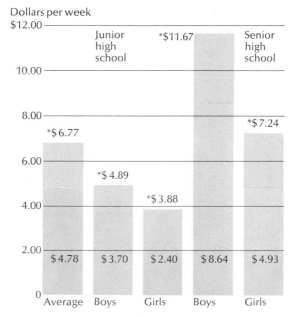

Figure 4-1   Average Income and Saving of Junior and Senior High School Students. Source: *Scholastic Magazine* survey, 1962.

nings of good money management, wise consumership, and responsibility to the family? This all leads us to the all-important responsibility of bringing up our children in an ever-changing money world.

Money Adulthood for the Teen-ager. Many teen-agers are not prepared to shoulder, in later years, their own important personal or family financial responsibilities because their parents neglected this part of their education. This neglect is understandable, because nothing that concerns a teen-ager is easy, and money training is no exception.

There is, however, one important fact that parents can use to good advantage. The world of money and finance is an adult world. A teen-ager longs for adulthood. And learning how to handle money is one of the steps that carries him into that proud estate. But how can this objective be achieved?

Because family beliefs and goals as well as family situations vary greatly, it is difficult to give tips on how to teach money management to a teen-ager in ten easy lessons. Nevertheless, the following suggestions, coming from experienced child-guidance experts and from parents who have experimented with their adolescent children, should be of considerable help to other parents.

1. The example the parents set will be as influential as any specific training. If the family makes no attempt to plan its spending, the youngsters can hardly be expected to do so.

2. Teen-agers should know the approximate family income and the major expenses.

3. In the light of the family income and major expenditures, children's allowances should be discussed in relation to expected responsibilities. Family income is not pocket money, but each member shares in the family funds. A child's share should include as much of the money spent on him as is known. It certainly should include most or all of the money normally used for his clothing expenses.

4. Let each child be responsible for his own money matters. Mistakes will be made. Let him learn from these mistakes. Almost overnight most youngsters will turn into thrifty shoppers. Advice, formerly unwanted and often viewed as nagging, will not only be accepted but sought.

5. When the occasion arises, help each child to understand the legal rights of the retailer and the legal rights of the consumer. Sometimes guarantees of goods are confusing to the uninitiated. He will need and want help in these matters and in many other intricacies of the business world.

6. Encourage children to use the services of a bank. Show them how to write a check, how to use charge accounts. Let them see how the family invests its money and how insurance is used to protect the family.

7. Encourage teen-agers to earn money outside the home. They should not be paid for doing their share of routine work in and around the house.

8. Do not discipline a child by withholding his regular share of the family income. Rather, investigate the real causes for the misbehavior or action.

9. Encourage each child to become an "expert" on certain expenditures for the whole family. This helps to build confidence as well as to give a child the feeling of contributing to the well-being of the family.

10. Do not treat matters that stem from more basic emotional and social problems of adolescence as money management problems. The two are easily confused.

Parental Attitudes in Money Training

Unfortunately, many parents show extreme immaturity when it comes to helping their children learn how to manage money. Mary S. Lyle, in her study of families in a rural-town community in Iowa, made the following conclusions.[14]

1. One hundred fifty-eight high school students, checking problems that troubled them most, mentioned "learning how to spend money wisely," "having to ask parents for money," and "having no regular allowance or regular income" more often than any other human relations problem. There were 330 problems listed in the check list.
2. Nearly half of these boys and girls were "very sure they were not getting (intellectual) stimulation in money management."
3. Less than one-third of their parents were providing stimulation for the children to learn to plan for and select most of their clothes within a given amount of money.
4. "Planning for the use of the total family income by all the family members mature enough to understand the situation was rather rare."

It was quite obvious that the parents of these 120 families were not helping their children to learn to handle money in the best way.

Why don't parents give their children a chance to handle the money that will be spent on them? Parents object to giving their children allowances for many reasons, such as:

"Money is a sordid business. I don't want my children to have to worry about it until they have to."
"I earned my own spending money when I was a boy."
"I'll give them money when they need it."
"My children spend enough money without giving them allowances, too."

All such arguments reveal poor insight with regard to the real purpose of children's allowances, and back of them are bits of family history, custom, folklore, inertia, and certainly lack of understanding.

Just how do most children get spending money? There are many schools of thought, each with its champions, on this question.

Whim of the Parent. "He who pays the piper may call the tune" sums up one point of view. What the children are given depends on the whim of the giver. Some parents use this to show their "power." Others use it to purchase love. Such a parent tries to purchase the affection of his children, substituting material things for understanding. He has little to offer his family in the way of human understanding, capacity for play, imagination, humor, or simple sociability. He has one major virtue—a source for money. This virtue is made to work overtime. Consequently, his children's attitude toward money often tends to succumb to parental standards or to rebel against them, and to become warped in either case.

[14]Lyle, op. cit., pp. 61, 66, 158. Reprinted with permission.

Money revealed to children only as a symbol of power and success may lead to feelings of inferiority, bitterness, and unhappiness in the parents. This same unhappiness and maladjustment tends to spread to the children. In such an atmosphere, money can easily seem to be the one good that has the power to dispel sorrow or, quite as falsely, become the root of some, if not all, evil.

Wheedling and Collusion.   A second approach is the one of wheedling father or mother into buying things that previously have been refused by the other parent. Sometimes there may be collusion between parent and child. Mother, for example, may say to her child, "I'd try asking your father for money after he has had his second cup of coffee."

At times, wheedling takes on a "cute" manner. In this case, children master certain tricks that net the biggest returns. Parents of such children may be educating them unknowingly for future trickery in business.

Money as Whip or Reward.   A third approach is to use money as a whip or means of enforcing discipline. "If you are a good boy, I'll give you a nickel." Should a child grow up believing that virtue always is rewarded by cash? Sometimes business deals are made for music practice, for getting good or even passing marks in school, or for household chores. Or a child is fined for poor schoolwork or for lying.

When John comes home late from baseball practice two nights in a row, mother suddenly announces that she will deduct 15 cents from next week's allowance. In such a case, the mother reduces the responsibilities of her child to a cash basis. John will have to decide, when challenged again, between 15 cents less cash or more fun playing baseball.

The real issue, personal responsibility with regard to other members of the family, is completely disregarded. In the second place, John is entitled to a part of the family income because he is a member of the family. Money should not be used as a club to discipline a member of the family. Using money to discipline a child confuses his thinking with regard to his family responsibilities, the value of money, and its proper uses.

Adults frequently are confused over how to settle accidents caused by a child's carelessness. Bill broke a neighbor's window. His father decided that the cost of the new window must come out of Bill's allowance, so much each week. Is placing a mortgage on a child's allowance because of a careless act a wise policy? In a clear case of an act of carelessness resulting in a material loss, the parents might preferably decide to pay for replacement of the glass.

The important issue concerns the attitude of the child. Most children are sorry when they destroy someone's property. With a child, the problem is to ease his conscience and to help him make his peace with all parties concerned. Help him without reducing the issue to monetary discipline, which may only confuse the problem of wrongdoing. For Bill, the important thing is forgiveness, that no one will hold anything against him, and that he will want to be more careful in the future.

Reward a Child after Accomplishment. When parents "purchase" better grades and honors, they confuse buying and bribery. Most parents know that there is no relationship between scholastic attainment and cash. It seems to be the path of least resistance. But are there not better ways of showing parental appreciation and for giving praise and approval? To pay cash for success in school, for accomplishment that is for the good of the child, is to give the child a false scale of values and relationships. For example, is an "A" in history worth the same as an "A" in grammar or arithmetic?

Why not celebrate after something has been done unusually well? Everyone loves a celebration. A gift or money in appreciation *after* the accomplishment might be a nice gesture. The important thing is that the child understands the difference between a spontaneous gift and a calculated contract, such as "If you get a 'B' in geography, I'll give you two dollars." It is preferable, after a child has accomplished a certain objective, for a parent to say, "Because you worked so hard to succeed, we are going to buy you that bicycle."

The problem is one of sharing, not making a deal. Those who have studied children have found that the way a child acts is not so important as *why* he acts a certain way. A child who usually carries out responsibilities within his ability range does so because he feels cooperative and because he gets parental approval. "We try to please those we love" is a more satisfactory approach to life than "We please those who pay us."

Should a Child Earn His Allowance? A fourth point of view of some parents is that children should not be given money unless they earn it. Such a parent says, "When a child needs money, make him earn it. He won't be handed money for nothing when he grows up." With as poor logic, you would refuse to button the dress of a 2-year-old because she will not be likely to have a maid when she grows up. After all, a small child is helped to do things until he can manage unaided. A healthy youngster wants to learn to do things alone. Children want to master buttons, to walk instead of being carried, because independence is an intriguing goal.

If a boy is taught that only earners can be spenders, is he likely to turn over most of his income to a wife for the family food, clothes, and rent? Grown up, he may feel that a full-time homemaker is not actually earning money and therefore is not entitled to a voice in how the family income is to be spent. A girl so taught may feel that as a housewife she is thwarted and be content only if she is actually receiving money earned outside the home.

If earning is to be the only source of a child's allowance, parents will find that they are paying for all home chores, since outside jobs available to children are strictly controlled by state labor laws. The family must decide which household jobs are to be done as a family team working together for the happiness of each member and which jobs can properly be paid for.

This is not a simple problem, because what is an outside hired job in one family may be just a family chore in another. Each family should discuss and come to an agreement on this matter. Usually it boils down to this proposition: "Here are some jobs we have to hire someone to do. If you want to do them, we'll pay you instead. How about it?"

Sharing Family Chores—Pay or No Pay.   This leads to the fifth point of view, the most sound, with regard to children's allowances and work—making a child feel that all the family should share in the family work, pay or no pay. It should not be hard to impress upon all members of the family that they must share the family work just as they share the total family income.

It is easy to point out that there is really no way of paying mother for the thousands of dishes she is washing for the entire family. Likewise, there is no way of paying father for making a living for the family. And there is no way of paying for the love and care that both parents give to a child, especially in sickness. These things are taken for granted because parents want to do them.

When the family income and work are shared by every member of the family, it is not unreasonable to conclude that:

1.   Every member of the family is entitled to a fair share of the family income, including an allowance, because he is a part of the family.
2.   Every member of the family should do certain chores in and around the home to keep the family life happy and successful.
3.   Jobs around the home that ordinarily involve hired help can be assumed by the children, according to their abilities and strength, for mutually agreed-on money payment.
4.   Jobs for pay, outside the family, can be undertaken if such work is beneficial for all the family.

Reactions Caused by Parental Attitudes

Inseparable from the children's allowance system is the way the parents manage the total family income. The spending pattern and the methods used by the parents are significant in terms of child development. First, family financial management determines the kind of living the child will experience for many years. Second, it influences his attitudes and feelings toward other people. Third, it sets before him a way of life in which relative values are revealed.

Most parents do not discover until a serious argument occurs that their attitude toward money is influencing all their relations with their children. In a study of 7,000 high school students, it was found that two-fifths of the quarrels between adolescents and their parents were over money matters.[15] In homes where money matters are permitted to become a focal point for argument, the children grow up with immature money concepts, which may continue for still another generation.

Here are some of the techniques resorted to by children in families with immature money management concepts.

[15] Evelyn Millis Duvall, *Keeping Up with Teen Agers*, Public Affairs Committee, New York, 1947, p. 77.

1.   Having to beg for every cent of spending money is not foreign to some homes. The variations of method depend on the degree of resistance on the part of the parents and often on the child's skill of playing one parent against the other. Such a child knows that it is especially hard to resist appeals for money if a visitor is within hearing distance or if mother is very busy.

2.   Some children take advantage of parents when on a shopping expedition. "Won't you buy me this?" pleads little Tommy. If mother refuses, Tommy says, "I'll lie down and scream unless you buy it." What should the mother do? Call his bluff in a crowded store? Give him a sound spanking right there? Lack of money education on the part of Tommy's parents, or possibly always giving in to the child's way of handling a situation, invited such a public display. It is a human relations problem, not a mere matter of money management, though money is the focal point of the dispute.

3.   In an effort to break through parental defenses, older children sometimes misuse the family charge account. This can be prevented by the parents, but too often the remedy comes after one or more bad experiences. For example, when a mother refused to give her daughter money for a birthday gift for a friend, the girl charged an expensive gift to the family account.

4.   Children sometimes resort to pilfering in stores. It may be candy, gum, small toys at first, later perhaps a baseball, a doll, or even a clothing item. Usually, they are personal items that could be purchased by an adequate allowance. A variation of pilfering is shaking coins from the child's bank, "borrowing" cash from mother's purse, or shortchanging the parents when making a family purchase.

5.   In some homes, the lack of an allowance system leads to seeking an outside job. This is not too bad if it is not forced on a child by parents who do not invite the child's confidence in money matters.

Today, youngsters spend more money than their parents spent in their day. Movies, soft drinks, milk shakes, and entertainment cost as much as the necessities of life may have cost a generation ago. But parents should remember that they helped to bring into existence these miracles of production and distribution. The problem cannot be solved simply by limiting a child's spending money or restricting it entirely. It must be met by helping a child to assume responsibility for spending his money intelligently—that is, teaching him to have money sense.

The Allowance System

Children learn how to swim and to play baseball, hockey, and other games by experience in each of these sports. Likewise, they can learn how to use money by experiencing the spending of money. The best way to distribute family money to normal children is via the allowance system.

An allowance gives a child a chance to handle some of the money that will be spent on him anyway. A child consumes food, clothes, and many other items from the time he is born. And he keeps this up on an ascending scale for many years.

Since youngsters must have certain essentials without actually earning them, why should money be an exception? Children should receive some money, then, just as they receive food and clothes. They can use such money to buy their own notebooks, paper, pencils, books, paints, and other personal items. This helps them to become acquainted with money, its limitations, potentialities, and value. They will learn money sense best by handling and spending money.

Even a preschool child can learn the use and value of money if he is permitted to hand the conductor the bus fare or to pay for things that mother buys in a store. In marketing, a child has the opportunity to see that mother has to make choices and decisions in buying.

Alice may say, "Mother! see the nice strawberries. May we have some for lunch?" Mother explains that those strawberries are expensive because they are out of season and she must plan to buy another fruit. Alice may be convinced after returning home if mother prepares another attractive dessert and compares its cost with the out-of-season strawberries. Add to these experiences, and soon even a preschool child begins to weigh the pros and cons of decisions in buying. Thus, when a child is put on an allowance and is confronted with the necessity for a decision, he will be more likely to weigh one desire against another.

What Is an Allowance?   An allowance is a specified sum of money given to a child at regular intervals, which is his to spend, save, give away, or even lose. It is cash received over and above any family income allotted for the child's normal care and necessities. As such, it should be set aside as a regular part of the family expenditures, like those for clothes, food, rent, and the car.

The allowance should not be treated as something earned or deserved; it should be distinct and separate from any form of discipline or parental desire. Also, it is desirable to avoid giving a child the feeling that his allowance is a gift from his parents. An allowance, no matter how small, should have no restrictions. Education, yes; but the child should have complete and exclusive control of the use of his allowance.

Restrictions, in place of information and education, reduce the experience to a point where the child is merely acting as a disbursing agent. This might rightly be called an allowance under false pretenses.

Guiding Principles for Allowances.   Planning an allowance is not unlike any other educational venture. Certain fundamental principles are important. In addition to those given above, educational experts generally agree on the following. [16]

1. Start a child on an allowance when he begins to make fairly regular requests for money for personal needs or desires. A child under 6 might need or desire such items as paints, crayons, ice cream cones, candy and chewing

[16] For more details, see especially Sidonie M. Gruenberg and Benjamin C. Gruenberg, *Parents, Children, and Money,* The Viking Press, Inc., New York, 1933; *Money Management: Children's Spending,* Household Finance Corporation, Chicago, rev. ed., 1955.

gum, Sunday-school money, gifts for others, children's books, and playthings. A child between the ages of 6 and 9 might begin to request money for magazines, movies, carfare, school lunches, box-top offers, and records, in addition to the items just listed.

2. The allowance should be matched with the child's ability to handle new responsibilities. Each child, even within the same family, is different. Usually you cannot handle two cases in the same way at the same age. A common mistake is to make the child assume too much responsibility or too little. Each year, additional responsibilities should be added, and corresponding increases in the allowance should be provided. By the time the child is of high school age, the allowance should cover most of his needs, including clothes.

3. The amount of the allowance should be determined after needs and costs have been listed by the child and discussed with the parents. Any cutting by the parents should be explained to the child and be fully understood and accepted by him. The amount will have to be based on the financial circumstances of the family. If possible, the sum should include a fair amount above and beyond such necessities as carfare and school lunch money; otherwise, the child has no opportunity to decide how to spend his own money for his desires as well as needs. He must get sufficient experience in making decisions.

4. The age and experience of a child will determine the length of time over which his money management has to stretch. If the family income is based on weekly payments, the allowance may have to fit into weekly spacing. Ordinarily, a young child, just beginning to have an allowance, might be paid twice a week; later, weekly or twice a month; and finally, monthly.

5. It is important that full payment be made on the day agreed on. All the rules must be known and agreed on in advance. Then stick to this agreement until changes are mutually made. This is a good time to invite a child to participate in an informal family discussion of the total income and spending setup. As years go by, more and more of such information can be revealed, until by the time he is about ready for college, he will know the total financial situation. The sooner this is done, other things being equal, the easier it is to get cooperation without unpleasant bickering.

6. After an allowance has been set up, the child should understand that part of it must be used for necessities and perhaps for savings, and the rest is his to spend as he chooses. Here is where parents need the patience of Job and the wisdom of Solomon. They must not expect too much. This might be illustrated by a remark that a student made in a money management conference: "When I was about twelve years old, my parents expected me to handle money as if I were thirty years old."

7. An allowance should not be tied to jobs done at home. The allowance should be distributed because the child is a member of the family and is en-

titled to it as such. Work at home should be divided according to age and abilities. This is a separate responsibility, and each child should be expected to do his part.

8. If a child requests more money, even though he understands the agreement, it is usually a good idea not to give him more money before his next allowance is due. While there are exceptions to all good rules in human relations, the exception can too easily become the rule. It might be wiser to say: "If your needs are more than your allowance, make a new list of them, and we'll talk it over again." Most children will consider that this is a fair attitude. At the same time, the parents are not placing themselves in the position of putting the child through a third degree. He, then, will have time to do a little adjusting for himself. This is sound psychology and good economics.

9. If a child loses his allowance, it is important to take time to learn all the facts in a calm discussion of the matter. If money is needed for necessities, replace it to that extent. The extra amount should be deferred until the next allowance is due. This may seem to be a little rough, but it is conditioning the child for similar experiences that he will have later.

10. If a child begins to hoard his money, observe whether it is a passing stage or whether it reflects maladjustment to living. Some children are influenced by their parents' attitude or by pressures and demands on them during their growing-up years. It may also be a symptom of personal insecurity.

11. When a child is eager to contribute money to an organization or a school or community group, it is important that he understand its purpose. He should not give money to inflate his ego or just to hold his status among his friends. He should not derive satisfaction out of proportion to his allowance.

12. Saving ought to be active and meaningful, not a routine stuffing of the child's bank. Saving can be encouraged if the objective is specific—for personal use or for a gift for someone the child loves—and the spending should not be delayed too long. A young child may save for a doll displayed in a window. A high school student may save for the annual dance. Saving for a rainy day—just putting away money—has no significance for a child.

A 4-year-old is not a saver. He must start with spending. In time, he may save to spend later. But the only way to learn this is by experience. When a child is 9 to 12 years old, he can begin to understand the principle of saving for future spending, but he must first discover the meaning of the future.

13. If a loan is made to a child, repayment should be arranged within a reasonable time, but without too much sacrifice. Borrowing and lending are constantly going on in our society. A child needs sympathetic guidance if requesting a loan that is out of proportion to his ability to pay. Disappointment can be accepted gracefully if parents use tact and display friendly counsel in such matters. It is not easy for parents to judge the value of the things for which children want money. A seemingly small want can produce intense emotional stress. Many parents still carry such emotional scars from their own childhood.

14. When a child is concerned because his friends have more money than he has to spend, two things are necessary. Discover what the allowances of the friends have to cover. Reexamine the child's needs and allowance. If the old agreement, or a new one, is consistent with the family income or with the needs of the child, he usually accepts it. Sometimes it is necessary to give him a clearer sense of values. Above all, a child must know why.

15. If a child has experience in handling money, by the time he enters high school, he is ready to assume more responsibility. The urge for independence is strong when a child is of high school age. He begins to resent any attempt to keep him young and dependent. He insists on making his own decisions. His money needs are greater, too. The allowance should grow, but so should the responsibilities. The child now should learn how to handle a checking account, how to order merchandise and pay bills, how to decide on tips, how to buy his own clothing and care for it.

16. Record keeping for a child is useless unless he can be made to feel a specific gain from the effort. A teen-ager may discover for himself that some records are necessary. This is especially true if he is granted increases in his allowance only on the basis of reasonably proved needs. Often this must take the form of evidence of where his money went.

Democratic Ways to Promote Happy Families

There is no substitute for happy, understanding family relationships. The best preparation for such relationships is for parents to teach their children to share the family chores, to cooperate in family discussions, and to handle money wisely. Children having such experience learn to face situations objectively, to analyze and solve difficulties and problems in later life.

This does not mean that children should be weighted down with family responsibilities before they are old enough to understand them. On the other hand, they should not be shielded or overprotected from the realities of family life. They should be allowed to join in family discussions and in final decisions as soon as they are old enough to understand what is involved.

QUESTIONS FOR DISCUSSION

1. What are your reactions to the following statements since studying this chapter?
   a. "If you are a good boy, I'll give you a dime."
   b. "I'm going to take fifty cents out of your allowance if you are late for supper again."
   c. "I had to earn my own spending money when I was a boy."
   d. "I'll give them money when they need it."

2. Do you agree that most of us are "born with money sense"?

3. When money is considered by parents as a symbol of power and success, what may be the effect on children in such a family?

4. When parents pay for better grades and honors in school, have they the best interests of their children in mind?

5. How can a child be made to understand that everybody in the family should share in the family work, not for pay, but because he is a member of the family team?

ACTIVITY PROBLEMS

1. Plan a class discussion or a recording of a discussion based on the topic "Parents and the Child's Pocketbook." Ask a father, a mother, a boy and a girl, ages 10 and 17, from different families, to participate in this project. See that illustrations of important principles in children's allowances, work in the home, human relations, school grades, and activities are brought into this discussion.

2. Ask several college students how they obtained things they wanted when they were living at home. Make a list of the techniques they employed. Discuss and evaluate these methods.

3. The question is often asked: "When should you start a child on an allowance?" An interesting way to gather evidence is to interview children in various age brackets. Ask them to name their regular personal money needs. Make a list of these needs, and classify them according to age groups, such as Under 6, Age 6 to 9, Age 9 to 12, Age 12 to 18.

4. How would you teach a child to save money? Begin by asking friends and classmates how they learned to save money. Perhaps they failed to learn how to save money. Analyze good and bad techniques.

5. Recall all the major experiences that you have had with the use of money. Keep in mind the principles involved in these experiences. Check these principles against a list of children's allowance principles that you consider sound. What changes would you make for your own children?

SUGGESTED READINGS

Bergler, Edmund: *Money and Emotional Conflicts,* Pageant Books, New York, 1959.

Butterfield, Oliver M.: *Planning for Marriage,* D. Van Nostrand Company, Inc., Princeton, N.J., 1965, chap. 14.

"Youth Leads the Way," *Business Week,* Jan. 18, 1964, p. 31. "Bring in the Kids, They Bring in the Family," Sept. 5, 1964, pp. 32-34.

Clare, Sister M. Paul: "Teen-age Attitudes toward Money Management," *Journal of Home Economics,* February, 1963, p. 124.

Remsberg, Charles, and Bonnie Remsberg: "Wooing the Dimply, Pimply," in *New York Times Magazine,* June 5, 1966.

Stewart, Alice M.: *Consumer Close-ups,* Cornell University, Ithaca, N.Y., May 29, 1967.

chapter 5

MONEY MANAGEMENT

There is something funny
That isn't so funny
To have too much month
At the end of the money

Family money is the hardest in the world to manage. Why? Families have not discovered the secret of converting dollars into contentment.

And what is the secret? Good money management, largely. Considering what money can do to your marriage, for better or for worse, this is a good time to get your money thinking straight.

When you marry, the marriage contract establishes an economic enterprise called a family. Like a business enterprise, a family sets out to operate at a profit. At the very best, it has to break even. If it doesn't, the enterprise goes under.

When a business fails, only the legal entity suffers. When a family goes under, human beings suffer. And, as we learned in earlier chapters, economic stress can put a marriage under great strain, and may even destroy it.

MONEY MANAGEMENT AND BUDGETING FOR COLLEGE STUDENTS

Adequate family income depends greatly on the education of the head of the family (Table 5-1). The largest single group is that in which the family head has completed high school but gone no farther in school. In 1966 this group comprised 30 percent of the families and the median income was 8 percent above the average. At the one extreme, where the family head had completed four or more years of college, there were 12 percent of the families and the median income was 56 percent above the average. In other words, the annual income for the head of the family with a high school diploma was $8,045 in 1966 compared to an income of $11,603 a year for the college graduate with four or more years of schooling. Education is one of the most important determinants of family income.

Education increases the income of women, too. After the excitement of the wedding day, parents may ask themselves if college was really necessary for their daughter. Rapidly rising college costs raise serious doubts for many parents. Research into this subject by the Institute of Life Insurance has found that a college degree for women is "likely to be valuable to her all her life." While most women find a college degree helpful in meeting the challenges of marriage and child-rearing, most would concede that it is not essential. On the other hand, the practical value of the college degree becomes evident later in life when the children are less dependent. At this time the woman may decide to enter the working world. The U.S. Department of Labor has found that among college-educated women 45 to 54 years old, seven out of ten now hold jobs, and the chances improve with a year or more of graduate work.

A new study by the U.S. Census Bureau estimates the worth of a man to his family. Assuming a 4 percent annual rise in earnings, and a 4 percent return on investments, the Census Bureau gives the following example for a man who was 22 years old in 1967 and works until retirement age of 65:

1. With an eighth-grade education, he would earn $445,000.
2. With four years of high school, the total earnings would be $623,000.
3. With four or more years of college, he would earn $1,125,000.

TABLE 5-1   FAMILY INCOME BY EDUCATION OF HEAD OF FAMILY, 1966* (PERCENT OF FAMILIES IN EACH GROUP)

| | SCHOOLING COMPLETED | | | | | | |
| | Elementary | | High School | | College | | |
Family Income	Less than 8 Years	8 Years	1 to 3 Years	4 Years	1 to 3 Years	4 Years or More	All Families
Under $3,000	35.9%	20.9%	14.2%	8.0%	6.4%	4.4%	14.3%
$3,000 to $4,999	22.8	19.3	16.3	11.3	8.0	5.2	13.9
$5,000 to $6,999	17.4	20.6	20.1	19.1	15.3	9.4	17.8
$7,000 to $9,999	14.8	21.8	25.9	29.3	28.2	20.8	24.4
$10,000 to $14,999	6.6	13.6	18.5	24.2	28.1	31.8	20.4
$15,000 and over	2.3	3.8	5.0	8.1	13.9	28.4	9.2
Total	100.0%	100.0%	100.0%	100.0%	100.0%	100.0%	100.0%
Thousands of families	6,462	7,792	8,986	14,740	4,950	5,992	48,922
Median income	$4,123	$5,966	$6,947	$8,045	$9,124	$11,603	$7,436

*From *Finance Facts*, 1968 Yearbook of the National Consumer Finance Association, Washington, D.C.
SOURCE: Bureau of the Census.

Dropping Out of College Is Not the End

About half of the entering college freshmen each year will probably drop out of college before receiving a degree. This 50 percent casualty rate has been constant since at least 1960.

This is not an entirely black picture, however. Even if a student does drop out of college, he is likely to return at a later date to finish his degree. The U.S. Office of Education reports that the one-out-of-two dropout rate is also balanced further by the fact that many of these students did not plan to go to college for the full four years.

A University of Illinois study reporting on the dropout problem says that more than seven out of ten men and women who enter state-supported colleges and universities eventually acquire their degrees, although it may take 10 years.

Many educators who have studied the dropout pattern are beginning to feel that four consecutive years of college may be economically or psychologically beyond the reach of a substantial number of students. For many youngsters an interruption provides needed cash or motivation to return to college to complete a degree.

Who Pays for College Education?

In a recent study reported in *Financing a College Education,* by the College Entrance Examination Board, one university indicated that its students paid approximately 25 percent of their college expenses from their own savings and earnings; parents paid 40 to 50 percent of the expenses from current income and another 10 to 15 percent, from savings and loans. The remaining 10 to 20 percent of the expenses came from various kinds of scholarships and gifts.

Most financial aid offices in colleges and universities are very familiar with the problems of parents whose income should be adequate to finance their children's higher education, who have every intention of providing for college, but who simply cannot meet college bills when they fall due. Typically, parents' lamentations are: "We thought we had planned well, but we just didn't save enough." "We never saved because we were sure our son would get a scholarship." Or, "We never imagined it would cost so much." Or, "We thought that by the time the children entered college the government would pay for it."

The fact is that, according to a recent study, [1] only two out of every five families with upper-middle income (mean gross income of $14,000) have any savings plan for college, and most of these plans are dangerously inadequate. The average amount saved was only $310. As Table 5-2 shows, this amount varied directly with the family's net income.

[1] Betty Lou and Wesley W. Marple, "How Affluent Families Plan to Pay for College," *College Board Review,* Spring, 1967.

TABLE 5-2   AMOUNT SAVED IN 1965 COMPARED WITH FAMILY INCOME

FAMILY INCOME	AVERAGE AMOUNT SAVED
$7,000 - $9,999	$185
10,000 - 11,999	211
12,000 - 14,999	335
15,000 - 19,999	353
20,000 - 24,999	438

The average amount saved and invested annually over 10 to 15 years might produce $2,000. But parents said that their savings would meet 40 percent of the college costs for one child. If college costs are around $3,000 per year or $12,000 over 4 years, savings should be $4,800 to meet the savings goal of 40 percent of costs. Clearly, actual savings are more than likely to fall short of the goal. Many parents seem unwilling or unable to save adequately to meet these costs. Unless affluent parents do a better job of saving and investing money for college education, most of them will continue having difficulty in meeting their children's college expenses. One obvious need is for parents to start saving 15 years in advance of the first year of college.

How to Pay for a College Education

Any boy or girl with average ability should be able to secure a college education in this country. Few parents can afford to pay all the college bills out of savings and regular income. But there is no need for panic. There are many ways to secure the funds. At least some can come from income, since parents will no longer have their child at home. The normal cost of essentials for a child at home is around $800 during the nine-month school period. Another part can come from the student's part-time and summer jobs. And some can come from the college, a local or national organization, a loan, or other sources.

The student himself can work, save, borrow, and be sensible about his expenditures and the choice of a college. Student employment is an important source of financial aid. So are "room and board jobs" and cooperative houses where students may live and possibly prepare their own meals or eat meals prepared for them. Normally, a student should not work over 15 hours per week when taking a normal college class load. Fifteen hours of work a week would pay a student $650 at $1.25 an hour.

The College Work-study Program.   The program for work and study in college, established under the Economic Opportunity Act of 1964, will provide many new and educationally related student employment opportunities. Any student demonstrating financial need is presently eligible for this program.

Student loans for higher education are available up to about $1,000 a year, carrying a very small interest rate. The National Defense Student Loan Program, established in 1954, was one of the largest sources of student loans. There are also state loan programs under the Higher Education Act of 1965 to encourage states to establish guaranteed loan programs. There are also commercial loan programs through banks, insurance companies, and finance corporations.

Colleges are the first source to which students should apply for scholarships. Most scholarships are based on financial need as well as scholarship. There are also state scholarship programs which should be investigated.

The Educational Opportunity Grants Program.   This program, established under the Higher Education Act of 1965, provides up to $800 annually to students who are admissible to college and who demonstrate "exceptional financial need."

GI benefits are presently available to some 3 million veterans whose service was after the Korean War. The major benefit to these veterans for financial aid for college is $130 per month, with added allowances for dependents.

Money Management for College Students

As a college student, you have the same reason as other individuals and families have for planning expenditures wisely. An intelligently planned budget will not deprive you of pleasure. On the contrary, it will help you to decide what to eliminate in order to have the things you need and really want.

If you are an unmarried college student, your family or guardian expects you—more or less—to manage your own expenditures during the college year. If you are a married college student, your budgeting problems will have to be centered around both family needs and college needs. Chapter 3 will be helpful in such a case. The married college student has, in fact, a double problem. He has to take care of all or most of the regular family budgeting problems in addition to his central purpose for the time being—education.

A good reason for devoting some serious attention to money management now is that you are setting habits that will stay with you during your entire lifetime. Good money management habits established now will pay dividends many times during your life. Some will say, "I'll wait until I'm married to set up a good money management program." Others will wait until the car is paid for or until the next raise comes along, or until . . . *ad infinitum.* Somehow they never get around to doing the job because they are always waiting for the right time. The best way to become an expert at managing money is to begin practicing *now.*

You may be one of that group of college students who are spending money not directly earned by them. Perhaps there has been little opportunity for you to learn to manage money well. You may be, however, among the few who are good consumers. If you are a good consumer, you insist on receiving value for your money. If you stick to that principle, you will probably be successful in managing all your resources—time, money, and energy.

You may be facing, for the first time, the full responsibility of deciding for yourself how to plan and spend your money. If so, you belong to the large group of college students who need counseling in the management of personal finances.

"How," you ask, "do I know whether I'm successful in handling my personal finances?"

The answer to that question is not an easy one. It is possible to make ends meet and yet not be successful in money management. It is likewise possible to be a careful buyer of consumer goods and services and not be a successful money manager. The person who is successful in money management is one who plans, buys, and uses goods and services in such a manner that he gets what he most desires from those goods and services.

MONEY MANAGEMENT AND BUDGETING FOR THE FAMILY

The accompanying questionnaire, Money Management IQ, will help you discover your "dollar sense"—help you evaluate your skill in money management.

If your score is below 55, you really need to develop your skills in handling money. If your score embarrasses you, do not be discouraged. Remember the first time you drove a car or tried to hit a little ball with a golf club? Everything went wrong. Then, almost without knowing when, you began making the right moves without consciously thinking of them. The same results will happen as you learn to handle your money in a planned way. You may think it time-consuming and unrewarding at first. Soon you will be making your money achieve the major goals that you set up.

Define Your Goals

There are two fundamentals of money management for college students. The first is to plan your own budget. It is your money. Establish your own spending pattern and be sure that your money is going where you want it to go. The second fundamental is to set up your own goals. Knowing what you are aiming for will give a positive approach to budgeting. When you define your goals, you have taken the first step toward reaching them.

As a college student, you have certain financial obligations that can be classified as fixed expenses, such as tuition, board and room, and possibly transportation. As a rule you must meet these fixed expenses at a particular time. Then there are many flexible expenses, such as supplies, books, snacks, clothes, grooming items, recreation. The important thing is to be clear about your goals—aims, obligations, immediate and remote wants. Then make a definite plan for spending your dollars to meet your personal needs and wants. Use your spending plan to reach your goals.

MONEY MANAGEMENT IQ

A SELF-TEST QUESTIONNAIRE ON PERSONAL SPENDING HABITS

This questionnaire, if filled out as accurately as your memory permits, will help you to discover your weaknesses in personal money management. Each "yes" answer rates 5 points. Add the points to find your money management IQ. If your score is

Over 75, consider yourself a *good* money manager.

Between 75 and 55, consider yourself *average.*

Between 55 and 35, you are *below average.*

Below 35, you are *very poor.*

1. Have you made a rough plan for your large expenses for the year?
2. Have you kept a written record of your expenditures for at least one month?
3. Have you examined your record of expenditures and made necessary changes?
4. Are you seldom "broke" before your next allowance or income is received?
5. When "broke" do you generally get along as best you can until your allowance is received?
6. Do you avoid making yourself miserable and unhappy by fretting about something you want but cannot afford?
7. Are you in the habit of spending moderately on personal grooming?
8. Can you generally be entertained without spending money?
9. Do you usually resist the spending pressures of friends?
10. Do you resist the spending of money according to your whim without regard to what you really need?
11. When "broke," do you tend to avoid getting an extra sum from your parents or guardian?
12. If you saw a clothing item in a store where you have a charge account, would you be likely to think about how to pay for it before you bought it?
13. Are you careful about not leaving cash in your room or carrying fairly large sums of money on your person?
14. Do you usually avoid buying clothes that you may wear only a few times?
15. Do you spend a moderate amount of money for food between meals?
16. Do you usually save ahead for something you want very much, such as a new dress or suit, a gift, a prom?
17. Do you make it a habit to go to more than one store to compare price and quality before deciding on a big purchase?
18. Would you say that about half your purchases are planned in advance and are not merely "impulse" buying?
19. Do you know whether your family carries personal belongings insurance, protecting such items as your luggage, clothes, jewelry, golf and tennis equipment?
20. Can you resist buying bargains just because they are advertised as bargains?
    Your score: The number of checks (   ) $\times$ 5 = (   ).

A Budgeted Spending Plan

The first step in preparing a college budget is to get a true picture of your expenses by keeping a record of spending for two to four weeks. At the end of each week, total the amount spent for "fixed" or necessary expenses. These always must be paid. Other expenses are "flexible," that is, they can be cut out or cut down, depending on your needs and income. You are the one to decide which of your expenses are fixed and which are flexible. An accurate spending record and classification of expenses into fixed and flexible items will help you set up a spending plan that works.

Table 5-3, A Budgeted Spending Plan, will help you differentiate between fixed and flexible expenses. Of course, you can add items or subtract any that you do not need to allow for in your own spending plan.

You will be one in a thousand if you can actually "balance the budget." But, like golf and tennis, even money management is a skill to be learned and practiced, and the attitude toward money management must be acquired. You can become quite efficient if you learn good management of your income while in college, and then continue using this skill in family income planning.

Financial Planning before Marriage

The marriage service is usually full of emotional and spiritual significance. Materialistically it is a contract. Although there is no mention of financial considerations in the ceremony, they are really implied in the terms of the contract.

What will be the economic future for your family? It depends on many things, but basically, there are two important considerations: the size of the family income, and how you use it. How much income are you likely to have the first year of marriage? Is it enough to support a family of two? If you are disturbed because your income may be a modest one, say $6,500, you are better off than you think. The median income (half below, half above) of families in 1966, according to the Bureau of the Census, was $7,436. Most of the families below $7,436 managed to make ends meet. It is well to remember that this figure is based on the entire population and includes families that have been established for years. And you are only a beginner.

For a college graduate, the chances are good that the first year's salary will be at least $6,000. Graduates in the sciences often have a beginning annual salary of $8,000 to $9,000.

Perhaps the wife-to-be has a job and will work after marriage. In early marriage, it is safer to include most of the second income in the regular budget; do not be too optimistic about how much of it to include. There are extra expenses attached to any job—perhaps as much as 40 percent. Then, too, the wife may become pregnant.

What about aid from parents? Attitudes and conditions vary so much that no general rule is possible. One caution is in order—assistance is one thing, dependency another. If a young couple depend on a parental financial prop too long, there will be trouble when the subsidy ends.

Most parents want to help their youngsters financially if such aid will strengthen the young family. Such help can be gracefully accepted and given.

TABLE 5-3   A BUDGETED SPENDING PLAN

INCOME	ESTIMATED INCOME	ACTUAL INCOME
Balance on hand (including amounts owed to you)	$_____	$_____
Regular weekly income	_____	_____
Additions to allowance	_____	_____
Earnings	_____	_____
Gifts	_____	_____
Total	$_____	$_____

FIXED EXPENSES	ESTIMATED FIXED EXPENSE	ACTUAL AMOUNT SPENT
Food	$_____	$_____
Room	_____	_____
Tuition	_____	_____
Transportation	_____	_____
Organization dues	_____	_____
Fees (laboratory, health, etc.)	_____	_____
Other	_____	_____
Total fixed expenditures	$_____	$_____

FLEXIBLE EXPENSES	ESTIMATED EXPENSE	ACTUAL AMOUNT SPENT
Recreation	$_____	$_____
School supplies	_____	_____
Books	_____	_____
Clothing	_____	_____
Contributions	_____	_____
Grooming	_____	_____
Snacks	_____	_____
Repairs (radio, watch, shoes, etc.)	_____	_____
Gifts	_____	_____
Laundry, dry cleaning	_____	_____
Cultural events	_____	_____
Health	_____	_____
Cigarettes	_____	_____
Beverages	_____	_____
Other	_____	_____
Total flexible expenditures	$_____	$_____
Grand total	$_____	$_____

Actual income $_____
Actual amount spent $_____
Balance left $_____

There are, however, many young families that never learn to live without financial aid from their in-laws.

Do You Need a Budget?   After marriage there are at least two persons to consider in using income. The spending patterns used when single cannot be followed successfully after marriage. There are different responsibilities, new motivations, a different kind of household. Before you establish a home, it is essential to have some idea of how far your money will go, where it will go, and who will spend it. As you contemplate marriage, you will probably think, "Other people need to budget, but we understand each other so well that we have no need to bother." Don't believe it! It is surprising how a financial quarrel can turn into a domestic crisis, and it is a shame not to take simple steps to avoid this *before* marriage.

The three most important areas in family finance are budgeting, buymanship, and credit. It is a good thing, therefore, to be sensible about money. It's a good idea to have a plan for spending and saving and to try to follow it. And this is true not just because good money management makes money do what you want it to do, but because a plan can mean more happiness, less preoccupation with money, and a better attitude toward life. It is helpful when young couples agree on the answers to the following questions.

Is the wife going to have a housekeeping allowance?
Exactly what is that going to cover?
Will the wife work for pay outside the home?
Who will keep the necessary income and spending records?
Who will pay what bills?
How much can be set aside for emergencies and savings?
How much can be saved for vacations? Baby expenses?
How much can be allowed for personal spending?

There will be other questions concerned with the particular way you are going to live, your job or jobs, transportation, insurance, and so on, which each couple can add to this list. But do settle these questions well in advance of setting up housekeeping.

Money Management after Marriage

Money management generally is mentioned as the most common cause, directly or indirectly, for marital discord. Family finance is often given as the most difficult problem in homemaking. It is one that causes much worry. The tendency of a young couple, very much in love, seems to be to expect that they will meet the financial problems *when they arise*. Such persons say, "When all is well, why plan?"

The tragedy among some families with this "meet it when it comes up" philosophy is that they refuse to meet or see the facts when the situation occurs. Other families, however, do meet the situation, but only by salvaging the results of their lack of planning beforehand. Such persons would not think of selecting a man to head a business or a surgeon to perform an operation unless he had had adequate training. Yet so many couples, deeply in love, are willing to go into marriage without knowing how to be wise managers of money.

People who cannot live within their income are, in general, poor managers. Money, like time and talent, can be wasted. Money has to be managed intelligently, or you will be on the losing side. And being on the losing side in money management is a serious matter, because you are playing a game for family happiness—for keeps.

How then do you prepare yourself for winning such an important game? The answer is training. Back of training, however, is attitude. The first prerequisite to wise management of money is attitude.

So much attention has been given to personality maladjustments as a cause of marital discord that we are likely to forget that normal people can achieve creative adjustments. A normal couple discover the facts, face them honestly, and seek an insight into their own pattern of behavior. We know from studies that happily married people are successful homemakers, not because they have no problems but because they face their problems and arrive at a working solution. An important attitude toward handling family finances successfully is the desire for joint planning, joint earning, and joint spending to the end that every member of the family gets the utmost satisfaction from the money spent.

Importance of Values and Goals.   The first step to successful money planning is to discuss the values you believe in and what you want out of life. This is a big order. It is important for family members to know, in general, what the family is working toward. Once you know the values you believe in, you will find a way of fitting them into your way of living.

Values determine the goals that give direction to living. Some values are ideals, such as loyalty, courage, and honesty. Religious values generally influence the moral tone of an individual. Other values, such as smartness, sophistication, popularity, cleanliness, comfort, and security, may not be dignified by the term *ideals,* but they influence behavior in an important way.

We learn our values at home, in school, in church, and in countless other places. Certainly one inescapable function of the home is to pass values on to the child, who in turn may accept or reject some of them. These values generally direct his actions without the necessity of making a new decision every time he is confronted with a new situation or problem. These values will change when some new value has greater appeal or worth for the individual or family.

Values, like democracy and authoritarianism, carry over to family behavior. In some families, the father is a "benevolent despot," "a dictator," or perhaps a senior member of a "democratic" family. Mass media—movies, radio, television, newspapers, and magazines—provide additional ways for people to share values. At times, these media lead people to accept values that in turn lead to conflict in the home. Romantic love stories portrayed on television and movie screens may lead to unrealistic concepts that make marital adjustments more difficult. On the other hand, these media have helped to improve parent-child relationships. Literature and art, scientific studies, and lectures have had direct influence in creating new values for many people. On the whole, values come from our family, our religious beliefs, our own peer group, our educational experiences, and our culture.

Values do change. Few of us escape the initial conflicts that generally accompany changing values. This conflict should be accepted as a part of growing up—maturing—which is characterized by the ability to acquire meaningful relationships from changing values. Until there is clarity and meaning in your value system, your individual and family goals are out of reach.

Goals Depend on Your Values.   Established personal or family goals will help you to realize the beliefs or values you hold. Long-term goals are related to your philosophy of living. Your beliefs or values, which determine your philosophy, are given priority in planning your life, depending on the importance you attach to them. It is the order of this priority, which may change, that determines the goals you set. If financial security is placed high in your value system, then financial security becomes a long-term goal. Saving a little each week or month and investing it immediately becomes a short-term goal whose basic value is financial security. Values are the "criteria against which goals are chosen."[2]

The value you hope to realize in attaining a certain goal becomes the goal value you will plan for and work toward. For example, parents who prize financial security for the family include this objective in such specific activities as planning a savings program; putting money in the bank; providing for various types of insurance; budgeting; securing information on good investments, annuities, and mutual funds; and investigating the reliability of the companies that offer such services. The goal values are the specific ones that are important to the objective—in this case, financial security.

A goal value must be clearly understood before it can be achieved. For example, you might say that the goal of the family is to achieve maximum happiness for all its members. This is too general. It is important to know how you intend to achieve your goal. One family may believe that happiness can be achieved by acquiring expensive clothes and cars. Another may believe that it is better to control expenditures at present and save money for education of the children. A third family may think of happiness in terms of good music, art, and literature. Each family must decide its own value goals, decide what things it wants to achieve with its time, energy, and financial resources.

[2] Talcott Parsons and Edward A. Shils, *Toward a General Theory of Action,* Harvard University Press, Cambridge, Mass., 1952, p. 429.

In general, individuals and families are more successful in achieving their goal values when they take these steps:

1. Make a plan based on the goal values sought.
2. Put the plan into action.
3. Evaluate the action periodically in terms of the goal values realized.
4. Make a new plan, if necessary, based on the evaluation of the old plan.

Long-term Planning Gives Goals for Happiness. The length of each stage will vary from family to family. If a family chooses, it can make long-term plans to meet the needs of these stages. Such planning should not be considered final. Perhaps the best that a long-term plan can provide is direction. One can see the inevitable financial problems that must be met in the various stages of the family life-span. By long-term planning, most families can get the greatest satisfaction from the spending of their income for the entire family.

What a young couple wants out of life is of major importance. These goals or mental standards create pictures of the kind of life one prefers to see develop in the family. Knowing what we want, even in the face of defeat, is an essential step toward achieving happiness. It certainly is a prerequisite to intelligent money management, because eventually goals must be translated into dollars-and-cents terms. Family goals can be achieved best through efficient financial planning.

Joint Planning to Eliminate Irritants. It is particularly important for a couple to learn how to plan together when they are first married. No bride from one family and a husband from another family can expect to have the same views on spending money. But they can learn to understand each other's views and to compromise. It is wise to remember that men and women do not always spend money in the same way. Men cannot understand why women say they have "nothing to wear" when the closet seems to be bulging with clothes. On the other hand, women do not understand why men appear to spend money as no woman ever would. So, understanding and compromise are necessary.

Bedeviled by Undisciplined Dollars. Said a young wife after her first year of married life, "I had no idea there were so many things to be paid for." Exactly true. And for so many it seems that there never is enough money. Many families are constantly worried about meeting their bills. But even if they manage to pay the bills, the family may not have a satisfactory spending plan.

Most families are worried from payday to payday. Many of them go through life forever bedeviled by undisciplined dollars. Such financial bedevilment may be due to one or more of the following reasons:

1. Overestimating family income
2. Underestimating expenditures
3. No long-term plans
4. Irregular or uncertain income
5. Too many fixed expenses
6. Not enough family participation in management

7. Arguing over who should be the manager
8. Divergent attitudes about money management
9. Differences in attitudes toward values
10. Poor buymanship
11. Paying high interest on debts

Many of these practices can be avoided or modified. Financial advisors at banks, insurance companies, and social agencies believe that in many instances people shy away from doing anything about their money mismanagement because they have so many misconceptions about family spending plans. Let's take a look at a few of these misconceptions.

Misconceptions about Budgets

Madelyn Wood interviewed a number of family financial counselors who had helped thousands of persons plan budgets. According to these experts, there are four major misconceptions about budgeting.

1. *A budget is not bookkeeping.* Mrs. Jones came to the bank, proudly bearing a bookkeeper's ledger representing a year's expenditures. "I've kept a record of every penny," she told the budget advisor. Entered in neat script were such items as "postage, 6 cents, phone call, 10 cents." "And still we can't save money," wailed Mrs. Jones. Tactfully the expert told her the truth; she had been wasting her time. She had made herself and her family miserable with the mistaken notion that budgeting means keeping a record of everything you spend. . . . Budgeting isn't bookkeeping. You can have a workable budget—without any bookkeeping.

2. *A budget is not a system of fixed percentages.* An earnest Chicago housewife told a budget expert that she had calculated everything scientifically. She knew the formula which said you were supposed to spend "x" percent on clothing, "y" percent on housing, and so on. This had called for changing the family's living habits, because they had been spending too much on housing. They had moved, and now their rent was lower. But they were no longer happy. The expert explained that nobody could say how much you "ought" to spend on housing. The fixed-percentage formula is a fallacy. There is only what you have to spend and what you want to spend. Every expenditure involves a choice—buy one thing and you can't buy another.

3. *A budget is not pinching pennies.* Mrs. Green was on the verge of a nervous breakdown when she came to an advisor. "When we worked out our budget," she explained, "we figured all kinds of ways to save money. John agreed to cut out two packages of cigarettes a week. Tom, our 15-year-old boy, said he could get along on half his usual allowance." She followed with a long list of deprivations, totaling $5 a week. But she admitted that everyone in the household was unhappy. She had the wrong idea. Budgeting is not nursing nickels and mortifying the flesh with painful forms of thrift.

4. *A budget is not only for people with small incomes.* A successful Washington physician asked his bank for a loan. The facts he laid before a financial advisor were shocking. His income was $24,000 a year, yet he "owed everybody." Extravagance? He didn't think so. He and his family had felt unable to afford a winter vacation trip. His teenage daughters complained that they weren't as well dressed as other girls at school. The doctor was keenly aware that something was wrong, but he honestly didn't know what. "Just a case of careless spending," the advisor said. "What you need is a budget."

What Is a Good Budget?

Let us begin with what a budget is not. It does not, will not, and cannot tell how to spend money. Furthermore, it is not designed to keep us away from the things we want. It is not an end in itself. It is not even a plan to restrict spending. What *is* it, then?

A budget is a plan for distributing income in order to give every member of the family the utmost satisfaction from the money spent. There are no restrictions except the ones the family makes. The plan will do for a family just what the members want. It is custom-tailored to fit individual family needs and desires. In the last analysis, a budget is actually a guide to acceptable choices.

Henry Bowman, in *Marriage for Moderns,* correctly compared a budget to a dam. He said the dam "holds back the undirected flow of the river in order to turn the waters into channels that supply power generators, so that electric current may be provided now here, now there, as needs arise."

Since a good family budget can do what a family wants it to do, there is no valid reason for not having one. The next question, then, is this: "How does one go about making a family budget?"

Family Lifetime Income Is Big Business

A typical American family, father having four or more years of college, with an income of $11,603, will spend at least $1,125,000 in the earning lifetime of 45 years from age 20 to age 65 for the head of the family. This is big business! And it will be bigger. Because family income is usually divided into weekly or monthly payments, and is so obligated in paying bills, it is easy to lose sight of how big the total is. What an important and worthwhile job it can be to manage the family income well!

As you shop for groceries, for example, you may think it of little value to save a few cents here and there. But in terms of the total amount of money spent for food in a month, year, or lifetime, the prospect of saving 5 or 10 cents on a dollar can begin to take on real meaning. This is indeed a good return on the investment of learning to be a good consumer. And the place to begin managing personal income is in sensible budgeting.

Family Income in the United States

The median income of families before payment of taxes in 1966 was about $7,436, according to the Census Bureau. A glance at Figure 5-1, Family Income, 1966, shows that 7 million families, or 14 percent of the 48.9 million families in the country, received money incomes under $3,000 in 1966; 11.9 million, or 24

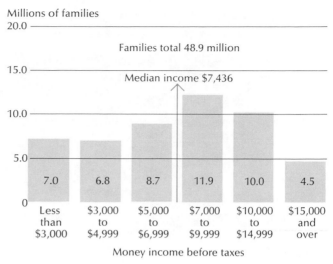

Figure 5-1   Family Income, 1966. Source: Bureau of Census.

percent, had incomes between $7,000 and $10,000. The remaining 14.5 million families, or 30 percent, are estimated to have received incomes of $10,000 or more.

The median income of families may be interesting information for comparison of family incomes. However, data on how much income it takes for a family to maintain an "adequate but moderate standard of living" and how such families spent their income are useful for making a family budget.

Making a Family Budget

There are many ways for families to budget. One way is to see how other families spend their money, then allocate the family income more or less accordingly. How much income, for example, does it take for a family of four, son age 13, daughter age 8, to maintain a modest but adequate standard of living in an urban center? How is the income allocated?

The latest study by the Bureau of Labor Statistics of the U.S. Department of Labor, completed in late 1967, shows that the annual cost of a moderate living standard for this "model" family of four averaged $9,191 in urban areas in 1966 (Figure 5-2). Honolulu was the city with the highest cost of living, $11,190, and Austin, Texas ($8,028), was the least expensive city among 39 cities studied. The cost of living averaged $9,376 in metropolitan areas and $8,366 in smaller cities. A study of Figure 5-2 shows expenditures for housing were 24 percent of income, for food 23 percent, for personal taxes and Social Se-

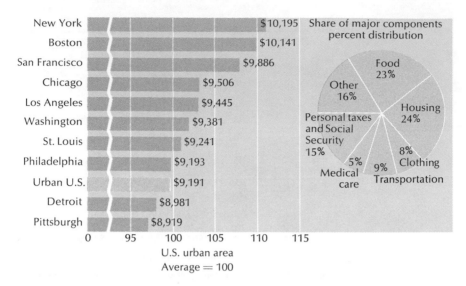

New York — $10,195
Boston — $10,141
San Francisco — $9,886
Chicago — $9,506
Los Angeles — $9,445
Washington — $9,381
St. Louis — $9,241
Philadelphia — $9,193
Urban U.S. — $9,191
Detroit — $8,981
Pittsburgh — $8,919

0   95   100   105   110   115

U.S. urban area
Average = 100

Share of major components
percent distribution

Food 23%
Other 16%
Housing 24%
Personal taxes and Social Security 15%
Clothing 8%
Transportation 9%
Medical care 5%

Figure 5-2   Cost of City Worker's Family Budget, 1966. Source: The Conference Board, Bureau of Labor Statistics.

curity 15 percent, for transportation 9 percent, for clothing 8 percent, for medical care, 5 percent, and for "other" expenses (includes occupational expenses, gifts, contributions, and life insurance) 16 percent.

Of the total costs, about $7,329, or 80 percent, is allocated to family consumption items—food, clothing, housing, transportation, personal care, medical care, and other items of goods and services. The other 20 percent represents allowances for gifts, contributions, life insurance, income and Social Security taxes, and occupational expenses. While it took $7,329 to purchase the consumption items listed above to maintain a family of four, a young couple without children would need only about $3,591. On the other hand, if the two children were of high school age, it would take at least $8,282. Or, if there were four children with the oldest under 16, the cost of goods and services to maintain the same standard of living would be about $9,674, according to the study.

The total costs for urban areas averaged about $800 higher for homeowner than for renter families. This figure includes about $450 in payments on mortgage principal—"savings" not included in the budget for renter families.

Food costs for a nutritionally comparable diet in the mainland urban centers ranged from 11 percent above the urban average in the New York area to 8 percent below the average in Nashville, Tennessee, in 1966. One major change is an upgrading of food standards to reflect more varied diets at home and more meals away from home. This accounts for the 23 percent for food cost in contrast to the more commonly noted 17 to 21 percent mentioned in some studies.

The new standard also recognizes the shift to homeownership for the first time by including homeownership for three-fourths of the budget families (the national average of homeownership was about 63 percent in 1967[3]).

Total costs for the moderate living standard in smaller cities average about 10 percent lower than in metropolitan centers.

This "model" family budget is not a yardstick to be compared with the average income or outlay of all types of families, since it applies to a very carefully defined family. Therefore, adjustments must be made before it can be applied to families of different size and age or where the wife works for pay outside the home. An equivalence scale is available from the Bureau of Labor Statistics in Washington.

One further observation is that consumer price changes vary considerably from city to city, putting varying degrees of pressure on the family budget. For example, New York's 2 percent increase in Consumer Price Index would add $204 to the family's cost, in contrast to the 3.4 percent jump in consumer prices in San Francisco, which would add about $336 to the index of year previous.

A study of income necessary in 1965 and 1968 to equal 1949 purchasing power (Figure 5-3) indicates that, to maintain the same purchasing power in 1968, a person who earned $5,000 to $10,000 in 1949 would in 1968 have had to earn over 50 percent again as much. A married couple with two children and having $5,000 income in 1949 would need $7,661 in 1968 to have the same pur-

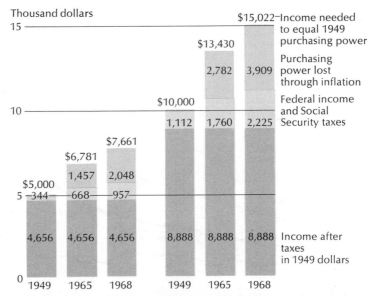

Figure 5-3   Income in 1965 and 1968 Necessary to Equal 1949 Purchasing Power. Source: The Conference Board and reported in *Finance Facts,* **July, 1968.**

[3] As reported in the *Savings and Loan Fact Book, 1968.*

chasing power. In other words, prices have increased about 44 percent, so that $2,048 has been lost through inflation. This inflation drain on income points up the importance of the monthly reports of the *Consumer Price Index.*

The Consumer Price Index.   The *Consumer Price Index* is a statistical measure of the changes in prices of goods and services bought by urban wage earners and clerical workers, including families and single persons. The index is really a "cost-of-living index." Essentially the index measures changes in prices, which are the most important cause of changes in the cost of living.

The index covers prices of everything people buy for living—food, clothing, cars, homes, house furnishings, household supplies, fuel, drugs, and recreational goods; fees to doctors, lawyers, beauty shops; rent, repair costs, transportation fares, public utility costs, etc. It deals with prices actually charged to consumers, including sales and excise taxes. It also includes real estate taxes on owned homes, but it does not include income or personal property taxes. A glance at Figure 5-4, consumer prices, from the *Consumer Price Index,* will show how consumer prices have increased since 1960 and particularly since 1966. The Consumer Price Index rose 4.1 percent between May, 1967, and May, 1968. The rapid increase in the cost of clothing, food, medical care, and real estate taxes led the way. What this means is that you need more income to break even. The *U.S. News & World Report* showed how a pay raise can disappear

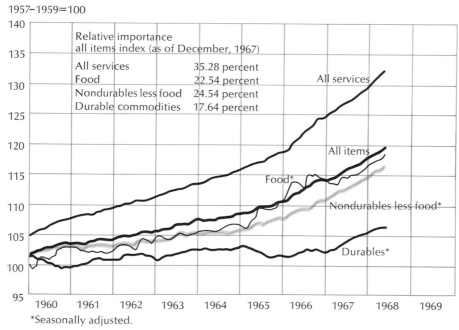

1957–1959=100

*Seasonally adjusted.

Figure 5-4   **Consumer Price Indexes: Commodities and Services. Source: Bureau of Labor Statistics, U.S. Department of Labor, latest data, May, 1968.**

Assuming 1967 pay is raised by 6% in 1968	Worker earning $7,000 a year		Worker earning $10,000 a year		Worker earning $15,000 a year		Worker earning $20,000 a year	
	1967	1968	1967	1968	1967	1968	1967	1968
Income:	$7,000	$7,420	$10,000	$10,600	$15,000	$15,900	$20,000	$21,200
Deductions:								
Federal income tax	$603	$673	$1,114	$1,217	$2,062	$2,240	$3,160	$3,450
Federal surtax		$50		$91		$168		$259
Social Security	$290	$326	$290	$343	$290	$343	$290	$343
State, local taxes	$592	$603	$806	$827	$1,087	$1,120	$1,489	$1,555
"Inflation tax" (rise in living costs, estimated at 3.8 percent in 1968):		$211		$297		$440		$571
Left over after taxes and inflation:	$5,515	$5,557	$7,790	$7,825	$11,561	$11,589	$15,061	$15,022
Change in buying power in 1968		Up $42		Up $35		Up $28		Down $39

Thus: Even a pay raise of 6 percent barely offsets the toll of higher and higher living costs this year.

Note: Examples are for a worker with wife and two children, assume 10 percent federal income tax deduction.

Source: Estimates by USN&WR Economic Unit, based on official data.

Figure 5-5 **How a Pay Raise Can Disappear. Reprinted from** *U.S. News & World Report.* **Copyright, 1968, U.S. News & World Report, Inc.**

(Figure 5-5).[4] A worker, for example, who had an income of $7,000 in 1967 and received a 6 percent raise to $7,420 in 1968 actually had only a $42 raise in terms of buying power. Why? Most of the increase in cost of living was due to inflation; the rest represented increase in state, local, and federal taxes. This is why a family should keep an eye on the monthly reports of the *Consumer Price Index.*

The Family Budget: An Individual Affair. The trouble with following a "model" family budget is that such plans include all kinds of families in all sorts of situations. No family is a national average family. Therefore, these percentages will not necessarily apply to your case. In fact, no family should try to

[4] The *U.S. News & World Report,* Aug. 26, 1968.

TABLE 5-4   MASTER   BUDGETS*

	SALARIED MAN		WAGE EARNER		YOU	
	$	%	$	%	$	%
Total income	9,742.41	100.0	6,777.59	100.0		
Income taxes	1,256.07	12.9	755.66	11.1	_____	____
Total take-home pay	8,486.34	100.0	6,021.93	100.0	_____	____
Food	2,407.85	28.4	1,831.41	30.4	_____	____
At home	1,915.49	22.6	1,791.89	29.8	_____	____
Away	492.36	5.8	39.52	0.6	_____	____
Beverages	80.55	1.0	57.98	1.0	_____	____
Housing	1,378.07	16.2	978.00	16.2	_____	____
Household operation	461.99	5.5	282.93	4.7	_____	____
House furnishings	330.51	3.9	216.86	3.6	_____	____
Clothing	756.33	8.9	503.54	8.4	_____	____
Man	248.10	2.9	136.21	2.3	_____	____
Woman	245.72	2.9	143.90	2.4	_____	____
Boy, 13	140.17	1.7	120.37	2.0	_____	____
Girl, 8	122.34	1.4	103.06	1.7	_____	____
Transportation	1,003.98	11.8	587.70	9.8	_____	____
Auto	850.33	10.0	570.08	9.5	_____	____
Carfare	153.65	1.8	17.62	0.3	_____	____
Medical, dental care	671.28	7.9	575.89	9.6	_____	____
Insurance	375.30	4.4	290.68	4.8	_____	____
Personal care	152.97	1.8	115.15	1.9	_____	____
Recreation	435.07	5.1	235.69	3.9	_____	____
Tobacco	119.08	1.4	119.08	2.0	_____	____
Reading	57.51	0.7	39.26	0.7	_____	____
Education	69.79	0.8	8.77	0.1	_____	____
Union dues	. . .	. . .	68.09	1.1	_____	____
Gifts, contributions	155.06	1.8	93.40	1.5	_____	____
Miscellaneous	31.00	0.4	17.50	0.3	_____	____

*The percentages of expenditure are close to those in the Bureau of Labor study of a City Worker's Family Budget of $9,191 for a moderate living standard for a family of four persons in urban areas.

operate on a national average or on another family budget. A family budget should be an individual affair. It must be geared to your goals and your personal needs. But it does help to know how other people live and how they divide their income as they try to make ends meet.

The two budgets devised by the Heller Committee for Research in Social Economics at the University of California, reproduced in Table 5-4, Master Budgets, reflect the actual living costs of two families of four persons at two income levels in the San Francisco Bay area. The blank column is for your use in estimating the distribution of your own income. Every household would not require the same data or use the same percentages. But those given in the first two columns of the table can help you to decide what items to include in your own budget.

The Monthly Ledger.   The division of your income according to the Master Budgets, Table 5-4, after many revisions, will testify to the care that went into preparing it. Once the final version is completed, you are ready to draw up a monthly ledger that will make your master budget work. This is the real workhorse of financial management. You may use an ordinary sheet of ruled paper or buy a ledger book for the purpose.

TABLE 5-5   MONTHLY LEDGER

ESTIMATE OF MONTHLY CASH INCOME

Annual income	$_____
Interest, dividends	_____
Other income	_____
Total	$_____
Deductions	_____
Spendable income	$_____

MONTHLY WORKING DETAILS

	(1) Balance Brought Forward	(2) This Month's Alloca- tion	(3) Total Avail- able	(4) Month's Spend- ing	(5) End-of- month Balance (+ or −)
Fixed Expenses					
Mortgage or rent	$0.00	$110	$110	$110	$ 0.00
Life insurance					
Savings					
Taxes					
Personal allowances					
Church, charities					
Variable Expenses					
Food					
At home	6.00	90.00	96.00	82.00	+14.00
Away					
Household operation					
Clothing					
Medical, dental					
Car upkeep, repair					
Fuel					
Light					
Water					
Recreation, entertainment					
Investments					
Christmas savings					
Vacation savings					
New furniture savings					

The Monthly Ledger, Table 5-5, is easy to follow. To find the amount for column 5, End-of-Month Balance, compare total spending in column 4 with the total available in column 3. If you spend less than allocated, enter the sum left over in column 5 as a plus balance. And, of course, enter any increased spending as a minus balance.

Then for the following month, copy the month-end balances from column 5 to column 1 for the new month as Balance Brought Forward.

There is nothing sacred about this system. Modify it to fit your family. One important merit is that the monthly ledger brings to light immediately both surpluses and deficits. It is, therefore, possible to make timely corrections in next month's spending.

Persistent surpluses or deficits in any one item will alert you to the defects in your budget estimates. Corrections can be made easily and accurately from year to year and thus provide for sensible flexibility in planning.

In any event, you do not have to be an accountant to manage your money as here described. All it takes is some skill in adding and subtracting, some ruled paper, and a desire. Budgeting cannot add dollars to your pay check, but it can make you richer in peace of mind and in real satisfaction.

The chances are that you will not have a definitive budget until after the first year. Some kinds of expenditures vary according to seasons, and some expenses, like mortgage payments and taxes, may occur only once a year. But once you complete a full year, you will know how your income should be distributed.

In attempting to cut these day-to-day expenses, do not scrimp too much on the little items. Do not deny yourselves comfortable allowances. Go after the more important economies.

How to Waste Money. During the first months of married life, you will discover that there is "too much month and not enough money." So consider the following common ways of wasting money before they can get a hold on the family income. Much of the material in this book will discuss the following wasteful habits and show how to prevent them.

1. Buying what you don't need—impulse buying, keeping up with others, compulsive buying, neurotic need
2. Buying worthless things, such as most gadgets, advertised medical concoctions, etc.
3. Being a victim of "something for nothing"—gimmicks like coupons, premiums, frauds, gyps, bait advertising
4. Wasting money when buying food
5. Wasting food in the home
6. Paying more for all types of purchases than you need to pay
7. Buying only the top-priced merchandise
8. Using household equipment, car, and clothing carelessly
9. Gambling—track, lotteries, games
10. Using installment credit unwisely
11. Selecting the wrong kind of life insurance
12. Buying a home before financially able

Fitting Large Expenditures into a Long-range Plan. Most families cannot afford more than one or two large extra expenditures in any one year. It may be for a downpayment on a house, for a baby, for an expensive piece of furniture, or for a college education fund.

Under such circumstances, it may be wise to stagger these items over a period of years. Obviously, a fund for a college education must be started early by most families. A television set may have to wait until next year because a refrigerator is needed this year. Saving a certain amount each year for specific purposes is the safest way for people on modest incomes to get what they want and can afford. A few items might be kept on that "nice to have but do not need now" list. When the family can afford it, these wants can be effectively met.

Families that can agree on these matters are not likely to be in the unhappy and embarrassing position of the family that has a $7,500 annual income but attempts to keep up with families in the $12,000 income bracket. In such a situation, the pressures, direct and indirect, are so great that a family with no financial plan is likely to spend far beyond its income. Such a family cannot escape certain inevitabilities.

The day comes when the unhappy financial condition must be faced. Family discord is almost automatic. The discovery is made too late of what should have been an accepted principle from the beginning of the family life—make spending fit income.

Effective plans for retirement are almost always made to fit into long-range planning. Unless a retirement program is planned carefully along with all other needs, a family may become "retirement poor." In other words, it is possible to put so much current income into a retirement fund, especially before the children have completed their education, that other essential needs are neglected. There are certain times in a family life cycle when additional money can be allowed for retirement without affecting the family's present standard of living.

Planning for Emergencies. Some families get into a financial jam because they failed to prepare in advance to meet the emergency "blockbusters." These are the expenditures that, as a rule, cannot be timed. They may be expensive surgery, a long siege of illness, or an unfortunate lawsuit.

Savings should be made for emergencies whenever possible. Savings may also take the form of paying off debts when income is more favorable. In this manner, loans are more easily available in times of need. Savings may take many forms, such as government bonds, insurance—especially covering death, illness, surgery, accident, and fire—real estate and homeownership, commercial stocks and bonds, and cash savings. Making a legal will can also help to reduce financial hazards for the family.

Methods of Handling Money. The method of handling money is not, perhaps, so much a question of who is the manager as it is a question of how the money is managed and to what end. Nor are all the methods of equal merit.

Some families have a financial dictator who makes all the decisions and doles out money for specific purposes. Then there is the kind of family that divides management responsibilities. The mother is responsible for managing food and clothes, and the father makes decisions in regard to investments, taxes, and insurance.

Some families have joint checking accounts, and others have separate accounts. Some rely on the envelope system—placing in envelopes money earmarked for specific purposes, such as rent, insurance, clothes. Since there is a chance of losing money kept in envelopes, some families write postdated checks. In this way, the check stubs are filled, and the records show that such money has been used.

There are other schemes. The important thing to remember is that the method decided on should accomplish what is intended.

Make Your Plan a Family Team Job.   It is easier to get cooperation on a family spending plan if the whole family helps to make it. There was a time when father thought that taxes, insurance, and investments were his own private headache. Mother worried about food and clothing prices all by herself. And too often the only thing the children heard about family expenses was the terse parental "We can't afford it now."

This is not true in many families today. Everyone except the tiny members has some part in planning the distribution of the family income. Parents have found that children are surprisingly cooperative, even eager, about giving up this and that demand on the pocketbook when they understand where the money goes. A plan made by and for the whole family has an excellent chance of succeeding. It is doomed to failure if any one member of the family makes a plan alone and tries to carry it out in the face of opposition or indifference. Therefore, make a family plan. But how?

The first step is to arouse the interest of the family in the plan. All the members should agree finally that a plan is needed, even if they have to be sold on the idea. When the plan has been explained and all questions have been answered, every member of the family should be willing to try it out. More than that, every member should have a responsibility, because responsibility, even if small at first, and a voice in the plan go hand in hand.

Common sense should be used in such a family council. Not all financial details can be entrusted to all children. Neither should the children be exposed to worrisome debts. At least, not until problems arise that necessitate revealing such information. Many families have discovered that even small children can be entrusted successfully with important family data. If such information creates worry and emotional distress, it may do more harm than good. Much depends on the approach taken by the parents and on the respect that children have for their parents.

When family financial planning becomes a reality, there is almost no resentment, no argument, no nagging. The results, in terms of improved human relations in the family, are so positive and good that one wonders why more families do not try it.

Joint planning, joint spending, and joint responsibility are an exciting idea. For those who join in the idea, there is understanding, friendliness, and cooperation. Such a family has the necessary financial foundation for a successful and happy life together.

Who Should Be the Manager?   A family, like a business enterprise, needs a manager with skill or one who is willing to learn. Managing successfully on a small or a large income is a real achievement. This takes planning, insight, and cooperation on the part of husband and wife. They must decide how the income will be distributed and who will be responsible for its distribution. Then they must cooperate fully in carrying out the plan.

Certain divisions of money distribution between husband and wife seem natural. In most American families, the plan as it relates to food for home consumption, clothes for the family, and household operation and equipment tends to give responsibility to the wife. On the other hand, in many families the husband takes care of insurance, investments, house payments, and the car. The wife's responsibility is usually great in paying the bills, in buying, and in keeping necessary financial records.

Ideally, the husband and wife share all financial plans together from the beginning. If both know all the financial facts and make joint decisions in regard to all important spending policies, much resentment and unhappiness is prevented. This method also enables the wife to be prepared to carry on alone in the event that it becomes necessary.

Newlyweds can expect to make changes from their first plans. Gradually, however, they will develop a pattern of joint planning and responsibilities that will fit their needs.

There are some men who still feel that they should handle all the family financial business. They prefer to write the checks, keep the records, and perhaps make all important spending decisions. If necessary, let them try it for a few months. Some men, after trying to handle the household exchequer, have gone to the other extreme. They have thrown the job into the wife's lap with the remark: "Here it is. You can have it, I don't want it." This, too, is unfortunate, unless they decide to be sensible and make it a cooperative affair.

There are a few men who, gallantly, feel that they should shield the little woman from the big, cruel business world. This is an old-fashioned idea. It has no place in modern life. Young people today discuss everything from sex to family finances. Moreover, many women have had considerable financial experience before marriage. In fact, a strong case can be made in favor of the argument that "money is a wife's business."

The Family Inventory.   At the end of each year, it is wise to take inventory of the family's assets and debts as shown in Table 5-6, Family Financial Statement. This is a good way to see what economic progress, if any, the family has

TABLE 5-6   FAMILY FINANCIAL STATEMENT   JANUARY 1 TO DECEMBER 31, 19......

ASSETS		DEBTS	
Cash on deposit	$ _____	Mortgages	$ _____
Market value of bonds	_____	Borrowed from life insurance companies	_____
Market value of stocks	_____	Borrowed from banks	_____
Market value of house	_____	Accounts at stores	_____
Market value of real estate	_____	Other debts	_____
Resale value of car	_____		
Social Security assets	_____		
Cash surrender value of insurance	_____		
Notes	_____		
Resale value of household goods	_____		
Other assets	_____		
Total assets	$ _____	Total debts	$ _____
Net worth (total assets minus total debts)	$ _____		

made. Such data are also useful in discussion of possible changes in the distribution of the family income, and they are helpful, even necessary, in applying for a loan for a large outlay of money—to build or buy a house, for example.

The net worth of the family may not be much during the first years of marriage. The important thing is to face whatever the condition is and decide how to increase the net worth. Note that the first three items in the Assets column of the Family Financial Statement are liquid assets. Is enough money being put into certain kinds of investments? Are the assets adequately insured? Discussion of the specific items in such a financial statement will eventually lead to changes that will increase the net worth of the family.

WHAT IT TAKES TO BE A SMART SHOPPER

In Chapter 2 we said that the task of learning how to become an intelligent consumer of goods and services has become ever more difficult because of the nature of the American market, the spectacular development of new products, the persuasive influence of advertising, and the lack of quality information at the point of sale. We have also pointed out that most colleges do a good job in preparing us for a job. But a good job is only half the battle. The other half is learning how to translate income into a satisfactory standard of living. In other words, learning how to buy a living is just as important as learning how to earn a living.

Description of a Careless Shopper

Contrary to some overoptimistic statements like, "Anyone can be a smart shopper," it unfortunately takes more than knowledge to be a smart shopper in today's marketplace. Sidney Margolius, a leading consumer authority and writer, emphasized this point in his recent best seller, *The Innocent Consumer vs. The Exploiters:*[5]

> Never in the 30 years I have been reporting on consumer problems has the public been as widely and steadily exploited as today . . . through diversion of income to excessive finance charges; unnecessarily high-priced food and medicine; excessively priced and sometimes even wholly deceptive home-improvement and car-repair schemes; unsatisfactory or high-priced insurance; outright rackets in medical gadgets; and a harrying of the public, even children, to spend for a constant stream of dubious new products, from presugared breakfast cereals to gold-plated percolators. . . .
>
> There are very few standards available or in use to assure you that a seller's "permanent-press" garment, horsepower rating, "bonded meat," or other claims of quality, capacity or performance, actually do measure up to an official yardstick.

When official national standards for consumer goods are not available at the point of sale, even the expert and experienced shopper is at a disadvan-

[5] Sidney Margolius, *The Innocent Consumer vs. The Exploiters*, Trident Press, New York, 1967, pp. 1-2, 6-7.

tage. This is not to say, however, that a beginner or a veteran shopper cannot improve her shopping skills. We have been told by Du Pont consumer buying habits studies and other studies that a typical woman in a supermarket makes most of her purchase decisions *after* entering the store; visits a supermarket three times a week and spends 27 minutes per visit; rarely buys the advertised specials; changes brands often; is unaware of increases in some food prices during the week; is a pushover for "cents off" and for new items; demonstrates a flunking grade in arithmetic; and plays the losing game of stamps and games of chance.

How a Careful Shopper Operates

Despite the many handicaps, and some impossible roadblocks to intelligent shopping, the beginner or veteran or in-between shopper can improve her purchasing techniques. It is easy for a skilled shopper to save $5 a week in buying groceries for a family; hundreds of dollars can be saved in buying a car or insurance, in financing a mortgage on a home, and in buying durable goods. The following principles for smart shopping will produce good dividends:

1.   Never expect something for nothing. A successful merchant cannot stay in business if his margin of profit is too low. So expect to pay a reasonable price.

2.   Make an expenditure plan for more expensive items like coats, suits, TV sets, and a new car. Many of these items can be purchased during regular sales, as indicated in the Shopping Calendar, Table 5-7. Saving money in advance and paying cash is money in the bank.

3.   Do not be an impulse buyer. No single habit can wreck a budget faster.

4.   Be an informed shopper. Compare prices in advertising, newspapers, and magazines. Check various kinds of stores—discount, mail order, chains, department stores, the small retailer, and cooperative stores. Check *Consumer Reports* and the *Consumer Bulletin*—both are nonprofit consumer testing organizations. You can save 10 to 30 percent by comparative shopping in food, and much more in other goods. High prices do not always assure high quality.

5.   Select commodities that will not go out of fashion in a short time—for items such as cars, clothing, furniture, and household accessories.

6.   Bargain for lower prices. Merchants and salesmen expect you to bargain for certain kinds of consumer goods, such as cars, appliances, cameras, furniture, sporting goods, and some clothing items. List prices for automobiles, for example, are the highest starting prices. Price reductions may be secured also by bargaining for higher price for your trade-in item or by securing more free services or extra accessories. Sometimes it is possible to secure price reductions through wholesale buying, from the employer, or through friends.

7.   Buy in quantity if the price is lower. But not all large quantities are lower in price than smaller quantities. Check the arithmetic carefully. Usually staple foods and some clothing items, such as men's shirts, have quantity discounts.

8.   Read labels and guarantees. File guarantees and warranties. Check the quantity. There are many ways to cheat on weight.

9.   Consider time and energy as well as money. A working wife may prefer higher-cost convenience foods.

10. Pay cash, and carry your own purchases. Cash is cheaper. Personal shopping is apt to be more satisfactory as well as cheaper.

11. Good shoppers will exercise their right to protest. If a guaranteed item is defective, bring it back. If the repair service on the car or appliance is poor or fraudulent, call this to the attention of the repair shop. If you have good reason to protest, you help not only yourself but many other consumers who may never exercise the right of protest.

TABLE 5-7 SHOPPING CALENDAR*

Here's the pattern that stores generally follow in setting up promotions throughout the year. Some are sales; others are special promotions that sometimes, but not always, include a sale on merchandise being promoted.

JANUARY	FEBRUARY	MARCH
White sales, storewide clearance, resort wear, fur sales, furniture sales (3rd week)	Furniture and home furnishings sales, Valentine's Day, Washington's Birthday, housewares	Housewares, china, silver, garden supplies, spring and Easter promotions

APRIL	MAY	JUNE
Spring-cleaning supplies, moth preventives, paints, housewares, fur storage campaigns, outdoor furniture	Mother's Day, summer sportswear, air-conditioning, fans, bridal business, garden supplies, outdoor furniture	Graduation, Father's Day, bridal gifts, sportswear, men's sportswear, camp clothes and supplies, vacation needs

JULY	AUGUST	SEPTEMBER
July 4th clearances, sporting goods, sportswear, furniture sales (4th week)	Furniture sales, fur sales, back-to-school, fall fashions, fall fabrics	Back-to-school, fall fashions, men's and boys' sportswear, home furnishings, china and glassware, accessories

SEPTEMBER	OCTOBER	
Back-to-school, fall fashions, men's and boys' sportswear, home furnishings, china and glassware, accessories	Women's coats, suits, and furs, men's and boys' outerwear, millinery and accessories, Columbus Day, home furnishings	

NOVEMBER	DECEMBER	
Christmas toys, pre-Christmas value promotions, Thanksgiving weekend sales, china, glassware, table linens, home furnishings	Christmas campaign, gift promotions, resort wear—north and south (4th week)	

*SOURCE: National Retail Merchants' Association.

These 11 criteria for careful shopping will be applied more specifically in the "shopping" chapters on food, clothing, credit, housing, and insurance.

When Financial Crises Come

You may wonder why an account of family financial crises is included here. The most important reason is that no family can escape financial crises. Virtually all families, at one time or another, face one or more of the following family crises: loss of a child, orphanhood, hospitalization, widowhood, non-support, infidelity, illegitimacy, desertion, suicide, imprisonment, homicide, divorce, loss of job, sudden increase in income, and so forth. To the price paid in emotional stress are added always dollars-and-cents charges.

Death, the crisis perhaps least talked about, will normally come to the average family several times. Sudden impoverishment hovers constantly over all families except perhaps the wealthiest. Sudden and appreciable increases in income are difficult for many families to meet and too often become the focal point in family quarrels.

Many of these crises are blows when they come, but they are a part of living and cannot be escaped. The sensible conclusion is to be prepared, as much as possible—to regard them as challenges. The main question, then, is not "How can family crises be avoided?" but rather "How can family crises be met?"

Would More Money Solve Your Problems?

The fact remains that, for many families, wants seem to be one jump ahead of income no matter how high the income. Some years ago a Gallup poll asked this question: "What do you want most for your family?" The answer, in overwhelming numbers, was "Ten percent more income."

That was in 1956. Apparently our economy rubbed Aladdin's lamp, and the responding genie worked overtime. The real income of the average American family rose not a mere 10 percent, but over four times that much. Measured in 1966 dollars, the average family that earned $100 a week in 1956 earned over $143 in 1966.

We are a lot better off financially. Most families have upgraded their standard of living. There is more money for homes, cars, appliances, color TV sets, new furniture, vacations, clothing, stereo, and motorboats. On the surface all is well. But probe a little deeper and you can see both boon and blight. Along with many material comforts have come financial woes of which our thrift-minded grandfathers never dreamed.

The astonishing contradiction of our time is the failure of a disturbingly large number of families to avoid financial stress in the face of continuously increasing real incomes. Money troubles beset many older families, but especially younger people just getting started.

At least half of our families owe money on possessions (not including homes).

The nation's installment debt was over $80 billion in 1967—about one-tenth of the total wealth produced in the country in one year. Add to this over $235.6 billion of home mortgage debts that still have to be paid off, and the outlines of the financial burden begin to become clear. All this affluence is by no stretch of the imagination bought and paid for.

A good part of the take-home pay is tagged for the bill collector even before it is received. Nationally, about $13 out of every $100 in take-home pay has a lien on it to pay installments due. Ten years ago, the figure was about $7. But creditors must be paid. If they are not, then a catastrophe like bankruptcy may come.

Bankruptcy in the United States

People are getting over their heads and going bankrupt at a rate that has become a cause of growing concern. A decade ago, about 63,600 bankruptcy petitions were filed by individuals each year. That was more than double the 1950 rate. In 1967, the official rate was about 188,600, about three times the figure a decade previous (Figure 5-6). Personal bankruptcies in the year ending June 30, 1968, declined from the previous year—the first decline in the last 16 years.

Alleged Causes of Bankruptcy.   Why is it that, in a period of unparalleled prosperity, so many people are going to federal bankruptcy referees to get a legal discharge from their debt burdens?   Dr. George A. Brunner, an authority on bankruptcies, states that "personal bankruptcies have until recently received very little attention."[6] The great increase in personal bankruptcies suggests the presence of some deep-seated malaise, the "cause and nature of which is not well understood," says Dr. Brunner.

Sudden, overwhelming expenses of illness or loss of income, the experts say, are causes in many cases. Some experts suggest that more people are becoming aware of how easy it is to go bankrupt, and are not too disturbed about the stigma that goes with that surrender. To many experts, the main factor is the lure of easy credit. "A dollar down and a dollar a week" has given way to "No cash and no payments for three months" or "No payments until spring." One leading authority, Linn K. Twinem, who for 8 years has been chairman of the Consumer Bankruptcy Committee of the American Bar Association, says that there are several reasons for the great increase in personal bankruptcies. He says many persons are misguided or misinformed on money matters. They just cannot look ahead and figure their future ability to pay. Some people, he notes, are simply indifferent and will buy what they want without any concern about paying up. The fact that about 17 percent of bankrupts are repeaters, says Twinem, seems to support the "indifference" argument.

Some federal bankruptcy referees think that most bankrupts are just "incom-

[6] George A. Brunner, *Personal Bankruptcies: Trends and Characteristics,* Ohio State University Press, Columbus, Ohio, 1965.

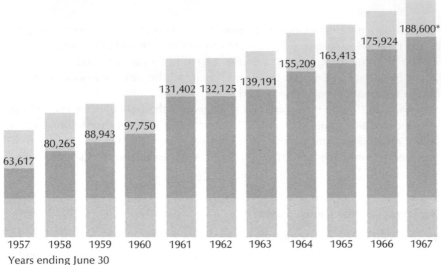

1957 1958 1959 1960 1961 1962 1963 1964 1965 1966 1967

Years ending June 30
*Official estimate.

Figure 5-6   The Rise in Personal Bankruptcies (New Cases Filed). Source: Administrative Office of the United States Courts.

petent"; credit is "too expensive"; some merchants are too aggressive in selling on credit; and harassment by bill collectors and, in some states, laws that make garnishment of workers' wages easy make families feel driven to bankruptcy as the only way out. For instance, in the states of Connecticut, Florida, Pennsylvania, and Texas, wages are not subject to garnishment, but wages may be attached in the states of California, Illinois, Ohio, and Oregon. There are comparatively few personal bankruptcies in the states that do not permit wage garnishment in contrast to the states having garnishment laws.[7]

Finally, the increases in personal bankruptcies are also due to laxity and an uncaring attitude upon the part of credit investigators, creditors, and referees in bankruptcy. Thus, negligence on the part of those most concerned allegedly encourages debtors to make use of the Bankruptcy Act even when relief is not needed.

Sudden Loss in Family Income

During economic depressions, more families experience serious income losses than at any other period. A major depression creates a crisis in family life, through loss of work and income, for which the family has no accustomed responses. The family may have to abandon certain plans, such as buying a home. It may not be able to continue membership in certain social clubs and thus no longer conforms to its social standards. It may not be able to pay bills on time, a standard in which it has always taken pride. It may experience the shifting of a dominant role from father to mother or to an older child. Not only is the entire

[7] *Ibid.,* p. 6.

family disorganized, but each member of the family may be personally disorganized over the loss of accustomed activities, over failure to meet financial responsibility, or over a feeling of lowered status.

The realization that the family cannot continue its past habits of social life usually causes severe emotional reactions. This period of acute emotional stress is terminated either by an adjustment to the situation or by the development of pathological reactions. If a family completely breaks or fails to adjust, the family life may disintegrate, or one member may be led to escape through mental illness, suicide, or running away.[8]

How can a family effectively meet a financial crisis? There are, say the experts, no pat answers. The following actions have aided some families.[9]

1. Face the facts as a family.
2. Agree on a temporary plan or procedure.
3. Clear the air of accusations with reference to "fixing the blame."
4. Cooperate in reducing expenses sufficiently.
5. Cooperate in pooling all family income for family use.
6. Discover together new cultural and psychological resources.
7. Look forward to reestablishing the business or profession.

Sudden Increase in Family Income

There are no adequate studies of the effect of sudden prosperity on families and their members. But most of us know families that have had such an experience. Perhaps we also know, in a general way, that disintegration often takes place among such families. Apparently, family happiness is not automatically achieved by a sudden increase in family income.

It is not a simple case of saying, "Now we can get what we have always wanted and do the things we have always wanted to do." Foster and Wilson, in reporting on the case study of 78 married women, concluded that "even when the income was increased, further obligations, a little exceeding the increase, were incurred."[10]

While we do not have sufficient accurate information on the effects of sudden prosperity, it may be that well-organized families remain organized, and disorganized families may tend to disintegrate further. Whether we agree with the above assumption or not, most of us will agree that any experience holds the potential of being either a destructive crisis experience or a constructive learning experience.

In the interest of reducing the chances of family unhappiness, we need to learn how to meet family crises. Crises involving decreases or sudden increases

[8] Ruth S. Cavan and Katherine H. Ranck, *The Family and the Depression,* The University of Chicago Press, Chicago, 1938, pp. 6-7.

[9] Howard Becker and Reuben Hill (eds.), *Marriage and the Family,* D. C. Heath and Company, Boston, 1942, pp. 531-533.

[10] Robert G. Foster and Pauline Park Wilson, *Women after College,* Columbia University Press, New York, 1942, p. 52.

in family income can disintegrate family life on the one hand or serve as the means of discovering or rediscovering a new and pleasant family relationship. Financial crises cannot be separated from other aspects of life. No problem is met in an isolated group of circumstances, but in relation to the total life of an individual.

The High Cost of Divorce

We are concerned here only with the dollar cost of divorce. This is not to suggest that the psychological, emotional, and personality costs are not as important as the financial price. Since all these aspects are interrelated, no single factor can be recognized as most important.

To the price paid in emotional stress in divorce must be added the dollar cost. Today, when one out of every four marriages ends in divorce, we need to know about some of the less-known facts of the economic costs of divorce.

Some wit has called desertion a "poor man's divorce." The high dollar cost of divorce works in the other direction at times. Rather than desert, and unable to pay for a divorce, the couple may decide to remain married.

We might as well try to answer: "How high is up?" as to attempt to give actual money costs of divorce. Every state has different divorce laws, and lawyers' fees are not standard. There are cut-rate divorces, but dangers are involved in these. Sometimes cases are handled dishonestly. Consequently, it is difficult to know whether one is legally divorced. Whatever the costs are, the final money arrangements will depend on the financial condition of the husband. If considerable money is spent seeking a divorce, less money is available afterward for the divorced couple.

A recent scale of bar association minimum fees for uncontested divorces showed that some New York counties have the highest figure—$500. The low of $75 was posted in some Texas counties. By region, the most expensive area is New York-New Jersey-Pennsylvania, where minimums range from $150 to $500. Cheapest is the Southwest, with its range from $75 to $250. Of course, actual fees usually exceed the minimum. In a Midwestern city, for example, the legal fees for a contested divorce case of a family with a modest weekly take-home pay of $136.81 amounted to $1,800. Another uncontested case in New York for a couple with only average income cost $2,000 in legal fees. These two families are not alone, but are among some 800,000 persons divorced annually in the United States in asking, "Why should a divorce be so costly?" Actually, many marriage counselors, clergymen, social workers, judges, and family service experts ask the same question. Men like Clark W. Blackburn, general director of the Family Service Association of America, believe that we need to reduce or eliminate the crushing financial burden on a couple dissolving marriage. These experts are not advocating "easy divorce," because they be-

TABLE 5-8

INCOME PER WEEK	ALIMONY (NO CHILDREN)	ALIMONY AND SUPPORT (CHILDREN)
$100	$ 40	$ 55- 60
200	75	100-120
311	105	140-165

lieve in thorough counseling to save the marriage. But once it becomes obvious that divorce is unavoidable, they recommend a quick, simple, and inexpensive termination.

Alimony plus Support.   The heaviest expenses in any divorce are alimony and the sum decreed for the support of children. In 1966 in the United States, there were over 3 million divorcees who received almost $5 billion in alimony. The following figures give a general picture of how much a divorce costs in alimony and support of children.

The amounts of alimony and support are usually based on the financial condition of the husband and wife; their earning capacity and property; the inheritance of either of them; the manner of living to which they are accustomed; the duration of their marriage; their age, health, and social position; and which of them is the guilty party and to what extent.

The real crux of how much a husband must pay, at least for the average-salaried person, is the time-honored phrase, "the manner of living to which they are accustomed." The courts generally will not let a wife improve her standard of living by getting a divorce. Most divorce lawyers have a form that provides them with fairly concrete proof of the standard of living to which a wife has been accustomed and of the money needed to support the children.

The ease of divorce in many states is an economic delusion to men of modest means. Some divorces are necessary, marriage experts say, no matter what the resultant hardships may be. But the impulsive divorce is not only a moral mistake but a financial one. Every available possibility for reconciliation should be thoroughly explored.

Emotional Cost of Divorce.   Divorce is never a clean break if children are involved. Every year, more than 225,000 children are affected by divorce in this country. If the mother and father fight for custody of the children, difficulty in visiting arrangements is inevitable.

The dollar costs, as well as emotional upsets, seldom end with the divorce. Young couples should be aware of these facts. It is unwise to assume that your case may be different. There is no such thing as an easy divorce. It costs more than emotional and psychological pain to all concerned, and especially to the children. It also costs more money than most people think. There is no such thing as a "bargain divorce."

SPEND FOR WHAT YOU REALLY WANT

A good budget should be your servant, never your master. The essence of successful money management is to get all the ideas you can from reliable sources but work out your own plan.

The important thing about your spending is the kind of life you are buying with your money and your savings. If you are buying family happiness and long-term security, your money management plan is a good one. If this is not the case, all the members of your family need to sit down together and work out another plan for spending the family income—a plan to fit your family and its income.

Some people spend their lives looking for the ideal place to invest money—where they can earn 5 to 10 percent or more. Few people realize that wise management of money in their day-to-day living and in their day-to-day purchasing decisions can net some of the best returns available. Each time the family spends nickels, dimes, and dollars, it is investing in a little piece of a way of living. Some find they have made a good investment, while others find they made their investment in such a haphazard, uninformed way that they have really made no gains in their way of life. The biggest investment that a person will ever make is in the way of life he purchases for his family.

QUESTIONS FOR DISCUSSION

1.   What importance would you attach to parental attitudes toward money management?
2.   What are some of the most difficult problems that many families experience in the handling of money?
3.   If you were contemplating marriage, how would you go about making a spending plan for the first year of married life?
4.   Do women, as a rule, manage family spending better than men?
5.   What are the implications of the remark that a family cannot escape financial crises?
6.   How does a divorce affect the family standard of living?
7.   What value is there in studying so-called "model family spending patterns"?

ACTIVITY PROBLEMS

1.   Ask several married persons these questions: "Do you have a family budget?" "What is the purpose of a family budget?" Record the answers. How many felt that the purpose of a family budget is to help the family get the greatest satisfaction from the use of its income.

2. What goals do you want for your family? Arrange these goals in the order of their importance to you. Which of the goals are short-term and which are long-term?

3. What kind of money manager would you prefer in your own home? A financial dictator? A benevolent despot? A compromiser? A dual manager?

4. Do you agree with the statement: "A carefully planned budget does not ensure a marriage free from money worries"?

5. In some of the larger cities, budgeting service is sold for a fee. Try to evaluate these services. What fees do they charge? Who seeks this kind of help? What are some of the techniques for helping a person in financial distress? How successful are they?

6. When financial crises hit a family, there is generally no accustomed response. If possible, check this assumption with people who have had financial crises. How did these families meet the problem. Do you think that these families met their problem successfully?

SUGGESTED READINGS

Annual Cost of Budgets for 3 Living Standards for a 4-Person Family, U.S. Department of Labor, Bureau of Labor Statistics, Spring, 1967.

Ferguson, Marilyn and Mike: *Champagne Living on a Beer Budget,* G. P. Putnam & Sons, New York, 1968.

"Getting by on $20,000 a Year: Almost All of Them End up in the Red," *Life,* Dec. 20, 1968.

The Heller Committee for Research in Social Economics: *Quantity and Cost: Budgets for Two Income Levels,* University of California Press, Berkeley, Calif., latest survey.

Herrmann, Robert O.: "Families in Bankruptcy—A Survey of Recent Studies," *Journal of Marriage and the Family,* Aug. 3, 1966.

———— : "Economic Problems Confronting Teen-age Newlyweds," *Journal of Home Economics,* February, 1965.

Margolius, Sidney: *The Innocent Consumer vs. The Exploiters,* Trident Press, New York, 1967, chap. 7.

Marple, Betty Lou, and Wesley W. Marple: "How Affluent Families Plan to Pay for College," *College Board Review,* Spring, 1967.

Morse, Richard L. D.: *Money Management Process,* Kansas State University, Manhattan, Kansas, 1966. Instructions and Worksheets.

"That Always Broke Feeling," *Changing Times,* March, 1966.

chapter 6

CONSUMER CREDIT
AND BORROWING MONEY

Let the seller make full disclosure.

President L. B. Johnson

Consumer credit is joked about and glimpsed in ridiculing caricatures. These are some examples: "To make time fly just buy something on the installment plan." Or this one, "The people that economists used to say were underprivileged are now described as overfinanced." And *Life* magazine editorialized on "Is Thrift Un-American?" Said the multimillionaire Texan, Sid Richardson, "Out here in Texas, we judge a man's wealth by how much he owes." And Vance Packard calls us a "credit-card society." One magazine writer chose for his article the title, "Are You a Credit Drunk?" A symbolic case is that of the clerk earning $73 a week who went on a $10,000 binge with his credit card. After he was caught by the "credit detectives," he wrote, "All of a sudden the credit card was just like an Aladdin's lamp and you didn't even have to rub it."

Charles Dickens gave the world one of its most famous harried consumers, Mr. Micawber, David Copperfield's friend. Micawber always had a terrible time making ends meet. But despite his inability, he knew where the trouble lay: "Annual income twenty pounds, annual expenditure nineteen pounds six, result happiness. Annual income twenty pounds, annual expenditure twenty pounds ought and six, result misery."

But there are two sides to modern consumer credit—good and bad. Wisely used, it can lead to a higher standard of living. Unwisely used, it can lead to misery. Not too many decades ago we used to boast, "Pay as you go or stay home." Of course, few Americans can make such a boast today. Charge plates, revolving charge accounts, installment credit, credit cards, and loan applications in hand, American consumers pay around $16 billion each year in pure interest to buy on credit goods and services that, on May 31, 1968, were worth over $100.3 billion.

WHAT IS CONSUMER CREDIT?

The terms "consumer credit," "consumer debt," "short-term credit," "installment credit," and "mortage credit" have been bandied about so much that some clarification of their meaning is needed. Essentially, of course, credit is the asset side of the ledger, and debt the liability side. Thus, "consumer credit" is money or purchasing power extended by the lending agencies to consumers, and "consumer debt" is money owed the lending agencies by consumers.

Indebtedness of individuals can be broadly broken into two classes: mortgage debt (or real estate debt) and shorter-term debt, which includes a number of types of commitments, usually payable within a period of 1 to 36 months. In many publications, the term "consumer credit" is confined to a consideration of the shorter-term obligations. It is in this sense that consumer credit is used here.

Short-term or intermediate-term consumer credit may be further divided into two large groups: installment credit and noninstallment credit. Credit to be repaid in a series of installments is of various types, for example, automobile paper, other consumer-goods paper—such as loans on refrigerators or furniture—home repair and modernization loans, and personal installment loans. The term "paper" used in connection with consumer credit means installment sales notes held by banks, other financial institutions, or retail outlets. Personal installment loans, frequently made by banks, are for unspecified purposes, as distinguished from installment notes for the purchase of automobiles and the like. They are frequently used for emergency medical care and other personal expenses, but they also may be used for the purchase of a car, modernization of a house, or the purchase of household equipment. They are also used for refinancing previous commitments, particularly in cases where a number of loans are being consolidated.

Noninstallment consumer credit consists of charge accounts, service credit—such as that extended by doctors, dentists, utility companies, and dry cleaners—and single-payment loans that are repaid in a single lump sum at the end of a specified time period.

THE CONSUMER CREDIT PROTECTION ACT OF 1968

The Consumer Credit Protection Act, known also as a "truth-in-lending" bill, signed by President Johnson on May 29, 1968, came only after a bitter and grueling eight-year-long struggle in Congress. The heart of this act was stated lucidly by President Johnson when he said, "As a matter of fair play to the consumer, the cost of credit should be disclosed fully, simply and clearly." The consumer legislative program of the Kansas Home Economics Association spelled out President Johnson's generalization aptly: "Easy credit, misleading advertising of interest rates and failure to disclose credit terms in standard simple terms prohibits efficient shopping for credit. 'Truth-in-Lending' legislation to require disclosure of credit costs both in dollars and in simple percentage rates is essential for efficient education for wise use of credit."[1]

This act is not perfect but, in general, it forces creditors to state in their contracts most of the information consumers need in order to buy wisely; and it takes some first steps toward protecting those most vulnerable to high-pressure credit merchants, who too often push people into debt over their heads and rely on the law to force them to pay. But a new era of truth-in-lending will dawn on July 1, 1969, July 1, 1970, and January 1, 1971. These are the dates when important parts of the new law are scheduled to be in effect.

Installment Loans and Sales

Starting on July 1, 1969, all lenders and credit merchants will have to disclose the full cost of finance charges in both dollars and annual percentage rate on installment loans and sales. The annual percentage rate will have to reflect not only the interest rate on the debt, but also the extra charges that would

[1] *Senate Hearings* . . . First Session on S. 5, Apr. 13 - May 10, 1967, p. 552.

not have been added onto a cash deal such as life insurance to cover the balance due. This section of the act is important because in recent years about 80 percent of consumer credit is on installment loans and sales.

Some minor concessions were necessary in order to get the act passed. The annual rate will not have to be computed on credit up to $75 if the finance charge is $5 or less, and on credit above $75 if the finance charge is $7.50 or less, or on a monthly charge account bill if the finance charge is 50 cents or less.

Every installment contract, however, will state in dollars the total of all finance charges, the purchase price of the goods or services being financed, any downpayment or trade-in allowance, the net amount being financed with credit, and the size of the weekly or monthly payments, as well as their due dates, and the total number of installments before the debt is paid up. Dollar cost of credit is important to the intelligent use of credit. But the annual percentage rate is the one indispensable piece of information that consumers need when shopping for the lowest cost for consumer credit.

Revolving Credit

The biggest battle in Congress was over revolving credit—the kind of buy-now-pay-later plan attached to store charge accounts, bank credit cards, and overdraft checking accounts. Revolving credit or open-end credit is increasing. In 1968, 21.3 percent of all consumer credit was revolving credit, in contrast to 11.1 percent in 1957.

Under the new law, all revolving-credit contracts and monthly bills must state the "nominal annual percentage rate." The use of the "nominal" part is part of a compromise with the retail merchants, who tried to escape from having to disclose their annual interest rates. The "nominal rate" on revolving credit will equal 12 times the monthly rate. Most retail stores and mail-order stores charge 1½ percent a month, and will, therefore, have to disclose a "nominal rate" of 18 percent a year.

But stores charging the same "nominal" rates can and do levy different revolving-credit charges. Unfortunately for consumers, the differences are concealed in the stores' various methods of arriving at the monthly balance on which credit is levied. Sears, Roebuck and Company, for example, applies its credit charge to your bill *before* deducting any payments you have made or credits for returned merchandise. J. C. Penney and Company, on the other hand, deducts all payments and credits; it charges you only for the amount of money you actually owe on the previous month's closing balance. An illustration is given in Table 6-1.[2]

Obviously, stores make more money charging by the Sears method than by the Penney method. Under this new law, therefore, revolving-credit lenders

[2] *Ibid.,* pp. 218-222.

TABLE 6-1

	OPENING BALANCE	PAYMENTS AND CREDITS	MONTHLY RATE OF FINANCE CHARGE	ACTUAL FINANCE CHARGE	ANNUAL RATE OF FINANCE CHARGE
Sears	$200	$100	1½%	0.015 × 200 = $3.00	36%
Penney's	200	100	1½%	0.015 × 100 = $1.50	18

may, if they wish, list not only the "nominal" percentage rate but also their yield rate, which will be labeled as the "average effective annual percentage rate." The optional methods permitted could result in disclosure of three different interest rate figures. A store could state its "nominal" annual rate at 18 percent, its "effective" annual rate at 10 percent, and its monthly rate at 1.5 percent.

Unfortunately, it appears that Congress intended to let retailers claim an "effective" rate that is lower than their "nominal" rate. Actually, as in the above illustration, the "effective" rate of some stores is higher than the "nominal" rate. The "effective" rate will distort, in the revolving creditor's favor, price comparisons with other forms of credit. Even so, the "effective" rate should permit consumers to recognize which revolving-credit bank plans and retailers offer the billing method most favorable to the customer. This is the basic purpose of the new law—to permit consumers to compare alternatives.

Retailers were given a concession in a provision that would allow them to exclude from the disclosure of finance charges a certain minimum monthly charge on small unpaid revolving-account balances.

Any class of credit transactions, however, may be exempted by operation of a Federal Reserve Board regulation if state laws subject them to substantially similar requirements.

Wage Garnishments

Unfortunately, the act does not contain any law on judgment (where creditors obtain court orders declaring debtors in default without giving them warning or opportunity for a hearing) and waters down the antigarnishment proposal. As of July 1, 1970, the first 75 percent of a debtor's take-home pay will become exempt from garnishment (a court order requiring an employer to withhold a certain sum or percentage of the weekly or monthly pay check for payment on debts of an employee). A weekly pay check of $48 or less, after deductions, will be untouchable by creditors. The law also says that an employee may not be fired the first time his pay has been garnished.

Representative Leonor K. Sullivan of Missouri, primarily responsible in the House for strengthening the bill, was disappointed with the wage garnishment section of the bill but called it "better than the wage garnishment laws in effect in roughly half of the states." In many states, therefore, debtors will get some relief beginning on July 1, 1970.

Other Provisions

Congress found that organized crime gets a big piece of income from loan sharking. When money lenders operating within the law will not lend you money, a loan shark probably will. His interest rate of 36 percent and up a year may look like a bargain to a person with poor credit. But his collection methods sometimes are pretty rough. Threats of injury or death are followed up, if necessary, by the real thing. Under this act, loan sharking becomes a federal offense. Federal prosecutors can obtain indictments and convictions, under the bill, without testimony from the victims.

Credit Advertising.   Another halfway provision in the law is its regulation of credit advertising. Bait advertising that falsely promises specific low installments or low downpayments will be banned. Advertising mentioning specific terms, such as size of installments, must tell the whole story, including the annual rate of finance charges and, in revolving credit, the billing method. But the law leaves merchants and lenders free to use generalized terms like "easy credit terms," "low bank rates," or "Pay nothing for two months." The Federal Reserve Board may have more to say about this when the regulations become effective.

Home Mortgage.   Another fight was waged and won to put home mortgages under this law. For the first time, mortgage interest will have to be figured to include any money you must pay as "points" or a discount or any other one-time extra charge beyond the stated interest. The mortgage lenders, however, exacted compromises from Congress. They will not, for example, have to disclose in a first mortgage the total finance charge in dollars. That sum would exceed the size of the mortgage itself in most instances, and the housing industry feared that many potential home seekers would be put off by knowing the stark truth that the interest on a 30-year mortgage may be nearly twice that on a 20-year mortgage. More on this in Chapter 10.

Home Improvements.   The new law affords protection to homeowners against fast-talking home-improvement salesmen and lenders promoting "easy-term" debt consolidation based on a second mortgage. Starting July 1, 1969, persons who sign such contracts will have the right for the next three business days to cancel the agreement without penalty. This "cooling-off" period will be required only in contracts containing real estate liens.

The Poor.   The truth-in-lending bill protects the poor and uneducated in our ghettos and in rural areas like anyone else. But no amount of written information will be enough to help them know what their rights are under the law until we have consumer advice centers easily accessible to the poor. England, to mention only one country, has had considerable success with their consumer advice centers. The poor in our ghettos are constantly preyed upon by a certain class of credit merchants who beckon day and night from their slum stores with television sets, clothing, and furniture on easy terms of only a few dollars a week. Studies reveal that the prices they charge, well concealed in their "easy payments," are often exorbitant. The Federal Trade Commission study in a low-income section of Washington, D.C., revealed that a television set available for $129.95 sold for $219.95 in the ghetto. The poor, who generally are the less educated, will need special help to protect them. Every effort should be made to improve consumer counseling in the ghettos.

   The Federal Reserve Board as Regulator.   It is up to the Federal Reserve Board to translate the law into concrete rules. As is true in almost all consumer legislation, success hinges on full and proper regulation. The FRB must write the rules in consultation with an advisory committee of credit merchants, lenders, and the public. The FRB is likely to be frustrated by the advisory committee every step of the way because merchants and lenders have a special interest which may be difficult to deny.

   Nine federal agencies will be responsible for enforcing the disclosure rules laid down by the law and the Federal Reserve Board. The Civil Aeronautics Board, for example, will enforce disclosure in air travel and the Department of Agriculture in meat selling; the Federal Trade Commission will have the difficult job of seeing that the whole truth about credit is told by retail stores, car dealers, consumer finance companies, mail-order houses, discount houses, and repair firms. And there is always the problem of securing sufficient funds to enforce the law and the regulations.

What Happens to Violators?

The law provides for criminal penalties of up to $5,000 fine and one year in jail. Consumers may recover in civil suits twice the amount of the finance charge (but not less than $100 or more than $1,000), plus legal costs, if a creditor fails to disclose any required information and if he cannot prove that the violation resulted from a bona fide error.

   This principle of self-enforcement of the law may not be good for the consumer. It asks more time, effort, and knowledge than the average person can or should have to supply. It may turn out that the federal agencies themselves must demand compliance, solicit consumer complaints, and act promptly against violators.

National Commission on Consumer Finance

The act establishes a National Commission on Consumer Finance. This commission is directed to study, among other things, the adequacy of existing protections against unfair credit practices. This commission comes at a critical time. Another group, the National Conference of Commissioners on Uniform State Laws, has presented a Uniform Consumer Credit Code to the state legislatures. The code has some serious shortcomings, according to some consumer-oriented lawyers. It is possible that the existence of the new commission may have the effect of preventing hasty adoption of the code by the states. It may recommend minimum standards of fair play for consumers in debt. Perhaps what is needed is a set of laws shifting more burden of risk onto the lender. Some credit lawyers agree with Abner Mikva, a Chicago attorney and a champion of credit protection for the poor who believes that the "penalty for over-extension of credit ought to be imposed on the overextender, rather than the purchaser."

Summary

The Consumer Credit Protection Act is one of the most important consumer laws passed in recent years. There are shortcomings, as has been pointed out. There may be more inadequacies due to poor regulations and inadequate funds. Nevertheless, it is indispensable legislation for a country that buys on the cuff and for an economy underpinned by an enormous installment debt. If credit helped propel our economy to ever-increasing heights, overextension of credit could be very serious. The new act, strengthened if necessary as experience dictates and effectively enforced, can provide the built-in controls needed for an orderly consumer credit market.

We are never going to stop some people from wanting things they cannot afford. But when they do buy, they should know what it is costing them in dollars and in simple, annual interest for using somebody else's money.

USING CONSUMER CREDIT

Education for More Effective Use of Consumer Credit

Good credit laws are not an end in themselves. Education for personal economic competence is also needed. Intelligent preparation to cope with the economic facts of life will save many of us the headaches that come from living by trial and error. Nowhere is this more true than in consumer credit. Young marrieds as well as old marrieds need the information and skill necessary to deal with the advantages and dangers in the use of consumer credit.

Practically everyone in this country uses credit in some form. In fact, four out of five young married couples with growing children are using installment credit for the purchase of durable goods.

Use of Consumer Credit in the United States

Total consumer credit outstanding in January, 1969, amounted to $112.1 billion, of which noninstallment credit was $22.6 billion. Of the $89.4 billion in-

TABLE 6-2   USE OF INSTALLMENT CREDIT IN 1967, BY AGE GROUPS (PERCENT OF FAMILIES REPORTING)

	TOTAL	OWED NO INSTALL-MENT CREDIT	OWED INSTALL-MENT CREDIT	AMOUNT OF INSTALLMENT CREDIT OWED				
				$1-199	$200-499	$500-999	$1,000-1,999	$2,000 or more
All families	100	52	48	9	8	9	12	10
Families where head of family was age:								
18 to 24	100	30	70	12	13	14	15	16
25 to 34	100	31	69	13	9	13	18	16
35 to 44	100	36	64	9	11	14	16	14
45 to 54	100	46	54	8	9	10	14	13
55 to 64	100	65	35	9	6	7	8	5
65 and older	100	88	12	5	3	2	1	1

NOTE: Parts may not add to totals because of rounding.

SOURCE: *1967 Survey of Consumer Finances*, Survey Research Center, University of Michigan.

TABLE 6-3 USE OF INSTALLMENT CREDIT IN 1967, BY INCOME GROUPS (PERCENT OF FAMILIES REPORTING)

	TOTAL	OWED NO INSTALL-MENT CREDIT	OWED INSTALL-MENT CREDIT	AMOUNT OF INSTALLMENT CREDIT OWED				
				$1-199	$200-499	$500-999	$1,000-1,999	$2,000 or more
All families	100	52	48	9	8	9	12	10
Families with income of:								
Under $3,000	100	76	24	12	6	3	1	2
$3,000 to $4,999	100	58	42	10	9	9	9	5
$5,000 to $7,499	100	45	55	10	12	12	12	9
$7,500 to $9,999	100	39	61	7	8	13	18	15
$10,000 to $14,999	100	41	59	7	6	11	18	17
$15,000 and over	100	55	45	3	7	7	9	19

NOTE: Parts may not add to totals because of rounding.

SOURCE: *1967 Survey Consumer Finances*, Survey Research Center, University of Michigan.

stallment credit, $34.0 billion was for automobiles, $24.6 billion for other consumer goods, $26.9 billion for personal loans, and $3.8 billion in repair and modernization loans. This is in contrast to $99.2 billion in total consumer credit by the end of 1967, of which $77.9 billion was in installment loans.[3]

Young families are apt to use installment credit more than any other age group. A study of Table 6-2, Use of Installment Credit in 1967, by Age Groups, shows that 70 percent of our families between 18 and 24 years of age owed installment credit. Only 12 percent of our families 65 and older owed installment credit. In terms of the amount of installment credit owed, $1,000 or more was owed by 34 percent of those 25 to 34 years of age, by 31 percent of those 18 to 24 years of age, by 30 percent of those 35 to 44, by 27 percent of those 45 to 54, and by only 2 percent of those 65 years of age or older.

The use of installment credit by income groups shows that 48 percent of all families in the United States owed installment debt in 1967 (Table 6-3). Sixty-one percent of families, the highest percentage, having incomes from $7,500 to $9,999 owed installment credit in 1967. Only 24 percent of families under $3,000 income owed installment credit in 1967—the lowest percentage of families by income groups. This low percentage is due largely to their inability to secure credit because of very low incomes. At the other extreme, 45 percent of families having $15,000 or more in 1967 owed installment credit, and 19 percent of them owed $2,000 or more.

The Cost of Consumer Credit Is High

The cost of credit, when the facts are known, is high, and sometimes shockingly high. Study after study has shown that for most kinds of consumer credit the equivalent annual interest rates can be as high as 30 percent or more. What is needed is a standard of comparison which consumers of credit can use so it will be possible to "shop for credit." To "shop for credit" requires that the information on total credit costs given to the consumer be truthful, standardized, and meaningful. Of equal importance, the consumer must be made aware of available credit opportunities or alternatives and their respective costs in dollars and interest rate on an annual basis. The passage of the Consumer Credit Protection Act of 1968 went a long way in disclosure of total consumer credit costs.

We cannot fully expect that all consumers will make better decisions because of the required disclosure of total credit costs. But with education and open publicity of credit costs, it is certain that many consumers will for the first time "shop for credit" in earnest. What is fundamental is that the consumer has the option of being able to compare credit costs and know what alternatives are available.

[3] Federal Reserve Board.

TABLE 6-4   TABLE FOR COMPUTING ANNUAL PERCENTAGE RATE FOR LEVEL MONTHLY PAYMENT PLANS

Number of Payments	ANNUAL PERCENTAGE RATE										
	10.00%	10.25%	10.50%	10.75%	11.00%	11.25%	11.50%	11.75%	12.00%	12.25%	12.50%
	FINANCE CHARGE PER $100 OF AMOUNT FINANCED										
1	0.83	0.85	0.87	0.90	0.92	0.94	0.96	0.98	1.00	1.02	1.04
2	1.25	1.28	1.31	1.35	1.38	1.41	1.44	1.47	1.50	1.53	1.57
3	1.67	1.71	1.76	1.80	1.84	1.88	1.92	1.96	2.01	2.05	2.09
4	2.09	2.14	2.20	2.25	2.30	2.35	2.41	2.46	2.51	2.57	2.62
5	2.51	2.58	2.64	2.70	2.77	2.83	2.89	2.96	3.02	3.08	3.15
6	2.94	3.01	3.08	3.16	3.23	3.31	3.38	3.45	3.53	3.60	3.68
7	3.36	3.45	3.53	3.62	3.70	3.78	3.87	3.95	4.04	4.12	4.21
8	3.79	3.88	3.98	4.07	4.17	4.26	4.36	4.46	4.55	4.65	4.74
9	4.21	4.32	4.43	4.53	4.64	4.75	4.85	4.96	5.07	5.17	5.28
10	4.64	4.76	4.88	4.99	5.11	5.23	5.35	5.46	5.58	5.70	5.82
11	5.07	5.20	5.33	5.45	5.58	5.71	5.84	5.97	6.10	6.23	6.36
12	5.50	5.64	5.78	5.92	6.06	6.20	6.34	6.48	6.62	6.76	6.90
13	5.93	6.08	6.23	6.38	6.53	6.68	6.84	6.99	7.14	7.29	7.44
14	6.36	6.52	6.69	6.85	7.01	7.17	7.34	7.50	7.66	7.82	7.99
15	6.80	6.97	7.14	7.32	7.49	7.66	7.84	8.01	8.19	8.36	8.53
16	7.23	7.41	7.60	7.78	7.97	8.15	8.34	8.53	8.71	8.90	9.08
17	7.67	7.86	8.06	8.25	8.45	8.65	8.84	9.04	9.24	9.44	9.63
18	8.10	8.31	8.52	8.73	8.93	9.14	9.35	9.56	9.77	9.98	10.19
19	8.54	8.76	8.98	9.20	9.42	9.64	9.86	10.08	10.30	10.52	10.74
20	8.98	9.21	9.44	9.67	9.90	10.13	10.37	10.60	10.83	11.06	11.30
21	9.42	9.66	9.90	10.15	10.39	10.63	10.88	11.12	11.36	11.61	11.85
22	9.86	10.12	10.37	10.62	10.88	11.13	11.39	11.64	11.90	12.16	12.41
23	10.30	10.57	10.84	11.10	11.37	11.63	11.90	12.17	12.44	12.71	12.97
24	10.75	11.02	11.30	11.58	11.86	12.14	12.42	12.70	12.98	13.26	13.54
25	11.19	11.48	11.77	12.06	12.35	12.64	12.93	13.22	13.52	13.81	14.10
26	11.64	11.94	12.24	12.54	12.85	13.15	13.45	13.75	14.06	14.36	14.67
27	12.09	12.40	12.71	13.03	13.34	13.66	13.97	14.29	14.60	14.92	15.24

29	12.98	13.32	13.66	14.00	14.33	14.67	15.01	15.35	15.70	16.04	16.38
30	13.43	13.78	14.13	14.48	14.83	15.19	15.54	15.89	16.24	16.60	16.95
31	13.89	14.25	14.61	14.97	15.33	15.70	16.06	16.43	16.79	17.16	17.53
32	14.34	14.71	15.09	15.46	15.84	16.21	16.59	16.97	17.35	17.73	18.11
33	14.79	15.17	15.57	15.95	16.34	16.73	17.12	17.51	17.90	18.29	18.69
34	15.25	15.65	16.05	16.44	16.85	17.25	17.65	18.05	18.46	18.86	19.27
35	15.70	16.11	16.53	16.94	17.35	17.77	18.18	18.60	19.01	19.43	19.85
36	16.16	16.58	17.01	17.43	17.86	18.29	18.71	19.14	19.57	20.00	20.43
37	16.62	17.06	17.49	17.93	18.37	18.81	19.25	19.69	20.13	20.58	21.02
38	17.08	17.53	17.98	18.43	18.88	19.33	19.78	20.24	20.69	21.15	21.61
39	17.54	18.00	18.46	18.93	19.39	19.86	20.32	20.79	21.26	21.73	22.20
40	18.00	18.48	18.95	19.43	19.90	20.38	20.86	21.34	21.82	22.30	22.79
41	18.47	18.95	19.44	19.93	20.42	20.91	21.40	21.89	22.39	22.88	23.38
42	18.93	19.43	19.93	20.43	20.93	21.44	21.94	22.45	22.96	23.47	23.98
43	19.40	19.91	20.42	20.94	21.43	21.97	22.49	23.01	23.53	24.05	24.57
44	19.86	20.39	20.91	21.44	21.97	22.50	23.03	23.57	24.10	24.64	25.17
45	20.33	20.87	21.41	21.95	22.49	23.03	23.58	24.12	24.67	25.22	25.77
46	20.80	21.35	21.90	22.46	23.01	23.57	24.13	24.69	25.25	25.81	26.37
47	21.27	21.83	22.40	22.97	23.53	24.10	24.68	25.25	25.82	26.40	26.98
48	21.74	22.32	22.90	23.48	24.06	24.64	25.23	25.81	26.40	26.99	27.58
49	22.21	22.80	23.39	23.99	24.58	25.18	25.78	26.38	26.99	27.59	28.19
50	22.69	23.29	23.89	24.50	25.11	25.72	26.33	26.95	27.56	28.18	28.80
51	23.16	23.78	24.40	25.02	25.64	26.26	26.89	27.52	28.15	28.78	29.41
52	23.64	24.27	24.90	25.53	26.17	26.81	27.45	28.09	28.73	29.38	30.02
53	24.11	24.76	25.40	26.05	26.70	27.35	28.00	28.66	29.32	29.98	30.64
54	24.59	25.25	25.91	26.57	27.23	27.90	28.56	29.23	29.91	30.58	31.25
55	25.07	25.74	26.41	27.09	27.77	28.44	29.13	29.81	30.50	31.18	31.87
56	25.55	26.23	26.92	27.61	28.30	28.99	29.69	30.39	31.09	31.79	32.49
57	26.03	26.73	27.43	28.13	28.84	29.54	30.25	30.97	31.68	32.39	33.11
58	26.51	27.23	27.94	28.66	29.37	30.10	30.82	31.55	32.27	33.00	33.74
59	27.00	27.72	28.45	29.18	29.91	30.65	31.39	32.13	32.87	33.61	34.36
60	27.48	28.22	28.96	29.71	30.45	31.20	31.96	32.71	33.47	34.23	34.99

SOURCE: "Regulation 2 Annual Percentage Rate Tables," *Truth in Lending*, Commerce Clearing House, Inc., Chicago, 1969, p. 7.

The federal act does not regulate interest rates or other charges, fees, et cetera, on consumer credit. Each of the states has credit law regulations. Usually the cost of using credit varies from state to state. But each kind of credit has a maximum rate set on the amount that can be charged. Consequently, it is as important as ever to be aware of the differences in credit cost. What the federal act does, after July 1, 1969, is to require lenders and merchants to give you the total cost in both dollars and annual percentage rate or, in the case of revolving-credit accounts, the nominal interest rate. If the federal law is carried out in credit transactions, the total dollar cost and the total cost in terms of annual interest rates will be available to you. It is, then, up to you to make use of this valuable information by shopping around for the most favorable credit cost. It is possible that some lenders and merchants may, through ignorance or planned dishonesty, misquote the total cost of credit. Under such circumstances it would be comfortable to know how to check the mathematics of the lender. (See Table 6-4.) The FRB has worked out a table to help consumers and businessmen determine the annual percentage rates to be disclosed in all types of credit other than open end (see Table 6-4). Creditors, however, may use other tables adapted to their particular needs.

Your Credit Rating

Is your credit "slip" showing? One way to find out is when you open your first credit account in a store. The store may open an account for you in less than an hour; sometimes it takes a day or longer. Behind the scenes of establishing credit is an elaborate national and international credit system. Your local credit bureau is at the center of the network. There are over 2,200 local credit bureaus in the United States. These bureaus are amassing data on everyone who uses credit. The facts come from many sources—banks, court and police records, press stories, directories, employers, other credit bureaus, personal references, other merchants, your neighbors and landlord, lending agencies, school and medical records, and legal records like judgments, bankruptcies, federal tax liens, and collections. In fact, you name it, and the bureau has it.

All this information is made available to all other credit bureaus through membership in the Associated Credit Bureaus of America. This means that your credit follows you wherever you go. You cannot clear your record, if it is not a good one, by moving to another town or state.

Are you a better credit risk when you make $10,000 rather than $8,000 a year? Not always. The right to credit must be earned. Stability of income counts for you. Table 6-5, How Your Credit Is Rated, shows the standards recommended for the use of bankers in a manual prepared by the American Bankers Association.

TABLE 6-5   HOW YOUR CREDIT IS RATED

	FAVORABLE	UNFAVORABLE
Employment	With good firm two years or more. Job involves skill, education.	Shifts jobs frequently. Employed in seasonal industry such as construction work. Unskilled labor.
Income	Steady, meets all normal needs.	Earnings fluctuate, depend on commissions, tips, one-shot deals. Amount barely covers requirements.
Residence	Owns own home or rents for long periods in good neighborhoods.	Lives in furnished rooms in poor neighborhoods. Changes address frequently.
Financial structure	Has savings account and checking account that requires minimum balance. Owns property, investments, life insurance.	No bank accounts. Few, if any, assets.
Debt record	Pays bills promptly. Usually makes large downpayment. Borrows infrequently and for constructive purpose.	Slow payer. Tries to put as much on credit as possible. Frequent loans for increasing amounts.
Litigation	No suits by creditors.	Record of suits and other legal action for nonpayment. Bankruptcy.
Personal characteristics	Family man. Not many dependents relative to income. Mature.	Large number of dependents. Marital difficulties. Young, impulsive.
Application behavior	Seeks loan from bank with which he regularly deals. Answers all questions fully and truthfully.	Applies for loan at banking office far removed from his residence or place of business. Makes misstatements on application. In great hurry to obtain cash.

SOURCES OF CONSUMER CREDIT

For installment credit services totaling $89.4 billion at the end of 1968, consumers were utilizing the facilities of commercial banks ($37.0 billion), sales finance companies ($18.1 billion), consumer finance companies ($8.8 billion), credit unions ($10.1 billion), and other financial institutions such as industrial loan companies, mutual savings banks, and saving and loan associations ($3.2 billion). Retail outlets, excluding their wholly owned finance companies, had outstanding loans of $12.1 billion.

Each of these specialized financial institutions was originally started to provide specific forms of credit: the consumer finance companies, to provide small loans; the sales finance companies, to provide for installment purchases, mostly of automobiles; and the credit unions, as cooperatives, to promote thrift and provide small loans to their members. Present credit holdings of these institutions, as well as of the commercial banks, which were latecomers to the consumer credit field, suggest that there has been much diversification and many shifts in the types of credit provided.

When You Need a Cash Loan

It has been estimated that nearly half of all consumer credit in this country is in the form of cash loans. Rare is the consumer who does not need to borrow at some time or other. Cash borrowing is generally made because of such hard-to-budget emergencies as operations, hospital and nursing bills, funeral expenses, a daughter's wedding, and a host of other expenses that can be otherwise financed only by careful planning and saving.

Most families have some savings. But savings are not easily accumulated and are usually modest sums. One serious illness, and the family savings are wiped out.

According to many surveys, the chief reason for getting a small loan is to consolidate debts previously contracted and to refinance them with a single loan. Then, and usually in this order, come loans for doctor, dentist, and hospital bills, followed closely by loans for clothing, fuel, food, and rent. Automobiles, furniture, and taxes are some of the other objects.

Most consumer borrowers are not prepared to cope with the various sources for cash loans. They are usually emotionally upset and are not armed with sufficient comparative facts about sources, rates, obligations, and budgeting. Consequently, the typical consumer looking for a cash loan is a rank amateur competing with a professional. Most of the unhappy endings to borrowing could have been prevented if the consumer had had a little basic knowledge about this business. It is important to be forearmed so that if the time comes to borrow a sum of money, you can go about the business in an efficient, knowing manner.

Before seeking a cash loan, analyze your situation. Compute how much money you need and what payment burden you can carry. Set up a plan to refinance yourself out of debt. Next come the general considerations.

1. Shop for cash just as you would shop for clothing or household equipment.
2. Do not shop with the attitude that you are in a bad spot and that the "loan sharks" have the advantage.

3. Offer the best security possible, because the best lenders give the lowest rate on good security.
4. Borrow the smallest amount of cash that will cover your need.
5. Be alert to compare the costs of borrowing money.
6. Avoid unlicensed agents.
7. If you are uncertain about a lending agency, consult the personal loan department of a commercial bank.
8. Listen to the agents who take time to discover the facts about your debts, your income, your ability to repay, and your budgeting plans.
9. Know the exact borrowing terms.
10. Get the total credit cost in terms of annual interest rate as well as in total dollar cost.

Where to Borrow Money

Every community has people who would like to lend money. Therefore, the secret of borrowing is to go shopping for money as you would for any other important commodity. It is all in knowing where to look and what to look for.

Let us assume that you are seeking a justifiable, moderate-size loan from a reputable lender. There are six major sources: a commercial bank, a life insurance policy, a credit union, an industrial bank or loan company, a small-loan company, and a pawnbroker. Before selecting the lender, examine the many points on which each differs from the others. Personal loans have many variations and are subject to state and local laws and conditions. Now for an inspection tour through each of the six major personal loan sources.

Commercial Banks. Suppose you need a few hundred dollars. The first place to go is your bank, if you do not belong to a credit union. There are three kinds of loans. An *unsecured loan* is one on which you give your personal note. If you borrow $200 for 90 days, the interest may be about 9 percent, or a total of $4.50. The principal falls due at the end of 90 days.

A second type of unsecured loan is an *unsecured installment loan*. The bank takes out the interest in advance—that is, it discounts the loan. You pay off the total in monthly installments. Thus, a $200 discount loan at 9 percent costs you nearly $36 a year net. The true rate of interest amounts to twice the discount rate, or about 19.9 percent a year. Many banks charge a fee also.

Another type of loan is a secured loan. It is possible to get a loan of up to 60 percent of the value of stocks, of the "bluebook" value of your car if fairly new, or of the cash value of life insurance policies. It generally takes a few days to complete such a loan. Interest rates on secured loans are lower than rates charged on unsecured installment loans, usually 8 percent true interest rate per year in 1970. This is less than the carrying charges for installment sales for one year.

Commercial banks are now the largest single source of installment credit. In 1967, commercial banks held 58 percent of the $31.2 billion in automobile paper and 27 percent of loans made for other consumer goods. Commercial banks led all other lenders in personal cash loans (36 percent).

Sales Finance Companies.   Sales finance companies purchase installment credit paper from retail merchants for cash. The sales finance company has the title to the car or other consumer goods purchased on an installment plan, collects the payments, and in case of default repossesses the car or durable goods, hoping to resell it for at least the unpaid balance on the loan. Sales finance companies supply almost one-third of the retail installment credit ($18.1 billion in 1968) and about one-fifth of the credit supplied for the purchase of other consumer goods.

Consumer Finance Companies.   These companies are sometimes called "personal finance" companies or "small-loan" companies. These finance firms sold less than 12 percent ($8.8 billion) of all installment credit, and about 25 percent of all personal cash installment loans, in 1968. Almost half of all these loans are unsecured. Most of the rest are secured by furniture mortgages. The companies are specially geared for persons without established credit. The better small-loan companies give personal budgeting counseling service. You apply for loans much as you do at a commercial or industrial bank. Your application, however, may go through faster. You sign a note for the amount you get. Each month you pay an installment on the principal, plus interest for the preceding month. As a rule, there are no other fees. Some may try to sell you life insurance. If you want it and need it, good. If you do not, go to another lending agency.

Credit Unions.   Credit unions are groups of people organized into cooperative thrift and loan associations chartered by either the state or the federal government. The members are likely to be employees of a corporation or firm, or they may be members of a church or other private or public community group. Each member deposits savings in the credit union, receives interest on his investment, and may borrow from his credit union.

At the end of 1968, the credit unions had about 19 million members having $10.1 billion in installment credit loans. Credit unions held 11 percent of all the automobile paper and 22 percent of all the personal cash installment loans in this country at that time.

In the recent effort to help the poor and less educated consumers, credit unions have been organized to serve the low-income people. More than 400 federal credit unions now serve low-income groups.[4] The Bureau of Federal Credit Unions and the U.S. Department of Health, Education, and Welfare are attempting to increase this number through their "Project Moneywise." With proper counseling and organization, credit unions can be successful even with the low-income group.

Other Financial Institutions and Retailers.   Other financial organizations, such as industrial loan companies, mutual savings banks, and savings and loan associations held $3.2 billion of installment credit at the end of 1968. Retail

[4] Federal Trade Commission, *Economic Report,* p. xv.

outlets (excluding their wholly owned finance companies) had outstanding loans of $12.1 billion at the end of 1968.

Pawnbrokers. Pawnbrokers do not play an important role as a source for loanable funds. The establishments of pawnbrokers range from dingy stores to plush emporiums that generally lend only on jewelry. Charges range widely from 2 to 10 percent a month true interest rate. Perhaps a common rate is about 3 percent a month. These loans represent exact dollar costs, since the loans are not repayable monthly: an average of 30 cents a month for each $10 owed.

A pawnbroker makes his loan on the personal property left with him for security. Ordinarily, he lends from 60 to 90 percent of the sale value of the pledge. When the loan is paid back, plus interest, the property is redeemed. If it is not paid, the pawnbroker has the right to sell the pledge. The interesting fact is that there is nothing to sign. Therefore, the borrower cannot be forced to pay back the loan or the interest, but the pledge is forfeit. In all fairness to pawnbrokers, there are not many other lenders who will hand out $5 for a few days or lend $150 on 10 minutes' notice.

A CONSUMER CREDIT CODE FOR LENDERS

The reform of archaic state credit laws is long overdue. But the proposed Uniform Consumer Credit Code (UCCC) prepared in 1968 by the National Conference of Commissioners on Uniform State Laws offers little in the way of relief for borrowers. The objective—uniform consumer credit laws in each of our 50 states—is, however, a good one.

The UCCC

The finance industry-dominated Uniform Consumer Code National Committee drafts a model code and makes an all-out effort to lobby it through the legislature of every state. The objective—uniform credit laws in each state to replace the present hodgepodge of state laws—is a good one. The draft of the present model credit law is not all bad. There is an effort, for example, to have something resembling the federal Consumer Credit Protection Act of 1968. There is also an attempt to make wage garnishments somewhat less oppressive. The main thrust of the draft is twofold: to raise interest rates and to remove some of the protection the public has under some of the existing state laws. Suppose you buy a refrigerator for $350, paying $50 down and the balance in 12 equal monthly payments. The maximum finance charge under California law is $30. Under the UCCC model law it would be $54—an increase of some 80 percent.

Nor would only Californians suffer should this model code go into effect. Table 6-6, below, shows interest rates on small loans in several major states, which may be compared with the rates allowed by the Uniform Consumer Credit

TABLE 6-6   MAXIMUM INTEREST RATES IN SEVERAL MAJOR STATES

	MAXIMUM RATE OF INTEREST ON LOAN OF		
	$300	$400	$500
California	28	27.0	26.4
Illinois	30	25.5	22.8
Michigan	30	26.25	24.0
New Jersey	30	24.0	20.4
New York	26	21.75	19.2
Pennsylvania	30	25.5	22.8
UCCC	36	32.25	30.0

Code. This comparison is especially important because actual interest rates on small loans tend to be the maximum allowed by law.

The table indicates that on a $300 loan the amount of interest a borrower could be charged would be boosted by 20 to almost 40 percent in the states shown; on a $400 loan from 19 to over 40 percent; and on a $500 loan, from 13 to 56 percent.

The laws on the books were themselves proposed by the loan companies about 30 years ago. They could use some strengthening. But now there is a real danger that the rates on small loans may increase. No one, however, should object to rates available at prices high enough for successful business operation but no higher.

CREDIT CARDS

Credit cards were used originally to replace the use of cash in buying. Usually there were no credit card charges because most people paid their bills at the end of the month. Retail stores were happy with this innovation because they retained their card customers longer, and their card customers purchased more goods than cash customers.

Instant Money

There are probably about 100 million credit cards in use in the United States today. Many people have several cards, despite the trend toward using one card for many kinds of stores. Oil firm cards, for example, are now used for food, lodging, and merchandise ranging from sporting goods to jewelry. So far the sponsors of the all-purpose credit cards, such as Diners' Club, American Express, and Carte Blanche, say they have not felt any impact from the recent oil card competition. It is estimated that there are currently about 70 million oil credit card accounts—about 40 percent more than 5 years ago. Industry officials claim that over $7 billion is charged on petroleum credit cards today. In contrast to most all-purpose credit cards (which may cost up to $11 annually for the first card and $2 annually for each additional card), oil company cards can be obtained free and have no annual fee.

Recently Sinclair distributed 2 million catalogs to its credit card holders, offering purchase of more than 200 items, including silver-plated coffee service and 17-jewel wristwatches. Orders are filled by a large premium house and Sinclair does the billing and collecting.

Banks are beginning to enter the credit card game with "instant money." The *Federal Reserve Bulletin* [5] reported that in December, 1967, 386 banks extended $211 million through credit cards, while 732 banks extended $116 million in check credit. The credit card tends to be a high-volume operation: one out of six banks offering credit cards had credit extensions of more than $500,000 in December, 1967, but only one out of 25 banks reached that volume with check credit.

Bank credit cards and check-credit plans are spreading throughout the country, but the largest concentration in terms of amount of credit outstanding is still in the San Francisco Federal Reserve District, with the Chicago and New York districts following in that order. Many local bank card plans are moving beyond former boundaries. The trend is toward multibank plans, ranging from regional to national in scope. Growth has resulted both from franchising arrangements and from interchange agreements among banks with their own cards.

Credit card plans, with credit outstanding on December 31, 1967, was reported by the Federal Reserve Board as follows:

CREDIT CARD PLAN	MILLIONS OF DOLLARS OF CREDIT OUTSTANDING
Bank credit cards (excludes check credit)	800
Oil companies (consumer portion)	1,000
Department store revolving credit	3,500
Retail charge accounts	6,550
Travel and entertainment cards (consumer only)	50
All other	150
	$12,050

Some Dangers in Credit Card Use

One bank advertises, "Forget about cash when you shop." To forget about cash is an example of the real danger. "Free credit," when it exists, is free only for 10 to 30 days. After the free time is up, you usually pay 1¼ to 1½ percent a month on the balance, which adds up to true annual interest rates of 15 to 18 percent.

[5] *Federal Reserve Bulletin,* June, 1968.

The other cost is hidden in adding the 3 to 5 percent sponsor's charge to the merchandise purchased. In most cases this extra charge is also added to the price charged cash customers, too.

Another danger is that the user of credit may accumulate bills more rapidly than he realizes. It is so easy to say, "Charge it."

The illegal use of stolen credit cards may be your loss unless you follow the directions of the issuing company. The customary procedure is to report the loss of the credit card immediately to the issuing company. Some insurance companies will cover certain credit card losses for a modest premium rate of around $8 for 3 years against a loss of up to $1,000.

Another recent problem, reported by *The Wall Street Journal*,[6] concerns illegal marketing of phony credit cards.

TEEN-AGE CREDIT

"Charge it" is a magic phrase to most adults. This magic phrase in the mouths of teen-agers is now an explosive buying weapon that adds to the already staggering problems of American families. Sharp warnings are being voiced in banking circles and in Washington.

Witnesses at hearings of a Senate banking subcommittee in 1961 reported that retail chains and some department stores were encouraging youngsters to sign up for revolving charge accounts. Junior charge accounts have been encouraged for several years by A. L. Trotta, manager of the Credit Managers Division of the National Retail Merchants Association. Mr. Trotta recommends the teen-age market as "a made-to-order opportunity for the sales-minded credit executive." As early as 1960, Sears Roebuck announced the opening of teen-age credit accounts in several of its stores.

The teen-age market is burgeoning at an astonishing rate. By 1970, when the teen-age population expands from the present 18 million to an expected 28 million, youngsters may be spending $20 billion annually—twice as much as in 1962. Many retailers, to get their share or more of this business, represent their juvenile charge accounts as "community services" and "living educational programs in money management." Ex-United States Senator Paul H. Douglas, on the contrary, brands teen-age charge accounts as "one of the unfortunate developments in consumer credit." The president of the Bowery Savings Bank, in New York City, says that such credit is "something like teaching the young to use narcotics."

Some credit plans do not require the signatures of parents. A few stores test teen-age credit cards. And one bank plan has three high school students acting as a teen-age loan board passing on loan applications from youngsters and issues loans without collateral or parental cosigners at 2½ percent interest.[7]

[6] *The Wall Street Journal*, Feb. 5, 1968.
[7] Reported in Lawrence Galton's column in the *St. Louis Post-Dispatch*.

Mrs. Helen Ewing Nelson, California Consumer Counsel, stated in 1962 that easy credit terms to teen-agers was creating a serious problem in California because "it is legal to charge at least $1 a month." Mrs. Nelson said, "The youngster may be paying interest which actually is greater than 30 percent."

Teen-age charge accounts can be good experience if the youngsters understand the high costs of credit attached to them. Parents, however, should think twice before they permit their teen-agers to open a charge account without proper understanding of the costs of credit and their responsibility in using such an account.

The rationale of the promoters is that teen-age charge accounts help a youngster to manage his money. But most stores are more anxious to sell than to educate. Usually there is a direct assault upon teens by credit sellers. Just prior to graduation time salesmen make a special drive to sell jewelry to boys to give to girl friends. And girls are pressured to buy flatware and stainless steel pots and pans at exorbitant prices.[8] The motto of our times could well be, "I want tomorrow today."

THE COST OF CREDIT

Credit, or the use of someone else's money, is a service that you must pay for. The amount that you pay for it may be called interest, carrying charges, service charges, or insurance, and may vary from one source to another. Interest and other charges may also vary with the amount of money used and the length of time taken to repay. Consumer borrowers pay about $10 billion a year for credit, and a big majority do not know the cost of the credit used.[9] The new Consumer Credit Protection Act will, in most instances, enforce the revealing of the total cost of consumer credit in dollars and in annual interest rate. This information was required after July 1, 1969. The credit shopper thus is not required to go through the difficult job of figuring the total dollar and total annual costs in specified percentage rates.[10]

Deceptive Credit Advertising

Table 6-7 tells the story of false, misleading, and deceptive advertising by lenders. The quoted rate (column 3 of this table) is the misleading and deceptive part of this sordid lending business. The true annual rate (column 2) is a more accurate cost of credit. This is why consumers desperately needed the recently

[8] Sidney Margolius, *The Innocent Consumer vs. The Exploiters,* Trident Press, New York, 1967, p. 63.

[9] Richard L. D. Morse, "Truth in Lending," Council on Consumer Information, University of Missouri, Columbia, Mo., 1966, p. 10.

[10] For those interested in consumer credit computations, the 1966 Council on Consumer Information pamphlet *Consumer Credit Computations,* by Dr. Richard L. D. Morse, is recommended.

TABLE 6-7   CREDIT RATES COMMONLY CHARGED BY LENDERS*

LENDER	TRUE ANNUAL RATE	QUOTED RATE
Revolving or budget charge accounts	12% to 18%	1 to 1½% per month on the unpaid balance.
Installment purchase— appliances, furniture	12% to 20% and more	Usually give dollar cost only.
Auto finance companies	12% to 24%	6% to 12% per year.
Small-loan companies	18% to 42%	1½% to 3½% per month on unpaid balance.
Commercial banks	6% to 16%	3% to 9% per year.
Credit unions	9% to 12%	¾ of 1% to 1% per month on unpaid balance.

*Alfred Stefferud, ed., *Consumers All,* U.S. Government Printing Office, 1965, p. 159.

enacted Consumer Credit Protection Act of 1968. After July 1, 1969, it was required that lenders disclose total costs in true annual rates and in total dollar costs for most credit transactions.

Life Insurance Loans

You can borrow directly from your life insurance company up to the full cash value of the policy. Rates range from 7 percent and up simple interest. Each permanent insurance policy has the exact terms spelled out. The loan can be arranged by your local insurance agent or by your writing to the home office.

Veterans having permanent life insurance can borrow directly from the federal government at only 4 percent—a low interest rate. There is a drawback, however, in borrowing on your life insurance via the company. It is easy not to repay the loan in regular payments, because the company adds the amount due to the debt (if there is enough cash value left). For some people it might be better, therefore, to use the policy as collateral and get a regular loan at a commercial bank, or at a credit union if you are a member.

Pay Cash or Pay Later?

There are many reasons for people buying on credit. Some of the more common arguments for using credit are these: (1) Consumers can enjoy the service or goods while paying for them; (2) using savings may result in nonreplacement of savings; (3) credit forces one to budget income; (4) credit is a convenience and an advantage in securing adjustments; (5) credit is useful in meeting emergency bills; (6) some credit transactions encourage wiser use of income, as in the case of the psychic satisfaction that a family receives from owning something now when their friends have the same; and (7) people ordinarily do not save in advance to enable them to pay cash.

TABLE 6-8   SAVE NOW AND BUY LATER*

	CASH PRICE	CREDIT CHARGE†	CASH PRICE PLUS CREDIT CHARGE	MONTHLY PAYMENT†	NUMBER OF MONTHS REQUIRED	
					To Pay Credit Price	To Save the Cash Price at Monthly Payment Rate‡
Range	$224	$44	$268	$10.50	25.5	21.3
Refrigerator	250	49	299	11.00	27.2	22.7
Washing machine	242	49	291	11.00	26.5	22.0
Clothes dryer	183	35	218	9.00	24.2	20.3
Dishwasher	160	26	186	7.50	24.8	21.3
Total	1,059	203	1,262		128.2	107.6

*Family Economics Review, June, 1964, p. 11.

†Based on the installment credit plan offered by a certain mail-order company for purchases of appliances. This plan allows 36 months to pay for a $500 purchase, with shorter periods for smaller amounts.

‡Smaller final payments are represented by fractional months.

All of the reasons given for using credit can be advantageous to consumers. The fact that there was $112.1 billion outstanding in consumer credit on January 1, 1969, seems to give support for the advantages of using credit. There is no doubt about the wide appeal of "Buy now, pay later." Saving ahead to pay cash has its appeal, too, because it means being able to satisfy more wants in the long run. It is the choice that might well be made by the family considering a purchase that is not an immediate necessity—say, a replacement for a still useful refrigerator, a new piece of furniture, or a new or a second car.

Save Now, Pay Later

Table 6-8 shows how the "Buy now and pay later" and the "Save now and buy later" plans would work in the purchase of five household items. In the "Buy now" plan, the items are to be purchased and paid for in monthly installments, as provided in a mail-order company's credit plan for the purchase of appliances. In the "Save now" plan, they are to be paid for in cash saved in monthly amounts equal to the installment payments.

The family that saved and bought for cash would have the five items (bought one after the other) in 9 years. The family that used the installment credit plan would need 20 months more than 9 years to pay for the same five items, because they would have an extra $200 to pay for credit charges. In this same 20-month period the first family, by saving at the same rate as the installment payments, could accumulate cash enough to buy an item like a television set or a room air conditioner in addition. "Save now and buy later" is a sort of "magic money" game that most of us have forgotten how to play. When we discover that this game of "Save and invest" for future planned purchases can be a winner for us, perhaps more families will play the game. After all, credit cannot add dollars to income, but saving and investing can.

Buying now and paying later does, of course, permit the purchase of something you need or want immediately. But buying on credit can be abused.

ABUSES OF THE USE OF CREDIT

Neither the Consumer Credit Protection Act of 1968 nor any other credit law will protect one from overextension of credit, from excessive charges for credit insurance, and from bad advice from debt adjusters and other abuses. It is up to you to learn how to use consumer credit wisely.

Concept of Collateral Has Evaporated

Many people are unaware of the changes that have taken place in the practices of debt financing of consumer goods and services in the last decade or so. Dr. Colston Warne, professor of economics at Amherst College, pointed this out to the Senate Banking and Currency Committee when he said, "The most significant change has been the transmutation of this financial device into a merchandising tool."

In the first place, according to Dr. Warne, the concept of collateral has evaporated. Even in automobiles, 36-month terms, together with rapid new-car obsolescence, have rendered the goods small surety for the loan. The resale value of other durables (white goods, TV sets, furniture, and the like) is so low in today's market that no lender considers them as collateral. Their repossession on delinquency is almost universally accompanied by a deficiency-balance charge that becomes, of course, a lien on any income or property of the debtor. Hence, credit contracts for these goods constitute at bottom little more than a disguised wage, chattels, or mortage lien—often unrecognized by the borrower. Finally, the great increase in the use of credit to finance the purchase of soft goods and services is incontrovertible evidence of the divorcement of consumer credit from any concept of the goods financed serving as collateral for the debt.

In short, consumer credit extensions are made singly and solely against the lender's expectations of (1) the consumer's ability to maintain current income, or (2) the lender's ability to exercise command over the borrower's assets via the courts. To put it another way, in their extensions of credit for consumption, lenders are, first, looking to the federal government's ability to maintain nearly full employment for surety, and second, depending on the police power at their command to tap existing equities in homes and cars. Thus, the theorizing of the past about the functions of consumer credit, which was based on the concept of pacing time units of consumption with payments over the period of use of the durables that secured the debt, fails to fit reality.

Retailers Acting as Agents for Lenders

A second concept of consumer credit that has evaporated, except in the case of a few of the largest retailers, says Dr. Warne, is the seller's responsibility for the loans disguised as sales. Although the courts and a good many state legislatures make a distinction between "carrying charges" and "interest," the practice that gave rise to that distinction is all but extinct. The retailer generally acts as an agent for a lender. Typically, the forms filled out by the consumer for the installment purchase of goods have been furnished the retailer by a lender. All conditions attending the loan, including a commission (kickback) for the retailer from a dealer reserve held out by the lender, have been set by a financing institution.

No longer does a retailer "carry the consumer" over a period of time, as the general store once carried the farmer between seeding and harvesting. As soon as the paper is signed, it is turned over to the lending agency. Only the old-style

30-day charge account offered by department stores can in any sense be called a retailer-carrying service, and this is the only form of consumer credit that has failed to increase.

The New Term—Credit Selling

The retail trade press has for a number of years been using a term that best expresses the present meaning of consumer credit. They speak repeatedly of "credit selling." Credit selling means two things: selling goods on credit, and selling credit as well as goods.

Credit selling is generally recognized as the core of present-day profitable retailing operations for four reasons. (1) The consumer buying on credit tends to buy higher-priced merchandise (he is easy to "trade up"), to buy more in volume, and to buy more frequently than the cash customer. (2) The credit customer does not shop around—he "marries" his seller-lender. (3) The amount of purchase per credit sale is typically enough larger than the cash sale to more than compensate for the extra overhead of credit selling. (4) Earnings on credit extensions frequently equal or better the net return from markups on merchandise. The National Automobile Dealers Association, for example, reported one year that the net profit from most dealers' operations was exactly equal to the small percentage return received by the dealers as a financing rebate from the lending agencies to whom they transferred their consumer paper.

Throughout retailing, therefore, there is a heavy and continuing pressure to sell debt. Salesmen in automobile showrooms and appliance stores are given larger commissions for credit sales. Department store employees are sometimes paid "spiffs" of $1 to $2 for each new credit customer signed up. Bank personnel are "spiffed" to bring in check credit, bank credit card, or personal loan customers. And, as one after another seller-lender has placed increasing promotional emphasis on loans disguised as sales, as new lending schemes tied to sales have multiplied (credit cards and bank schemes), the traditional lender to consumers—the small-loan company—has accordingly been forced to greater promotional efforts. Thus, the advertising of debt as a way of life has expanded into a national propaganda effort of phenomenal proportions.

Overextension of Credit

Installment selling has added another tool to the selling arsenal of salesmen. This rather new selling tool has enticed many unsuspecting and trusting consumers to incur more debt than they can afford. Thousands of families are forced into bankruptcy or on welfare because they are snared by deceptive sellers. To sellers it is simply business. They can tell you that it is legal; that it is necessary to keep the economy going; that after all, a salesman has to make a living; and that his employers have to meet quotas, budgets, and expenses. Large corporations are driven by the "growth" complex—if they do not grow rapidly, their stock will not be rated as a "growth stock." Most retailers do not carry their own paper. They sell it to banks and other big lenders at a discount price. This forces a consumer to deal with an institution, probably in another city, other than the original seller.

There is no accurate way of knowing the extent of overindebtedness. Morris Rabinowitch, president of Financial Counselors in San Francisco, at an annual meeting of the American Association of Credit Counselors on August 29, 1968, said that "More than one-third of all American families are overextended in their debts and are on the brink of serious trouble."[11] At the same meeting, Dr. William Regan, dean of the Business School, University of San Francisco, termed the American society one in which "everybody owes," and that there were 41,000 personal bankruptcies filed in California in 1967. Dean Regan felt that a "consumption ethic" has replaced the "work ethic."

Families that use installment credit comprise 65 percent of all American families. The *National Consumer Finance Association Yearbook for 1968* reported that on June 30, 1967, 191,709 personal (nonbusiness) bankruptcy petitions were filed in the United States—an increase of 45 percent over 1962 figures.

The University of Michigan Survey Research Center found that 10 percent of families have installment obligations exceeding the 20 percent of income usually considered a danger point. Ten percent of our families in financial trouble adds up to about 6 million families.

Margolius pointed up a local example of overindebtedness at the large Washington, D.C. Naval Base. The commanding officer at the base found that 7 to 8 percent of the civilian staff was in debt to an extent requiring intervention with creditors.[12]

Many professional financial counselors blame our society's financial sickness on automobile loans and an ever-increasing number of personal loans. They recommend an intensive program of financial education for the consumer and the merchant. Young marrieds, in particular, are in need of financial education because this age group (age 25 to 34) has the highest percent of disposable income committed to repayment of installment credit. This group, and most of us, must learn our credit limit, and the merchant must learn he can survive only with a healthy consumer.

Debt Consolidation and Debt Adjusters

An ad in the paper reads, "Consolidate your debts; borrow $2,000 at 6 percent, pay back $14.33 a month." Sounds easy, but the 6 percent rate adds up to 15 to 40 percent when brokerage fees, closing costs, credit reports, insurance premium, and other costs are included. Such dishonest debt adjusters, and there

[11] *U.S. News & World Report,* Sept. 16, 1968, p. 81.
[12] Sidney Margolius, *op. cit.,* p. 50.

are many, do not loan money. They try to keep their victims in bondage for many years. Abuses have been so bad that commercial debt adjusters have been banned in 22 states and regulated in 12 states.[13] Sixteen states have no regulation at all.

Most of the commercial debt pooling businesses are "just plain vultures," a credit manager said. A lawyer said, "They can't do any more for you than you could do for yourself." A priest suggests, "You'd be better off going to a nonprofit consolidator."

More and more people in serious debt trouble consult honest debt consolidators or adjusters. This service is rendered usually without charge by some counseling groups and for a modest fee of about 10 to 12 percent of the indebtedness. Charles Neal, who has had much experience in private debt counseling, has doubts about creditors counseling debtors. In his book, *Sense with Dollars,* he wrote, "There is a serious conflict of interest. . . . It may be similar to asking the Tobacco Institute to help us curb our smoking. Those who helped you get into trouble in the first place qualify poorly as experts to help you get out."

Honest, nonprofit debt counseling ranges from the Michigan League Budget Service, which operates a chain of nonprofit counseling offices, to Family Debt Counselors of Phoenix, one of the oldest nonprofit counseling groups in the country. St. Paul, Minnesota, has the credit counseling service of the Credit Bureau and the Family Service Social Agency. The Legal Aid Society operates a financial counseling service in many cities (Chicago, Atlanta, Cleveland, Buffalo, and many more). A union member can go to his AFL-CIO Community Service Activities for free help.

If you are deeply in debt and do not qualify for a consolidation loan, an honest financial counselor or your lawyer will study the facts and make recommendations. He might, for example, recommend use of the Wage Earner Plan (Chapter XIII of the Bankruptcy Act) for debtors who want to pay their creditors out of future earnings. In hopeless cases, he may advise straight bankruptcy as a last resort.

Credit Insurance Misuse

Margolius is of the opinion that "one of the most widespread devices for sweating more money out of innocent—or desperate—consumers is excessive charges for 'credit' insurance."[14] There are probably 70 million such policies in force, totaling over $70 billion, says Margolius. Investigations have shown many instances of high charges—as much as $2 per $100 of debt. Dean Sharp, Senate

[13] According to the *New York Times,* Feb. 26, 1968.
[14] Sidney Margolius, *op. cit.,* p. 73.

Antitrust Committee Assistant Counsel, estimates the annual overcharge at $100 million. The Michigan State Insurance Commissioner found that lenders make a profit of 60 to 70 percent in a fee of 75 cents per $100 of debt. [15]

Montgomery Ward told half of its 6.5 million credit customers that life insurance would be automatically added to their bills at a rate of $1.20 a year per $100. At this rate Ward's could pocket $3 out of every $4 it collects. A pretty neat profit, if you can get it. The public, and Senator Proxmire of Wisconsin, reacted swiftly and successfully. Other retailers made a profit at only 33 cents per $100, according to testimony before the Senate Antitrust and Monopoly Subcommittee in 1967. Ward's finally said that customers did not have to pay for credit insurance unless they wanted it.

Credit insurance is really quite a cozy arrangement by which stores and lending agencies insure the lives of their credit customers, at the latter's expense, for the balance due on their payments. The store or lender is both policyholder and beneficiary. It automatically gets its money if the debtor dies. The debtor is a secondary beneficiary in that his estate will not have to pay the debt. For this joint benefit the debtor pays the entire premium.

USE CREDIT WISELY

How Much Consumer Debt Can You Carry?

There is no easy answer to the question of how much debt you can carry. There is constant controversy on this question. Families with the same income may differ as to number of dependents, ages, future plans, and the way they earn their money. Statistics show that the national consumer debt keeps increasing.

YEAR	TOTAL OUTSTANDING	AVERAGE PER ADULT
1956	$ 42.3 billion	$406
1958	45.0 billion	425
1960	55.8 billion	513
1962	58.5 billion	527
1963	69.9 billion	569
1968 (July)	102.4 billion	849

But personal incomes are also increasing, and the debt burden is not growing quite so fast.

[15] *Ibid.,* p. 74.

YEAR	INCOME AFTER TAXES	CONSUMER CREDIT (PERCENT OF INCOME)
1956	$292.9 billion	14.4
1958	317.9 billion	14.2
1960	349.4 billion	16.0
1962	381.8 billion	15.03
1967	626.4 billion	15.1

Though the consumer debt as a percentage of personal income appears favorable, many individuals are carrying too much debt, and bankruptcies are increasing.

YEAR	PERSONAL BANKRUPTCIES PER 100,000 ADULTS
1956	48
1958	60
1960	82
1962	72
1967	98

The administrative office of the United States courts report the following figures for personal bankruptcies.

YEAR	PERSONAL BANKRUPTCIES
1945	11,051
1960	94,750
1963	139,191
1967	208,329

In most cases these personal bankruptcies were due to people carrying debts beyond their financial ability to make satisfactory payments. Quite typical of the bankrupt persons or families was the case of a family with a monthly take-home pay of $214 but fixed monthly payments to nine creditors amounting to $216.

Yardsticks. Credit men generally feel that the total amount you owe should not exceed 20 percent of the take-home income for the family for any one year. This excludes mortgage on a house. If the take-home income is $4,800, the debt limit would be about $1,000. Actually, hard-and-fast rules cannot be applied to all families. Obviously, a man with five children to support on an average family income might have to keep his outstanding debt around 10 percent of his yearly take-home income. A young married couple with no children may stretch their outstanding debt to 25 percent or more of their joint income.

Another yardstick would set the limit at about 10 percent of take-home income over an 18-month average. Thus, on $4,800 take-home income, the debt limit would be around $720.

A third yardstick suggests limiting total debts to about a third of discretionary income for the year. *Discretionary income* is that part of family income that is *not* spent for food, clothing, and housing (including utilities). To apply this test, let us assume that the above items in a budget come to $3,000 for the year. Discretionary income, the balance, is $1,800 for a family with take-home income of $4,800 annually. One-third of $1,800 is $600, the debt limit according to this yardstick.

These yardsticks indicate that the maximum family debt, exclusive of mortgage on the home, for a family having take-home income of $4,800, should be between $600 and $1,000.

Lenders will usually help you determine your debt limit. They are likely to subtract expenses and savings from monthly take-home income and set the amount left over as the sum you can safely afford to pay in monthly installments on your total debt.

Lenders usually follow certain standards when granting credit. Here are a few illustrations.

Charge Accounts.   Most retail merchants will obtain a credit bureau report on you. They may limit you to credit equivalent to two weeks' or a month's pay on a 30-day charge account.

Installment Accounts.   The limits of your monthly payments are figured as a percentage of your monthly income. A credit manager does not like to grant installment credit of more than 10 percent of monthly income. He will scan most carefully that part of the credit report that shows steady employment and ability to keep up payments on past long-term accounts.

Car Loans.   This is an easy loan to negotiate because the loan is secured by the value of the car. The loan balance is seldom more than the cash value of the car. The loan is paid off faster than the car normally depreciates. The borrower has to carry insurance, which further protects the lender against loss. Many credit people believe that car loan payments can safely run from 15 to possibly 30 percent of the monthly take-home income.

Personal Loans.   Personal loans are usually less than $1,000. One general rule used by small-loan companies is that the amount of the monthly repayment should be no more than about 6 percent of monthly income. They figure that the total amount of the loan should not be more than 10 to 20 percent of annual income.

It Is How You Manage Credit That Counts

As you understand by now, consumer credit is intricate and deceptive. A few conclusions may be helpful.

1. Use credit only when necessary or where benefits justify the cost and risk involved.

2. Assume no more debt than you can safely repay out of current income.

3. Shop for the best credit bargain. None of the credit terms are easy.

4. Go to a bank or your credit union first to investigate the possibilities.

5. Know your lender or dealer.

6. Do not expect too much from creditors. After all, their main concern is to collect your debt.

7. Use 30-day charge accounts intelligently. Do not use them to spend next month's income, or charge accounts will become real debts.

8. Do not let an installment debt run so long that the psychological enjoyment of "having it now" wears off before the debt is paid.

9. When buying major items, such as a car and expensive appliances, it is not wise to sign up for terms that will have you owing more than the resale value of the article you bought. In some car deals, the buyer's debt exceeds the value of the car for 15 or more months in the case of a small downpayment and 36 months to pay.

10. In general, make the downpayment as large as possible and the repayment period as short as possible. The lower the downpayment, the greater the percentage of cars that have had to be repossessed.

11. Avoid *balloon notes,* in which the installments pay off only a part of the debt and after the last installment is paid the balance is due in one payment. When you cannot handle the lump-sum payment, you are in difficulty.

12. Finally, let yourself be "sold down." The merchant or lender "sells down" when he believes that you are assuming too big a debt risk and suggests that you make a larger downpayment, postpone the purchase, or use a layaway plan instead. The chances are such businessmen, though rare in this day of selling credit as well as goods, know what they are talking about.

13. Shop around for credit. Since July 1, 1969, consumers have the advantage of knowing both the total dollar cost of credit and the total cost of credit in annual percentage rate on installment purchases. Take full advantage of this valuable information by shopping around for the best terms.

Whatever your reasons, using credit is not necessarily good or bad. It is the way you use it that counts. You have to manage credit. If you do not, your debts will manage you. Someone wisely said, "Credit is a good servant but a bad master."

"Easy Credit" Hurts the Poor

According to a massive study by the Federal Trade Commission (1966) of 96 retailers with sales of $226 million, which represented 85 percent of the sales of furniture, appliance, and department store retailers in the District of Columbia, the poor did pay more.[16] FTC found that low-income market retailers used

[16] *Economic Report on Installment Credit and Retail Sales Practices in the District of Columbia,* Washington, D.C., March, 1968.

installment credit in 93 percent of their sales, against 27 percent for general market retailers. On the average, goods purchased for $100 at wholesale sold for $255 in the low-income market stores, compared with $159 in general market stores. Furthermore, the poor paid, on the average, 24 percent for credit compared to an average of 20 percent for general market customers. This suggests that the marketing system for distribution of durable goods to low-income consumers is costly. Their markups are very much higher than those of general market retailers, as pointed out, but the low-income market retailers do not make particularly high net profits. Furthermore, the high prices charged by low-income market retailers suggest the absence of effective price competition. What competition there is takes the form of easier credit availability. Hence, the poor depend upon easy-credit merchants. And easy-credit merchants take "early action" against default rather than using such action as a last resort.

FTC recommends for the poor that (1) free financial, professional counseling be given in their neighborhood, (2) reasonable credit be made available, (3) legal rights of buyers and creditors be equalized, (4) chain stores be encouraged to enter the low-income area, and (5) consumer protection activities be intensified to eliminate fraud and deception in advertising and credit.

A CASHLESS, CHECKLESS SOCIETY?

Changing Times magazine wrote in October, 1967, that "soon you'll never see money at all." Instead of money, they said, "you'll use a plastic card and a telephone." This would be a convenience and could be a boobytrap for your budget.

The Trends

There is no doubt about the trend. A revolution is going on right now. Bankers are presently working up the details of a checkless society by using computers and other technological tools. According to the American Banking Association, over 2,000 bank credit cards were in operation in 1968. More than $2 billion in retail sales would be charged with credit cards. The Bank of Delaware was using for each patron a plastic card with punched holes corresponding to his account number. Then four stores were equipped with Touch-Tone telephones into which the plastic card could be slipped. When a customer purchased an item, the clerk would slip the card into a phone and dial instructions to the computer as to how payment was to be handled. The computer would even answer by voice "Yes" or "No" as the customer's credit standing. Soon 50 million persons will have centralized credit files.

Preauthorized payment of bills is another task that will be taken over by computers. This service will include payments for mortgage, car payments, rent, insurance premiums, and others.

A checkless society may be inevitable. Already there are 50 billion checks written each year. Checkwriting activity has been increasing 7 percent a year. Before 1980, at this rate, the banking system will be choked. It is estimated that the banking system spends over $3 billion annually to process present checks.

Is This an Invitation to Trouble? How you will manage under this checkless, cashless system will depend on your understanding of the system. You undoubtedly will find the new system more convenient, or you might find it an invitation to trouble. After all, credit doesn't add dollars to your income. And this system makes it too easy to spend and borrow. Some financial counseling experts believe that the easier it is to get credit, the more people will run into financial trouble. In the last 10 years the average family income has increased about 50 percent, but family borrowing has gone up 100 percent. And personal bankruptcies went up 200 percent in the same period. In 1949 the average family paid out about 11 percent of its total income for debt repayment and interest charges, including mortgage installment, charge account cost, etc. Today it pays out over 22 percent. At this rate, what will it be by 1975? Perhaps by 1975 most of us will be in hock forever at 18 percent!

Discount for Cash?

So the cashless, checkless society may be here sooner than we think unless so many people get into a financial mess that somebody starts a 5 or 10 percent discount for the use of cash instead of credit. Perhaps some group could popularize cash instead of credit. Members could be issued official identification cards. The person with a card will patronize cooperating businesses, pay in cash, and get a discount for so doing. On the other hand, it may be too late to even dream about a cash-and-carry discount system. And it may also be too late to request credit cards to carry this warning: "Caution. Excessive use of credit cards may be hazardous to your economic health." Most of us can appreciate the advice of the *Lothian Mirror* (Texas): "It isn't buying on time that's difficult; it's paying on time."

QUESTIONS FOR DISCUSSION

1. What are the various purposes for which consumers use credit?
2. What sources of credit are available in most communities?
3. What would you include in a list of "do's and don'ts" for users of consumer credit?
4. When families use credit or borrow cash, does it mean that they are poor money managers?
5. How sound is the assumption that installment selling is necessary for a healthy, prosperous economy?

6. How do you account for the increased interest of commercial banks in the consumer credit field?

ACTIVITY PROBLEMS

1. Make an analysis of the sources of consumer credit in your community. For each credit source, find out (a) how to apply for credit, (b) amount of money you can borrow, (c) time limit on the credit, (d) method of repayment, (e) true annual interest rate charged, and (f) any conditions, penalties, or special privileges attached to the loan.

2. When analyzing the various purposes for which consumers use credit, name specific cases under each classification where you would rate the using of credit wise, and name other cases where it would be wiser to pay cash.

3. Obtain sample installment contracts for cars, furniture, or jewelry. Then find in each case the cash price, the dollar cost of credit, and the annual cost rate. Are the advertised rates accurate?

4. Introduce yourself at a bank as one who would like to know how the commercial bank serves small borrowers. Ask such questions as: "What questions are asked?" "What are the terms and the cost of small loans?" "Is the interest deducted in advance? If so, how does this affect the cost of the loan?"

5. Visit a local General Motors or Ford dealer and obtain information on the cost of financing a new car, assuming your trade-in allowance of $550 on your old car as the downpayment on the new car. Compare total credit costs with those offered at a commercial bank or a credit union.

SUGGESTED READINGS

American Home Economics Association: *Proceedings of a National Workshop on Consumer Credit in Family Financial Management,* 1967.

"Don't Get Careless about Your Credit," *Changing Times,* June, 1968.

Hearings before the Subcommittee on Consumer Affairs of the Committee on Banking and Currency, House of Representatives, First Session, on the "Consumer Credit Protection Act," U.S. Government Printing Office, 1967, 1968, parts I, II.

House of Representatives Committee on Government Operations: "Consumer Problems of the Poor: Supermarket Operations in Low-income Areas and the Federal Response," *House Report,* Aug. 7, 1968, U.S. Government Printing Office, 1968.

Morse, Richard L. D.: *Consumer Credit Computations,* American Council on Consumer Interests, Columbia, Mo., 1966.

———— : *Truth in Lending,* American Council on Consumer Interests, Columbia, Mo., 1966.

"No, Charge Accounts Aren't All Alike," *Changing Times,* January, 1969.

Truth in Lending. Draft of Proposed Regulation Z. Effective July 1, 1969, Board of Governors of the Federal Reserve System, Washington, D.C., Oct. 16, 1968.

U.S. Consumer: A Bi-monthly News Sheet, Washington, D.C., Feb. 7, 1968.

"What Makes You a Good Credit Risk?" *Changing Times,* February, 1966.

chapter 7

FOOD SHOPPING
BEGINS AT HOME

A first-class soup is more creative than a second-class poem.

Food problems exist in almost every family regardless of income and home production. And food problems arise even in connection with the pleasant things in family life. In fact, the busier and happier a family becomes, the greater the increase of food problems. Home, husband, children, friends, and social and business contacts are all dependent on the strength and vitality that are on a direct line with the kitchen and the marketplace. And no matter where or how a food problem originates, a woman faces it in the kitchen and to a large extent in the market.

Food management is therefore one of the most important jobs in the home. The health and happiness of the family are directly dependent on the skill and information used in the kitchen and in the marketplace. The family pocketbook is affected, too, because food is the largest single expense most families have in their budgets.

Getting along on poor diets takes its toll in chronic fatigue, shifting aches and pains, and digestive disturbances. These discomforts may not keep a person in bed. They do, however, cut down on efficiency. Inadequate diets also lower natural resistance to infection. They destroy the sense of well-being, the joy of being actively alive and able to work and play hard.

BUYING NUTRITIOUS FOOD

American families spend about one-fifth of their income for food. Of course, they can spend much more, but they can be well nourished by spending much less than this amount. To get the most food value for your dollar, you must have knowledge about foods and stores and you must plan and buy carefully the food your family needs and likes. Everyone needs the same basic foods. How much each person needs depends largely on age, sex, occupation, and general health.

The first step toward buying nourishing foods is to learn the type of nutrients that are essential to the family's health and well-being. The second step is to learn which foods are good sources of these nutrients.

Nutritionists generally divide foods into groups to show how to select the right foods for good health. The U.S. Department of Agriculture Leaflet no. 424, *Food for Fitness,* suggests these four groups:

1. Milk group. Includes milk and dairy products like cheese and ice cream. This group gives calcium, protein, vitamin A, and riboflavin. These nutrients are so important that they should be supplied daily as follows:

Adults	2 or more cups
Teen-agers	1 quart at least
Children	3 to 4 cups
Pregnant and nursing mothers	1½ quarts at least

The alternatives and equivalents to milk on the basis of calcium furnished are:

1-inch cube cheese equals ⅔ cup milk
½ cup cottage cheese equals ⅓ cup milk
½ cup ice cream equals ¼ cup milk

2. *Meat group.* Includes meat, eggs, dry beans; provides protein, iron, and B vitamins. Two or more servings of beef, veal, pork, lamb, poultry, fish, or eggs should be provided daily. Alternates are cooked dry beans, peas or lentils, nuts, peanuts or peanut butter, soya flour, grits, and soybeans. The amount of one serving is two or three ounces of lean meat, poultry, fish, or lentils, four tablespoons of peanut butter, or two eggs.

3. *Vegetable and fruit group.* Provides chiefly vitamin A and vitamin C plus calcium, iron, and some of the B vitamins. Four or more servings should be provided daily for everyone. Serve at least every other day a citrus fruit or some other fruit or vegetable with lots of vitamin C and a dark green or deep yellow vegetable for vitamin A. But don't ignore potatoes and many other good vegetables and fruits.

4. *Bread and cereal group.* Four or more servings in any form that is either whole

TABLE 7-1   BASIC NUTRIENTS AT VARIANT COSTS

THE AVERAGE ADULT CAN GET A WHOLE DAY'S SUPPLY OF . . .

Vitamin C		*Vitamin A*	
By Eating or Drinking . . .	At This Cost	By Eating or Drinking . . .	At This Cost
1½ c raw cabbage	4¢	—¼ c carrots	2¢
1 orange	4¢	½ c kale	3¢
¾ c canned or frozen orange or grapefruit juice	4¢-5¢	¼ c spinach	3¢
		1 c broccoli	9¢
⅔ c broccoli	7¢	⅓ cantaloupe	12¢
1⅓ c kale	7¢	—2 c canned tomato juice	15¢
2¼ c cooked cabbage	11¢	– 3 tomatoes	26¢
— 2 c canned tomato juice	15¢	5 c green snap beans	36¢
¾ c frozen strawberries	20¢	3-4 c canned peas	36¢
— 2½ tomatoes	20¢	—2 lb (2 compact heads) lettuce	40¢
⅔ cantaloupe	21¢	4 c canned peaches	44¢
5 c mashed potatoes	22¢	2½ c fresh asparagus	48¢
3¼ canned pineapple juice	27¢		
Calcium		*Protein (⅓ of a Day's Supply)*	
By Eating or Drinking . . .	At This Cost	By Eating or Drinking . . .	At This Cost
—2½ c nonfat dry milks	5¢	1½ c cooked dry beans	4¢
2½ c evaporated milk	10¢	⁓ ½ c cottage cheese	7¢
2½ c skimmed milk	12½¢	—5⅓ T peanut butter	11¢
3 c buttermilk	15¢	— 3 oz Cheddar cheese	12¢
3 oz Swiss cheese	15¢	3 large eggs	15¢
4 oz Cheddar cheese	16¢	2⅔ c milk	16¢
3 c whole milk	18¢	3⅓ oz beef liver	17¢
— 3½ c cottage cheese	49¢	3⅓ oz chuck roast	18¢
5 c ice cream	70¢	3 oz halibut	18¢
		11 strips bacon	28¢
		3½ oz rib roast	29¢
		3½ oz pork chops	29¢
		3½ oz ham	33¢

grain, enriched, or restored provide other B vitamins, iron, calories, and roughage. One serving equals one slice of bread, or a like amount in the form of crackers or baked goods, one ounce of dry cereal, or one-half to three-fourths cup of cooked cereal, corn-meal, grits, macaroni, noodles, rice, or spaghetti.

Fats and sugars, added in cooking and at meals, provide calories for energy.

Good Nutrition Is Not Expensive

With nutrition as the basis for decision, a well-balanced diet can be planned at comparatively low cost. Table 7-1, Basic Nutrients at Variant Costs, shows how the average adult can get a whole day's supply of vitamins C and A from different quantities of vegetables and fruits. Compare the costs per serving. Although prices may change, the principle that good nutrition need not be expensive is valid.

TABLE 7-2   MENU PATTERNS WITH EXAMPLES OF LIGHT AND HEAVY MEALS

MENU PATTERN	LIGHT MEAL	FOOD GROUP	HEAVY MEAL	FOOD GROUP
		Breakfast		
fruit	orange juice	(3)	half grapefruit	(3)
cereal, milk	cereal, milk	(4, 1)		
egg or meat			bacon, eggs	(2)
bread, butter	cinnamon toast	(4)	toast, butter	(4)
milk (children)	hot chocolate	(1)	hot chocolate	(1)
coffee or tea	coffee		coffee	
		Lunch		
soup	chicken salad			
main dish } Choose	sandwich	(2, 4)	broiled ground beef	(2)
salad } 1 or 2	carrot sticks	(3)	green salad	(3)
fruit	apple	(3)	peach halves	
bread, butter			(canned)	(3)
			muffins, bread	(4)
beverage	milk	(1)	milk	(1)
		Dinner		
main dish	meat loaf	(2)	pork chops, gravy	(2, 1)
potato			baked potato	(3)
vegetable	broccoli, cheese			
	sauce	(3, 1)	spinach	(3)
salad	chef's salad,			
	French dressing	(3)	cabbage slaw	(3)
bread, butter	bread, butter	(4)	bread, butter	(4)
dessert	oatmeal cooky	(4)	frozen lemon	
			custard	(1)
beverage	milk (children)	(1)	milk (children)	(1)
	coffee		coffee	

The second part of the table shows that eggs, cheese, dry beans, and pea-nut butter are all good substitutes for the higher-priced protein foods. Dry beans and peas are especially good bargains, but should be used in combination with a small amount of meat to best satisfy nutritional needs.

Prices are nationwide averages prepared by the U.S. Department of Agri-culture, and the amounts for one day's supply are based on recommendations of the National Research Council's Food and Nutrition Board.

Menus can be planned that will provide well-balanced meals from a large variety of foods, as shown in Table 7-2, Menu Patterns with Examples of Light and Heavy Meals, prepared by the Institute of Home Economics, U.S. Depart-ment of Agriculture.

Tasty Tips for Meal Planning.   Feeding the family is first a mental process, beginning with the planning of meals and menus and extending through the selection of the right markets on to the actual buying of the food items. It also includes proper storage of food supplies, daily preparation of meals, appetiz-ing service to the family, proper restorage of food, and even changes in plans for the next meal or two.

Daily meals should be appropriate, attractive, satisfying, and nutritious, and should fit the family pocketbook. This is a big order. Let us begin with a few practical suggestions in planning the menu.

1. Choose methods of food preparation suitable to the persons being served.
2. Plan menus that can be prepared in the time available for each meal.
3. Include some foods that do not require last-minute preparation.
4. Plan baked foods that require the same oven temperature as others that must be prepared at the same time.
5. Use only one or two foods that are difficult to digest in the same meal.
6. Plan for a contrast in texture, such as crisp and soft foods.
7. Balance the different types of food in each meal.
8. Serve the same food only once in the same meal.
9. Serve no more than one strong-flavored or highly seasoned food at one meal.
10. Plan pleasing combinations of acid, bland, and sweet foods.
11. Plan colorful meals in which the colors harmonize.
12. Use natural shapes.
13. Do not introduce two new foods at the same meal.

QUALITY OF DIETS IN THE UNITED STATES

The U.S. Department of Agriculture made a nationwide survey of household food consumption in 1965. Diets were rated "good" that met the Recommended Dietary Allowances set by the National Research Council's Food and Nutrition Board for seven nutrients—protein, calcium, iron, vitamin A value, thiamine, riboflavin, and ascorbic acid. Diets were rated "poor" that furnished less than two-thirds of the allowance for one or more of these nutrients. The survey shows that

1.   One-half of the diets were good and one-fifth were poor in both urban and rural areas (Figure 7-1).
2.   Diets were poor in more households in the North Central and Southern regions than in other regions.
3.   More high- than low-income families had good diets, although there were poor diets at high-income levels (Figure 7-2).
4.   Diets in 15 percent of the families were below allowances for three or more nutrients.
5.   Diets were most often below allowances in calcium, vitamin A value, and ascorbic acid.
6.   Relatively fewer families had good diets in 1965 than in 1955 (Figure 7-3).
7.   Calcium, vitamin A value, and ascorbic acid were the nutrients most often below allowances in both 1955 and 1965, but more often in 1965.

Increased consumption of milk or other good sources of calcium, vegetables, and fruit is needed to improve our diets. Awareness of the foods that make up a good diet, a desire to eat these foods, and enough money to buy adequate food are necessary if most families are to have good diets.

Teen-age Nutrition

All the recent nutritional studies show that the family's worst-fed member is the teen-age girl—and that the older the child, the poorer the diet. Furthermore, as youngsters move from elementary to high school, from childhood to teen age, the number with careless eating habits increases sharply. Even teen-agers who eat a lot are undernourished, investigator after investigator found.

Dr. Evelyn B. Spindler, nutritionist with the U.S. Department of Agriculture, reported the startling and disturbing fact that "6 out of every 10 girls and 4 out of every 10 boys have poor diets."[1]

Why are America's teen-agers so poorly fed? Here, summarized by Dr. Spindler, are the main reasons: (1) They skip breakfast. A study of 2,000 Flint, Michigan, high school teen-agers found that nearly two-thirds regularly ate no breakfast. In an Illinois study, more than five times as many girls as boys ate no breakfast. Most of the girls missed breakfast for weight reasons. (2) They select snacks unwisely. One-fourth of teen-agers' calories come from snacks, according to an Iowa study. (3) They drink little or no milk, the important source for calcium. A major study in eight Western states found insufficient calcium intake in half of the girls and in one-fifth of the boys. (4) They are indifferent to meals. Why? Partly because of social pressures, their growing independence, and their hurried schedules. A study of Guilford, North Carolina, high school students found 15 percent missed at least one meal daily. A University of California study found a large percentage of teen-agers "who never really had one organized meal." (5) They fear fat. Many adolescent girls go on fad or crash diets. The result is they often deprive their bodies of much-needed nutrients. More teen-age

[1]"Report on Teen-age Nutrition," March, 1965, issue of *Clubwoman,* General Federation of Women's Clubs.

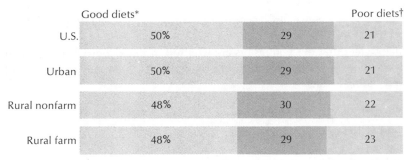

*Met recommended dietary allowances for seven nutrients.
†Had less than ⅔ allowance for one to seven nutrients.

Figure 7-1 **Urbanization and Quality of Diets. Source: Nationwide Household Food Consumption Survey, Spring, 1965, U.S. Department of Agriculture, Neg. ARS 5876.68 (2) Agricultural Research Service.**

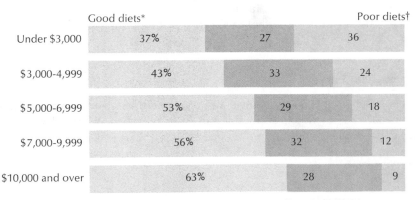

*Met recommended dietary allowances for seven nutrients.
†Had less than ⅔ allowance for one to seven nutrients.

Figure 7-2 **Income and Quality of Diets. Source: Nationwide Household Food Consumption Survey, Spring, 1965, U.S. Department of Agriculture, Neg. ARS 5878.68 (2) Agricultural Research Service.**

*Met recommended dietary allowances (1964) for seven nutrients.
†Had less than ⅔ allowance for one to seven nutrients.

Figure 7-3 **Quality of Diets. Source: Nationwide Household Food Consumption Survey, Spring, 1955, and Spring, 1965, U.S. Department of Agriculture, Neg. ARS 5882.68 (2) Agricultural Research Service.**

girls than boys are overweight, according to studies of 15- and 16-year-olds in Oregon, Iowa, and Maine.

We like to feel that our youngsters are well fed in this country. But research on teen-age diets in this country confirms the ugly fact that many of them need improved eating habits.

FOOD EXPENDITURES

The purchase of food is one of the most important expenditures families make; it accounts for about 18 percent of per capita disposable income (income after taxes). Food is purchased more frequently than any other item of family spending; it is nondurable, and it is one of the few items for which families usually pay cash. At the same time, food is necessary for the health of each family member.

For these and other reasons, families are concerned about food costs. Price has generally been one important factor in selecting a food store in which to shop.

Concern about Prices

What was behind this increased evidence of concern about food prices? After a period of time in which disposable family income had increased at about twice the rate that retail food prices increased, families experienced a period

TABLE 7-3   ANNUAL PER CAPITA DISPOSABLE PERSONAL INCOME AND FOOD EXPENDITURES, 1960-1967*

| | PERSONAL INCOME | | | EXPENDITURES FOR FOOD | |
Year	Disposable Personal Income	Percent Change From Year Before	Actual	Percent Change from Year Before	Proportion of Disposable Income
1960	$1,937		$388		20.0%
1961	1,983	+ 2.4	392	+ 1.0	19.8
1962	2,064	+ 4.1	398	+ 1.0	19.3
1963	2,136	+ 3.5	404	+ 1.5	18.9
1964	2,273	+ 6.5	418	+ 3.5	18.4
1965	2,411	+ 6.1	439	+ 5.0	18.2
1966	2,584	+ 7.2	472	+ 7.5	18.3
1967	2,747	+ 6.3	485	+ 2.8	17.7

*Economic Research Service, U.S. Department of Agriculture, *Marketing and Transportation Situation,* Government Printing Office, February, 1966, and November, 1967; also *National Food Situation,* February, 1968.

TABLE 7-4   COST OF FOOD AT HOME ESTIMATED FOR FOOD PLANS AT THREE
COST LEVELS, MARCH, 1968, U.S. AVERAGE* (1965 BASE)

Sex or Age Groups: Families	COST FOR ONE WEEK			COST FOR ONE MONTH		
	Low-cost Plan	Moderate-cost Plan	Liberal Plan	Low-cost Plan	Moderate-cost Plan	Liberal Plan
Family of two:						
20 to 35 years	$16.40	$20.90	$25.60	$71.30	$ 90.50	$110.90
55 to 75 years	13.40	17.50	20.90	58.40	75.40	90.40
Family of four:						
Preschool children	23.90	30.30	36.90	103.50	131.50	159.50
Schoolchildren	27.70	35.40	43.30	120.30	153.30	187.60

*Family Economics Review, June, 1968.

when food prices and disposable income expanded at nearly the same rate.
Table 7-3 points up this situation rather clearly. Families found it necessary
to spend more total dollars for food than they had been accustomed to spending.

Food cost about 17.7 percent of disposable personal income at the end of
1967 (Table 7-3), which was a decrease of 2.3 percent from 1960. But this decrease in percentage figures can be deceiving. The increase in the dollar cost
of food between 1947 and 1967, inclusive, was about 26 percent, according to
the federal government's cost-of-living index. Actually, since the 1957-1959
base period, food prices have gone up more than other commodity groups.
It has not increased, however, as much as all services, largely because of the
rise in costs of medical services and recreation.

When the food industry points to the low 17.7 percent of personal disposable income spent for food and says, "Consumers never had it so good," they
need to be reminded that the decline was, in part, due to the nearly universal
principle that as personal incomes rise, people tend to spend a smaller percentage of it for food. Some credit is, therefore, due to increased earnings of husband and wife in the last 17 years. Furthermore, the 17.7 percent figure taken
from the Department of Commerce includes expenditures of nonprofit institutions and single persons as well as families. In contrast, the Bureau of Labor
Statistics data on the annual cost of food for a moderate living standard in the
autumn of 1966 of a family of four—husband and wife, boy age 13, and a girl
age 8—were 23.3 percent of the city worker's family budget of $9,191.[2] Only
housing costs (24.1 percent) exceeded food costs for the average urban family of four persons. Food is hardly a "bargain." Fortunately, good food planning,
intelligent marketing, and proper cooking and preserving of food at home can
reduce food costs considerably.

[2] Bureau of Labor Statistics, U.S. Department of Labor, news release, Oct. 25, 1967.

Cost of Food at Home

A continuing up-to-date report on the cost of food at home at three cost levels is published quarterly in the *Family Economics Review,* a publication of the U.S. Department of Agriculture. A family of four, including two schoolchildren, for example, could have a weekly "low-cost" food plan for $27.70, a moderate-cost plan for $35.40, and a liberal-cost plan for $43.30 a week (March, 1968 prices). (See Table 7-4, which gives food cost plans for a family of two and a family of four with preschool children.) These quarterly reports also give food costs for individuals of all ages and for both sexes.

  Food Costs in Ghettos.   It has been estimated that there are 29.7 million Americans, or about 15 percent of our population, living in poverty. The overall expenditure of all our people for food at home as a percentage of disposable income is about 17.7 percent. Estimates of poor households for the cost of food at home generally range from 29 to 36 percent. [3] This points up the fact that any discrimination in the retail sale of food hits the poor the hardest, since they spend a greater percentage of their budget on food than does the population at large.

  The evidence to date to support the charge that the poor pay more for food in the ghettos is not clear at all. In inquiries conducted by the House Subcommittee on Government Operations, the Bureau of Labor Statistics was asked to find out whether merchants charged higher prices in low-income neighborhoods than in high-income areas in six large cities. They found no significant discrepancy in prices between these areas. But the poor paid more for food if they shopped the small independent stores. The study fails to answer the question whether prices were higher in chain-store outlets in both income areas for the reason that food chain stores are scarce in low-income neighborhoods. Also the two weeks' notice given to the managers of stores surveyed renders the findings of questionable value. [4]

  Professor Carlton E. Wright, of Cornell University, made a survey of food prices in July, 1967, involving 1,418 New York City stores in low- and middle-income areas. He found that a 20-item food basket in the low-income areas averaged $9.47, against $8.97 in middle-income neighborhoods. This is about a 5.5 percent difference. [5]

  Some evidence was submitted to the House Subcommittee on Government Operations that in August and September, 1967, food prices were 9.1 percent higher in three stores serving large numbers of welfare recipients than in six stores serving middle- to upper-income families. [6] It appears that some

[3] Committee on Government Operations, House of Representatives, *Consumer Problems of the Poor: Supermarket Operations in Low-income Areas and the Federal Response,* U.S. Government Printing Office, 1968.

[4] *Ibid.,* p. 9.

[5] *Changing Times,* August, 1968, p. 44.

[6] *Op. cit.,* p. 17.

food stores in low-income areas increase food prices on the days welfare checks are issued and the largest number of food stamps are spent.

Efforts are being made to correct any abuses with respect to price and quality of food purchased in the ghettos. In the heart of a Miami, Florida, ghetto, for example, a nonprofit food supermarket sells food at wholesale prices, according to an AP news report dated September, 1968. The Food Fair supermart offered this store top technical personnel to help it get started. In due time, the store will be turned over to black people, who will own it and run it. Similar operations have proved successful in Mississippi, New York City, San Francisco, and Canada.

Changing Patterns of Family Food Spending

The Bureau of Labor Statistics reports that between March of 1959 and March, 1967, food bought to be prepared in the home increased 12 percent compared to 28 percent for food eaten away from home (Figure 7-4). The main reason for the steeper rise in food costs away from home was the increased cost of labor involved in preparing and serving food in restaurants, hotels, and other commercial eating places. The BLS estimates that food at home accounts for about four-fifths and food away from home for one-fifth of the total food expenditures. Approximately $30 billion was spent for food away from home annually out of a total expenditure for food of about $100 billion in 1968. The trend since 1965 has been in the increase of home consumption of soft drinks, punches and ades, potato chips, crackers, doughnuts, ice cream, candy, and

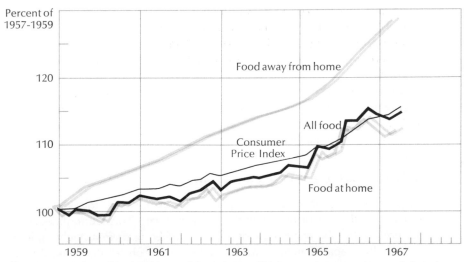

Figure 7-4   Prices of Food at Home and Away. Source: BLS data on city wage earners and clerical workers. U.S. Department of Agriculture, Neg. ARS 67 (8)-5867 Argricultural Research Service.

peanut butter. Incidentally, the increase in consuming snacks is very expensive, since the markup on this kind of food is high. *The Progressive Grocer* reports that snack sales have boomed 390 percent in the last 15 years.

The pattern for consumption of basic foods per capita has changed since 1950. According to the U.S. Department of Agriculture, consumers in 1967, in contrast to 1950, consumed 14 percent more meat, over 89 percent more poultry, about 10 percent less dairy products, almost 4 percent less fruits and vegetables, 12 percent less cereal products, and about 50 percent more vegetable oil. In other words, consumers have increased their consumption of relatively higher-priced foods, such as meat, and commercially processed foods as opposed to fresh or relatively unprocessed foods. These changes, in turn, are probably due to increased incomes, changes in relative prices, changing tastes, and mass advertising.

Nonfood Items.   The spending for nonfood items in grocery stores is increasing. Food costs, of course, should never include nonfood items purchased in food stores. The annual survey of grocery store sales, conducted by Conover-Mast Publications, shows that about one-fourth of the amount spent in food stores in 1966 was for nonfood items, including alcoholic beverages.[7]

HOW FOOD MONEY CAN BE WASTED

Impulse Buying

The first rule is to avoid impulse buying. Careful surveys of consumer buying habits in food supermarkets reveal that well over one-half of all food purchases are impulse buying. The National Commission on Food Marketing reported: "Impulse-buying is common." Some experts claim that you can save as much as 25 percent of your food costs if you purchase only the food on your buying list.

If we buy with a child in a food supermarket, we may reach the check-out counter with cookies, gum, and candy. We start for bread and end up buying cookies and doughnuts because the fragrance proves overwhelming. Solution— stick to your marketing list.

Convenience Food: Economy or Extravagance?

The food industry is succeeding in converting inexpensive ingredients into costly processed foods or providing them in a new convenience form, such as prebuttered vegetables and cheese slices, and marketing them at higher prices. Most partially prepared items—frozen corn on the cob, stuffed baked potatoes, cheese in a spray can, and frozen dinners—will cost more than the fresh.

[7] *Family Economics Review,* June, 1968, p. 6.

Some convenience foods, like frozen concentrated orange juice, frozen green peas, canned orange juice, fruit cocktail, and some cake mixes, are often cheaper than their fresh counterparts.

Built-in Maid Service.   Many of the convenience or "built-in maid service" items have startling prices if you figure the real value. The innocent consumer, for example, pays $1.07 a pound for sugar in some presweetened breakfast foods; about 15 cents a pound more for sliced cold cuts of meat—and even more for cheeses sliced, grated, or wrapped in foil; over twice as much per pound for frozen beef patties; broccoli spears in butter sauce at 3.9 cents an ounce in contrast to frozen broccoli spears at about 1.8 cents an ounce; about twice as much per ounce for peas in butter sauce as for frozen peas in polyethylene bags. The same doubling or further multiplication in price occurs in many other convenience foods. It is strange that many consumers buy "diet" margarine at a price about three times that of ordinary margarine though the leading ingredient in the "diet" version is water. The fairly recent twist of cornflakes with strawberries or some other fruit is an expensive food. At 55 cents for an eight-ounce package, you get about 20 cents' worth of cornflakes and about 15 freeze-dried strawberries worth about 20 cents. The price is approximately $1.10 a pound for cereal with dried fruit.[8]

Some Nutritional Value Lost.   A matter of as much concern as increased cost of most convenience foods is the reduced nutritional value of many prepared and processed foods. Many of the processed food and meat products have cheap fillers, extenders, and a considerable amount of water. Consumers Union, for example, tested 25 brands of frankfurters in New York City and found excessive use of extenders, the misuse of coloring agents, and mislabeling. One of the most widely used convenience foods—dehydrated mashed potatoes—costs about twice as much per serving and has only approximately 50 percent as much vitamin C as fresh mashed potatoes. Some of the vitamin B also is lost in dehydrated potatoes. Likewise, a slice or two of "balloon" bread (air added when baking in larger pans) provides considerably less nutritional value than fine-grained bread for youngsters' sandwiches. Many other examples of loss of nutritional value can be found in other convenience foods, notably TV dinners, frozen meat and poultry pies (need have no more than 25 percent meat), frozen and canned chow meins (need have only 4 to 6 percent deboned meat), and chopped poultry "with broth" (which can have as much as 50 percent added liquid without specifying the amount of water). In 1967 the USDA regulation required that canned and dry soups may not be labeled "chicken" or "turkey" unless they contain at least 2 percent of these poultry meats when ready to serve. This was not a very impressive nutritional victory for consumers. One wonders why frozen breaded shrimp need be only 50 percent shrimp, and frozen deviled crab only 22 percent crabmeat. The popular 11-

---

[8] See chap. 8 in Sidney Margolius, *The Innocent Consumer vs. The Exploiters,* Trident Press, New York, 1967, for more examples of waste in food money.

ounce TV dinner package of "meat loaf with potatoes and peas" costs about $1 a pound for meat loaf that is more loaf than meat.

Time Saved versus Money Lost. Unfortunately, the USDA has not been very helpful in exposing the truth of the high cost of most processed and convenience foods and the loss in nutritional value. THE USDA literature has emphasized the amount of "time" saved when using convenience foods. And time is saved because they reduce the amount of preparation required at home. Consumers, however, need more information than the "time" saved. Consumers cannot make intelligent decisions in the marketplace unless they have information on exact amounts of all ingredients in processed or convenience foods. This kind of information is more important today than it was a decade ago. Dr. Gordon Bivens, professor of family economics at the University of Missouri, pointed out the fact that in 1965 the expenditures for 32 convenience foods averaged 30 percent of the total amount spent for food at home in one week in United States homes in contrast to about 27 percent in 1955; and that families with low incomes "increased their expenditures for the 32 convenience foods more than higher income families."[9]

The question about the use of convenience foods boils down to this: Is the time saved in preparation of the meal or the package lunch worth the extra cost (sometimes 100 to 200 percent more) and the loss in nutritional value?

National Brands versus Store or Private Labels

National brands of food are products sold under manufacturers' advertised brands. Similar food products sold under retailers' or other distributors' brands are called "private" or "store" labels. In a research study of 174 large food retailers, conducted by the National Commission on Food Marketing in 1966, private labels had been adopted by practically all of the major food retailers. David Call, professor of food economics at Cornell University, concluded that there were very few consumers who did not have an opportunity to shop in retail stores where private food-label programs were offered.[10] Yet, some 50 percent of consumers do not understand the basic concept of private label programs, according to the findings of the Food Commission. This unfamiliarity with private labels is unfortunate because their economic advantages to the consumer are considerable. Table 7-5 clearly shows lower prices for store brands than for advertised national brands. Foods of equal quality, to the extent possible, were compared in this study. On the average, the advertised national brand was priced 21.6 percent higher than the private-store brands. Private-store brands are frequently used as "specials" on weekend sales. These "specials" should attract a sizable share of the consumer's dollar to their brand. The Food Commission study showed that the retailers' gross margins on

[9] Family Economics Review, December, 1967.

[10] "Private Label and Consumer Choice in the Food Industry," Journal of Consumer Affairs, Winter, 1967, pp. 149-160.

TABLE 7-5   AVERAGE RETAIL PRICES PER CASE FOR SELECTED PRODUCTS

PRODUCT	PRIVATE LABEL	ADVERTISED NATIONAL BRANDS	PERCENT DIFFERENCES
Frozen orange concentrate	$ 8.74	$11.57	32.4
Frozen green beans	4.84	6.42	30.0
Canned green beans	4.57	6.46	41.3
Canned green peas	4.76	5.54	16.4
Canned cling peaches	6.24	6.54	4.8
Canned Bartlett pears	10.86	13.00	19.7
Canned applesauce	3.29	3.65	10.8
Catsup	4.46	5.51	23.5
Evaporated milk	6.52	7.49	14.9
Tuna fish	12.72	15.46	21.5
Average, 10 foods	6.71	8.16	21.6

13 private-store brands of foods were reduced by 50 percent, on the average, when on "special" sale at retail stores. In addition to definite price advantage of store brands of similar-quality food compared to nationally advertised food brands, store brands have provided a competitive limitation on unnecessary advertising and premature cost raising, of nationally advertised brands. This is a healthy situation in the food industry, where great efforts are made by nationally advertised brands to eliminate price and quality competition.

Vitamin and Dietary Supplements

Americans spend over half a billion dollars annually on vitamins, minerals, and other types of food supplements. All of the nutrients essential to the maintenance of health in a normal individual are supplied by an adequate diet, according to the Council on Foods and Nutrition. Food is the best source for vitamins.

In his talk to the National Congress of Medical Quackery, the Food and Drug Commissioner said:

> The most widespread and expensive type of quackery today is the promotion of vitamin products, special dietary foods, and food supplements. Millions of consumers are being misled concerning their need for such products. Complicating this problem is a vast and growing "folklore" or "mythology" of nutrition which is being built up by pseudo-scientific literature. Especially disturbing is the tendency shown by some big and hitherto respected food concerns to use quackery in their sales material.

On June 20, 1968, the FDA began holding hearings on a labeling proposal aimed at reducing the excessive promotion and sale of certain vitamin, mineral, and special dietary food products. The FDA wants to require the following words to be added to most of these products: "Vitamins and minerals are supplied in abundant amounts by commonly available foods. Except for persons with special medical needs, there is no scientific basis for recommending routine use of dietary supplements." The FDA argued that many consumers spend large sums of money needlessly, and excessive amounts of certain items can be harmful. More than 100 leading drug and food firms attacked the proposed label regulations. Behind their objections was a well-founded fear of loss of sales.

Diets to Lose Weight. In connection with taking vitamin preparations without a prescription or taking a pill to help lose weight, Dr. Milford O. Rouse, president of the American Medical Association in 1967, said, and most authorities agree, that there is no way for a normal person to lose weight except by eating fewer calories than he uses up expending energy. He said, "There is no tablet, . . . no pill . . . no chewing gum . . . no tonic . . . that will reduce you while you eat all you want." He said that "crash diets . . . can be dangerous to your health."[11] Two of the better-known crash diets, the Air Force and the Mayo Clinic diets, are not authorized by the organizations named. Dr. Frederick Wolff, director of research at the Washington Hospital Center, said at a Senate subcommittee hearing that "diet pills do more harm than good." He explained that they may cause some people to become addicted to them, since most of them are simply pep pills made up of amphetamine compounds.

Trading Stamps and Other Gimmicks

The National Commission on Food Marketing reported that food chains spent less than $1 million on trading stamps in 1950 and $680 million in 1964. Waddell[12] estimates that the stamp industry's annual sales amounted to about $1.1 billion in 1966. Sperry and Hutchinson had about 75 percent of the total stamp business.

There is an increasing controversy over the effects of trading stamps on consumers, on retailers, and on the prices that stamp-giving retailers charge customers. The consumer, however, is primarily interested in this question: "Do stamps really save money?"

Sperry and Hutchinson concedes that stamps must produce at least 12 percent increase in sales for stamps to pay their way. Retailers unable to increase their sales by at least 12 percent must operate at a loss until the stamp contract expires or raise their prices. Grocers operate on a narrow net profit margin of about 1¾ percent of sales. In a national survey in 1966 by the USDA Agriculture Marketing Service, 75 percent of supermarket operators reported increased operating expenses after introducing stamps. Fewer than 10 percent of the store managers were able to absorb the increase; 26 percent raised their prices; 44 percent used fewer specials; and 38 percent reduced their expenditures on advertising.

The Supermarket Institute claims that the use of stamps "costs a supermarket

[11]Reported in *U.S. Consumer*, Sept. 20, 1967.

[12]Frederick E. Waddell, in his article in *The Journal of Consumer Affairs*, Summer, 1968.

between $25,000 and $35,000 a year, a price roughly double the profit margin that it hopes to wring from its sales."[13] *Business Week*[14] summed it up, "Promotion has lost its competitive edge because it just doesn't pay if everyone gives stamps." S & H, however, did well on profits of 7 percent of sales in 1965. It would appear that stamp companies are practically the only ones who gain in this game of entrapment. Retailers are beginning to resent being in the middle between increasing operating costs (partly from trading stamps) and growing consumer resentment of higher and higher food prices. Mrs. Marlene Chapla, spokesman for the Denver, Colorado, supermarket boycotts, said, "We're sick and tired of excuses, and we're fed up with free dishes, bingo games, and trading stamps. All we want is lower prices." A Denver food chain responded with this advertisement, "Trading stamps and Gimmicks, No? Lower prices, Yes? But you can't have both."[15]

It does seem that supermarkets are beginning to drop trading stamps. The Supermarket Institute in 1966 reported that up until 1961, 78 percent of supermarkets were giving trading stamps, whereas in 1966 only 55 percent were doing so. The attitude of most supermarket managers was summed up by President Clarence Adamy of the National Association of Food Chains in 1966 when he said, "There is not a retailer who likes the games or stamps."

Consumers may also feel like Mr. Adamy when they realize that "trading stamps raise the price of groceries about 2 percent," according to a congressional study. [16]

Short-weighting

Short weights are common in many prepackaged foods. Before the days of prepackaged foods (now 85 percent of family food), the consumer had to watch the "butcher's thumb" or worry about inaccurate store scales. That old problem is still with us, but supermarkets need to weigh only about 15 percent of their food products.

In the spring of 1959, the Food and Drug Administration made a survey of 107,000 packages of 35 commonly purchased prepackaged foods. [17] The most significant shortages were in cornmeal, butter, margarine, oatmeal products, rice, coffee, sugar, macaroni products, liquid salad dressings, and vegetable shortening. About the only products not significantly short-weighted were frozen fruit juice concentrates and fruit and vegetable baby food preparations. Losses in butter for the consumer are estimated at about $25 million annually. In 10 of the 35 most commonly purchased foods, short weight occurred in 32 to

[13] Reported in *Duns Review,* July, 1962.

[14] Sept. 4, 1965.

[15] Waddell, *op. cit.*

[16] Reported in *Marketing Insights,* Nov. 14, 1966.

[17] Reported in the *Industrial Union Department Digest,* AFL-CIO, Washington, D.C., Fall, 1960.

54 percent of the commodities checked. In all, 39 percent of the 32,225 packages of the 10 foods mentioned were short in weight.

Also in the spring of 1959, the Wisconsin Weights and Measures Division checked 318 food stores in 114 cities, involving 16,181 prepackaged items of fresh meat, poultry, and potatoes, and found that 44 percent of the fresh meat, 48 percent of the fresh poultry, and 37 percent of the potatoes were short-weighted below the tolerance level permitted by law. Instances of overweight were so uncommon that they had no statistical significance.

More evidence of cheating on weight of food in retail stores was presented in 1966 at the House of Representatives hearings on fair packaging and labeling. In a survey of 1 million packages checked in Pennsylvania, 14 percent were short-weighted. The Weights and Measures Division in Louisville, Kentucky, found 13,000 packages were short-weighted. The attorney general's office in Michigan found 4 out of 10 meat packages underweight.[18] In 1968, the Consumers League of Ohio checked packaged meat in 33 supermarket stores in Cleveland, Ohio, and suburbs. In all, 19 of the 33 stores were overcharging for fresh packaged meat. The percentage of loss to consumers ranged from a modest 1 percent to 32 percent.[19]

Non-price Competition

Consumers have a large stake in effective competition in the food industry. Price competition, or lack of it, affects the consumers' real income. The National Commission on Food Marketing was sufficiently concerned about non-price competition in the food industry to investigate this area. Dr. G. E. Brandow, of Pennsylvania State University, was executive director of the National Commission on Food Marketing. According to Dr. Brandow, the commission found much that was favorable about the food industry but that there were areas of poor performance, notably in price competition.[20]

The commission study found that competition in the food industry produces excessive emphasis on efforts to sell products and services. This excessive cost takes the form of high advertising and other promotional costs and extensive use of salesmen or brokers to push retail sales. Retailers use trading stamps, games, and other selling devices. It all costs money, and the consumer pays for it.

The cereal manufacturers, for example, spent more for promotion, packaging, and color than on ingredients. About 20 percent of the price the consumer pays for breakfast cereals goes to persuade her to buy a particular brand. The cost of advertising and promotion was 36.5 percent of the retail price of breakfast cereals. Net profits before taxes averaged 14.1 percent of the retail

[18] Hearings on Fair Packaging and Labeling, U.S. Government Printing Office, 1966, part 2, p. 1035.

[19] Reported in *The Commuter*, Cuyahoga Community College, Apr. 4, 1968.

[20] See the Brandow article in *The Journal of Consumer Affairs*, Winter, 1967.

price of the cereal.[21] Brandow concludes that "it is not conceivable that information or other value to consumers justifies this cost." The great increase in advertising and promotion costs of food manufacturers was estimated to be $2.2 billion in 1964, in contrast to $560 million in 1950, according to the Food Commission study. Four of the 10 largest advertisers now are manufacturers of supermarket products. The *Food Industry Yearbook, 1964-1965,* stated that General Foods spent $101 million on advertising; National Dairy $53 million, Campbell $37 million, Kellogg $34 million, Corn Products $33 million, General Mills $32 million, and National Biscuit $33 million annually. The 1964 net profit on invested capital, according to a *Fortune Magazine* study, was high on the whole for food manufacturers—General Foods had 17.1 percent, National Dairy Products 11.8 percent, Corn Products 14.5 percent, and National Biscuit 16.8 percent, to mention a few.

Antitrust and Monopoly Prices.   It is difficult for government to break monopoly prices in the food industry because a few national chains do over one-half of the retail food business, and only a few very large food manufacturers produce most of the basic food sold at retail stores. The market power of these giants is apparently so great that they dominate the price of many food commodities. Evidence of their dominance can be seen by reviewing antitrust cases against such giants as Swift and Company, National Dairy Products, Borden's, Foremost, and Ward Bakery Products (to mention a few) and food chain stores such as Safeway and A & P.[22]

The lack of price competition in some foods is blamed on "leadership" prices— if one chain lowers or increases prices, they all lower or raise prices, says the Federal Trade Commission. Brandow recommends "vigorous antitrust policies . . . to maintain a structure of the industry conducive to effective competition." The Food Commission emphasized antimerger policy—a mild form of antitrust restraint—as one means of maintaining price competition. The Federal Trade Commission has recently laid down guidelines on mergers by large food retailers. Consumers could help themselves, within limitations, if they became expert buyers of food. It is difficult, however, to become an effective buyer of food unless there are quality standards of food products at the point of sale to the consumer.

Deception in the Market

Federal law requires that only pure fruit juice can be labeled "juice." This means that when the word "juice" and the name of the fruit are listed, you get the natural juice with natural flavor, color, and sugar—nothing added.

In the last few years, however, beverage manufacturers have been having a field day with diluted drinks that are little more than sugared water with a

[21] Hearings on Fair Packaging and Labeling, 1966, part 2, p. 1035.
[22] Hearings, *ibid.,* part 2, pp. 1037-1043.

little vitamin added. There are no accepted standards or requirements to reveal the percentage of real fruit juice. The 1967 Fair Packaging and Labeling Act does not require a percentage of fruit juice in such mixtures unless the expensive ingredient (juice) is "promoted as significant to the value of the food." Beverage manufacturers have a perfect escape-mechanism setup for themselves. They can continue to sell "orange drink," "ades," "punches," and "nectar" without giving the percentage of ingredients.

The Food and Drug Administration has recently proposed standards for various types of juice drinks, with percentages of genuine fruit juice to be prominently listed on the labels. For example, the FDA wants pineapple-grapefruit drink to declare on the label that it contains not less than 50 percent fruit juice; orange juice drink to be at least half orange juice; orangeade to be at least 25 percent orange juice, and orange drink to be at least 10 percent orange juice.

The sudden flood of objections from industry sources shows how the public is being misled in these products. If you look at the list of ingredients, sugar and water lead the parade. The cost of these diluted drinks is about 30 percent higher than the cost of using frozen orange juice concentrate and adding water, according to the New York Cooperative Extension Service. If children like these drinks, the inexpensive thing to do is to use powdered drinks like Tang and Kool-Aid. At least, you are not paying store prices for carting home water.

"Unfoods"—Do You Know What You're Eating?

"Unfoods" is a general term used to identify "imitation milk" products which cannot be called pure milk, "imitation bacon," and imitations of yogurt, various cheeses, and all the creams from sweet and sour to ice. And there will be others on the food shelves shortly.

Most of the milk imitations are nonfat dry milk reconstituted with water and vegetable oil. Some imitations use no nonfat dry milk but depend on sodium caseinate, a chalklike chemical equivalent of milk solids, plus coloring, flavoring, and other nonmilk ingredients. When labeled "imitation milk" and bearing a full list of ingredients, they cannot be banned from interstate commerce. If, however, the product is based on nonfat dry milk, it must be labeled "filled milk" and cannot be shipped across state lines as yet.

Imitation milk products have captured 5 percent of the dairy product sales where they have been introduced, according to a *U.S. Consumer Newsletter.*[23] There is a high profit margin, estimated to be nearly 50 percent, in contrast to about 20 percent for regular milk. People seem to look at the lower price, 33 to 40 cents per half-gallon in contrast to 50 to 56 cents for milk. There is a longer shelf life for imitation milk) about three weeks—and a reduction or elimination of butterfat. Consumers will have to be alert because the pro-

[23] *U.S. Consumer Newsletter,* Dec. 13, 1967.

motion and advertising that are sure to accompany these higher profit-making products may lead to their buying less nutritive food for the family. On the other hand, some of the imitation foods may have all of the nutrients that are in the pure product. There is a big battle going on within the dairy industry. The trouble is that some of the giant companies make both imitation and pure products. This leaves the dairy farmer with the higher-priced but often tastier and possibly more nutritive natural product.

Freezer-meat Fraud

Many families seeking to reduce high food prices are often trapped by "beef baiters." These shockingly overpriced freezer-meat contracts are the nation's biggest food swindle today. The freezer-meat operators sell frozen meat in hundred-pound lots at come-on prices of 29 to 39 cents a pound. They are known in the trade as "beef baiters" for their use of "bait-and-switch" selling. The June, 1968 issue of *Consumer Reports* comments in detail on how the racket works. Here are some of the tricks of the trade. The local newspaper ad is the bait. A typical ad may show a profile of a beautiful black Angus steer with copy which proclaims: "Government Inspected—Tender—Delicious BEEF SIDES. No money down, 31¢ lb. Includes: All cuts of beef, steaks, roasts, etc." The first switch occurs when the salesman walks you past good-looking beef, ending at a carcass covered with a thick, heavy layer of yellow fat. Then he shows you good-looking meat at twice the price. The better meat comes only in larger quantities than you intended to buy. Therefore, the beef baiter sells it to you on credit. He sells the contract to a finance company, thus escaping any obligation to adjust your complaints. The finance company, probably a thousand miles away, won't listen, either.

There are other extra costs. A legitimate freezer provisioner will trim from a side or quarter of beef about 25 percent of its hanging weight in fat and bone; a beef baiter will trim as much as 50 percent. He resells the trimmings to others. Thus, beef priced at 79 cents a pound may cost you $1.58 trimmed.

Solutions

What about protection from your government agencies? The U.S. Department of Agriculture, in what may be a landmark case, has charged Bruhn's Freezer Meat of Chicago, which operates from at least 25 locations under almost as many names, with using beef-baiter's false and deceptive advertising tactics and other violations of the Packers and Stockyards Act. The case is already four years old (since 1966). If the USDA examiner finds Bruhn and its owners guilty, they will most certainly take the case to the federal courts. Years will go by before the final decision. Meantime, the beef-baiters' ads keep appearing in our best and most respectable newspapers from coast to coast.

THE FAIR PACKAGING AND LABELING ACT

For five years Senator Philip A. Hart of Michigan had been urging a law to make it easier for consumers to see how much they were getting for their money. Before deceptive packaging became common, consumers could depend upon our weights-and-measures laws. At that time many foods were sold from bins and weighed out at the store, usually in half-pound and pound amounts. Implicit in this basic assumption was recognition also of the consumer's right to examine the product and compare it to other similar products, her right to name the quantity she chose to buy, and her right to compare prices. The consumer could recognize these rights when she bought in bulk. Modern packaging has eroded the consumer's right to examine the product and compare prices. The consumer's inability to compare prices of the same or similar products means that she cannot achieve rational choice.

Packaging Deceptions

The consumer testimony at the Hart hearings came as a surprise to the industry. Sellers had ignored the effect of their conduct on consumers. However, as one witness after another cited packaging malpractices in baby foods, cereals, cooking oils, canned goods, cake mixes, frozen foods, cookies, candy, crackers, fruit juices, bread, bacon, and many other foods, the point got across.[24] Even *Advertising Age* was moved to comment:

> We must confess that, as consumers, our sympathy lies with the statements of Senator Hart's subcommittee which concern deception, and particularly deceptive packaging. It would be nicer to live in a simple world in which "pound" packages contained 16 oz., and not 15 or 14½; in which "quart" bottles were actually quarts, not fifths, or even 25 oz., in which packages containing the same weight or volume didn't look as though one were twice as big as another . . . and so on. . . . A little standardization might help everyone.

Other trade papers were also impressed. *Food and Drug Packaging,* for example, described the testimony as the "rumblings of consumer discontent erupting into a full-blown packaging controversy." But it was not the trade comment that jolted the $100 billion industry. It was what occurred in the public press and on television and on radio.

"A Story for Our Times"[25]

Consumer issues seldom receive much attention in the mass media. This time the media did report the issue. Deceptive packaging made good pictures.

[24] See five volumes of Hearings . . . held by the Senate and the House for specific details.

[25] For a full report, see *Consumer Reports,* March, 1965.

Figure 7 - 5   Readers taken in by this gimmick told CU that they had reached for Birds Eye beans, a General Foods product, as they wheeled by, thinking the big "17¢" (see package at far right) was a lower price, only to find at the check-out counter that the "17¢" referred to coupons, not beans. The beans actually cost more than they did in the regular carton, near right. Reprinted from *Consumer Reports,* March 25, 1965. Copyright, 1965. Consumers Union, Inc.

So deceptive practices were shown on a few television screens, and headlines like "The grocery cart is being used to take shoppers for a ride" topped news stories.

Many newspaper editorials called Senator Hart silly ("our housewives are too smart to be fooled") or ("regulation will curb the freedom of enterprising packagers"). But the food industry, so accustomed to a docile press, was not looking for a dialog. The trade paper *Packaging* pointed out in its August, 1962 issue, "If we don't smother all this talk about how the consumer is being deceived and cheated, our whole economy will emerge 'sell' shocked."

Food Industry Fought Packaging Law.   By this time, after the second year of Senate hearings, the food industry decided to oppose *any* packaging law. And it certainly did not want any more exposure of its misdoings. Yet, a few months before the second set of hearings in early 1963, Paul Willis, president of the Grocery Manufacturers Association, was given the job to make the food industry's position clear to the nation's news media. He told his audience at the Television Bureau of Advertising's annual meeting that he had met with 16 top management people from national magazines. He suggested to the publishers "that the day was here when their editorial department and business department might better understand their interdependency relationships as they affect the operating results of their company; and as their operations affect the advertiser—their bread and butter."

The magazine people, he said, had understood. They had begun to run articles to create "a favorable public attitude" toward food advertisers. He regretted, however, that he could not say "similar nice things about the relationship of our advertisers with television." He said television received about "65 percent of their advertising revenue from GMA members." "These advertisers," he said, "have seen some television newscasts where they seemingly took great delight in bellowing out stories that were critical of this industry." He closed his speech with a question: "What can you do additionally that will influence your advertiser to spend more of his advertising dollar with you?"

The broadcasters, with one or two exceptions, got the message. On radio only Edward P. Morgan (ABC) gave news about the hearings. Since the speech, several scheduled television appearances of Senator Hart were canceled. So the food industry entered the 1965 legislative year with its trade groups coordinated and the news media under control.

Let's Keep Politics out of the Pantry.   In the January 26, 1965, issue of *Look*, the editorial pages displayed the by-line of an advertiser: Charles C. Mortimer, chairman of General Foods, as author of an article, "Let's Keep Politics Out of the Pantry." In the article he salutes the American housewife as a shrewd and happy woman—shrewd because "when it comes to clever buying," she "can give lessons to a Yankee horse trader," and happy because "she takes it for granted that what she has bought is the purest, most nutritious, easiest-to-prepare food the world has ever seen." (Recorded against his own food company are 28 violations in the last 25 years against one of our regulatory laws, the Federal Food, Drug and Cosmetic Act.)

What further disturbed Mr. Mortimer is that American housewives probably do *not* know that their good fortune as a food shopper results from "the machinery of free competition." The informed reader will find his eulogies of competition even more interesting than his protestations on behalf of existing government regulations over food. For he is chairman of a food combine that is the nation's largest and prime example of what the Federal Trade Commission called "economic power and market concentration created by the great merger movement." It markets 250 products, and has challenged an FTC order to dissolve a more recent merger; and the earnings from its many merger-acquired companies are such that it commands over $100 million worth of advertising power a year.

Since there was another side to the packaging issue than the one Mr. Mortimer presented, Senator Hart asked whether he might not be given an opportunity to clarify some of these matters for readers of *Look*. Gardner Cowles, editorial chairman of *Look*, answered by taking full-page ads in other magazines, to publicize its sponsorship of Mr. Mortimer's article.

This has to be one of the great stories of our time on the freedom of the press when pressure is brought to bear on the big advertising revenue of mass media. And, despite this all-out, no-holds-barred drive to defeat the Fair Packaging and Labeling Act, a fairly good packaging and labeling law was finally passed in 1966. This act, like most proposed consumer laws, was largely defensive. Even *Advertising Age* commented that it would be nice to be able to buy something in an even pound again.

The Fair Packaging and Labeling Act of 1966

This act became effective theoretically in July, 1967. It will aid consumers by requiring that packaged or labeled consumer products in interstate commerce be honestly and informatively labeled. The law requires that the label of a consumer product must:

identify the commodity and give the name and place of business of the manufacturer, packer, or distributor.

contain a statement in a uniform location on the principal display panel of net contents in units appropriate for the product.

be free of such terms as "jumbo pound," and "giant quart."

give the net quantity per serving if number of servings is stated.

authorizes government to establish additional regulations, on a product-by-product basis if this is necessary to prevent deception or facilitate value comparisons.

authorizes government to establish and define standards for describing package sizes that may be used to supplement the label statement of net contents.

regulate bargain-price labeling such as "cents off."

require (except for food) that the label give the common name of the product and list the ingredients in order of decreasing predominance.

prohibit packaging the product with an unnecessary amount of packing material or air space.

gives the Secretary of Commerce responsibility for requesting industry agreements on *voluntary* standards of weights, measures, or quantities for packaging when he finds a commodity is sold in an unjustified number of package sizes.

The Fair Packaging and Labeling Act does not apply to certain drugs, or to tobacco, meat, and poultry products and other products that are covered by other federal laws. In general, provisions of the act that affect foods, drugs, devices, and cosmetics will be enforced by the Food and Drug Administration, and those affecting other products by the Federal Trade Commission.

Implementation. Not much has been done so far. Part of the trouble is the weakness of the law. The key section on proliferation of package sizes depends on the willingness of industry to initiate the standard-setting machinery. The FDA and the FTC are in the throes of issuing regulations to implement the law. So far, there has been little progress. By September, 1968, the terrible jungle of confusion in package sizes had been reduced for only 14 products—toothpaste in 5 sizes, instead of 57; cooking oils in 7 quantities, rather than 15; green olives in 15 container sizes, down from 50; dry detergents in 6 sizes, formerly 24; paper towels in 8 sizes, instead of 33; cereals in 16 sizes, rather than 33.

Unfortunately, there is little evidence of change in packages on the shelves of retail stores, according to surveys by Charles A. Vanik, member of the House. Four days before the effective date of the Fair Packaging Law (July 1, 1967), a survey of a large food supermarket in Washington, D.C., revealed no evidence of how much constitutes a "serving." Another continuing problem was the confusion in the number of package sizes. Surveyors found 24 different package weights for dried cereals from 4⅞ ounces to 1 pound 4 ounces.[26] They also found continuing evidence of hidden price increases built into new and sometimes "improved" packages. Vanik reported that the American Beauty can dropped from 16 ounces to 15 ounces between August 31 and September 18, 1967. And there was no public announcement and the price remained the same.

Another survey of 44 food supermarkets in the Lake Worth, Florida, area on a visit in October, 1967, and another visit to the same stores in December, 1967, uncovered continuing abuses of "servings" in 13 instances and continuing use of "cents off" in 9 instances.[27] Apparently, the food industry is in no hurry to implement the new packaging law.

Another handicap in enforcement of the recent packaging law is the lack of funds to administer the act. The FDA, for example, did not receive any extra funds to enforce the new packaging law. It was forced to dump enforcement into the laps of nine regional offices, which were already overburdened.

Undue Delays Permitted.   When will we get truth-in-packaging? Dr. Leland Gordon, a leading authority on packaging and labeling, concluded that the packaging law itself "contains built-in procedural delays." He said the "finalizing of regulations is a time consuming process"; that the "food industry never seriously considered voluntary standards during the five year period when the hearings and debates took place." Gordon also stated that "industry groups which fought the packaging bill . . . are determined not to yield anything they do not have to yield."[28] Certainly, the law and the procedures pertaining to undue proliferation permit undue delay. The procedures seem to invite procrastination—even deliberate refusal to comply. If the concept of voluntary standardization has any validity, it will be because the ultimate alternative is the threat of amendments to the original bill. This threat of amendments is quite unlikely. Even granting amendments favorable to consumers, Congress can shut the door on enforcement by refusing funds to the four federal agencies responsible for enforcement of the law. According to Stanley E. Cohen, of *Advertising Age,* the House Appropriations Committee told the FDA: "If you are pinched for funds, give truth-in-packaging a low priority."[29]

Gordon concluded, "Never in this century has so complicated a law been enacted, with enforcement and administrative responsibility divided among several agencies. It will take years to achieve full implementation."[30]

[26] See table in *U.S. Consumer,* Jan. 10, 1968.

[27] *Ibid.*

[28] *Fair Packaging and Labeling—When?* Consumers Union, Inc., Mount Vernon, N.Y., July 15, 1968, p. 21.

[29] *Ibid.,* pp. 20-21.

[30] *Ibid.,* p. 2.

Sleepers in the Act. The new Packaging Act, however, does establish a significant principle. Section 2 of the Declaration of Policy of the act states that "Informed consumers are essential to the fair and efficient functioning of a free market economy." This is the first time that a federal consumer law has established the principle that the way you spend your money or are led to spend your money affects the nation's economic welfare as well as your own. Up to now, consumer legislation has been passed to protect the public against deception, fraud, or unsafe products.

The new Packaging Act has another provision of considerable significance. The declaration of policy in the original bill stated that one purpose was to help consumers make price comparisons. Industry representatives objected, saying that there was more to a purchase than price and quantity. And they are right. There is also the quality of a product. Accordingly, Congress agreed to change the term "price comparison" to "value comparison." This change "opens the door to consideration of legislation such as grade labeling and government testing of consumer products," according to Senator Hart, the chief sponsor of the Packaging Act. Historians may consider this declaration of policy to be as important as the provisions of the legislation itself, said the Senator. Consumers, however, may have to wait a long time, many years perhaps, before Congress will have the courage to enact grade labeling against the nearly united opposition of the industry.

HOW TO GET MORE FOR YOUR FOOD DOLLAR

Buying Rationally in a Stamp-happy Market

When all the stores have stamps, what then? If most of the stamp plans are approximately equal in exchange value, the competing merchants are back where they were before stamps became icons. They have to go back to price and quality competition and to become better merchants again.

How, then, can homemakers buy rationally in a stamp-happy marketing area? Ignore stamp offers, and try to buy on the basis of price and quality. Take the stamps, if offered. If food is selected on a price-and-quality basis first, chances are that the stamps will cost the thoughtful homemaker less and offer more in the long run than they do to people who buy to satisfy "inner satisfactions" that have nothing to do with competitive price-and-quality analysis. Compare food and quality prices at cooperative and discount food stores, if such stores are available in your marketing area. Cooperative patronage dividends average around 3 percent on total purchases today.

Use the Food Ads

Food shopping begins at home. Studying the food ads in the local papers and listening to local radio food programs will often suggest the best daily or weekly buys. Comparing food costs *before* marketing is both economical and time-saving.

Place all the desired ads before you, with your grocery list handy. When comparing the price of veal shoulder roast, for example, circle the best buy and double-circle the next-best buy. Jot down the name of the retail store opposite the particular food on your list.

After an experience or two in comparing prices and knowing what you want before you leave home to shop for food, you will find that you have saved as much as half an hour or more in the marketplace—and been much easier on your pocketbook.

Weekend Food Shopping: Does It Pay?

Generally, it pays to market for food on weekends. In national food chain stores, most price reductions occur on Thursday, Friday, and Saturday. On Monday, prices frequently increase. In one survey of retail national food chain stores, about 86 percent of the fresh fruits and vegetables were reduced on Thursday, Friday, and Saturday. Spot surveys also indicate that some food prices are increased in the latter part of the week.

Independent food stores seem to have a more flexible price policy than many national food chain stores. There is evidence to support the conclusion that food prices are also reduced in many independent stores during the weekend. Like the national chain food stores, independent stores tend to increase some prices on Monday. One may conclude, therefore, that shoppers can make their best buys in the latter part of the week.

One result of weekend price reductions is the heavy concentration of shoppers and consequent crowding, particularly in afternoons and evenings. Some competent marketing observers have concluded that marketing costs could be reduced if sales were more evenly distributed throughout the week. In view of the pressure of retail competition and force of habit on the part of the retailers themselves, any corrective measure is likely to make slow progress.

The Stanford University Food Research Institute, a few years ago, in Palo Alto, California, compared 1,546 price observations of 225 food items advertised as specials. They found that in 96 food items (1) the consumer could have saved over 20 percent if he had purchased all the specials; (2) most of the specials offered were standard foods commonly purchased weekly; (3) the stores with the lowest-priced specials generally maintained higher prices on other food products than their competitors.

Food Cost-cutters

Marketing research firms have reported that since 1965, consumers' desire for low prices on groceries has replaced desire for quality and freshness of meat as the number one factor in supermarket shopping. This change of desire from quality and freshness to low prices may have been due to rapidly increasing cost of food since 1965. Although food is usually the largest single expense in a family budget, you can generally reduce the amount you spend for food in the following ways:

1.   Making a shopping list, and sticking to it unless you switch when the price is right.
2.   Looking at the labels and checking the weights.
3.   Shopping for advertised specials and planning menus around them.
4.   Willingness to substitute and try new recipes for good ways to prepare lower-cost foods.
5.   Avoiding fancy canned whole tomatoes for making soup or French beans for everyday family meals.
6.   Keeping a notebook of prices of foods used regularly if you are really serious about saving money.
7.   Buying in quantity whenever it is more economical.
8.   Watching for combination sales, especially in frozen foods just before the fresh item reaches the market in volume.
9.   Buying the right amounts for family use. We waste too much on leftovers unless we plan meals carefully.
10.   Taking time to prepare finished foods. Avoid the more expensive convenience foods unless you are a working wife and time is worth more to you.
11.   Using less glamorous foods, such as dried beans, for good, nutritious, but less expensive meals.
12.   Comparing costs and buying food in the form—fresh, frozen, canned, freeze-dried—that gives the most savings for the money.
13.   Using USDA grades whenever possible.
14.   Taking advantage of seasonal abundances.
15.   Preventing food waste by proper storage and by cooking methods that conserve nutrients.
16.   When buying meat, consider the lean meat in the cut, not the cost per pound.
17.   Using eggs whenever possible because they are usually a less expensive source of nutrients than most meats.
18.   Using cereals you cook yourself are almost always less expensive and usually more nutritious.
19.   Avoiding cold cereals in multipacks of small boxes, sugar-coated cereals, and dried fruit mixed with cereals because they are much more expensive.
20.   Baking at home usually costs less than buying ready-baked foods.
21.   Buying nonfat dry milk and evaporated milk because they cost considerably less per quart when reconstituted than whole fluid milk and supply comparable amounts of calcium and protein.
22.   Considering family likes and dislikes when planning meals and shopping. Every now and then—not too often—try a new dish on the family.

Dial-a-Number Best Food Buys

New York City consumers can dial a number (presently 349-0949) and obtain information about the best food buys, according to the *New York Times*. Perhaps in the near future more communities will have such a service. In the foreseeable future we will be able to dial a service number from any home and

TABLE 7-6   CALENDAR OF THE BEST FOOD BUYS

MONTH	MEAT, FISH, ETC.	DAIRY PRODUCTS	VEGETABLES	FRUIT	MISCELLANEOUS
January	Chicken (broilers & fryers), pork and pork products, eggs		Potatoes, cabbage, onions, lettuce	Oranges, apples, tangerines, grapefruit	Tree nuts, raisins, honey
February	Eggs, better-grade beef		Lettuce, celery, potatoes, cabbage	Oranges, grapefruit	Tree nuts, raisins, honey
March	Chicken (broilers & fryers), frozen fish, eggs		Dried beans, potatoes	Canned & frozen citrus fruit, juices	Raisins, prunes
April	Chicken (broilers & fryers), pork and pork products, eggs	Cottage cheese	Cabbage, carrots, potatoes, spring greens, celery	Apples, oranges	Raisins, prunes
May	Chicken (broilers & fryers), eggs	Butter, milk, cheese, cottage cheese	Asparagus, onions, lettuce, cabbage, spring greens	Strawberries	
June	Chicken (broilers & fryers), fresh fish	Butter, milk, cheese, ice cream	Potatoes, onions, lettuce, snap beans	Berries, cantaloupe	
July	Chicken (broilers & fryers), turkey (fryers & roasters)	Cheese, ice cream, cottage cheese	Cabbage, tomatoes, potatoes, local vegetables	Lemons, peaches, watermelons, cantaloupe, limes, plums, apricots	

Month			Local vegetables		
August	Fresh fish	Ice cream		Grapes, pears, watermelons, peaches, plums	
September	Stewing chicken, lamb	Cottage cheese	Onions, carrots, cabbages, tomatoes, corn	Grapes, pears	Rice
October	Stewing chicken, turkey, lamb, pork	Cheese	Potatoes, onions, sweet potatoes, cauliflower, dried beans, pumpkins, cabbage	Apples, pears	Honey
November	Turkey, pork and pork products		Potatoes, onions, sweet potatoes, cauliflower, cabbage, pumpkins	Cranberries, apples	Tree nuts, raisins, honey
December	Turkey, pork		Onions, sweet potatoes, potatoes	Grapefruit, cranberries, oranges, dried fruit	Honey, tree nuts

secure best buys on food and most other basic consumer products. Consumers Union, publisher of *Consumer Reports,* is presently experimenting with such a service for consumers. But until this kind of service is generally available, most consumers will have to learn to use the information presently available.

Buy by the Calendar

Food prices go through seasonal cycles that can be plotted by the calendar. Use Table 7-6 above, worked out by *Changing Times,* as a general guide, subject to the changes that can be brought on by an unexpected freeze or a prolonged drought.

Nutritious Food Habits Still a Major Family Problem

Feeding the family nutritious and interesting food remains, as yet, one of the major family problems. Our food habits are not ruled by the desire for health. Dietary surveys and other evidence reveal the embarrassing fact that one-third of American families are eating below the optimum level for proper nutrition.

We know now, thanks to the science of nutrition, what foods will maintain good health for the entire family. It remains to put this information to use. Eating habits of Americans have improved somewhat in terms of consumption of fruits, vegetables, and dairy products, but unfortunately the eating of grain products and potatoes has decreased.

The first important job for the homemaker is menu planning before going to market. But good planning at home must be followed by intelligent marketing. This, in turn, must be followed by proper preparing of food for the table and its conservation for use throughout the week, as well as adequate storage.

The next chapter will introduce you to the fascinating but complex world of supermarkets.

QUESTIONS FOR DISCUSSION

1. Keep a record of the kind, quality, and quantity of all the food you eat during one week. Then evaluate your diet according to the data in this chapter. What foods should be added or changed and in what quantity, to give you an adequate diet?

2. Can food habits be changed? Is it hard to give up poor food habits? Why?

3. Do the national trends in eating habits indicate that American families are improving their diets?

4. Does spending more money for food automatically improve the diet?

5.   In many countries, the major food problem is a shortage of food. In the United States, it is a matter of poor selection of foods in most families. What are the implications of these two statements?

6.   How effective has the Fair Packaging and Labeling Act been in correcting abuses in your local food stores?

ACTIVITY PROBLEMS

1.   A famous physiologist told a House committee investigating the use of chemicals in foods: "We feed our best grains to hogs and cattle—we eat the poorest part." What are the implications of this statement?

2.   Using *Consumer Reports* and *Consumers' Research Bulletin,* compare the price and quality of various brands of the same kind of food. Are the best buys always the most expensive?

3.   Some nutritionists claim that the day can be started with a breakfast that will improve efficiency and well-being but not necessarily add pounds. Investigate this claim, and report to the class.

4.   It is generally difficult to get people to buy the foods that are most plentiful at certain times. Some food experts claim that if you "eat by the calendar," you can cut food costs by as much as 20 percent. Investigate this statement, using local markets as the chief source for information.

5.   Make a study of the food habits of several persons you know. Are these people eating well-balanced meals? List their poor and good food habits.

6.   With a typical weekly shopping list, visit a supermarket. Study the location of the various departments in the store. Then arrange the list so that you need not backtrack for items. Keep this in mind when making such shopping lists hereafter.

7.   Make a survey of food bargains as featured in the local ads. Are these items bargains? How do you know?

SUGGESTED READINGS

Bivens, Gordon E.: "Household Use of Convenience Foods," *Family Economic Review,* December, 1967.

Call, David: "Private Label and Consumer Choice in the Food Industry," *The Journal of Consumer Affairs,* Winter, 1967.

Fox, Harold W.: *The Economics of Trading Stamps,* Public Affairs Pamphlets, Washington, D.C., 1968.

"The High Price of Being Poor," *Changing Times,* August, 1968.

"How Much Do You Spend for Groceries?" *Changing Times,* January, 1968.

Margolius, Sidney: *The Innocent Consumer vs. The Exploiters,* Trident Press, New York, 1967.

Tatkon, M. Daniel: *The Great Vitamin Hoax,* Macmillan, New York, 1968.

Waddell, Frederick C.: "The Case Against Trading Stamps," *The Journal of Consumer Affairs,* Summer, 1968.

"Weights and Measures and Your Money's Worth," *Changing Times,* March, 1968.

chapter 8

FOOD SHOPPING IN THE MARKET

Shopping for food is a complex problem. All the information that is valuable to consumers cannot be condensed into one chapter. It is necessary to select what experienced home economists have found to be the most useful advice for a typical family. When consumers have done a good job of mental food planning at home, they will not want to lose that benefit by poor buying in the market. To have tasty, nutritious food at all times at an economical price, one must give constant attention to food costs to win the "battle of the budget."

The right quality and quantity of food for the family depend mainly on the buying practices of the homemaker, on her information and skill in choice making, on her willingness to shop at the stores where the best buys are available, and on her actual selection of the food. She must decide:

1. What to buy.
2. Where to buy.
3. When to buy.
4. How much to buy.
5. Whether to buy bulk or package, canned or fresh, frozen or dehydrated foods.
6. How to pay.
7. What quality or grade to use for specific purposes.
8. Who will buy.

This sounds like a full-time career in itself.

MANAGEMENT OF TIME FOR FOOD SHOPPING

The management of time for family food shopping has become increasingly important. Experienced shoppers have their time for marketing well organized. A study of food-shopping activities, made by Deanne Suneson at Cornell University, may still be useful to experienced shoppers, and young housewives can surely profit by this study.[1]

To study the management of time for family food shopping, a random sampling procedure was used to select 100 families in the Ithaca, New York, area. The major food shopper in each family was interviewed with questions pertaining to the food shopping done by the family during the week prior to the interview. Information was obtained about the time used for all the activities connected with family food shopping: planning and preparation, shopping in the markets, transportation to and from the markets, and storage of foods purchased.

Almost one-half of the major shoppers felt that food shopping was a pleasure; only 11 major shoppers felt it to be a chore. The remainder said that shopping was just a routine that could not be avoided.

Planning for the major shopping was done by a written list in over three-fourths of the families. One-half of the families used the newspaper in planning for food shopping, mainly to look over specials and bargains.

[1] Deanne Suneson, "Use of Time for Family Food Shopping Activities," unpublished master's thesis, Cornell University, Ithaca, N.Y., 1961.

Eighty-six percent of the families made a major food shopping trip once a week. Two-thirds of the families did their major shopping on Thursday or Friday, mainly because time was available or the pay check came then. The hours during which the major shopping was done showed a fairly even distribution as to morning, afternoon, and evening.

Families made an average of about three shopping trips per week; on an average, one of these three shopping trips was unscheduled or unexpected. Forty-three families made no unscheduled trips, however. There was a significant difference in the total number of shopping trips made by employed homemakers and full-time homemakers, with the latter making slightly fewer trips.

Most of the families went to the market by car for the major food shopping; only six families walked to the market from home. Most of the families lived within three miles of the most distant food market they had shopped in during the week. Almost one-half of the families combined the major shopping trip with another errand or activity, while the other half went on the major trip with food shopping as their sole purpose.

All the households in the study had mechanical refrigerators; one-fourth of the households had separate freezers for food storage. In over three-fourths of the households, between 6 and 20 linear feet of cupboard space were available for storage of dry groceries.

Sixty percent of the families received no home deliveries of food. More full-time homemakers than employed homemakers had home deliveries of food. Three-fifths of the families had done no home production of food of any type during the previous year, and over two-thirds of the families had not purchased food in quantity during the previous year.

The total time used for all shopping activities by the two groups, employed homemakers and full-time homemakers, was nearly the same.

An increase in the time used for all food-shopping activities was noted in families that reported the following:

1. More persons eating in the home regularly
2. More meals prepared in a week
3. More shopping trips made in a week
4. Greater complexity of meals
5. Greater household workloads for tasks done daily and for tasks not necessarily done daily
6. More family members participating in food shopping
7. More money spent for food in a week
8. Negative attitude of the major shopper toward food shopping
9. Age of the major shopper being over 60 years

THE SUPERMARKET REVOLUTION

In the last 20 years, the marketplace has undergone an amazing transformation. Technological advances and streamlined marketing methods have made more goods available to more people more efficiently than anyone would have dreamed possible a generation ago.

The Commission Report

Then, on June 27, 1966, the report of the National Commission on Food Marketing went to Congress, after two years of diligent study on every phase of food marketing. It had been like a rigorous medical examination of a patient who believed he was healthy but whose doctor thought he detected dangerous symptoms. Is our largest industry as well as it claims to be, or is it malfunctioning, and if so, where, and what can be done about it? The 113-page diagnosis, plus 10 separate technical studies, had a lot to say for both sides.

The commission report raised many doubts as to whether the supermarket, as now operated, fulfills the promise which it initially held out to consumers. Some of the problems stem from new facts of economic life of the last 20 years: the swing from a production to a marketing orientation, the startling technological changes in agriculture and food processing, the population growth, and the emergence of a new, well-to-do consumer.

The first result has been to threaten the balance of competition within the industry. The commission reported an increased concentration in retailing and manufacturing, shown in and aggravated by the extinction of 133,000 small- to medium-sized stores during the period 1948-1963, and by the rising number of mergers. Large firms have been gobbling up small- or medium-sized ones; retailers have been moving into food processing and processors into food production, and all at an accelerated rate since 1954. Today, concentration is most extreme among retail and wholesale food buyers and among manufacturers of baby food, coffee, cake mixes, shortening, crackers, cookies, and soap, where 50 percent or more of the market is held by the four largest firms. Some of the biggest companies, especially among retailers, have grown beyond the size needed for maximum efficiency. Medium-sized firms are just as competent to process and distribute. The only edge held by the giants is in advertising, promotion, and sales, where their superior resources reduce competition.

Promotion Costs.   There are areas of poor performance. The commission report found, for example, that the competitive process produces *excessive* emphasis upon efforts to sell products and services. This takes the form of high advertising and other promotion costs, extensive use of salesmen or brokers to push retail sales, and other selling devices. Retailers use gimmicks like trading stamps, games, cents-off, and advertising to attract customers. It all costs money, and the consumer pays for it. The consumer pays about 20 cents of the dollar she spends for breakfast cereals to persuade her to buy a particular brand in a particular store. It is not conceivable, says the report, that information or other value to consumers justifies this cost (some of it goes to pay for television programs, trading stamps, etc.).

These expensive selling efforts have a powerful effect on consumers' decisions, as demonstrated by a study of brands made by Dr. David Call for the commission (mentioned earlier in Chapter 7). You recall that highly advertised national brands of food, costing about 20 percent more than retail or store brands of comparable quality, outsold store brands by a considerable margin. This situation could not persist if consumers had the information to buy on the basis of price and quality.

The drive to sell the product has wide-ranging effects. It is the chief incentive to develop new products, which is good when the products are genuinely new and useful but costly when it produces merely proliferation of trivially differentiated products. Emphasis on selling diverts attention from efficiency in processing and distribution, and it often adds costs other than the promotional costs directly involved.

Advertising Costs. Food manufacturers' advertising, now running at $2.2 billion, wastes too much money simply urging housewives to buy brand A instead of brand B (Table 8-1). New products often cost 57 percent of their first year's sales for advertising. These costs must ultimately be paid for by the public.

Inadequate Labels. The only other major consumer gripes, says the commission, concerned packaging and inadequate information on food, particularly the quality of food. The commission recommended that the federal government might usefully go further than it has to increase the amount of objective information for consumers about foods they buy. Possibilities include reasonable standardization of packages (the Fair Packaging and Labeling Act may help), requiring more informative labeling, additional standards of identity, and mandatory consumer grading of important packaged foods where this is feasible. One cannot give the food industry high marks for its willingness to recognize consumers' problems. On the other hand, consumers should be willing to inform themselves about the economics and technology of the food industry, and should play an active role in making constructive, workable proposals.

"Sticky" Prices. Vigorous antitrust policies are also warranted to maintain competition. There are virtually no benefits to the consumer from permitting domination of any part of the national food industry by a few large firms. The Food Commission recognized this and emphasized the need for a more vigorous antimerger policy.

The Food Supermarket Today

The typical supermarket today is far from being the efficient store it was in the 1920s and 1930s. The point that stands out today is that retail margins in food have been advancing. The rise of costly promotion, the duplication of supermarkets on costly sites, the big inventory, the use of expensive equipment,

TABLE 8-1 WHERE CONSUMERS' FOOD DOLLARS GO*

	FARMER (%)	LABOR (%)	PACKAGING (%)	ADVERTISING (%)	TRANSPORTATION (%)	PROFIT (%)	OTHER COSTS (%)	TOTAL (%)
Breakfast cereals (1 lb.)	10	20	12	20	5	13	20	100
Canned corn, 303 can	13	23	21	6	3	10	24	100
Canned tomatoes, 303 can	16	28	25	4	4	3	20	100
Apples—Wash. Delic. (lb.)	18	29	11	2	12	4	24	100
White bread, 1 lb.	19	40	7	5	3	5	21	100
Processed fruits & veg. (lb.)	21	24	14	6	4	4	27	100
Oranges, Florida (lb.)	24	31	6	3	10	4	22	100
Ice cream, ½ gal.	24	28	10	5	6	4	23	100
Fresh fruits & veg. (lb.)	33	26	6	2	14	3	16	100
American cheese, ½ lb.	41	17	6	4	4	10	18	100
Milk—home del., ½ gal.	41	31	5	2	9	3	9	100
Milk—evap., 14½ oz.	43	9	20	6	5	5	12	100
Milk—store, ½ gal.	45	21	6	3	5	5	15	100
Pork (lb.)	51	28	2	3	3	3	10	100
Veal (lb.)	52	21	2	3	4	3	15	100

*National Commission on Food Marketing Report, June, 1966, pp. 14-15.

and the higher labor costs have all contributed to this mounting-cost picture. The net of it is that much of the one-time efficiency is fading from the supermarkets.

Merchandising is no longer a simple transaction of buying bread, butter, and beans. It is surrounded by the siren voices of radio and television that seek to imbue a brand consciousness in listeners. At the check-out counter the buyer presents a miscellany of coupons and receives a miscellany of stamps, bingo cards, and pictures for matching. Coupons come through the mails offering products at "cents-off" prices. Off from what price, we never know! Favorable shelf space is often leased to the highest bidders—a sort of second-cousin merchandising "payola." The very arrangement of the products accents high markups.

Less Cost Advantage.   In this setting, supermarket food retailing has lost some of the cost advantage it once possessed. Willard Mueller, director of the Federal Trade Commission Bureau of Economics, reports that in 1947-1952 three large food chains operating at high efficiency took only 15 percent of the dollar consumers paid for food. From 1952 and on, the margin began a steady rise, reaching 20.6 percent in 1963. This was an increase of 37 percent in their share of your food dollar. Another survey of large and small food chain stores showed an increase from 18.1 percent in 1955 to 22.2 percent in 1963. Clarence Adamy, president of the National Association of Food Chains, said that if extra services like check cashing, carry-out boys, and night openings were discontinued, retail prices could be brought down 6 to 9 percent. The economic facts are clear. Food supermarkets are not the efficient, economical stores that they were in the early decades of food supermarketing. Also, it takes more time and physical effort to shop for food now than it did before the supermarket appeared on the scene. And since the food supermarket now has a margin requirement of over 20 percent on food, it is hardly offering food on a basis so much lower than was traditional in the service stores many years ago as to justify the shopper's extra time and effort. More and more shoppers will be asking, "Why am I doing this, and for cash?" Some day shoppers will conclude: "I'll shop from my home, by telephone, by catalog, or from in-home sellers." Perhaps there will be a supermarket without a store. There is a supermarket without a store in Stockholm, Sweden, the Hemkop (Home Shop), which never sees a customer yet has grown into a major distributor in 10 years.[2] You merely dial in your shopping list from the store's biweekly catalog, and rapid delivery service is provided. The order is taken down, channeled into a delivery route, and filled by a conveyor-belt system. The store's customers, who give it about 3 percent of the Stockholm area food sales, save time, energy, and money. The operating cost, exclusive of cost of the food, is only 12.5 percent of sales.

Food shoppers in Sweden have a big advantage over American shoppers in the United States. Most of the food in Sweden is quality-graded so the shopper can telephone the standard quality grade and the brand name.

[2] *Business Week,* Jan. 11, 1964, p. 100.

Factors in Selecting Food Stores

Several economic factors are involved in the intelligent selection of food stores, such as quality of food, price, convenience, and service.

A *range of quality foods* at various prices is usually desirable. Some stores deliberately cater to one class of consumer. The quality factors also include cleanliness of the store and personnel and a rapid turnover, particularly of perishable foods.

Prices and Values.   It is smart to be conscious of *price and values* when selecting food stores. It is one thing, however, to be conscious of paying higher prices for elaborate service and atmosphere and quite another to be unconscious of the extra dollars it takes to trade in such retail stores. It is wise to shop around until you discover which stores give good value at reasonable prices. The price range should match your pocketbook.

Almost always it is necessary to shop from three to five food stores to get quality, price, and value when buying food. The stores that sell at higher prices are not necessarily handling the better foods. Likewise, the store with low prices is not necessarily selling lower-quality goods. You must learn by intelligent appraisal—by being objective and not too easily taken in by persuasive salesmanship, conspicuous display, and catering to your ego.

Convenience to markets is also a consideration in selecting food stores. Sometimes the distance to the best food marts, or the parking problem, is so great that one must shop the more expensive small neighborhood stores. Usually, however, when shopping is done on a basis of once a week or so, it pays to go farther to the large supermarkets.

The *services* rendered by salespeople and by store policy constitute another important factor. Some stores cut down expenses by having a small "consumer-aid" staff and lower the prices of their products. Other stores reduce personnel costs but do not pass on the savings to the consumer. It is smart to discover these things and to identify the store accordingly.

Some stores have elaborate service for customers. As a rule, such stores subordinate price appeal to pleasing service. They usually take telephone orders, deliver food to the home, and extend credit. This service costs money. Consumers buying in these stores must expect to pay more.

Ethics.   There is still another factor that wise buyers should consider—honesty and fair business ethics. An honest merchant can be judged by the following business ethics.

1.   He gives consumers accurate information about his products—in his advertising, in the reliability of the labels on the containers and packages of food that he features, and in the guidance of his salespeople.

2.   He makes fair adjustments. Most merchants try to be fair in this matter. If the merchant is evasive or tends to argue about his rights, perhaps it is time for a change of market.

3.   He provides good working conditions and fair wages for his employees.

Shopping the Supermarkets

Supermarkets are advantageous for knowledgeable shoppers, but confusing and expensive for the uninformed and impulsive buyer. The uninformed and disorganized buyer drifts around the place almost in a trance. A noted designer, Gerald Stahl, claims that these types "are in a mild hypnotic trance induced by mass displays, lights, signs, slogans, pictures, and brilliant colors." This may be slightly exaggerated, but have you ever gone into a supermarket for a dozen eggs and come out with a jar of olives, a new anchovy spread, and a gadget can opener?

Bend down at the dairy case for milk, and your eyes come level with jars of fresh fruit salad or imported Swiss cheese—impulse items ready for you even when stooping. Make a turn around the corner, and you nearly collide with red tomato ketchup bottles, so you take one. Red always attracted you. Another retailing stratagem is to place big-profit items in several different places in the store. For the toddlers (heaven help you if you have one with you!), the lowest shelves are baited with cereals, cookies, candies, and everything advertised on children's TV programs.

Aisles are arranged to direct you into sections you didn't intend to visit. Steaks are often surrounded with green leaves because they make the meat look redder, more appetizing. Women, say color specialists, are likely to fall for packages that feature turquoise, yellow, or pink, So watch out, the payoff is at the check-out counter!

How, then, should the wise consumer shop a supermarket? Successful shoppers say:

1. Study the food ads before leaving home.
2. Have a shopping list.
3. Organize the items by departments so that you do not need to retrace your steps.
4. Select stores where prices in relation to quality are lower.
5. Jot down the price of each item on your list.
6. Ask for help when you need it.
7. The best bargains are the foods that are plentiful in the market.
8. Store brands are likely to be a better buy than manufacturer brands.
9. Buy according to use. (In canned goods, half peaches for an attractive salad; sliced peaches for other purposes.)
10. Look for the U.S. Department of Agriculture grade stamp on fresh meat.
11. Read all labels.
12. Check the checker. (They do make mistakes.)
13. Pay cash.

Kinds of Food Stores. [3] Judging from the many types of food stores—supermarkets (doing an annual sale of over $1 million), discount stores, superettes,

---

[3] Based on "Food Retailing by Discount Houses," *Marketing Research Report* no. 785, Economic Research Service, U.S. Department of Agriculture, 1967.

gourmet shops, grocery stores, meat markets, fish stores, convenience stores, cooperative stores—the consumer food market is a many-segmented market. Moreover, consumers patronize a specific store or stores for many reasons, such as price, convenience, variety, and assortment of merchandise. The initial merchandising appeal of the depression-born supermarket was price. However, the supermarket has matured as a retailing institution, and price, though still most important, has become only one of its many appeals.

The number of small food stores has been decreasing in the last 15 years, and the number of supermarkets has been increasing. In 1965, supermarkets did about 60 percent of all the retail food business in the United States. Almost all of the food supermarkets are classified as national chains, independent chains and discount chains. Food cooperatives, though important in a few communities, have less than 1 percent of the retail food business. The most rapidly growing supermarkets in terms of retail food sales are associated with discount houses. The combined sales of food via discount stores was almost 11 percent of 1965 retail food sales.

Lowest Prices.   Most consumers are still price conscious when buying food. Most food is purchased in three kinds of supermarkets. These supermarkets— national chains like A & P, Safeway, and Kroger; independent chains (voluntary associations) like IGA, Red & White, and Clover Farm; and discount stores like Gem, Two Guys, and Gibson's—are available to most families in urban and suburban communities. Which of these kinds of stores have lower prices on identical foods? How can one kind of supermarket have lower prices than the others? The Economic Research Service of the U.S. Department of Agriculture studied supermarket chain, independent, and discount stores in metropolitan areas from Philadelphia to Los Angeles, and from Minneapolis to Dallas. The findings of this study were:

1.   Discount food stores carried a smaller variety of merchandise than the national chains and the independent chains, but they sold identical food at lower prices and with lower margins than stores of the national chains and the independent chains.
2.   The discounters' average weekly sales were a third larger than those of stores of the national food chains, and 88 percent larger than those of the independent food supermarkets studied.
3.   The discounters sold more units per dollar of sales than the national chains and the independent chains because their margins of profit were lower.
4.   The discounters' wage rates were not significantly lower than those of the other stores studied, but the discount supermarkets' labor costs as a percentage of sales were significantly lower. This was the result of greater labor productivity linked with more effective employee scheduling and use of labor.

The chief advantages that discounting has over conventional food retailing, as seen by the discount store managers, are directly related to costs:

Selling at lower prices
Lower overhead

No food stamps
Larger sales volume
Offering one-stop shopping
Lower labor costs
Carrying a smaller variety of merchandise

National chain store and independent chain store officials say that they take one or more of the following actions to meet this competition:

Reduce prices.
Increase promotional activity.
Increase advertising.
Stress personal service.
Introduce trading stamps.

Most of the chain stores and independent chain operators try to reduce prices.

Food Discounting and the Future. One indication of how the trade views discounting can be obtained from members of Super Market Institute (SMI). The institute reports that one-fourth of all new supermarkets planned by SMI members for 1966 were to be discount stores.[4] Slightly more than half of these would be component parts of a discount house; the balance would be a separate food supermarket. These plans indicate confidence in discounting's future.

All indications, according to the *Economic Research Service Report* of the U.S. Department of Agriculture, point to the continued growth of food discounting. Expansion into food discounting by conventional food retailers has been inhibited by their already large investment in conventional food facilities and their desire to maximize returns from them. The rapid growth of discount food supermarkets indicates that conventional food retailers are likely to accelerate their entry into discount food retailing with a faster overall rate of growth for the discount food industry as a result.

FOOD STANDARDS

Thirty years ago the typical American food store stocked only 700 different food items. Today, the typical supermarket offers between 6,000 and 8,000 different food items. And about 85 percent of all food sold in food stores is prepackaged. This means that the consumer must rely on food standards and on important information on the label. The processing and labeling of these foods are subject to federal, state, and local regulations. To make the best use of the information on packaged foods, you need to understand food laws, standards, and labels.

[4] *The Super Market Industry Speaks, 1966*, Super Market Institute, 1966, p. 19.

The food label on a package or can tells the kind of food, its type and quality, all ingredients, added nutrients and seasonings, and often suggestions for use. By studying and comparing these labels, you can select the brand and type that is best for a certain use, with the seasonings your family prefers. Thoughtful selection will give you the best return for your money.

Three kinds of food standards have been established: (1) standards of identity, (2) standards of quality, and (3) standards of fill of container. Specifically exempted by Congress are most fresh and dried fruits and vegetables.

Standards of Identity

Standards of identity define what the product is. Under federal regulations, processed foods containing two or more ingredients must either meet the established "standard of identity" or list the ingredients in order of predominance. These standards are not fully revealing, even with familiar products like cheese, fruit preserves, and salad dressing. Who remembers that Cheddar cheese must have 50 percent milk fat and not more than 39 percent water (moisture)? That breaded shrimp means 50 percent shrimp, that lightly breaded shrimp means 65 percent shrimp? That chili con carne is 40 percent meat but chili con carne with beans is only 25 percent meat? That vegetables and beef are 35 percent beef but vegetables with beef only 20 percent beef? Where water is listed as the second ingredient in franks or bologna, you never know how much water is included. If this information were given on the label, we would have some basis for knowing what we are getting for our money. In other words, standards of identity are far too minimum. The public, apparently, was not adequately represented when standards of identity were created. Most of the federal standards of identity were established by the U.S. Food and Drug Administration after consultation with interested industry and private groups. Poultry standards of identity, likewise, were established by the U.S. Department of Agriculture after consultation with interested industry. There is, no doubt, tremendous pressure on the U.S. Department of Agriculture and the Food and Drug Administration by industry in the formulation of standards for food sold at the retail level. Present requirements for standards of identity are no longer adequate today because of the increase in variations of food and inadequate information on the labels.

Standards of Quality

Standards of quality have been established for a number of leading varieties of canned fruits and vegetables. These are minimum standards for such qualities as tenderness, color, and freedom from defects. They do not provide a basis for comparing foods as grades do, but they fix minimums. Canned foods that fall below standard in appearance must be labeled "Substandard" or

"Below Standard in Quality," or "Good Food—Not High Grade" with the reason—"excess peeling" or "excessively broken."

Unfortunately for the consumer who wants to cut food expenses, such products seldom appear in retail stores. "Below Standard" foods are wholesome and entirely satisfactory. Where only appearance and texture of the food are lost, there is no loss in nutritional value.

Minimum quality standards are a step in the right direction. The next step should be "U.S. grades" as recommended by the National Commission on Food Marketing.

Standards of Fill of Container

These standards apply chiefly to canned fruits and vegetables, tomato products, and shellfish. They were set up to prevent deception of consumers. Packers must adhere to regulations on how full containers must be to avoid prosecution for "slack filling." Similar standards have been set up informally for many other foods, such as olives, pickles, and spices. Cheating of the consumer still exists, but it is not as common as it used to be.

Standards for Enriched Products and Dietary Regulations

Usually, food standards are thought of as devices for protecting the consumer's pocketbook—for example, the fact, mentioned above, that Cheddar cheese must contain at least 50 percent milk fat (moisture-free) and not over 39 percent moisture. But these standards also ensure that a food has the required nutritional value, as in enriched flour, cornmeal, farina, macaroni products, oleomargarine, evaporated milk, and rice. However, the purpose of the standard originally was to promote "honesty and fair dealing" among processors.

The law guarantees uniformity of enrichment as well as a substantial amount of enrichment. A regulatory action by the FDA is in order if the "enriched" flour or meal does not contain the specified proportions of thiamine, riboflavin, niacin, and iron or if margarine does not contain the required amount of vitamin A.

Regulations have also been established by the FDA regarding foods for special diets. Such foods include low-calorie and low-sodium products, foods designed for infant feeding or for persons with an allergy, and foods to be used for their mineral and vitamin content.

Families who follow Jewish dietary laws can look for authorized symbols on the labels of processed foods. These symbols indicate that the products have been certified as kosher. About 1,000 foods have been identified as kosher by the use of the letter "K" or "U" of the Union of Orthodox Jewish Congregations.

In addition to the services of the FDA, which sets the rules for labeling foods, drugs, and cosmetics that move interstate, the Meat Inspection Division of the U.S. Department of Agriculture has authority to require that all meat and meat food products intended for interstate commerce be approved before they are sold to consumers. Likewise, the Poultry Division of the Agricultural Marketing Service requires fresh and frozen ready-to-cook poultry and canned poultry and frozen poultry products to be inspected and marked correctly. Standards for certain prepared fish products, including fish sticks and ready-to-cook shrimp, are established by the Bureau of Commercial Fisheries of the Department of the Interior.

Label Reading Is Important

It pays to develop skill in label reading. The brand name is not enough. Learn to compare ingredients, amounts, and costs of various products. Choose the ones best suited to your family needs and your food dollars.

Label reading in the supermarket is difficult. It is better to practice in the kitchen with packages and cans already purchased. You may be surprised to note that of three brands of chicken pie, one brand has five vegetables, another has three, and a third has only one vegetable. One brand of oyster stew may use skim milk, whereas another brand may use whole milk. At any rate, develop the habit and the skill to read the labels. There is a difference in foods as a general rule.

The Need for Quality Standards

The basic role of standards is simply to supply a common language understood and respected by both seller and buyer. Standards function as the language of careful description in the production and exchange of goods in somewhat the same way that mathematics is the language of the sciences. It is unfortunate that when it comes to most consumer goods, foods included, we have few standards available to the ultimate consumer. We seem to be caught up in a social time lag.

Standards of identity are limited only to "minimum quality," as we learned earlier. The next step is to take minimum standards the rest of the way and establish additional grades of quality. With some education on the meaning of grades, it would seem that all our needs would be met by grade labeling. All the products of the same grade would have virtually the same quality, and our purchase could then be made on the basis of style, cost, availability, brand name even, and other factors easy to determine.

A recent law requires the federal government to set quality grades for automobile tires, an exciting development we are watching with interest. During World War II, when food was scarce, the federal government established quality grade standards for food at the consumer level. If quality grade standards were useful then, why not now? Our neighbor to the north, Canada, has for several years required quality grades on food. Many other countries have quality grades placed on the label of the food product.

In our country, there are now standardized and recognized quality grades in use. Private-branders often specify them to suppliers. But these quality grades rarely get on the labels of foods. In 1966, the National Commission on Food Marketing, established by Congress, recommended wider use of grade labeling. Thus far, Congress has not heeded the recommendation of that commission, nor has private industry.

Grade Labeling versus Descriptive Labeling. Standardized descriptive labeling, endorsed by the National Canners Association, is not a complete alternative to grade labeling. Both kinds of labeling can be used on the same food label. This is evident from the practice of private brand-grade labeling by the canning industry, which has opposed A, B, C grade labeling. Dr. Richard L. D. Morse, an authority on grade labeling, favors A, B, C or 1, 2, 3 grade terms on labels for products in which an ordinal or successive arrangement of product quality is possible.[5] Morse is of the opinion that consumer grades are of primary concern to those who wish to improve the efficiency of the marketing system and to improve the effectiveness of the price mechanism for communicating consumer preferences to producers of products. Grading can also assist consumers in buying more intelligently in the marketplace.

HOW TO BUY MEAT

Meat is the largest single item in your food budget, usually taking 25 to 30 percent of the family food dollar. At times you have to defend your food dollar by looking for better values in meats and by relying on other animal protein foods, such as cheese, milk, eggs, poultry, and fish. It is wise to use these high-protein foods to stretch the food dollar rather than starchy extenders, such as bread, potatoes, and cereals, which do not provide the complete proteins you get from animal foods.

Meat, dairy, and poultry products are the only sources of proteins containing the amino acids that are essential in the diet. In terms of protein count, for example, bacon is usually about 50 percent more expensive than rib roast. Cheddar cheese is one of the lowest-priced protein-yielding foods on the market, while bacon is one of the more expensive protein foods.

Thrifty Use of Larger Cuts

A larger cut of meat is frequently an economy. But the larger cut does not have to be cooked all in one piece. One pot roast, for example, with a little help from the meat man, can be easily divided at home into cuts for beef stew, Swiss

[5] Unpublished paper on "Need for Consumer Grades," presented at the National Marketing Service Workshop in Louisville, Nov. 11, 1964.

HOW TO GET THREE FRESH-COOKED MEALS FROM ONE POT ROAST

1. Beef Stew

2. Pot Roast

3. Swiss Steak

With a simple bit of meat cutting in your kitchen you can get three different meals from a thick round-bone pot roast like this.

From the round end of the roast, cut a piece to use for meal number one. Cut this boneless meat into cubes for a beef and vegetable stew.

Cut a piece from the center for a chunky pot roast. It will be thick, for best results in cooking and easy carving, too.

With a sharp knife and a saucer under your hand for safety, you can easily split the remaining piece to make two attractive Swiss steaks.

HOW TO MAKE FOUR FRESH-COOKED MEALS FROM HALF A HAM

1. "Boiled" Dinner

2. Baked Ham

3. Fried Ham Slices

When ham is on your shopping list, it's a real economy for the average size family to get a full-cut shank half, large enough to make four meals as shown here.

Have your meat-man saw off a generous shank end for lots of flavor in a "boiled" dinner. Simmer it with carrots, onions, potatoes and wedges of cabbage.

You can easily divide the center part of the ham half into two portions as shown here. Bake the piece with the bone. The slices will be small, but no less delicious.

The remaining piece is easily sliced with a knife. Cut fairly thick slices from the larger end to fry or broil.

4. Ham and Scalloped Potatoes

Cut the smaller end into thinner slices. Use them in alternating layers with sliced potatoes to make a dish of scalloped ham and potatoes.

HOW TO MAKE THREE FRESH-COOKED MEALS FROM ONE PORK BUTT

1. Pork Roast

2. Pork Steaks

3. Chop Suey

It's a real economy purchase to get a whole fresh pork shoulder butt (5 to 7 pounds) and cut it at home as shown.

A pork shoulder butt has only one bone. It extends only part way through the piece. Cut with a sharp knife, as shown in the diagram, to divide easily into two pieces. The piece with the bone is your smaller, one-meal roast.

The remaining piece is clear, solid meat. From it you can cut boneless steaks about one-half inch thick. Braise the pork steaks just as you would pork chops. Make a panful of gravy with the drippings.

As you get to the small end of the boneless piece, cut the remaining meat into small half-inch cubes. Use the diced pork for a meat stretching dish of chop suey or, if you prefer, a casserole of corn and pork.

Figure 8-1   Thrifty Use of Larger Cuts.

HOW TO GET STEAKS, A ROAST, A STEW FROM ONE LEG OF LAMB

For three freshly cooked meals, buy a full-cut leg of lamb. Ask your meatman to cut off a few lamb steaks and to cut through the shank, leaving about a pound of meat on the bone.

1. Lamb Steaks to Broil

Broil the lamb steaks just as you would loin chops. Serve sizzling hot with broiled pineapple slices.

2. Lamb Roast

Here's your Sunday roast—just the easy-to-carve center portion of the leg. Make a panful of gravy and serve with potatoes and peas.

Remember, you'll get more juicy slices and less cooking shrinkage if you roast lamb at a low oven temperature (no higher than 325°F.).

3. Stew or Casserole

Later in the week, cut the meat from the shank into cubes for another freshly cooked meal. Use these tender, boneless cubes of lamb in an Irish stew—or a more glamorous dish such as lamb curry or shish kebob (marinated pieces of lamb grilled on skewers along with green pepper, onions, and tomatoes).

HOW TO GET THREE FRESH-COOKED MEALS FROM A PORK LOIN ROAST

To use this method for getting three very different meals—all fresh-cooked—select the more economical rib cut of pork loin. The larger your family, the larger the cut you will need.

1. Meaty Barbecued Backbones

Have your meatman saw through the ribs high enough to leave an inch-thick layer of meat on the backbones. Ask him to chop these "country style" backbones into serving-sized pieces. Cook as you would spareribs.

2. Pork Chops and Gravy

Later, cut enough chops for another meal from the remaining piece by slicing between the ribs. You'll find that this is now easy to do because the backbone has been removed.

3. Easy-to-serve Pork Roast

You still have a piece left to cook as a pork roast for your third fresh-cooked meal. Be sure to cook pork thoroughly. Use an oven temperature of 325-350° F. and roast about 40 minutes to the pound.

HOW TO MAKE A RIB ROAST DO DOUBLE DUTY

Here's a thrifty trick that lets you get not only a fine party dinner from that handsome beef rib roast but also another fresh-cooked meal of braised short ribs. And you can depend on it, that man in your life goes for short ribs.

1. Braised Short Ribs

Here's what you do. Have your meatman saw through the bones at A and B as in the picture. You can then cut between the ribs to make individual servings of short ribs. Braise them slowly with vegetables to stretch their good meat flavor further in the meal.

2. Juicy Roast Beef

Now, for your roast, you have just the tenderest "heart" of the piece you bought. To make it juicier—and to get more servings from it, too—keep oven heat at 325° F. to cut shrinkage to a minimum. One hour before done, put peeled potatoes in the pan to brown in the drippings.

steak, and pot roast. Likewise ham, pork butt, leg of lamb, pork loin, and rib roast can be divided for different purposes. Figure 8-1, Thrifty Use of Larger Cuts, shows how larger cuts may be divided for cooking and serving as different meat dishes.

An expensive American habit is the preference for only six to eight cuts of meat from each carcass. From each 1,000-pound steer, for example, about 465 pounds reach the retail counter. Only about 75 of the 465 pounds constitute the most purchased, expensive cuts: porterhouse, T-bone, club, and sirloin steaks. Another 45 pounds comprise the popular rib roasts. This leaves 345 pounds of less expensive cuts: round, chuck, blade, rump, hamburger, and stewing meats. These are lower priced but make tasty and nutritious meat dishes. Add to this the nutritious and usually lower-priced variety meats: heart, kidney, liver, tongue, tripe, and oxtail.

Meat Tips

Price variations from month to month and season to season also represent possible savings. Round steak, pork chops, bacon, and eggs usually show more than a 10 percent change in monthly price averages during the year and should be used often during periods of low prices. Rib roast, whole ham, fryers, and chuck roast show a monthly price range from 5 to 10 percent. Frankfurters, cheese, and hamburger vary slightly in price during the year. In general, beef bargains in September and low-cost pork in December save money for the consumer. Watch for the weekly or monthly reports on meat prices in the food section of your daily newspaper.

Here are tips worth remembering when buying meat.

1. Get on buying terms with the many cheaper cuts of beef, pork, veal, and lamb.
2. Price has nothing to do with the nutritive value of meat. The lower-priced cuts are usually as tasty and rich in vitamins, protein, and other nutrients as the higher-priced cuts.
3. Buy grades and cuts of meat according to intended use.
4. Look for the largest amount of lean meat for your price. Fat and bone are useful, but they can be purchased at a lower price.
5. Buy United States-inspected and graded meats for health and economical reasons, because the grades and inspection marks provide information to assist in selecting cuts for wholesomeness and quality.
6. Buy the cheaper varieties of liver, kidney, and heart.
7. Purchase canned meat for variety. Canned meat packed with vegetables is not an economical buy.
8. The lean meat from cheaper cuts of meat from the same carcass is just as nutritive as the lean meat from the expensive cuts. The higher price paid is for tenderness.
9. Meats showing streaks of fat are more flavorful because fat helps to distribute flavor.
10. The percentage of waste, when figuring the cost of lean meat, varies from nothing in flank steak and tenderloin to about 11 percent in porterhouse, 16 percent in sirloin, 20 percent in chuck, and about 27 percent in rump with the bone left in.
11. Improper cooking of meat can offset gains in wise planning and shopping.

12.   Buy roasts large enough to serve for two meals. Small roasts dry out in cooking and do not carve well.

13.   The price of meat is generally lowest when the supply is largest.

14.   For hamburger, meat loaf, and stews, Standard or Commercial beef may be just as satisfactory as Choice or Good and is usually more economical.

Cost of Cooked Lean Meat

The principal considerations in finding good meat buys are the yield of cooked lean meat and the price per pound. Thus, you need to compare the cost of equal amounts of cooked lean meat from the various cuts and types of meat available. Table 8-2 shows the approximate cost of 3-ounce servings of cooked lean meat from selected kinds and cuts of meat at various retail prices per pound. Locate in the table the kind and cut you plan to buy, then follow the line on which it appears to the column headed by the price nearest the current price at your markets. The figure at this point is the approximate cost of a 3-ounce serving of cooked lean meat. For a 3-ounce serving of lean meat from a chuck roast—bone in—priced at 50 cents a pound, the cost would be 22 cents, and from ground beef at 55 cents a pound, the cost would be 14 cents.

Variety Meats

It is wise to include variety meats—glands and organs—in the weekly menu because they supply excellent nutrients and, comparatively speaking, are lower priced.

Calf liver is preferred by most families, and therefore costs more than other kinds of liver. Pork liver is richer in iron and as rich in vitamin D as calf liver and beef liver.

Usually, lamb kidneys are the highest in price, then come veal kidneys, with beef and pork kidneys usually the lowest in price.

Brains are very low in price, comparatively. They are sold whole by the pound and sometimes by the pair. Brains should be firm.

Beef, veal, lamb, and pork hearts should be firm and full, with fat surrounding the muscles. Beef heart is the largest, but is less tender than the others.

Beef tongue is generally less expensive than the smaller veal, lamb, and pork tongues.

Sweetbreads are the thymus glands of the calf or lamb. These are often purchased by the pair. The part near the heart is preferred.

U.S. GOVERNMENT INSPECTION AND GRADING OF MEAT

Consumers Are Confused

In 1967 the U.S. Department of Agriculture and the National Livestock and Meat Board made a joint study of what consumers knew about inspection and

TABLE 8-2   COST OF A 3-OUNCE SERVING OF COOKED LEAN MEAT FROM SELECTED KINDS AND CUTS OF MEAT AT SPECIFIED RETAIL PRICES*

KIND AND CUT OF MEAT	PRICE PER POUND OF RETAIL CUTS (CENTS)											
	30	35	40	45	50	55	60	65	70	75	80	85
Beef												
Roasts:												
Brisket, bone in	16	18	21	23	26	29	31	34	36	39	42	44
Chuck, bone in	13	16	18	20	22	25	27	29	31	33	36	38
Chuck, bone out	10	12	14	16	17	19	21	23	24	26	28	30
Ribs—7th, bone in	13	16	18	20	22	25	27	29	31	33	36	38
Round, bone in	10	12	13	15	17	18	20	22	23	25	27	28
Round, bone out	9	11	12	14	16	17	19	20	22	23	25	27
Rump, bone in	13	15	17	20	22	24	26	28	31	33	35	37
Rump, bone out	10	12	14	15	17	19	20	22	24	26	27	29
Steaks:												
Chuck, bone in	13	16	18	20	22	25	27	29	31	33	36	38
Chuck, bone out	10	12	14	16	17	19	21	23	24	26	28	30
Club, bone in	17	20	23	26	28	31	34	37	40	43	45	48
Porterhouse, bone in	16	18	21	23	26	29	31	34	36	39	42	44
Round, bone in	10	12	13	15	17	18	20	22	23	25	27	28
Round, bone out	9	11	12	14	16	17	19	20	22	23	25	27
Sirloin, bone in	13	15	17	19	21	23	26	28	30	32	34	36
Sirloin, bone out	12	14	16	18	20	21	23	25	27	29	31	33
T-bone, bone in	17	19	22	25	28	30	33	36	39	41	44	47
Ground beef	8	9	10	12	13	14	16	17	18	20	21	22
Shortribs	18	20	23	26	29	32	35	38	41	44	47	50
Pork, fresh												
Roasts:												
Loin, bone in	15	18	20	23	25	28	30	33	36	38	41	43
Loin, bone out	10	12	14	16	17	19	21	23	24	26	28	30
Picnic, bone in	16	19	21	24	27	29	32	35	37	40	43	45
Chops:												
Loin	13	16	18	20	22	25	27	29	31	33	36	38
Rib	15	18	20	23	25	28	30	33	36	38	41	43
Pork, Cured												
Roasts:												
Butt, bone in	11	13	14	16	18	20	22	23	25	27	29	31
Ham, bone in	10	12	14	16	17	19	21	23	24	26	28	30
Ham, bone out	8	9	10	12	13	14	16	17	18	20	21	22
Picnic, bone in	14	16	18	21	23	25	27	30	32	34	37	39
Picnic, bone out	11	12	14	16	18	19	21	23	25	27	28	30
Ham slices	9	11	12	14	16	17	19	20	22	23	25	27
Lamb												
Roasts:												
Leg, bone in	12	15	17	19	21	23	25	27	29	31	33	35
Shoulder, bone in	14	16	18	21	23	25	27	30	32	34	37	39
Chops:												
Loin	14	16	18	21	23	25	27	30	32	34	37	39
Rib	17	19	22	25	28	30	33	36	39	41	44	47

*Yield data from U.S. Dept. Agr., HERR no. 31, *Proximate Composition of Beef . . .*, and U.S. Dept. Agr., AH no. 284, *Purchasing Guide.*

PRICE PER POUND OF RETAIL CUTS (CENTS)

90	95	100	105	110	115	120	125	130	135	140	145	150	155	160	165	170
47	49	52	55	57	60	62	65	68	70	73	76	78	81	83	86	89
40	42	45	47	49	51	54	56	58	60	62	65	67	69	71	74	76
31	33	35	36	38	40	42	43	45	47	49	50	52	54	56	57	59
40	42	45	47	49	51	54	56	58	60	62	65	67	69	71	74	76
30	32	33	35	37	38	40	42	43	45	47	48	50	52	54	55	57
28	30	31	33	34	36	38	39	41	42	44	45	47	48	50	52	53
39	41	44	46	48	50	52	55	57	59	61	63	66	68	70	72	74
31	32	34	36	38	39	41	43	44	46	48	49	51	53	55	56	58
40	42	45	47	49	51	54	56	58	60	62	65	67	69	71	74	76
31	33	35	36	38	40	42	43	45	47	49	50	52	54	56	57	59
51	54	57	60	62	65	68	71	74	77	80	82	85	88	91	94	97
47	49	52	55	57	60	62	65	68	70	73	76	78	81	83	86	89
30	32	33	35	37	38	40	42	43	45	47	48	50	52	54	55	57
28	30	31	33	34	36	38	39	41	42	44	45	47	48	50	52	53
38	40	43	45	47	49	51	53	55	57	60	62	64	66	68	70	72
35	37	39	41	43	45	47	49	51	53	55	57	59	61	62	64	66
50	52	55	58	61	64	66	69	72	75	77	80	83	86	88	91	94
23	25	26	27	29	30	31	33	34	35	36	38	39	40	42	43	44
53	56	58	61	64	67	70	73	76	79	82	85	88	91	94	96	99
46	48	51	53	56	58	61	63	66	69	71	74	76	79	81	84	86
31	33	35	36	38	40	42	43	45	47	49	50	52	54	56	57	59
48	51	53	56	59	62	64	67	70	72	75	78	80	83	86	88	91
40	42	45	47	49	51	54	56	58	60	62	65	67	69	71	74	76
46	48	51	53	56	58	61	63	66	69	71	74	76	79	81	84	86
32	34	36	38	40	42	43	45	47	49	51	52	54	56	58	60	61
31	33	35	36	38	40	42	43	45	47	49	50	52	54	56	57	59
23	25	26	27	29	30	31	33	34	35	36	38	39	40	42	43	44
41	43	46	48	50	53	55	57	59	62	64	66	68	71	73	75	78
32	34	35	37	39	41	42	44	46	48	49	51	53	55	57	58	60
28	30	31	33	34	36	38	39	41	42	44	45	47	48	50	52	53
38	40	42	44	46	48	50	52	54	56	58	60	62	65	67	69	71
41	43	46	48	50	53	55	57	59	62	64	66	68	71	73	75	78
41	43	46	48	50	53	55	57	59	62	64	66	68	71	73	75	78
50	52	55	58	61	64	66	69	72	75	77	80	83	86	88	91	94

grading of meat. The study revealed that 73 percent of homemakers correctly related inspection to wholesomeness, but 45 percent incorrectly related it with quality or grading, and 2 percent did not know.

Most of the homemakers (70 percent) correctly related grading to quality, but some of these (43 percent) also incorrectly related grading to wholesomeness or price. Twelve percent of the homemakers incorrectly related grading to inspection, and another 6 percent just did not know.

Fifty percent of the homemakers stated incorrectly that pork was graded, 44 percent did not know, and only 6 percent stated correctly that pork is not graded. All pork cuts are tender, and grades are therefore not necessary.

There was, also, confusion about names used to designate USDA grades of beef. Only about 21 percent could identify grades of beef (Prime, Choice, Good, Standard, and Commercial).

The data indicate that many homemakers are confused about meat inspection and grading.

United States Inspection and Grades

All meat shipped interstate has a federal government inspection stamp on it, a purple circle. This is important because it means that the animal was healthy when slaughtered. The U.S. Department of Agriculture has also established grades for the quality of meat in beef, veal, lamb, and mutton. Pork is usually not graded because all the cuts are tender. Grades are not measures of nutritive value or wholesomeness.

The beef grades used are:

U.S. Choice (highest retail grade)
U.S. Good
U.S. Standard (from younger beef)
U.S. Commercial (from mature beef)
U.S. Utility
U.S. Cutter (used in processed meats)
U.S. Canner (used in processed meats)

The grades for veal, lamb, and mutton are:

U.S. Choice
U.S. Good
U.S. Commercial
U.S. Utility
U.S. Cull

The U.S. Department of Agriculture amended the Federal Meat Inspection Regulations in 1962 to require that certain essential information for consum-

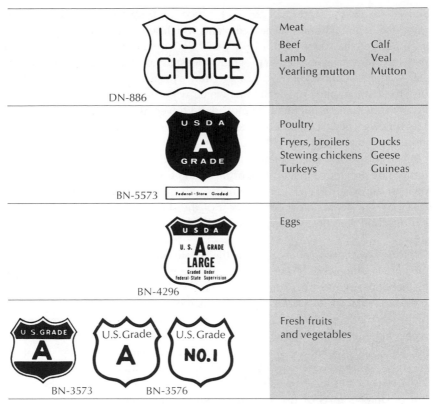

Figure 8-2   USDA Grade Marks and the Foods on Which They Are Used. The grade names on the various grade marks shown here are merely illustrative. There is a range of grades for each of these products, but different grade names are used. For a list of grades, see "Grade Names Used in U.S. Standards for Farm Products" (AH-157) and "Shopper's Guide to U.S. Grades for Food" (HG-58). Source: U.S. Department of Agriculture.

ers remain intact on the labels of federally inspected meat and meat food products. The amendment applies to such products after they leave the packing or processing plant and are available to buyers at the point of sale.

Although this label requirement has long been a part of the Meat Inspection Act, the Federal Meat Inspection Regulations had not pinpointed the requirement as it applies to a product *after* it leaves the packing establishment. The amendment to the regulations did this. (The regulations serve as a detailed guide for processors and inspectors.)

It is also illegal to remove, mask, or tamper with a label so that the information is concealed or the product misrepresented. Allowance is made for unavoidable damage to marks or labeling in the normal cutting, slicing, or other handling of a product.

The Wholesome Meat Act of 1967. The Wholesome Meat Act of 1967 will ultimately assure consumers that meat is always federally or state inspected.

Under this law, the states will conduct inspection programs for meat products processed in non-federally inspected plants which sell meat within state boundaries. Each of the states has up to 2 years, or 3 if significant progress is being made, to develop an inspection program at least as good as the federal program. USDA officials conduct a review of the state's inspection organizational structure, the number and types of plants which will come under state inspection, the personnel and equipment employed, and even the personnel policies the state follows. The USDA will also check such things as the water disposal system and the sanitation of the plant equipment.

When this review is completed, a report is made indicating any deficiencies in the state program. Finally, state officials and USDA sign a cooperative agreement to establish financial arrangements and other necessary provisions. The USDA pays up to 50 percent of the cost of the state's inspection program.

If the state does not do the job, the federal government is authorized to take over.

A little-noted "sleeper" section in the wholesome meat law may prove significant. It empowers USDA to write standards and regulations concerning the handling of meat and meat products as they move from packinghouse to the supermarket check-out counter. This means that the USDA can set minimum standards of refrigeration, temperature maintenance for frozen meats, honest labeling, nomenclature for meat cuts, and shelf life in the store, and that the standards can be written into law. Enforcement, however, is left to the states—with standby powers for the USDA if any state is lax.

The USDA can thus establish a frozen-meat handling code—something Consumers Union's tests of frozen meat products have repeatedly demonstrated to be badly needed to prevent quality deterioration.[6]

Enforcement Problems.   Like most new laws, the Wholesome Meat Act depends for effectiveness on the spirit and vigor of its enforcement. The USDA inspectors seem generally to do a good job of enforcement. But the consumer has sometimes been hurt in the writing of the rules. The classic example was the watered-ham case. The USDA yielded gradually to big-packer pressures to change its regulations against adding water to cook-before-eating types of ham. First, it granted packers permission to use pickling chemicals that help ham to absorb water. Then it permitted hams with water added to be sold under the label "imitation" ham. Finally, in 1960, it permitted the addition of up to 16 percent water in ham without a label addition.

When a public furor developed, the USDA tried to close the floodgates by reinstating its rule that watered ham must be labeled "imitation." The courts overruled the USDA. Today, however, according to the USDA, products labeled as "Ham, Water Added" may contain up to 10 percent added water, while those labeled "Imitation Ham" contain over 10 percent water.[7] Unfor-

[6] See "Frozen Dinners," *Consumer Reports,* October, 1967.

[7] *Agriculture Marketing,* March, 1966.

tunately, the public is unaware of the maximum water permitted to be injected into ham because this information is not required to be on the label.

Comparative Costs of Canned and Fresh Meats

All canning of meat for retail selling is federally inspected. The costs of canned and fresh meat may be compared by keeping in mind that 12 ounces of canned meat equals 15 to 18 ounces of raw boneless meat.

Not all canned meats are better buys than fresh meats. Some are in the luxury class. Those that usually offer good comparative value over fresh meats include canned corned beef, canned hamburgers and beef without gravy, canned luncheon meats, and canned lamb and pork tongue.

Comparisons are based on the cost of meat per pound, taking comparative quality and estimating waste of trimmings and shrinkage of fresh meats during cooking. Some experts estimate that trimmings account for 6 percent of an average roast; shrinking accounts for 19 percent more; and in serving, the bones and fat account for 32 percent more waste.

Imported Canned Meats

Before any country can ship meat products to the United States, its meat inspection system must be approved by USDA as being comparable to that required in this country. Veterinarians from USDA regularly check the foreign government's system and exporting plants. When a shipment of meat products leaves a country destined for the United States, a veterinary official of that country's meat inspection system signs an official meat inspection certificate. At the port of entry here, USDA inspectors recheck each shipment for wholesomeness.

Canned meat must meet strict tolerances for net weight and description on the label. Samples are tested in the USDA laboratories. In 1966, 3.4 million pounds of foreign canned meat products were refused entry.

Prepackaged Meat

In most food stores, retail meats are offered in prepackaged form on a self-service basis. They include a variety of fresh cuts, cold cuts, variety meats, frozen meats, smoked and cooked sausage products, and other cuts. The meats are wrapped and sealed in transparent film and displayed in self-service refrigerated cases.

The labels on fresh meat packaged in plants under United States inspection must meet requirements of federal inspection. The label should show the name of the cut, price per pound, total weight, and cost of the package of meat.

A survey showed that discoloration is the retailer's major problem with some fresh cuts of meat. Rewrapping packages, especially roasts and steaks, is some-times necessary because of handling by customers. Prepackaged meat either must be trimmed to remove much of the surplus fat and bone, or it must have most of the fat and bone clearly visible. The quality throughout the package should be as high as that of the meat that can be seen.

The Fair Packaging and Labeling Act of 1967 specifically exempts packaging of fresh meat. The USDA continues to have jurisdiction over meat products. According to the USDA, their meat inspectors are required to examine pack-aging to make sure it will prevent contamination. And the weight of the product is verified. The USDA regulations state that transparent packaging of meat and poultry products should not be of such a color or design as to be misleading or deceptive. For instance, red lines would not be permitted on cellophane covering bacon or pork sausage, to avoid giving a false impression of leanness.

"Angry Complaints." There are weaknesses in the administration of the prepackaged meat program. The President's consumer adviser, Mrs. Esther Peterson, told the American Meat Institute in 1964 that she had received "angry complaints" by housewives in regard to packaged meat confusion. In 1964, only 20 states had adopted the policy of putting the price per pound on pack-aged meat. Today there may have been some progress in putting not only the price per pound but also the net weight and cost of the meat on a particular package. For some reason, the USDA has been negligent in effectively promot-ing this important information on the meat package. The USDA has also neglected to require prepackaged meat to be packaged in transparent pack-aging. The buyer, too often, discovers that fatty and aged sections are not exposed to view. Furthermore, the fat-to-lean ratio is not regulated. Bacon, for example, is usually cooked down to an edible value of 25 percent or less. There is nothing in USDA regulations to prevent water being pumped into bacon before it is cured. Excessive water in bacon, as in ham, is pretty expensive water. Does this mean that USDA does not establish standards that would be useful to con-sumers if industry interest is lacking?

Terms and Grade Labels for Poultry

Poultry is an expensive meat to purchase, as a rule, because there is only a small percentage of meat in a dressed bird. The Department of Agriculture has com-piled the percentage of meat in six kinds of dressed bird. To figure cost per pound, divide the price per pound for a dressed bird by the percentage given here.

	PERCENT		PERCENT
Fattened roasting chickens	63	Unfattened broilers	54
Unfattened roasting chickens	57	Fattened hens	64
Fattened broilers	61	Turkeys	68

| Graded
ready-to-cook | Graded and inspected
ready-to-cook | Inspected for
wholesomeness
ready-to-cook | Graded dressed |

Figure 8-3   Poultry Grade Levels and Inspection Marks. Source: Agricultural Marketing Service, U.S. Department of Agriculture.

If you need only a few pieces of chicken, it may be cheaper to buy just those you want. Breasts from roasters contain about 72 percent edible meat; drumsticks yield about 75 percent. If you want a turkey meal without eating turkey all week, buy turkey cuts.

On January 1, 1950, a revised program of the U.S. Department of Agriculture for the grading and inspection of poultry went into effect. Although a voluntary program, the regulations apply to those members of the poultry industry who request inspection and grading services of the department.

An important part of the program deals with the requirements for the sanitation of dressing plants. Since January 1, 1951, all ready-to-cook poultry prepared in official plants approved by the Department of Agriculture have been processed under the same sanitary standards.

Broiling and frying chickens are now one class and may be termed *broilers* or *fryers*. Stewing chickens may be described as *hens, stewing chickens,* or *fowl*. The term *dressed* is used for birds that have been bled and picked, but not drawn. *Ready-to-cook* describes poultry that has been fully drawn, or eviscerated.

The official grade label, in the form of a shield, states the quality (U.S. Grade A or U.S. Grade B), the style of processing (dressed or ready-to-cook), and the class (stewing chicken). The label also states that the product is government graded.

Ready-to-cook poultry that has been inspected for wholesomeness by a federal veterinarian but not graded for quality carries an inspection mark in the form of a circle. Ready-to-cook poultry that has been both graded and inspected carries a combination label, a shield within a circle.

Inadequate Poultry Labeling.   The USDA declines to require separate weights for the poultry and the stuffing in each package. The stuffing weight often exceeds 25 percent of the total weight of the bird and the stuffing. Is the consumer not entitled to know the true quantity of the product he is buying? The label should show the net weight of the turkey unstuffed and the combined weight of poultry and stuffing.

Present grading standards of USDA consider the birds' conformation, fleshing, fat covering, and defeathering; cuts, tears, and gouges; broken bones and missing parts; discoloration of the skin and flesh; and freezer burns. From these largely visual factors, the birds are graded A, B, or C. Most of these factors merely indicate marketability, not flavor and tenderness. It is true that the label must show young, old, or mature, which are factors in tenderness. But processing techniques also affect tenderness, and judging by Consumers Union test results, there are "clear differences in quality among birds labeled Grade A."

The Wholesome Poultry Products Act of 1968.   This law amends the poultry products inspection law. The amendments provide for extension of federal jurisdiction to state poultry-inspection programs that do not measure up to federal standards within 2 years. The new measure will affect an estimated 1.6 billion pounds of poultry, or about 13 percent of the nation's output. That portion is not federally inspected because it is not shipped across state lines. Congress was told that a spot check of retail markets in 16 states had shown that one out of five chickens not federally inspected was unfit for human consumption, according to Dr. Mehren, Assistant Secretary of Agriculture. Thirty-two states had no poultry inspection in 1968; 11 states had voluntary inspection; and 7 states had some mandatory features in their inspection laws.

In due time, possibly by 1970, most of our poultry products will be inspected by qualified federal or state inspectors. The same standards will be used by federal and state inspectors. If adequate funds are appropriated to implement the new poultry law, we can be assured that the product has been government inspected (is clean, wholesome, and unadulterated) and properly graded.

How Fish Is Marketed

Fish may be purchased fresh, frozen, or canned. It also pays to know the most common ways fish are marketed.

Whole or round. This term refers to fish just as they come from the water. Before cooking, internal organs must be taken out and scales removed. Remove the head, tail, and fins except on some small fish or fish to be baked. For broiling or frying, the fish may need to be split or cut into serving portions.

Drawn. Internal organs are already removed. Prepare for cooking just as whole or round fish.

Dressed or pan dressed. Internal organs and scales are removed. Most dressed fish also have head, tail, and fins removed.

Steaks. These are cross-sectional slices of the larger dressed fish. Steaks are ready to cook as purchased. A cross section of the backbone is usually the only bone in a fish steak.

Fillets. These are meaty sides of the fish, cut lengthwise away from the backbone. Fillets are practically boneless and require no preparation for cooking. Sometimes the skin, with scales removed, is left on one side of the fillet; other fillets are completely skinned.

Sticks. These are pieces of fish cut from blocks of frozen fillets into portions of uniform dimensions, usually about ½ inch wide, 3 inches long, and ⅜ inch deep, weighing approximately 1 ounce.

Whole fish may be cheaper than steaks, fillets, or sticks, but include considerable waste. Steaks have little bone or waste, and fillets and sticks have none at all.

Fish Product Inspection. There is much misunderstanding about fish product inspection. Few people realize that there is no mandatory federal inspection program for fishery products yet. There is a voluntary program run by the Bureau of Commercial Fisheries, but it covers only about 20 percent of all fish products sold. The FDA spot-checks imported products and domestic plants, and the Public Health Service conducts a certification program to ensure cleanliness of shellfish. There is need for required inspection of all fish products.

In 1966 there were more recalls of contaminated fish products than in most recent years. Inspection of smoked fish-processing plants by FDA, for example, showed that all but two were operating under conditions described as dangerously unsanitary. As a result Senator Philip Hart introduced a bill in 1968 to set up broad inspection of fish products, but the bill met so much opposition that it did not get out of committee. And yet, preliminary studies show that the 2,200 fish-processing plants in the United States are inspected "an average of less than once a year," that "virtually no fishing vessels are inspected," and that imported fish, which constitute about 50 percent of the total fish consumption here, enter the country almost entirely uninspected.

MILK AND MILK PRODUCTS

Grades and Kinds of Milk

The U.S. Public Health Service Milk Ordinance standards have been adopted by most American cities. This ordinance provides for three grades of fluid milk.

1. Certified milk: Very rigid sanitary requirements; sold only by licensed dealers; expensive.
2. Grade A, pasteurized: Must not contain more than 30,000 bacteria per cubic centimeter; must have hooded caps; must be kept below 50 degrees at all times.
3. Grade B, pasteurized: May contain as many as 50,000 bacteria per cubic centimeter when delivered to the consumer; need not have hooded caps.
4. Grade C, pasteurized: Is below Grade B requirements.

The ordinance also provides for three grades of raw milk, A, B, and C.

Grade A pasteurized milk is the most common form of milk for table use. Milk delivered to the home costs from 2 to 4 cents a quart more than when purchased at milk stores in gallon and half-gallon quantities.

Homogenized milk is processed so that the fat does not separate and rise to the top of the bottle. It is thought to be more digestible, but authorities are still battling over this assumption. Some pediatricians believe that only in the case of infants is there value in homogenization, since it softens the curd of milk. There are no extra food values in homogenized milk, but the consumer pays 1 to 2 cents a quart more for it, though the process costs are very low.

As yet, science has discovered no milk substitute. It is possible, however, to reduce the cost of milk without decreasing the food value. This can be done by using evaporated milk.

Evaporated milk mixed with an equal volume of water is whole milk slightly above the average for the composition of bottled milk. Some evaporated milk is enriched with vitamin D. One pint of evaporated milk (before water is added) is equal in food value to a quart of fresh milk, at a little more than half the price. A 14½-ounce can of evaporated milk selling for 15 cents is a cheaper source of milk than a quart of whole milk that costs 24 cents.

Many homemakers prefer evaporated milk for cooking, and it is recommended for cream sauces, gravies, cream soup, chowder, scalloped vegetables, custards, puddings, dessert sauces, cakes, cookies, breads, frozen desserts, and candy. Undiluted evaporated milk is used by many families in coffee, candy, and frozen desserts, and as an emulsifier in mayonnaise. When thoroughly chilled, it can be whipped like cream.

Dried milk (powdered milk) is used largely for cooking purposes, in the proportion of ¾ cup of dried milk to 1 quart of water.

Skim milk (nonfat milk) can also be used for cooking purposes. The cost of this product may be from 15 to 19 cents a quart.

Milk Equivalents in the Diet. Here are some substitutes for fresh whole milk in mathematical terms, which will help in calculating food values.

1 quart of skim milk plus 1½ ounces of butter equals 1 quart of fluid milk.
1 pint of undiluted evaporated milk equals 1 quart of fluid milk.
⅓ pound of Cheddar cheese equals 1 quart of fluid milk.
¼ pound of dried whole milk equals 1 quart of fluid milk.

Filled and synthetic milk is available at from 8 cents to 10 cents cheaper than a half-gallon of whole milk at 1969 prices.

Filled milk is a combination of dairy and nondairy products. It is presently made from either skim or nonfat dry milk, but the butterfat has been replaced by less expensive vegetable fat. The true synthetic milks replace both the butterfat and the nonfat milk solids with soybeans or soya protein combined with sodium caseinate, which is derived from real milk.

Filled milk under federal law cannot be shipped from one state to another. Synthetic milk can be if it meets legal labeling standards.

Are these so-called "fake" milks as good as real milk? Some experts say that filled milk is, if vitamin A has been added to it. There is some disagreement about synthetic milk. Apparently, it is not yet nutritionally equivalent to real milk. Some scientists say there is no reason why synthetic milk cannot be as nutritious as real milk.

Ice Cream

Ice cream continues to be one of the best buys. The Consumer Price Index shows that the price of ice cream is just slightly below its cost 10 years ago. All other dairy products increased about 19 percent in price in the last decade.

The standards for ice cream vary from state to state but generally conform to federal regulations. According to federal standards, "ice cream" must have at least 10 percent milk fat and 20 percent milk solids; "ice milk" must have at least 2 percent but not more than 7 percent milk fat, and at least 11 percent milk solids. (Milk solids include proteins, milk sugar, minerals, and vitamins.)

How to Buy Cheese

The most food value for the money is in *American Cheddar cheese*. About 5 quarts of milk are required to make 1 pound. Thus all the proteins, fats, minerals, and vitamins found in whole milk are found in Cheddar cheese.

There are over four hundred varieties of cheese made in this country. The fancy processed cheese is generally Cheddar, processed with inexpensive fillers and water.

Sharp cheese costs more than mild cheese because it is aged.

Cheese is not a complete substitute for meat or eggs because it is low in protein, although high in butterfat.

The federal government has established the following quality grades for American Cheddar cheese, and some manufacturers use them.

	QUALITY SCORE
U.S. Extra Fancy	95 and above
U.S. Fancy	92-94
U.S. No. 1	89-91
U.S. No. 2	86-88
U.S. No. 3	83-85
Culls	Below 83

Cottage cheese is usually the next best buy in food value. It is made from skim milk, and therefore has no butterfat or vitamin A. It cannot replace whole milk in the diet. No U.S. grades have as yet been produced for cottage cheese, but rigid specifications have been set to cover its manufacture and quality. Cottage cheese may carry a shield stating that it is "Quality Approved" by the U.S. Department of Agriculture.

Grades of Butter

Butter is the dairy product most widely sold on the basis of U.S. grades. The letters "U.S." before the grade mark on the carton or wrapper indicate that the butter has been graded by an authorized grader of the U.S. Department of Agriculture.

The letters AA, A, B, or the numerical score, 93, 92, 90, without the prefix "U.S." on the package indicate that the butter has not been certified by a federal butter grader.

Some states have enacted a law requiring that butter be grade labeled, and in these localities the letters or grade names on butter cartons denote state standards, applied by state graders. Such state grades do not carry the prefix "U.S.," but may show the state name or seal.

A grade mark on the package without the prefix "U.S." or state identification reflects the manufacturer's or distributor's own standard of quality. This butter may be of good quality, but since it is not federally graded the consumer must necessarily rely on the distributor's statement that it meets the quality designation on the package.

U.S. grades for butter include U.S. Grade AA (U.S. 93 score), U.S. Grade A (U.S. 92 score), and U.S. Grade B (U.S. 90 score). "Score" refers to the total number of points allotted a sample on the basis of the quality of several factors—chiefly flavor, but also including body, texture, color, and salt.

To be rated U.S. Grade AA, butter must have a fine, highly pleasing aroma and a delicate, sweet taste. Americans like butter, though it is comparatively expensive. It takes from 10½ to 11 quarts of milk to produce 1 pound of butter.

Standards for Margarine

Oleomargarine, or margarine, as it is more generally called, when fortified with vitamin A has as much food value as butter, according to the American Medical Association. In addition, margarine does not become rancid as quickly as butter. Margarine is a genuine food, made from refined food fats, such as cottonseed oil, soybean oil, peanut oil, and meat fats. These oils are blended with pasteurized cultured skim milk and salt for flavor. The retail price of margarine is usually less than half the price for the same weight of 92-score butter.

Many laws, both state and federal, have been passed in the last 50 years to protect the butter interests. Congress finally repealed the 64-year-old antimargarine taxes and license fees and permitted the sale of yellow margarine in interstate commerce on July 1, 1950.

The quality and purity of margarine that enters interstate commerce are guarded by two federal agencies. For instance, margarine that contains animal fats is inspected by the Federal Meat Inspection Service. Margarine that contains only vegetable oils comes under the supervision of the Federal Food, Drug, and Cosmetic Act. Margarine must contain 80 percent fat, which corresponds to the 80 percent fat requirement for butter.

EGGS

Know the Eggs You Buy

The alert consumer always considers value in purchases more than price. When prices are high, it is especially important to know where and how to get the most for your egg money. To get the best buy, know quality or grade, know size or weight, know about shell color, and know their food values.

In many places, eggs are sold by grade, and the quality is stated in terms of grade on the label of the egg carton. An egg in one of the top grades, AA or A, should have a large amount of firm white and a round, upstanding yolk. Eggs of such quality are preferred for poaching, frying, and cooking in the shell.

Grade B eggs, just as satisfactory for scrambling and for baking and cooking, have thinner whites and somewhat flatter yolks. They offer the same food values as the top grades. Grade B eggs may cost as much as 10 or 12 cents a dozen less than Grade A eggs of the same weight.

In terms of value on a scale, the size of eggs means the same as weight. A dozen jumbo eggs weigh not less than 30 ounces. A dozen eggs labeled "Extra Large" must weigh at least 27 ounces, and eggs of the more common size, Large, weigh not less than 24 ounces to the dozen.

Let us stop here a minute: 24 ounces equals 1½ pounds. That is worth remembering when you consider relative prices of eggs, meat, fish, cheese, and other protein foods that are purchased by the pound. It takes only 8 large eggs, two-thirds of a dozen, to make a pound, and they cost two-thirds the price of a dozen. But you buy eggs by the dozen unit, and you get 1½ pounds of a meat-alternate food in 12 large eggs.

If you pay 60 cents for a dozen large eggs (weighing 24 ounces or more), you are actually paying only at the rate of around 40 cents a pound, because the shells, the only waste, weigh very little. This waste is especially small when compared with that of many other protein foods.

Medium eggs run 21 ounces or more per dozen eggs, and small or pullet eggs weigh 18 or more ounces per dozen. The small eggs are seldom on the market except in late summer and fall, when they are usually good buys. Any time of year, it pays to figure the relation between the price of eggs and their weight or size. Table 8-3, Comparative Values in Grade A Eggs Based on Weight, will help you to compare egg-weight values.

Comparing the prices of eggs of the same size (large, for example) but of different qualities (Grades AA, A, B) is also worthwhile. For instance, such a

TABLE 8-3   COMPARATIVE VALUES IN GRADE A EGGS BASED ON WEIGHT

When Large Grade A Eggs, at Least 24 Ounces per Dozen, Cost	Medium-sized Grade A Eggs, at Least 21 Ounces per Dozen, Are as Good a Buy or Better at	And Small Grade A Eggs, at Least 18 Ounces per Dozen, Are as Good a Buy or Better at
$.46 - $.50	$.40 - $.44	$.34 - $.38
.51 - .55	.45 - .48	.39 - .41
.56 - .60	.49 - .52	.42 - .45
.61 - .65	.53 - .57	.46 - .49
.66 - .70	.58 - .61	.50 - .52
.71 - .75	.62 - .66	.53 - .56
.76 - .80	.67 - .70	.57 - .60
.81 - .85	.71 - .74	.61 - .64
.86 - .90	.75 - .79	.64 - .68
.91 - .95	.80 - .83	.69 - .71

comparison may show that Grade B and Grade C eggs are priced from 10 to 15 cents a dozen lower than higher-quality eggs of the same weight.

Finally, know the food values that eggs have to offer: high-quality protein, iron, vitamin A, riboflavin, thiamine, and some vitamin D, all stored inside an eggshell. Eggs rate as a protective food along with meat, poultry, fish, dry peas, and beans. And of them all, none of these protein foods is so versatile as eggs. They fill the bill for young and old alike at any meal—as a main dish, in soup and salad, or in the beverage or dessert.

FRUITS AND VEGETABLES

Increase Family Use of Fruits and Vegetables

Nutrition experts figure that about 21 percent of the family food costs should go into the purchase of fruits and vegetables. This is probably far above typical family expenditures, because most families usually do not have enough of these foods in their diets.

Modern science has discovered that fruits and vegetables are valuable to the diet in many ways. First, leafy vegetables, skins, and fibers provide needed roughage. Second, fruits and vegetables are rich in vitamins that are essential to good health. Third, some fruits and vegetables are good sources of minerals. And finally, some fruits and vegetables are rich in fuel content.

Generally, green and yellow vegetables, such as green lettuce, sweet potatoes and tomatoes, peaches, and apricots, are rich in vitamin A.

Oranges, lemons, grapefruit, tomatoes, limes, and tangerines are rich in vitamin C. Since vitamin C cannot be stored in the body, we need a fresh supply every day.

The B family of vitamins (thiamine, riboflavin, niacin) are found in apples, apricots, bananas, cabbage, kale, and dried peas. Iron is supplied by the green leafy vegetables, such as broccoli, chard, spinach, and lettuce.

How to Buy Fresh Fruits and Vegetables

There are many ways in which you can get more for your money when purchasing fresh fruits and vegetables. The following suggestions are used by wise shoppers.

1. Select fruit and vegetables the family likes.
2. Select fruit and vegetables that are most plentiful in the market.
3. Use fruit and vegetables that are in season.
4. By using a variety of fruit and vegetables, it is easier to keep costs down.
5. Purchase in as large quantities as use and storage without loss permit.
6. If possible, shop personally and as early in the day as demands on your time permit.
7. When handling fruit (the touch system), be careful, because careless handling increases spoilage and adds to the price that consumers pay.
8. Low price is not necessarily an indication of poor quality. There may be an oversupply of that particular product.
9. The most expensive quality may not be the best buy for a particular use. For example, topless carrots sold by the pound are just as good for stews and soups or served raw, and they are cheaper than bunch carrots.
10. Blemishes on fruit may affect the looks but not the eating quality. Shriveled, wilted, and discolored vegetables, however, are usually poor buys.
11. Buy by weight rather than measure whenever possible, because numbers, pints, or quarts do not have consistent meaning. Cauliflower heads, for instance, may vary from 25 to 50 ounces.
12. Sometimes packaged fruits have poor-quality specimens in the lower layers, and fruit or vegetables in bags are not always all of the same quality.
13. Carrots, kale, collards, spinach, and green cabbage are often the least expensive vegetables, but they have high food value.
14. Compare prices in the food advertisements and in the stores.
15. Compare the costs of fresh, canned, frozen, and dried fruit and vegetables.

Grading Is Permissive

The U.S. Department of Agriculture has established standards at the wholesale level for some 70 fresh fruits and vegetables. There are 12 consumer level standards at retail stores. All federal inspection is based on these standards, but their use is permissive.

Each fruit and vegetable has its own set of quality grades. The principal United States grades are U.S. Fancy, U.S. No. 1, U.S. No. 2, U.S. Commercial, and U.S. Combination. The quality grade is marked on the container, which speeds the handling of the produce. Some use has been made by homemakers of standard grades in the purchase of apples, grapefruit, oranges, peaches, and potatoes in quantity.

One reason that consumers do not see the grade quality is the fact that by the time the consumer gets the fruit, a lot graded U.S. No. 1 may have deteriorated to U.S. No. 2. This is, of course, no argument in support of keeping the consumer ignorant of grade classifications. It is merely a reason given by many retailers.

Sizes of Apples and Citrus Fruits.   Boxes of apples are usually stamped with numbers to represent the count per standard box. Here are the sizes that are found in the market.

48	80	100	125	163	210
56	88	104	138	165	232
64	96	113	150	180	252
72					

Likewise, the size of citrus fruit is indicated by the count of fruit in a box. The size of fruit packed in a California box will be a little smaller than that packed in Florida or Texas. This variation is due to the California box capacity being 1⅗ bushels and the Texas and Florida box capacity being 1⅘ bushels. The following sizes are found in the market.

GRAPEFRUIT		LEMONS		ORANGES		TANGERINES	
28	80	180	420	64	220	48	150
36	96	210	432	80	226	60	168
46	112	240	442	96	250	76	176
54	126	252	490	100	252	90	192
64	150	270	540	112	288	96	200
70		300	588	126	324	100	210
		360		150	344	120	246
				176	360	144	294
				200	392		
				216	420		

Processed Fruits and Vegetables

Processed foods may be canned, frozen, dehydrated, or dried. Each of these processes has an effect on food values and on the price paid by the consumer. Generally, the most food value in relation to the cost is found in fresh fruits and vegetables in season and properly cared for; then, in the following order: dried and dehydrated foods, canned foods, and frozen foods. This generalization needs to be checked from time to time, because processes improve, and consumer demand is an uncertain factor at best.

Dried and Dehydrated Foods

Dried foods are usually more economical buys, because they are the least expensive to handle and ship. The Food and Drug Administration standard for dried fruits does not permit more than 24 to 26 percent moisture in fruits that are dried in a dehydrator. When not more than 5 or 6 percent moisture remains in the fruit, they are called "dehydrated" foods.

The food value in dehydrated foods varies, but generally the minerals and calories do not vanish in the water. Some vitamins, however, are lost. As yet, dehydrated foods are not very popular because the process needs improvement.

The process of drying fruits changes the food values to a considerable extent. Fuel value is greatly increased, and mineral value is increased to a less extent. In some cases, vitamin value is also increased. Nearly all dried fruits are excellent sources of vitamin A. Dry beans are often used as a substitute for meat, but they need to be supplemented by animal proteins, such as milk, eggs, fish, or cheese.

The federal standards for dry edible beans and peas are widely used by the trade, but the grades rarely appear on consumer packages.

Grades for beans and peas are based on such factors as color, presence or absence of defects, foreign material, and beans or peas of other classes. Defects may be those caused by weather, disease, insects, or mechanical means.

There are special "handpicked" grades for beans, which are well adapted for consumer sales. The top grade is U.S. Choice Handpicked, followed by U.S. No. 1 Handpicked, U.S. No. 2 Handpicked, and U.S. No. 3 Handpicked. In other than the handpicked grades, grades for beans are simply numerical. Grades for dry peas, both whole and split, are also numerical.

Frozen Fruits, Juices, Vegetables, and Precooked Frozen Foods

One of the major problems is in the mishandling of frozen foods before they reach the consumer. During the past decade, food and drug officials and the frozen food industry have become increasingly disturbed over the mishandling of frozen foods. There has been little effort to alert consumers to this problem, despite their need to know about damage to the quality of frozen food by temperatures above 0 degrees Fahrenheit.

Freeze-dried Foods

Freeze drying is one of the greatest techniques known for drying foodstuffs, causing far less damage to flavor, texture, and color than conventional heat drying. In freeze drying, food is first frozen; then, in a partial vacuum, the ice crystals thus formed in it are transformed directly into vapor without melting. When processing is done carefully, the cellular structure of the food remains intact, little shrinkage or shriveling results, and nutritive values are fairly well preserved. Because the dried product is nearly full size and is porous, reconstitution is quite easy.

The advantages are obvious. Food does not have to be refrigerated, and weight is reduced. It is claimed that products resume the taste, texture, and appearance of fresh foods when they are reconstituted.

This is a promising new process. The process has worked only on fairly thin pieces of food, half an inch or so thick. Some foods (broccoli) do not freeze-dry well, and others (carrots) are better dried by conventional methods. The process is still quite expensive, and packaging problems are keeping prices up.

The first of such foods to be widely distributed for retail stores was Lipton's chicken-rice soup and meats in some of Campbell's Red Kettle soups and in Armour Star Lite outdoor foods. There are others entering this market, a market that the *Reader's Digest* billed as "the greatest breakthrough in food preservation since the invention of the tin can." Time will tell. In 1968, freeze-dried coffee became quite popular although expensive.

Canned Fruits and Vegetables

Canned fruits and vegetables are very popular with the homemaker. In canning there are, however, minor losses of minerals. Water-soluble nutrients are dissolved in the liquid in which the food is canned. Thus, it is wise to use all the liquid in the can.

Vitamin A is only slightly affected in canning. There is some loss of thiamine and riboflavin. The retention of vitamin C is higher in citrus products than in tomato juice and canned vegetables. In some cases, food analysts have found canned vegetables superior in nutrients to fresh produce that has been allowed to stand in a market, especially in sunlight or warmth, or that has been washed.

Brand Identifications and Grade Labeling.   Brand identifications do not give consumers the information needed to make an intelligent selection. Adequate label information should accompany brand names. The permissive standardized labeling program promoted by the National Canners Association is an attempt to "describe" the contents in addition to the statements required by law under the Federal Food, Drug, and Cosmetic Act.

Descriptive labels do not give information about quality, except in general terms not based on accepted standards. To select canned foods wisely, consumers need, in addition to brand names and standard descriptions, standard quality grades. Some canneries and large chain stores and consumer cooperatives have included standard graded canned fruits and vegetables.

Grade-labeling Facts for the Wise Shopper.   For the wise shopper who wants to buy by standard grade rather than by guess and by grab, here are the necessary facts.

Grade A or Fancy stands for "excellent." Use it for special occasions.

Grade B, Choice or Extra Standard, is for "good." Use it for every day.

Grade C or Standard is for "fair." Use it for thrift.

All grades have the same food value, but each serves a different purpose and has a different price. Over 40 fruits and vegetables now have standards worked out by the cooperative efforts of the U.S. Department of Agriculture and private canners.

The U.S. Department of Agriculture inspects and certifies these products as to quality and condition on requests of processors, buyers, federal and state purchasing departments, or other interested parties. These applicants pay the cost of inspection.

Some canners, freezers, and distributors use grade designations on their labels. Labels may also carry additional information descriptive of the product, such as the number of halves in canned peaches or pears, the sieve size of peas,

SLICED PEACHES

U.S. Grade **A** (Fancy)

Selection Information

No. 2½ size   1 lb. 13 oz.
3½ cups   6 to 8 servings

U.S. GRADE B SLICED CLING-STONE PEACHES are well-ripened—reasonably good color —reasonably uniform in size and symmetry—reasonably tender—with normal peach flavor.

USE them as they are for desserts—in combination with other fruits in cocktails or salads—spiced or pickled as meat accompaniment—in shortcakes and upside down cakes. Try peaches spiced and baked with ham.

PREPARATION: Store unused portion covered in refrigerator. The syrup may be mixed, flavored, colored and served as an appetizer, or frozen into sherbets. Boiled down it may be used to sweeten desserts, gelatins, sauces, and beverages —as well as a syrup for basting meats—or adding to other cooked fruits—or combined with lemon and raisins for a special dessert sauce.

Brand offers a complete line of U.S. Grade B Fruits and Vegetables for U.S. Grade A and C-use

All packed under the continuous inspection of the U.S. Department of Agriculture.

U.S. Grade **B** (Choice)   U.S. Grade **C** (Standard)

Figure 8-4   Source: Production and Marketing Administration, U.S. Department of Agriculture.

HALVES

BARTLETT PEARS

In Water   Slightly Sweetened

BELOW STANDARD IN QUALITY

Mixed Sizes—Unevenly Trimmed

Figure 8-5   Source: Production and Marketing Administration, U.S. Department of Agriculture.

ings, cooking instructions for frozen vegetables, or special statements for dietetic foods.

Any processor or distributor may use the terms "Grade A," "Grade B," and "Grade C" on labels to describe the quality of his products, whether or not they have been inspected. However, products thus labeled must meet the specifications of the Department's standards for the grade claimed; otherwise, the products may be considered mislabeled.

Some processing plants operate voluntarily under continuous inspection—a service offered by the U.S. Department of Agriculture at a nominal fee to packers. These plants have been carefully selected and thoroughly inspected to make sure that they meet strict sanitary requirements. Processors who operate their plants under U.S. Department of Agriculture continuous inspection may use the prefix "U.S." before their grade designation on their label (such as U.S. Grade A), as well as the statement "Packed under continuous inspection of the U.S. Department of Agriculture."

A wise shopper will look for the brand and a reliable standard grade. Grade labels are not common in food stores because they are in the developmental stage. Consumers can cast an economic vote for grading by patronizing the stores that stock graded foods. Let your store know that you appreciate graded foods, because this is the best way of convincing the producers and the food store owners of the importance of graded labels.

Some hints for buying canned fruits and vegetables are:

1. Compare different brand prices for the same grade.
2. Find the brands and the grades best suited to your family uses.
3. Buy the largest size of can that you can economically use.
4. Purchasing in quantity—case lots—saves from 5 to 10 percent.

5. Look for the special sales, especially just prior to the appearance of the new crop in cans. Last year's crop in the cans is just as nutritious and good as ever.
6. Buy by grades according to intended use of the food.

YOUR MONEY'S WORTH IN FOOD: A RECAP

If your family is typical, very likely 40 to 50 percent of your money for food goes for meat, dairy products, and eggs. About one-fifth of this is spent for vegetables and fruit. The rest is nearly equally divided among the grain products; the fats, oils, sugar, and sweets; and such items as vinegar, spices, leavening agents, coffee, tea, and other beverages.

Question: "Do you wonder if your money for food is spent to the best advantage?" A good way to determine this is to compare foods in each of the groups by their yield in nutrients as well as by their price. A few examples will point this up.

Meat, poultry, fish, and eggs are important for their high-quality protein, iron, and the B vitamins. To make worthwhile savings, judge them on a comparative basis. Some meat has bone and gristle. Buying the less expensive cuts of meat can save money with no loss in food value, provided the cuts do not have large amounts of bone, fat, and gristle. Dry beans or peas as a main dish is an economical substitute for meat. Buy lower-grade eggs for scrambling or baking. Small eggs are as economical as large ones when they are at least one-fourth cheaper.

As for the dairy products, everybody needs milk in some form because it is the best source for calcium and an important source of protein and riboflavin. One serving of fluid whole milk, evaporated milk, buttermilk, skim milk, or dry milk furnishes about the same amount of nutrients but at widely different costs. Dry milk generally costs least and fluid milk the most per serving. Cream cheese is more expensive for the value received than most other milk products, except butter and cream. Cottage cheese is a bargain for protein and riboflavin. Cheddar cheese is a more economical source of calcium than cottage cheese.

Vegetables and fruits furnish a large share of the vitamin A value and most of the vitamin C. Certain vegetables and fruits, however, are better buys than others, although prices vary with locality, season, and form or processing. Usually, the best buys for vitamin A—dark green or deep yellow vegetables—are carrots, collards, kale, spinach, sweet potatoes, and winter squash. Most other common fruits and vegetables, including light green and pale yellow ones, are usually more expensive sources of vitamin A because they contain only small amounts. It would take about 7 cups of corn to give as much vitamin A value as $\frac{1}{4}$ cup of carrots, and would cost about 10 times more than the carrots.

Oranges, grapefruit, and raw cabbage generally supply the most vitamin C for the money. Some dark green leaves, potatoes, and sweet potatoes—properly cooked—also give vitamin C at moderately low cost. Tomato juice and canned tomatoes usually are cheaper sources for vitamin C, except possibly fresh tomatoes in season. Most other common fruits and vegetables furnish less vitamin C and cost more. Some vegetables and fruits have both vitamins A and C—tomatoes and sweet potatoes—and may be good buys.

Canned, frozen, dried, and fresh fruits and vegetables vary considerably in price per serving. As a rule, these foods in canned and dried form are cheaper. The safest way, however, is to make a comparison of price per serving.

Whole-grain, restored, or enriched cereals and bread can mean extra food value for the money. Natural whole grains are significant sources of iron, thiamine, riboflavin, and niacin. Many breakfast foods have nutrients, lost in milling, "restored." There is no federal standard for restored cereals. It is, therefore, safer to purchase enriched bread or flour, because the federal standards require a minimum amount of iron, thiamine, riboflavin, and niacin for enrichment. If breads of various types cost the same or a few cents more per pound of bread, the whole-grain or enriched kinds are the best nutrient buys for the money. The same is true of cereals. Cold cereals are not as good nutrient buys as cereals that have to be cooked.

It is well to remember that many convenience foods are still more expensive, if you discount the time element, than those prepared at home from the ingredients. Canned and frozen fruits and vegetables are often best buys, because they are canned and frozen when supplies are large and prices low. There is also none of the waste that occurs in the handling and storage of perishable produce.

Pay cash for food. Credit costs money, and you will pay for the extra cost. In selecting supermarkets, compare prices for food value. Remember that gimmicks like trading stamps, premiums, and the forms of lottery or games of chance increase the cost of food. When you spend almost one-fifth of your income for food, it pays to get the most value per dollar for your family. You can still be well nourished if you spend considerably less than this amount. These last two chapters were designed to help you plan and select (1) food that keeps your family well fed, (2) food that is economical and nutritionally good, and (3) food that pleases your family.

QUESTIONS FOR DISCUSSION

1. What is the implication of the statement that we "tend to buy where the ego psychology is stressed"? Is this good or bad?

2. Make a careful survey of differences in the retail prices of a dozen commonly used foods. Select half a dozen different kinds of food markets. Which store has the lowest prices for similar grades or quality of the food items you selected?

3. How can you cut the cost of milk and milk products without reducing quality and nutritive value?

4. Are frozen foods economical buys? What can be done about the mishandling of frozen foods?

5. Most families know from experience that meat costs can easily wreck the food budget. How can you reduce the proportion of money spent for meat and yet serve nutritious and interesting meat dishes?

6. Are convenience foods economical buys?

ACTIVITY PROBLEMS

1. At current prices, from what cuts of meat does the homemaker get the most lean meat for the dollar she spends for meat? You might select five cuts each of beef, veal, pork, lamb. Use Table 8-2.

2. What protein foods can be used in place of meat to cut costs and yet not jeopardize health? Be sure to get scientific facts and make accurate current cost calculations.

3. Keep a record of the kinds and quantity of food that you eat for seven consecutive days. Evaluate the diet. List the deficiencies and indicate the foods that should be added. Remember that health experts say you need balanced food for each meal.

4. Select certain foods and make an investigation of the most economical buys in terms of quality, quantity, and price relationship. You might like to compare fresh, canned, dehydrated, and frozen fruit. Be accurate.

5. Assume that you are married with no children as yet. Plan menus for all meals at home for seven consecutive days. Prepare a grocery list of the food you need to purchase. List the kinds of food, quantity, brand, and price, and the name of the food store or stores where you might purchase the items. Since you want to have balanced, nutritious meals at the most economical cost in sufficient quantity and food that is liked, check all essential facts. How much will the food cost? Have you used all the tips and information given in the text about selecting food stores, selecting food for specific purposes, quantity buying, prices, and quality?

SUGGESTED READINGS

Bivens, Gordon E.: "An Exploration of Food Price Competition in a Local Market," *The Journal of Consumer Affairs,* Summer, 1968.

Brandow, George E.: "Consumers and the Food Industry," *The Journal of Consumer Affairs,* Winter, 1967.

"Frozen Dinners," *Consumer Reports,* October, 1967.

"Frozen Turkeys," *Consumer Reports,* November, 1967.

"One and One-half Cheers for Congress," *Consumer Reports,* February, 1968.

Padberg, David I.: *Economics of Food Retailing,* Cornell University, Ithaca, N.Y., 1968.

"Price Competition among the Retail Food Stores," *Journal of Farm Economics,* August, 1966.

Weiss, E. B.: "Retailing in 1975," *Advertising Age,* March, 1966.

chapter 9

FAMILY CLOTHING MANAGEMENT

There are no norms for choice in clothing as there are in the nutritional needs of the body. Clothing problems in a family must be analyzed in terms of the individual in a group setting. Style, fashion, and fad need to be adapted to individual differences within the financial limits of the family.

In addition, the way we wear our clothes is as important as what we wear. Being well dressed for the occasion, and being aware of it, benefits all members of the family psychologically, physically, and socially. It helps a person to be self-confident, to act and speak more effectively in public. People who are well dressed in the sense of having used good taste in the selection of their clothes are more readily accepted in most social situations.

But the managerial problems of clothing the family so that all members are properly dressed for all occasions are numerous and often difficult. Adequate income does not always solve clothing problems. Even families with luxury incomes are not necessarily style conscious and may not use good sense and taste in costume coordination.

For moderate-income and low-income families, clothing expenditures are not regular. Seasonal demands and sudden disintegration of garments make it difficult for every member to have an adequate wardrobe at all times. And even the best-planned clothing budget can be ruined by unexpected expenses, such as medical and housing bills.

Right Clothes Are a Mental Stimulant

Whether we like it or not, a girl gets more flattering masculine attention if she is attractive and knows how to wear clothes than if she has a Phi Beta Kappa key. A lady's looks and general grooming are a powerful magnet, and, no doubt, women appraise men in the same way. We hasten to add that attractive dress is not enough in the long run to hold the attention of others, but the right clothes, worn well, give a mental stimulus to the wearer, to the family, and to personal friends and promote an air of confidence.

If there is truth in the assumption that our innermost life tends to become evident in the choices we make, it might follow that a glance at a family's wardrobe may be more revealing than a composite diary of its members.

Some women, especially mothers devoted to their children, seem to stand still in the matter of dress when the world about them moves forward. Often a wife allows herself to look dowdy and perhaps, as a result, considerably older than her husband, because she has let household duties absorb all her interest. But the husband's contacts with the business and professional world may have kept him alert and well groomed in keeping with his position and associates. On the other hand, a man who allows himself to slip in his grooming may be slipping in his business and social life.

Other women of a retiring nature are perhaps too conservative in their dress. Still others wear too youthful or extreme clothes or makeup in a conspicuous manner. Generally, conspicuous dress emphasizes rather than conceals age in either sex. If a woman's dress or hat, or a man's suit or tie, dominates the picture, that person is not well dressed in spite of the fact that those items originally may have worn a high price tag.

Family Happiness Is Involved

The family attitudes toward dress, especially on the part of the mother, are important to the good mental health of each member of the family. Good grooming, good taste in dress, and an active interest in style, fashion, and even fads are assets to family happiness.

The clothing one wears plays an important part in adjusting to the social group. Clothing management, as such, is largely a psychological problem, because it affects the personality development and happiness of each member of the family. No one but the family or close friends may observe our eating manners and food standards, but as soon as we step outside the door, our clothes and how we wear them are appraised by those we meet. Much of this appraisal is unconscious. Perhaps we need to build a consciousness of good dress without creating the value that good dress is everything.

Parents who allow their children to feel unhappy about their methods of dress may be responsible for personality maladjustments later in their lives. The clothing needs of children differ because of individual differences in personality and in physique. A study made by the Bureau of Home Economics on measurements of children shows that many children of like age have entirely different body proportions and dimensions.[1] Ignorance of this fact often results in unhappy relationships between mother and children. It is of utmost importance to help a child to feel no different from others, even when the body is developing in a different way.

Considerable unhappiness can be needlessly generated if, for example, a mother insists on dressing a rather tall, early-teen-age daughter in below-knee-length dresses, with hair in long braids, when the girls in her set are wearing shorter skirts, sweaters, and long hair. Insistence on "bucking the crowd" usually produces a weepy, irritable, unhappy youngster. At the same time, parents need to help youngsters understand that there is not an unlimited amount of money for clothing.

It is wise to let children gradually assume responsibility in selecting their clothes. By intelligent discussion of their personal assets and liabilities, children can develop skill in self-analysis and in selecting or creating clothes that are acceptable to others and that at the same time accentuate their individual personalities.

[1]Ruth O'Brien and Meyer A. Girshick, *Children's Body Measurements for Size in Garments and Patterns,* Bureau of Home Economics, U.S. Department of Agriculture, Miscellaneous publication 365, 1939.

Training Children to Select and Care for Clothing

Children who are accustomed to an environment of good grooming and common sense in dressing are not likely to fail to acquire these good habits. They may go through certain stages of refusing to wear suitable footwear, for instance, or adequate clothes on the pretext that such things are not "in style." At times, they may wear the most illogical clothes because these happen to be the fad. High school and college-age youngsters are usually the worst offenders in this respect. In time, sense and intelligence in dressing will return, plus an individual style and air—the reverse of the herd instinct.

Even preschool children can be taught how to select, wear, and care for their own clothing. If a young child is going to attend a birthday party, let him select what he will wear. Let him choose from among several around-home garments. Then, let him select from two pairs of shoes that are acceptable for the occasion but quite different in appearance. At a store, let him select from two or three garments first picked out by the parent.

As the child grows in responsibility, allow him to plan his clothing needs for six months, then perhaps for the next 12 months. Follow this by allowing absolute independent action with parents as permissive consultants only. By this time, the child should have a monthly or annual clothes allowance; so make him responsible for living within his clothing budget and for selecting and caring for his personal clothing.

No one child should be favored above some other member of the family in sharing the family clothing budget. This is almost a certain invitation to family squabbles and possible maladjustments. The manner in which these group problems are handled reveals the kind of spirit that exists in the family. If the family has succeeded in creating individual responsibility in budgeting the family income, the stage is set for continuance of this frank and friendly policy in determining individual clothing expenditures and responsibility for care and upkeep of clothes.

In some homes, proper family attitudes toward sharing space for clothing must also be developed.

Developing Skills in Clothing Management

For a vast majority of families, an adequate wardrobe for every member is possible only by intelligent management. Here is the most practical way to plan and carry out a clothing budget.

1.   Know the maximum amount of money available for the family clothing.
2.   Analyze the characteristics of each member of the family as applied to clothing needs.
3.   Plan, even two and three years in advance, the wardrobe needs of the family.
4.   Select the best stores for values, and shop the sales.
5.   Select the right garments for specific uses.

6. Use all available information concerning quality, workmanship, shrinkage, color-fastness, suitability, care, and upkeep of clothes.
7. Teach children good clothing habits in terms of care and upkeep.
8. Teach teen-age budgeting for clothes.
9. Discover family resources for home production of clothing items.

All these problems involve information, correct family attitudes, some skills, and time and energy, particularly when the family income is inadequate. But a limited income can be offset by skill in planning (1) how to buy, (2) when to buy, (3) where to buy, (4) care and upkeep, and (5) home production.

How Much to Spend for Family Clothing

Everyone wants to be well dressed, but it is difficult to agree on what it should cost to achieve this objective. This is a good time to turn to the figures compiled by budget experts. It is well to keep in mind, however, that no family is "average" in its expenditures. It depends on the age, sex, and number of persons in the family; on the climate; on personal taste, social needs, and occupations; and, importantly, on the family income.

A 1967 publication of the Bureau of Labor Statistics gives a wealth of information about the clothing expenditures of individuals living in urban centers, based on the Survey of Consumer Expenditures in 1960-1961. Although the expenditures themselves may seem out of date now, they show some basic relations in clothing expense that are of lasting interest because they change relatively little over time. In other words, the generalizations about the cost relationships in clothing expense among members of the family are applicable today. The number of dollars spent in 1960-1961 and now are quite different. The difference in dollars spent for apparel in July, 1968, and in 1957-1959 was reported in the Consumer Price Index as follows:

	JULY, 1968	1957-1959 ($=$ 100)
All clothing and upkeep	120.3	100
Men's and boys'	120.7	100
Women's and girls'	116.4	100
Footwear	132.5	100

According to the U.S. Department of Commerce, yearly per capita expenditures on clothing and shoes reached an all-time high of $205 in 1966. This was about 9 percent of expenditures for personal consumption. Between 1960 and 1966, per capita expenditures for clothing and shoes—in constant dollars—increased a whopping 26 percent.

The following generalizations on clothing expenditures of urban families have not changed over the last several years even though the number of dollars paid out has increased considerably:

1.   Average clothing expenditures increase as a child grows older, peaks at young adulthood (18 to 24 years), then declines with advancing age.
2.   Clothing expenditure for adults 18 to 64 years old differed with their family status, interests, and financial pressures.
3.   Clothing expenditures increased as family income increased, but at a slower pace.
4.   The response of clothing expenditures to an increase in income appears in the statistic that women and girls increased their expenditures more than men and boys increased theirs.
5.   At all income levels, clothing for a child 2 to 5 years old cost the family about half as much as that for a man.
6.   The average clothing expenditure was generally highest in the Northeast region and lowest in the South.
7.   For females, the average price paid per garment increased with the age of the person and was highest for the oldest group.

PLANNING AND BUYING THE FAMILY'S CLOTHING

Pay Cash for Clothing

When buying clothing, you have the choice of paying cash or using credit. Generally, it is best to pay cash. The best method, however, depends in part on your situation. Families with irregular incomes have more of a payment problem than families with regular weekly or monthly income. Regardless of the nature of the income, there is a compelling principle related to the decision of how to pay for clothing. It is this: clothes are consumer goods that do not earn income for the buyer and therefore should be paid for in cash. Credit can be used with some justification, other things being equal, for clothing that outlasts credit payments. Credit costs, however, are high for typical credit plans.

Ideally, a family should allocate some percentage of its income for clothing, thus making cash more readily available for clothing. The percentage of cash set aside for clothing will vary with different families, but 10 to 12 percent is a reasonable allocation in terms of the most recent studies on clothing expenditures.

The Power of Fashion

Fashion, style, fad, craze, and good taste have various meanings to various people. Paul H. Nystrom, in his classic *Economics of Fashion,*[2] defines these terms as follows:

[2] Paul H. Nystrom, *Economics of Fashion.* Copyright 1928 by The Ronald Press Company, New York, pp. 3-7. Reprinted with permission.

"Style is a characteristic or distinctive mode or method of expression, presentation or conception in the field of some art."

"Fashion is nothing more or less than the prevailing style at any given time." Whenever a style is accepted or followed it is the fashion.

"A fad is merely a miniature fashion in some unimportant matter or detail."

"A craze is a fad or fashion accompanied by much crowd excitement or emotion."

"Taste . . . is the ability to discern or appreciate what is beautiful or appropriate." Good taste is present when one makes the most artistic use of current fashions.

Fashion, says Nystrom, seems to be the result of powerful forces in human nature. We laugh, sometimes, at fashion, but generally we accept it. Strangely enough, the influence of fashion is such as to make a style, when accepted, seem beautiful, no matter how hideous it might have appeared at other times.

Fashion is perhaps the most extravagant force in clothing selection, for imitation and conspicuous consumption play important roles. As fashion changes, garments become socially obsolete. And conformity tends to become so important, if you want that well-dressed appearance, that all other values are rejected. This is especially important during the teen-age period. If necessary, teen-agers will sacrifice health, comfort, economy, and even becomingness to achieve conformity and social acceptance.

The following account of a shopping expedition of a college freshman girl exemplifies the force of fashion.

I have been contemplating the purchase of a brown cardigan sweater for almost a year now (sounds impossible but very true), since that's the general procedure I have to go through before coming through with a major purchase. My indecision came when trying to decide between a cashmere, which was more durable but far more expensive, and a good-quality wool sweater. Before coming to college there would have been no question. I would have simply purchased a wool sweater, since I hadn't come into contact with the cashmere-conscious students. Well, I made the rounds of all the stores comparing the different cashmere and wool sweaters and trying desperately to decide, or rationalize, which would be the more satisfying for the amount of money in the long run.

I couldn't decide! Was a cashmere worth three times more than a wool one? If I got *one* cashmere, would it go well with my wool pull-overs? If I got one, would I ever be satisfied with anything else but cashmere? Yet, I figured—everyone has cashmere and admires it and would comment on mine, if I got one. I could wear it on a casual date and be much more in style and would possibly make a better impression. But would it be a false impression? Could I afford to continue buying sweaters of that quality?

Time was short! I had to decide. My eyes wandered and suddenly landed on a cashmere sweater in a shade of green that I just loved. It was deep and striking. I asked to see the sweater. It happened to be a turtle-neck. I shouldn't wear such high-necked things but, on the other hand, many people did, and it *was* different from anything else I had. Well, I was all keyed up to the point where I *had* to buy something, preferably a sweater, and since I couldn't decide about the brown cardigan, I bought the green one that I had no intention of buying.

The final factor in determining this purchase was the girl's feeling of conformity and of social acceptance by her group.

Wardrobe Planning by Inventory

An adequate wardrobe is not dependent on how much money you spend. It depends as much or more on careful planning and good management of the clothing dollar. The first step in having an adequate wardrobe on a modest income is in knowing what you have and what you need—in short, a common-sense clothing inventory. To dress each family properly, there must be no last-minute hasty buying and needless mistakes.

There is really no average family. Each individual and each family lives a slightly different life from other families, and their clothing requirements are bound to differ. Income, occupations, social life, climate, vacations, and travel plans must be taken into account. For most families, the clothing dollar needs to be spent for comfort, usefulness, good style, and quality, rather than for quantity. It is necessary to buy with foresight and not fall into temptations of the moment or be led astray by whims—purchasing a dress, for instance, because "it looked so lovely in the window."

Each purchase should be backed by reason rather than rationalization, although the latter may be fun for the moment. Everyone enjoys a nonsensical fling once in a while, but it is wise to control such flings by channeling them into the inexpensive and less basic clothing items.

Buying new clothes without first knowing what is in the clothes closet is like buying food without knowing what is in the pantry. For good wardrobe planning, it is necessary to be on spending terms with the six clothing inventory principles given on page 265. Accompanying this list of principles are two clothing replacement inventories, one for the husband and one for the wife. Similar inventory lists can be prepared for each child in the family.

Analyzing Flops and Successes.   The value of analyzing the flops and successes in your clothes closet depends, to a great extent, on the insight gained from the analysis. One mother, on analyzing the items and cost, found that she had spent five times as much for little-used garments that hung in the closet as for those she used regularly. She decided to spend more of her share of the family clothing money for good suits, versatile dresses, and semiformal or informal dresses, and less on vacation and formal clothes that she seldom wore. With the money saved, she could afford accessories for each costume and a much-needed casual coat.

Another mother, analyzing the clothing inventory of her two grade-school boys, discovered that one child was spending twice as much for clothes as his brother, because he was careless and destructive. This mother had a job outside the home. In checking on her own clothing expenditures, she decided that too large a percentage was being spent on luxury underwear and hose. She switched to simple types of underwear and daytime sheer hose for general wear, and transferred the difference to good dresses and suits.

A third family had two fashion-conscious girls whose associates had much more money than they had to spend for clothes. When the mother and the girls studied their clothing inventory, they realized that they obtained pleasure and

CLOTHING REPLACEMENT INVENTORY—HUSBAND

ANNUAL REPLACEMENT COST $____   TOTAL COST $____

Present Items	Stock	Annual Replace- ment	Unit Price	Annual Cost
Hats:				
felt	_____	1	$10.00	$10.00
sport	_____	_____	_____	_____
straw	_____	_____	_____	_____
Overcoats	_____	⅓	60.00	20.00
Sweaters	_____	_____	_____	
Suits:				
business	_____	_____	_____	_____
tuxedo	_____	_____	_____	_____
Slacks	_____	_____	_____	_____
Shirts:				
dress	_____	_____	_____	_____
collar attached	_____	_____	_____	_____
Socks	_____	_____	_____	_____
Underwear:				
shirts	_____	_____	_____	_____
shorts	_____	_____	_____	_____
Bathrobes	_____	_____	_____	_____
Pajamas	_____	_____	_____	_____
Shoes:				
dress	_____	_____	_____	_____
sport	_____	_____	_____	_____
business	_____	_____	_____	_____
House slippers	_____	_____	_____	_____
Ties:				
bow	_____	_____	_____	_____
other	_____	_____	_____	_____
Gloves	_____	_____	_____	_____
Bathing trunks	_____	_____	_____	_____
Emergency	_____	_____	_____	_____
Annual upkeep cost:				
Cleaning overcoat	_____	_____	_____	_____
Cleaning suits	_____	_____	_____	_____
Pressing suits	_____	_____	_____	_____
Blocking hats	_____	_____	_____	_____
Repairing shoes	_____	_____	_____	_____

1. All usable clothes are listed. Discarded clothes are made wearable. Individual replacement needs are made known, and their approximate costs are listed.
2. The total clothing allotment is subdivided to suit the needs of each individual member of the family.
3. Purchases are made in the order of urgency before desirability.
4. Purchases may be made with a long view for coordination and economy, and may even be based on a 3-year plan for the most expensive items, such as a winter overcoat or a fur coat.
5. Plans are made for upkeep and general care of clothing.
6. A flexible balance is left, even if small, for unforeseen emergency requirements.

ANNUAL REPLACEMENT COST $____   TOTAL COST $____

Present Items	Stock	Annual Replacement	Unit Price	Annual Cost
Hats:				
winter	_____	_____	$_____	$_____
summer	_____	_____	_____	_____
casual	_____	_____	_____	_____
Coats:				
fur	_____	_____	_____	_____
winter cloth	_____	_____	_____	_____
casual	_____	_____	_____	_____
Suits:				
wool	_____	_____	_____	_____
other fibers	_____	_____	_____	_____
Blouses:				
cotton	_____	_____	_____	_____
other fibers	_____	_____	_____	_____
Sweaters	_____	_____	_____	_____
Dresses:				
evening	_____	_____	_____	_____
dinner	_____	_____	_____	_____
afternoon	_____	_____	_____	_____
casual	_____	_____	_____	_____
house	_____	_____	_____	_____
Slacks	_____	_____	_____	_____
Lingerie	_____	_____	_____	_____
Foundation garments	_____	_____	_____	_____
Bathrobes	_____	_____	_____	_____
Housecoats	_____	_____	_____	_____
Nightgowns	_____	_____	_____	_____
Stockings:				
sheer	_____	_____	_____	_____
semisheer	_____	_____	_____	_____
Shoes:				
evening	_____	_____	_____	_____
dress	_____	_____	_____	_____
sports	_____	_____	_____	_____
Slippers	_____	_____	_____	_____
Rainwear	_____	_____	_____	_____
Bathing suits and beachwear	_____	_____	_____	_____
Gloves:				
leather	_____	_____	_____	_____
fabric	_____	_____	_____	_____
Handbags:				
evening	_____	_____	_____	_____
street	_____	_____	_____	_____
Emergency	_____	_____	_____	_____
Annual upkeep cost:				
Cleaning and glazing fur coat	_____	_____	_____	_____
Cleaning and pressing garments	_____	_____	_____	_____
Repairing shoes	_____	_____	_____	_____

use from a wide variety of garments. They decided to buy jackets, sweaters, skirts, and blouses that could be alternated and changed by scarves, costume jewelry, and similar accessories. They could double the value of their dress allowances by making each garment serve a double duty wherever possible. They learned to use many style-right ideas that took little time and money.

Teen-age Clothing Budget. If there are teen-agers in the family, the mere fact that a family clothing inventory has been made does not necessarily mean that the family has solved its clothing problems. The subject of clothes can be one of the greatest little peace wreckers in any modest-income household. Teen-agers believe that clothes are about the most important things in the world. They are at the age when classmates are playing the game of trying to outdress each other. This game usually results in tears and much unhappiness for parents and children. When this happens, a family meeting is in order.

If children have not been brought up on a family budget based on increasing consumer responsibilities as they grow older, it may not be too late to lay the problem wide open and honestly face it. Let them know how much money is available for clothes for each youngster, and why. If everybody agrees, for example, that the teen-agers may each have $150 a year for their clothes, including repairs and cleaning bills, the chances are good that they will jump at the opportunity of making their own decisions. The clothing budget will have a personal meaning because they have a voice in deciding on what they need.

For inexperienced youngsters, it is better to give the clothing allowance in quarterly payments, because they are likely to go wild at first. It is also wise to insist that they (1) buy sturdy shoes for school wear, (2) keep supplied with rainy-weather equipment, (3) do not wear ragged underwear and socks to save money, and (4) do not expect that the next quarterly allowance will be advanced if they have spent their money unwisely.

Many youngsters under such a clothing budget have tracked down bargains like hunting dogs. The girls think twice before buying junk jewelry, a scarf that will not launder, a blouse that might require dry cleaning. They learn that a cheap sweater that will not launder is no economy even if it costs only half as much as a good sweater. Boys are likely to develop amazing caution about buying a sports jacket that does not look well with more than one pair of slacks.

Both boys and girls are more likely to keep their best clothes for dress occasions and to take better care of all their clothing. Shoes are taken to the repair shop before it is too late; girls take better care of blouses and sweaters. The lost-clothing problem will probably end abruptly. And, perhaps best of all, in some families the youngsters will forget to remind parents "what the other kids get." This, indeed, would be welcome in many homes.

Combine Buying Skill with Care of Clothing

There is no satisfactory substitute for the feeling of being properly dressed for the occasion. This, in turn, contributes to personal happiness. It is not necessary to spend a lot of money to have an adequate wardrobe for the family. How well the homemaker plans and how skillfully she buys and oversees the buying of all members of the family are as important as the amount of money spent.

The first requirement for a satisfactory wardrobe is to take stock of what you have and make a list of what you need for the year. Be sure they are necessary items. Extras can follow the essentials. One hundred dollars well planned can bring more satisfactions than $200 unplanned.

Your money interest, however, does not cease with a well-planned wardrobe. Proper care of clothes can prolong their life. Managing the care of clothing, however, is more successful and costs less money if skill and all possible information are used in the selection of clothing in the market.

Good Buying Principles

Gains that may come from wise planning of the family wardrobe can be easily lost through careless shopping in the stores. Getting your money's worth depends on intelligent shopping for the wardrobe you planned at the prices you expect to pay.

The following seven shopping principles can help you save money and get lasting satisfaction from the purchases that not only are necessary to clothe the family but actually keep its members happy and contented.

Compare Values.   Clothing stores vary in price, even on similar items. Some stores change some of their prices daily and weekly. The higher-priced suit, for example, is not always the best buy in terms of value and style. No two stores have identical operating costs; therefore, their margins of profit are different. The more efficient stores often sell goods of equal quality and style at lower prices. Experienced professional comparative shoppers say that it is necessary to shop at least five stores before purchasing expensive clothing items, such as a coat, suit, or good-quality dress.

Select Basic or Classic Styles.   Classic styles almost always mean simple styling, which can mean better-quality fabric and finish. Many stores now feature such styles with the suggestion that they do not become dated. In addition, their appearance can be changed by different accessories. Simple lines also mean lower cleaning costs. One manufacturer of women's clothing put a date on his labels so that purchasers could see how long a particular line remained in fashion.

Buying Clothes That Fit Your Needs.   Do not develop a case of "bargainitis." Do not buy an article merely because you like the color or because the price has been reduced. It is difficult to resist a bargain, but no garment is a bargain unless it fits your needs. The color that you found irresistible in the store will soon cease to delight you if it does not harmonize with your wardrobe.

Purchase Middle-price Items.   Most stores have several price ranges for all types of clothing. Salespersons, especially those on commission, may attempt to "trade up" customers to the highest-priced group, but this group may not have enough additional value and style to offset its high price. The lowest-priced goods usually cut costs by using cheaper-quality raw materials, resulting in unsatisfactory wear. The middle-price lines are usually safest to buy because good-quality materials may be used and costs saved by eliminating nonessentials do not affect good styling and wear.

Shop Store Brands.   It is possible to save up to 25 percent on many clothing items of the same quality and style as the nationally advertised brands. Some manufacturers make identical clothes that are sold under several brand names at different price levels. Large retailers, such as department stores and mail-order houses, have their own store brands. They can often sell clothes more cheaply than smaller competitors who handle nationally known brands, because costs of a wholesaler and of national advertising are eliminated. Store brands exist because prices for nationally advertised clothing are seldom reduced after the items have won public acceptance. Money-saving store or private brands have made considerable headway, especially in the staple clothing, hosiery, and shoe lines.

Shop Regular Store Sales.   When you know your clothing needs in advance and plan for cash purchases at reliable sales, it is possible to save up to 50 percent on some clothing purchases. Get acquainted with the months for such sales in your locality, as suggested later in this chapter.

Pay Cash.   You get more for your money at stores that have strictly cash terms, unless the customer buys on the installment plan and pays a reasonable interest rate. Installment buying is expensive and should be avoided if possible. Some credit stores mark up clothing prices considerably to pay for the cost of credit and, in some cases, for their delivery costs. Some cash clothing stores can sell an identical dress, for example, for 25 percent less than a competitor who offers credit.

How to Select Clothing Stores

There are many kinds of clothing stores to serve the variety of tastes of consumers. Since methods of merchandising vary, the problem is to discover the stores that serve your purposes most satisfactorily.[3] The general answer is found in the answers to these five questions.

Does the Store Stock a Fairly Wide Range of Qualities at Different Prices? Some retail stores cater only to one class of customers. Thus, an exclusive women's apparel store may offer dresses at $50 and up. Or a men's clothing store may offer suits at a top price of $29.50. Neither store is seeking to interest all consumers. In addition, a good store will have a wide variety of styles, colors, and sizes.

[3] For an excellent source for selecting clothing stores, see Sidney Margolius, *The Consumers' Guide to Better Buying,* New American Library of World Literature, Inc., New York, 1963.

Does the Store Give Good Value for the Money? Intelligent consumers are price-conscious and value-conscious. Some consumers like an expensive atmosphere and settings and are willing to pay more for such a shopping environment. This factor constitutes value for them. Others prefer to have the value in goods rather than in atmosphere. Nevertheless, almost everyone tends to shop around for the stores that give the most value for the money spent.

The store that charges the highest prices does not necessarily offer the best goods. The outlet with low prices may not be sacrificing quality. Some stores have low prices but offer poor-quality merchandise. The consumer needs to develop skill in buying to see through the camouflage of atmosphere or of too persuasive selling.

Is the Store Conveniently Located? Most people are willing to accept some inconvenience in terms of distance and accessibility when shopping for the more expensive clothing items, because this occurs only a few times a year. They are willing to drive to a larger city or to shopping centers where there are branches of large city department stores.

Mail-order houses offer a convenience that appeals to consumers who want good-quality merchandise at medium prices. The catalogs are attractive and, on the whole, carry accurate descriptive information.

What Kinds of Service Are Offered by the Store? Besides convenience in terms of distance a store should have enough salespeople to serve customers promptly. Some stores reduce their sales force, but pass on the savings to the consumer. The appeal in such stores is based on price rather than on quick service. Other stores emphasize delivery service, charge accounts, liberal policy on returned goods, comfortable lounges, and even nurseries for the children. These services cost money. But some people are willing and can afford to shop such retail establishments.

When shopping in such stores, remember that you are paying for service in addition to your actual purchases. But also remember that you can save money by shopping around and comparing price and quality values.

These four considerations—quality level, price level, convenience, and service—are the most important economic factors in selecting clothing markets. There remains another quality that may be just as important when selecting a store—fair business ethics.

Does the Store Practice Honesty and Fair Business Ethics?[4] The best merchants are not satisfied unless they can help their customers get their money's worth. Shrewdness and trickery have no place in a good store.

The merchant who serves you best gives expert guidance concerning all important information about clothing items. Examine his advertising. Is it accurate and sufficiently informative? Read the labels. Do they tell you everything

---

[4] See your Better Business Bureau, financed by business in most cities of the country, for investigations of sharp and tricky practices.

you want to know? Observe the salespeople. Are they well informed and competent, and do they show a desire to serve you?

Know the adjustment policy of the store. Are they reasonably fair in making adjustments? If they hide behind every legal right, or if they are evasive, give some other store your business and economic vote.

Some consumers are interested in the way stores treat their help and in other personnel policies. Union members, in particular, prefer to buy in stores that sell merchandise produced and sold by union labor.

All other things being equal, an honest, informative merchant is your best bet in the continuous struggle to get the most value for your money.

Shopping Facilities

Table 9-1, Shopping Facilities, describes the various kinds of available shopping facilities, comparing their advantages and disadvantages. You have probably noticed also the following trends in retail business.

1. Variety stores, supermarkets, and drugstores carry clothing items, usually the lower-priced goods.
2. Drive-in stores sell shoes and clothing.
3. Some stores are now self-service, and there are self-service departments in regular department stores.
4. Door-to-door selling is used by some department stores.
5. Shopping centers are established within easy distance of residential centers.
6. Discount stores have been established, and there is discount selling in regular department stores to meet this competition.
7. Vending machines are set up in convenient places for quick and easy service and round-the-clock selling.

Typical Margins of Department Stores

You may be a better shopper by knowing approximate markups of important clothing items. The margin or markup percentage varies from store to store and from item to item. For example, *Changing Times* magazine published margins used by department stores with annual sales of $2 million to $5 million. The percentages came from a report of the National Retail Merchants Association.

Only part of this margin is profit because the markup has to cover the expenses of the store. Nevertheless, the margins help you to figure approximate price reductions. For example, a 15 percent cut on an item with a 25 percent margin is better than a 15 percent cut on an item with a 77 percent margin.

Usually, stores figure markups on a percentage of the retail price rather than on the wholesale cost. An item that costs 40 cents and sells for 60 cents may have a margin of 33⅓ percent (20 cents divided by 60 cents).

TABLE 9-1   SHOPPING FACILITIES

OUTLETS	DESCRIPTION	ADVANTAGES	DISADVANTAGES
Retail stores: Business establishments engaged in selling merchandise to consumers	Department: Chain or independent store merchandising a large variety of goods, divided into departments for purchasing, promoting, and selling	Many services are usually offered. One-stop shopping is possible. A wide selection of goods is provided in every price range. Merchandise may be returned.	The size of the store and location of departments may make it difficult to find what you want. Department stores are often located in areas beyond your neighborhood.
Chain: Member of a group of stores with similar goods and policies	Specialty: Chain or independent store specializing in a limited type of merchandise, such as children's wear, shoes, clothing, books, furnishings, or groceries	There is greater variety within the area of specialty than in general stores. A wide range of prices is available in the specialty items. Salespersons are usually trained, and their knowledge of the specialty results in good service and advice.	One-stop shopping is not possible. Prices may be higher than in larger stores.
True chain: Owned and operated by one company			
Voluntary chain: Independent stores associated for common buying and promotional activities	Variety: Chain or independent store selling a variety of consumer goods usually in a low price range and with a high amount of self-service and open counter display	Merchandise is openly displayed. Self-service is speedy. The price range is low. Great variety is available.	Salespeople may not be well trained. Shopping traffic may be heavy. Few services are provided.
Independent: Operated by the owner	Discount: Chain or independent store selling some known lines of merchandise at low prices	Parking is convenient. Self-service is speedy. Prices may be lower than other retailers. Stores are usually open for night shopping.	Usually little effort is made to display merchandise attractively. Service is limited. Return privileges are limited. Little or no home service on appliances or equipment is provided. Location may be inconvenient. There are usually few salespeople.

		Advantages	Disadvantages
Nonstore retailers: Businesses established to sell goods to consumers on a nonstore basis	Direct door-to-door: Selling in the consumer's home	Shopping at home is convenient. Often the product is demonstrated for you. Offers the opportunity to see or use items in your home before purchasing them.	There is little opportunity for comparisons of products and prices. Investigating the qualifications of the salesman is up to you. Salesman may come at an inconvenient time. There is limited selection and price range.
	Mail order: Selling through orders received and delivered by mail	Armchair shopping is convenient. Saves time and energy. Return privileges are offered. Prices are usually reasonable. Catalog descriptions are usually accurate and helpful. It is quick and easy. It offers 24-hour service.	There is no opportunity to see and inspect merchandise before buying. You pay the cost of delivery. The time lapse between ordering and delivery may be inconvenient.
	Vending machines: Providing goods through a coin-operated machine on a self-service basis		There is limited opportunity to inspect products. Machines are impersonal. No returns or services are possible.
Cooperatives: Associations created and jointly owned by their members, operated for their mutual benefit	Consumers cooperatives: Formed by private consumers to buy products and services jointly at favorable prices for selling to members	Profit is divided among members. Prices compare with and are often lower than those in retail stores.	The amount and variety of merchandise may be limited. There may be a lack of professional retailer know-how. Services may be limited. Location may be inconvenient.

SOURCE: Reproduced with permission from Household Finance Corporation, Money Management: Your Shopping Dollar, Chicago, 1962, pp. 20-21.

ITEM	AMOUNT ADDED ON AS PERCENT OF WHOLESALE COST
Costume jewelry	81.8
Handbags, small leather goods	70.9
Women's, children's gloves	72.1
Women's shoes	77.6
Children's shoes	70.0
Women's, misses' coats and suits	67.5
Men's clothing	71.8
Boys' clothing	61.0
Men's, boys' shoes	69.2

Discount Stores

Legitimate discount stores have forced a change in prices and in merchandising goods. Some large department stores have reduced personnel and expensive services, and have cut prices to meet this new competition. A few department stores have rented space in their own stores to regular discount chains. Others have set up their own discount units or stores.

Do you usually get lower prices for comparable quality in discount stores? Studies indicate that, on the whole, prices in discount houses are lower than prices in standard department stores and independent specialty stores. But in highly competitive areas, the specialty and department stores often meet discount prices. Some discount stores may have a few items marked higher than those in other competing stores. Successful discount stores usually sell fast-moving items and may offer less variety in size, color, style, and quality. A few manufacturers will not sell to a discount house or will sell the same item under a different label. Often, discount stores make a "special purchase" deal with a manufacturer and then offer an exceptional bargain to consumers.

Nondiscount stores are increasing their "private label" brands. These retailers also purchase "distress" goods—surplus stocks of manufacturers, wholesalers, and other stores—and offer them at much lower prices built around a "special purchase." However, some of these "sales" are fictitious.

Textile Fiber Products Identification Act

Consumers have a new shopping aid when buying clothing, rugs, curtains, slip-covers, and various household textiles. This federal law, which became effective March 3, 1960, requires that all textile products carry a label stating the exact percentage of each fiber in the fabric. Furthermore, when trademarks and trade names are used on labels, the generic name [chemical family category] must also appear "in immediate conjunction therewith and such trademark and generic names must appear in type or lettering of equal size and conspicuousness." If it is a two-sided label, the front side must show clearly the words "fiber content on reverse side."

Consumers must become acquainted with the generic names that are on textile labels. Most consumers know the properties and characteristics of the natural textile fibers—cotton, wool, silk, and linen—but many of the synthetic fibers were known only by their trademarks or trade names. Now the more than seven hundred trade names for man-made fibers are classified within one or more of the 16 generic groups that have been defined by the Federal Trade Commission. The qualities of these generic groups, when understood, serve as guides to proper washing, drying, pressing temperatures, and the durability of the fabrics.

To aid consumers in understanding the generic groups of man-made textile fibers, a list of properties, trade names, and use is presented in Table 9-2, A Quick Guide to Synthetic Fibers.

PROBLEMS CONSUMERS FACE IN CLOTHING AND TEXTILE STANDARDS AND LABELING[5]

Much of the information presented in this chapter in regard to planning, buying, care of, and paying for clothing and shoes could be even more useful to the consumer if there were better standards of labeling. The contemporary revolution in textiles and clothing, with all its salient benefits, brings problems, too. First came rayon, and then nylon, followed by dozens of other man-made fibers and yarns. Chemical manipulation also modified familiar natural fibers into substantially new products—cotton that has some of the characteristics of synthetics, and wool that does not shrink and retains a crease. New finishes have been created. New ways have been discovered to weave fabrics and to manufacture garments using almost every combination of these components. And the revolution is still going on.

Complexity of Modern Textiles

Consumers have fallen hopelessly behind in their understanding of modern textiles. Even the most knowledgeable people have trouble identifying the fabric of which a garment is made, and even when given this information they cannot adequately predict the garment's performance. Fiber and fabrics producers often publish information about their products, but it tends to be highly promotional or technical, beyond the comprehension of the average customer, salesperson, and merchant alike.

[5] For details see Consumer Advisory Council, *Consumer Issue '66*, U.S. Government Printing Office, 1966; *Consumers Union Report for the President's Committee on Consumer Interests,* April, 1966.

TABLE 9-2   A QUICK GUIDE TO SYNTHETIC FIBERS

CHEMICAL GENERIC NAME	SOME TRADE NAMES	PROPERTIES
Acrylics	Acrilan, Vyleran, Orlon, Zefran, Creslan	Soft hand, lightweight, bulk (warmth without weight); resistant to sunlight; wrinkle-resistant; good dimensional stability; dries fast; pleats and creases can be heat-set permanently.
Modacrylics (modified acrylic)	Dynel, Verel	Similar to acrylics but nonflammable; very sensitive to heat; subject to piling.
Polyesters	Dacron, Kodel, Vycron	Wrinkle-resistant; pleats and creases can be permanently set by heat; dimensionally, stable; good body, drape, and hand; little or no ironing necessary, so adds easy-care qualities; favored for its worsted hand.
Nylon	Nylenka, Banlon, Chemstrand, Agilon, Du Pont, IRC	Strongest of all fibers even when wet, yet lightweight; resists abrasion; wrinkle-resistant; dries fast; dimensionally stable; resists perspiration damage; good elasticity; wear and tear resistance; easy care; pleat retention in a multiplicity of fabrics.
Olefin	Olane, Prolene, Reevon	Auto seat covers; outdoor furniture; marine rope, belts; handbags. Strong and lightweight; highly resistant to rubbing and stretching; easily cleaned.
Nytril	Darvan	Deep-pile women's coats; soft, resilient quality; used in sweaters.
Saran	Dawbarn, Velon	Excellent resistance to soiling and staining; resistant to acids and alkalies and to attack by bacteria and insects. Principally used in screens, upholstery, fabrics, and carpets, and in blends with other fibers for drapery and casement cloth.
Spandex	Tycron, Vyrene	Elasticity; softer than rubber but having many of the same properties; extremely lightweight; used in foundation garments and swimwear.
Vinal	Vinylon	Reported to be useful in a wide variety of textile applications, including all forms of wearing apparel, blankets, curtains, sheets, carpets, tire cord, fish nettings, tents, and ropes. High softening temperature; high dry strength.
Vinyon	Vinyon, Rhovyl T	Resistant to moths and mildew; nonflammability (melts but does not flame); low melting point, can be easily molded.
Rayon	Tyrex, rayon, Fortisan, Super L, Corval, Topel	Absorbency; washability; will shrink unless treated for shrinkage; easy ironing with a fairly hot iron. No resistance to wrinkling; special finish required if resistance is desired. Flammability if napped; fabric should be treated for flame resistance.

CHEMICAL GENERIC NAME	SOME TRADE NAMES	PROPERTIES
Acetate	Arnel, Avisco, Celanese, Estron	Little absorbency, so dries rather quickly. Heat sensitivity, so fabric must be pressed with a cool iron to prevent fusing at thick places. Triacetates will stand higher ironing temperatures. Some wrinkle resistance. Poor resistance to fume or gas fading (color change due to atmospheric conditions). Spun or dope dyeing developed to overcome this problem. Tendency to accumulate static electricity.
Azlon		Fabrics made from protein fibers. Following properties are usually contributed by these fibers: softness, elasticity, absorbency, dimensional stability.
Glass	Fiberglas, PPG, Uniformat	Little absorbency, so can be washed easily and dried quickly. Flame-resistant; resistant to fungi, microorganisms, moths, acid, and rot. Little resistance to flexing, having tendency to break along crease lines. Freedom from odor.
Metallic	Lurex, Reymet, Fairtex, Mallora, Lame, Metlon	Metallic fibers coated with plastic; widely used as ornamental fibers in clothing and household textiles; do not tarnish with wear or use. Plastic coating has tendency to stick to iron if too high heat is used.
Rubber	Polyisoprene	Core for covered yarns used in a wide variety of fabrics; foundation garments, suspenders, garters, and similar garments. Yarns vary greatly in tensile strength but have great elongation and 100 percent elastic recovery. Do not absorb moisture and are moderately resistant to heat. Should not be exposed to excessive sunlight or heat, or to oils, fats, or greases (lotions or creams).

One special problem in textiles is premature marketing of innovations by which the consumer does the testing. Prematurity often involves exaggerated claims. The classic example was wash-and-wear a few years ago. A similar situation seems to exist with the new "durable press" or "permanent press" garments. There is also a considerable amount of fabric failure in washing and dry cleaning.

Some of these problems stem straight from the new materials and processes. Others are the same old problems that we failed to solve before the revolution and that have now become more acute as a result of it.

We need to give more serious attention to safety, size, dimensional stability (shrinkage), colorfastness, performance claims, care and maintenance, and durability and workmanship.

Flammability

No one should be asked to decide for himself about the safety of any fabric in the market. Yet synthetics have in some instances complicated the safety question instead of alleviating it.

In 1953 Congress passed the Flammable Fabrics Act as a reaction to the tragic stories of young girls burned by sweaters so highly flammable that they exploded into flames in the presence of a lighted match or cigarette. But the act was limited to wearing apparel, although hosiery and interlinings were excluded. A particularly glaring omission from regulation is blankets and other bedclothes. Who would believe that "receiving blankets" for babies do not have to meet flammability limitations?[6] Electric blankets and carpets are also excluded from this act, although they have shown themselves to be highly flammable according to tests by Consumers Union.

1967 Amendment to the Flammable Fabrics Act.   The Flammable Fabrics Act of 1953 was amended in 1967. While the enactment of this amendment will not provide an immediate solution, it will provide the federal government with the necessary tools—broader research; investigation and standard-setting authority—to help reduce the number of persons who are victims of hazardous flammable fabrics, according to the report from the Safety Commission hearings in 1967. A weakness in the amendment is in the time it takes for testing products, producing standards, holding hearings with textile and clothing manufacturers, judicial review, and final acceptance by the industry and government. Until new standards are instigated, the amendment remains only a future promise of safety.

Size

The size tag is not reliable. The situation is especially chaotic with women's and children's wear. Many items, such as blouses, underwear, and shirts, often come packaged in sealed plastic packages that discourage people from trying things on before buying them. Thus an unsatisfactory fit is not discovered in the store.

Rational sizing schemes can be developed. After a study by the U.S. Department of Agriculture and the garment industry involving 36 measurements of about 150,000 children and 58 measurements of almost 15,000 women, commercial standards for apparel sizing were established. Despite these standards, unreliable size tags crop up in independent testing. Consumers Union found manufacturers disagreeing by as much as an inch on the waist measurements

---

[6] Story of tests of "receiving blankets" in *Consumer Reports,* October, 1964.

corresponding to a given age-size. Studies by the American Association of University Women have confirmed widespread dissatisfaction with size fits.

Dimensional Stability

Shrinkage is a perennial problem with textiles. But great strides have been made in solving it. Preshrinking of woven textile products is widely practiced. Wool can now be stabilized somewhat. There is very little shrinkage in synthetic-fiber fabrics. Even some knit goods are now advertised as maintaining their size after proper laundering.

The consumer's problem in the midst of these advances is that he must learn how to distinguish the garments that are stable from those that are not. Shrinkage behavior of garments with no shrinkage designation is completely unpredictable. Some processes, such as Sanforizing, are fairly reliable. Some manufacturers, while using fabric that is properly stabilized, will use thread or other components that shrink, causing seams to pucker. But how is a consumer to tell what the shrinkage will be in a product that merely says "preshrunk"? In the absence of standards, "preshrunk" can mean anything.

In the case of stretchy knit fabrics and garments, the shopper faces a chaos of meaningless claims. Even the new synthetic-fiber stretch fabrics pose many problems. Neither industry standards nor consumer standards exist to define the stretch in stretch fabrics.

Standards for dimensional stability are essential to consumer satisfaction. If voluntary standards cannot be agreed upon by industry, consumers, and the federal government, the FTC ought to ask the National Bureau of Standards to develop standards. After standards have been established and agreed upon, the label should be required to state the type of care and maintenance necessary to maintain the dimensional stability of the product.

Colorfastness

In the present market there is no way for a consumer to know the degree of colorfastness of any item or textile. Technology exists by which the consumer could be given full information. American Standard L-22 (performance requirements for textiles) defines a minimum degree of colorfastness and a standard test procedure for about 75 basic end uses for fabrics. A majority of the industry agreed to use these important standards. Today, however, L-22 remains unknown to the consumer.

In the fall of 1969, by order of the FTC, the United States of America Standards Institute, Inc., name was changed to the American National Standards Institute, Inc. (ANSI). The chief function of the ANSI is not development of standards, but the adoption of standards formulated by its member organizations. The ANSI is presently making efforts to get its members to adopt a revision of L-22 standards. This information certainly could and should be given to consumers.

Performance Claims

The performance of textile products is their basic claim to utility. But when manufacturers write about performance in ads and on labels, they usually use the same superlatives. It would be rare to see a manufacturer state that his product performs less well than that of his competitors. Nevertheless, product performance often does differ among competing products. It must mean that similar words have different meanings from one manufacturer to the next. Consumers Union, for example, tested water-repellent topcoats reported in *Consumer Reports,* April, 1966. Standard tests showed clear differences among the coats tested. But the manufacturer does not put this important information on the label. There are many other examples. How permanent are the new "permanent press" finishes? How warm are "winter-weight" blankets? How resistant is "stain-resistant" finish?

Words should have clearly defined meanings, and ways should be found to get this information to the purchaser.

Care and Maintenance

Many hang tags on textile products that give specific and accurate instructions on care and maintenance. Unfortunately, these are usually disposed of with all the miscellaneous tags and wrappings that come with each purchase. When the time comes to wash or clean a garment, the consumer does not know how. For this reason consumers and retailers have been urging wider use of sewn-in care labels.

Some positive steps were taken in 1966 when the President's Committee on Consumer Interests asked Mrs. Esther Peterson, the President's Special Assistant for Consumer Affairs, to appoint an Industry Advisory Committee on Textile Information. This committee, made up of some 36 representatives of every part of the textile fabrics business community, was given a mandate to come up with recommendations for care labeling information. In April, 1966, they recommended permanently attached care labels on all textile products where special-care instructions are needed. Many countries—Sweden, England, and the Netherlands, among others—already have permanent care instructions and, in addition, information on material, colorfastness, and shrinkage. So far, nothing has happened in this respect here.

Durability and Workmanship

Before the advent of the new finishes, synthetic interlinings, and other hidden components of contemporary clothing, a knowledgeable consumer could make a fairly intelligent judgment on tailoring and workmanship. He could also recognize the fabric as wool, cotton, linen, or silk, and thus estimate its durability pretty well. Today, however, it is difficult even for an expert with laboratory facilities to evaluate textile products. The advertisements proclaim the new miracles. In the absence of experience or expertise, the consumer is bewildered by all the claims and counterclaims. In the ready-to-wear shop, how can he know whether a suit will lose its shape after a few dry cleanings, or whether an attractively woven fabric of some unpronounceable fiber is going to pill? Such information on estimated service is nowhere available on the labels and tags. Quite obviously, people need this information.

WHAT NEEDS TO BE DONE IN STANDARDS AND LABELING?

What needs to be done, then, to help the consumer? All the other problems discussed, except safety, may be considered to stem from inadequate communication between seller and buyer. Communication implies language, and language implies definition. Thus, when the consumer asks about sizes, a reply should be possible in universally accepted terms; when he asks about colorfastness to light, a reply should be possible on the basis of a definition of "colorfastness to light" adhered to by every manufacturer.

Standards

In some circles these definitions are called "standards" and the process of developing them is called "standardization." Critics of standards falsely equate them with potentially rigid uniformity of manufacture or product design. What standardization does connote is uniformity of meaning, or, simply, a definition. The more complicated concepts must often be defined in terms of test methods. For example, the flammability of a textile product can be described meaningfully only by specifying the kind of flame to which it will be exposed, the duration of exposure, the condition of the product at the time of exposure (dry, brushed, etc.), and so on. The item that fails to sustain a flame under these conditions meets the definition for nonflammability.

It would be immensely helpful to consumers if the textile industry would agree on sets of definitions for all the important properties of textile products and would use the defined property characterizations in describing their products. There is no good reason why industry, together with government and consumer representatives, should not be able to take such a step voluntarily rather than under compulsion. Only those properties affecting the safety of the user clearly need to be set by law. But if industry proves itself unwilling or unable to agree on some voluntary definitions, compulsory ones should then be imposed.

Actually, a reasonably good start has been made toward formulating standards for the characteristics of many textile products. There are some products, however, for which research remains to be done on the technical background upon which standards should be built. But this should present no obstacle. In the 1930s, the National Bureau of Standards performed exemplary work of this kind. It developed standards and specifications (groups of standards, sometimes including required levels of performance for each characteristic) for blankets, women's hosiery, carpets and rugs, and other products. This kind of work should be resumed by the Institute of Applied Technology of the Bureau of Standards.

Voluntary Standards.   Like the "no-law" law, standards which are not used are "no-standards." There is a long history of commercial standards (on size, for example) that are not used, even by those who have signed them. ANSI standard L-22 (Performance Requirements for Textiles) has lain dormant since its adoption several years ago; it might have laid the basis for a system of informative end-use labeling. Some people argue that these standards are not dormant but are used by the industry internally, even though the consumer never knows it. But what the consumer does not know will not help him. As we have pointed out, the problem is to tell him what he needs to know. What does it matter that one producer's product conforms to L-22 specifications and another's does not, if the consumer cannot single out the conforming product? It does no good to assure him that "a large part of the industry conforms to L-22." Nor does it help to say that many producers are using the sizing standards of Commercial Standard CS 215-58, without telling the consumer exactly what producers are so doing.

Solving the consumer's textile problems means not merely establishing definitions or standards. Equally important, it means letting him in on the secret of product characteristics. Various methods for conveying this information have been proposed.

Standards Definitions.   One proposal—the most modest—would require that any descriptions of properties of textiles on labels or in advertisements must be in terms of the agreed-upon definitions. Policing would have to be provided. Perhaps, if their procedures could be speeded up, it could fall under the normal jurisdiction of the FTC, which would at last be given firm criteria for determining when advertising is deceptive. But such a proposal, while quieting fake or meaningless claims, would fall far short of full disclosure. It would leave each producer free to decide which properties, if any, he would publicize. Some manufacturers would probably decide to remain mute on the most important properties of a product, promoting some other about which his competitor was silent. The consumer would then be left with his present inability to compare the quality of competing products.

Informative Labeling in Sweden and England. A more effective approach is the Swedish Varudeklarationsnamnden (VDN) labeling system, established in 1951 and still going strong. The VDN is financed and administered by government, business, and consumer groups, whose representatives meet to agree on the essential information needed by the consumer. Each product characteristic is defined and, when necessary, made verifiable by reference to a standard test method devised by a standards-making agency. Labels of quality are also established, when appropriate, for each characteristic. Once all this has been done, a manufacturer may apply for use of the standardized label on his product. He pays a small fee for the right to do so, but his expense is offset by the value of the label in attracting buyers. The VDN authority, on its part, publicizes its labels as a trustworthy source of consumer information. Although the manufacturer must put on the label only a required minimum of information, all characteristics of his product he chooses to label must conform to the standard terminology.

The British Tell-Tag System is modeled on Sweden's system. But in England the manufacturer must include all the defined characteristics on his labels, using the standard terminology and grade levels. In each country, the labeling agency itself polices the system.

The consumer in Sweden and England is thus in the enviable position of being able to get reliable information at the point of sale on the essential characteristics of the product he wants, and to get it in a form that makes direct comparison easy and accurate. He can translate price differences into precise quality differences, and he can make an intelligent decision about whether to pay more or less, depending on his own particular needs.

The Consumer Selects. Under the Swedish and British systems, the consumer is required to evaluate the level of quality of each characteristic on the label of one brand of product against the comparable information on another. For example, in shopping for a blanket, he might find one labeled:

Colorfastness to laundering, excellent;
dimensional stability, fair;
durability, good;
piling, poor.

Another blanket might state:

Colorfastness to laundering, fair;
dimensional stability, excellent;
durability, fair;
piling, good.

Manufacturers who adopt the VDN label must include all the information required in the specification. A Swedish VDN informative label on curtain fabric might have the following characteristics:

VDN
CURTAIN MATERIAL

Width:
   See separate label.
Material:
   100% cotton.
Colorfastness:
   To light, 6-8
   To washing, 4-5
   (Highest rating is 4-5, except for fastness
      to light, where it is 6-8.)
Shrinkage:
   0% in length.
Washing:
   Method—Colored fabrics, 60° C.
   (Manufacturer's name and address here.)

Assuming that all the blankets or curtain fabrics are the same in other important characteristics, and assuming that the consumer knows and understands the labeling definitions, his chances of making a wise decision are definitely better than they would have been if all he had to go on were store claims such as "The best blanket ever sold" or manufacturer claims such as "Gorgeous colors . . . heavenly . . . Zephyrlike." But the decision on which blanket or curtain to buy is still a difficult one.

   Standards of Quality.   If the L-22 standard were used as a basis for certification, we would, in fact, right now have a "minimum standard of grade" scheme.

   Many manufacturers, in opposing the use of L-22, argue that the minimum tends to become the maximum, and that, anyway, their products are well above the minimum and would be competing with others at the minimum, both carrying the L-22 certification, so that the consumer could make no distinction.

   These arguments have some validity. The answer to them would be a multiple "standards of grade" system. True, it would be most complex to devise, but it would also be the easiest for the consumer to use. Again, we have a prototype in wide use—the USDA food grading scheme. The Department of Agriculture says: "USDA grades for food are a dependable, nationally uniform guide to quality and a means of making valid comparisons of quality and price." USDA grading schemes have been established for more than 300 farm products—meat, poultry, eggs, dairy products, and fruits and vegetables, among other foods. They are voluntary grades "unless required under State or local law or an industry program."

   Textile grading, like food grading, would define several grades of overall quality for each product. A product could not receive a top-grade designation unless it met the requirements for top grade for each characteristic entering into the overall quality definition for that product. The consumer, having learned the meaning of the grades, could make selections far more easily than under any other scheme. Once he knew that two products were of the same grade, he could limit his comparison to color, style, special features, and price. How much easier and more rewarding shopping would become under such conditions!

Why Oppose Standards?   Why, then, do we not have such schemes for some kinds of textile products, at least? P. G. Agnew, that giant figure in the standards movement, probably puts his finger on the right answer when he says:

> Perhaps [the manufacturers] attitude may be fairly summarized by saying that insofar as they are aware of the movement they see it simply as a feeble and ill-advised attack upon the institution of trade brands. Because trade brands and the tremendous volume of advertising based upon them constitute the very citadel of modern merchandising, the attitude is that the movement for consumer standards is to be ignored if possible; but if it cannot be ignored, it must be fought.

And Jessie Coles sees it this way: "Their real reason is that they fear the effects of standards . . . upon the quasi-monopolistic positions they have developed through advertising and use of brands. Many apparently fear the effect which public knowledge of qualities of their goods would have upon their sales."

There are, to be sure, difficult technical problems to be solved. Standards need to be developed; overall quality and grade levels must be defined. Says Jessie Coles: "The development of such information may require much specialized research and considerable time and effort. However, the absence of adequate information does not constitute a serious or permanent obstacle, since its development can be accomplished if such a program is consciously planned and seriously pursued."

The fact is that on an industry level in some cases such standards of quality already exist. Manufacturers make and sell different quality lines, using their own definitions of quality. As in other standards endeavors, obstacles to agreement among different interests will crumble in the face of determined effort. If many foods can be graded, textile products can also be graded.

Certification List.   The government, through the General Services Administration, buys many consumer products, and these are tested for conformance to GSA purchase specifications. It has been proposed that conforming products should be certified by the GSA. Such certification lists could give standing to many otherwise unknown brands, bringing small manufacturers into effective competition with highly advertised brands. Thus the work of governmental technical efforts would be used doubly—for its own purchasing and for the benefit of the consumer.

WHAT IS MY CLOTHING IQ?

1. Have you any costly clothing mistakes hanging in your closet?
2. Do you make an annual or periodical replacement inventory of all your clothing?
3. Do you set aside a certain amount of your income for clothes and keep within that limit?
4. Do you save money in advance and shop the genuine clothing sales?
5. Do you generally buy clothing that fits your needs?
6. Do you shop several stores and compare quality, value, style, and fit?
7. Do you generally compare the store brands and the nationally advertised brands?
8. Do you know what to check when shopping the more expensive clothing items?
9. Do you avoid "bargains" when you have no immediate need for the merchandise?
10. Do you know how to combine friendliness, courtesy, and good buying techniques when consulting a salesperson?
11. Do you always read the clothing tags and labels that are available?
12. Do you take the time to tell a salesperson who is helping you that it would be a good idea to have more informative labels?
13. Do you handle clothing in a store carefully to prevent damage and to minimize waste?
14. Do you realize that credit and delivery add to the cost of clothing purchased in stores that offer these services?
15. Do you always purchase clothing with the intention of keeping it and return goods only if they have material defects?
16. Do you buy clothing when you are bored or when you are angry or upset about something?
17. Do you think about the upkeep cost when buying clothing?
18. Do you build your wardrobe around two or three color schemes or around many colors?
19. Can you clearly describe to a salesperson exactly what you want?
20. Do you ask to see more than one quality level for comparison to get the best value for the money or possibly save money?
21. Do you avoid buying clothing in chain stores and department stores?
22. Do you generally buy clothing at the highest price level that your budget can stand?
23. Do you file for later reference valuable information that teaches better buymanship?
24. Do you file for future use any tags and labels that explain how to care for garments that you purchase?

QUESTIONS FOR DISCUSSION

1. How do you rate on What Is My Clothing IQ?

2. Have you ever anaiyzed your reasons for purchasing a certain item? Try it. Search below the surface for underlying motives.

3. When shopping for clothes, do you generally get all the information necessary to make an intelligent selection? Can you get most of this information from the label attached to the merchandise, or is the salesperson competent in answering your questions?

4. Using the Clothing Replacement Inventory suggested in this chapter, can you determine what minimum annual sum and garments you need to keep your present wardrobe up to a standard that is satisfactory for your way of life?

5.   Check labels on clothing for evidence of the effectiveness of the Textile Fiber Products Identification Act and the 1967 Flammable Fabrics Amendment.

ACTIVITY PROBLEMS

1.   Organize a class project on how to buy clothing. Let each student select a clothing item in which he is interested. Use information prepared by competent persons. Give all the sources used. An editorial committee of three persons might collect all the investigative reports and prepare a mimeographed collection that can be distributed to each person in the class.

2.   Report on a recent clothing purchase. Name the garment purchased; considerations given to fashion, style, color, fabric, workmanship, cost, use, brand, and advertising; stores visited; observations; examination of article; decision and reasons for it; and method of payment.

3.   Collect several clothing labels and analyze the statements on each label.

a.   What is the item made of?
b.   What treatment or finishes have been given to the material?
c.   What service can be expected from it?
d.   What special care will it require?
e.   Who makes or sells it?
f.   How could each label be more helpful?

4.   College women can compare and discuss the cost of making their own clothes with the price they would have to pay in the retail stores. Keep accurate records of all costs, even of the thread used.

5.   If you live in a large city, compare the price of the same garment in two or more stores owned by the same company. Why would the cost of the same garment differ in stores owned by the same company?

6.   Ask a good shoe merchant to demonstrate the characteristics of good and poor shoe construction. He may be willing to take an old shoe apart to identify the following: upper, sole, insole, toe, lining, shank, counter, box, and heel.

7.   Stage a fashion show for the class or for a larger audience and include illustrations of poor clothing choices, each followed by a superior choice.

SUGGESTED READINGS

Anspack, Farlyne: *The Way of Fashion,* Iowa State University Press, Ames, Iowa, 1967.

"Care Labeling Guide Labeled Unsatisfactory," *Consumer Reports,* February, 1968.

"Clothing Expenditures for Individuals," *Family Economics Review,* March, 1968.

"Flammable Fabrics," *Consumer Reports,* February, 1968.

"International Care Labelling of Textiles," International Organization of Consumers Unions, The Hague, The Netherlands, 1968.

"Purchases of Various Types of Clothing for Men, Women, and Children," *Family Economics Review,* September, 1968.

A Report from the Industry Advisory Committee on Textile Information, May, 1966, President's Committee on Consumer Interests, Washington, D.C., 1966.

Rosencranz, Mary Lou: "Clothing Symbolism," *Journal of Home Economics,* January, 1962.

chapter 10

A HOME FOR YOUR FAMILY

What do young married couples want most after they are married? Their own home. But the shelter problem is not a simple one. There are many complex factors in the economics and sociology of housing. Modern fixtures and hidden costs present technically subtle and expensive options. Schools, neighborhood, and other environmental factors in the urban centers present complicated and future mobile risks for the family that is tied to an owned home.

High carrying charges and unexpected tax assessments for modern municipal developments put a premium on foresight about ability to pay for a house out of regular income. Mortgage companies and other links of the modern corporate housing industry involve technicalities with which few persons are prepared to deal intelligently and safely. Dozens of risks, big and little, are smothered under sales talks. One of the major risks is deciding how much to budget for shelter.

INTRODUCTION

Problems Facing Young Marrieds

The following questions represent the problems that must be decided and overcome by young couples who wonder whether it is wiser to keep renting the family shelter or to begin planning for ultimate purchase of a home.

Should we buy or rent quarters?
How much can we afford to spend on housing?
If we purchase a house, how can we finance it at the least cost?
What are the legal pitfalls and problems?
How do we go about selecting a good site or location?
How difficult is it to rent if you have small children?
What are the advantages and disadvantages in owning or renting a home?
Is it cheaper to own than to rent?
Where can we get reliable information in settling these problems?
Are there many unexpected expenses when moving into a new home?
How much will hazard insurance cost on a home?
What is involved when working through a real estate broker?
Is the home that is being considered in keeping with future family needs?

There is an almost universal prejudice against children on the part of landlords. Some young married couples postpone having children because they are unwilling to subject themselves to the indignities often encountered in searching for adequate living quarters for a growing family. In the first place, rental charges are too high. And in the second place, even with sufficient income to rent modern quarters in a good neighborhood, landlord prejudice against young children limits the rental possibilities.

Families that are forced to buy or build homes under these two pressures are likely to find it difficult to regain the flexibility of rental status without inconvenience, loss of equity, or both, if they cannot carry the expense of their purchase.

Your Housing Goals

Finding the best place to live is one of the most important decisions an individual or family makes. The values responsible for choices in housing vary from family to family and for one family for different periods in its life cycle. Even though few families can achieve all their housing goals, a more satisfying decision can be made if a family is aware of the goals it desires the most.

Many families want reasonable privacy, comfort, health and safety, facilities for leisure-time activities, convenient and accessible stores and good schools, prestige (good address and the right playmates for the children), congenial neighbors, churches, good playgrounds, and other goals.

When thinking about your housing goals, picture your family's daily needs and activities. Children need play and study space, breadwinners need to relax, and the family needs space and facilities to live together as a unit. The more you plan how you want to live, the more likely are the prospects of knowing what kind of living space to rent, buy, or build.

Housing and the Family Life Cycle

The requirements of a family home change during the life of the family. These changes, moreover, parallel changes in the family life pattern. Also, family members undergo many changes: financial; physical and mental; culture interests; children growing up, then leaving home for schooling, then getting married. These and other changes affect family life from beginning to end, dividing the family cycle into the (1) beginning family, (2) expanding family, (3) launching family, (4) middle-age family, and (5) old-age family.

The modern home, in whatever form, is usually the center of family life. There have been changes in the functions of the home, but basically most American homes provide space for cooking, eating, sleeping, recreation—play, hobbies, listening—carport or garage, personal hygiene, laundering, and storage. Most people never own a home in which they live out the entire family cycle from early marriage to death. Why? For one reason, we are a "mobile people." The United States Chamber of Commerce has reported that in one year 35 million people, 21 percent of the population, moved to different homes—23 million to different homes in the same county, 7 million to a different county in the same state, and 5 million to a different state or out of the country. For another reason, American families strive to become more affluent, and their wants and desires include better or more expensive housing when there is increased ability to pay for it. All in all, selecting housing for a family is a highly complex problem that should not be taken lightly.

Basic Concepts in Housing

When considering the various alternatives in family housing, use the following basic concepts as guidelines.

1.   The choice of a home is related to family goals.
2.   The consumer considers alternative ways of securing shelter.
3.   Housing requires large amounts of capital.
4.   Homeownership is ordinarily a long-term investment.
5.   Housing investment is sensitive to future trends.
6.   Fixed charges and operating expenses are significant factors of homeownership.
7.   Houses are relatively immobile (5.5 million people live in 2 million mobile homes).
8.   Housing is beginning to benefit from mass production techniques.
9.   Construction materials are shortest when demand is greatest.
10.   Restrictive practices sometimes prevent use of new, economical designs, materials, and construction methods.
11.   Housing may involve a "do-it-yourself" program.

HOMEOWNERSHIP AND RENTING

In 1890 almost half of the families in the United States owned their own homes. The Great Depression during the early 1930s reversed the trend, causing homeownership to fall to an all-time low of 43.6 percent in 1940. By 1960 the homeownership rate had increased to 61.9 percent. Since then, homeownership has continued to advance, reaching a record of 63.6 percent in 1967, according to the *Savings and Loan Fact Book, 1968.*

A 1967 Census Bureau report shows that of the 59 million families in the United States, about 1.55 million families own second homes, which they use fairly regularly through the year. The picture of the family unit that owns and uses a second home is still one of affluence and older age, but not so wealthy and old as was once true.

Why Do Families Buy a Home?

A recent survey conducted by the United States Savings and Loan League indicated that the dominant reasons for homeownership were noneconomic. A minority of homeowners responding, however, felt that buying a home enabled them to build an equity in real estate, and some stated that buying a house was cheaper than renting. The majority of homeowners, however, felt that homeownership provides a better environment for the children, privacy, and freedom to improve the property and fills the need for more space. A few said that their wives wanted to own a home.

Age and Income Differences

Homeownership is concentrated in the middle and older age groups. Almost three out of four persons in the age group 35 to 64 years own their homes. Although older people provide much of the demand for apartments, about two-thirds of those 65 or older either live in or continue to hold title to their homes.

New Ownership Patterns

Homeownership is usually identified with a single-family house. However, relatively new kinds of housing extend ownership to the apartment dweller. The older and widely used arrangement is the cooperative apartment. A newer type of unit ownership is the condominium.

Cooperative Housing

Under the cooperative-apartment type of ownership the apartment dweller owns shares in a nonprofit corporation which holds title to the building, and he has a long-term proprietary lease on his individual apartment. The real estate taxes and operating costs are prorated among the owners, and the cooperative makes all disbursements and assessments. The transfer of the apartment unit is accomplished by a transfer of shares in the corporation.

At present there are some 640 housing cooperatives in this country serving some 165,000 member families and doing an annual business of $235 million, according to *Coop Report* for September, 1968. Over 15,000 families of moderate income live in cooperative apartments in New York City. Under construction (1969) in the East Bronx is a $300 million, 15,200-unit Coop City. Another housing cooperative enterprise rising in Brooklyn will house 6,000 persons in Twin Pines Village.

Most cooperative housing is produced for middle-income families (usually for incomes under $7,400), although Congress has enacted the rent-supplement program for the low-income family.

Cooperative housing can be found in most states in this country. Present cooperative housing in smaller cities and towns averages about 200 units and in large cities 1,000 or more units.

It is possible to get better housing at less cost through nonprofit cooperative housing. A recent independent survey by the Peoples Gas Company of Chicago covered 29 projects, including 15 rental projects and 14 cooperatives in eight cities. The conclusion was that cooperative housing is available at a lower monthly charge than rental housing. The average figures were as follows:[1]

	COOPERATIVE MONTHLY CHARGE	RENTAL MONTHLY CHARGE
1 bedroom	$63	$ 86
2 bedrooms	83	99
3 bedrooms	91	107

[1] *Owners, Not Tenants,* Foundation for Cooperative Housing, Chicago, 1968.

In the cooperative housing there was an average down payment of $258. In the rental projects, a security deposit equal to one month's rent was customarily charged.

Condominium Housing

The condominium is a newer type of unit ownership in a multifamily structure. Under this arrangement the apartment dweller holds direct legal title to the apartment in which he lives and a proportionate interest in the common areas and the underlying ground. Ownership rights in an individual unit are the same as if it were a single-family dwelling. Rules and regulations for managing the property are set forth in the deed and are binding upon the owner. In most states, when a unit is sold, ownership is conveyed by a transfer of title.

With land becoming scarcer and the desire to own real property continuing, interest in condominiums is increasing. This new kind of homeownership will be a factor in maintaining a high rate of owner occupancy in the years to come.

Cooperative and Condominium Tax Benefits

Cooperatives and condominiums offer the prospect of combining the economic and tax benefits of homeownership with the convenience of apartment living. Yet, there are important differences between the various forms of real estate investment, particularly in their tax treatment. One should get professional advice before making a purchase.

Generally, both cooperatives and condominiums offer considerable tax advantage because local taxes and interest on the mortgage can be deducted from income taxes. Also, capital gains taxes can be deferred if a home is sold and the money is reinvested in a cooperative or condominium. And there is the big nontax benefit of building up an equity.

If one buys a cooperative apartment he, in effect, buys stock in a corporation. He does not own his apartment outright. This arrangement complicates tax deductions. For example, a husband who puts up *all* the money to buy a cooperative apartment but enters into a joint ownership situation with his wife may wind up owing gift taxes. The gift-tax law says the creation of a husband-wife joint tenancy in real estate is *not* a gift—which includes a house as well as a condominium. But a cooperative apartment is considered personal property, not real property, and the exemption does not apply. There are ways to overcome this tax responsibility.

Homeownership versus Renting

We will be concerned here only with the economics of homeownership and renting. Between 1960 and 1964, the cost of homeownership and rent for urban wage earners increased at about the same rate as "all items" in the Consumer Price Index—about 1 percent a year (Figure 10-1). Beginning in 1964, however, rents have risen less rapidly and homeownership costs more rapidly than the all-items index. In 1967, the index for rents was 112, for homeownership 120, and for all items 116 (1957-1959 = 100). In the December, 1967, Index, the five homeownership costs had the following relative importance (expressed as percentages of the homeownership index): insurance, 3; property taxes, 13; mortgage interest, 21; maintenance and repairs, 22; and home purchase, 41. In general, the rise in the prices of homes reflects higher prices for land and used homes and much higher construction costs. Property taxes also rose as local governments needed more revenue. Between 1965 and 1968, mortgage interest rates rose 11 percent as a result of the tight money market. Another interest rate increase occurred in 1969.

In general, the factors that make homeownership costs rise also increase rents. However, rents tend to adjust more slowly. Leases account for some of the lag. Also, landlords may not pass on to their tenants all of the increased cost when the rental market is poor. Rental vacancy rates, however, have been relatively high much of the time since 1960. They averaged 7.5 percent between 1960 and 1965, then dropped. In 1967, the vacancy rate was 6.4 percent.

Obviously, no family is a statistical average. Yet, the Consumer Price Index does reveal the increase or decrease in the various components of the cost-of-living trends—in this case, the trends in cost of homeownership and renting. A more accurate method of figuring the cost of homeownership of a *specific* house and renting a *specific* dwelling or apartment is to compare the actual

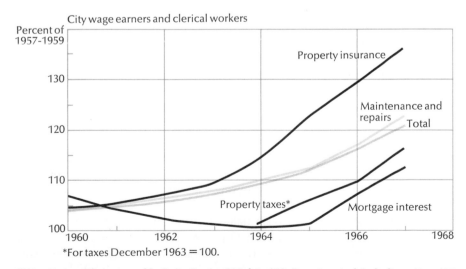

Figure 10-1   Homeownership Costs. Source: BLS data, U.S. Department of Agriculture, Neg. ARS 5874-(68) 2 Agricultural Research Service.

costs. Let us say you have a house in mind that costs $25,000, with $10,000 down payment and a $15,000 first mortgage at 6¼ percent interest for 20 years. The financing (principal and interest) is about $120 per month on the loan. An apartment in a good neighborhood and with a comparable number of rooms rents for $250 a month. The facts seem overwhelming. Apartment, $250. House, $120. The actual costs in owning this home were considerably more than $120 a month.

The details of owning this house were these:

OWNERSHIP EXPENSE	BUDGET PER MONTH
Financing (principal, interest)	$120
Real estate taxes	35
Insurance (hazard, personal, property, liability)	8
Maintenance, repairs, improvements	75
Heating fuel	20
Electricity	15
Water	8
Garbage, trash collection	3
Telephone	7
Loss of interest at 6 percent on $10,000 down payment	50
Total	$341
Apartment budget	
Rent	$250
Telephone	7
Total	$257

As the rundown shows, these out-of-pocket and other costs are a far cry from $120 a month. They total $341 a month, quite a different piece of change. Many homeowners forget to include the interest they could earn each year on the downpayment. In the illustration cited, the $10,000 down payment at 6 percent would net about $50 a month while they owned it. It is reasonable to add loss of interest to the cost of living in the house. The accumulation of equity in the house is less than many people think. In a typical 20-year mortgage there is comparatively small equity accumulation during the first 7 to 10 years because most of the payments go to paying interest and very little into equity or principal.

No form of housing is a bargain unless it affords you contentment as well as shelter. Some people are "apartment people" by temperament, inclination, and style of living. Other people by temperament are inherent householders. For the latter, living in a house of their own is a source of self-fulfillment and satisfaction, and higher costs may not be an important factor in the choice.

Mobile Homes

Would you like a new, two-bedroom home completely outfitted with furniture and appliances for $6,000? And you'll get a house, not a trailer. This mobile home will have wheels, but you may never use them because the home may be nearly 60 feet long and 12 feet wide, with an expandable living room. The old-fashioned trailer home is about 32 feet long and 10 feet wide and can be pulled by a car. Over 10 percent of mobile homes sold today are double-wides or expandable and are not movable except by commercial transporter. In 1966, units 10 feet wide and over 54 feet long accounted for 7.6 percent of all mobile home shipments. Larger units 12 feet wide and over 54 feet long accounted for 39.9 percent of deliveries.[2]

Popularity of Mobile Homes. in 1967, delivery of mobile homes rose to 240,980 in number from 90,200 in 1961. These deliveries equaled 19 percent of all private nonfarm housing starts and 29.3 percent of all new single-family units. This suggests that these preengineered units are being widely accepted. Product development and construction of over 25,000 attractive parks have also contributed to the popularity of these mobile homes. Most of the units contain standard major appliances, furniture, draperies, lamps, wall-to-wall carpeting, hardwood paneling, wood floors, prefabricated fireplaces, walk-in closets, cedar closets, built-in stereo systems, and control heating and air conditioning. No wonder that more than 5,500,000 people live in more than 2 million mobile homes across our country.

Mobile homes have special appeal to young marrieds under 34 years of age (they purchase 43 percent of all mobile homes) and the elderly and the retired (they purchase 25 percent of all mobile homes). Such advantages as their convenience, their very small maintenance costs, being supplied completely furnished, their expandable features that provide a 24- by 14-foot living room and two or three bedrooms, and their low cost are important to these age groups.

Financing Mobile Homes. While the average mobile home 60 feet long and 12 feet wide costs about $6,000, you can buy new mobile homes for as little as $3,000 or as much as $15,000 or more. The average site-built home costs between $14 and $19 per square foot, in contrast to between $7.50 and $10 per square foot for a mobile home, complete with furniture and equipment.

In 1968 most sales required about 20 percent to 25 percent down payment, although 10 percent might be possible. The balance was financed like an automobile loan. You had 5 to 7 years to complete the payments. The quoted rate of 6 to 7 percent add-on really cost you from 11 to 15 percent simple interest. A $5,700 mobile home with a $700 down payment at 6 percent add-on over 7 years cost about $85 per month. If you could have gotten regular home mortgage-type financing, your monthly payments would have been around $73.

There are, of course, costs in parking your mobile home. In a high-quality park, with about 3,200 square feet per space, monthly rents without utilities

[2] *Savings and Loan Fact Book, 1968,* p. 29.

average $40. Water, sewage, electricity, gas, playgrounds, swimming pool, phone service, mail service, fire and police protection, and garbage collection are all available.

The average buyer of a mobile home depends on the dealer for financing and for information about the home. Some dealers are dependable. A dealer belonging to the Mobilehome Dealers National Association (MDNA) indicates that he subscribes to the group's code of ethics. Only one in six dealers were members of this organization in 1967. The MDNA also adopted construction standards for materials, equipment, and workmanship. These codes take some of the risk out of buying a mobile home.

Advantages of a Conventional Home

Because emotions alone must not be the guide, this most important single financial decision in the life of the average family—buying and owning a home—merits thoughtful, logical analysis. First, let us examine the 10 arguments for homeownership.

1. It is said that homeownership stabilizes the annual cost of a family's housing, because you can figure the immediate and future costs and thus keep housing costs at a set amount. This is an advantage when figuring the annual family budget.

2. It is contended that homeownership is a fairly safe form of investment. It is claimed that rent money is spent money. Why not pour the rent money into your own house? At the end of 15 or 20 years, you have the house and lot as an investment from your rent money. If the value of your home increases, you can sell your property at a profit.

3. There are possible income tax advantages in homeownership. You may deduct taxes and interest charges on your loan. For example, you may be paying a loaning agency $800 a year for your house—$130 may represent property taxes, and $310 may represent interest on the mortgage. Both these payments are proper income tax deductions.

4. There is more incentive to save when you own your home. According to this widespread belief, a family puts in a safe place savings that might tide them over hard times. With a home to pay for, the family will even forgo other pleasures or needs. Some families might not save a dime if not forced to do so by the fact of homeownership.

5. Homeownership improves the credit status of the family. The equity in the home investment is good collateral for an emergency loan.

6. Homeownership gives the family a sense of increased security, especially for old age. Once a home is owned clear, it may afford cheaper housing than renting, and if a drop in income comes with old age, the family will at least have a roof over its head.

7. The desire to provide a better home environment encourages many families to buy a home. It is believed that the children will have more favorable circumstances for play and work.

8. Closely connected with the preceding argument is another—that homeownership strengthens the general social and financial prestige of the family. This is regarded by some people to be likely if the house "shows well." Professional people are likely to be house-proud. This value placed on property ownership is based, in part, on middle-class emphasis on property as an index of social and economic status. Many homeowners like the feeling of homeownership.

9.   Some people buy homes to free themselves from the authority of landlords. The homeowner is his own master. The rent cannot be raised. He will not be evicted. The owner can make any alterations he can afford. The home can be changed to suit the way of living.

10.   Homeownership has also been cloaked with the virtues of good citizenship. Homeowners are supposed to have a greater feeling of civic interest. As a local tax-payer, the homeowner has a protective interest in the management of his town or city.

The above reasons sound convincing. Each of these 10 arguments has played a part in the decisions of millions of Americans to own their homes. But prospective homeowners should also investigate the *problems* of homeownership.

Disadvantages of Conventional Homeownership

There are, of course, some disadvantages in homeownership. The upkeep of house and property takes time and work and additional money, besides the expense involved in the original purchase.

1.   There is work and expense in maintaining the house and grounds. Time must be given to cutting grass, trimming shrubs and hedges, gardening, painting and decorating, and other tasks. Some families do not find these tasks burdensome, but rather enjoyable, a refreshing change from normal employment. But other families lose interest in this work in time, and deterioration sets in and lowers the value of the property.

2.   There must be constant maintenance of a house, the amount depending on its age and construction. A sum of money should be set aside each month to provide for whatever comes up that needs renewing or repair.

3.   As time goes on there will be reasons, perhaps, for wanting extra space—finishing a room or two in the attic, remodeling the basement recreation space, adding new kitchen equipment. Of course, this extra expense is offset by family happiness and contentment because of the increased livability of the home.

4.   Besides the mortgage and interest payments and the fees in connection with the original purchase, there will be monthly utility bills and real estate taxes; also, hazard insurance must be arranged.

5.   There is a strong tendency for families to overestimate their ability to pay for a new home. Too often, costs of maintenance and depreciation are never considered or figured beforehand.

How Much Housing Can You Afford?

This is the crucial question once you have made the decision to buy a conventional home. Experts have devised general rules of thumb to guide a family that is planning homeownership. One rule is that a family can afford a home that costs 2½ times their annual income; another rule is one week's pay out of each month's salary.

These are only general rules. They never fit a specific family's way of living, size of family, or income. To find out how much of your income you can af-

TABLE 10-1   YOUR INCOME FOR HOUSING

Total monthly income	$ _____
Total monthly wage or salary deductions, such as withholdings for income taxes, retirement, Social Security benefits, hospitalization insurance (subtract the second figure from the first)	_____
Total take-home pay	$ _____
Expenses:	
Monthly savings budget $ _____	
Food and clothing _____	
Medical care _____	
Life insurance _____	
Recreation _____	
Utilities and fuel _____	
Transportation _____	
All other expenses (membership dues, contributions, charge account and installment payment, etc.)	
Total expenses (subtract from take-home pay)	_____
Your income for housing	$ _____

ford toward buying a home, first make a list of your expenses and income. (Do not include the wife's income if it is expected to be temporary.) Table 10-1, Your Income for Housing, will give you an idea of what to include in your list.

You now have the approximate sum available for your housing on a monthly or yearly basis. Locate your housing income figure in Table 10-2, How Much Housing Can You Afford? to find the amount of the loan you can afford. The data in the table include principal and interest charges on a mortgage and allowances for taxes and insurance. Taxes have been estimated at $18 and insurance at $3 annually for every $1,000 loaned. Make adjustments to conform with your situation.

Suppose your income available for housing is $150 a month. According to the table, you can afford a home loan of $16,515 plus your down payment, at 6¼ percent for a 20-year mortgage. This sum does *not* include costs of maintenance, which vary greatly.

FHA Housing Expense Chart.   The FHA Housing Expense Chart, Figure 10-2, sets forth the relationship of dollar amounts of total housing expense to amounts of mortgagor's net effective income for a large sample of cases processed and approved throughout the United States in 1957, 1958, and 1959. To use the chart effectively, it is necessary to understand the terms used.

Mortgagor's effective monthly income is an estimate of the amount of dependable income (after deducting federal income tax) that is likely to prevail through the first third of the mortgage term. The estimate is made by deducting from current earnings any income that may be temporary, such as overtime, bonuses, and room rent. The income of the wife is included only when it is reasonably certain and is an established characteristic of the family.

Prospective monthly housing expense includes mortgage principal and inter-

TABLE 10-2   HOW MUCH HOUSING CAN YOU AFFORD?

INCOME FOR HOUSING		AT 5 PERCENT			AT 5½ PERCENT		
Monthly	Annual	10 Years	15 Years	20 Years	10 Years	15 Years	20 Years
$ 40	$ 480	$ 3,245	$ 4,140	$ 4,800	$ 3,180	$ 4,035	$ 4,615
50	600	4,055	5,170	6,000	3,975	5,040	5,770
60	720	4,865	6,205	7,200	4,770	6,050	6,920
80	960	6,485	8,275	9,600	6,360	8,070	9,230
100	1,200	8,110	10,345	12,000	7,950	10,085	11,540
125	1,500	10,135	12,930	15,000	9,935	12,605	14,425
150	1,800	12,160	15,520	18,000	11,920	15,125	17,310
175	2,100	14,190	18,105	21,000	13,910	17,650	20,190
200	2,400	16,215	20,690	24,000	15,895	20,170	23,075
225	2,700	18,245	23,275	27,000	17,880	22,690	25,960
250	3,000	20,270	25,860	30,000	19,870	25,210	28,845
INCOME FOR HOUSING		AT 6 PERCENT			AT 6¼ PERCENT		
Monthly	Annual	10 Years	15 Years	20 Years	10 Years	15 Years	20 Years
$ 40	$ 480	$ 3,115	$ 3,935	$ 4,485	$ 3,075	$ 3,870	$ 4,405
50	600	3,895	4,920	5,605	3,845	4,840	5,505
60	720	4,675	5,900	6,730	4,615	5,805	6,605
80	960	6,235	7,870	8,970	6,155	7,740	8,805
100	1,200	7,790	9,835	11,215	7,690	9,675	11,010
125	1,500	9,740	12,295	14,020	9,615	12,095	13,760
150	1,800	11,690	14,755	16,820	11,540	14,515	16,515
175	2,100	13,635	17,215	19,625	13,450	16,935	19,265
200	2,400	15,585	19,670	22,430	15,385	19,355	22,020
225	2,700	17,530	22,130	25,235	17,310	21,775	24,770
250	3,000	19,480	24,590	28,035	19,230	24,195	27,525

SOURCE: Courtesy of United States Savings and Loan League, *What You Should Know before You Buy a Home,* p. 8.

est, insurance premium on mortgage, service charges, hazard insurance, taxes, assessments, cost of maintenance and repair, heating, air conditioning, and other utility costs.

The general principle followed is that the relationship of a mortgagor's prospective housing expense to effective income should be kept within those limits found to be favorable through experience in insured mortgage lending.

Generally, prospective housing expense falling above Curve E will indicate too high a risk, especially for the lower income ranges. Each case, however, is handled individually.

For consumers the chart has real value. For example, if income (after taxes) is $500 a month, a reasonably safe median housing expense is about $118 per

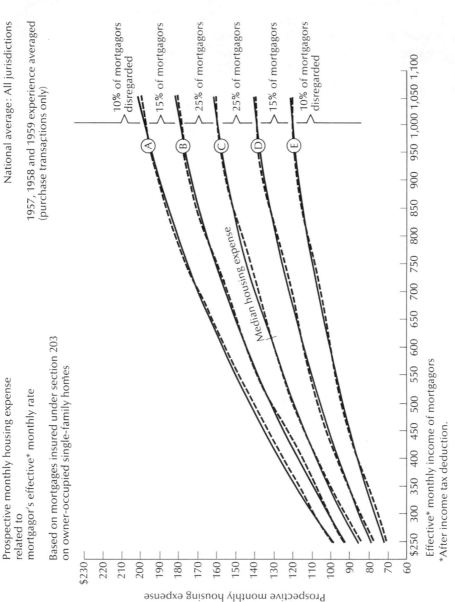

Figure 10-2   FHA Housing Expense Chart. Source: *Estimating Ability to Pay for a Home*, **Federal Housing Administration, Washington, D.C., rev. ed., November, 1962.**

month. If this family elects to spend over $140 for all housing costs, it may be in financial trouble. In budgeting, such a family may have to cut corners elsewhere to carry the heavy housing costs.

None of these "How much can you afford?" systems are perfect. You can use them only as guides. The trouble is that too many families disregard the realities of homeownership costs. The alarming increase in foreclosures is one consequence of family budget mismanagement.

Shopping for a New Home

If you have made up your mind to buy a house and have figured the maximum sum you can use for total costs of housing, you are prepared to look for a home. It is best to have a fairly good idea of what you want in housing before selecting a real estate broker.

Professional appraisers consider the following factors important in judging the merits of a house and neighborhood.

1. Neighbors who are of the same social, educational, and economic background
2. Physical attractiveness of the neighborhood
3. Proximity to community facilities (schools, buses, playgrounds)
4. Adequate transportation
5. Taxes within your income

In selecting a house, it is well to keep in mind that "no house is perfect." But there are four important things to check in any house that you are considering.

1. Size—at least 1,000 square feet. Check size of all the rooms.
2. Design should be functional and pleasant, provide privacy, and save steps.
3. Lot size and orientation. Check distance between houses, drainage, exposure of various rooms, trees, shrubbery.
4. Construction. Check cracks, squeaky floors, trim around doors and windows, insulation, weather stripping, heating and hot water units, electrical outlets, roof and gutters for leakage, air-conditioning system.

As there are other things to check in selecting a house, it is wise to hire a reliable home builder to go over any house you are considering thoroughly.[3] This is good insurance against possible later unlooked-for expense.

Consulting a Real Estate Broker and an Appraiser

It is wise to consult a real estate broker. If you do not know a reliable broker, get at least three A-1 names, perhaps from your bank. Then be candid in telling a broker how much you can afford as well as the type of house you prefer.

[3] See *Home Buyer's Check List,* Southwest Research Institute, San Antonio, Tex.

The more the broker knows about your wants, the better service he can give. This will save time that would be wasted in looking at houses that are beyond your income. The broker's fee is usually 7 to 10 percent of the selling price, and it is paid by the seller of the house.

If you want to know the present real worth of a house before buying it, the best way to get it is from a professional appraiser. The cost of an appraisal is around $25. The final estimate will be a fair judgment of what the house can be sold for. An appraisal for mortgage loan purposes will estimate its future value over many years. What you get is an opinion only, but it is an informed one, carefully reasoned, based on factual data, and unbiased.

On Finding "The" House

When you have decided on your house you will be asked to sign an "agreement to purchase," in which you agree to buy at a specified price, subject to certain conditions. Usually you have to put up a deposit, or "earnest" money—possibly $1,000. This contract will permit a return of your money if the specified conditions are not met; for example, if you are unable to get mortgage money, or if there is not a clear title to the property. The agreement should cover sales price, amount of cash payment, manner of financing, date of delivery of property, right to inspect the property, delivery of clear title, and possibly a survey. It should also specify what goes with the house—perhaps carpeting and draperies—provisions for prorated payment of taxes, and special assessments, if any.

It is a good policy to have an attorney inspect the property and offer advice *before* you sign any instruments of sale. He should pass on the "title" and the "abstract," and should be on hand when the parties are "closing the deal." The attorney's fee, usually a modest one ($25 to $35), will pay for itself over and over again.

FINANCING YOUR HOME

The cheapest and safest way to purchase a home is to pay cash. If a mortgage is placed on a house, you may lose both the house and past payments in the event you cannot make the payments on time. However, most families, particularly younger families, purchase a home with a minimum down payment and a mortgage.

Mortgaging a Home

To finance your house, you will need a mortgage loan. A *mortgage* is a conditional assignment of the property to the lender, which can be put into effect if the borrower fails in the terms of the contract. Most home loans are made by savings and loan associations, savings banks, commercial banks, insurance companies, and individuals. More than 90 percent of the families who buy homes do so with a mortgage loan. Of the three types of institutions, only the savings and loan associations specialize in making home loans exclusively. Currently they finance about 44 percent of all homes in the United States.

If you wish to do business with an insurance company, you will have to deal with a local real estate broker or an insurance agent. A loan may be secured from an individual, but it may cost more than from a financial institution.

An *amortized loan* requires the borrower to make a fixed monthly payment that not only includes the interest (and possibly taxes and insurance) but also reduces the principal of the mortgage debt after each month's payment. The earlier monthly payments include mostly interest. It is possible, therefore, to make payments for several years with only a small proportion going into your equity in the house.

In a 5 percent, 20-year amortized loan, more than 63 percent of the first payment is interest. In the seventh year, payments are split about fifty-fifty between interest and principal. While you may think you are paying yourself instead of a landlord as in the case of renting, this is not quite true during the first few years of an amortized loan.

Taking over an Old Mortgage. You may be fortunate enough to qualify for taking over a mortgage that is old enough to be a low-cost mortgage. Sometimes an old mortgage can be taken over for 4½ to 5 percent instead of 5¾ to 7¼ percent, or more. Incidentally, but important to the seller, if you assume the old mortgage, the seller is still responsible in case you default.

In some states, a mortgage cannot be assumed without the lender's consent. It is also well to remember that the previous owner has a sizable equity to recover. So you may have to make a bigger down payment than under a new mortgage. Balance a larger down payment against lower interest charges to see if the deal is worthwhile.

Accessories to the Mortgage. Before shopping for a mortgage loan, it is wise to know the terms, or language, of the lending trade.

An *open-end mortgage* allows you to borrow more money in the future without rewriting the mortgage in case you want to repair or enlarge the house.

A *prepayment privilege* grants you the opportunity to prepay the mortgage before maturity without penalty. You may wish to refinance at lower rates or to pay it off completely.

A *packaged mortgage* covers the cost of household equipment as well as the house itself.

A *deed* is the written instrument that transfers the title of property from one party to another. There are two principal kinds of deeds.

A *quitclaim deed* conveys to the grantee whatever title the grantor may have had and throws the risk on the grantee.

A *warranty deed* conveys title, and the grantor warrants that his title to the property and his right to transfer it are not defective. The grantee can go to court to recover from the seller in the event of breach of the warranty.

An *abstract* is one of four methods of checking the safety of a title to property. This involves a history of the ownership of the property. Most or all liens, legal transactions, deeds, mortgages, sales, etc., are recorded in the abstract. It provides reassurance for the buyer.

Title insurance is a guarantee for a fee against any defects. *Certificate of title* is a certification by an attorney that he has examined the records of the property and in his opinion there are no unsettled or prior liens or claims.

The *Torrence certificate,* used largely in big cities, is issued by a governmental unit evidencing and registering title to real property.

Kinds of Mortgage Loans. There are three possible choices for a mortgage loan: conventional loan, VA (Veterans Administration) loan, and FHA (Federal Housing Administration) guarantee loan. All three types are available from the same sources—savings and loan associations, commercial banks, savings banks, insurance companies, and mortgage bankers.

In a *conventional loan,* you offer only two kinds of security: the mortgaged property and your own credit and investment worth. There is no third party to back the loan, which explains why such loans are more conservative. Most mortgage loans are conventional loans, which represent the basic forms of wholly private financing. But these loans vary widely in form.

In a *VA loan,* the federal government guarantees payment of a large portion of the loan. This means extra safety to the lender, so the cost is generally less than for the other kinds of loans. Only qualified veterans can apply for VA loans.

There is an important difference between VA and FHA guarantee loans and conventional loans. The object of the VA loan guarantee is to help veterans buy homes. VA appraisals are usually very strict, because the federal government does not want a veteran to be overcharged. VA appraisal, therefore, serves as a good guide to a fair price for a home.

FHA-insured Mortgage. The Federal Housing Administration does not actually make loans. It agrees to insure the lender against loss in case of default. It insures mortgage loans made by banks, savings and loan associations, mortgage companies, and other lending institutions approved by the FHA.

The borrower pays ½ percent premium for this insurance on the unpaid balance of the loan. This added security usually makes it possible for a buyer to finance a home on more liberal terms than would otherwise be available—a larger loan with longer time to pay, probably at a lower interest rate.

You can apply for an FHA-insured mortgage loan to any approved lending institution. The lender will supply the necessary forms, help you to complete them, and, if willing to make the loan, will submit your application to the FHA insuring office.

When your application reaches the FHA office, the staff must process it.

FHA processing involves a thorough analysis of the entire transaction—your qualifications as a mortgagor; the property's estimated value and conformance to FHA minimum property standards for location, design, and construction; and the suitability of the mortgage terms for you and for the FHA.

After the lending institution notifies you that the FHA has approved the application, it arranges with you for the closing of the loan. At closing, the FHA endorses the mortgage for insurance. Closing costs consist of such items as the lender's service charge, the cost of title search and insurance, and charges for preparing, recording, and notarizing the deed and mortgage.

The chief requirements for the borrower are a good credit record, the cash required for down payment and closing costs, and a steady income to make the monthly mortgage payments without difficulty.

The FHA has no arbitrary rules with respect to age or income. It does consider these factors, but only in relation to ability to repay the loan over the period of the mortgage. Each application received by the FHA is considered individually on its own merits. There are guidelines, but they are not rigid. No two families have exactly the same circumstances. Family obligations, responsibilities, future prospects, and ideas on spending all differ widely.

Long-term Mortgages and Interest Costs. The availability of long-term mortgages with their lower monthly payments, along with progressively lower down payments, has doubtless been an important factor in the increase in homeownership. In 1940, 44 percent of all United States families owned the homes they occupied; by 1950, this had increased to 55 percent, and by 1967 to 63.6 percent.

By using a long-term rather than a short-term mortgage, a family with a specified amount available for shelter each month can buy a more expensive house, or a family buying a house at a specified price can make smaller monthly payments. However, the investment or equity in the house builds up very slowly with a long-term mortgage, and it will cost much more for interest by the time the mortgage is paid off.

For example, Table 10-3, FHA-insured Mortgages—Length of Term, shows that the total amount of interest a family would pay on a $15,000 loan at 5¼ percent would be $17,823 if it took 35 years to pay, and $9,264 if it took only 20 years—a difference of over $8,500. The monthly payments on these mortgages would be $78.15 and $101.10, respectively. Total interest costs on a 5¼ percent mortgage exceed the original amount of the loan when it takes more than 30 years and 3 months to pay off the loan.

With the 35-year loan for $15,000 at 5¼ percent, only $12.53 of the first monthly payment of $78.15 is repayment of principal. Moreover, less than half of each payment goes to principal for almost 22 years. If the 20-year loan is used, $35.40 of the first monthly payment of $101.10 applies to repayment of principal, and less than half of each payment is for principal for almost 7 years.

If the interest rate on a $15,000 loan is 6 percent instead of 5¼ percent, the total interest cost would be $20,923 for a 35-year mortgage and $10,793 for a

TABLE 10-3   FHA-INSURED MORTGAGES—LENGTH OF TERM

MONTHLY PAYMENT AND TOTAL INTEREST COSTS ON
$15,000 LOAN AT 5¼ PERCENT ANNUAL INTEREST

Term of Loan (years)	Monthly Payment on Principal and Interest	Approximate Total Interest Costs*	First Date Payment on Principal Exceeds Payment on Interest
20	$101.10	$ 9,264	6 years and 11 months
25	90.00	12,000	11 years and 10 months
30	82.95	14,862	16 years and 9 months
35	78.15	17,823	21 years and 11 months
40	74.85	20,928	26 years and 11 months

*Calculations are based on the assumption that the regular monthly payment will be required for the final month to discharge the obligation. Overpayment each month due to rounding of the monthly payment to the nearest cent may be sufficient to reduce or eliminate the last one or two payments.
SOURCE: Housing and Home Finance Agency, Washington, D.C.

20-year period. The effect of even this small increase in the interest rate on the total cost of interest emphasizes how important it is for the prospective purchaser to shop for the best credit terms available.

Disclosure Exemptions.   It is of interest at this point to recall that the Consumer Credit Protection Act of 1968 exempts first mortgages on houses from disclosure of all the real costs. It is true that mortgage interest is already stated as a true annual rate. But certain fees are usually left out of the rate picture—such as mortgage placement and appraisal fees, credit report fees, and discount points. According to recent figures from the Federal Home Loan Bank Board, placement fees and points on conventional new-home mortgages mentioned above are now averaging 1 percent of the amount of the loan. In effect, the interest rate is higher than you think. One of the reasons for omitting disclosure of these extra costs and the cost of the interest on the loan from the truth-in-lending act was the fear lenders had that disclosure would show, in many instances, the extra costs exceeding the mortgage itself. Lenders and the housing industry feared that many potential home seekers would be put off by knowing the stark truth that the interest and other costs may cost more than the original mortgage loan.

Down Payment.   It is usually wise to make as large a down payment as possible. With a loan of a given amount, the price paid for a home varies according to the down payment. If you can afford to pay $100 per month on a 20-year mortgage at 6 percent, you can borrow about $14,000. A $6,000 down payment would allow you to purchase a $20,000 home. A smaller down payment, say $3,000, would allow you to purchase a $17,000 home. There will be variations in the above illustrations depending upon the types of loans. In recent years, down payments on conventional loans (no FHA guarantee) on new houses have averaged 25 percent, and on used houses the average down payment has been approximately 27 percent. The down payment on FHA and G.I. loans is considerably less.

The advantage of a larger down payment is that the total interest paid over the life of the loan is considerably less.

Amortized Mortgage. The amortized or direct-reduction mortgage is the best type of loan. Both the federal government and most private mortgage financing agencies insist on the amortized mortgage. The borrower, using the amortized method, makes a fixed monthly payment which includes the interest (and, in some cases, taxes and insurance) and reduces the principal of the mortgage.

The earlier monthly installments include mostly interest and only small amounts of principal repayment. (See Table 10-5.) As the principal is gradually reduced, a larger percentage of the monthly payment is applied to repayment of principal until the loan is repaid. This method is cheaper than the old straight mortgage because the part of the monthly payment which is applied against the principal reduces the base on which the rate of interest is computed.

Table 10-4 shows the monthly payments to pay off a $1,000 monthly amortized loan in from 10 to 30 years with varying interest rates.

The monthly payments to liquidate a loan of any amount can be obtained from Table 10-4 by multiplying the monthly payments shown by the number of thousands borrowed.

An Amortization Schedule. For each mortgage loan an individual amortization schedule is given to the borrower. An example of such a schedule is shown in Table 10-5. This schedule covers a loan of $15,000 at 5 percent for 25 years. The required monthly payment is $87.75; number of payments, 300. The schedule shows how much of the monthly payment goes to interest, how much to repay principal, and what the balance of the loan is. Only portions of the schedule will be reproduced because of space.

It is interesting to note that the payments on interest in this schedule are larger than on principal until payment number 134 (after 11 years and 2 months). It is obvious that equity accumulation may be quite disappointing to the owner of the house if he sells the house in the first 10 years of the 25-year mortgage.

TABLE 10-4   MONTHLY PAYMENTS TO AMORTIZE A LOAN OF $1,000

PAYMENT PERIOD	INTEREST RATE				
	5%	5½%	6%	6½%	7%
10 years	$10.61	$10.85	$11.10	$11.35	$11.61
15 years	7.91	8.17	8.44	8.71	8.99
20 years	6.60	6.88	7.16	7.46	7.75
25 years	5.85	6.14	6.44	6.75	7.07
30 years	5.37	5.68	6.00	6.32	6.65

TABLE 10-5   AN AMORTIZATION SCHEDULE

PAYMENT NUMBER (MONTHS)	INTEREST	PRINCIPAL	PRINCIPAL BALANCE
1	$62.50	$25.25	$14,974.75
4	62.18	25.57	14,898.36
12	61.32	26.43	14,689.96
24	59.97	27.78	14,364.06
134	43.85	43.90	10,480.90
298	0.94	86.81	138.19
299	0.58	87.17	51.02
300	0.21	51.02	0.00

Discount Points.   In response to tight money, interest rates on all types of loans increase. In late 1965 and early 1966, for example, interest rates on conventional home loans rose from 5.91 percent to 6.55 percent. In 1967, interest rates on conventional loans moved up and down from 6.23 percent in June to 6.41 percent in December. In early 1969, interest rates rose to about 7½ percent.

The interest rate on home loans that lenders can charge on mortgages insured by FHA is lower at times than the yield desired by lenders in the market. For this reason lenders are likely to "discount" FHA mortgages. In other words, if you want to sell or buy the house, you may have to pay the lender a commission, commonly known as a "discount" or as "points." A point is a charge of 1 percent of the loan. This charge can be assessed against the buyer, the seller, or both.

How Discount Points Work.   When a borrower pays points, the money is deducted from the total of the loan. If you pay four points on a $20,000 loan, you get $19,200 ($20,000 × 0.04% = $800), but you pay interest on the full $20,000. If Bank A charges 6¼ percent but no points on a 20-year mortgage, and Bank B charges 6 percent interest plus 4 points, which is the better deal for you? Look at Table 10-6, prepared by *Changing Times* magazine, June, 1967, calculated on the basis of 6 percent interest rate payable over 20 years. Bank B's nominal 6 percent interest rate goes up to 6.51 percent—a little higher than the 6½ percent—if you pay 4 points. And if you sell the house in 5 years, the effective rate will be higher—7.02 percent. You would do better in this case with Bank A, even though its nominal rate is higher than Bank B's. Incidentally, points you pay are not tax-deductible.

Settlement or Closing Costs

Settlement day is when the property officially becomes yours. Among the papers you will sign are likely to be the following: a note (promise to repay the loan); a mortgage or deed of trust (rights of lender to enforce payment); a title insur-

TABLE 10-6 MORTGAGE COSTS WHEN CHARGED INTEREST PLUS POINTS

20-YEAR MORTGAGES

Nominal Interest Rate	Number of Points Charged	EFFECTIVE RATE IF LOAN IS REPAID AFTER:			
		5 Years	10 Years	15 Years	20 Years
6%	1	6.25%	6.16%	6.13%	6.13%
	2	6.50	6.31	6.26	6.25
	3	6.76	6.47	6.40	6.38
	4	7.02	6.64	6.54	6.51
	5	7.28	6.80	6.67	6.65
	6	7.55	6.97	6.82	6.78
	7	7.82	7.14	6.96	6.92
	8	8.09	7.31	7.10	7.06
	9	8.36	7.48	7.25	7.20
	10	8.64	7.66	7.40	7.34
6.25%	1	6.50	6.41	6.38	6.38
	2	6.76	6.57	6.52	6.50
	3	7.01	6.73	6.65	6.63
	4	7.27	6.89	6.79	6.77
	5	7.54	7.06	6.93	6.90
	6	7.80	7.23	7.07	7.04
	7	8.07	7.40	7.22	7.18
	8	8.35	7.57	7.36	7.32
	9	8.62	7.74	7.51	7.46
	10	8.90	7.92	7.67	7.61

25-YEAR MORTGAGES

Number of Points Charged	EFFECTIVE RATE IF LOAN IS REPAID AFTER:				
	5 Years	10 Years	15 Years	20 Years	25 Years
1	6.24%	6.15%	6.12%	6.11%	6.11%
2	6.49	6.30	6.24	6.22	6.21
3	6.74	6.45	6.36	6.33	6.32
4	6.99	6.60	6.49	6.45	6.44
5	7.25	6.76	6.62	6.56	6.55
6	7.51	6.92	6.74	6.68	6.66
7	7.77	7.08	6.87	6.80	6.78
8	8.04	7.24	7.01	6.92	6.90
9	8.31	7.40	7.14	7.04	7.02
10	8.58	7.57	7.28	7.17	7.14
1	6.50	6.40	6.37	6.36	6.36
2	6.74	6.55	6.49	6.47	6.47
3	6.99	6.70	6.62	6.59	6.58
4	7.25	6.86	6.74	6.70	6.69
5	7.51	7.02	6.87	6.82	6.81
6	7.77	7.17	7.00	6.94	6.92
7	8.03	7.34	7.13	7.06	7.04
8	8.30	7.50	7.27	7.18	7.16
9	8.57	7.67	7.40	7.31	7.28
10	8.84	7.83	7.54	7.44	7.41

ance policy (protection against defect in title); a copy of the survey of the land. You should receive five documents: note, mortgage, deed, survey, and the title insurance, plus receipts for all payments you make. Ask for copies of all papers.

Closing costs are likely to be higher than you figured—from $250 to $500. Not all lenders make the same charges. Fairly typical charges might run as follows:

Attorney fees	$ 50.00
Credit report	3.00
Recording fee and stamps	15.00
Appraisal fee	25.00
Title insurance	175.00
Mortgage service charge	150.00
Prepaid hazard insurance	30.00
Total	$448.00

If you deal with a bank, you may have *origination charges* of around $100. This sum covers bank expenses in securing the loan, lawyer's fee, cost of drawing note or bond, mortgage, and so on. Under VA procedures, these costs are limited by law—at present to 1 percent of the sale price of the house.

First-year Expenses of Homeownership

Outfitting a new house or moving from one home to another costs money. Besides moving expenses, you are likely to need several items for making the home livable. Few people budget enough money for these purposes. The Uni-

TABLE 10-7   FIRST-YEAR EXPENSES OF HOMEOWNERSHIP

	VALUE OF HOUSE		
ITEMS	*$10,000 to $15,000*	*$15,000 to $20,000*	*Over $20,000*
Power lawnmower	$ 60.00	$ 55.00	$ 93.00
Fencing	207.00	197.00	257.00
Carpets, carpeting	190.00	186.00	1,085.00
Draperies, curtains	72.00	105.00	432.00
Furniture, living room	217.00	173.00	780.00
Furniture, bedrooms	240.00	133.00	579.00
Furniture, dining room	150.00	250.00	—
Furniture, den	92.00	116.00	566.00
Shrubbery	104.00	78.00	266.00
Patio	90.00	—	217.00
Furniture, outdoor	53.00	57.00	83.00

versity of Houston surveyed 218 new homeowners and found they spent an average of $1,580 on new furniture and equipment the first year. The main items are shown in Table 10-7, First-year Expenses of Homeownership, in relation to the value of the house.

Some of this spending may not be necessary immediately or at all. The fact remains that there will be costly items to buy other than air conditioner, kitchen appliances, and laundry equipment that you normally foresee and plan for. Watch out for these budget busters. If you are moving from a rented apartment, chances are that you will need yard tools, grass seed, fertilizer, and other such items not in your budget. It may, therefore, be wise to provide about 10 percent of the cost of the house for planned and unplanned expenditures the first year.

SELLING A HOUSE

It costs money to sell a home, too. If you lived in your house for several years and desire to sell it, the selling price of the house is likely to be higher than when you purchased it because of inflation in real estate values. It looks like a good "deal" for you. It may not be such a profitable sale when you discover that even a very modest house appraised at $15,000 may cost over $1,600 to sell.

You should hire a lawyer (the usual flat rate runs from $35 to $50) even if a reliable real estate broker will be handling the sale. The lawyer should be experienced in real estate transactions.

Usually it is wise to let a reliable real estate agent sell your house at about 6 percent commission. Unless conditions are very favorable—a seller's market, mortgage money available, house in a popular neighborhood, ample time to sell—a good Realtor can probably sell it faster, for a better price, and with fewer problems.

Most owners will spend a little money in fixing up the house—painting, papering, and doing small repair jobs—and get good returns for spending $200 or $300.

To the inexperienced seller of a home, "point" charges, mentioned earlier, may be imposed on the seller and on the buyer. Five points on a $20,000 loan at 1 percent of the loan would come to $1,000. At present, FHA and VA loans cannot be charged more than one point. If other points are charged with any of these guarantee loans, the seller has to pay them. Point charges change rapidly, so find out what the going rate is in your area.

If your mortgage is to be retired before due, you may have to pay a prepayment penalty unless the contract permits prepayment without penalty.

In most places taxes are paid on the current year, but not always. In some localities taxes run a year behind. The seller must pay all current taxes up to the time of sale.

Some of the closing costs may be yours to pay. Other expenses you might be asked to pay in part or in whole are surveying fees, appraisal and inspection, and possibly termite inspection.

Finally, you have the expense of moving from the old home into another home. This cost could be several hundred dollars, depending on the distance, hours of work, and other services connected with moving.

THE COST OF MOVING

Population Mobility

About 35.2 million persons, or nearly one-fifth of our population, moved in the year ending in March, 1967. Persons moving locally (within counties) numbered 22.3 million, a drop of 1.9 million from the 24.2 million who moved in 1966. This decline in local mobility was concentrated in metropolitan areas and appears to be related to difficulties in financing real estate caused by the tight money market.

Persons who moved between counties in the year ending March, 1967, numbered 12.9 million, of whom 6.6 million moved between states. Total number of movers (35.2 million) was 18.3 percent of the population—the lowest rate in the last 20 years of Census Bureau Surveys. This low rate was due to a drop

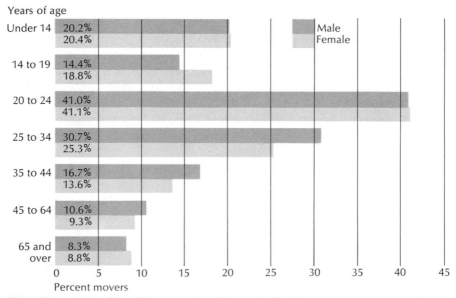

Figure 10-3   Age and Sex of Movers in United States, March, 1966, to March, 1967. Source: Bureau of the Census.

in local mobility rate. Longer-distance movers constituted slightly over 6.5 percent of population—about the same rate as in the previous year.

Mobility rates reflect several phases of the life cycle as well as varying economic status. Peak mobility rate is in the age group 20 to 24 years (Figure 10-3). Below age 35, married persons have higher mobility rates than single persons, but above that age the rates for both groups are the same. Men are slightly more mobile than women. The unemployed are more mobile than the employed. Men who worked less than 50 weeks in the survey year had higher local mobility rates than those who worked 50 weeks or more, and men with incomes of less than $5,000 had higher mobility rates than those with incomes of $5,000 or more.

The Moving Industry

There is only one mover per 14,000 people. To service the one-fifth of our population that is "on the move," there are only 12,000 movers. About one-fourth of these are certified to operate by the Interstate Commerce Commission. In practice, the ICC usually follows the decisions of the American Movers Conference, the chief industry association, which is controlled by the largest movers. Since the AMC is a subsidiary of the powerful American Trucking Association, the ICC has not been in the habit of lifting an interstate license from a large mover because of a violation. An illustration of the attitude of the ICC can be seen in the agency's effort to pass long-needed new regulations in 1960. The big trucking firms fought these mild proposals bitterly, even through court suits, and in the end the ICC backed down until the final regulations were a mere shadow of the original mild proposals.

ICC's jurisdiction also has declined. The biggest loophole, for example, has to do with the "commercial zone." Any community is entitled to set up such a zone, usually corresponding to metropolitan areas and at times including parts of two or more states. Movers are exempt from ICC regulation in such zones. Consequently, in these places movers can charge what the traffic will bear in contrast to regulated rates.

Estimates and Costs of Moving

Once a family has decided to move and has contacted several movers, each moving company will send a representative to the home to make an estimate of the cost. According to the American Movers Conference, every effort is made to keep the final bill within 5 to 10 percent of the estimate.

There are several factors involved in making an estimate of costs—distance, intrastate or interstate, special handling needs, value protection, timing, and scheduling—and other factors. Charges for intrastate are usually regulated by a public service commission in each state. Interstate rates are under the jurisdiction of the ICC and are based on distance and weight. Whatever the charges for moving, the mover usually insists on being paid before he unloads your goods. He can accept only cash, traveler's or certified checks, and money orders, unless some other method of payment has been prearranged.

Insurance

According to the AMC, one in every four shipments involves a claim of some kind. Twenty-five percent of shipments suffer some damage. The average claim is probably around $42. The losses are probably much higher than settlements because the interstate mover is liable for only 60 cents per pound! It may pay to take out additional insurance.

The ICC has no authority to compel movers to settle claims for loss or damage, but it will provide names of insurance companies. Thus, there is no machinery for the settling of disputes except the long, involved court procedures. But there may be an answer to this problem if Senator Warren Magnuson, Chairman of the Senate Commerce Committee, has his way. He plans to hold public hearings and may introduce legislation to give consumers better protection.

Major Complaints

The chairman of the ICC, after making a six-month investigation of consumer complaints in 1968, found that the major consumer complaints concern: (1) loss and damage claims, (2) inordinate delays in settlement, (3) inadequate compensation, (4) underestimates of moving costs, and (5) failure to meet delivery schedules.

The 1967 ICC Rules.   Under the ICC rules that took effect in 1967, moving companies must:

1.   Give at least 24 hours' notice when charges are going to be 10 percent or $25 more than the estimate, whichever is greater.
2.   Pay a minimum of 60 cents a pound for lost or damaged articles rather than the former rate of 30 cents a pound.
3.   Notify the customer, at company expense, at least 24 hours in advance if delivery is going to be a day or more late.
4.   Acknowledge damage or loss claims within 30 days and pay up or otherwise respond within 120 days.
5.   Bear liability for the declared value of the shipment if the customer requests it and pay 50 cents per $100 of estimated value, which must equal at least $1.25 per pound shipped. A 4,000-pound load, for example, must be valued at $5,000 and the charge would be $25.
6.   Give customer a copy of "General Information for Shippers of Household Goods," a leaflet explaining consumer rights.
7.   Reweigh the load if you have reason to question the actual weight, but this may incur an extra charge if the difference does not exceed 100 pounds or 2 percent of the lower net weight.

A Few Moving Pointers

Before contracting for moving, check with your own insurance agent concerning your household insurance. It is likely to give some coverage in case of moving. Then consider the following precautionary measures.

1.   Before moving, sell as many goods as possible—especially heavy, outdated items.
2.   Very low bids are likely to be unrealistic.
3.   When awarding the job, get a copy of the contract stating the rate to be charged, liability, and dates of pickup and delivery.
4.   Choose insurance from other sources than the van company. Insure against major damage or loss. Check your present coverage first.
5.   Keep a list of what is in each box or package.
6.   Make a complete inventory of all items.
7.   When loading, challenge any written statement by the van mover that a piece is already "marred and scarred" if it is not.
8.   Count all crates, boxes, and barrels as they leave the house.
9.   Get from the local agent the name and address of the destination agent, the file number and van number of your shipment, and the driver's name.
10.   Request advance notice of lateness and immediate notice of actual charges. Better have a certified check for 50 percent more than the estimate of the costs.
11.   If the van is overdue, contact the local agent and keep a record of all resultant expenses.
12.   After the van arrives, examine the bill of lading carefully. Note weight before paying.
13.   When unloading, tell where to put the various items. Insist that all disassembled pieces be put together.
14.   When unloading is over, indicate any damage or lost articles before signing. You may write in: "Accepted subject to concealed loss or damage." Later, when damaged goods or lost articles are identified, file damage and loss claims. State the original value, because the company will depreciate the value. If you do not get action, report the matter to the Interstate Commerce Commission, Washington, D.C. 20423. As a last resort, a letter from your lawyer to the van line's headquarters may help.

HOW TO INSURE YOUR HOME

At one time you had to buy home insurance in pieces—a fire policy, "extended coverage," a theft policy, a liability policy, and so on. Now you can buy all your home protection needs in one package and save premium costs.

The Homeowner's Policy

A homeowner's policy is a complicated contract. It also comes in several types of protection. Since it is a fairly recent kind of protection, today's policy may differ a little from the policy of a year or so ago.

There are two major parts to a homeowner's policy. The first part consists of four types of property coverage:

1. The "dwelling" includes the structure and extras such as patio, air conditioner, lawnmower, furniture, and outdoor equipment.
2. "Appurtenant private structures" includes other buildings on the lot, like a detached garage and tool shed.
3. "Unscheduled personal property." This refers to household contents, such as chairs, tables, dishes, clothing, carpets, and a boat if stored at home, which are not scheduled by name.
4. "Additional living expense," in case you have to live off the premises while your house is being repaired.

The second part of the homeowner's policy covers three other areas:

1. "Personal liability." This section protects you in the event you are sued by a visitor or neighbor who was injured on your property, or off your property in certain cases.
2. "Personal medical payments" will pay expenses of people injured by you, your family, or your pets, at or away from home.
3. "Physical damage to property" covers damage to the property of others, even though you may not be at fault.

Homeowner's Policy: Protection Varies. In most states five kinds of protection are sold:

1. MIC 1, a "standard form."
2. MIC 2, the "broad form."
3. MIC ¾, a combination of the "dwelling special form" (MIC 3) and the "residence contents broad form" (MIC 4).
4. MIC 4, the "tenants form," used for people who rent a home or apartment.
5. MIC 5, the "comprehensive form."

All of these policies provide the same liability protection: up to $25,000 for personal liability; $500 for medical payments to one person; and up to $250 for damage to someone else's property. Once you go beyond the liability protection, the policies begin to differ, primarily in the amount of insurance on the house. The protection varies with the type of property and the policy, as shown in Table 10-8.

If you insured your house for $20,000 with MIC 2 (broad form), the insurance company will pay up to $2,000 for buildings other than your house; $8,000 for personal property at home; $4,000 for living expenses; and $1,000 for trees, shrubs, and plants. There is also $1,000 minimum for property away from home.

The above allowances are ample for most situations. You can reduce the limit on personal property in all policies except MIC 5. Other allowances can usually be cut only by reducing the coverage on the house.

TABLE 10-8   HOMEOWNERS' PROTECTION ACCORDING TO POLICY TYPE

	POLICY TYPE				
	1	*2*	*¾*	*4*	*5*
Appurtenant structures	10%	10%	10%	. . . .	10%
Personal property at home	50	50	50	$4,000	50
Personal property away from home (percentage of personal property at home)	10	10	10	10	100
Additional living expenses	10	20	20	20	20
Damage to trees, shrubs, plants (limit, $250 per item).	5	5	5	—	5

Specific Coverage.   MIC 1 covers 11 perils: fire and lightning; damage to property removed from the house; windstorm and hail; explosion; riots; damage from aircraft; damage by vehicles not owned or operated by the insured person; sudden and accidental damage by smoke; vandalism; theft; and breakage of windowpanes.

MIC 2 covers the above 11 plus losses from falling objects; weight of ice, snow, and sleet; collapse of building; sudden and accidental tearing asunder, cracking, burning, or bulging of a steam or hot water system and appliances for heating water; accidental discharge, leakage, or overflow of water or steam from a plumbing, heating, or air-conditioning system; freezing of plumbing, heating, or air-conditioning systems and domestic appliances; and sudden and accidental injury to electrical appliances, devices (excluding TV and radio tubes and transistors), fixtures, and wiring from artificially generated electric currents such as short circuits.

MIC 5 covers all risks except those excluded in the policy.

MIC ¾ gives the all-risk coverage of MIC 5 for the house and other structures and the MIC 2 coverage for personal property.

Exceptions.   Look at the section headed "Special limits of liability," such as a limit of $100 for loss of money or coins, $1,000 for manuscripts, $1,000 for any fur or single piece of jewelry, and $500 for boats, boat trailers, and outboard motors. There are other exceptions.

The above exceptions may make it necessary to take out additional insurance known as a "floater." Each item is listed and valued in this policy. Any item covered in the floater, however, is *not* covered by your homeowner's policy.

The MIC 1, 2, and ¾ policies do not mention "mysterious disappearance"—a situation in which something disappears but you cannot prove it. This coverage can be added if you pay a higher premium.

Deductible. Many policies are sold with a deductible feature. In about half of the states a $50 deductible is required on hail and windstorm losses. As a rule, it is usually wise to accept this deductible because it will save you about $20 a year.

In the homeowner's policy the $50 deductible is not applied to losses over $500; and on losses between $50 and $500, the company pays 111 percent of the remaining loss. If you have a $100 loss, for example, the company pays 111 percent of $50 ($100 minus $50 deductible), or $55.50. The MIC 5 policy pays 125 percent of the amount over the deductible sum.

Some Guidelines. The homeowner's policy is probably the best one for homeowners. But the policy needs revision from time to time. The desire for protection should be balanced against cost. The premium as well as the coverage goes up from the MIC 1 to MIC 5. For example, in one community it costs $263 to insure a $25,000 home for 3 years without deductible under MIC 1, $338 under MIC 2, and $365 under MIC ¾. The MIC 5 costs $495 even with a $50 deductible. Which one do you really need? MIC 1 offers a lot of protection against basic risks.

The second suggestion is to use the current market value of the house. On big losses, you are entitled to full replacement cost if the insurance is kept up to 80 percent of the cost of replacing the house. If you insure for less than 80 percent of the replacement value of the house, the company will pay only a part of the cost figured on the basis of the ratio of the insurance to the amount of insurance you should have had under the 80 percent rule. If you do not have coverage that automatically increases a homeowner's insurance as property values rise through inflation (using U.S. Department of Labor cost-of-living indices), you are probably underinsured. If you are underinsured, see your insurance agent and get coverage up to the 80 percent rule of current value of the house. The replacement cost feature applies only to buildings.

The third reminder is that payment for property other than buildings is reduced by an allowance for depreciation, regardless of how much insurance you have.

Fourth, as a rule one company's homeowner's policy is identical to that of another company. Premium rates vary on the type of house (frame construction costs more than brick or masonry). The kind of fire protection in the community makes a difference in premium rates, too. Some companies offer discount rates. But equally as important as the premium rate is the reputation of the company for paying claims. In the final analysis, your policy is only as good as the company.

Personal Property "Floater"

An ordinary homeowner's policy may not adequately cover your personal property. It usually limits coverage on the valuables. Most property insurance policies are written on a "named peril" basis. It covers only losses caused by something specifically listed in the policy, such as fire, or theft, or windstorm. Floaters are issued on an "all risk" basis. They cover all losses except those specifically excluded. For example, a camera would be protected by a floater policy if the camera were lost, stolen, run over by a car, dropped in a lake, damaged by wind, hail, or storm, or shattered by a fall. In other words, you would be unprotected only if the damage came from a cause specifically ruled out.

Exclusions.   There are some excluded areas of protection. A standard floater does not insure against wear and tear, inherent defects, vermin damage, or losses from military actions and a few other risks. Accidental breakage of a fine arts object is excluded if you, the owner rather than a thief, dislodged the object from a table or shelf.

There are several ways of using a floater. A single object such as a piece of art may be insured. It can be added to another floater. For example, a homeowner's policy can cover ordinary personal belongings, and highly valuable articles can be protected on the floater. This "scheduling" of special articles can be attached to the basic policy.

You can also protect your wedding presents by a floater for a given number of days while you are on your honeymoon.

Cost of a Floater.   The premium depends upon where you live, the value of the article insured, and the kind of object insured. Usually, there is a minimum charge. As a rule the more goods you insure, the less the cost per $100 of face value of the articles. Here are some standard rates for a pay-in-advance three-year floater:

TABLE 10-9   STANDARD RATES FOR A PAY-IN-ADVANCE THREE-YEAR FLOATER

ARTICLES	ANNUAL RATE PER $100	MINIMUM PREMIUM
Jewelry	$1 to $2.40, depending on location	$10
Silverware	$0.25	5
Stamps, coin collections	1.00	10
Musical instruments	0.75	10
Wedding presents	0.75	10
Furs	$0.30 to $1.80, depending on location	5

DO NOT PLUNGE INTO DEBT FOR A DREAM HOUSE

Next to food, housing is the greatest need of every family. Today, families spend from 25 to 35 percent of their total income on shelter. When such a large percentage of income must be spent for housing, it is wise to give close attention to the problems of securing satisfactory shelter at an economical cost. Every family must decide whether to rent, buy, or build a home.

Since a home is the base of family operations, it deserves high priority in the family spending plan. It is wise to investigate whether renting a house or apartment, or buying or building a house, is the intelligent choice for your family. The maximum amount that can be expended for shelter and still leave adequate income for other aspects of family living must be figured before allowing dreams to plunge the family into debt.

QUESTIONS FOR DISCUSSION

1.   Is it cheaper to own a house or to rent?
2.   What would you include in a check list to aid a young married couple in selecting a house?
3.   Study a house lease and then name some of the legal responsibilities of the lessor and the lessee.
4.   What reactions do you have to the following statements?
     a.   "You have to build two houses before you get what you want."
     b.   "Never build a house before employing an architect."
     c.   "All contractors must be watched carefully."
5.   Why is it important to carry fire insurance on the structure of a house amounting to at least 80 percent of the present value of the property?

ACTIVITY PROBLEMS

1.   Study a standard lease used in your community when renting a home. Make a report to the class on the legal information necessary for renters.
2.   Prepare a check list for a young married couple to aid them in selecting a house for renting and for owning. Are the things to check different if you plan to buy a house rather than rent one? Are the problems different when selecting a rural home? A suburban residence?
3.   Interview a homeowner you know. Ask such questions as: "What were your biggest problems in acquiring a home to fit your family needs?" "How did you solve these problems?" "What advice would you give to others who are contemplating owning a home?" Evaluate the answers to these questions. Ask yourself, for example: "Could these problems have been solved better?" "How?"
4.   A family buys a house costing $20,000. A down payment of $4,000 is made. A 6¾ percent mortgage loan is made for the balance of $16,000 over a 15-year period. What monthly payments will have to be made to retire the loan? What will the actual total cost of the house be at the end of the 15-year period? Will income tax deductions of the interest reduce the total cost of this house?
5.   Observe a house under construction. From time to time, talk to the ar-

chitect or general contractor about the important stages in the construction of the house. Try to discover any problems of the owner during the period of construction.

SUGGESTED READINGS

Addington, Wendell G.: *Housing the Disadvantaged,* Foundation for Cooperative Housing, Washington, D.C., 1967.

———— : *Mutual Ownership,* Foundation for Cooperative Housing, Washington, D.C., 1967.

———— : *Owners, Not Tenants,* Foundation for Cooperative Housing, Washington, D.C., 1968.

"A Brand-new Home for $6,000," *Changing Times,* April, 1968.

"Buying a House: the 9 Most Common Questions," *Changing Times,* February, 1966.

"Cooperatives and Condominiums," *Changing Times,* January, 1969.

"Highway Robbery," *McCall's Magazine,* January, 1969.

"How Much Can You Afford to Pay for a House?" *Changing Times,* June, 1968.

"How Much Your Mortgage Really Costs," *Changing Times,* June, 1967.

"How to Insure Your Valuables," *Changing Times,* July, 1965.

"It Costs to Sell a House, Too," *Changing Times,* October, 1968.

"Moving Problems," *U.S. Consumer Newsletter,* June 12, 1968.

Savings and Loan Fact Book, annual editions; *What You Should Know Before You Buy a Home,* latest edition, United States Savings and Loan League, Chicago.

Shelton, John P.: "The Cost of Renting Versus Owning a Home," *Land Economics,* February, 1968.

"Up, Up/Away: Moving," *Consumer Close-ups,* Cooperative Extension, Cornell University, New York, N.Y.

chapter **11**

FAMILY TRANSPORTATION

The automobile has broadened our horizons. No longer are we satisfied with public transportation. More and more of us own one or more cars. Over 100 million Americans are licensed car drivers. Our social patterns have been influenced by mass ownership of automobiles. Car ownership has changed our pattern of recreation, increased our standard of living, and brought us many conveniences and new services. Drive-in restaurants and theaters, multi-million-dollar shopping plazas, country inns, and suburban bowling alleys are dependent upon people with cars. Many public and private beaches and parks have come into existence because their patrons have cars.

Owning a car has become a necessity for many, a convenience for some, and a pleasure for most of us. Why do over 80 percent of American families own cars? More families can afford a car today because their real incomes have increased and their work hours have decreased. By use of a car more people can live farther from their place of work. Furthermore, installment financing of cars, with payments stretched from 12 to 36 months, brought automobiles within reach of middle-income and even below-middle-income people. And for some, a car took them away from the miserable surroundings of their homes. Then there are those who want tomorrow today.

AUTOMOBILE OWNERSHIP: A STATUS SYMBOL

Auto Ownership Statistics

According to data from the University of Michigan Survey Research Center, almost 80 percent of all American families owned one or more cars in 1966. And about 25 percent of these owned two or more automobiles (Figure 11-1). Single-car ownership varied between 24 percent of families with annual incomes of $1,000 or less to about 95 percent of those with incomes of $10,000 or more.

Ownership rates in 1966 were not greatly different from 1965 except that there was a slight reduction in proportion of car owners among income groups below $4,000 and an increase in proportion of multiple-car owners among families making $15,000 or more.

What Price Status?

Year after year, the automobile moves farther out to a center-stage position in the minds of most Americans as just about the most exciting thing in their lives. The cost of purchase and upkeep ranks about third in the average family's budget, yet few people ever raise an eyebrow about the wisdom of such an expenditure. In our national thinking, we assume that automobile ownership is as necessary to adequate living as indoor plumbing and good shelter.

Why is this so? Why does a car mean so much? What intense gratification does it provide to create this remarkable desirability? It is, of course, a means of transportation. The automobile also emerges as a powerful symbol of personal mastery and control of basic human impulses. The car is a mass of enormous energy, and, because the driver is controlling all this power, he knows

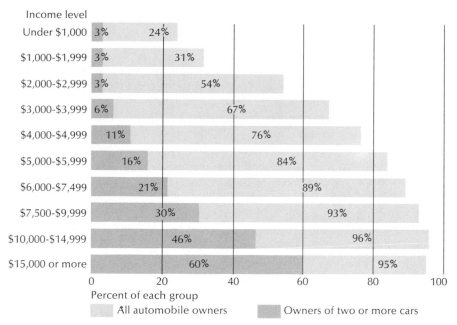

Figure 11-1   Automobile Ownership by Annual Income Levels. Source: University of Michigan Survey Research Center.

the pleasures and fears of handling major drives. Any driver senses that he is directing potentially powerful forces. The social meanings surrounding a car should be apparent: how much the car is being involved with people being together—as for family vacations, or for driving to work with a friend. Social companionship is a powerful motive. Yet it is important to recognize how much the automobile in American life has come to be used as an indicator of the individual's social status, his position, his place in the scheme of things. Regardless of whether this is utterly illogical, we unconsciously classify every car and use it as a yardstick for determining how important a person is in our society. When we observe a stranger getting out of a car, our behavior in considerable part is determined by the make and the year model of his car. Furthermore, the car is a portable symbol of status. Only a few people can be aware of my bank balance, my investments, my wife's fur coat, my country-club membership. But the car is a useful device for carrying my position and accomplishments with me for all to see.

For many reasons, then, and in many ways, a car gives us the feeling of "being somebody." The man who owns a car, or even the teen-ager who is driving a car, feels more important, more successful, more achieving, perhaps more masculine, than the man or teen-ager without a car. In short, the car tells us what we are or want to be as a person—or what we think we are.

SHOULD A TEEN-AGER HAVE HIS OWN CAR?

The Teen-ager: Wheels of His Own

There is little doubt but that teen-agers evaluate the status of boys and girls partly by whether they have a car. Boys feel it is difficult to date without wheels of their own.

For most youth it is much more important to arrive at driver's-license age than at voting age. The car is technology in their hands, a machine to command, power at the touch of a toe, danger, skill, privacy from family, privacy with his date, courtship. They are probably the true pleasure drivers. They can drive around for hours, never bored or tired. When they return home and parents ask what they did, their answer is like a child's. Instead of "Nothing," they reply, "Oh, just drove around with the boys."

Most girls can get along without a car of their own. But to most boys a car of their own can be almost a necessity. Without a car, a boy feels handicapped socially. His need is not merely transportation, because way down deep he wants the status, independence, and manhood that go along with wheels of his own.

A teen-ager with his own car can be dangerous because his exposure to traffic would be increased. The nation's 21 million under-24 drivers, about 20.6 percent of our driving population, were involved in 33.4 percent of the accidents and suffered 33.1 percent of the fatalities.[1] That makes the car the number one killer of teen-agers, deadlier than all diseases combined.

Why a Teen-ager Should Not Have a Car of His Own [2]

After completing a driver-training course and satisfying a state driver examiner, your teen-ager may know a lot about driving, except how. He will learn more about how to drive by being given errands to run. Until he convinces you that he is a responsible and fairly skilled driver, he has not earned the privilege of having his own car. There are other reasons why he may not earn the right to own a car. There is evidence that his schoolwork may suffer. There is evidence, as noted at the University of South Carolina, that after freshmen were forbidden to have cars, their grades went up, but older students who had cars continued to have academic problems.

Another consideration is this—a youth who owns his own car usually will not account for his whereabouts while he is gone. You will end up knowing less about his companions than ever before.

His expenses increase rapidly. Insurance alone can cost up to several hun-

[1] *Changing Times,* October, 1968.

[2] Committee on the Judiciary, House of Representatives, *Auto Insurance Study,* Oct. 24, 1967, U.S. Government Printing Office, 1967, pp. 4-5.

dred dollars annually. It is a good idea to check on insurance costs, since they vary greatly from state to state. In some states a youngster can secure only limited insurance, particularly in liability coverage. Girls have better accident records, and most companies have lower rates for them than for boys. Too, teen-agers log more in-town driving than most parents, and the cost of operating the car will be higher per mile. For these and other reasons, should you flatly deny him a car of his own?

An Alternative Choice

Let him have his car, but try to reason with him along these lines. Try to steer him away from a "bargain" car with souped-up engine, drag-racing shift, and wildly changed suspension. These can be and often are roaring beasts on wheels or a lethal weapon in the hands of youth. Why not discuss a standard car with a stick shift and clutch (boys prefer this)? The youth might be less tempted to reach cruising speed by spinning the rear wheels even on dry pavement if he had a column-mounted shift lever, which costs less and is cheaper to repair. He should have a mechanically safe car, whether new or used. So, go along with him on his search for that "dream" car. Parents are likely to have to be in on the deal anyway if he is under legal age in the state. It might be well to hire a reliable car mechanic to take the car on a test drive and to examine the vital parts carefully before buying the car. After purchase and use, it might be a good idea to give the car an occasional check and inspection yourself.

FAMILY SPENDING FOR TRANSPORTATION

With higher incomes and increased leisure, individuals and families have chosen to spend more and more dollars for transportation—largely, automobiles. In 1967, about 13 percent of family take-home pay was used for transportation.[3] Only food and housing costs exceed the cost of transporting the family members today.

The average cost of transporting family members can be misleading because of variable factors such as income, cost and age of car, number of cars, annual mileage, number and age of drivers, urban or country driving, and kind of driving. A family of two nearing retirement age is apt to use fewer dollars in transportation, whereas a young family is likely to spend above the national average of 13 percent of take-home pay. Families with net income of over $5,000 spend, on the average, 14 to 17 percent of their income on transportation, and most of it is for the family car. Some estimates indicate that driving a standard-sized American car may cost from 11 to 13 cents per mile.

[3] U.S. News & World Report, quoted in the Congressional Record, Aug. 1, 1967.

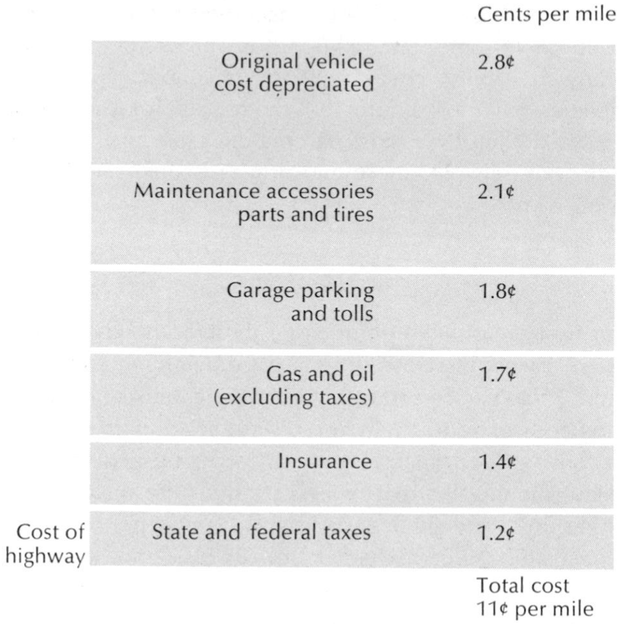

Cents per mile

Original vehicle cost depreciated	2.8¢
Maintenance accessories parts and tires	2.1¢
Garage parking and tolls	1.8¢
Gas and oil (excluding taxes)	1.7¢
Insurance	1.4¢
State and federal taxes	1.2¢

Cost of highway

Total cost
11¢ per mile

Figure 11-2   Cost of Operating an Automobile. An analysis of automobile operating costs by the Bureau of Public Roads of the Federal Highway Administration, U.S. Department of Transportation, shows that the cost of highways (taxes) is only 1.2 cents of the total 11.0 cents per mile it costs to own and operate an automobile. The analysis is based on a $2,800 car driven 100,000 miles over a 10-year life-span. Source: U.S. Department of Transportation, Federal Highway Administration, rev. January, 1968.

The Cost of Operating a Car

Automobile costs include much more than the original purchase price. Other costs for operation and maintenance may range up to $1,500 or more per year.

The amount spent for maintenance of a car may vary greatly from one person to another because of distances driven, general car care, and the conditions of driving.

The American Automobile Association estimates in 1967 indicated that it cost 13.6 cents a mile to operate and maintain a late-model car. This is a 1.8-cent-per-mile increase since 1965. The AAA 1967 figures per year are:

Variable costs (gasoline, oil, tires, and maintenance)	$ 380
Fixed costs (insurance, taxes, license, registration, and depreciation)	980
	$1,360

These figures are based on expenses incurred for a medium-priced, full-size, four-door, eight-cylinder Chevrolet sedan. They are costs for the car in its first three years, assuming the owner will subsequently trade it in on a new model.

By dividing the 10,000 (average mileage per year) into $1,360, AAA comes up with the average operating cost in 1967 of 13.6 cents per mile. In 1965, they estimated cost per mile to be 11.8 cents.

The Bureau of Public Roads of the Federal Highway Administration figures that the average motorist spends 11 cents per mile to own and operate a car (Figure 11-2). The study was based on a typical $2,800 car driven 100,000 miles over a 10-year period. Although many drivers do not keep the same car 10 years, the Bureau indicated that this is the life-span of the average automobile in this country. The study includes cost of the car, gas, oil, tires, tubes, maintenance and repairs, parking, insurance, tolls, and all taxes. These costs do not include interest or financing costs.

The average person may not realize the fact that, except for buying a home, he will never purchase anything nearly as expensive as his car. He probably has only a vague notion of how much his car costs to own and operate. He would be shocked to learn that the man who signs a contract for a new $3,000 automobile is, in effect, signing a contract for $11,000 for 3,500 pounds of steel, glass, and plastic to be moved 100,000 miles over a period of 10 years (Table 11-1). To do this he will have to spend $2,230 for 7,000 gallons of gasoline, pay $1,415 for insurance, $1,763 for maintenance and repairs, and more than $1,800 for parking and tolls. His bill for state and federal taxes will amount to $1,172. If he had sold or traded the car at the end of 1 year (14,500 miles), depreciation would be a whopping $842 or about 5.81 cents per mile. If he sold the car at the end of 2 years, depreciation would be $1,431 for both years or 5.2 cents per mile (total mileage, 27,500). Keeping the car the second year saved him $253 minus anything spent for tires and spark plugs or other replaced parts. Depreciation is by far the greatest single cost of owning a car. Year by year, as the car gets older, depreciation decreases; but the maintenance costs go up. If the car has been kept in good condition and driven properly, some experts feel that a typical family car (averaging 10,000 miles a year) should be kept 4 or 5 years before trading. One of the major arguments in favor of this conclusion is the tremendous depreciation during the first 2 years of operating a new car. A careful study of the dollar costs will be most rewarding to the average driver, particularly young drivers and young marrieds. It is easy for youth to overestimate their financial ability to own a car.

Car Repair Costs

A Senate subcommittee investigating the automobile repair business in December, 1968, and early 1969 was attempting to find out whether the annual $10 billion car repair business for 81 million automobiles might be reduced.

TABLE 11-1   ESTIMATED COST OF OPERATING AN AUTOMOBILE*

Costs Excluding Taxes				TOTALS AND AVERAGES FOR 10 YEARS	
				Total Cost	Cents per Mile
Depreciation				$ 2,806	2.81¢
Repairs and maintenance				$ 1,788	1.79
Replacement tires and tubes				232	0.23
Accessories				82	0.08
Gasoline				1,497	1.50
Oil				227	0.23
Insurance				1,415	1.41
Garage, parking, tolls, etc.				1,805	1.80
Total				$ 9,852	9.85¢

Taxes and Fees	State	Cents per Mile	Federal	Cents per Mile	Total Taxes	Cents per Mile
Registration	$100	0.10¢	. . . .	. . . .	$ 100	0.10¢
Titling	86	0.09	. . . .	. . . .	86	0.09
Property	50	0.05	. . . .	. . . .	50	0.05
Gasoline	454	0.45	$280	0.28¢	734	0.73
Oil	. . . .	. . . .	6	0.01	6	0.01
Auto, tires, tubes, etc.	. . . .	. . . .	196	0.19	196	0.19
Total	$690	0.69	$482	0.48¢	$ 1,172	1.17¢
Total of all costs					$11,024	11.02¢

*Four-door sedan; cost new, $2,806 excluding taxes. Assumed life-span, 10 years, 100,000 miles. Date of estimate, January, 1968. Courtesy of Bureau of Public Roads, Federal Highway Administration, U.S. Department of Transportation.

The committee had preliminary information indicating that certain factors operating in the car repair business were causing the consumer to pay unreasonably high prices or to get unreasonably bad work. Some of the evidence raises the following questions:

1.   Could repair costs be reduced if the auto industry designed "repairability" into its products?
2.   Are the books that the service manager consults in making out the repair bill a proper guide to labor charges?
3.   Are cash customers, who spend $6.5 billion of the $10 billion annual repair bill, subsidizing such privileged customers as the fleet owners and automobile insurance companies?
4.   Do dealers permit or encourage slipshod warranty repair work in order to spend more time and more money on nonwarranty repairs?

The subcommittee memorandum showed that labor costs for auto repairs had increased 53 percent since 1961 (in 7 years). Parts costs had increased 52 percent during the same period.

The flat-rate manual mentioned is the book published by the car manufacturer and private sources that lists the time required to make every kind of auto repair. There appears to be evidence that these repair list prices, published by private sources, often inflate the required repair prices several times over those listed by the car manufacturers. Seldom is any consideration given to the fact that the shop often can beat the book time. Thus, there is little benefit to the consumer from the skill and efficiency of the better mechanic. As a matter of fact, there seems to be an incentive program in the business that motivates the mechanic not to beat the book time. For example, in Washington, D.C., investigation by the committee staff showed that the hourly rate charged for labor in auto shops was $8. Approximately half of the $8 went to the mechanic. The good mechanics are not making the $160 you would expect for a 40-hour week, but more likely $200 to $210.

As for the subsidization by cash customers of the insurance companies and big fleet owners, staff sources said they would produce witnesses to testify that "insurance companies insist on a 10 to 20 percent discount on their work." Because warranty work and parts cost less, the staff memorandum said this "would tend to discourage a dealer from wanting to do the work or to get it out of the shop soonest." One way to accomplish this is to get the work done in less than book time while charging book rates, by the simple expedient of replacing rather than repairing defective parts.

The investigators' report implied that rushed-up repair work may be a significant factor in the hazards of driving. The major concern over the flat-rate manual is that it "tends to act as a price-fixing agreement, and the consumer would normally waste his time if he shopped for prices on repairs among the competing dealers."

Another witness, Louis Baffa, president of the Auto Body Association of America, told the Senate Antitrust and Monopoly Subcommittee that repair costs could be reduced considerably if parts were designed on a more practical basis. Bumpers, for example, "can reduce repair costs if they are designed for their function—to absorb bumps—rather than primarily for beauty."

Along with the evidence of hanky-panky in repair shops, the subcommittee detected definite changes in automotive tastes. Senator Hart, chairman of the Senate Antitrust and Monopoly Subcommittee, told the American Association of Body Engineers in 1968 in Detroit, "Consumers are no longer happy merely to have the biggest, chromiest, coolest car parked in their driveway, to the envy of the Joneses." He said:

> [The] automobile isn't the status symbol it used to be. Today's consumers are more likely to brag about how little they spent—not how much. They are becoming more concerned with quality, durability, dependability, ease of maintenance—in short a very full value for their dollar—in items they buy. It is only natural that they begin

to scrutinize minutely a purchase which may account for one-third of a year's income. . . . One thing stands out clearly. Consumers want repairability built into their cars. . . . Chances are [that the] Federal Government will have more to say about cars in the next 20 years than it did in the past 20 years. [The people] will insist on it.

Possibly something will come out of this investigation that will reduce repair bills on cars and make them safer.

Leasing a Car

To decide whether leasing a car for family use is advantageous, you will have to do a little pencil work. Assume, for example, that you are interested in a medium-priced 4-door sedan, 8 cylinders, air-conditioned, power brakes, automatic transmission, power steering, and radio. The car dealer assumes all the risks, depreciation, repairs, sales tax, license costs, personal property tax, insurance premiums, and all maintenance costs for 2 years and a maximum of 30,000 miles during the 2-year period. You pay for the gasoline and oil changes.

The first problem is to get some facts on the total costs for operating a medium-priced car as described above. The U.S. Department of Transportation prepared an estimate of operating a new 1968 medium-priced car for the first 2 years (Table 11-2).[4]

These costs of operating a new, medium-priced 1968 automobile are estimates considered to be in the middle range by the Transportation Department. You may have to change some costs, depending on local and state taxes, insurance rates, and other variable factors. Even so, the total costs of $1,821.81 the first year and $1,465.85 the second year are probably fairly accurate figures to use. Changes in cost after 1968 will, of course, have to be made.

Now look at a 2-year lease contract. In 1968 you could probably have leased a similar model for about $130 to $140 per month for a maximum of 30,000 miles of driving. Assuming a leasing cost of $130 per month, the total cost for 2 years would be $3,120. Using the U.S. Transportation Department study of the costs of operating a new 1968 medium-priced car as described above, the total costs for 2 years will add up to $3,287.66. Other things being equal, it appears that you will save a small sum by arranging for a 2-year lease rather than to buy and trade in. But this is not the whole story. There are several less obvious points to consider when you lease.

You might buy a "lemon" and have expensive repair bills not included in the warranty. Warranties for 1969 are for only 1 year in contrast to 2-year guarantees in previous years. You also take a chance on the trade-in allowance.

[4] "Estimated Cost of Operating an Automobile," U.S. Department of Transportation, Washington, D.C., 1968.

TABLE 11-2   ESTIMATED COST OF OPERATING A CAR (2 YEARS)

ITEM	FIRST YEAR (14,500 MILES) *Total Cost*	SECOND YEAR (13,000 MILES) *Total Cost*
Costs excluding taxes:		
Depreciation	$ 842.00	$ 589.00
Repair—maintenance	58.10	120.50
Replacement, tires—tubes	—	—
Accessories	24.51	17.14
Gasoline	216.99	194.55
Oil	32.99	29.48
Insurance	181.00	170.00
Garage, parking, tolls, etc.	207.73	198.65
Total	$1,563.32	$1,319.32
Taxes and fees, state:		
Gasoline	$ 65.91	$ 59.09
Registration	10.00	10.00
Titling	85.68	—
Property	5.00	5.00
Subtotal	$ 166.59	$ 74.09
Federal:		
Gasoline	$ 40.56	$ 36.36
Oil	0.85	0.76
Auto, tires, tubes, etc.	50.49	35.32
Subtotal	$ 91.90	$ 72.44
Total taxes	$ 258.49	$ 146.53
Total all costs	$1,821.81	$1,465.85

At the time you are ready for a trade-in, the market may be soft; or extra heavy driving may cut down your trade-in.

In leasing you may avoid a lump-sum outlay and thus keep your money free for investment. If this is true, and say you can earn $250 in investing over 2 years, the overall purchase price goes up accordingly.

In leasing, as in buying, it pays to look around. You can do better in leasing a smaller car provided it suits your needs. You may also prefer to lease a car by the month or by the day.

A final word—if you lease, be sure to read the contract carefully. Contracts are not standard. Automobile manufacturers are presently encouraging dealers to push leasing of cars. Leasing may be to your advantage. You better know exactly what you are getting in return for the monthly payments.

SHOPPING FOR A CAR

How to Buy a New Car

The January through April issues of *Consumer Reports* will contain the ratings of new models. But before you shop around for a new car, sit down with your family and decide what sort of car will fit your needs and budget.

But no matter how hard you bargain, you will probably pay more for next year's model than you would have paid for last year's equivalent.

In contrast to the way the big three auto manufacturers administer prices, the automobile salesroom operates much like a Levantine bazaar. You must go prepared to bargain or risk being fleeced. With few exceptions, new cars carry no set selling price.

Dealer strategy in many a sales booth is to play down the price of the car and play up the trade-in deal and the financing terms. Don't play that game. Insist on negotiating one deal at a time. First, isolate the price of the car together with the optional accessories you want. It is wise to decide in advance on the make, model, and equipment you want. Essentially, the same automobile, sold with variations in trim and nameplate, may be delivered with a range of sticker prices as wide as $560.

Remember that the sticker price is not the selling price on most cars. Cars customarily sell for less than the total on the sticker.

If you are negotiating for a car already in the dealer's possession, read the sticker, deduct the freight charge, and then apply a discount of 22 percent for a full-sized car or 18 percent for a compact or intermediate. The result should be quite close to the dealer's cost. If the car must be ordered, have the salesman itemize the sticker price anyway, including the accessories you want.

Here's the way the figures would work out. Say the sticker price for a full-sized V8 was $3,270 with automatic transmission and power steering. Deducting 22 percent, you arrive at a wholesale price of $2,551. Figure $150 to $200 for the dealer, and set your bargaining sights on a final price in the $2,700-to-$2,750 range. If you are dickering for a car that wholesales for $3,500 or more, figure on $300 to $400 over wholesale. You will also, of course, have to add shipping charges and local sales taxes to the final agreed-on price.

Whether or not you can bring yourself to bargain, you make the salesman put his price in writing. The time to do so is before you put down a cash deposit or give him the keys to your old car. Get from him on his company's standard order form an itemized statement of the model you are buying, number of cylinders, engine size, accessories, transportation and makeready charges, sales tax, registration fees, and any special features (such as color) the salesman has promised. Then request that the statement be signed by an official of the firm. That way, a salesman will not be able to "low-ball" you—quote a lower price than he will demand when you come for the new car, on the excuse that the official would not approve his price quotation. And he probably will not try to "pack" the final price with phony or unordered extras.

If you intend to trade in your present car, start out with some idea of its value on the used-car wholesale market. One source of such information is the *Annual Buying Guide* issue of *Consumer Reports,* which lists retail prices for many of the previous years' models and explains how to update them and reduce them to wholesale.

The best self-defense in car buying is the time-honored one of comparison shopping. Get several dealers' prices on the car you want and on the trade-in allowance. Sign no document until every part of the deal is down on paper.

It will be worth a few extra dollars' purchase price to buy from a dealer where you have reason to believe the service department may treat you as a possible regular customer rather than as an outcast.

If you are among the 60 percent of new-car buyers who will have to borrow money on the deal, steel yourself against any temptation to accept the car dealer's terms without further investigation. Shop the banks, too, and your credit union, if you belong to one.

Since you will be investing a sizable amount of money, make sure that every detail of the car you choose is exactly what you want. If you are not completely satisfied with the new cars, consider a good used car as an alternate choice.

Shopping for a Used Car

Most used cars are on the market because the owners were dissatisfied with them. Nevertheless, a carefully chosen used car can provide relatively low-cost transportation because its high early depreciation has already taken place. Most repairs are likely to cost less than the yearly depreciation on a new or nearly new car. But the older the car, the more likely it is to be in need of repairs.

For average family use, choose from recent models of the compact, intermediate, or lower-priced standard-size cars. Such cars are likely to provide a maximum of trouble-free service per dollar spent; they should burn less fuel than larger cars; and when repairs are needed, the cost is less. Stick to the simple cars—without power-operated options, extra carburetors, boosted compression ratios, and other features.

Do not be fooled by odometer readings or by shiny appearances. Used-car dealers are more likely to spend money on paint, polish, and new floor mats than on mechanical repairs.

Used-car guarantees take various forms. The dealer may guarantee the cost of repairs, including or not including replacement parts, for a specified period, usually 30 days. Or seller and buyer may agree to share repair costs. Whatever the form of guarantee, it should be signed by an officer of the firm. If you are financing your purchase, here are some points to remember:

Carrying charges on used cars nearly always are higher than for new cars.
Shop around for your financing loan. Usually the best source is a commercial bank or credit union.

Buy your insurance separately, not as a part of the time-payment sales contract.

Read the whole contract carefully. Do not sign until all details are written in and you understand them all. Never, of course, sign a blank contract.

Get a signed copy of the contract and file it. If, later, you feel the dealer did not act in good faith, get in touch with your local Better Business Bureau, the frauds division of the attorney general's office, or a lawyer.

If you are not acquainted with average prices on used cars, see the most recent *Annual Guide* of *Consumer Reports.* Dollar figures are usually given for used cars for the last 5 or 6 years. The *Annual Guide* will also advise you on on-the-lot tests, driving tests, and a list of used desirable models and undesirable models. For the person not mechanically minded, it may be worthwhile to invest in a final examination by a reliable garage, auto diagnostic center, or independent mechanic. The charge is usually modest, $5 to $25. If there are defects, the mechanic can offer suggestions and give you reliable repair estimates and help you decide whether the car is a good buy. Whether you buy or reject the car, consider his fee as good insurance and continue your search.

Some states require annual and semiannual inspection of all cars using public roads. If your state has inspection requirements, ask the used-car dealer to present evidence for the last inspection. It may be that the previous owner decided to sell the car rather than make all the repairs needed to continue driving the car.

It may be that your state requires used cars to be inspected within seven days or so of registration, but that they do not legally have to be inspected *before* they are sold and registered. If the latter is true, a buyer of a used car may be faced with spending more money to put it into safe operating condition. A car that has been inspected usually carries an inspection sticker. Look for this sticker before buying.

FINANCING A CAR

The most economical way to finance a car is to pay cash. The next best way is to pay as much down as possible in addition to your trade-in allowance. Then arrange to pay the balance in as short a time as possible. The shorter the interest period, the less you pay.

What Price Credit?

The price you must pay for money to buy a car will vary with the age of the car, where you live, the lender you deal with, and the going rate at the time. The cost of a car loan is generally quoted either as a percentage discount rate or as a finance charge of so many dollars.

After July 1, 1969, the Consumer Credit Protection Act of 1967 required the lender to disclose the cash price of the car, the down payment or trade-in allowance, an itemization of all other charges, the total money actually borrowed, the total finance charge, the number of payments and their amounts and due dates, any extra charges for late payments, and a description of any lien or other security interest kept by the lender on your property. The yardstick for comparing prices will be a figure labeled "Annual Percentage Rate." This rate for credit deals will usually look about twice as high as the rates mentioned or advertised. For example, a credit charge of $10 per $100 of debt per year, to be repaid in regular installments, was, before July 1, 1969, misrepresented as a rate of 10 percent. It is not now and has never been 10 percent because the $10 does not buy the use of $100 for a year. It buys the use of diminishing portions of that $100. If the declining monthly balances are averaged, the result is around half of the original amount borrowed or financed. So the true annual interest rate is about 20 percent.

If $10 per year is deducted in advance (discounted) from each $100 borrowed, the Annual Percentage Rate (rounded to the nearest quarter of 1 percent) is:

20% for one year
22.5% for two years
24.75% for three years

If you receive the entire $100 you need and repay the $10-per-year finance charge as part of each monthly installment (an "add-on" loan), then the Annual Percentage Rate for 1, 2, or 3 years is about 18 percent.

If the above explanation is not entirely clear, the new Consumer Credit Protection Act requires the lender to give you the dollar amount of the finance charge and the annual percentage rate. These facts will enable you after July 1, 1969, to shop separately for the lowest-price credit. As a general rule, banks and credit unions are likely to charge lower interest rates than dealers. Pick the deal most advantageous to you.

CAR WARRANTIES

After 50 years of giving a 90-day guarantee on parts and workmanship, the auto industry discovered a new selling tool—the extended warranty. In 1963, Ford started the race with its "24—24" (24 months or 24,000 miles) warranty. Then Chrysler boosted its sales over the next 3 years with a hard sell for its 5—50 on its "drive-train" guarantee—engine, transmission, suspension systems, wheels, and wheel bearings, or 50,000 miles, whichever came first. The rest of the car, with some exclusions, was covered for 2 years or 24,000 miles. Parts and labor on warranty parts were supposed to be supplied free.

But when the 1968 cars were introduced, the hedging began. All the car manufacturers offered the same basic warranty. But they put a limit on the transfer of the warranty when the car was sold to second or third owners. This did reduce the resale value of cars from $100 to $500, according to *Automotive*

News. By 1970, no 1968-model car, however low its mileage, had a manufacturer's warranty coverage to offer a third owner.

The 1969 warranty will be good for only one year or 12,000 miles, whichever comes first, and then it is only good to the first owner of the vehicle.

The Nature of a Warranty

The Federal Trade Commission uses the terms "guarantee" and "warranty" interchangeably. The word "warranty" is a written assurance of quality which will specify the manufacturer's responsibility to the buyer in terms of replacement, repair, and servicing. Therefore, when you buy a new car, it is important to read the warranty carefully. The car warranty "giveth and it taketh away." One of the conditions it places on the owner is to have the car serviced in the manner and at the intervals set down in the car manual. You cannot just leave it to the dealer to do what he thinks is best. If, for example, the dealer forgets to change the oil filter, the warranty is voided. On the other hand, some dealers try to do more nonwarranty work on the car than is necessary. *The Wall Street Journal* reported in 1967 that keeping the warranty in effect costs car owners about $75 a year for work not needed.

According to the warranty, required servicing need not necessarily be done by authorized dealers. Independent mechanics can do it so long as they give you an invoice showing you that the manufacturer's specified parts, oil, and lubricants were used. You must show the invoice to the car dealer once a year.

The overindulgence in warranties has caused a three-way headache. The manufacturers have found their warranty costs rising sharply. In the 1966 and 1967 models, they have built those costs into price increases.

At the same time, the dealers are complaining that the carmakers do not reimburse them well enough or fast enough. The dealers also find that assembly negligence is so common they cannot afford the time or money for proper "dealer servicing."

But car owners probably feel the most pain. Examples of unhappy car-warranty service is common. The plague of new-car defects grows more serious year by year. In the annual questionnaire of *Consumer Reports* readers, 35 percent of car-owning respondents said their car was delivered in "unsatisfactory condition." The dissatisfied respondents went on to report major problems in getting defects repaired: 25 percent said repairs were not made satisfactorily under the warranty. Similar complaints poured into the offices of the President's Special Assistant for Consumer Affairs and the members of Congress.

In 1968, open warfare broke out between car dealers and manufacturers over the plague of defects and the costs of repairing them under warranty. In 1967, *Automotive News,* a trade journal, canvassed dealers on what changes they preferred in new-car warranties. More than 70 percent wanted the scope and length of coverage decreased.

Senators Warren Magnuson and Carl Hayden have introduced legislation that will set up standards and grievance-solving machinery for warranties. Until some sort of "truth-in-warranties" act is passed, your best protection is a careful reading of the warranty. You should keep a careful record of work done and a copy of all correspondence with dealer and manufacturer. A lawyer who is willing to make a phone call or write a letter would be helpful. Meantime, the courts are beginning to protect the consumer.

"Implied Warranty"

Consumers have a right to collect damages for personal injuries resulting from defects in cars regardless of any time or parts limitation imposed by the warranty, according to the Federal Trade Commission and recent court decisions. Philip Elman, of the FTC, said:[5]

> Section 5 of the FTC Act, prohibiting unfair practices in interstate commerce, precludes automobile manufacturers from using time and mileage limitations, exclusion of successive purchasers and other restrictions and conditions in new car warranties, to limit their liability to remedy any defects in manufacture, whenever and wherever they appear.

Court decisions are supporting Mr. Elman's interpretation in personal injury cases and in the right to obtain satisfaction for repairs authorized by the warranty. In 1967, the owner of a $6,700 Lincoln Continental sued Ford and its dealer in Miami, Florida, for recovery of the price of the car because, he claimed, it was a "lemon." Ford defended itself by quoting the limitations of liability in its warranty. But the Florida Supreme Court ruled that, despite the expressed warranty, the customer may recover damages "on the basis of implied warranty of a product due to its defects and lack of fitness and suitability."[6] The owner of a Chrysler Imperial who took the car back to the dealer 38 times over a 60-day period to fix a rain leak collected $2,800 from Chrysler Corporation.[7]

It seems that consumers have more legal rights than they think they have. Of course, the consumer is not likely to get the protection he needs unless he sues until Congress enacts some legal remedies, such as some sort of inexpensive compulsory arbitration procedures for settling warranty disputes.

AUTOMOBILE INSURANCE

Consumer discontent with increasing costs, long settlement periods, and policy cancellations has led to discussions and investigations of the present system of automobile insurance. Government inquiries, at both the federal and local levels, have been initiated. More will be said about auto insurance re-

[5] *U.S. Consumer,* Nov. 27, 1968.
[6] *Consumer Reports,* April, 1968.
[7] *U.S. Consumer,* Nov. 27, 1968.

form proposals following a review of how to shop for car insurance policies which are presently available.

Kinds of Insurance Coverage

There are five kinds of insurance coverage that a prudent person should weigh carefully: liability, medical payments, uninsured motorist, collision, and comprehensive. Liability and collision insurance are the most expensive.

Liability Insurance.   Liability insurance covers bodily injury liability and property-damage liability. Bodily injury liability coverage pays the sum for which the car owner becomes legally liable if his car injures someone. Property-damage liability pays the amount for which the car owner becomes legally liable for damage to property—another car, a telephone pole, a building. Liability insurance is the heart of an automobile insurance policy. No prudent person would drive even temporarily without liability insurance, and in some states it is compulsory. Liability insurance also pays the cost of legal defense. The practical question is what liability limits to carry.

The insurance company pays no more than the amounts specified in a policy. Liability limits are usually described by a series of three numbers separated by diagonal lines—for example, 10/20/5. This set of numbers describes a policy that pays a maximum of $10,000 for bodily injury to one person, a maximum of $20,000 for bodily injury to more than one person, and a maximum of $5,000 for property damage in one occurrence.

Insurance companies offer liability up to 300/500/100 and even higher. The difference in the cost of liability of 10/20/5 (around $100) and liability of 50/100/5 coverage is usually small. No matter where you live, be sure to meet the requirements of the financial-responsibility laws of the states in which you drive.

The relative costs of various liability coverages are:

If 10/20/5 liability coverage costs $100, then—
20/40/5 coverage will usually cost about $109
25/50/5 coverage will usually cost about $112
50/100/10 coverage will usually cost about $119

Medical Payments Insurance.   This insurance ($2,000 coverage may cost around $10) pays medical and hospital bills, and funeral expenses if there is a death in an automobile accident, regardless of fault. This is good insurance since it protects all passengers in the car. It is not a duplication of your medical and hospital insurance.

Comprehensive Physical Damage Insurance.   This insurance pays for loss if your car is stolen, damaged, or destroyed by fire, hail, hurricane, and most other causes, and also pays for losses due to vandalism. This policy does not pay for collisions, mechanical breakdown, wear and tear, or freezing.

Driving without comprehensive insurance is a gamble, but full comprehensive coverage is quite expensive. A $50 deductible provision (the car owner pays the first $50 loss) may be available at about 55 percent of the full-coverage rate. The cost of such a policy depends on where the car owner lives and on the age of the car.

Collision Insurance.   This insurance covers damages to a car if it is upset or hit by another car or fixed object. Collision coverage is primarily valuable for losses due to an upset that is not the fault of someone else or where the question of fault is debatable.

Full coverage on collision is expensive. Collision rates vary with the age of the car. The rate for new models is based on the original factory price of the car. Last year's models may pay off at only 87.5 percent of the original factory price. The premium remains the same. A point is eventually reached where the premium is out of all proportion to the coverage. Consequently, a car more than four years old may have too little coverage compared to the premium paid.

Full collision coverage is rarely offered and is very expensive. Coverage with the first $50 or $100 of the damage deductible is generally purchased—in which event you pay the first $50 or $100 of the repair costs and the company pays any balance.

> If full-coverage collision insurance is priced at $300, then—
> $50 deductible coverage will cost about $75
> $100 deductible coverage will cost about $45 to $60
> If $100 deductible collision insurance is priced at $50, then—
> $250 deductible coverage will cost about $30
> $500 deductible coverage will cost about $30

Uninsured Motorist Insurance.   This more recent form of coverage insures the driver and passengers against injury by a driver who carries no insurance or by a hit-and-run driver. It is automatically included in some policies. The premium is small because the risk is small.

Premiums Based on Classes of Drivers

Insurance companies set up classes of drivers and assign each class a rate based on its own accident and claims record. The class depends on the use made of the car and on the age of the male driver. Premiums vary also according to the place of residence, and for comprehensive and collision coverage they vary with the value of the car.

Premiums are generally lowest if the car is driven only for pleasure, with no male driver under 25 years of age. A single male driver under the age of 25 will pay about two or three times as much as a single male driver over 25.

Preferred Risks.   For years many insurance companies have cut rates for drivers who passed stiff eligibility tests. The criteria among companies vary, but these are the most common: (1) driving record, (2) occupation, (3) driver under 25 years or over 65, (4) alcoholism or physical handicap, (5) condition of car, and (6) merit rating if the insured has avoided traffic trouble. Discounts in premium, if a driver qualifies, generally range from 10 to 25 percent below the company standard rates.

Special or Package Policies

Some insurance companies offer a package of various kinds of insurance, which usually costs less than if selected separately. Strictly speaking, however, the differences in premiums on standard policies and on the special or package deals are not comparable because of the differences in coverage. Then, too, maybe a car owner wants only liability coverage. The premium for a standard liability policy would be less than the package would cost. On the other hand, if a car owner wants to combine comprehensive and collision insurance, the package savings may run to around 15 percent.

Some companies combine the special or package deal and the merit-rating plan. In 1962, one large automobile insurance company announced that good school grades would get California students and their parents a 20 percent discount in auto insurance. California was selected as the first state for the program because state laws there permitted immediate introduction of the new plan.

What Insurance Coverage Do You Need?

If insurance is purchased through the dealer who sells the car, you will usually get only collision and comprehensive coverage. If the car is a late model, buy liability insurance before driving it off the lot. Here is the order in which some automobile experts rate the need for various kinds of coverage.

1. *Liability.* A must for all drivers. Awards of $50,000 are common, and verdicts run much higher at times. Buy 50/100/5 if you can afford it.
2. *Comprehensive physical damage.* A must on a new car. You might omit comprehensive on an old car if you can absorb the loss. Repair costs are usually higher than the value of an old car.
3. *Collision.* A good idea for a late-model car that you own outright. Repair costs run high. If you need to economize, you might omit it for an older car. If you need this insurance, buy a $50 or $100 deductible policy.
4. *Medical payments.* Some motorists can do without this protection. It may be worth the premium if the family is large or in case of carpool driving.
5. *Uninsured motorists.* Inexpensive but the risk is very small.

Shopping for Insurance Rates

To aid you in comparing automobile insurance rates, make out a chart (similar to Table 11-3, Policy Specifications Chart) for each company you select

TABLE 11-3   POLICY SPECIFICATIONS CHART

TYPE OF COVERAGE	FAMILY OR INDEPENDENT POLICIES	SPECIAL OR PACKAGE POLICIES
Liability	Limits: ____ / ____ / ____	$____,000
Medical	$500	$____,000
Uninsured motorist	Yes	Yes
Collision	$____ deductible	$____ deductible
Comprehensive	Full coverage	Full coverage
Towing	Yes	Included with collision or comprehensive
Other	None	None

SOURCE: *Consumer Reports,* June, 1962.

for bids. Then select the coverages you want. When asking for and comparing rates, be sure that they are for the same coverage.

After receiving the bids, record them on a blank similar to Table 11-4, Rate Comparison Blank. The lowest rate quoted is not necessarily the best buy. Give some consideration to membership fees, service, discount for two or more cars, premium rates, cancellation and renewal record. Also check on the financial stability record of each company in *Best's Insurance Guide.* The Consumers Union recommended list of automobile insurance companies will be useful.[8]

Safe Driver Policies.   Other things being equal, including comparative costs, give some preference to a policy *without* a Safe-driver or Merit Rating plan, says *Consumer Reports.* The magazine points out that you could easily lose the advantage of a lower rate. These plans charge lower rates to drivers with good records and raise the rates of others. Many of these plans base your rate on the driving records of members of your family over a period of 2 or more years. Some plans raise the rate on the basis of accidents or claims. Some exclude certain types of accidents which are not your fault. Your driving record may thus earn you the minimum rate under one plan and subject you to large surcharges under another.

Many companies use a point rating system for each chargeable accident, and one, two, or three points for serious traffic-law violations. Under this system, your rate might be set as follows:

POINTS	EFFECTIVE RATE
0	None
1	30% surcharge over base rate
2	70% surcharge over base rate
3	120% surcharge over base rate
4 or more	180% surcharge over base rate

[8] *Consumer Reports,* June, 1962.

TABLE 11-4   RATE COMPARISON BLANK

Name of company						
Safe-driver or merit rating (yes or no)						
Liability	$	$	$	$	$	$
Medical	$	$	$	$	$	$
Uninsured motorist	$	$	$	$	$	$
Collision	$	$	$	$	$	$
Comprehensive	$	$	$	$	$	$
Towing	$	$	$	$	$	$
Total	$	$	$	$	$	$
Membership fees	$	$	$	$	$	$

SOURCE: *Consumer Reports, June, 1962.*

A few companies allow discount rates to drivers with unblemished records. Under such plans, your average rate through the years may (with good luck) be a little lower than the rate initially quoted.

Family versus Special Policies.   The family policy is a uniform policy form developed by the Insurance Rating Board and the Mutual Insurance Rating Bureau. Since 1959, most of the old-line insurance companies have introduced into most of the states a policy form known as the "special policy" or "package policy" in addition to the usual family policy. Usually the special or package policy will cost less than the comparable approximate coverage which the same insurer sells under its family policy contract. The savings may be 10 percent or more. There are some differences in extent of coverage. For example, special policies set a liability limit—$25,000—rather than the usual split liability, such as 10/25/5. There are other limitations or advantages that should be weighed carefully before making a decision as between family and special policies.

The Auto Insurance Dilemma

There is little doubt that we will be reading and hearing much more about revising or changing automobile liability insurance laws. Complaints from motorists are streaming into congressional mailbags and state insurance departments. In 1967 the antitrust subcommittee of the Committee on the Judiciary in the House submitted a report on its automobile insurance study. Now the Committee on the Judiciary is investigating car insurance. So is the U.S. Department of Transportation. In short, public discontent is shaping itself into demands for reform of the system for compensating traffic injury victims.

The nature of the complaints includes company cancellations of policies on the flimsiest of pretexts or, without explanation, refusal to renew them. People have had policies canceled because they were divorced, behind in their debts, parents of teen-agers, or inducted into the Army—or for no stated reason at all. Insurance companies are becoming very selective about whom they will insure. Agents are instructed to look twice at a prospect who is young or old, who lives in the center of a city or ghetto, or who works as a musician, barber, doctor, or undertaker. The job of the agent is to skim the cream off the market—the cream being a middle-class, middle-aged suburbanite with no children of driving age and preferably with a record of few if any accidents.

Extremely high premium rates are another cause of motorist discontent. Rates go up each year as the cost of living increases but at double or triple its rate of ascent. The average price of auto insurance rose, from 1960 through 1966, 26 percent, against 10 percent for the overall Consumer Price Index. A recent congressional survey[9] found the premium on liability coverage for a family

[9] Subcommittee on Monopoly and Antitrust of the Committee on the Judiciary, House of Representatives, *Automobile Insurance Study,* U.S. Government Printing Office, 1967.

car (driven occasionally by an 18-year-old son) up between 1960 and 1966 by 128 percent in Lansing, Michigan; by 134 percent in Des Moines; by 107 percent in Indianapolis; and by 90 percent in Sacramento. Those were changes in ordinary rates.

The underlying problem has to do with the very nature of automobile accidents. Liability claims are payable only if one party admits fault, or if the insurance company concedes fault on the part of its policyholder, or if one driver can prove the other was negligent. In many cases, negligence is not a factor or cannot be proven.

Many accident victims are not compensated or are not fully compensated for their injuries. In a Michigan study of 86,000 persons injured in traffic accidents, 57 percent did not file claims, companies paid claims of 29 percent of the victims, and 14 percent retained lawyers. In Michigan, legal expenses of collecting claims added up to 25 percent of all the liability insurance settlements won with or without the help of a lawyer. Thus do legal expenses go hand in hand with the fault system of car insurance.

The system incurs other costs. It clutters the civil courts with litigation. In urban areas, it takes about 2½ years for a suit to reach trial. In Chicago, the delay is 5 to 6 years.

The Michigan survey, mentioned earlier, indicates that insurance companies, when they pay claims at all, commonly award much more or much less than full monetary losses to seriously injured victims. Figure 11-3 divides the Michigan injured who received insurance payments into four groups, according to monetary loss. Of those with losses under $1,000, about half were paid all their losses. Of those with losses of $1,000 to $4,999, only 40 percent recovered in full. Some claimants were overpaid. Oftentimes they won "nuisance

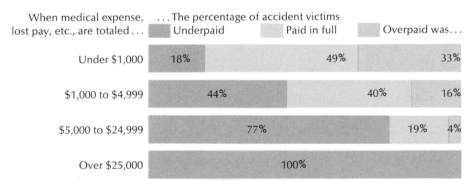

Figure 11-3   How Much Accident Victims Recover When Liability Insurance Pays the Claim. This graph compares actual economic losses to people seriously hurt in auto accidents with the percentage of loss they managed to recover from a faulty driver's liability insurance company. The data, taken from a study of crashes in Michigan in 1958, covers only those victims who collected some money and thus, theoretically, only those with valid injury claims. Source: Conard, Morgan, Pratt, Voltz, and Bombaugh, *Automobile Accident Costs and Payments,* **University of Michigan Press, 1964. Courtesy of** *Consumer Reports,* **January, 1968.**

settlements," meaning it was cheaper to pay the claim than fight it in court. Liability insurance paid only a small fraction of the losses of most Michigan victims where injuries cost them $5,000 or more.

Americans pay $4.5 billion a year in premiums for automobile bodily injury liability insurance, and the system returns net benefits of about $2.2 billion to *some* of the injured, according to *Consumer Reports* of January, 1968. The high proportion that claim settlement expense bears to a total real payout settlement has generated lively controversy and has resulted in severe criticism of the industry for inefficiency. For example, why does about 25 percent of the total payout to the automobile injury victims studied go to legal fees when only about 5.5 percent of the payouts in workmen's compensation is paid to claimants' attorneys? The State of New York reports that 42 percent of the claim expenses goes to attorneys.[10] Figures compiled by the Subcommittee on Monopoly and Antitrust reveal that in the past 37 years, auto insurance companies paid out in claims only half the $120 billion they received in premiums. For each dollar received by mutual and stock companies charging bureau rates in 1966, 12.3 cents went to investigate and fight claims, 20.6 cents went for selling expenses, 5.7 cents went for company operating expenses, and 2.3 cents for state taxes and fees. The rest (58.2 cents) was available for claims and profits.[11]

What can be done about this mess? Almost everybody in the car insurance business and independent experts agree that some other system must replace the present one. One hope for lower automobile insurance rates may be group auto insurance through a labor union or a credit union or through an employee group. The Michigan Credit Union, The United Auto Workers Union, the University of Pennsylvania, and General Electric Company are interested in this proposal.

Another answer may be in a plan proposed to be like workmen's compensation. Accident victims may be able to collect from auto compensation boards no matter who is at fault, and lengthy trips through courts with their costly litigation fees would be eliminated.

"Basic protection" is a third major proposal. This plan is proposed by two law professors, Robert E. Keeton, of Harvard, and Jeffrey O'Connell, of the University of Illinois. As in medical payments, collision, and fire insurance, claims under their plan would be paid because a person was "injured in a traffic accident, not on the basis that somebody else was at fault." Claims would be submitted to your own insurance company, not the other driver's, and payments would be made, not in one lump sum, but monthly as loss occurred. Duplicate benefits, such as those granted by sick-pay or Blue Cross coverage, would be eliminated. Compensation could not be paid for "pain and suffering" in most cases but only for measurable loss—for example, injury, physical damage, and time lost from jobs.

[10] *Ibid.*, p. 16.
[11] *U.S. Consumer*, July 24, 1968.

The Keeton-O'Connell plan is designed to spread the benefits more widely and more efficiently without upsetting the industry's private enterprise structure. It would partially replace negligence liability insurance with direct loss insurance, payable without regard to fault. The only costs it would not pay are those of injuries a driver intentionally inflicts on himself.[12]

You cannot as yet buy "basic protection" car insurance.[13] Before insurance companies can sell it in your state, the legislature must enact a law setting up a new auto insurance system making basic protection compulsory for all motor vehicles. As of 1969, no state has passed the necessary law. Several large insurance companies, however, are supporting the basic protection plan. Independent experts tend to favor the plan. About the only thing we can be sure of at this time is that the old car insurance liability system is not satisfactory and that a new system will eventually replace it. In October, 1968, for example, the American Insurance Association, an organization of 160 firms writing about 40 percent of car insurance in this country, endorsed a plan to pay medical expenses of persons injured in automobile accidents without regard to liability. The National Association of Independent Insurers, comprising 480 firms providing over half of the car insurance written in our country today, acknowledged that serious problems exist in the present system which warrant remedial action. The NAIS expects to make a recommendation of changes. Meantime, the suggestions made earlier in this chapter should be useful in helping you select the best car insurance plan available to you at this time.

AUTOMOBILE SAFETY

The Automobile Insurance Study by the staff of the House antitrust subcommittee in late 1967 stated that by the end of 1966, 102 million licensed American drivers drove 96.1 million registered vehicles 935 billion miles. During the course of this driving, there were 13.6 million accidents in which 53,000 people were killed, and 3.7 million were injured, and 24.3 million vehicles were damaged—about one accident for each 68,000 miles of vehicle operation. The 53,000 fatalities occurred in 44,200 accidents. The National Safety Council estimates that motor vehicle accidents in 1966 cost the American people $10 billion; wage losses of $2,600 million; medical expenses of $600 million; and insurance industry administrative costs of $3,500 million.

Notwithstanding the statistics that underscore the seriousness of car accidents, the probability of an accident during any individual operation is low,

[12] These two authors have published two books on this plan: *After Cars Crash* (Dow-Jones-Irwin, 1967); *Basic Protection for the Traffic Victim* (Little, Brown and Company, 1965).

[13] Tests of "no fault" car insurance plans are being conducted in parts of Illinois and New York.

and even though the economic loss suffered by any particular accident victim is likely to be minor, in some accidents the result may be catastrophic to the individuals involved. Although he may survive the accident, the victim may have permanent injuries. In addition, hospital and medical expenses in serious accidents may be substantial and may continue after all savings benefits have been consumed. Moreover, extensive damage to the car may be a major economic loss to the family.

We have already expressed opinions from car insurance officials and from the public to the effect that the system of automobile insurance in this country does not work well. The National Safety Council reports that special studies show that drinking may be a factor in one-half of the fatal motor vehicle accidents.[14] It is difficult to create a safe driver. Perhaps we should concentrate on producing safer cars.

In recent years, there is the opinion that the car industry has found it easier to sell visible style than engineering substance. Some engineers are advancing the idea that improved vehicle safety is the most sensible and efficient means of preventing accidents and casualties. They say that, with proper design, car accidents can be *safe*. It may be easier to make a car safe than to create a safe driver. It is far more feasible to change the engineering to adapt to the needs of vehicle safety than to expect drivers to behave properly at all times and under all conditions, and particularly when operating a vehicle that is often unstable and unsafe.[15]

The New York State-financed car safety feasibility studies carried out by the Republic Aviation Corporation showed that a safe, attractive, and reasonably priced car suitable for mass production can be developed—one that would protect the driver from almost any injuries at collision-impact speeds of up to 50 miles per hour and make higher-speed collisions at least survivable.[16] Safer cars, then, may be an area of research that may help in preventing serious casualties.

Motor Vehicle Safety Act of 1966

In carrying out the safer-car idea, the federal law requires the National Highway Safety Bureau to write standards of safety in vehicles that are "reasonable and practical." The first safety standards for cars were supposed to be issued on or before January 31, 1967, covering 1968 cars, and before January 31, 1968, to cover 1969 and 1970 cars. No more such restrictive deadlines exist for new-car standards. Henceforth the bureau can initiate new standards at its leisure. The bureau policy is to seek out standards in areas where something can be accomplished quickly. Tamperproof odometers and radiator caps were not

---

[14] *Automobile Insurance Study, op. cit.,* p. 4.

[15] Interview with Ralph Nader in *Playboy,* October, 1968.

[16] *Ibid.*

very important requirements in improving the safety of the car. The bureau works now on basic needs, such as requirements for bumper effectiveness, for auto-body energy-absorption and crush characteristics, and for limiting intrusion of the car structure into the interior. Engineers also say that there is need for new standards for steering performance, for greater protection to occupants in rollovers, against penetration of carbon monoxide into the passenger compartment, and for tire standards, to suggest a few. Ralph Nader, crusader for safer cars, wrote a letter to the bureau in September, 1968, in which he accused the bureau of laxness in determining compliance with its tire standards, seat belts, outside rear-view mirrors, and brakes. This delay in carrying out needed changes to make cars safer may be due to lack of funds for research and enforcement as much as to inertia and pressure from the automobile industry. At any rate, there has been some progress.

Safety Progress

In some respects, the 1968 and 1969 cars are safer than the 1967 models, and much safer than the pre-1966 models, according to automotive engineers at Consumers Union. But the April, 1968, issue of *Consumer Reports* finds that the set of 20 Federal Motor Vehicle Safety Standards now in effect, and the changes made in cars to comply with them, represent only an awkward first step down the road to an automobile as safe as even the current state of car engineering permits.

Since early 1969, both industry and government have been busy on the car safety front. Federal highway officials have issued new safety standards and changes in existing standards, all effective after January 1, 1970. The new standards require concealed headlights to remain open automatically if malfunction occurs, a second latch to prevent front hoods from opening accidentally, and a device to warn drivers when a door is open or the key left in the lock. The amendments tighten requirements for windshield wiping, washing, and defrosting systems, and for making door latches and locks safer.

In the years 1960-1966, 19 percent of all new cars in the United States were recalled for safety defects. Between September, 1966, and April, 1968, our car makers recalled more than 4.8 million defective vehicles.[17] To encourage the auto industry to move faster in remedying defective new cars, and to implement bureau safety requirements, the Transportation Department will require car makers to supply new-car owners with certain safety information on brakes, tires, and other equipment on new cars.[18] It is the biggest step yet toward requiring manufacturers to translate safety information into meaningful terms for auto buyers. The proposed rule will be effective after August 1, 1969, and should be effective for the 1970 models. The information will allow consumers to compare safety features of various makes of cars in regard to braking

[17] The *Washington Post,* Apr. 26, 1968.
[18] The *Wall Street Journal,* Oct. 8, 1968.

performance, tire performance, vehicle resistance to intrusion of passenger compartments during side crashes, and illumination and glare produced by head lamps. Also required will be information on mirror views, acceleration and passing capabilities, steering ratio, and flammability of interior materials.

The car manufacturers have been reluctant to introduce their own safety devices. A rare exception occurred when General Motors introduced side "guard rails" on most of its 1969 cars. The device, a steel bar that looks like a typical highway guard rail, is inside the door panels, out of sight.

But if consumers really want safer cars, they have the obligation to speak up more strongly and more often. At least, this is the gist of a report recently made by a consulting firm to the National Highway Safety Bureau.[19] The report said the public could make auto makers comply with safety standards faster and more effectively by demanding more factual information about new cars instead of accepting "implied promises of instant happiness, increased prestige and virility."

"Can the United States," asks the report, "remain aloof from concern with a system of design, manufacture and selling which perpetuates a mishap rate that . . . remains 10 times as dangerous per passenger mile to drive as it is to fly?"

In due time, car makers will have to accept safety as a factor in the manufacture and selling of vehicles.

NEEDED: ONE PLAN FOR ALL TRANSPORTATION[20]

Because of the U.S. Department of Housing and Urban Development, a "think-tank" team at Stanford University Research Institute (SRI) studied and proposed a possible solution to unsnarl our urban transportation system as a whole. The urban transportation 806-page proposal seems fantastic now, but the plan is realizable. It will be costly—maybe up to $60 billion if adopted nationwide over the next dozen years. Clark Henderson, team captain, estimates it will save you from death by traffic strangulation and save the country as much the first year as the cost of implementing the program.

The SRI Proposal

The SRI proposed five separate approaches. The first proposal is a fleet of three-passenger automatically controlled vehicles running on guideways at 15 miles per hour that can be shunted off and onto tracks without interfering with the main flow. Such guideways could be elevated so they would not interfere with the street-level truck and cab traffic.

Second, as a replacement for the manned taxi and the big urban bus, the

[19] U.S. Consumer, May 15, 1968.
[20] UPI News, St. Louis Post-Dispatch, Dec. 16, 1968.

plan proposes a public automobile system. You could use a telephone to dial a 20-passenger bus, or use a miniature pocket-radio transmitter to ask the bus to pick you up and carry you on a designated but flexible route. Dial buses would be radio-dispatched.

If you drive and care to pick up a car anywhere, then you could secure the use of an electrically powered car capable of speeds of 25 miles per hour that would carry four persons. To make it go, you would insert a credit card in a meter in the car and take it out at your destination, where you would leave the car.

The drive-a-car proposal is tied to a complicated whole-area transport system. Three network (NET) systems are proposed. The first would consist of independent loops of guideway tracks, each with a captive fleet of four-passenger or larger vehicles. There would be no switching. Rather, the lines would cross at different levels and passengers would change cars at interchange points.

The second NET system would allow the cars to switch from one loop to another. Thus, you could ride all over the system in one car.

The third NET alternative proposes cars that would be both operated on NET guideways and driven on the streets as in the public automobile system.

All the NET vehicles would be rubber-tired and the guideways would be air-cushioned. Speed of the vehicles on the guideways would be 70 miles an hour.

For commuter transportation, the Stanford plan envisions Fast Traffic Link (FTL) trains of 20 to 80 passenger cars operating at 150 to 250 miles per hour on air-cushioned guideways without wheels.

Far-fetched? Impossible? Not so, say the transportation experts. In fact, the strangulation of traffic is so critical in and around large urban centers now that big changes must come soon.

Proposals like the Stanford plan will and must reduce the use of personal cars in and around large urban centers. The plan must speed passengers swiftly and more cheaply. The Stanford think-team believes these objectives can be achieved.

SOCIAL RESPONSIBILITIES OF TRANSPORTATION CHANGE

The most remarkable and pervasive of all convenience devices is the automobile. In the very short span of two-thirds of a century, it has redrawn the map of this country. It has altered the distribution of our population, the shape of our cities, and the pattern of our lives.

The car has also brought with it some by-product problems. Its extensive use and abuse have resulted in widespread death, disability, and destruction of property. Its extensive use has resulted in serious pollution of the air. The highway systems and parking systems, or nonsystems, designed to accommodate it have scarred the land and created deserts in the midst of our urban centers. Even the simple act of disposing of the discarded product turns out to be not so simple at all.

In recent years the voice of the consumer is being heard in the land. Society is making an organized effort to attack these problems. Safety, mentioned only in whispers until fairly recently, is becoming a major preoccupation of the new national Transportation Department. Safety will soon become a major essential in automobile design and production. Also, devices to reduce pollution by cars are becoming mandatory. Even beautification of the landscape along our highways is becoming an acceptable target for major effort. Soon billions of dollars will be spent to solve the complex vehicle strangulation in and around all large urban centers.

Clearly, we still have a distance of ground to travel before we can have the automobile's convenience free of insult. But we are moving in that direction, and the fact that we are moving testifies to the growing strength of the consumer's voice.

ACTIVITY PROBLEMS

1. Do drivers in your state with good safety records get a break in lower car insurance premiums? Investigate carefully, because in some states the system is so out of date and unfair that even drivers with good safety records prefer standard policies (higher rates) rather than safe-driver policies.

2. You have just passed the tests for a license to drive a car. Visit with your father's car insurance agent on the subject of increase in insurance premium rates because you are not married and are under 25 years of age. What have you learned?

3. In the *Congressional Record* for Sept. 25, 1968, at p. S 11354, there are 17 pages of figures on the cost of manufacturing cars and optional equipment. This is the first time such information has been made public. Dealer-suggested markups are also stated. The class may be interested to hear a report on your findings.

4. "Most girls can get along without a car. To many a young male, wheels can be almost a necessity." Does this statement make good sense today?

5. Some of the evidence gathered by the Senate Antitrust and Monopoly Subcommittee in 1968-1969 indicates that "auto repair fleeces the public." After becoming acquainted with the evidence, investigate your local car repair situation.

6. After getting acquainted with information on how to buy a used car, visit with salesmen in your local used-car lots. How do the salesmen react to the information? Are you disillusioned or not by their attitude? What have you learned from this experience?

7. After the new car models appear in your local market, make a study of the safety features added to the new models. Which of the safety features are required by federal standards? Have the car makers added safety features voluntarily?

SUGGESTED READINGS

"Auto Insurance," *U.S. Consumer Newsletter*, July 24, 1968, and Oct. 30, 1968.

"Auto Insurance: Big Blow-up Ahead," *Changing Times*, February, 1967.

"Automobile Insurance Study," House of Representatives, Antitrust Subcommittee of the Committee on the Judiciary, U.S. Government Printing Office, 1967.

"Auto Insurance Report," *Consumer Reports*, January, 1968.

Auto Repair Business, Senate Antitrust and Monopoly Subcommittee, U.S. Government Printing Office, 1968.

The *Buying Guide* Issue (see Annual December issue), *Consumer Reports*.

"Car Insurance," *Consumer Close-ups*, Feb. 26, 1968, and Mar. 18, 1968, Cooperative Extension of Cornell University, New York, N.Y.

"Car Repair Costs," *U.S. Consumer Newsletter*, Dec. 11, 1968.

"Consumers Union Auto Insurance Project," *Consumer Reports*, March-June, 1962.

"Cost of Manufacturing Cars," *U.S. Consumer Newsletter*, Oct. 2, 1968.

"Financial Auto Mechanics," *Consumer Close-ups*, Sept. 25, 1967, Cooperative Extension of Cornell University, New York, N.Y.

"Guarantees," *Consumer Close-ups*, Aug. 26, 1968, Cooperative Extension of Cornell University, New York, N.Y.

Keeton, Robert E., Jeffrey O'Connell, and John H. McCord: *Crisis in Car Insurance*, University of Illinois Press, Urbana, Ill., 1968.

Lewiston, Robert E.: *Hit from Both Sides—An Exposé of Our Auto Insurance System*, Simon & Schuster, Inc., New York, 1967.

"Safety in the '69 Cars," *Consumer Reports*, January, 1969.

"Should a Teen-ager Have His Own Car?" *Changing Times*, October, 1968.

"Warranties," *Consumer Reports*, April, 1968.

"Warranties," *U.S. Consumer Newsletter*, Nov. 27, 1968, and Jan. 22, 1969.

chapter 12

BUYING GOOD HEALTH CARE
AND SERVICES

Buying good health is not the same as spending money for food, clothing, and shelter. These needs can be budgeted, because their cost facts are constant. But health and medical costs are uncertain and unpredictable. It is possible for a young family to budget $30 a week for food expenditures, but who can say that the health and medical expenditures of this family will average $3 or $15 a week? For this reason, the cost of ill health is, for most families, the hardest of all expenditures to face. A large percentage of families live in constant fear of loss of income resulting from disability. Earnings are usually reduced or stopped completely during an extended illness or recuperation from an accident.

Family budget experts have sometimes said that the medical expenditures of the average family should not exceed 6 to 8 percent of the net income. There are, as yet, no complete reliable statistical data on medical and health needs to aid in constructing accurate premium rates. Meantime, unpredictable medical costs confront families and sometimes lead them to make costly bargains for health by becoming victims of faddists and charlatans—even of superstitions.

THE CONSUMER AND HIS HEALTH CARE

Health Misinformation

American consumers bought more than $2 billion worth of dieting aids, headache remedies, cold preparations, vitamins, and many other health-related proprietary cures for ill-health in 1966. In that same year, American drug manufacturers spent almost $300 million advertising those same products.[1] In many cases, products with marked similarity were advertised as possessing unique or unmatched qualities. Many were accompanied by claims that medical science has proved are dubious at best and sometimes dangerous if accepted as a substitute for proper medical care.

A careful reading of *The Medicine Show* will put to doubt most of the health claims of health quacks and faddists.[2] But health education is a very slow process, despite efforts of the Food and Drug Administration, the American Medical Association, and other legitimate health organizations to inform the public. Their efforts are not aided by the editorial climate advertising dollars can buy. Disappointingly rare among the magazine, newspaper, radio, and TV media are exposés of questionable health products or regimens that are identified by brand name.

Editorial Policy. Even editorial neutrality is not enough for some magazine and newspaper advertisers. Warne, for example, makes this quite clear in quot-

[1] Colston E. Warne, "Health Information for the Consumer," a paper presented before the National Health Council Conference on Health Information and Misinformation, Nov. 3, 1967.

[2] Rev. ed., published by Consumers Union, Mount Vernon, N.Y. 10550.

ing Robert E. Launey, of Launey Advertising, addressing the American Business Press. Mr. Launey noted:

> In the interest of sound advertising relations, every editor owes his advertisers the courtesy of primary editorial consideration. Nothing is blinder, more outmoded or unfair than the sacred cow of overdone editorial integrity. Rather than total objectivity, an editor owes the advertiser at least a modicum of favorable prejudice. After all, the advertiser is the guy who puts the bread on the table.

Of course, the press, as a whole, has not lost all conscience or sense of responsibility. In recent years there are some signs that indicate more newspapers are becoming willing to name the product, the manufacturer, the seller, or the advertiser who has been called to account by government regulatory action. While we may applaud such disclosures, we should remember that their continuance depends on editors being supplied with prompt and authoritative notices of government actions. In this connection, it is disturbing to note recent attempts to curtail the flow of such information. For example, the FDA's decision to permit drug manufacturers to send Dear Doctor correction letters, as a substitute for the old policy of seizure, with its national publicity, seems to imply that consumers will be given less opportunity to learn about drug manufacturers' mistakes.

Small-scale Victories. The FDA is perhaps the best friend the consumer has had among the major federal agencies. While regulatory action may, after many years of delays, succeed in banning a Hoaxy Cancer Cure or a Micro-Dynamometer, we know that these are momentary, small-scale victories. While a Dr. Taller may finally be called to task for misinforming readers about nutrition, we know that a mass of equally fallacious information is still misleading consumers. Nor can we pretend that the antidotes reach readers who have been exposed to misinformation. How many readers of Adelle Davis' book, *Let's Have Healthy Children,* are aware that the *Journal of the American Dietetic Association* called it a "confusing mixture of fantasy, half-fact, inconsistency and outright error"? And you can be just as sure that few readers of Gaylord Hauser's pitch for yogurt and blackstrap molasses ever saw the corrective information published by the American Dietetic Association on these so-called "health goods."

Cigarette Smoking. But what about excessive cigarette smoking? The Surgeon General's report, documented with massive evidence and the most expert opinion available, pointed out the real dangers of cigarette smoking. The recent attack on this report by the Tobacco Institute came in the form of a nationwide barrage of advertisements featuring a front-page editorial from *Barron's National Business and Financial Weekly.* In this editorial, *Barron's* dismissed the Surgeon General's report as "suspect" and as providing dubious "proof."

Yesterday's patent medicine salesmen would be green with envy if they could witness the ability of commercial interests to outshout expert medical opinion. Witness the campaign for new, longer, 100-millimeter cigarettes. L & M invites you to experience "a happening." And Chesterfield tops this by offering a new 101-millimeter, longer cigarette. Midst all this fanfare, few of us can hear the voice of medical experts who warn that the greater length of the new cigarettes will increase the danger to the health of smokers.

Basic Measures in Keeping Well

How, then, can a person provide optimum health at reasonable cost for himself and his family? There is no easy answer, because the basic requirement for good health does not depend entirely on doctors and hospitals, important as doctors and hospitals are today. Indeed, there are important health protection virtues in a good standard of living, in adequate housing, in proper nutrition, in exercise and recreation, in education, and in sound personal hygiene. In fact, keeping well depends more on these and other protections than on medical care. Appropriate patterns for healthful living will serve as a guide in reaching maximum health for yourself and your family.

There are several valuable health measures that go far toward preventing acute and chronic disorders: (1) good nutrition, (2) moderation in smoking, (3) regular exercise, (4) avoidance, or at least careful use, of proprietary drugs, and (5) periodic health examinations.

The importance of a well-balanced diet of natural foods must not be underestimated. Eating too much leads to obesity, which in turn aggravates vascular and other diseases. It is well to remember that medical authorities on the "battle of the bulge" say that there is no painless road to effective, long-term weight reduction. No dietary aid, no drug, no passive-exercise device can substitute for a supervised program of diet, moderate exercise, and psychological support.

In the light of much research, moderation in smoking is a good rule to follow. Excessive smoking of cigarettes is definitely one of the factors causing cancer of the lung and aggravating coronary artery heart disease and peptic ulcer.[3]

Regular exercise, all year around, has not been appreciated. Long, brisk walks, cycling, and skating can be practices the year around.

Avoidance of proprietary drugs and devices is also wise. Intelligent people, as a rule, avoid self-treatment with patent medicines. Beware of medical frauds like "dietless" reducing schemes; "sure cures" for cancer, arthritis, skin troubles, baldness, and lost manhood; and medical quacks who deal in "atomic" medi-

[3] *The Consumers Union Report on Smoking and the Public Interest,* Consumers Union of U.S., Inc., Mount Vernon, N.Y. Also the *Surgeon General's Report on Smoking and Health,* Superintendent of Documents, 1963.

cines and "electronic" claptrap devices with flashing bulbs, ticks, and buzzes. The Food and Drug Administration tries to track down these quacks and their wares. A study of over 500 cases since 1938, however, shows that most of these violations do not come to the attention of the FDA until months or years have elapsed.[4] Unfortunately, the chief witnesses die before the cases reach the courts.

Periodic Health Examinations.   Everyone should have a periodic health examination. Disorders detected early are usually easy to treat and reduce sickness and economic loss. Cost, however, is an important barrier against periodic checks by the family physician or an internist. Most people are already struggling with paying for medical care for existing common illnesses and find it difficult to pay the cost of routine comprehensive examinations for the entire family. Life extension examiners charge about $35 for a standard periodic examination.

The typical fee for one visit at the doctor's office may range from $3 to $25. Routine blood and urine tests and chest X-ray tests cost from $10 to $20. Microscopic examinations, blood sugar test, sedimentation test, and stool examination add another $20. An electrocardiogram costs about $25. Such an annual outlay of $75 or over for each member of the family is a serious barrier for a majority of families. When hospitalization is needed, the cost is nearly prohibitive for most families. Twice-a-year dental examinations for each member of the family further add to the serious problem of paying for the needed services to keep healthy.

Unfortunately, even regular medical and dental checkups cannot give absolute health security or prevent vulnerability to major acute or chronic illnesses. But next to keeping the body healthy via proper eating, sleeping, exercise, and other personal health measures, routine physical examinations are valuable preventive medicine.

Budgeting for Health

The big budgetary question is: How can the family pay for adequate medical care for all its members? It means little to the average family to say it should budget about 6 to 8 percent of take-home pay for health. Rather, a budget for health should include (1) a reserve fund for routine health expenses and minor unexpected expenditures and (2) protection against major medical costs, for serious long-time illnesses can wreck any family budget.

To get the maximum return from your health dollars, (1) follow the recommended good-health practices, (2) know where and how to get the best professional medical help, and (3) protect the family with health insurance, especially against the cost of major and prolonged illness and disability.

[4] *Consumers Can Protect Their Own Health.* American Council on Consumer Interests, University of Missouri, Columbia, Mo., p. 28.

General Physicians and Specialists

The right choice of a family physician is very important. He should be well trained in the science and art of medicine. The possession of a medical degree does not necessarily mean that a doctor is competent. It means only that he has completed the minimum requirements of a medical school.

A good general physician is trained to treat a wide variety of bodily illnesses and is likely to have specialization in general medicine. The American Academy of General Practice requires two years of hospital training as a prerequisite for membership and also requires that a member complete 150 hours of postgraduate work every three years for continuation of membership. Today, the internist is taking the place of the former general practitioner as the family doctor. He is likely to have a certificate from the American Board of Internal Medicine.

A specialist is a physician who has general medical training but, in addition, has concentrated on a special area of the body or a special branch of medical practice. Specialization requires 2 to 5 years of postgraduate training. Here are some specialists you may consult for treatment in their fields.

1. Internist—general field of diagnosis and treatment of physical diseases
2. Surgeon—operations for a variety of physical ailments
3. Obstetrician—medical care during pregnancy and birth
4. Pediatrician—medical care of children
5. Ophthalmologist—diseases of the eye
6. Otolaryngologist—ear, nose, and throat diseases
7. Dermatologist—skin diseases
8. Psychiatrist—diseases of the mind
9. Neurologist—diseases of brain, spinal cord, and nervous system

A well-trained doctor can be identified not only by his professional degrees, hospital associations, and bedside manner, but also by his office procedure. A good physician, on the first examination of the patient, takes a detailed history of the family. He needs to know the nature of the patient's occupation and personal and family problems. He is then ready for a thorough examination, which includes a pelvic examination for women and a rectal examination for men and women. The urine is tested and the hemoglobin concentration of the blood is determined, and there are other laboratory tests. The physician then discusses the findings and recommendations with the patient.

Hospitals and Hospital Services

Most patients enter whatever hospital their doctor recommends. It is usually a good recommendation. The ideal time to choose a hospital, however, is when you are searching for a good internist. There are three important questions to ask about a hospital. (1) Is the hospital accredited by the Joint Commission on Accreditation of Hospitals? (This is a minimum safeguard against substandard hospital care.) (2) Is it a "teaching hospital"? (A hospital is more likely to provide good medical care if the level of teaching doctors is high.) (3) Is it a voluntary, nonprofit community hospital or a privately owned, proprietary hospital? Many good doctors prefer the voluntary, nonprofit community hospital because it is dedicated to good medical care on a nonprofit basis.

The basic charge for hospital service is figured on day-to-day use of private, semiprivate, or ward accommodation and includes general nursing care and meals. Charges for the operating room, anesthesia, commonly used drugs and dressings, laboratory tests, X rays, physical therapy, special medicines, and other special services are added to the regular day-rate charge.

Hospital bills may be presented weekly, monthly, or at the time the patient leaves the hospital. When a patient enters the hospital, his credit is likely to be investigated if he does not have an insurance company credit card or a card from a hospital service plan such as Blue Cross. He may make advance payment or show other evidence of ability to pay. As a rule, credit is investigated after admission to the hospital.

Nursing Homes

Nursing homes or recovery wings of a hospital provide care for patients who are chronically ill or recovering from illness or injury. They do not require the more expensive costs of regular hospitalization. As the costs of regular hospital care have increased (more rapidly than the general cost of living), attention has been given to the construction and operation of nursing or general recovery homes. Your physician can be helpful in selecting a nursing home with good standards.

The Medically Needy

Community and tax-supported health services are available in most communities for medically needy individuals and families. Most of these people are able to finance ordinary expenditures. A variety of health services and clinics are available at little or no cost through local or state health departments, welfare departments, medical schools, large business organizations, and other sources, such as: mental hospitals, armed forces facilities, child-guidance clinics, dental clinics, treatment clinics, employees' health clinics, preventive public devices, eye clinics, prenatal clinics, vocational rehabilitation centers for physically handicapped persons, and privately supported organizations like the Red Cross, Junior League "Homemaker Services," and Medicaid.

Solo Practitioners and Fee-for-service System

The "fee-for-service" system, long upheld by the medical fraternity, is under fire. Yet most physicians still cling to this system of payment.

Historically, the physician is presumed to adjust his fee according to his own notion of what the patient can afford. As a method of payment, say competent medical leaders, such fees may have been suited to the era of family doctor and home visits, but it is not satisfactory in these days of specialization, better hospital care, complicated surgery, necessary laboratory tests, and medical teamwork. Dr. James Howard Means, a former president of the American College of Physicians, made this observation:

> Doctors by and large tend to work too long and too hard either for their own good or for that of their patients. The competitive nature of their work is largely responsible for this situation. The fee-for-service method of payment, in my opinion, is the chief source of trouble. Under that system of private practice, the more fees he collects the better off the doctor is. Naturally he works hard to get them and charges what the traffic will bear. . . .
>
> Fee-for-service is scientifically indefensible, because it makes little if any provision for preventive medicine, and because it actually makes the patient reluctant to call the doctor even when really ill. For most laymen it makes medical expense unbudgetable. Organized medicine nevertheless clings to it and is willing to fight to the last ditch to retain it.[5]

A prime reason that physicians are able to command fees that often are inordinately high is the shortage of doctors in the United States. In 1900, there was one doctor for every 578 persons; by 1967, there was only one doctor for about 938 persons. Even these figures tend to overstate the actual number of physicians available to patients, because doctors doing research or otherwise not actively practicing medicine are included.

The shortage of physicians has become so acute, and the pressure for government action so great, that the American Medical Association has tried to ward off federal funds for tuition and subsidization of medical students by developing its own plan, which would create about 50 medical school scholarships annually. This modest proposal will not solve the problem of the shortage of doctors in our country.

Medical Group Practice

Medical leaders are of the opinion that group practice or teamwork is the rational approach to the tremendous growth of medical knowledge, the increase of medical specialties, and new techniques that are far beyond the ability of a solo practitioner. In group practice, each doctor can turn to his colleagues for consultation. The information of specialists is shared.

Many doctors prefer group medicine. In addition to other great hospitals, such institutions as the Mayo Clinic in Rochester, Minnesota, the Lahey Clinic in Boston, and the Ochsner Clinic in New Orleans, and such famous hospitals as Johns Hopkins in Baltimore and Massachusetts General in Boston are evidence that the medical profession has long recognized that group practice is

[5] *Doctors, People, and Government*, Little, Brown and Company, Boston, 1953.

the logical way of making better medical care widely available, of bringing new medical knowledge and techniques to medical practice.

Group medical practice, if available in your community, would likely be under one of three categories:

1.   Clinics and medical centers, which offer you a choice of physician and the services of other doctors in the group. You may be treated in the clinic, the hospital, or your home.
2.   Referral or specialty clinics, which offer diagnosis and treatment relating to a particular disease, such as heart disease or cancer. Your personal doctor is likely to be the one to refer you to this clinic.
3.   Prepaid group medical practice, which offers a combination of group practice with a "prepayment" plan. Preventive and curative health services in office, hospital, or your home are usually offered at a stated monthly fee. Since prepaid group medical plans are about the most promising in our country in terms of care and preventive medicine at reasonable cost, we will present more details on them later in the chapter.

RISING COSTS OF HEALTH CARE AND SERVICES

According to a report by the Department of Labor released on October 29, 1968, hospital bills have more than tripled and doctors' fees have more than doubled in the past 21 years. The overall rise in medical prices during the 21 years was 50 percent greater than the general rise in living costs (on the basis of the Consumer Price Index).

High Cost of Drugs and Medical Services

Drug prices have remained relatively stable, says the Department of Labor report. On the other hand, drug prices are higher, in many instances, than they need be as a result of causes that will be made clear later in the chapter.

The report also said that since 1946 hospital room rates have skyrocketed 354 percent and doctors' fees have climbed 107 percent. All medical costs averaged out to a rise of 125 percent. This compared with a rise of 71 percent over the same period for all living costs measured by the Consumer Price Index, including food, housing, clothing, transportation, recreation, medical care, and other family expenditures.

The increasing demand for hospital services has forced hospitals to expand both their facilities and their staffs, pushing costs upward. But while wage costs account for some 65 percent of hospital operating costs, their rise is due more to a vast expansion in number of workers than to high wages, the report said. Also, advanced medical technology, more expensive equipment, and specialization by doctors—all adding up to better medical care—have also been responsible for some of the rapidly rising costs.

The report noted that doctors' fees rose 7.8 percent in 1966, while dentists increased their charges 4.6 percent that year. One possible reason for the disparity may be the fact that few consumers have insurance covering dental care while over 80 percent of the population have some kind of coverage for physicians' fees.

Finally, the federal government support of Medicare and Medicaid programs have prompted more doctors to send patients to hospitals.

Nursing Home Costs

Nursing homes provide care to patients who are chronically ill or recovering from illness or injury or who need assistance in carrying on their daily living but do not need hospitalization. A registered or a licensed practical nurse is usually in attendance to carry out instructions for medicines, treatment, and care ordered by the attending physician. Cost of care in a nursing home varies greatly with the accommodations, the services available, the condition of the patient, and the amount of care needed. Most of the recently built nursing homes are too expensive for average family or individual incomes at the present time. Medicare, too, has some serious limitations in caring for patients in nursing homes.

Under Medicare, your doctor may have you admitted to a nursing or convalescent home. If your doctor arranges to have you admitted to a nursing or convalescent home within 14 days of your discharge from the hospital, after you have been hospitalized for at least three days, the present hospital insurance program of Medicare will pay for up to 20 days of care. With your doctor's permission, you may stay an additional 80 days and the insurance will bear the cost of the stay after you are charged $5 a day for the additional days. In short, costs of the nursing home will be borne by the Medicare insurance program only up to the 100-day limitation.

Before choosing a nursing home, check with your doctor or health department. Find out if the home is licensed or registered by a local, state, or federal agency. Ask about the qualifications of the attending medical staff, the type of medical attention available, and the nature of the general care of patients. If possible, visit the nursing home you are considering. Look at food service, safety, comfort, privacy, sanitation and cleanliness, recreation facilities, and attitude of personnel. The Joint Commission on Accreditation of Hospitals publishes a list of nursing homes that meet the Commission's standards.

The Dilemma about Drug Costs

The truth about drug costs is gradually emerging, and the evidence to date indicates that this publicity will have a good effect on the consumer's pocketbook.

The average consumer does not have the time to read the reports of Senate probes on prescription drugs conducted earlier by Estes Kefauver and in recent years by Gaylord Nelson, and the recent one-year study by the Task Force on Prescription Drugs for the Health, Education, and Welfare Department which was released in 1968.

Task Force Report. The Task Force says (in contrast to the Bureau of Labor Statistics report that drug prices declined 11 percent in the last 10 years) that the cost of prescriptions is a more accurate measure than the cost of a few drugs, as in the BLS report. The average number of actual prescriptions per person in the United States, the Task Force reports, was 2.4 in 1950 and 4.6 in 1966. During the same period, it says, independent surveys show the average cost of a prescription ranged from $1.66 to $2.03 in 1950 and from $3.26 to $3.59 in 1966. For the elderly, the average prescription price in 1966 was $3.91. Consumer expenditure for prescription drugs reflects the average number of prescriptions per person times the average price of the prescription. Thus, taking the median or midpoint of the two price ranges above—$1.85 in 1950 and $3.43 in 1966—and multiplying by the average number of prescriptions per person, the average cost of medical drugs per person was $4.44 in 1950 and $15.78 in 1966. This, says the Task Force, means the increase in drug costs was actually 255 percent more rather than an 11 percent decrease. The Task Force does not dispute that some individual drug prices have dropped. It depends on which drugs you use. It would appear that the Task Force study of the prescriptions actually used per person is the more accurate method of arriving at consumer cost of drugs. The average family (4.2 persons) spent approximately $66 a year for prescription drugs in 1966. The cost for each succeeding year is likely to be more, because the number of prescriptions has been increasing each year in the last 10 years.

The Task Force also confirmed the great disparity between prices of widely advertised brand-name drugs and their lesser-known unbranded (generic) counterparts. It also found the tendency of brands to replace generics.

The Task Force also confirmed the findings of the earlier Kefauver and the recent Nelson Senate investigations as amounting to a sweeping indictment of the drug makers and the medical profession. The drug makers are accused of excessive profits (the industry as a whole was the nation's profit pacemaker of 21.1 percent on invested capital), and the medical profession of failing to combat this profiteering by relying too much on the information supplied by drug advertising and promotion ($800 million or $3,000 per doctor per year in promoting drugs).[6]

Same Brand, Different Prices. Most doctors are not aware of the price disparities which do exist in many drugs. A recent survey concludes that "Commercial sources of information form the major, and probably a predominant, part

[6] Senator Gaylord Nelson, "The Public Must Demand Lower Drug Prices," *Everybody's Money Magazine,* Autumn, 1968.

of the physicians' means of keeping informed about new drugs."[7] This is one reason why patients receive so little help from their doctor on the lowest price for a particular prescription. Doctors' ignorance about comparative drug prices is not the only problem.

Complex Drug Prices.　The Senate Monopoly and Antitrust Subcommittee investigation of drug prices in 1967 found many cases of the same drug sold at different prices. Prednisone, for example, is a drug used for arthritis. The best-known brand was being sold under the name Morticorten. The subcommittee found that at the same time the drug maker of Morticorten was selling the drug to pharmacists for $17.90 for 100 tablets wholesale, it was selling the same drug for one-fourth the price to overseas druggists, offering to sell it to New York City for $1.20 for 100 tablets and then to our Defense Department for 82 cents for 100 tablets. Other brand companies sold Prednisone for about $2.25 for 100 tablets, and it could be purchased generically for 59 cents for 100 tablets wholesale. Soon after these facts were made public, the company reduced its price to pharmacists to $10.80 for 100 tablets. Shortly afterward, another drug maker of the same drug (brand name Paracort) slashed its price to $3.45 for 100 tablets—an 80 percent drop!

The Senate subcommittee also found that this drug could be produced for about 50 cents per 100 tablets. The manufacturer testifying disclosed that the breakeven point was about $1.36. Adding 25 percent profit and 10 percent for research costs realizes a total of $1.84. Yet the price the drug maker charged pharmacists was $17.90 for 100 tablets.

This is one dramatic illustration of how the writing of prescriptions with brand names rather than the generic raises the cost of prescription drugs. Only public hearings of a Senate subcommittee brought the facts to the public and forced a reduction in price.

Generic versus Brand Names.　This is a complicated issue.[8] One fact, however, seems to be quite clear. There is a wide disparity between prices of widely advertised brand-name drugs and their lesser-known unbranded (generic) counterparts. The Task Force (HEW), mentioned earlier, found that among 409 frequently used drugs, 379 were brand items, 30 were generic, and the average price of the branded drugs was $4.11 against $2.02 for the generics.[9]

With over 1 billion prescriptions written each year, consumers are becoming more aware of the rising cost of drugs today. Their problem is not limited to

[7] Raymond A. Bauer and Laurence H. Wortzel, "Doctor's Choice: The Physician and His Sources of Information About Drugs," *Journal of Marketing Research*, February, 1966.

[8] For a good but brief discussion of the issues, see *Consumer Close-ups, Newsletters* for Sept. 23 and Oct. 29, 1968.

[9] "The Drug Users," background paper by the Task Force on Prescription Drugs, Health, Education, and Welfare Department, Washington, D.C., 1968.

prices but includes why the costs are high, who determines prices, and what alternatives are open to consumers.

Dr. William S. Apple, director of the American Pharmaceutical Association, said: "With prescription drugs, the consumer cannot weigh the alternatives, so others must do it for him." He thinks the professional pharmacist can provide "greater help in drug selection [in regard to cost] than the various sales promotions of the pharmaceutical firms."[10]

The Pharmaceutical Manufacturers Association say that "generic identity . . . is a futile goal, for it does not guarantee uniform therapeutic effect of finished products in all patients."[11]

Dr. Thomas H. Hayes, director of the Department of Drugs, American Medical Association, says that the AMA policy in prescribing is that "physicians should be free to use either the generic or brand names in prescribing drugs for their patients; and to encourage physicians to supplement medical judgment with cost considerations in making this choice."[12]

Solutions. If the physician is to carry out cost recommendations, he must have an easy-to-use, up-to-date, and complete compendium on the cost of the drugs he is prescribing. The Pharmaceutical Manufacturers Association is conducting a pilot project now concerning this problem.

Another suggestion is that the federal government, possibly the FDA (Food and Drug Administration), should continue comparative tests of the brand-name and generic drug products and compare prices for identical generic and brand-name drugs. This information should be included in a compendium available to all doctors and pharmacists. A news report in the *Washington Post*[13] stated that by a 7–to–2 vote, doctors backed the federal government's publishing the relative costs of all prescription drugs, generic and brand-named.

Meantime, What Can You Do? Do not be afraid to discuss this matter with your doctor before he writes the prescription. It pays to shop around, but it takes time and energy that should not be imposed on people. *Consumer Reports*[14] gives a report on the American Medical Association's drug price survey in the Chicago area for 686 prescriptions.

There are several mail-order prescription institutions filling prescriptions. David Shakariau, a Pittsburgh pioneer, entered the prescription business because so many of his diet customers complained about high drug prices.

The California Pharmaceutical Services, Incorporated, a nonprofit prepaid prescription organization started by professional pharmacists, offers its services

---

[10] *Consumer Close-ups,* Sept. 23 and Oct. 29, 1968.

[11] *Ibid.*

[12] *Ibid.*

[13] *Washington Post,* Dec. 9, 1968.

[14] *Consumer Reports,* October, 1967, issue.

to unions and other employee groups. In a statewide plan, the Colorado Prescription Service members pay a small semiannual fee and receive reduced rates for prescriptions. Consumer groups, cooperatives, and labor unions have found that buying drugs in large quantities can result in considerable savings when they use their own drugstore prescription service.

Other mail-order prescription services are the Senior Citizens Direct Drug Service, sponsored by the National Farmers Union, Greenbelt Consumers Service, and the National Council of Senior Citizens.[15] This drug service claims to offer savings of from 20 to 50 percent. This service recommends that the patient ask his doctor to prescribe by generic name for even greater savings. Most of the mail-order drug services take pride in their ability to fill and mail a prescription order on the same day it is received.

MEETING TODAY'S RISING COST OF HEALTH CARE

Your health care insurance is important to your family's security and well-being. It enables you to plan ahead for the unexpected and sometimes heavy expenses of illness and injury.

Health Care Insurance

Health care insurance helps protect you and your family against two economic risks: (1) the cost of hospital, surgical, and other medical services; (2) the loss of income due to disability of the major breadwinner. Most Americans cannot afford to be without health care and loss-of-income protection.

Health care insurance and services today are undergoing vast changes. Health and medical insurance continues to change to keep up with social legislation such as Social Security benefits, workmen's compensation, state-sponsored disability benefits, Medicare, and Medicaid, and to adjust to the family needs in meeting the costs of better health care. So it is desirable to understand not only what protection you have, but to review it periodically. In this way you can make certain that your health insurance is in step with your family's current situation as well as with present costs of health care and the advances made in medical services. Family health care insurance, therefore, requires careful planning to be well balanced and effective.

Types of Health Care Plans.   Health care insurance is not intended to cover the small expenses which most families can budget for, such as regular checkups, inoculations, and the like. There are, however, nonprofit, prepaid group plans that encourage and provide for regular physical checkups at no extra

[15] National Council of Senior Citizens, 1627 K Street, N.W., Washington, D.C. 20006.

expense. For costly and unexpected bills, however, protection is provided through: health insurance, offered by about 1,000 private insurance companies; nonprofit prepayment plans, such as Blue Cross and Blue Shield; panels of doctors practicing in a group arrangement; nonprofit, prepaid, independent-group health plans; and tax-supported programs, such as the federal Medicare program, largely for the aged, and the various state Medicaid programs for low-income people who are unable to pay for health care.

Group or Individual Policy.   There are two principal ways a family can have insurance to share the costs of health care: (1) Group plans are usually offered by employers, unions, and other associations, such as colleges. Most such plans protect your dependents as well. Group insurance has certain advantages—like lower premiums. The employer usually pays all or part of the premium, and individuals are eligible regardless of their physical condition. (2) Individual policies are usually obtained by those who are not eligible for a group plan, or, if they are eligible for a group plan, they may wish to supplement its benefits. Individual plans are usually more expensive than group plans. Individual plans have the advantage of flexibility whereby they can be tailored to fit the particular requirement of the individual or family.

New Types of Health Insurance.   New kinds of health care problems are always in a developing stage. Among these are specific protection against the costs of dental care; costs in a nursing or convalescent home; coverage for mental illness; costs of out-of-hospital drugs; costs in such areas as eye or vision needs; group travel insurance; and credit insurance in the event of death or disability. There will be more kinds of coverage in the foreseeable future.

Extent of Voluntary Health Care Insurance.   In the United States over 87 percent of the civilian, noninstitutionalized population below age 65 were

TABLE 12-1   NUMBER OF PEOPLE UNDER 65 COVERED BY PRIVATE HOSPITAL INSURANCE (DECEMBER 31, 1967) (000 OMITTED)

TYPE OF INSURER	HOSPITAL EXPENSE	SURGICAL EXPENSE	REGULAR MEDICAL EXPENSE
Insurance companies:			
Group insurance	71,279	72,583	56,909
Individual insurance	35,650	26,965	10,848
Deduction for duplication	10,698	9,209	4,798
Net total	96,251	90,339	62,959
Blue Cross, Blue Shield, medical security plans	63,330	55,671	52,314
Other plans	7,020	8,375	8,180
Deduction for duplication	12,833	11,557	6,788
Net total persons covered	153,768	142,828	116,665

SOURCE: Health Insurance Council, New York, August, 1968.

TABLE 12-2   PRIVATE HEALTH INSURANCE BENEFITS PAID TO PERSONS UNDER
65 (DECEMBER 31, 1967) (MILLIONS OF DOLLARS)

TYPE OF INSURER	TOTAL	HOSPITAL EXPENSES	SURGICAL AND MEDICAL EXPENSES	DENTAL EXPENSES
Insurance companies	$4,504	$2,800*	$1,663*	$41
Blue Cross, Blue Shield,				
medical society plans	4,149	2,772	1,377	—
Other plans	625	256	339	30
Total	9,278	5,828	3,379	71

*Includes benefits paid by major medical policies.
SOURCE: Health Insurance Council, New York, August, 1968.

covered by private hospital expense insurance by the end of 1967. The number covered, 154 million, was up by 5.2 million over those covered in 1966 (Table
12-1).

Hospital expense benefits during 1967 to people under age 65 totaled $5,828
million, $271 million more than was paid in 1966 (Table 12-2).

Surgical expense benefits covered nearly 143 million persons under age 65
at the end of 1967, 5 million more than in 1966 (Table 12-1), and paid over
$3.3 billion in benefit expenses (Table 12-2).

Regular medical expense protection, such as cost of physicians' visits, covered 117 million persons under age 65 at the end of 1967, 6 million more than
in 1966 (Table 12-1).

Major medical coverage helps pay for nearly all kinds of hospital and medical care prescribed by physicians. It is designed to provide protection for catastrophic or prolonged illness. At the end of 1967, over 66 million persons
in this country were covered by major medical and comprehensive, nonprofit group plans. [16]

About 2.3 million persons were covered by dental insurance at the end of
1967 and received about $41 million in benefits from the for-profit insurance
company plans, according to the Health Insurance Council. Many more persons are covered by nonprofit plans like Blue Cross and Blue Shield.

Some 57.9 million people—7 out of 10 in our labor force—had loss-of-income insurance or some other form of formal protection against loss of income
at the end of 1967, according to Health Insurance Council data.

The health care coverage of our civilian population has been improving each
year in the number of people covered and benefits received. Despite this progress, there are many serious gaps and inadequacies in our voluntary health

[16] Health Insurance Council, August, 1968; Cooperative League of the U.S.A., *Coop
Report*, September, 1968.

insurance cost and coverage. More will be said about these inadequacies later in this chapter.

Health Insurance Costs

To begin with, you can get health care insurance from three different types of organizations. There are the private, for-profit insurance companies; the Blue Cross-Blue Shield plans; and the independent plans run by communities, medical practitioners, employer-union groups, and comprehensive group health practice.

Blue Cross and Blue Shield are doctors-and-hospitals-administered, nonprofit plans. Their activities are coordinated nationally, but their insurance plans are slightly different in each community or area. Blue Cross covers hospital bills for the most part; Blue Shield covers surgeons' and physicians' bills largely. Blue Cross and Blue Shield are usually separately run, but they work together to provide package policies for both hospital and some doctor bills. On the whole, Blue Cross and Blue Shield nonprofit groups pay more benefits per premium dollar than the for-profit private insurance companies.

Insurance companies and Blue Cross offer a wide variety of policies with widely different benefits. Generally, you can select the amount of benefits you want for a specific price. For example, you can raise a standard $10-a-day hospital benefit to $20 or more a day by paying an added premium.

You may have a choice of individual or group policies, too. The health insurance you get through your union, employer, or business or professional society is usually a group policy. The benefits and premiums in a group policy are fixed in a master policy. It costs the insurer less to sell and administer group policies than individual policies, so group policies usually provide more liberal benefits.

Policies pay off in terms of either service benefits or indemnity (cash) benefits. In service-type policies, the plan pays for the service itself regardless of the cost. In indemnity or cash benefit plans, a flat sum of money is paid directly to you toward particular expenses. Blue Cross, for example, pays all the cost of a semiprivate hospital room. That is a service benefit. Insurance companies usually provide a set sum of $10 a day toward the cost of a hospital room. That is an indemnity benefit.

The group practice, prepayment comprehensive plans originate with groups of doctors who practice medicine as a team in their group-owned hospitals and clinics. You pay on a monthly level-premium basis just as you pay for insurance. For this premium, you or your family receive comprehensive health care, from periodical checkups to diagnosed treatment and surgery. The key benefit in comprehensive medical practice is "preventive medicine." As a rule, comprehensive group practice yields more benefits per premium dollar than most plans available to the public as a whole.

Who Gets Your Health Dollar?

For the average family, physicians' bills were the largest single health expense in 1966, with hospital bills a close second. The druggist gets about half what the doctor gets and the dentist a third as much. This is how the spending goes over the course of the year:

Physicians	30%
Hospitals	29
Drugs/sundries	16
Dentists	10
Health insurance premiums	5
Eyeglasses, other medical appliances	4
General professional services other than physicians' and dentists'	3
Nursing home care	3

The Five Big Protections

There are five basic kinds of health care insurance available to you. These kinds of protection are hospitalization, surgical-physician expenses, major medical, accidental death and dismemberment, and disability.

1. Hospitalization.   In general, these benefits help pay for two types of services or costs: daily room and board, routine nursing, minor medical supplies, and additional related services such as laboratory tests, X rays, anesthesia and its administration, use of operating room, drugs and medications, and local ambulance service. Blue Cross plans pay for all the cost of a semiprivate room (a service benefit). Insurance companies pay an indemnity like $10 per day for 31 days toward room and board cost, plus $100 miscellaneous hospital expenses. A man, age 35, for example, might pay $44-a-year premium for $10 a day for 31 days in the hospital plus the $100 miscellaneous expenses. Since the average cost of a semiprivate room in a hospital today is about $44 per day, a man age 35 may want $20-a-day benefit by paying a premium of $58 a year, no deductible. A man and wife, age 35, for a $20-per-day board and room benefit would pay about $128 premium per year. Insurance company premium rates for women are higher than for men. If there are children or other dependents, the insurance company rates are higher.

Blue Cross hospital rates cover all the board and room charges. In a large city, the Blue Cross premium rate for a family (includes all dependents up to age 18) may average $16 per month for 120 days of care. In rural or small-town areas, where hospital costs are lower, the Blue Cross family premium rate might be as much as 40 percent lower.

When investigating various kinds of hospital benefit insurance policies, find out:

How many days in the hospital does your policy cover?

How much does the policy pay per day for room and board?

How do these daily benefits compare with hospital room and board charges in your community?

How much does the policy pay for related expenses in the hospital—X rays, anesthesia and its administration, and the like?

Are there waiting periods before certain conditions are covered?

Is there a deductible which you must pay toward hospital expenses before benefits start?

Is the policy renewable?

What are the limitations or exclusions in the policy?

2. Doctor Bills. Surgical insurance and physician's expense insurance are usually available only in combination with a hospital expense policy, if provided by insurance companies, or as a Blue Shield contract supplementing a Blue Cross hospital contract. Benefits for surgery run as high as $500, or higher for a particular operation. Physician's expense benefits pay for a specific number of in-hospital visits—possibly as many as 50 visits—at $5 per visit.

The maximums paid by two private insurance companies, for example, with a $300 limit for any one surgical procedure, were as follows: Company A, for removal of gallbladder, $165, in contrast to $175 by Company B; hysterectomy, Company A, $180 and Company B, $250.

Most Blue Shield plans cover X rays, therapy, and other benefits in addition to surgery expenses.

Check on the following points before deciding on surgical-physician's expense benefits:

Are the benefits in line with physicians' and surgeons' fees in your community?

What types of surgical and physicians' services does the policy help pay for?

What are the limitations or exclusions in the policy?

How much does the policy pay for each doctor visit in the office or in the hospital?

How many such visits are allowed per confinement?

Are you covered for house calls?

Is there a deductible before benefits start?

3. Major Medical Insurance. Major medical coverage is the fastest-growing type of health coverage in the country. It is sold by private insurance companies and by nonprofit Blue Cross - Blue Shield. It is designed to handle costs of serious illnesses and accidents. These policies cover expenses ranging from $10,000 to $20,000 and higher, for every type of care and treatment prescribed by physicians both in and out of the hospital. Most major policies are written with a deductible of $250 to $500 which the policyholder must pay before the benefits begin. After the deductible, these policies also have a "coinsurance" provision, which means that the insurance pays 75 to 80 percent with the policyholder paying the balance.

Many families have major medical coverage as a supplement to their "basic" plan. Other families have their basic and major medical protection combined into a single policy, called "comprehensive" major medical insurance.

This is how major medical coverage works. Let's say a patient has an illness costing $5,000 with a major medical policy with a $500 deductible and a 25 percent coinsurance clause. The patient would pay the $500 deductible, plus the coinsurance amount, or $1,625 in all. If he had basic coverage, it would pay the $500 deductible. The insurance company would pay $3,375. A typical policy of this kind with a $15,000 benefit maximum might cost a person, age 35, with his wife and two children also covered, approximately $175 annually. If he had a smaller deductible, say $250, the premium rate would be higher; and if the deductible were $750, the premium rate would be lower. The reason for having deductible and coinsurance is to reduce the premium costs to a point where most individuals and families can afford to buy this important health care protection.

Check the following points before buying major medical insurance:

What is the maximum amount your policy will pay?

Will the maximum benefit be in effect again for you upon recovery?

How large a deductible must you pay?

Is there a deductible for each claim for a different illness or injury? Or is it on a calendar-year basis, with one deductible in a given year charged against the total bills?

What percent of the total cost above the deductible does the policy pay—75 percent? 80 percent? What percent do you pay?

What provisions exist for renewing your policy?

What top benefits limits, if any, exist for such expenses as hospital room and board, surgery, or other specialists' consultation and treatment?

4. Accidental Death and Dismemberment.   This is the earliest kind of health insurance. Basically, the policy pays a flat amount for injury and death caused by an accident. The protection is not expensive. For about $8 to $10 a year, a person can buy a policy that will pay: (1) $5,000 for accidental death; the loss of both hands, or both feet, or the sight of both eyes, or the loss of one foot and one hand; (2) $3,750 for loss of an arm or a leg; (3) $2,500 for the loss of a foot or a hand, or the sight of one eye.

Accident policies can be expanded to include greater protection and other benefits. School districts offer accident policies with some medical provisions for children attending school. Adult policies are usually combined with disability income insurance.

5. Loss of Income.   Loss-of-income protection helps replace loss of wages, salary, and other earned income incurred through disability resulting from illness or injury. Some 57.9 million persons, 7 out of 10 in the labor force, had loss-of-income insurance at the end of 1967, according to the Health Insurance Council.

Payments usually do not begin until after you have been disabled for a specified "elimination period." Your protection depends not only on the benefits but on how the company defines disability. For example, does "total disability" mean incapacity to engage in your usual work, or incapacity to work for which you are suited by education and training, or incapacity to perform *any* work at all?

Women are considered poorer disability risks than men and may have difficulty securing disability insurance or as much as they may need. Men ordinarily can buy monthly benefits which do not exceed 60 percent of their monthly earnings. Higher benefits may discourage policyholders from returning to work.

A policy for a man, age 35, in the lowest-rate occupation category can get a $100-per-month policy to age 65, with a waiting period of 30 days, for about $60 premium rate a year. Some policies have shorter waiting periods, but the shorter the waiting period, the higher the premium rate. Benefits, however, usually begin on the first day for accident and the eighth day for illness. Benefit payments may continue anywhere from 13 weeks to lifetime for accidents and to age 65 for sickness. Be sure to take into account the length of time your earnings and any other income will continue. This will enable you to evaluate the "waiting period" in your policies—and will help you to better budget against loss of income.

The following questions will help you select disability income insurance that will fit your needs:

Is there a waiting period before benefits begin?

Does the waiting period vary depending on whether sickness or an accident is involved?

How does the policy define total disability?

Will it pay benefits for partial disability?

Is it a requirement of the policy that you be confined to bed at home, or confined to your home, for benefits?

What is the amount of weekly or monthly benefits?

How long do the regular payments continue for accident? For illness?

What provisions exist for renewing the policy?

What exclusions or limitations exist in your policy?

How will workmen's compensation, or Social Security, or disability income from your employer affect income from your insurance policy?

Dental Care Insurance

The Health Insurance Council in August, 1968, reported that 2.3 million Americans were covered by insurance company dental insurance policies at the end of 1967. This is one of the newest kinds of health care protection offered by insurance companies. The coverage is written on either a scheduled or a comprehensive basis. Most policies sold were protected by scheduled plans.

Getting teeth straightened can put a big kink in your budget. Visits to an orthodontist for two years may cost anywhere from $800 to $2,000!

Dental insurance pays all or part of the cost of dental care. Coverage, however, varies from policy to policy. You may have to pay the first $25 of a year's dental bills, and then the insurance policy pays a percentage of the remaining costs, commonly 75 to 80 percent. With other policies, you are reimbursed for each service according to a schedule—$6 for each filling, for instance. Usually there are limits on the benefits you can receive in a year.

Virtually all dental coverage today is group insurance. Usually the coverage is arranged by an employer, a union, or a state medical society (Blue Shield).

There are a few differences between dental insurance and other kinds of health care protection. Unlike accident insurance, dental insurance is not protection against a possible disaster that may never occur. Most people know they will need dental care. The premiums, therefore, tend to bear a direct relationship to the benefits in any one year.

There were over 500 groups insured in 1968. These groups range from 10 or so employees to 100,000 in a large corporation. Their policies are purchased from insurance companies, from dental service corporations, through dental clinics, and from Blue Shield.

If you belong to group practice clinics, the oldest dental insurance plan, you go directly to the dental clinic or to the offices of contracting dentists for your dental care. Insurance companies offer protection in group policies, although individual coverage is sold by some insurance companies. Dental service corporations sell dental service much as Blue Shield sells medical service. They are nonprofit, chartered by the states in which they operate. The main difference between insurance companies and a state service company is that dentists control the service corporations. Another difference is that an insurance company pays you and you pay the dentist; most service corporations pay the dentist directly. Several states presently have dental service plans—California, Hawaii, Washington, Oregon, Colorado, Michigan, Ohio, Connecticut, and New York—to mention a few. A national dental service association has recently been organized by the American Dental Association. It will not merchandise policies as the national Blue Cross does, but it will serve as a coordinating agency for state organizations.

How Dental Insurance Works.   The Wisconsin Physicians Service of the State Medical Society of Wisconsin, a Blue Shield plan, currently writes dental plans for groups of 25 or more. WPS pays 50 percent for orthodontics on a nondeductible basis or offers options under which the patient pays the first $25, $50, or $100 with WPS paying 50 percent of the remainder or matching these amounts. Anyone can join without regard to need for dental care.

A dental service corporation in Michigan covers the whole family, with the employer paying the premium. The employee pays $25 per person, not over $50 per family; then pays 25 percent of additional costs. Maximum benefits per patient are $750 a year.

A union in San Francisco protects all children under 15 years of age in a union family. The employer-employee contributes to the fund to cover the entire cost of this dental care. The benefits cover most dental services except extractions, oral surgery, and orthodontics.

Comprehensive Dental Care. The number of people having dental care protection is small, as we noted earlier. There are a number of forces at work to expand the group insurance program. The U.S. Public Health Service and the American Dental Association like the prepayment plan because it means better dental care for more people. The University of Maryland School of Dentistry is studying the feasibility of installing a prepayment plan through which parents may pay a fixed yearly rate on a voluntary basis and receive comprehensive dental care for their children, as well as orthodontic and surgical care. Private dentists would perform the dental services, and the university's school of dentistry would supervise the program.

All one can say at this time is that dental care plans are few but there is progress. The need for better dental care is great. Untreated dental conditions in this country are among the most common of all diseases afflicting our people. One study claimed that there are, on the average, four unfilled cavities per person. [17] Consumers need to weigh the possible advantages of dental health care plans and encourage their professional associations, unions, and other organizations to investigate and report their findings to their respective constituents. A number of prepayment plans have been organized by state dental societies. [18]

HOW EFFECTIVE IS PRIVATE INSURANCE COMPANY PROTECTION?

The HIAA Study

The Health Insurance Association of America made a study of some 40,000 of their group policy claims. [19] The study showed that:

> Four-fifths of the expenses incurred by insureds for items of health care against which insurance was purchased was reimbursed.
>
> Group plans reimbursed about 88 percent of the hospital charges in semiprivate rooms and 81 percent of charges for private-room accommodations. For all types of accommodations, 86 percent of covered expenses were reimbursed—83 percent for room and board and 89 percent for ancillary expenses.

[17] W. D. Young, *Dental Health,* American Council on Education, Washington, D.C., 1961.

[18] For more information, ask your local dental society or write to the American Dental Association, 211 E. Chicago Avenue, Chicago, Ill. 60611. For names of insurance companies selling dental policies, write to the Health Insurance Institute, 277 Park Avenue, New York, N.Y. 10017. You might also encourage your Blue Shield organization to include dental care benefits like those of the Wisconsin Blue Shield plan mentioned earlier.

[19] Health Insurance Council, *Viewpoint,* August, 1968.

For other health care expenses, the relationship was as follows:

Percent of covered charges reimbursed:	
Surgery	77%
Anesthetist	84
X Ray, Laboratory	76
Doctor visits in hospital	70
Doctor visits at home or office	60
Private-duty nurses	73
Prescribed drugs	61
Other expenses	77

The percent of expenses reimbursed varies by diagnosis and by type of claimant. As examples, only 74 percent of the covered charges for nervous and mental conditions were reimbursed, compared with 81 percent for other sickness. Of the covered expenses incurred by dependent children, 85 percent was reimbursed, compared with only 77 percent for male employees.

COMPREHENSIVE NONPROFIT PREPAID GROUP HEALTH PLANS

In 1967, John Gardner, Secretary of Health, Education, and Welfare, prepared a *Report to the President on Medical Care Prices,* in which he concluded:

> Group practice, especially prepaid group practice, should be encouraged. . . . Groups of doctors practicing together can make more efficient use of equipment, auxiliary personnel, and consultation than doctors practicing alone. Where the patient has paid in advance for comprehensive medical care under a group practice plan, less incentive exists to use high-cost hospital services where lower cost alternatives would meet the patient's needs just as well.

Dr. William H. Stewart, Surgeon General of the U.S. Public Health Service, said: "The American people . . . want to know when and how they shall receive better health care at prices they can afford to pay. We who believe in group practice have an answer. It is not the whole answer, nor the only answer, but it represents a valid and important approach."[20]

In the April, 1968, issue of *Group Health and Welfare News,* Dr. W. Palmer Dearing, executive director of the Group Health Association of America, said: "Group practice prepayment plans provide a rational organization of medical services with good quality and cost control."

The question is: Is this a promising route?

[20] Quoted in "Who Can Afford to Be Sick?" *Look* magazine, Oct. 15, 1968.

Comprehensive Prepaid Group Health Care

Group Health Association estimates that there are about 5 million Americans presently receiving this kind of health care in some 196 group plans that have some of the following characteristics: [21]

1. Group practice. This simply means doctors practicing as a team, general practitioners and specialists together.
2. Prepayment. You pay for health care (generally monthly) on a "level-premium" basis just as you pay for insurance.
3. Comprehensive care. You go to the medical center on some regular basis and the doctors' job is to take care of your health *before* you get sick. This is called "preventive medicine." If medical attention—treatments, surgery, etc.—is needed, all of the costs are paid for by your monthly premiums.
4. Consumer control. Generally, a group health association or foundation is formed and a board of directors (usually doctors) is selected which hires an administrator who hires the staff. The doctors have full charge of the practice of medicine.

Some Group Plans. Among the 196 group plans, the following organizations are especially noteworthy: Health Insurance Plan of Greater New York (HIP), which has some 750,000 enrollees; Group Health Cooperative of Puget Sound, which cares for 95,000 members; Community Health Association of Detroit, 80,000 members; Group Health Association of Washington, D.C., 65,000 members; Community Health Foundation of Cleveland—only 3 years old in 1968—33,000 members. The latter is now ready to build a $10 million, 128-bed general hospital in nearby Independence, Ohio.

Federal Government Interest. Why was the federal government interested in group health plans? The answer largely is: costs. On July 1, 1966, the federal government began picking up the health care tab for millions of Americans over 65 years of age. It found that it did not have good answers to basic questions such as: How much does it actually cost to provide good medical care? What are fair and reasonable rates for the government—and others—to pay? Meanwhile the Bureau of Labor Statistics study showed that, whereas all items in the Consumer Price Index rose 16 percent in the years 1965-1966, medical care costs rose 42 percent.

Genuine nonprofit, group health plans provided the best cost guidelines available to the federal government. For example, studies of various health care plans in which federal government employees are enrolled (over 7 million) show that consistently those in group plans spent less time in hospitals during a 14-month contract period ending December 31, 1965. In the indemnity benefit (insurance company) plans, federal employees spent 11.1 days in the hospital per utilizer; Blue Cross-Blue Shield federal members, 9.4 days per

---

[21] *Coop Report,* September, 1968.

utilizer; and Group Practice Plan federal members, only 8.3 days in the hospital.[22]

The importance of this is evident in the fact that hospital care in most cities costs $40 or more a day, and one reason for the difference is believed to be the regular checkups—preventive care—that members of group health plans receive.

There was more significant evidence in favor of group health plans. The annual benefits per covered person provided to the members of group health plans were the highest of all plans. Furthermore, group health plans had less than half the surgery rate of 4 million Blue Shield enrollees. And the appendectomy rate for insurance company plans was twice that of group health plan enrollees.[23]

Medical Society Opposition.   The Community Health Foundation of Cleveland, Ohio, is an illustration of medical society opposition. This group health plan—only 3 years old in 1968, with 33,000 members—700 new members each week in 1968—illustrates why group health plans have modest growth. In the first place Ohio (and 16 other states) passed laws barring group health plans. The main issue against group health plans centered around the opposition of the medical society to the free-choice concept of physician. The Ohio Medical Society claimed that patients do not have a choice of doctors. This point of view was quickly settled at a state senate committee hearing when one senator queried the representative of the medical society: "If I were to select you as my physician," the legislator wanted to know, "do you have to treat me?" The doctor admitted that he could refuse. Whereupon the senator concluded that free choice was a rather one-sided affair and had little meaning. He decided that the right of a subscriber to select a physician from a roster of doctors in a group plan had more validity. The new law passed 101 to 11, and the way was opened for Cleveland's Community Health Foundation. In 3 years, it had 33,000 subscribers. A family premium costs $29 per month and covers the whole family. CHF offers private medical care, with doctors available 24 hours a day, 7 days a week, for emergencies, and with full hospitalization and surgery when needed. Each family can select from a roster of doctors one to serve as a personal physician and a pediatrician to look after the children. Because CHF doctors stress regular checkups and practice preventive medicine, subscribers need only half as much hospitalization as other Clevelanders.[24]

Unfortunately, comprehensive group health care is not available to most Americans. As we said earlier, in 1968 17 states had legislation preventing organization of group health. Furthermore, in states permitting group health plans,

---

[22] *Group Health and Welfare News,* Special Supplement, October, 1968.

[23] *Ibid.,* November, 1968.

[24] *Look* magazine, Oct. 15, 1968.

the growth has been slow, largely because of the opposition of some medical societies.

Encouraging Alternatives

In the *Report to the President on Medical Care Prices* in 1967, we find two important recommendations. Recommendation 1: "Group practice, especially pre-paid group practice, should be encouraged." To implement this recommendation, the report said:

1. The Federal Government should encourage group practice prepayment plans by amending Title XIX of the Social Security Act to require States to allow medical beneficiaries to use such plans.
2. The Department of Health, Education, and Welfare should encourage the States to use Title XIX funds to foster and extend the group practice of medicine.
3. The National Center for Health Services Research should provide "seed money" to encourage incipient group practice prepayment plans, and to evaluate their ability to provide quality care efficiently.
4. The Department of Housing and Urban Development and the Department of Health, Education, and Welfare should make maximum use of the Group Practice Facilities Mortgage Guarantee Program.

Recommendation 2: "Comprehensive community health care systems should be developed, demonstrated, and evaluated." To implement this proposal, the report said:

1. The Federal Government should take the lead by creating a National Center for Health Services Research and Development in the Department of Health, Education, and Welfare. The center would offer technical assistance and financial support for the development of model comprehensive systems. These model systems would make available intensive care, hospital care, extended or convalescent care, nursing home care, outpatient care, and organized home health services. Doctors would be encouraged to choose the least costly appropriate service for their patients.

THE MEDICARE PROGRAM

When reviewing your health care program, it is necessary to take into account other elements in your family's financial security. One of the most important of these programs is Medicare. Under this Social Security program, benefits are provided to individuals when they reach age 65 to help pay hospital and, in 1967, nursing home charges. For a fixed monthly premium, Medicare also provides benefits for physicians' charges and other health services.

Many insurance company plans, Blue Cross-Blue Shield, and other insurance plans have policies which pay for costs not covered in Medicare, or which supplement its benefits. Although Medicare benefits people age 65 and older, this program is important for young people, too.

How Medicare Works

Although Medicare went into effect on July 1, 1966, it was amended by Congress in late 1967. It is likely that other changes will be made by Congress from time to time. Consequently, we will concentrate on basic benefits and limitations of the program.

There are two kinds of health care insurance in Medicare.

1. Hospital insurance helps pay the bills when you are hospitalized. The program also provides payments for nursing care and other services in an extended care facility after hospitalization, outpatient hospital diagnostic services, and home health services. This insurance is financed out of special contributions paid by people while they work, with matching contributions from employers, so that people will not have to pay premiums when they are old and not working.

2. Medical insurance helps you pay the bills for doctors' services and for a number of other medical costs and services not covered under the hospitalization insurance program. Unlike the hospital program, the medical insurance program is *voluntary* at this time. You decide whether to enroll for protection under the medical insurance plan. You can have this important protection at a low cost ($4 monthly) because the federal government will match your monthly premium.

Hospital Insurance Benefits

You are presently entitled to up to 90 days of bed patient care in any participating general care, tuberculosis, or psychiatric hospital. For the first 60 days, hospital insurance pays for all covered services, except for the first $44. For the next 30 days, hospital insurance pays for all covered services except for $11 a day.

Also, you have a "lifetime reserve" of 60 additional hospital days, You can use them if you need more than 90 days of hospital care in the same benefit period. For each "lifetime reserve" day used, hospital insurance pays for all covered services except for $22 a day. Private-duty nurses are not covered by Medicare.

Medicare also pays for all covered services in a participating extended care facility for the first 20 days in each benefit period, and all but $5.50 per day for up to 80 more days in the same benefit period. There are also some limitations on the extended care benefits.

Hospital service pays for as many as 100 days' home health visits furnished by a participating home health agency for up to a year after your most recent discharge from a hospital or a participating extended care facility.

You can now see why additional hospital insurance *is* needed to supplement this program. Blue Cross-Blue Shield, insurance companies, and other health care plans have policies that plug the gaps of Medicare.

Medical Insurance Benefits

This optional medical insurance coverage for a small monthly premium (presently $4) gives a lot of protection per dollar. This premium is reviewed annually. It was only $3 per month at first. The premium is likely to increase as medical costs increase. The federal government, you recall, must match your monthly premium.

This is how it works. For each calendar year, medical insurance does not pay for the first $50 of reasonable charges for covered services ("reasonable charge" is the prevailing charge by local doctors). After the first $50 for a calendar year, medical insurance will pay 80 percent of the reasonable charges for covered services for the rest of the year. There are some special additional limitations for certain services like mental treatments furnished outside the hospital. There is only one $50 medical insurance deductible each calendar year, although medical expenses in the last three months of one year can sometimes count toward the $50 deductible for the next year.

Medical services are covered no matter where the doctor treats you. You select your own doctor.

Limitations

Medical insurance does not pay for routine medical checkups, routine foot care, eye refractions, examinations, and prescribing or fitting eyeglasses, hearing examinations and prescribing and fitting, immunizations unless directly related to an injury or a risk of infection, and for services of chiropractors and naturopaths. Medical insurance does not cover dental services unless the services involve surgery of the jaw or related structures.

Ambulance charges are paid for only when such services are medically necessary. After the $50 deductible, medical insurance takes care of 80 percent of the reasonable charges for outpatient hospital services you receive.

Supplementary Health Insurance

The federal government estimates that Medicare will care for about half of your medical expenses, if you include everything from aspirin to major surgery. But it will pay a much higher proportion of the big costs like hospitalization, convalescent care, doctors' bills, diagnostic tests, home health treatments, and the like. Sometimes a patient who stays in the hospital will pay as little as 10 percent of the bills.[25]

[25] *Changing Times,* June, 1966.

Should You Buy Supplementary Insurance?   Your decision should be based on what is *not* covered by Medicare (hospitalization and medical costs). If you decide that more coverage is desirable, you can buy "Medicare-Extended" from most Blue Cross-Blue Shield organizations. They will not, of course, pay for services for which you are compensated by Medicare or other insurance. Present premium rates for "Medicare-Extended" run from $46 to $60 a year.

Private-insurance supplementary health insurance policies cost from $96 to $150 a year, depending on the extent of the coverage. Women pay a little more than men.

If you should decide to buy supplementary health care coverage, compare several policies (Blue Cross-Blue Shield, comprehensive prepaid group plans, insurance company policies, and others). If you select an insurance company, be sure to select one licensed to do business in your state. Also, read the policy carefully. Look for such things as "inside limits" on the sum a company will pay for certain services, the deductibles, and the terms on which the policy may be renewed. Some companies are very slow to pay claims. It is a good idea to talk to people who have had experience with them.

PLANNING FOR FAMILY HEALTH NEEDS

All of us want to be prepared if we are faced unexpectedly with doctor and hospital bills and termination of income due to extended illness or injury. This, of course, requires planning ahead on our part to determine how we can best meet health care expenses when they arise.

The first thing to do is to evaluate your health care needs and then set up a plan for health care protection and for loss-of-income protection.

Setting up a Plan for Medical Expenses and Loss of Income

This is not such a difficult job if you keep in mind the basic principles. *First,* budget for the usual or routine expenses. Concentrate your insurance on the big, unpredictable costs. *Second,* buy a group policy, of possible. *Third,* get a blanket coverage. Avoid limited policies covering named diseases or accidents. *Fourth,* plan your basic protection around hospital and surgical costs. *Fifth,* select major medical insurance with deductible and coinsurance features. *Sixth,* add income disability insurance with emphasis on long-term total disability. Finally, keep a detailed record of what the family spends for health care through the year.

If you can do all this, you can stop worrying about the blockbusters that may hit your family and begin worrying about the premiums—by far the lesser of two worries.

WHAT ABOUT FUNERAL COSTS

Regardless of our skill in giving our loved ones the best health care possible, death is an inevitability. Consequently, a family should be knowledgeable about the cost of services and merchandise provided by the funeral director, burial receptacles, interment or cremation, monument or marker, and miscellaneous expenses for flowers, burial clothing, transportation of the body, and so on.

Cost of Services and Merchandise

The National Funeral Directors Association, representing some 14,000 of the 25,000 funeral directors in the nation, said that the average adult funeral in 1966 cost about $820. About 15 percent of the funerals cost over $1,000, according to the same source.[26] These figures do not include vault, cemetery or crematorium expenses, monument or marker, or items like honorarium for the clergyman, flowers additional transportation charges, burial clothing, or newspaper notices. The cost of shipping a body by train or plane, for example, is twice the cost of a first-class ticket or more. *The Exchange,* a florist trade journal, puts the total average flower cost at over $300 per adult funeral when flowers are suggested.

The U.S. Department of Commerce figures for the cost of a "regular adult funeral" in 1964 would average out at $1,160.[27] Regardless of the difference in the price of funerals, the fact remains that "one funeral director has the same things to sell that another one has." So said Charles L. Arnold, vice president of the Missouri Funeral Directors and Embalmers Association, when testifying before the Senate Subcommittee on Antitrust and Monopoly. He said: "The difference in price is in overhead. The funeral director determines his overhead costs by dividing annual operating costs by the number of adult funerals he performed in a year."

The Senate subcommittee got information for comparative figures from one funeral home in Missouri that performed between 100 and 200 funerals annually. This home had 12 types of caskets, ranging from a low-priced wooden casket to mahogany and fiber glass. He reported that the price of the cheapest casket was $50 and the price of the basic service with that casket was $150.

Progressing upward in cost, he reported these figures, giving the wholesale cost first and the basic funeral price second: $54 and $150, $72 and $397, $120 and $863, $167.50 and $939, $175 and $997, $246 and $1,237, and finally, $439.15 and $1,989. So the "operating spread," or difference between casket cost and funeral price, reported by this funeral firm ranged from $96 to $1,549.85.

[26] *What About Funeral Costs?*

[27] U.S. Senate Hearings, Subcommittee on Antitrust and Monopoly, part 1, *Antitrust Aspects of the Funeral Industry,* U.S. Government Printing Office, 1964, p. 1.

Interment or Cremation.   Interment or cremation charges are in addition to the basic costs paid to the funeral director for goods and services he provides. In most cemeteries, the cost of an individual grave space, says the National Funeral Directors Association leaflet, ranges from $75 to $350. Costs of opening and closing the grave run from $45 to $150, and the price of individual crypts in indoor mausolea start at about $600. Outside garden crypts begin at about $350. Vaults of metal or concrete cost from $100 upward.

The cost of cremation ranges from $35 to $100. Urns to hold the ashes or remains cost from $50 to $250. Columbaria niches to hold such urns range from $35 to $750.

Monument or Marker.   Bronze markers vary in price from $75 to $300, and stone monuments begin at $60. The cost can run very high, depending on material, design, and craftsmanship.

Miscellaneous Expenses.   The cost of flowers, burial clothing, transportation of the body, additional limousines or flower cars, honorarium for the clergyman, and newspaper death notices make up some of the miscellaneous items paid through the funeral director or directly by the family.

The Funeral Industry and Its Problems

The National Funeral Service Journal, a trade journal, stated that a funeral director "must condition the public mind to associate established funeral customs with all that is desirable in the American way of life." The basis for doing this, the writer said, lies in "cultivating certain subconscious opinions regarding the funeral service." And he added that "chief of these is the acceptance of the funeral as a valid status symbol—which in fact it is." In short, it is argued, with some justification, give the public what it wants.

There seems to be little doubt that the funeral industry as a whole has some special difficulties. The death rate, for example, is going down, and the funeral market is limited by the death rate. Meanwhile the number of funeral homes grows. Some 25,000 funeral homes share 1,750,000 deaths annually, for an average of 70 funerals each. In fact, 60 percent of the funeral homes average one funeral a week, while the famous Forest Lawn Memorial Park in Los Angeles has about 6,000 funerals a year.

There is no doubt, too, that the funeral industry faces increasing costs. Chapels are luxuries with wall-to-wall carpeting, expensive organs, "slumber rooms," and the "selection room" where coffins and burial garments are displayed. A hearse costs about $15,000 to $20,000. Labor costs have increased. Furthermore, calls have to be answered around the clock. According to NFDA (the National Funeral Directors Association), the average funeral home represents an investment of $116,459 for land, buildings, equipment, cars, inventory, and service charges outstanding. The total annual pretax income for the owner of an average funeral home comes to $20,671, says the NFDA.

Prefinanced Burial Plans. Funeral directors have other problems that need attention. Many of them have been accused by the Federal Trade Commission of using high-pressure promotion in getting people to sign up for prefinanced funeral plans and burial plans. The abuse, said the FTC, was that the first 20 percent went to the sales firm; 80 percent went into a trust fund. Income from the trust also went to the sales firm, and the sales firm in due time split some of the income with the funeral home named in the burial agreement. Some firms, say the FTC, pay half of the first 20 percent to the salesmen. The NFDA and the Better Business Bureaus have opposed this kind of preneed plans.

There is nothing wrong with preplanning a funeral and burial. Consumers have been well-advised to engage in careful preplanning. Clearly, the consumer should be aware of, and perhaps should be protected by, state laws against being high-pressured by promoters into making hasty decisions to buy prefinanced plans. Certainly, a salesman deserves some commission for services rendered. But the interest on the payments in the trust fund should go back to the trust fund, just as in mutual fund investment. Furthermore, for the protection of the people involved, trust funds should be carefully regulated and supervised by the state.

Advertising. Another problem concerns the right of a funeral director to advertise truthful pricing information.[28] A case in point receiving national attention occurred in Wisconsin. A Wisconsin funeral home prepared a simple 3- by 5-inch printed card showing the range of prices it had charged for 1,036 adult funerals conducted over a period of time. The funeral home director said he wanted to inform the public about funeral prices. The printed card was available to visitors at the funeral home. The cards were also available at civic and community meetings.

After prolonged discussion, the Wisconsin Funeral Directors Association (membership in the National Funeral Directors Association) finally suspended the funeral home from membership in WFDA. Later, the NFDA took similar action by reaffirming the price advertising prohibition contained in their code of ethics.

In 1964, the U.S. Justice Department announced a proposed consent judgment intended to encourage price competition among funeral directors in advertising their services. The judgment prohibiting the National Funeral Directors Association from engaging in any activity to limit advertising of prices for funeral services was accepted by the association. The judgment also provided for local and state groups to offer readmission to any funeral director who had been expelled or suspended or who had withdrawn because of restrictions on price advertising.[29]

[28] Senate Antitrust Hearings, *ibid.,* pp. 12, 43.
[29] *Wall Street Journal,* July 18, 1968.

Public Protests against High Costs

With all the built-in extravagance attached to the rites of death, is it possible for a prudent person to have a dignified and inexpensive funeral? Many people think it is possible. Doctors, lawyers, clergymen of all faiths, union officials, cooperative organizations, and consumer groups are protesting against funeral practices that are needlessly costly and often relegate spiritual values to a place of minor importance.

In 1962, *Medical Economics,* a national physicians' journal, carried an article entitled "Fighting Fancy Funerals." In May, 1963, the *Stanford Law Journal* featured an article, "Funeral Prearrangement: Mitigating the Undertaker's Bargaining Advantage." The National Council of the Churches of Christ in the U.S.A. has a report on burial costs. Booklets have been issued by the Union of Orthodox Jewish Congregations of America, the Protestant Episcopal National Council, The United Presbyterian Church in the U.S.A., the Unitarian and Congregational churches, and the Quakers—all of them giving aid and direction in dignified and inexpensive funerals.

Reducing Funeral Costs

Here are suggestions for the average consumer confronted with arranging for a funeral.

1.   Discuss the funeral arrangements with your minister, rabbi, or priest. It is generally wise for the clergyman to accompany a member of the family to the funeral parlor to help resist any pressure toward overspending.
2.   Arrange for the service to be held at your church.
3.   Select an inexpensive casket and consider limiting or omitting flower displays.
4.   Omit embalming and hold the service as soon as possible.
5.   Arrange for cremation or for delivery of the body if it has been willed to a medical or scientific society. These methods of disposition appeal to many public-minded and sophisticated persons today.
6.   Permit the funeral to center around the spirit rather than the body by having the casket closed during the service. Many families prefer to have the casket removed from the actual service.
7.   Keep the graveside service, if any, private—only for the family and close friends.
8.   Request the funeral director, in advance, to provide a detailed, itemized estimate of the funeral costs.
9.   Join a memorial association if possible.

Most families who have given thought to the subject agree with the Jewish decree that the funeral should be conducted with "dignity, sanctity, and modesty."

Memorial Associations.   Membership in a memorial or funeral society can be a solution if there is such a society in your community. In 1950, there were about eight memorial associations in the United States and Canada, and in

1964 there were about 115 in these two countries, with a membership of some 200,000 persons.

Memorial societies[30] are nonprofit, and life membership fees average $5 for an individual and $10 for a family. A few societies are merely educational, acting as sources for information; others contract with funeral homes to provide a dignified, simple, and modest burial. The cost of embalming and cremation, without a formal ceremony, may average $250. With a modest coffin and private burial before a memorial service, the charge is usually around $350, not including a cemetery lot. More elaborate ceremonial arrangements are negotiated with the funeral home.

The society assists members in advance planning, helps with subsequent memorial services, and may be of aid in case of contractual misunderstandings.

QUESTIONS FOR DISCUSSION

1.   To what extent is health a national problem? A state problem? A local problem? A personal or family problem?

2.   How would you decide whether to join a nonprofit voluntary prepaid health insurance group or buy a health policy from a commercial company?

3.   If you were selecting health insurance protection from a commercial company, what provisions in the contract would you consider important? Does your opinion agree with that of authorities?

4.   What important questions must be answered when examining your own present and future health protection needs?

5.   Why is it hard to find a good disability income insurance contract?

6.   How would you go about planning a funeral and burial with "dignity, sanctity, and modesty"?

ACTIVITY PROBLEMS

1.   Study a disability insurance contract, according to the following questions.

   a.   When does the policy go into force?

   b.   What are the benefits for loss of income?

   c.   Are there any other benefits, such as payment of hospital bills and so on?

   d.   Are diagnostic services included?

   e.   Under what conditions are benefit payments made? How much? For how long?

---

[30] Information on memorial associations may be obtained from the Continental Association of Funeral and Memorial Societies, 59 E. Van Buren Street, Chicago, Ill. 60605.

f.   Are the first 5 to 10 days excluded in benefit payments?

g.   Are the benefits reduced if you are not in continuous confinement?

h.   Are both partial and total disability provided for?

i.   Does the policy cover accidental death?

j.   Are benefits reduced at certain ages?

k.   Does the policy cover traveling outside the boundaries of the United States? Traveling in private or chartered planes?

l.   Are there occupational and other restrictions and exceptions?

2.   Send for the leaflet entitled "Our Family's Health Insurance: Do We Know the Answers?" from Department W Health Insurance Institute, 277 Park Avenue, New York, N.Y. 10017. With cooperation from your family, fill in parts 1 and 2. You will learn much and your family will likely be most grateful for this useful evaluation of their present health care protection.

3.   What do you make of the generic versus brand name drug battle?

4.   Are we the healthiest nation in the world? The World Health Organization, an agency of the United Nations, collects information on the status of health in over 100 countries. You may be in for a shock! See also *Consumer Reports,* March, 1965; *Look* magazine, Oct. 15, 1968.

5.   Write to one of the comprehensive prepaid growth health care organizations mentioned in this chapter. To get you started, write to Health Insurance Plan of Greater New York, 625 Madison Avenue, New York, N.Y. 10022, for information on coverage, cost, professional standards, and so on.

SUGGESTED READINGS

Berry, William F., and James C. Daugherty, "A Closer Look at Rising Medical Costs," *Monthly Labor Review,* November 1968.

Funeral Service Facts and Figures, National Funeral Directors Association, Milwaukee, Wis., 1968.

"The Generic and Brand Name Drug Issue," Part 1, *Consumer Close-ups,* Sept. 23, 1968, and Part 2, *Consumer Close-ups,* Oct. 28, 1968.

Health, Education, and Welfare Department: *The Drug Users,* U.S. Government Printing Office, 1968.

_____: *John Gardner's Report to the President on Medical Care Prices,* Feb. 28, 1967, U.S. Government Printing Office.

_____: *Report of the Task Force on Prescription Drugs,* U.S. Government Printing Office, 1968.

_____: *Your Medicare Handbook,* latest edition, U.S. Government Printing Office.

_____: *Your Social Security,* latest edition, U.S. Government Printing Office.

"Health Insurance Costs," *Consumer Close-ups,* Dec. 25, 1967.

"Hospital Bills Go Up and Up and Up," *Changing Times,* July, 1968.

"How Unbranded Drugs Could Save Consumers $41,159,000," *U.S. Consumer Newsletter,* Nov. 13, 1968.

"Insurance for Dental Bills," *Changing Times,* October, 1965.

"Medicare and Health Insurance, Too?" *Changing Times,* June, 1966.

Memorial Associations, What They Are—How They Are Organized, Cooperative League of the U.S.A., Chicago.

Morgan, Ernest: *A Manual of Simple Burial,* Celo Press, Burnsville, N.C.

"The Truth About Drug Costs," *U.S. Consumer Newsletter,* Sept. 18, 1968.

"What Kind of Health Insurance Should You Have?" *Changing Times,* May, 1967.

chapter 13

BUYING PROTECTION:
SOCIAL SECURITY, LIFE INSURANCE,
AND ANNUITIES

Every year in the United States, 200,000 more men die than women, and the ratio is increasing. In every adult age group, women already outnumber men. One reason is that medical science seems to have benefited women more than men. Deaths connected with childbearing, which used to help balance the hazards of being a man, have been reduced to near zero. More women are staying alive.

What about the men? Twenty percent more men than women die of cancer. While this disease kills more women in their middle years, it strikes the men when they are under 30 and over 55. Still more important is heart disease, which is responsible for 40 percent of all deaths. Between ages 40 and 75, nearly twice as many men as women die of heart disease.

Accidents account for more than three-fourths of the extra male deaths between ages 10 and 35. Between ages 20 and 24, more than six times as many men as women die in accidents—largely because of automobile accidents.

By 1975, at the present death rate, women will outnumber men in the United States by 3,600,000. Life insurance agents say that wives, generally, object to the purchase of life insurance because they do not want to think about the possible death of their husbands. But no widow objects to the life insurance payment when such death occurs. In a way, it is not life insurance that costs money; it is the things that the widow and children will need, and life insurance can provide that cost money.

THE CONSUMER'S INTEREST IN BUYING PROTECTION

But, some say, there is little or no need for personal life insurance because of pension plans, employee group life insurance, and Social Security. It is true that most families have one or more of these protections in the event of premature death of the major breadwinner. But the fact remains that these protections are only minimal.

Social Security—No Cure-all

Employee group insurance seldom reaches $5,000 in protection, and then only while the breadwinner is employed by the company. Retirement or a change in employment usually ends employee group insurance protection.

Present Social Security benefits will not meet the minimum needs of the average retired couple, and the cash grant of $255 for burial is hardly enough for this purpose. Social Security is not enough insurance against death unless the covered breadwinner dies before the children are 18 years of age. The widow under 62 could then in 1969 receive a maximum of $327 a month for herself and one child, and a maximum of $434 a month for herself and two or more children under 18 years of age. When the children reach their eighteenth birthday, all payments in their behalf cease.

Social Security will not pay off all of a man's illness and burial expense; it will not pay off his mortgage or other debts; it will not pay income to a widow under 60 unless she has a child under 18 or unless she is disabled at 50; it will not provide educational funds for children after age 18 unless they stay in school or college. Benefit payments will continue until age 22 if the children continue their education. Social Security will not supply money for emergencies or opportunities; it will not pay a retirement income to a man who wants to retire before 65 nor to a wife before age 62; it will not allow income benefits to be taken in a lump sum; and it will not allow invasion of principal in case of emergency.

Social Security, however, can do a great deal. Social Security, as presently constituted, is not intended to be a complete financial protection program. Social Security does provide for "basic" protection for a modest retirement income (really insurance), disability income insurance, and Medicare. So Social Security occupies a vital part in family financial planning. No family can plan its life insurance program intelligently without figuring out the size and duration of the Social Security benefits. But overestimating Social Security benefits is more dangerous than underestimating them.

Defense against the Threat of Insecurity

Elmo Roper, a leading authority in measuring public opinion, concluded on the basis of 12 years of opinion polling that what the average American wants most in life is a sense of security.

No two families can successfully work out the same security program. But they can begin by noting the major hazards to security and then find the best means for protection against them. The major hazards to financial security and the most common defenses employed are these.

Unemployment: Unemployment compensation; a savings fund for contingencies

Illness: Medicare; health and medical insurance; a savings fund for emergencies

Accident: Social Security; accident insurance; in special cases, state workmen's compensation; a savings fund

Old age: Social Security old-age insurance; retirement pensions; a savings fund; annuities

Premature death: Life insurance; survivors' insurance under the Social Security Act

The particular needs of each family will be apparent to its members. For example, a government employee protected by civil service may not need unemployment insurance. A carpenter, on the other hand, is constantly faced with seasonal unemployment. Most professional people, such as teachers and doctors, usually have continuous work and should build their financial defenses around other insecurities than unemployment.

The needs of a family with several children are large compared with the needs of a childless couple. The latter could minimize its life insurance expenditures and build up larger emergency and retirement income funds.

The first important step, then, in planning a security program is to evaluate each hazard in terms of a family's particular needs. Then select the defenses that will best protect against the insecurities. This is, of course, easier said than done. But few informed persons would disagree with the following statements.

1.   Protection of family dependents through insurance should be the first consideration. In purchasing insurance, the primary objective should be to get the most protection for the lowest cost that safety permits.
2.   Investment for the education of children and for retirement should be a second but important consideration.
3.   The financing to meet the minimum needs of a family should be the safest and best that is available—namely Social Security, United States savings bonds, and insurance.

Financial Security Goals

Every family has a level of basic living costs. How much it can save is determined by the difference that exists between this level and its income. The closer these two come together, the more difficult it is to save.

How much you can save is primarily controlled by how determined you are to save for future use. One thing is certain: unless you plan to save early and methodically, you are not likely to achieve your goals. There can be no evasion in setting aside the sum agreed on for savings.

No one is likely to argue that the savings pattern should be the same for all families having similar net incomes and spending units. For some families, it is important to concentrate on certain kinds of savings because they will sacrifice many things before touching these savings. Some families are unable to save at all, while some go to the other extreme and deny themselves daily "good living." It goes without saying that a happy medium between reckless extravagance and niggardliness makes for greater satisfaction and happiness.

1. Insurance.   There should be life insurance and disability insurance on the breadwinner to protect the family from loss of income in case of death or of partial or permanent disability. Health and medical insurance is necessary to protect the family group against hospital and surgical-medical bills.

2. Emergency Fund.   A cash reserve fund should be built up to a minimum sum equal to two months' income.

3. Educational Fund.   Since most families hope to give their children a college education, the way to build such a fund is to begin as early as possible, but after goals 1 and 2 have been achieved.

4. Retirement.   Old-age benefits under Social Security are a base for retirement, but not sufficient to maintain the standard of living to which most families are accustomed. Therefore, Social Security should be supplemented by investments and perhaps an annuity purchased just prior to retirement.

5. A Mortgage-free Home.   Some families may aim to achieve this before adding to a retirement fund.

SOCIAL SECURITY

The United States, in its early history, was a developing country with a vast frontier and a predominantly agricultural economy. One of the early forms of "social security" was the availability of up to 160 acres of free land, given by the government to any person who wished to be a farmer. American citizens have always been encouraged to provide their own security, to take advantage of the opportunities in a young nation, rich in natural resources and with a rapidly growing population.

That everyone should plan for his own security remains a cherished heritage of the American people. Essential to the purpose is an economy that provides full employment at a high wage level. Today the great majority of Americans have savings, life insurance, a home, and other forms of personal property that contribute to security as well as to a high standard of living.

Individual effort by itself, however, is not sufficient protection against the insecurities of a society now highly industrialized and urbanized. Such a society, while increasing the productive capacity of the nation manyfold and providing the basis for an ever-increasing standard of living, has created a dependence on cash income that was unknown in the earlier history of the United States. Also, the small, mobile family of today, while well suited to an urban-industrial economy, is less able than the three- or four-generation family of the past to provide mutual care and support.

Therefore, the American people acted through their government to establish a Social Security system that protects against the risks common to all and against which citizens as individuals are unable to provide adequate safeguards. The system serves as a foundation on which individuals may build additional protection through their own efforts and with the help of their employers.

How Social Security Works

The basic idea of Social Security is a simple one: During working years employees, their employers, and self-employed people pay Social Security contributions, which are pooled in three special funds. When earnings stop or are reduced because the worker retires, dies, or becomes disabled, monthly cash benefits are paid from these funds to replace part of the earnings the family has lost.

Part of the contributions go into a hospital insurance fund; and when workers and their dependents reach 65, money from this fund helps pay their hospital bills.

Voluntary medical insurance, also available to people 65 or over, helps pay doctor bills and other medical expenses. Money to pay medical insurance benefits comes from a fourth special fund. Half of the money in this fund comes from the premiums paid by people who have signed up for medical insurance, and the other half is paid by the federal government.

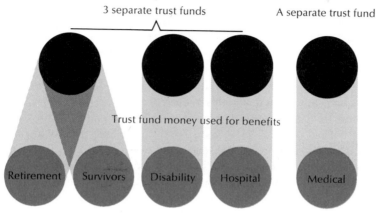

How Social Security Works

Retirement, survivors, disability, and hospital insurance

Voluntary medical insurance

Contributions paid during working years by: employers, employees, self-employed people

Premiums by people 65 or over who sign up— equal contribution by government

3 separate trust funds

A separate trust fund

Trust fund money used for benefits

Retirement Survivors Disability Hospital Medical

Figure 13-1   How Social Security Works.

About 24 million men, women, and children were receiving monthly cash Social Security benefits in early 1968. Their total included about 1.2 million disabled workers and nearly 1 million of their dependents. Nearly 2.4 million children of deceased workers were receiving benefits at that time, and about half a million widowed mothers were receiving benefits because they were caring for their children entitled to benefits. About 2.8 million older widows and dependent widowers were also receiving benefits.

Protection Stays with You

The Social Security protection you earn stays with you when you change jobs, when you move from city to city, when you move to another state.

More than nine of every ten working people in the United States are building protection for themselves and their families under the Social Security system. Almost all other people are either covered by another federal, state, or local government retirement system or are protected under Social Security as dependents of other workers.

Nearly any job you take is covered by Social Security; your earnings from any business you go into are covered, too; and you earn protection under Social Security while you serve in the armed forces. Through 1967, only your military basic pay counted toward Social Security benefits. Beginning with January,

1968, additional earnings credits, generally amounting to $100, were counted for each month of active duty. No additional deductions are made from your pay for these additional credits.

Financing Social Security

Social Security retirement, survivors', and disability benefits and hospital insurance benefits are paid for by contributions based on covered earnings.

If you are employed, the contributions are deducted from your salary, and your employer pays an equal amount; if you are self-employed, you contribute at about three-fourths the combined employee-employer rate for retirement, survivors', and disability insurance. The hospital insurance contribution rate is the same for employers, employees, and self-employed persons.

The maximum amount of yearly earnings that can count for Social Security and on which you pay Social Security contributions under present law is $7,800 for 1968 and years thereafter. The maximum in past years was: $3,000 a year for 1937-1950; $3,600 for 1951-1954; $4,200 for 1955-1958; $4,800 for 1959-1965; and $6,600 for 1966-1967.

How Protection Is Earned

For a worker and his family to get monthly cash payments if he becomes disabled or retires or dies, he must first have credit for a certain amount of work under Social Security. This credit may have been earned at any time after 1936.

If a person stops working under Social Security before he becomes insured, credits for the earnings reported for him will remain on his Social Security record. He can add to them if he later returns to covered work. No benefits based on his earnings can be paid to him or his family, however, until he has credit for enough earnings to become insured.

Certain types of benefits are payable if a person is currently insured, fully insured, or meets the special requirements for disability insurance protection. The first two types of insured status are explained below.

1. Currently insured. Even if a worker is not fully insured, certain kinds of benefits may be paid to his survivors if he is "currently insured" when he dies. He is currently insured if he has credit for at least 1½ years of work within 3 years before his death.
2. Fully insured. If you are fully insured when you reach retirement age, you and certain members of your family can get monthly benefits. If you are fully insured at death, benefits can be paid to certain members of your family.

No one can be fully insured with credit for less than 1½ years of work, and a person who has credit for 10 years of work can be sure that he will be fully insured for life. Having credit for sufficient work, however, means only that certain *kinds* of benefits may be payable—it does not determine the amount.

The amount will depend on the worker's average earnings covered by Social Security.

How Benefits Are Figured

The amount of your monthly retirement or disability payment is based on your average earnings under Social Security over a period of years. The monthly payments to your dependents or to your survivors in case of your death also depend on the amount of your average earnings.

The exact amount of your benefit cannot be figured until you apply for benefits. This is because all of your earnings covered by the law are considered. The Social Security Administration will, of course, figure your exact benefit (Table 13-1).

A Retired Worker's Earnings.   The 1967 amendment to the Social Security Act provides for no loss of cash benefits to a retired person on current earnings up to $1,680 a year, loss of 50 cents in benefits for each $1 on earnings on the next $1,200, and for the loss of $1 in benefits for each dollar earned in excess of $2,880. Retired people 72 and over can earn any amount without losing benefits. The law also provides that, regardless of annual earnings, no benefits are withheld for any month in which a person earns no more than $140 and does not do substantial work in self-employment. Finally, the law does not reduce benefits because of investment income, a company pension, or royalties. Congress is likely to increase the permitted earnings of a retired person without loss of Social Security benefits.

A Working Wife versus Nonworking Wife.   Many working wives wonder what benefits they will receive in return for the Social Security taxes they pay. It depends on how long they work and how much they make, but their benefits will be substantial.

Take the case of a wife 40 years old who has earned at least the maximum amount covered by Social Security, and what she would receive in retirement benefits compared with a nonworking wife as of 1969—

If this working wife continues on the job, she can get $202 a month at the age of 65, or $155.22 at 62, regardless of whether her husband is receiving benefits. The most a nonworking wife can receive is $105 a month, and that is payable only if her husband is retired and drawing benefits.

The same working wife of 40, if she quits work at 55, would be eligible for $171.80 at the age of 65, or $137.50 at 62. If she should quit at 50, she could receive $148.90 at the age of 65, or $119.20 at 62.

Any wife who has 10 or more years under Social Security can collect some retirement benefits at age 62 even if her husband still is working. When her husband retires, she can switch to wife's benefits if they are higher.

There are added protections for working wives. In the event of a working wife's death, her children would receive benefits no matter how much the father continued to earn.

TABLE 13-1   MONTHLY CASH BENEFIT PAYMENTS*

AVERAGE YEARLY EARNINGS AFTER 1950	LESS THAN $900	$1,800	$3,000	$4,200	$5,400	$6,600	$7,800
Disabled worker	$55.00	$88.40	$115.00	$140.40	$165.00	$189.90	$218.00
Wife under 65 and 1 child	27.50	44.20	87.40	140.40	165.00	190.00	214.00
One child of disabled worker	27.50	44.20	57.50	70.20	82.50	95.00	109.00
Widow under 62 and 1 child	82.50	132.60	172.60	210.60	247.60	285.00	327.00
Widow under 62 and 2 children	82.50	132.60	202.40	280.80	354.40	395.60	434.40
One surviving child	55.00	66.30	86.30	105.30	123.80	142.50	163.50
Two surviving children	82.50	132.60	172.60	210.60	247.60	285.00	327.00
Maximum family payment	82.50	132.60	202.40	280.80	354.40	395.60	434.40

*Generally, average earnings are figured over the period from 1950 until the worker reaches retirement age, becomes disabled, or dies. Up to 5 years of low earnings (or no earnings) can be excluded. The maximum earnings creditable for Social Security are $3,600 for 1951 - 1954; $4,200 for 1955 - 1958; $4,800 for 1959 - 1965; and $6,600 for 1966 - 1967. The maximum creditable in 1968 and after is $7,800, but average earnings cannot reach this amount until later. Because of this, the benefits shown in the last two columns on the right generally will not be payable until later. When a person is entitled to more than one benefit, the amount actually payable is limited to the larger of the benefits.

In case of disability, a working wife with at least 5 years of coverage could get benefits for herself and her children, regardless of her husband's earnings. Young wives require even fewer years in covered employment.

Unmarried Women.   Based on equal coverage, benefits would be as much as for a man, or slightly more. That applies to both retirement and disability pension. In the event of disability or death, dependent parents also could get benefits.

There is no simple table showing what working wives, single women, or men would receive in Social Security under the many thousands of possible combinations. But a worker can get estimates, based on his or her own coverage, from his local Social Security office.

Adequacy of Social Security

Our Social Security system, best known as a retirement income scheme, is far more than that. Its initials, OASDI, stand for Old-age, Survivors, and Disability Insurance. To a middle-income wage earner or self-employed person with a wife and young children, OASDI represents, among other things, over $75,000 of decreasing term life insurance in a unique form. Each time a child is born, the father's Social Security life insurance is automatically restored to its maximum face value, and its term is automatically restored to a potential 21 years.

But Social Security is more than life insurance. In 1969-1970, for example, the premium for that "insurance," plus disability income insurance, a modest retirement insurance, and Medicare, was at most $686.40 a year. An employee earning $7,800 or more a year paid $374.40 in Social Security withholding tax in 1969-1970, and his employer paid a matching amount. A self-employed person with $7,800 or more income paid $538.20 a year. So, for all of this protection—life insurance, disability income insurance, retirement insurance, and Medicare—you have the best protection per dollar premium available in this country.

We said earlier that Social Security protection was not intended to pay for all retirement, disability, life insurance, and medical needs of a person or family. Social Security provides only a minimum subsistence protection for survivors. Yet, no family can plan its life, health, and disability insurance program intelligently without figuring out the size and duration of its Social Security benefits.

LIFE INSURANCE

Social Security provides a minimum subsistence for survivors. It is intended to keep them from actual minimal need, not to give them all the basic comforts of life. Life insurance will help complete a protection program. In evaluating family needs, these questions are pertinent:

1. Which family members should be insured?
2. How much insurance should be carried?
3. What kind of insurance is best?
4. Which insurance companies should be selected?

But first, something about the nature of life insurance and the money value of the major breadwinner.

The Lengthening Life-span

Longevity in the United States has changed but little in recent years. The average length of life in 1965 was 70.2 years, the same as in 1964. It had previously reached that figure in 1961, after which an unusually high prevalence of acute respiratory disease resulted in slight setbacks for 2 years.

The improvement since the turn of the century has been great. Based on today's mortality conditions, three-fourths of the newborn may be expected to reach their sixty-third birthday and half may attain 75 years of age. Around 1900, according to mortality conditions prevailing at that time, less than half the newborn were expected to reach age 63 and only a fourth had prospects of living to 75. However, the bulk of this progress was achieved in the earlier part of the century, in sharp contrast to the relatively stationary situation in the past decade. Between 1900 and 1956, expectation of life at birth, for all persons, increased by over 20 years, but since then it has improved by less than a year.

In 1965 the expectation of life at birth for white females was 74.7 years, an increase of only a year since 1956. Among white males the corresponding figures were 67.3 years in 1956 and 67.6 in 1965, a gain of just three-tenths of a year. White men 20 years old in 1965 had, on the average, 50.2 years of life ahead of them.

The longevity of nonwhite persons is considerably less than that of whites. Among nonwhites the expectation of life at birth in 1965 was 61.1 years for males, the same as in 1956. Among nonwhite females the figure rose from 65.9 years in 1956 to 67.4 years in 1965, increasing by 1½ years.

Sharing Risks

Insurance is a plan by which large numbers of people, each in some danger of unforeseen loss, are brought together for mutual protection so that when one person suffers a loss, it can be made good by the premiums of all the others in the group. For example, term insurance is a year-to-year wager on survival. The insurance company statisticians, from a study of life expectancy tables and interest rates over the years, have figured out a system that works like this:

Of 1,000 men, age 30 and apparently healthy, two will die within the next year. If each of these men buys a $10,000 policy good for 5 years, insurance companies can sell it to each of them for about $55 a year. This will put enough money in the "kitty" to pay the salesmen's commissions, the insurance companies' overhead, and $10,000 to each of the 10 men who will die within the 5 years. The total 5-year premiums of around $275 each, for those men who continue to live, remain in the "kitty."

The odds on the term insurance bet change each year as a man gets older, and the premiums have to go up at 5-year intervals for a 5-year term contract. At the age of 40, a $10,000 term contract costs about $85 a year; at age 50, about $160. Other kinds of life insurance, like ordinary life, have built-in savings in the policy, so the statisticians have to include interest in the cost calculations.

The principle of the law of probability, or the law of averages, is basic in figuring premium rates. Insurance companies have actuaries—skilled mathematicians—who study the proportion of people who die at certain ages. They figure rates of mortality based on hundreds of thousands of cases and the results are compiled in mortality tables, which insurance companies use as the basis for figuring the rate to charge for a particular kind of insurance policy.

When to Buy Life Insurance

If a man is single and has no dependents, the only life insurance needed is enough to cover debts and final expenses. It is true that the younger a man is when buying life insurance, the lower the annual premium for any policy. This argument has several weaknesses. In the first place, the final cost remains about the same because the younger a man is when buying insurance, the longer he pays. Buying early may mean several years of needless expense if there is no need for protection. The odds are almost 65 to 1 that a healthy man of 20 or 25 will live at least 5 years.

On the other hand, delay in buying life insurance risks the development of some health condition that may make it impossible to get insurance other than group insurance, or makes it necessary to pay a higher premium as a poor medical risk. From the standpoint of insurability, then, the sooner you buy, the better.

It might be better for a single person, in reasonably good health and with no dependents, to delay purchasing life insurance (except enough to cover debts and final expenses) unless he is eligible for one of the United States government life insurance programs for veterans.

For a newly married couple, with the wife working, about the same protection is needed as when single. If the wife is not working but could, some income should be provided for the readjustment period. In case there are sizable debts, it would be wise to cover them with reducing term insurance.

Here is one case. A young couple have been married a year or so. The wife is a college graduate but has never worked. They have purchased a home with a small down payment and a large, economy-size mortgage. A baby is on the way. Do they need life insurance? The question appears silly. A better question would be "How much life insurance?" Failure to insure the husband's life to a reasonable amount would be an unpardonable irresponsibility in this case, because there are dependents who need financial protection.

Consider another case. This young couple have been married a year. The wife taught high school before marriage. Her folks are moderately wealthy. They expect no child as yet; they rent an apartment and have no big obligations. Do they need life insurance? There is probably no immediate need for life insurance unless each of them thinks it advisable to have a $2,000 ordinary life policy for funeral purposes. Conditions can change, of course. In the second example, if their present situation continued for many years, they might be considered irresponsible if they did not methodically and prudently invest each year to supplement their Social Security retirement or disability income.

Insurance Needs of Children

As a family increases in size, it may be necessary to add more insurance on the father to protect each new dependent. When the children are young, more life insurance may be needed on the father to protect the mother during the period before she can return to work.

Experts on family economics have found that the period when children are still dependents is a difficult one in which to protect a family adequately on a modest income. For such families, the following recommendations may be useful.

First, concentrate the insurance on the life of the breadwinner or breadwinners. Some insurance experts advise against insurance on the wife (if she is a full-time mother) and on the children. Others recommend a joint ordinary life policy of $3,000 for husband and wife to meet burial expenses or a separate $2,000 policy on the wife.

Second, many experts recommend, in addition to veterans' life insurance if available, the purchase of renewable term insurance during this period. A 20-year decreasing term insurance, for example, guaranteeing a stated income during the remainder of dependency in case of the breadwinner's death, would give dependents the most protection at the least cost.

Third, buy all the group life insurance and veterans' life insurance for which the breadwinner can qualify because it is the cheapest protection available.

The Most Economical Use of Life Insurance

When buying a car, you have many models to choose from. Life insurance also comes in many models. Though the basic principles of life insurance are relatively simple, the many models offered may be confusing to the average consumer. This confusion often ends in the selection of the wrong kind of insurance for a good objective—either in increased cost of insurance without appreciable increase in protection, or in being underinsured by policies that are too expensive.

Fundamentally, life insurance is economic protection for dependents against the possibility of death of the breadwinner. This is the most economical use of life insurance. It is *not* a savings plan; it is *not* an investment plan. Savings can be built up faster, and with reasonable safety, through prudent investments. Also, life insurance is *not* a plan to send a child to college. True, it is sold for all these purposes, but there are better ways for knowledgeable couples to attain certain necessary objectives than through life insurance.

Here are the financial problems a family must face on the death of the breadwinner, arranged in order of importance: death expenses, dependency income for the children, temporary income for the wife, adjustment fund (1 to 3 years), paying up the house mortgage, college education fund, gifts, and grants to charity. Wealthy families can afford to carry life insurance for all these objectives, but most families would not have sufficient money to live on if they tried to cover all of them.

Four Basic Types of Life Insurance Policies

Despite the many differing policies offered by life insurance companies, there are only four types of life insurance policies: (1) term, (2) straight life or ordinary life insurance, (3) limited payment life insurance, and (4) endowment insurance. All these types have in their contracts one or two elements. Term insurance is pure protection in the event of death. The other three types have one additional feature—savings. It is the savings feature, primarily, that makes these other types more expensive. So forget about the advertising or selling gimmicks like "modified life," "whole life special," "special protection policy," "pure endowment," "joint life," "last survivor life," "family protector," "contingency life," "retirement income," "family income," "preferred risk," and many other catchy but confusing terms.

Remember the basic principle when planning a life insurance program for your family—to gain the most protection at the lowest cost. Table 13-2, What Various Policies Cost, shows that term insurance gives much more short-term protection per premium dollar.

TABLE 13-2   WHAT VARIOUS POLICIES COST ($1,000 POLICY), A MUTUAL COMPANY

TYPE OF POLICY	AGE AT ISSUE		
	25	35	45
10-year renewable term	$ 4.93	$ 6.84	$12.89
Straight life (ordinary)	12.71	17.07	25.18
Payment to 65	14.37	20.79	35.30
20-payment life	23.33	27.97	35.30
Endowment at age 65	16.94	24.97	42.64
20-year endowment	39.35	39.73	42.64

Term Insurance—Maximum Protection at Low Cost. Term insurance is so named because it is sold for a term—usually for a period of 1, 5, 10, or 20 years, often with option to renew without another physical examination. Such policies are called "renewable term." The rate is increased at the beginning of each new term because the rates are based on the age of the insured, and because there are no extra premium charges for savings, as there are in all other contracts.

In term insurance, there are no savings or investment features. It cannot be used as loan collateral or be surrendered for cash. You pay premiums only as long as you keep the protection. But this kind of insurance gives the family the highest protection for a limited period for the least cost, and it can be made the backbone of protection for dependents in event of premature death of the breadwinner. It provides almost twice as much protection per dollar cost as ordinary life—the next cheapest policy—during the early years of family life.

It is generally wise to purchase renewable term insurance rather than non-renewable insurance because it is adaptable to situations where temporary or decreasing protection is needed. Term insurance is best planned on a reducing basis so that it may be reduced or terminated as dependents no longer require a large amount of protection. It should be increased to maximum protection as each child is born and decreased to the point of no insurance on the father for the children after they are economically independent, perhaps around the age of 22.

The maximum protection of the wife in the early years of marriage may be reduced gradually to zero when the husband reaches his retirement age at 65

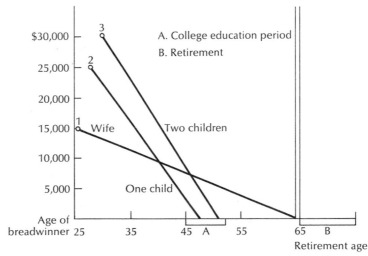

Figure 13-2   Life Insurance Program Using Reducing Renewable Term Insurance.

or earlier. Then he could give up all life insurance with the possible exception of a $2,000 ordinary life policy (for last illness and burial) acquired shortly after marriage.

Figure 13-2, Life Insurance Program Using Reducing Renewable Term Insurance, shows how the purchase of renewable term insurance works out.

Before Buying Term Insurance. The breadwinner should fully understand a reducing term insurance program before embarking on it. It does not build up an educational fund for the children in the event that the insured person lives. Nor does it necessarily provide a retirement fund or funds for other purposes. Additional savings must be used to plug these gaps in family financial planning. But the savings in excess premiums that would otherwise go into more expensive life insurance can be placed in more productive kinds of investment.

The theory of term insurance is that the family would have insurance for less money plus a larger cash fund if needed. But there are these questions to consider: Will the family save and invest the difference between level premium insurance, such as ordinary life, and reducing term insurance premiums? Will they be able to save beyond Social Security benefits, which are inadequate for comfortable living during retirement years?

If the breadwinner is uncertain about carrying out the use of reducing renewable term insurance, it is better to pay a little more for combined term insurance and ordinary life and a savings plan, described later. However, the family would get about the same benefits by the purchase of renewable term insurance and separate ordinary life policies, or by purchasing all renewable term insurance with the privilege of converting to ordinary life insurance without a physical examination after the children are financially independent.

Buying Term Insurance. After considering the problems involved in a term insurance program, keep the following main points in mind when buying term insurance.

1. Purchase only renewable and convertible term insurance.
2. Buy several term policies rather than one or two large ones. This gives greater freedom in dropping policies that are no longer needed and allows more convenient distribution of premium due dates.
3. Be examined by your own doctor before applying for term insurance. The physical examinations are usually more severe than for other contracts. If possible, you want to avoid rejections by the company doctor. A good agent can be helpful in this matter. If you have once been rejected, other companies will know it because your record will be on file at the Medical Information Bureau, created by the insurance companies.
4. Since there are no loan values on term insurance, maintain an emergency fund to pay the premium in case you fall ill or lose your job.
5. Compare the net cost of policies sold by several companies, because the final cost varies considerably among a few companies.
6. Select agents who are trained to give honest, intelligent technical help in servicing your general plan.
7. Select insurance companies that are sound financially and have a record of efficiency in selling the kind of insurance contract you want. Some companies are very

efficient in selling one kind of contract and less efficient in selling other kinds of insurance policies. Never accept the trite statement that all the good companies charge about the same premium rate.

8. Compare premium costs between stock and mutual companies. Do not assume that a mutual company has lower-cost insurance because it has regularly returned a good dividend. Likewise, do not assume that a stock company policy is cheaper because the premium is lower. A stock company's premium is net and final—no dividends.

Buy Term, Invest the Difference. Is the family better off in protection of dependents and with more cash-in value at age 65 of the breadwinner? Yes, if the difference in the cost of straight life and a decreasing term policy is invested. Interesting details discovered by *Changing Times* magazine (October, 1962) are shown in Table 13-3, which compares "Straight Life" with "30-year Decreasing Term" and "Term-to-65 plus Mutual Fund Investment."

The buyer is age 35. In case A, he buys a $10,000 straight life policy for $237 a year and leaves the dividends to gather interest. In case B, he buys a $10,000, 30-year decreasing term, for $76 a year. In case C, he buys a term-to-65 policy for $120 a year. In both B and C, he invests the difference between the cost of the straight life policy and the two kinds of term insurance in a mutual investment fund that charges an 8 percent sales commission. Dividends and capital gains are reinvested in the fund.

In case of death, the conclusions are: (1) death proceeds would be greater by a wide margin under the term-to-65 policy than under straight life; (2) straight life would yield a little higher death proceeds than decreasing term in the early years unless the mutual fund investment yielded more than 10 percent interest compounded annually; (3) the term-to-65 is likely to produce more death benefits than the decreasing term.

If the breadwinner lives, the conclusions are: (1) both term programs will amass a nest egg much larger than the toal value of the straight life (30-year-term, $27,374; term-to-65, $19,542; straight life, $8,853). *Warning:* The difference in premiums must be invested each year without fail, and earnings and dividends must be plowed back.

Ordinary Life or Straight Life Insurance.   Ordinary life or straight life insurance is ·payable at death of the insured, but one need not die to win on this contract. The same premium is paid as long as the insured lives.

Since ordinary life is a combination of term plus savings, a reserve is accumulated, and in a few years the policy has cash-surrender, loan, and other values. Consequently, the premium is about twice as expensive per $1,000 as term insurance, when first taken out.

Generally, the cash value at age 65 is ample to provide a paid-up policy equal to all the paid premiums. Many companies permit the cash value to be used to provide a guaranteed annuity, if by the age of, say, 70 to 75 there is no longer the need for protecting a dependent in event of the death of the insured.

A *family income policy* combines decreasing term with ordinary life insur-

TABLE 13-3   INVEST THE DIFFERENCE

A. STRAIGHT LIFE—IF BUYER DROPS POLICY AT END OF YEAR

Age at Start of Year	Premiums Paid to Date	This Cash Value	Plus These Dividends
35	$ 237	0	0
50	3,792	$2,940	$ 923
64	7,110	5,600	3,253

Results at 65:

Total outlay	$ 7,110
Insurance in force if premiums continued*	$10,000
Insurance in force if premiums stopped	$10,000 for 15 years, or $ 7,330 for life
Cash if insurance surrendered	$ 8,853

B. 30-YEAR DECREASING TERM PLUS MUTUAL FUND INVESTMENT

Age at Start	Premiums Paid to Date	Amount Invested to Date	Insurance in Force	Savings at 10 Percent
35	$ 76	$ 161	$10,000	$ 163
50	1,216	2,576	5,000	5,853
64	1,824	5,286	383	27,374

Results at 65:

Total outlay	$ 7,110
Insurance in force if premiums continued	_____
Insurance in force if premiums stopped	_____
Cash value of mutual fund	$ 27,374

C. TERM-TO-65 PLUS MUTUAL FUND INVESTMENT

Age at Start of Year	Premiums Paid to Date	Amount Invested to Date	Cash Value of Policy	Savings at 10 Percent
35	$ 120	$ 117	0	$ 119
50	1,920	1,872	$740	4,271
64	3,600	3,510	0	19,542

Results at 65:

Total outlay	$ 7,110
Insurance in force if premiums continued	_____
Insurance in force if premiums stopped	_____
Cash value of mutual fund	$19,542

*Plus $3,253 in dividends.

ance. It provides, in addition to the regular life insurance payment, income payment to the beneficiary if the insured dies within the stated period. The payments begin at death of the insured and extend to the end of the period. If the insured is living at the end of the period, the premiums usually decrease.

The advantage in this policy is that while the children are young there is greater protection than the family usually can afford on a permanent basis. The highest income is provided for the dependents during the first 20 years, when the need is greatest in case of premature death of the breadwinner. If the policyholder lives, the term insurance ends 20 years after purchase of the policy, and the premium is reduced accordingly. Only the ordinary life insurance remains permanently in this contract.

Limited Payment Life Insurance.   Limited payment life insurance is payable only at death of the insured. The premiums are payable only for a stated number of years or until the insured reaches a certain age, such as 60 or 65. Payments are usually limited, however, to 10, 20, or 30 years. Thirty-payment life, for example, provides for premiums to be paid for 30 years, after which the policy is paid up. The face value, however, is not paid until the insured dies. The premium rate must be considerably higher on this kind of policy than on ordinary life because it is fully paid up in a stated number of years.

Policies of this type are considered to be more appropriate for persons whose incomes may be expected to decrease appreciably in later life. It is not suitable for most young married couples, because the premium is so costly that they cannot afford to buy enough for adequate protection for dependents. Term insurance, in particular, and ordinary insurance will give a young family much more protection at lower cost at a time when the highest protection is most needed—the first 20 years of married life.

Endowment Insurance.   Endowment insurance is a combination of temporary life insurance and periodic savings. If the insured dies, the beneficiary receives the face value of the policy. If the insured lives, however, the face value or amount is paid to him, or to some designated person, either in a lump sum or in the form of income. The protection offered not only is small compared to the cost but ceases when the policy matures.

This kind of policy should not be considered as permanent protection for dependents. It provides the least protection for a given premium, but includes the highest investment element of the above general types of policies.

Endowment policies can be purchased on a basis of 10, 15, 20, 25, or 30 years, or to mature in cash at specified ages. Since the company must have the stated amount (say $2,000, in a 20-year $2,000 endowment) available for payment at the end of 20 years, the premium rate must be higher than on a 20-year family income policy.

In the latter case, the company might not have to pay the beneficiary for several years after the insured had stopped making premium payments, provided the insured continued to live. The company could use these funds to earn additional interest. The endowment policy, on the other hand, calls for payment at the expiration of a certain number of years. Consequently, higher premiums are necessary for endowment policies.

Settlement Terms of Life Insurance Policies

The method of payment of life insurance policies is important. There are several options, and choosing the right settlement option helps to accomplish the purpose of the insurance. Before purchasing an insurance policy, the settlement terms that are available should be discussed with a competent life insurance underwriter. Most policies have the following four optional settlement plans, which may be decided by the insured or by the beneficiary.

Option 1. The beneficiary may receive a lump sum. This may be a good option if the money must be used to pay expenses for sickness, taxes, and burial. On the other hand, a lump sum coming into the hands of a beneficiary who cannot manage it carefully may prove to be an unsatisfactory option. It is easy for the beneficiary to become a victim of poor investments suggested by well-meaning but uninformed friends or even by an investment counselor.

Option 2. The principal sum is retained by the company, and interest (about 2½ percent) is paid to the beneficiary for a certain number of years or for life. At the end of the period, the principal is paid to the children, or according to the terms of the contract—a good option, as it is not final, and allows time to consider.

Option 3. A third option provides for the payment of insurance in installments—annual, semiannual, quarterly, or monthly. Usually, the company will specify the minimum installment or the minimum number of payments it guarantees. It might be, for example, a guarantee of $100 a month for 30 years, or that principal and interest will be paid until exhausted. This option may fit nicely for the protection of children.

Option 4. The annuity or life-income settlement provides regular life income to the beneficiary. The company may guarantee either a specified number of payments or payments that will equal the principal. If the beneficiary dies before the guaranteed payments have been made, the remainder goes to the estate, or as directed. Guaranteed payments cost more, however, because the risk is greater to the company.

Table 13-4, Monthly Installment Payments for Each $1,000 of Insurance, shows the amount due under options 3 and 4, as reported by an American life insurance company.

If option 3 is selected, the guaranteed income to a beneficiary will be $6.53 a month for 15 years for each $1,000 policy. A $15,000 policy would provide an income of $78.36 a month for 15 years.

If the widow is age 65 and is eligible for full Social Security coverage, she may wisely elect a monthly life annuity of $4.67 per $1,000 of insurance. A $15,000 policy would provide $70.05 a month for life, which would be in ad-

TABLE 13-4   MONTHLY INSTALLMENT PAYMENTS FOR EACH $1,000 OF INSUR-
ANCE

OPTION 3		OPTION 4		
Number of Annual Payments	Amount of Payments	Attained Age of Payee		Monthly Life Annuity
		Male	Female	
1	$84.19	20	25	$2.69
3	28.69	25	30	2.89
5	17.59	30	35	2.96
7	12.84	35	40	3.13
9	10.21	40	45	3.34
11	8.53	45	50	3.59
13	7.38	50	55	3.88
15	6.53	55	60	4.24
17	5.88	60	65	4.67
20	5.16	65	70	5.20
25	4.34			
30	3.80			

dition to her monthly Social Security benefit. The monthly life annuity would cease on her death.

There is no single option, of course, that will fit all needs. These four options, however, are planned to meet all possible choices.

Restrictions and Double-indemnity Clause

Before buying a particular policy, compare the contract with policies of other companies. Policies vary with regard to restrictions and advantages. Some companies, for example, will not accept the risk of death in air travel. Others will accept financial responsibility for travel on regularly scheduled commercial planes.

Some companies, for an extra premium, will include a double-indemnity clause that will pay double the face value of the contract in case of accidental death.

In case of total or permanent disability before age 60, some contracts provide for waiver of future premiums.

The disability income payment, not common any more, pays a stated income in case of total or permanent disability. This kind of contract is far more expensive.

Loan Value and Dividends

Most level premium policies have a loan value after the second year or so. The loan value and the rate of interest charged are stated in the policy. Sometimes a loan can be obtained from a commercial bank at a lower rate of interest than most insurance companies charge. Consequently, it is a good idea to compare the total interest charges of a bank and of the insurance company before a decision is made for a loan on a life insurance policy.

If it is difficult to pay the premium, some policies contain an automatic premium-loan provision. If the policyholder takes advantage of this provision, the loan should be repaid as soon as possible; if long continued, the interest, usually 5 or 6 percent, can destroy to a considerable extent the protection value of the policy. Consequently, borrowing on life insurance should be a last resort.

Dividends may be paid by mutual or participating companies. The policyholder may use them in any of four ways: (1) accept them in the form of cash, (2) allow the company to retain them at interest, (3) apply them to future premiums, or (4) use them to purchase more life insurance.

HOW MUCH LIFE INSURANCE SHOULD YOU BUY?

Independent insurance advisors say that Americans lose millions of dollars annually because they do not know how to plan a protection program to fit their needs and pocketbook. Many families get a poor insurance deal because they (1) carry more insurance than they need, (2) carry a too expensive type of insurance, (3) carry too little insurance, (4) purchase too cheap insurance, (5) insure the wrong members of the family, (6) borrow on their insurance from the insurance company, (7) select poor companies and agents, or (8) fail to relate life insurance to total family savings and protection needs.

Wife

If there is no financial risk involved in the premature death of members of the family who are not breadwinners, there is no urgent need for buying life insurance for those members. For example, it is questionable to buy a large amount of insurance for a wife when the husband is the breadwinner. It is preferable in such case to limit life insurance on a wife to a $2,000 burial policy. This reasoning is based on the assumption that a wife or mother cannot be called a substantial financial risk in most families.

Minor Children

Minor children, likewise, are not financial assets to most families. Burial insurance for children is a doubtful need for most families. Some insurance salesmen have been too enthusiastic in selling life insurance for unimportant or nonexistent needs. Most persons would never think about buying fire insurance on a house if they did not own a house. Why then buy life insurance on members of the family who do not have financial dependents?

Life insurance dollars should protect dependents. If there are no dependents, it is preferable to put the savings into good investments.

Practical life underwriters have worked out rough-and-ready rules for determining the amount of life insurance one should carry. These estimates are general enough to fit nearly everybody's case but not particular enough to fit any case exactly. Though the most important reason for taking out life insurance is protection of dependents, it is not necessary to provide income for dependents indefinitely. For many families, the monthly income need is around 50 to 65 percent of present income.

How Much Life Insurance Do You Need?

Consumers Union, publishers of *Consumer Reports,* hired insurance experts to study this complex problem and reported the findings in a *Report on Life Insurance.* [1]

Step 1. Take inventory of your assets:

Life insurance: Include amounts payable at death of all policies of the major wage earner. Deduct from face value any loans against the policies.

Widow's pension benefits: If there is a death benefit for an employee's beneficiary, enter that lump sum below.

Cash on hand: Enter total deposits in savings and checking accounts and present value of U.S. savings bonds.

Equity in real estate: Enter the present value of all real estate after subtracting the amount due on mortgages.

Securities: Enter present market value of stocks, mutual shares, debentures, and other commercial bonds.

Other: If there is a ready market for antiques, jewels, and art work, enter present sale value. Money in trust funds should be counted, but omit a possible future asset like a possible inheritance from someone now living.

TABLE 13-5   INVENTORY

FAMILY ASSETS	FAMILY LIABILITIES
Life insurance _____	Family income fund _____
Widow's pension benefit (omit Social Security) _____	Education fund _____
Cash on hand _____	Widow's retirement fund _____
Equity in real estate _____	Widow's income fund _____
Securities _____	Uninsured debts (omit home mortgage) _____
Other _____	
Total _____	Total _____

[1]Consumers Union, Mount Vernon, N.Y., 1967. The author wishes to give credit to Consumers Union for some of the excellent material used in this section of Chap. 13.

TABLE 13-6   SURVIVOR'S INCOME*

YEARS OF INCOME NEEDED	MULTIPLIER	YEARS OF INCOME NEEDED	MULTIPLIER	YEARS OF INCOME NEEDED	MULTIPLIER
1	12	16	148	31	229
2	23	17	155	32	233
3	34	18	161	33	237
4	45	19	168	34	241
5	55	20	174	35	245
6	65	21	180	36	248
7	75	22	185	37	252
8	84	23	191	38	255
9	93	24	196	39	258
10	102	25	202	40	261
11	110	26	207	41	264
12	118	27	211	42	267
13	126	28	216	43	270
14	134	29	221	44	272
15	141	30	225	45	275

*Table 13-6 was prepared by Consumers Union insurance experts and can be found in their *Report on Life Insurance.*

Step 2.   Now take inventory of your liabilities. But first you have to figure out the monthly income your life insurance funds would have to contribute at future periods to meet your family income goals. You will also have Social Security income before age 62 if you are a widow with children under 18 or 22 or if children are in college. After one child graduates from college, Social Security income decreases. Therefore, insurance income must be planned to fill in the gaps. Information on Social Security benefits can be secured from your local Social Security office. The worksheets prepared by Consumers Union in their *Report on Life Insurance* will be especially useful at this stage of planning.[2]

Step 3.   The next step is to convert long-term income and education funds into present values. You may wish to provide $100 a month for 120 months. This does not mean that you need $12,000 worth of insurance, because the insurance is likely to be paid in a lump sum and the diminishing principal can earn interest. Therefore, the insurance sum need not be $12,000. The present value—the face value of the life insurance necessary to produce it ($100 per month for 120 months)—is a discounted amount. Table 13-6 will be useful in helping you to find out your survivor's income need.

Step 4.   After you have decided how much monthly income you will need in addition to Social Security, and for how long, find the desirable number of years in Table 13-6. Then apply the multiplier to the monthly income figure.

[2] See worksheets beginning on page 113.

The resulting sum is what you need to provide that monthly income. Table 13-6 is constructed on the assumption that the lump sum will be invested at a modest 3½ percent net annual interest after income taxes. Thus, to provide $100 a month for 10 years starting now, you would need $100 × 102, or $10,200.

Table 13-6 shows the proper multipliers for determining how much money at 3½ percent interest will be needed to create a fixed monthly income for any number of years up to 45. Simply apply the appropriate multiplier to your monthly income goal. Example: To figure out the lump sum needed to provide $100 a month for 20 years, look up the 20-year multiplier in Table 13-6. It is 174. The lump sum needed is $17,400 ($100 × 174).

Table 13-7 shows the interest discount factors to which an entire fund may be reduced if it will not have to be touched for some years. Example: If the $17,400 income fund would not be needed until 5 years from now, look up the 5-year factor in Table 13-7. It is 0.84. The lump sum needed now is $14,616 ($17,400 × 0.84).

If your heirs are not to start spending certain insurance funds for a number of years, these funds should be discounted for the interest they can earn in the interim. In Table 13-7, find the number of years before the income will be needed. Then multiply the adjacent discount factor by the lump sum needed. The result is the amount that, when invested at 3½ percent net, will grow to the lump sum needed in the appropriate number of years. Thus, to provide $8,000

TABLE 13-7   DISCOUNT FACTORS FOR MONEY NEEDED LATER*

YEARS BEFORE INCOME IS NEEDED	DISCOUNT FACTOR	YEARS BEFORE INCOME IS NEEDED	DISCOUNT FACTOR	YEARS BEFORE INCOME IS NEEDED	DISCOUNT FACTOR
0	1.00				
1	0.97	16	0.58	31	0.34
2	0.93	17	0.56	32	0.33
3	0.90	18	0.54	33	0.32
4	0.87	19	0.52	34	0.31
5	0.84	20	0.50	35	0.30
6	0.81	21	0.49	36	0.29
7	0.79	22	0.47	37	0.28
8	0.76	23	0.45	38	0.27
9	0.73	24	0.44	39	0.26
10	0.71	25	0.42	40	0.25
11	0.69	26	0.41	41	0.24
12	0.66	27	0.40	42	0.24
13	0.64	28	0.38	43	0.23
14	0.62	29	0.37	44	0.22
15	0.60	30	0.36	45	0.21

*Table 13-7 was prepared by Consumers Union insurance experts and can be found in their *Report on Life Insurance.*

for college—but starting 16 years from now—your insurance policy should supply only 0.58 × $8,000, or $4,640.

How to Use the Four-step Plan

An Illustration for Planning Your Own Insurance Needs.   We will follow the methods used in the Consumers Union study. The Smith family is made up of Tom, age 25, his wife Mary, 23, and two children, Johnny, age 2, and Amy, age 2 months. Tom earns $7,500 annually and nets $530 a month after deductions.

This family plans that, in the event of the father's death, the mother would stay at home until Amy, her 2-month-old, is 18 years old; that's when the mother's own Social Security income would stop unless Amy goes to college. The mother would support herself after that until she retired at age 62.

The insurance objectives of the Smith family: $400-a-month family income for 18 years; an $8,000 college fund for each of the two children; and a $250 a month retirement fund for the mother.

The father's Social Security survivors' benefits were $368 a month (1967) for his widow and two children under 18; up to $252 a month for his widow and one child under 18; $126 a month for a child age 18 to 22 in college (using the conservative figure of 40 benefit months, or about $5,000 for each of the two children); $138.60-a-month lifetime income for the mother beginning at age 62.

Figure 13-3 projects the Smiths' Social Security benefits. Note that if John goes to college, his mother and Amy will not receive the full $252 a month for widow and one child. This is because their maximum monthly income was $368; with John receiving $126, $242 is left for his mother and sister.

The Smiths figured their family income, education, and widow's retirement fund as follows:

FAMILY INCOME FUND
Monthly income needed: $400
Number of years: 18
Social Security monthly income for first 16 years: $368
Monthly balance needed ($400 minus $368): $32
16-year multiplier (from Table 13-6): 148
Lump sum needed now ($32 × 148): $4,736
(Note: No interest discount factor from Table 13-7 is used because income drawn
    from this fund would be needed as soon as Tom Smith died.)
Social Security monthly income starting 16 years from now and continuing for about
    two years: $242
Monthly balance needed ($400 minus $242): $158
Two-year multiplier (from Table 13-6): 23
Lump sum needed 16 years hence ($158 × 23): $3,634
16-year discount factor (from Table 13-7): 0.58
Lump sum needed now ($3,634 × 0.58): $2,108
    Total lump sum needed now ($4,736 + $2,108): $6,844

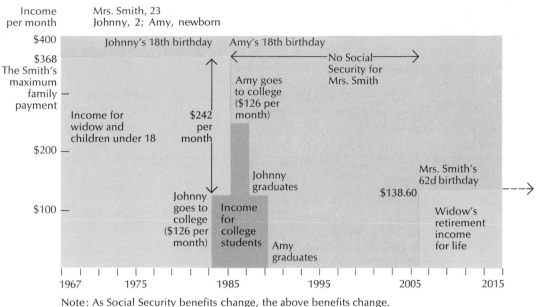

Note: As Social Security benefits change, the above benefits change.

Figure 13-3   The Smiths' Social Security Income. Courtesy of Consumers Union.

EDUCATION FUND
For son Johnny (now age 2 years): $8,000
Social Security's contribution: about $5,000
Balance needed: $3,000
Number of years before it will be needed: 16
16-year discount factor (from Table 13-7): 0.58
Lump sum needed now ($3,000 $\times$ 0.58): $1,740
For daughter Amy (now two months): $8,000
Social Security's contribution: about $5,000
Balance needed: $3,000
Number of years before it will be needed: 18
18-year discount factor (from Table 13-7): 0.54
Lump sum needed now ($3,000 $\times$ 0.54): $1,620
  Total lump sum needed now ($1,740 + $1,620): $3,360

WIDOW'S RETIREMENT FUND
Monthly income needed: $250
Age when it would begin: 62
Number of years: rest of life
Social Security monthly income: $138.60
Monthly balance needed ($250 minus $138.60): $111.40
20-year multiplier (from Table 13-6; using this multiplier gives roughly the price, at
  age 62, of a life annuity): 174
  Total lump sum needed now ($111.40 $\times$ 174): $19,384
Note: Although this income will not be needed for 39 years, the fund should not be
  reduced by the interest discount factor in Table 13-7. Its interest should be dedi-

cated to coping with inflation, and some of its principal could be spared for emergency use.)

The Smiths' Balance Sheet

If we assume that the Smiths' present assets consist of $3,000 in group life insurance and $1,500 in checking and savings accounts and they have no sizable debts, their balance sheet looks like this:

FAMILY ASSETS		FAMILY LIABILITIES	
Life insurance	$3,000	Family income fund	$ 6,844
Cash on hand	1,500	Education fund	3,360
		Widow's retirement fund	19,384
Total	$4,500	Total	$29,588
Deficit to be made up with new life insurance ($29,588 minus $4,500)			$25,000

Although Social Security survivors' benefits will provide much of the Smiths' income needs, a part of the new life insurance could be used for the father's funeral expense. As future life unfolds, there is great flexibility in how the balance might be used during Mrs. Smith's middle years (Mrs. Smith would be 41 when Amy is 18) until she retired at age 62, a 21-year period without Social Security income. And at age 65 she will be eligible for Medicare (hospital and medical insurance).

Can the Smiths Afford $25,000 of New Life Insurance?   It seems a lot for a young father making $7,500 a year. According to insurance industry data, the average insurance coverage for insured heads of families with an income like the Smith family was less than $13,000.

If Mr. Smith selects the right kind of life insurance, he can afford to buy $25,000 of it.

What could $25,000 of life insurance cost each year?

KIND	ANNUAL COST
Ordinary or straight (nonparticipating)	$322.50
"Modified Ten" (ordinary life):	
Low premium the first 10 years	206.50
Higher premium the rest of the years	402.50
25-year decreasing term insurance	84.75

Although Mr. Smith can buy $25,000 of the 25-year decreasing term life insurance, the death benefit goes down to zero in 25 annual steps. The family goal, however, was to obtain adequate coverage for the present when the family needs the most protection, and this policy provides it.

In the event Mr. Smith remains healthy for 10 to 15 years longer, his insurance needs may increase if there is another child—or substantial increases in his salary and, with it, an increase in his standard of living, such as purchasing a house. As long as Mr. Smith remains insurable or his firm provides group life insurance for employees, he can cope with new insurance needs as they arise. He can buy more decreasing term insurance. A more flexible way, as we learned earlier, would be for Mr. Smith to start out insuring himself with $25,000 of 5-year *renewable* term insurance for about $106.50 annually, and the death benefit will not decrease unless he wants it to decrease. Every 5 years the policy can be renewed at its full amount or at any smaller amount selected by the policyholder down to a minimum of $5,000. Generally, however, the price of the policy goes up at the end of every 5 years.

An important feature of this kind of insurance is that it is guaranteed renewable until age 65. The company must renew this policy without requiring another medical examination.

The Smiths' Selection. This type of policy may be the best kind for the Smiths. This type of policy (5-year renewable term) goes up in price very slowly at first (in fact, the premium goes down the second 5-year period at Mr. Smith's age). The sixth through tenth annual premiums would be $101.75; at age 35, the premium would rise to $175.50; at age 40, down to $158.25. In later years, the premium goes up steeply, but by then Mr. Smith has possibly passed the peak of his financial responsibilities. The chances are that increases in income have enabled him to pay for most or all of his home, or to have invested some savings in stocks or bonds. At this stage of his life he actually needs less life insurance because the children are on their own economic power, and the parents will soon be eligible for modest Social Security income and very likely a company pension. The sensible policy would be for the Smiths to reduce their insurance coverage as each child leaves home, and to carry only a modest amount of insurance when both children are on their own. After the father reaches his early fifties, very little insurance is needed because there are only a few years left before they reach age 62 or 65 for Social Security and age 65 for a company pension and Medicare.

It Pays to Shop around for Life Insurance

Consumers Union made a price-comparison study of participating 5-year renewable term policies. Table 13-8 compares 20-year premium costs of policies from six conventional insurance companies and four other sources open only to certain qualified people. The prices shown are based on standard rates in 1966 for a man age 35, and the insurance was for $50,000 or the maximum coverage available if under $50,000. The companies were selected to show the rather wide price range of 5-year renewable term policies.

In comparing prices, each person must construct a set of comparisons based on his own age and insurance needs. National Life Insurance Company, whose

TABLE 13-8   PARTICIPATING 5-YEAR RENEWABLE TERM POLICIES

	POLICY SIZE	20-YEAR GROSS PREMIUM	20-YEAR DIVIDENDS*	20-YEAR NET PAYMENT	AVERAGE ANNUAL NET PAYMENT	AVERAGE ANNUAL COST PER $1,000
New York State mutual savings banks	$30,000	$ 5,041.50	$1,950.30	$3,091.20	$154.56	$5.51
Massachusetts mutual savings banks	43,000	6,815.50	2,337.48	4,478.02	223.90	5.21
Institute of Electrical and Electronics Engineers (Washington, D.C.) group plan	50,000	8,412.50	2,903.77	5,508.73	275.44	5.51†
National Life Insurance Co. Montpelier, Vt.)	50,000	9,750.00	2,882.50	6,867.50	343.38	6.87
Teachers Insurance and Annuity Assn. of America (New York City), individual policy	50,000	9,815.00	2,653.50	7,161.50	358.08	7.16†
Connecticut Mutual Life Insurance Company (Hartford, Conn.)	50,000	9,572.50	1,736.50	7,836.00	391.80	7.84
National Life Insurance Company (Columbus, Ohio)	50,000	12,347.50	4,159.00	8,188.50	409.43	8.19
Berkshire Life Insurance Company (Pittsfield, Mass.)	50,000	11,655.00	3,269.50	8,385.50	419.28	8.39
Prudential Insurance Company of America (Newark, N.J.)	50,000	11,515.00	2,916.50	8,598.50	429.93	8.60†
Metropolitan Life Insurance Company (New York City)	50,000	11,280.00	2,665.00	8,615.00	430.75	8.62†

*Based on 1966 dividend scales.
† Includes waiver of premium for total disability.

5-year renewable term insurance compared well in Table 13-8 with those of other commercial companies, listed, sells insurance in all 50 states. This comparatively low price might be used as a benchmark for comparing costs of companies other than the few listed in the above study. But you must be specific about requesting information on the same kind of term insurance from each of the companies.

The lowest-price policies shown in Table 13-8 tell an interesting story. The best buys in life insurance are not available from agents of commercial insurance companies, whose overhead of heavy sales promotion, advertising, and commissions must be included in the price of the product they sell. Whether you find a bargain depends on who you are, where you work, and where you live. Here are some of the possibilities to investigate:

Savings Bank Life Insurance.   Any person who lives and works in New York, Massachusetts, and Connecticut can, if he passes the medical examination, buy a limited amount of low-priced life insurance from mutual savings banks. You could purchase up to $5,000 in Connecticut, $30,000 in New York, and $43,000 in Massachusetts as of 1968.

Wisconsin State Life Fund.   This state-operated life insurance company will sell to anyone "who is within the state at the time the insurance is granted." The 1968 ceiling was $10,000. A medical examination may be required.

Association Group Insurance.   Most professional, fraternal, and alumni associations offer their members group life insurance underwritten by life insurance companies. Table 13-8 lists one such company—Institute of Electrical and Electronics Engineers. This is a low-cost insurance. Members can buy up to $50,000 of 5-year renewable term insurance if they are under 45 years of age, or up to $30,000 if they are 45 to 54 years of age.

Teachers Insurance and Annuity Association of America (TIAA).   Staff members of colleges, universities, independent schools, and certain other nonprofit, tax-exempt educational and scientific institutions are eligible to purchase this insurance. The price is toward the low end of those written by private companies, as you can see in Table 13-8. TIAA group life insurance plans are available at prices lower than for the individual policies.

Employers' Group Life.   Most private companies provide, automatically, a group life policy covering all employees. This is usually a group, term policy. It is an excellent buy because the company usually pays all or part of the premium. If the company offers you more than the minimum amount covering everybody, you probably would do well to take all you can get.

Veterans' Insurance.   Veterans of World Wars I and II and the Korean War were fortunate in that they were permitted to keep up to $10,000 of their GI life insurance as a cash-value or term policy at very low rates.

To date, veterans of the Vietnam War are not included in this favored group. In 1966, a group insurance plan, called Servicemen's Group Life Insurance, cost GIs only $2 a month for a $10,000 policy while in uniform. But they cannot take it home with them to civilian life.

Unfortunately, this group insurance can be converted only to the more expensive kind of life insurance—either ordinary life or a higher-cost cash-value insurance of a private insurance company at regular premium rates for the buyer's age at time of conversion. You cannot, unfortunately, convert it to term insurance.

All things considered, you may have to buy some life insurance in the general commercial market. The question then is, Shall it be a participating or a nonparticipating policy? Some 36 percent of all life insurance in force now is nonparticipating. Premium rates for it are generally lower than for dividend-paying participating policies. Again, the only way you can be sure about the cost of participating and nonparticipating policies will be to compare prices for the same kind of term policies. There is no substitute for shopping around for the lowest-cost life insurance.

ANNUITIES: SHOULD YOU BUY THEM?

Life insurance and annuities are exact opposites. Life insurance pays the beneficiary on the death of the policyholder. An annuity pays the policyholder for life. In life insurance, the company is betting that the policyholder will live. In an annuity, the company is betting that the annuitant will not live. This means that if a family is young and growing up, life insurance protection for the family comes first.

The word *annuity* implies an annual payment. Today, however, any fixed periodic payment—yearly, monthly, or weekly—for a given period of time or for life is an annuity. The essential feature of annuity payments is their payment as long as the annuitant lives. The annuitant pays a certain amount per month for a given number of years, or pays a lump sum just prior to retirement, and in return receives an income for life, or variations of a deferred annuity.

No medical examination is required because the insurance company counts on the annuitant's death earlier than statistics indicate. The purchase price for women is higher than for men, because women usually live about five or six years longer than men.

The more frequent the payments to the annuitant (monthly, quarterly, or yearly), the higher the purchase price. The annuity policy is primarily for the benefit of the annuitant and only secondarily of benefit to others. One can, however, select a "joint and survivorship" form that pays an income for life to two or more persons.

Kinds of Annuities

All annuities have three variables: how you pay for them, when you collect, and how you collect. Similarly, every annuity has a three-part name. A glance at Figure 13-4, What Kind of Annuity? shows these three classifications and the various types of annuities available.

An *immediate annuity* is paid for in one lump sum, and annuity payments begin without delay. For example, to buy such an annuity for $100 a month

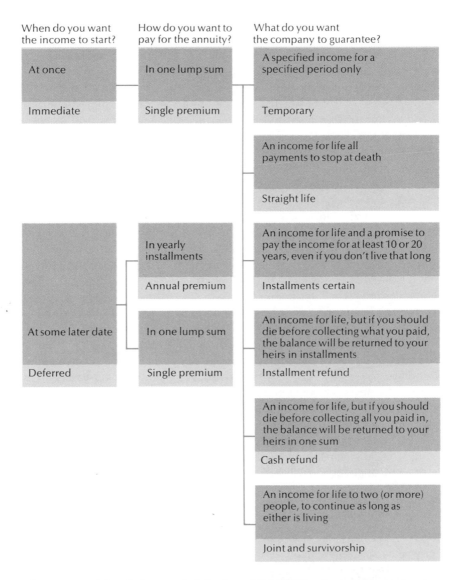

When do you want the income to start?	How do you want to pay for the annuity?	What do you want the company to guarantee?
At once	In one lump sum	A specified income for a specified period only
Immediate	Single premium	Temporary
		An income for life all payments to stop at death
		Straight life
	In yearly installments	An income for life and a promise to pay the income for at least 10 or 20 years, even if you don't live that long
	Annual premium	Installments certain
At some later date	In one lump sum	An income for life, but if you should die before collecting what you paid, the balance will be returned to your heirs in installments
Deferred	Single premium	Installment refund
		An income for life, but if you should die before collecting all you paid in, the balance will be returned to your heirs in one sum
		Cash refund
		An income for life to two (or more) people, to continue as long as either is living
		Joint and survivorship

Figure 13-4   What Kind of Annuity? Check one label in each column, string together three you have checked, and you will have a description of the type of annuity that suits your plans. (Annuity experts might use shortcut descriptions, or rearrange the three elements, but these will do.)

at age 65, a male annuitant would have to spend approximately $13,750. Generally, people buy an immediate annuity just prior to retirement, to continue as long as they live.

A *deferred life annuity* is one that begins to pay the annuitant at a later specified date, say at age 65. As in the immediate life annuity, it can be purchased in one lump sum years before benefits begin, or by installments covering perhaps many years.

Sometimes a deferred life annuity is paid to the annuitant until he dies, and then the remainder is paid to a named beneficiary until the entire cost of the annuity has been recovered. In other instances, if the annuitant dies, a lump sum is paid to a named beneficiary. The lump sum paid is the difference between the income payments received and the total premiums paid by the annuitant.

Both immediate life and deferred life annuities may be *joint and survivorship annuities*. Under this annuity policy, an income is guaranteed during the joint lifetime and is continued until the death of the survivor. This plan may fit a man and wife who have no other dependents but may not be a good one for a husband with an invalid wife. It may not be a good policy if the annuitant had been rejected for life insurance, which might indicate that he may not need financial assistance after age 65 or so.

In any event, it is wise to have a thorough physical examination before taking out an annuity, especially if the annuity is to be taken out shortly before retirement or before the beginning of payments to the annuitant. For healthy persons reaching age 65 or older, it may be advisable to purchase an annuity just prior to retirement, because the older the annuitant, the higher the return.

One of the principal advantages of a joint life-and-survivorship annuity is that most of the need for life insurance (beyond the great need when children are still on the family payroll) is eliminated. For example, if husband and wife have an annuity or a combination of annuity, Social Security, and some income from stocks, bonds, or real estate, which provide sufficient income, they need carry only permanent insurance (straight life) to cover funeral expenses, because the wife will be supported by the annuity income even after the husband's death. This arrangement eliminates paying heavy life insurance premiums during the retirement period when income is usually less than in the earning years.

Cost of Annuities

The cost of annuity is based largely on the amount of income it will pay. Annuity rates are usually quoted in either of two ways: the amount of income the annuitant receives per unit of premium, or the amount the annuitant receives per unit. Table 13-9, The Cost of Annuities, gives some averages of costs from both points of view. The amount the annuitant pays for a given income depends on the income plan selected, on the age when payments begin, and on the sex of the annuitant.

TABLE 13-9 THE COST OF ANNUITIES

IMMEDIATE SINGLE PREMIUM ANNUITY (Income to Begin at Once)

Age		Each $1,000 Buys This Monthly Income			Each $10 of Monthly Income Costs		
Male	Female	Straight Life	10 Years Certain	Installment Refund	Straight Life	10 Years Certain	Installment Refund
50	55	$4.93	$4.88	$4.73	$2,030	$2,050	$2,110
55	60	5.51	5.41	5.20	1,838	1,847	1,920
60	65	6.30	6.08	5.81	1,605	1,644	1,721
65	70	7.36	6.87	6.56	1,375	1,455	1,524
70	75	8.80	7.73	7.50	1,145	1,293	1,331

DEFERRED ANNUAL PREMIUM ANNUITY (For Men Age 65 When It Starts*)

Age at Issue	Each $100 a Year Buys This Monthly Income			Each $10 of Monthly Income Costs This Much a Year		
	Straight Life	10 Years Certain	Installment Refund	Straight Life	10 Years Certain	Installment Refund
30	$33.17	$31.33	$30.38	$ 30.15	$ 31.92	$ 32.92
35	26.49	25.01	24.50	37.75	39.98	40.82
40	20.57	19.42	19.03	48.61	51.49	52.55
45	15.34	14.49	14.20	65.19	69.01	70.42
50	10.71	10.12	9.92	93.37	98.81	100.81
55	6.62	6.26	6.13	151.06	159.74	163.13

*A woman would receive 15 to 20 percent less in annuity income per $100 of annual premium than a man of comparable age at issue.

SOURCE: *Changing Times.*

It is well to remember these facts about costs: (1) A woman pays more than a man because she lives longer; (2) for each dollar of income, a cash-refund joint life-and-survivorship plan costs most, and a straight life plan costs least; (3) the older the annuitant when the income begins, the less he will pay, as in the case of an immediate annuity; (4) with a deferred annuity, the younger the annuitant when he buys, the smaller the annual premiums will be; (5) a straight annuity is the cheapest. The more generous the guarantee, the greater the cost.

Why Buy an Annuity?

An annuity is really an investment. You have to compare annuities with stocks and bonds, savings accounts, and other kinds of investment in order to pick out the advantages and disadvantages. The chief advantages are these:

1.   Annuities are the safest way to obtain a retirement income. You get guaranteed payments that cannot be reduced.
2.   You are freed of the job of managing your investments.
3.   You can never outlive your capital.
4.   A deferred annuity makes it easier to save for old age, and more difficult to use your savings.
5.   There can be tax advantages, because your annuity premiums draw interest during your working years, but you delay paying an income tax until you collect it. By then your tax bracket is apt to be lower.

The chief disadvantages are these:

1.   Your income will not increase if inflation erodes the dollar's value, unless you select a "variable" annuity described later in the chapter.
2.   You will leave less to your heirs because you use up your capital.
3.   You earn a comparatively low rate of interest on your investment.
4.   You cannot get at your capital in an emergency once annuity payments begin.

Annuities versus Investments

If you are about to retire and need an income of $100 a month in addition to Social Security and other investment income, you will be interested in putting a large part of your capital into either an annuity or investments. Table 13-10 will be useful when making this decision.

Should You Buy an Annuity?

The answer depends on your investment skills and temperament and your financial circumstances. Keep these points in mind:

1.   Have enough life insurance before you invest in annuities—first things first.
2.   You may consider buying an annuity just prior to retirement rather than paying

TABLE 13-10 ANNUITIES VERSUS INVESTMENTS

START WITH YOU.		SUPPOSE YOU BUY AN ANNUITY.	SUPPOSE YOU INVEST OR BANK THE SAME AMOUNT AND TAKE $100 A MONTH TO LIVE ON.		
If you are:	Your life expectancy is:	$100 a month guaranteed for life costs:	You can live on dividends or interest only if your money earns:	With lower earnings, you can tap both interest and principal and your money will last:	And if still living, your life expectancy will then be:
A woman age 62	19½ years (49% live at least 20 years)	$17,300	7%	At 3%, 19 years At 4%, 22 years	At 81, 9 years At 84, 7½ years
A man age 65	14½ years (27% live at least 20 years)	$13,750	8¾%	At 3%, 14 years At 4%, 16 years	At 79, 7½ years At 81, 7 years

SOURCE: *Changing Times.*

monthly premiums during your working years because the interest from annuities is comparatively low.

3. Figure your retirement income before buying annuities—how much you may need and where it will come from.

4. You can make more money through the regular investments during your working years.

5. Consider variable annuities, because with these most of your premium money is invested in common stocks. Common stocks keep up with inflation or go even higher, and you get a larger monthly annuity as the earned income increases.

6. If you have enough money, diversify. Put some of your savings into other investments and some into annuities just prior to retirement.

Combination of Annuities and Investments

Should you put most or all of family savings into annuities? There are limitations to the judicial use of annuities. The major limitation is that they provide for a *fixed income* unprotected from inflation. For the same reason, placing all savings in investments might be too risky.

By judicious combination of annuities and investments, a greater fixed income could be obtained as well as a hedge against inflation. For example, if an elderly couple had $40,000 available at a retirement age of 65 (for the husband) and 62 for the wife, they might invest all the money at 5 percent, which would net an annual income of $2,000, hardly sufficient to live on. Their income could be divided as follows:

	ANNUAL YIELD
$17,300 for straight life annuity for wife (at age 62)	$1,000
$13,750 for straight life annuity for husband (at age 65)	1,000
$9,250 in good common stock yielding 6 percent	550
Total	$2,550

Thus a greater income can be obtained by a combination of annuities and other investments.

Another way to achieve the same objective has been in operation since 1952. In that year, the Teachers Insurance and Annuity Association offered college teachers the opportunity to place three-fourths of their pension contributions into selected common stocks through the College Retirement Equities Fund (CREF) and the remainder in regular annuities (TIAA).

This way to finance retirement has been called "inflation-proof annuities." The combined annuity (*fixed* dollar annuity plus the *variable* annuity based on the purchase of common stocks) has produced more income since its inception than the fixed income annuity. This was to be expected because stocks went up between 1952 and 1969.

Variable Annuities—Pro and Con

Despite the arguments, pro and con, over the variable annuity, offered by security dealers, investment bankers, mutual funds, and insurance companies, the two most important considerations from the buyer's point of view concern the tax angle and the final cost in making the investment.

When you buy a variable annuity, the dividends and capital gains are reinvested nearly tax-free by the insurance company. That makes the capital grow faster than is possible when you buy stocks or invest in mutual funds, because in these instances you pay taxes on capital gains and dividends in the year of purchase.

As for cost, variable annuities will probably carry a commission charge, or load, of around 12 percent over a long period of time. This means that about 12 percent of the premiums would go into commissions and expenses. For ordinary life insurance the figure is over 15 percent. On most mutual funds, the load ranges between 4 and 9 percent. On common stock purchased on a major stock exchange, the commission is much lower, running less than 2 percent on purchases over $500.

By 1969 over 212,000 persons were contributing to the College Retirement Equities Fund. An ever-increasing number of large corporations are also providing variable pensions for their employees, including Warner-Lambert, Boeing Airplane, Pan American Airways, and New Jersey Power and Light, to mention a few. Among the major life insurance companies, Prudential is offering variable annuities on an individual or a group basis.

A survey at year-end of 1966 showed that 90,000 Americans were covered by 178 group plans providing variable benefits from life insurance companies.[4]

How the Variable Annuity Works.   If a buyer decides to set aside, say, $25 each month over a number of years for a variable annuity, the funds would be invested in common stocks. Each payment, after deduction of expenses, would be credited to the buyer's account units, determined by the current dollar value of a unit. The dollar value would go up or down depending on the market value of the stocks; the company makes no guarantees. When the buyer retires, all his variable contract account units would be converted into a fixed number of units. But instead of paying him each month in a *fixed* number of dollars, the variable contract provides for the *current* value of the units credited to him. Thus the dollar value of an annuity unit would change each month according to the investment results on the account.

The potential hazard of the variable annuity, then, is that stock prices may decline and the investor may get back less than he put in. But in testimony before the Securities and Exchange Commission in 1962, the Prudential Insurance Company argued that the danger is minimal; that the payments into a variable annuity over any modern 15-year period would have provided a greater return than fixed annuities. One reason for the delay in launching the variable

[4]*Life Insurance Fact Book,* 1968, p. 36.

annuity programs is that they have been ruled by the courts to be subject, not only to state insurance regulations, but to SEC regulations also.

The chief advantage of the variable annuity is that it serves as a hedge against diminished purchasing power due to inflation. The chief disadvantage is that income may be reduced during a period of stock market decline.

What If Stocks Go Down? A variable annuity is backed by a broad selection of common stocks. Therefore, the monthly income of annuitants moves rather closely with stocks as a whole. The long-term trend of common stocks has been steadily upward, and this trend appears to be continuing.

The stock market can have some strong ups and downs, and no one can rule out completely a protracted slump in our economy. This is why the financial institutions who use variable annuities team them with a fixed-dollar annuity. In the TIAA-CREF plan for colleges, for example, a participant must have a part of his contribution put into a fixed annuity. The variable annuity, however, provides an income advantage, as can be seen in Figure 13-5.

It is well to remember, however, that it is not quite fair to compare a variable annuity with investments like stocks and mutual funds. When you buy

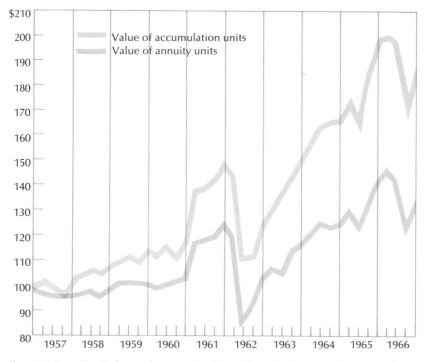

Figure 13-5 **How Values and Income Can Vary. The color line shows how the value of a \$100 net payment made on a variable annuity on January 1, 1957, varied over the years through 1966. The gray line shows how the monthly income from a variable annuity, starting at \$100 in January, 1957, varied over the years through 1966. Figures are based on the actual results of a representative variable-annuity company. Source:** *Changing Times.*

a variable annuity, you are buying not only management but also the "annuity principle"—that is, a guarantee of an income continuing as long as you live.

Where Can You Buy a Variable Annuity?   A few life insurance companies are presently selling most of the variable annuities. A few special variable annuity companies, like Variable Annuity Life Insurance Company of America and Equity Annuity Life Insurance Company, both located in Washington, D.C., make an effort to sell to individuals, although they also sell to groups.

There are legal obstacles to buying variable annuities. Over two-thirds of the states either prohibit their sale or permit their sale only to organized groups. Securities and Exchange Commission rules make it difficult for life insurance companies to sell individual contracts to anybody anywhere. This situation may change, because a few variable annuity companies now sell these policies to individuals in some 14 states and are building sales forces to move into other states. When this happens, it is a good time for you to learn about this new kind of financial policy and see whether it fits into your own planning.

QUESTIONS FOR DISCUSSION

1.   How do you account for the fact that many Americans do not plan an intelligent life insurance program for their dependents?

2.   Why do many life insurance agents recommend ordinary life insurance rather than term life insurance?

3.   How would you modify, if at all, the insurance program for this family?

The father is an engineer, 37 years old, and his wife is 35. They have two children: Jack is 8 and Peggy is 4. Their annual income is $10,000, but this may increase to a maximum of about $20,000. They own their home, but there is a $2,500 unpaid mortgage. The father's employer does not offer group life insurance and does not have a private pension plan. The father is fully covered by Social Security.

This family owns, at present, $28,000 in life insurance. All the policies are on the life of the father, the only breadwinner in the family. His insurance program is as follows:

DATE PURCHASED	AGE	AMOUNT AND KIND	ANNUAL PREMIUM
1951	21	$ 5,000 whole life	$ 72
1955	25	10,000 whole life	158
1959	29	7,500 family income	202
1963	33	1,000 whole life	21
1963	33	4,500 20-year term	46

4.   Determine the benefits you might receive from the present Social Security law by creating your own hypothetical case.

5. Under what conditions might it be wise to purchase an annuity as part of a retirement program? What kind of annuity?

ACTIVITY PROBLEMS

1. Obtain the rates of a typical life insurance company for renewable term insurance, ordinary life insurance, 20-payment life insurance, 20-year endowment insurance, and an annuity purchased just prior to retirement at age 65, for a man at ages 25, 35, and 65. On the basis of the information obtained, which type of insurance would you recommend in each of the following cases?

    a. A man, recently married, age 25, whose dependent wife will need about $200 a month for life in the event of the death of her husband during the first 5 years of married life.

    b. A man 35, with dependent wife and two children ages 8 and 12.

2. Ask a life insurance agent how he would answer these questions and statements.

    a. "All my savings are going into investments. Why bother about life insurance?"

    b. "I have no dependents. Why should I buy life insurance?"

    c. "I don't believe in buying life insurance on my children."

3. Suppose a widow is left with $35,000 from life insurance. She is debating whether to take it in a lump sum and invest it or to take a definite amount each month for as long as she lives. What are your arguments for and against each course?

SUGGESTED READINGS

Goodwin, Dave: *Stop Wasting Your Insurance Dollars,* Simon and Schuster, New York, 1969.

Health, Education, and Welfare Department, Social Security Administration: *Financing Your Social Security,* 1967.

———— : *Recent Improvements in Your Social Security,* 1968.

———— : *Social Security Benefits,* 1968.

———— : *Social Security Benefits for Students Up to Age 22,* 1966.

———— : *Social Security Benefits for Young Families,* July, 1968.

"Inflationproof Insurance," *Changing Times,* February, 1967.

Life Insurance and Annuities, American Institute for Economic Research, Great Barrington, Mass., latest edition.

Life Insurance and Annuities from the Buyer's Point of View, American Institute for Economic Research, Great Barrington, Mass., latest edition.

Margolius, Sidney: *How to Make the Most of Your Money*, Meredith Press, New York, 1966.

"Optional Extras They Sell with Insurance," *Changing Times*, March, 1968.

Report on Life Insurance, Consumers Union, Mount Vernon, N.Y., 1967.

"Which Kind of Term Insurance?" *Changing Times*, September, 1964.

chapter 14

SAVINGS AND INVESTMENTS:
ESTATE PLANNING, WILLS, AND TRUSTS

We might as well admit, at the start, that saving money is not easy. So many people feel like the wife who said: "But why should we save for the future, Roscoe? If there is anything we want in the future, it'll be available on the credit plan."

Saving money takes discipline, planning, cooperation, and plain hard work. But it is so important to family security and happiness that it is worth this effort. Savings based on a well-planned and purposeful program, balanced with present needs, can be an exciting experience when a family has agreed on its financial security goals.

THE IMPORTANCE OF SAVINGS TO THE CONSUMER

Every family needs to accumulate funds for use during the more expensive stages of the family life cycle—especially the high school and college period—and for recreation, pleasure, rewards, vacation, household furnishings and equipment, or new furniture. In addition, every family needs to build a reserve fund for the expenses of illness, death, loss of income, and other unforeseen emergencies. It needs savings to ensure financial security in old age or for protection should the breadwinner become incapable of further earning. The payment of life insurance and disability insurance premiums and payments toward the purchase of a home are usually classified as protection for the family.

Putting the American Way of Life into Action

The major goal of family savings is to achieve family happiness through protection. There is, however, another desirable reason why a family should plan its own financial security above the minimum Social Security benefits. A family that plans its own financial security program—insurance, emergency fund, educational fund, retirement, and possibly its own home—and begins to accumulate its own wealth is not likely to fall for the philosophy, "Let the government take care of us."

A family that has planned and saved, sometimes even at the expense of better current living, has too much at stake to support legislation that may substitute government funds for family funds. In other words, family-planned and -earned financial security is one of the concrete ways by which we can put into action our belief in the American way of life.

What Are Savings?

An economist might describe saving as "accumulating wealth through the postponement of consumption." He looks at savings as the first step in creating wealth—that is, the first step in increasing the economy's ability to produce more and better things.

If you decide to bank some of your money for later spending, the bank will lend a part of it to a manufacturer who needs more capital to install new machinery. This is a form of savings that diverts your present spending to new machinery to produce more goods for everyone. This is one function of savings.

What if you, and most Americans, decide to spend all your income in buying things? This would result in less money for producers who want money to expand, and the demand for savings would exceed the supply. This, in combination with other factors, can produce inflationary pressure.

What if you, and most other Americans, decide to double your savings at a time when business does not want to expand? The supply of savings exceeds demand. This, in combination with other factors, can produce a recession.

This is an oversimplified description of the role you play when you drop coins in a piggy bank or put dollars in your bank account. We can draw several useful conclusions from all this.

> 1.   Saving as an operation has an overriding public significance as well as a personal and private one.
> 2.   Savings are not "money not spent." They are money spent at one time instead of another time.
> 3.   The important idea is that savings consist of money that is not spent for "current consumption."

What has this to do with you and your spending patterns? For one thing, it leads to the idea of what savings are: the difference between your current consumption expenses and your current income. Thus, money you spend for food, clothes, and taxes is not savings. Another lesson to learn from the economist's approach is that of choosing how to spend. When most people choose to save, it actually means choosing to spend more on capital goods, as when you buy a house or stocks, or on future enjoyments, such as college education for your children, retirement, or a trip around the world later on. When you save, you deny yourself something you could have now in order to have something later.

Why Families Save

The greatest incentive to save is provided when savings have a purpose, such as for an emergency fund, an education, homeownership, or a new car—those objectives in life for which money is necessary. Families with the foresight to establish both short-range and long-range goals for the use of money are the ones who seem to get ahead most rapidly. They find that planning helps them place the proper emphasis on the desired goals.

According to researchers, there are three basic purposes for which families save:

> 1.   Short-term spending plans—saving for something wanted badly in the near future, a car, a home, a vacation
> 2.   Long-term spending plans—college education for children, retirement, buying into a business
> 3.   Financial security—a rainy-day fund, investments, an estate for children or grandchildren, retirement

According to research in the behavioral sciences, a family's major future obligations for retirement and for the education of children may lead to concern but not always to saving.[1] Families may have some long-range concerns, but except for the major contractual commitments in insurance, mortage, and retirement programs, may appear to be operating on a relatively short-run strategy. According to the researchers, a substantial number of persons are unable to plan. Those who say they are unable to plan are less likely to have hospitalization insurance or liquid assets. They also have less education.

Families with higher incomes do most of the saving and hold most of the assets. Families in the middle range of incomes, $5,000 to $7,500, do less saving, apparently because they prefer to have a higher standard of living immediately—a new car every other year, shrubbery for the yard, a bedroom for the new baby, a long vacation trip, and so on. Often, however, the choices are not this clear-cut.

Who Are the Savers?

Families that have received a substantial increase in income are likely to be savers. Their living has been adjusted to a certain standard, and it takes time before they move up to a higher standard of living.

There are other factors that influence a family's ability or desire to save.

1.   Occupation. More lower-income wage earners and clerical workers on steady jobs eke out savings than professional and salaried people—perhaps because of the fear of losing their jobs. High-income salaried people often save quite a bit.

2.   Medical expense. Families having constant large medical bills are not savers. The fewer the medical bills, the higher the savings.

3.   Age and family cycle. Generally, young single persons and people past 65 produce relatively few savers. The heaviest proportion of families with savings comes from the 35-to-64 age bracket. Couples under 45 with young children and persons over 45, with or without children, are those who seem best able to save.

4.   Once a person gets into the habit of saving money, he tends to retain the habit. Conversely, a person who is used to satisfying impulses of the moment and to avoiding choices and decisions finds it hard to save.

5.   Contractual savings is the easiest way to save for many people. Commitments to mortgage payments, insurance premiums, pension contributions, and regular monthly investment plans almost always produce continued savings.

6.   The big influence on the nature of savings is the great change in the financial tools that families have to work with. Two or three decades ago, the family that did not save might find itself on charity and in the county poorhouse. But private pension plans, Social Security, and other government financial aid programs have reduced the need for saving to prevent poverty. Families now plan protection largely by investing in life insurance, disability income insurance, and medical aid insurance. In a strict sense, Social Security taxes and health insurance premiums are not savings, but the benefits from these affect retirement and emergency fund requirements and savings.

[1] James N. Morgan, "Planning for the Future and Living with Risk," *The American Behavioral Scientist,* May, 1963, p. 40.

Increase in Personal Savings

Over-the-counter savings (including savings at financial institutions where transactions are conducted across a teller counter) increased from $131.7 billion in 1957 to $362.7 billion at the end of 1967. Over-the-counter savings (not including securities and bonds) at the end of 1967 in selected savings institutions were as follows:

	BILLIONS OF DOLLARS
Commercial banks	$166.8
Savings associations (all types)	124.6
Mutual savings banks	60.1
Credit unions	11.1

Postal Savings went out of existence in 1966 because of lack of interest on the part of depositors. This savings institution had about $50 millon on deposit in 1967. Commercial banks have garnered an ever-increasing volume of over-the-counter savings. Their annual gain rose from $9.9 billion in 1961 to $20.5 billion in 1967, while savings associations' gain rose from $8.7 billion to $10.7 billion. [2]

What to Do with Your Savings

People use various savings instruments to meet different objectives. Usually, the higher the return on savings, the less safety of the principal. If you want liquidity (getting cash quickly), do not expect long-term growth. If you want certainty of income, do not expect a high yield.

A study of Table 14-1, Comparative Savings Instruments, can help you to decide on what to do with your savings. Surveys of consumer finances by the University of Michigan, Ann Arbor, indicate that people generally buy government bonds for safety of principal and a fair return on their investment, growth common stocks as a hedge against inflation and a chance for long-time growth, and real estate mortgages for a reasonably high rate of return. As might be expected, people with fairly low incomes and small assets select savings bonds and savings accounts, while the proportion who prefer common stocks is largest among the spending units with large incomes and considerable assets.

How Much Do You Want to Save?

Why not try this idea: Save Now, Pay Later. Decide how much you need for specific objectives—a trip to Europe, a college fund—you name it. Then find

[2] *Savings and Loan Fact Book, 1968.*

TABLE 14-1 COMPARATIVE SAVINGS INSTRUMENTS

SAVINGS INVESTMENT	PRINCIPAL	INFLATION	RATE OF RETURN, %	CERTAINTY OF CONTINUED RETURN	SMALLNESS OR LACK OF SELLING CHARGE OR OTHER FEES	LIQUIDITY UNDER ALL CONDITIONS	CHANCE FOR LONG-TERM GROWTH
Cash	Exc.	Poor	0	. . . .	. . . .	Exc.	None
Life insurance	Exc.	Poor	3/4-4	Exc.	Fair	Exc.	Poor
United States savings bonds	Exc.	Poor	4 3/4	Exc.	Exc.	Exc.	Poor
Savings account in commercial bank*	Exc.	Poor	4	Exc.	Exc.	Exc.	Poor
Bank savings certificates	Exc.	Poor	5-5 1/2	Exc.	Exc.	Exc.	Poor
Mutual savings bank*	Exc.	Poor	5	Exc.	Exc.	Exc.	Poor
Federal savings and loan association*	Exc.	Poor	4 3/4-5 1/4	Exc.	Exc.	Good	Poor
Credit union	Exc.	Poor	4-4 1/4	Good	Fair	Good	Poor
Corporate bonds	Good	Poor	4-7	Good	Fair	Good	Poor
Corporate stock	Fair	Exc.	3 1/2-4 3/4	Poor	Fair	Fair	Good
Growth common stocks	Good	Exc.	1-2 1/2	Fair	Fair	Fair	Exc.
High-grade preferred stocks	Good	Poor	4 3/4-6	Good	Fair	Fair	Poor
High-grade convertible preferreds	Good	Good	4-4 1/2	Good	Fair	Fair	Good
Convertible bonds	Good	Good	3-4 1/2	Good	Fair	Good	Good
Investment companies (mutual funds)	Poor	Good	3 1/2-5 1/2	Poor	Poor	Fair	Good
Common trust funds	Fair	Fair	2-3 1/2	Fair	Fair	Good	Fair
Real estate mortgages (as investments)	Fair	Poor	6 1/2-7 1/4	Poor	Poor	Poor	Fair
Unimproved real estate	Fair	Good	. . . .	Poor	Poor	Poor	Exc.
Your own home	Fair	Good	0	. . . .	Poor	Poor	Good

* Insured up to $15,000.

SOURCE: Adapted from "What to Do with Your Savings," *Changing Times.*

in Table 14-2 the amount of money you must set aside monthly, at various rates of interest, to reach your goal. To accumulate $2,000 in 5 years at 5 percent interest, for example, you need to invest $29.75 a month for 5 years.

The two assumptions built into this table are these: interest is compounded semiannually and the money does not earn interest until six deposits have been made. Quarterly deposits will put your goal ahead of schedule.

How Long Will Your Savings Last?

Solving problems like these is complicated for most people. You can get a quick answer from Figure 14-1. It is based on a $10,000 fund, but you can adapt it to

TABLE 14-2   HOW MUCH DO YOU WANT TO SAVE?

FIND YOUR SAVINGS GOAL IN THIS COLUMN	HERE IS THE REGULAR MONTHLY SAVING NEEDED TO REACH THAT GOAL IF YOUR MONEY IS INVESTED AT							
	3%	3½%	4%	4½%	5%	6%	7%	8%
$ 500 in 5 years	$ 7.80	$ 7.70	$ 7.60	$ 7.50	$ 7.45	$ 7.25	$ 7.10	$ 6.95
10 years	3.60	3.50	3.40	3.35	3.25	3.10	2.95	2.80
15 years	2.20	2.15	2.05	1.95	1.90	1.75	1.60	1.50
20 years	1.55	1.45	1.40	1.30	1.25	1.10	1.00	0.90
30 years	0.85	0.80	0.75	0.65	0.60	0.50	0.40	0.35
$1,000 in 5 years	$15.55	$15.40	$15.25	$15.05	$14.85	$14.55	$14.20	$13.90
10 years	7.25	7.05	6.90	6.70	6.50	6.20	5.90	5.60
15 years	4.45	4.25	4.10	3.95	3.80	3.50	3.25	2.95
20 years	3.10	2.90	2.75	2.60	2.45	2.20	1.95	1.75
30 years	1.75	1.60	1.45	1.35	1.25	1.00	0.85	0.70
$2,000 in 5 years	$31.15	$30.80	$30.45	$30.10	$29.75	$29.05	$28.40	$27.75
10 years	14.40	14.05	13.70	13.40	13.05	12.40	11.80	11.20
15 years	8.85	8.55	8.20	7.90	7.60	7.00	6.45	5.95
20 years	6.15	5.80	5.50	5.25	4.95	4.40	3.95	3.50
30 years	3.45	3.20	2.90	2.70	2.45	2.05	1.70	1.40
$3,000 in 5 years	$46.70	$46.15	$45.65	$45.15	$44.60	$43.60	$42.60	$41.65
10 years	21.60	21.10	20.55	20.10	19.55	18.60	17.65	16.80
15 years	13.30	12.80	12.30	11.85	11.40	10.50	9.70	8.90
20 years	9.20	8.75	8.30	7.85	7.40	6.65	5.90	5.25
30 years	5.20	4.80	4.40	4.00	3.70	3.05	2.55	2.10
$4,000 in 5 years	$62.30	$61.55	$60.90	$60.20	$59.50	$58.10	$56.80	$55.50
10 years	28.80	28.10	27.40	26.75	26.10	24.80	23.55	22.35
15 years	17.75	17.10	16.40	15.80	15.20	14.00	12.90	11.90
20 years	12.30	11.65	11.05	10.45	9.90	8.85	7.90	7.00
30 years	6.95	6.35	5.85	5.35	4.90	4.10	3.40	2.80
$5,000 in 5 years	$77.85	$76.95	$76.10	$75.25	$74.35	$72.65	$71.00	$69.40
10 years	36.00	35.25	34.25	33.45	32.60	31.00	29.45	27.95
15 years	22.20	21.35	20.55	19.75	19.00	17.50	16.15	14.85
20 years	15.35	14.55	13.80	13.05	12.35	11.05	9.85	8.75
30 years	8.65	7.95	7.30	6.70	6.15	5.10	4.25	3.50
$6,000 in 5 years	$93.40	$92.35	$91.30	$90.30	$89.20	$87.20	$85.20	$83.30
10 years	43.20	42.20	41.10	40.15	38.10	37.20	35.35	33.55
15 years	26.60	25.60	24.65	23.70	22.75	21.00	19.35	17.85
20 years	18.40	17.45	16.55	15.70	14.85	13.25	11.85	10.50
30 years	10.40	9.55	8.75	8.05	7.35	6.15	5.10	4.20

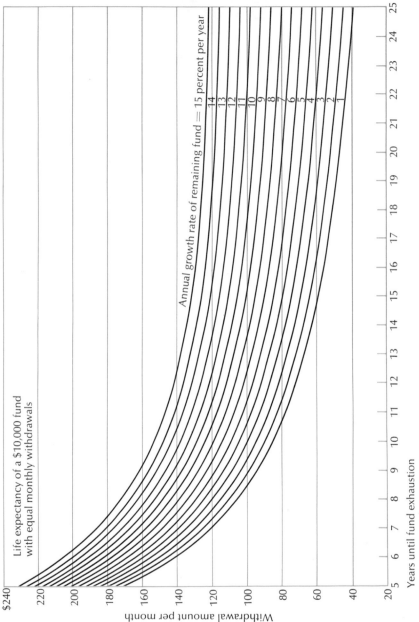

Figure 14 - 1   How Long Will Your Savings Last? Reprinted by permission of *Changing Times, The Kiplinger Magazine*, April, 1966. Copyright by the Kiplinger Washington Editors, Inc.

other amounts. How long will $10,000 earning 5 percent a year last if you withdraw $150 each month? Find $150 on the left-hand margin, then draw a horizontal line over to the curve representing the 5 percent growth rate. From this point drop a vertical line to the bottom scale, and find the answer, 6½ years.

You can handle other amounts with the aid of a ratio. If, for example, you want to find out how long a $25,000 sum will last if you want to withdraw $150 a month. Set up a ratio: $25,000 is to $10,000 as $150 per month is to $X per month. You will discover that X works out to $60. So your answer will be the same as for $60-a-month withdrawals from a $10,000 fund—about 23 years.

If you want to use a $10,000 sum for a fixed monthly amount for 20 years, assuming the fund grows 10 percent a year, locate 20 years on the bottom scale, then draw a vertical line up to the 10 percent curve. From there draw a horizontal line over to the left margin. You will find it hits $94 per month. This is what you can withdraw.

If the sum were $25,000 instead of $10,000, you would multiply $94 by 2½ times, since $25,000 is 2½ times $10,000. The answer—$235 a month.

The fund will remain the same if your withdrawals equal the monthly earnings. The data below show the maximums that you can withdraw each month from a $10,000 sum without running out of money. By using ratios again, you can figure the monthly amounts for sums larger or smaller than $10,000.

PERCENT GROWTH PER YEAR	MAXIMUM MONTHLY WITHDRAWAL THAT WILL MAINTAIN CAPITAL
1%	$ 8.30
2	16.52
3	24.66
4	32.74
5	40.74
6	48.68
7	56.54
8	64.34
9	72.07
10	79.74
11	87.34
12	94.89

SAVINGS INSTITUTIONS

Only those savings media which are generally known as savings institutions—savings and loan associations, commercial banks, mutual savings banks, and credit unions—are considered in this section of the chapter. These savings institutions are differentiated from other kinds of investment by their relative liquidity and safety, and by the fact that they are under state or federal control. These institutions have as their major purpose the safekeeping of savings of individuals and institutions. Savings in these institutions, as a group, are not well protected against inflation because they provide for a return of a fixed number of dollars of principal plus interest regardless of the value of the dollar.

Savings and Loan Associations

The savings and loan associations had their origin in 1831, in a suburb of Philadelphia, in the form of a home-building society. In this society each of six members would give a certain sum each month until there was enough to build a home. The house was built and auctioned off to one of the members. Later, one could become a member by simply opening a savings account or by borrowing to finance a home.

At the end of 1967, there were 6,115 savings and loan associations in the United States with assets of more than $124.6 billion, representing the savings of over 44 million shareholders. Among savings institutions, only commercial banks have more total savings on deposit—$166.8 billion at the end of 1967.

The whole purpose of savings and loan associations is to assemble loan capital for homeownership. Over 80 percent of their assets are invested in first mortgages on real estate—mostly one- to four-family homes. The balance in assets, not in cash, is invested in government bonds. Every third home in this country is financed through a savings and loan institution.

Operation of Savings and Loan Association.   Since 1933, when Congress enacted legislation providing for federal savings and loan associations, federally chartered associations have grown until there are presently 2,056. There are 4,059 with state charters. Most savings and loan associations are mutual organizations. The saving members of the association are the owners. Borrowers also may become owners.

A small number of associations (about 12.7 percent) have organized as stock corporations. No permanent stock is issued except in 23 states, including California, Ohio, and Illinois. In the case of all federally chartered associations, and some organized in several states, each member is entitled to one vote for each $100 in his savings account, with a maximum of 50 votes. In federal associations, each borrower has one vote.

There are two major types of accounts. The "savings account" may be opened with any amount of money. All transactions are recorded in the account holder's passbook. Additions and withdrawals can be made. Dividends are credited either quarterly or semiannually. "Investment accounts" can be opened and added to with $100 or in even multiples of $100. Dividends are generally paid quarterly.

Except for checking accounts, many savings and loan associations offer regular banking services, such as Christmas savings accounts, renting safe-deposit boxes, cashing bank checks, selling money orders, redeeming Series E savings bonds, and advising on investments.

How Safe Are Savings and Loan Associations?[3]   Because these associations specialize in high-return type of investment—first mortgages on homes currently bearing interest at 7 to 8 percent—and enjoy some tax advantages, they usually pay dividends that are higher than the interest on bank savings accounts. In 1969, the associations were paying from 4¾ to 5¼ percent per year, compounded quarterly. How safe are the savings in the savings and loan associations that pay high dividends?

All federally chartered associations are members of the Federal Home Loan Bank System, a chain of 11 district banks that provide some of the funds to member associations. Accounts are insured in all 2,056 federally chartered associations up to $20,000 per account in any one institution by the Federal Savings and Loan Insurance Corporation (FSLIC). State-chartered institutions may belong to the Federal Home Loan Bank System (2,431 in 1967). Being members, they have to operate under the same regulations as federal associations; thus savings are just as safe as in federal associations.

A few state associations belong to the bank system without carrying the insurance coverage, and some are neither system members nor insured. A few state systems have accounts insured by private insurers. Unfortunately, a few of these uninsured or poorly insured associations, notably a small group of organizations in Maryland in the guise of savings and loan associations, mulcted several thousand people of their savings in 1961-1962. All these organizations were state-chartered in Maryland; none held a federal charter; none was insured by the FSLIC, the federal government agency that underwrites accounts up to $15,000 in 4,487 federally and state-chartered units.

But what of the savers in other savings and loan associations? Are they running the risks that occurred in these few Maryland units? A review of the record of the FSLIC, created in 1934, can provide reassurance. In all its history, only 70 associations out of 4,487 needed financial assistance in 34 years. In 60 of these cases, the FSLIC made direct contributions to the distressed unit. In only 10 cases was it necessary to go into receivership, and in those cases, insurance was paid to the savers.

On the basis of this fine record, it might be reassuring to put your savings in an association protected by the FSLIC. Over 60 percent of the 6,115 savings and loan associations were federally insured, covering about 96 percent of all assets in all savings and loan associations.

Liquidity. Although insured savings and loan accounts compare favorably with savings in banks for safety, there is a difference in liquidity (right to get your money when you want it). In a bank you can withdraw your savings when

[3] All statistics are from Savings and Loan Fact Book, 1968.

you want them on short notice. When you withdraw savings from a savings and loan association, you are really selling shares to the association.

A savings and loan association has the bulk of its money tied up in long-term mortgages. An association could be perfectly sound yet be unable to meet all withdrawal requests if presented at one time. So it must reserve the right to go on a "notice basis." Under normal conditions, you would have no trouble getting your money. Enough money keeps coming in daily to take care of normal dividends and withdrawals. The association can call on the Federal Home Loan Bank System for aid in a pinch. It would take an emergency affecting all associations at the same time to bring about the "notice basis"—a delayed payment program. The typical notice that could be required is 30 days. Commercial banks, too, can require 30 days' notice.

Dividends.   Dividends depend on earnings. Back in 1958, a year typical of that decade, savings and loan associations paid a return on savings accounts of about 3.38 percent, topping commercial banks by about 1.7 percent. Beginning with 1961 and up to 1969, the advantage began to narrow as banks pushed up their rates on time and savings deposits. The average dividend yield on savings at associations was 4.63 percent in 1967, in contrast to 4.27 percent paid by commercial banks. This narrow differential, coupled with the one-stop, department-store type of services by banks, tipped the competitive advantage in their favor in recent years.

The savings and loan associations paying the highest dividends (insured by the Federal Savings and Loan Insurance Corporation) are located in California and the Southwestern states. In 1967-1969, most of the California FSLIC-guaranteed savings and loan associations were paying 5 percent dividends on passbook savings and $5\frac{1}{4}$ percent on savings certificates (accounts left with the association for a minimum period, usually 1 year to 3 years). Many commercial banks pay $5\frac{1}{4}$ percent on savings certificates today, which makes the competition for your guaranteed savings a tight one at the present time.

Dividends are usually credited to your account, so you get the benefit of compound interest. This is very important, because without compounding annually, it would take longer to double the amount of your accumulated capital. This advantage can be seen in Table 14-3.

"Before You Invest, Investigate."   You can help protect your savings in a savings and loan association by following these suggestions.

1.   Find out whether the association is operating under a federal or state charter. In most cases, either form of organization is safe.
2.   Be sure that the accounts are insured, preferably by the FSLIC.
3.   Find out the current dividend rate, how long the present rate has been in effect, when it is paid. Beware of too high a dividend rate.
4.   Investigate the management.
5.   Look over several recent financial statements. (A good association will be from 13 to 15 percent liquid; about 80 percent of its assets will be in first mortgages; not over 5 percent of its assets will be in borrowed money.)

RATE OF RETURN, %	APPROXIMATE NUMBER OF YEARS	RATE OF RETURN, %	APPROXIMATE NUMBER OF YEARS
1	70	6	12
2	35	6½	11
2½	28	7	10¼
3	23½	7½	9½
3½	20½	8	9
4	17½	9	8
4½	15¾	10	7¼
5	14¼	11	6⅔

The Mutual Fund Bill.   The $150 billion savings and loan industry is seeking to enter the mutual fund industry. Now, the savings and loan industry is primarily in the conventional home mortgage business (85 to 87 percent of their funds).

The mutual fund bill, which passed the Senate in late 1968, allows commercial banks and mutual savings banks to get into the lucrative fund business, but it makes no mention of savings and loan associations. Savings and loan officers feel they are entitled to share in the mutual fund business if their commercial and mutual savings bank competitors are permitted to sell mutual funds.

If the present proposal passes Congress and is signed by the President, a savings fund, to be called Fund for Mutual Depositors, Inc., would be offered to the public with little or no sales charge and with an investment management fee substantially below that now prevailing in the mutual fund industry.

Commercial Banks

We are primarily concerned here with your savings in commercial banks. Banks perform so many services that they are known as "department stores of finance." Most of these services are known to undergraduates—loans, checking accounts, safe-deposit boxes, investment services, collection services, issuing travelers' checks and letters of credit, selling and redeeming United States savings bonds, performing trust functions, and so on.

There are more than 13,000 commercial banks in this country having various kinds of savings accounts. Over 45 million depositors have over $166 billion in these banks. On these savings accounts (called "time" deposits), commercial banks paid an average annual interest of 4.2 percent in 1967. On these time deposits or savings accounts, banks may require a waiting period of 30 to 60 days for withdrawal of money, but this is seldom carried out.

Safety and Liquidity.   No saver of an insured account has lost his money since 1935. In the event there are heavy withdrawal demands and the insured bank's cash and liquid securities are used up, the bank can borrow from the Federal Reserve Bank to pay depositors. If the bank is still unable to pay all depositors, the bank goes into receivership, and the Federal Deposit Insurance Corporation (FDIC) makes funds available to the depositors.

Over 90 percent of commercial banks are insured. The law limits insurance to $15,000 per depositor in any one bank, but does not prohibit a person from having several deposits of $15,000 in several insured banks.

Interest on Savings.   Commercial banks are not as generous as savings institutions in their interest returns, largely because they have more expenses, not the least of which is expected profits for their stockholders. Thus, most commercial banks pay from 4 to $5\frac{1}{4}$ percent interest currently.

The interest is usually credited to the account every six months and is compounded, as in the savings and loan associations. There are several ways of determining interest. It is possible for six different banks to state that they pay interest at the rate of 1 percent per annum, but the variations in returns to the depositor may be as extreme as $3.96 to $7.88 for a six-month period.

It pays to select a bank that uses the best interest method.[4] If there is a choice, select the plan that provides for interest to be paid semiannually, computed on the lowest monthly balance for each month. By this method, interest can be earned on sums withdrawn between the semiannual payment dates.

Savings Certificates.   A savings certificate is a fairly recent document on which the savings institution records receipt of your money and pledges to repay the face amount plus a stated interest or dividend after a period of time. Most banks and savings and loan associations offer them.

By regulation subject to change, banks can pay up to 5 percent on certificates under $100,000 and up to 4 percent on regular passbook accounts.

Similarly, federal regulations currently limit to $5\frac{1}{4}$ percent the annual dividend rate by those savings and loan associations with passbook rates of $4\frac{3}{4}$ percent or less. Most associations authorized to pay a passbook rate of 5 percent are limited to 5 percent on certificates as well. To secure 5 percent on certificates, some associations require savings certificates to be held 3 years.

The minimum deposit for a savings certificate at most savings and loan associations is $1,000. Depending on the bank's policy, minimums range from $500 to $1,000 or more. Future deposits must be in fixed multiples of $100, $500, or $1,000.

Earnings are usually paid at maturity. Banks do not have to pay before maturity, but they may do so if you explain in writing that you have an emergency. And then you will have to forfeit all or a part of your interest. Demanding payment of a savings and loan association certificate before maturity will probably reduce the interest to the regular passbook rate or possibly lower.

[4]*Methods and Procedures in Computing Interest on Savings Deposits,* Savings and Mortgage Division, American Bankers Association, New York.

Mutual Savings Banks

Mutual savings banks are defined as banks of deposit, without stockholders, having as their basic mission the continuous promotion of true thrift at the local or community level. The first savings bank was established nearly 150 years ago. In 1968, there were 522 such banks located in 17 states, with over $60 billion of deposits and over 24 million depositors.[5] They have successfully weathered wars, panics, and depressions. No new institutions have been chartered since 1934, owing largely to the rapid development of savings and loan associations and to certain changes in commercial banking.

These banks are termed "mutuals" because they are owned and operated for the benefit of their depositors. None of these banks is chartered by the federal government. The depositors do not have any rights in management. Most state charters invest management in a self-perpetuating board of trustees. Most members of these boards are civic-minded persons with no financial interest in the institution, and they serve without salary.

Safety of Deposits in Mutual Savings Banks.   All mutual savings banks are regulated by state banking departments. Most of them are permitted to purchase farm mortgages, real estate mortgages, railroad and public utility bonds, state and municipal bonds, and federal government bonds. A few states permit them to invest in industrial bonds, consumer loans, bank stocks, and FHA Title I loans. Mortgage loans, however, account for about 60 percent of the assets; then, in order, come federal government securities and private corporation securities. Such a variety of investment opportunities gives these banks more flexibility in their investments than most savings institutions are allowed.

Deposits in a savings bank are recorded in a passbook. The depositor can withdraw sums at any time, although the bank has the right to require a notice of from 30 to 90 days of intention to withdraw. In practice, savings banks pay immediately.

Many kinds of accounts can be opened in savings banks, such as "individual account," "joint account," "organization account," "school savings account," "payroll deduction account," "special account," "Christmas club account," and "vacation club account." Fewer than 30 of the 522 banks have service charges.

Most of these banks have been very prudent in their investment policies. They are also carefully supervised by state banking departments. Furthermore, 234 of the 522 mutual banks are members of the FDIC, with deposits insured up to $15,000 per deposit. No depositor has suffered a loss in an insured bank since the FDIC was established.

Comparison of Dividend Return.   Since these banks are mutuals, they pay

[5] Connecticut, Delaware, Indiana, Maine, Maryland, Massachusetts, Minnesota, New Hampshire, New Jersey, New York, Ohio, Oregon, Pennsylvania, Rhode Island, Vermont, Washington, and Wisconsin.

dividends, not interest. Dividends accrue on deposits. Since most of their investments are long-term, like mortgages, the returns are relatively high—generally higher than on savings in commercial banks, and usually slightly lower than on savings in savings and loan associations and in credit unions. Most mutual savings banks have paid between 2 and 4 percent annually on savings. The average annual dividend in 1967 was 4.8 percent.

Credit Unions

A credit union is a cooperative association organized to promote savings among its members and to provide for them short-term consumer loans at relatively low interest rates. At the close of 1967, 19 million people had joined 23,207 active credit unions in this country.[6] Credit unions have actually doubled their membership since 1950.

The average credit union in the United States has an average membership of 822. Most credit unions are small in terms of total assets. At the end of 1967, credit unions held assets averaging $549,360. Most of these assets are in the form of loans to members.

Credit union membership is predicated on a common bond. People who are united by employment, by membership in church or association, or by living in the same well-defined neighborhood can easily operate a credit union because they are usually well acquainted with each other. Employee groups account for 85 percent of all credit union accounts. In the United States, over 32 percent of all credit unions serve employees in manufacturing industry alone, with government employees accounting for over 13 percent of the total.

Compared to savings already listed for competing savings institutions (commercial bank savings of about $166.8 billion, savings and loan of about $124.6 billion, mutual savings of about $60.1 billion), credit unions held only $11.2 billion of the personal savings in all savings institutions in the United States at the end of 1967. Credit unions have actually grown faster than other financial institutions since World War II, but they still own only a small portion of personal savings.

Federal and State Supervision.   The credit union movement in this country began in 1909, when Massachusetts passed the first credit union law. Today, most states and the District of Columbia permit credit unions. The Federal Credit Union Act was passed in 1934, permitting the chartering and supervision of federal credit unions.

There are now over 23,207 active credit unions, with 19 million members, and about half of the credit unions elect federal government supervision. In most states, the state banking commission supervises state-chartered credit unions. All laws treat credit union operations in substantially the same way. Under them, credit unions are strictly regulated, and each one is examined regularly by the government.

[6] *The 1968 International Credit Yearbook,* CUNA International, Madison, Wis., 1968.

Government examination is backed by auditing by an elected committee composed of credit union members. This committee must examine the books, verify member accounts, and check the cash and investments at frequent intervals. Larger credit unions employ public accountants for this auditing.

In many states, credit unions are required to buy surety bond coverage, which protects the credit union against dishonesty and robbery. In many areas, credit unions have banded together to set up a stabilization fund, which is available when needed. Credit unions, unlike some of the other savings institutions, do not have the safety feature of federally sponsored insurance of accounts. Despite this, the safety record has been good.

Bad debt losses have been low and almost always adequately covered by reserves. Credit unions are required to set aside a reserve against losses. Federal credit unions must transfer to the legal reserve 20 percent of each year's net earnings until the reserve equals or exceeds 10 percent of the amount paid in on shares. Furthermore, the treasurer must be bonded. Adequate security is required on all loans over $400.

Surplus funds of the federal credit unions are invested in government securities, in loans to other credit unions, or in shares in federally chartered savings and loan associations. Furthermore, all federal credit unions are examined and supervised by the Bureau of Federal Credit Unions. Funds of a federal credit union must be deposited promptly in a bank insured by the FDIC.

Membership in a credit union is usually obtained by purchasing at least one share, normally for $5. In many instances, employers have a payroll deduction plan for the purchase of shares. Shares of credit unions are not transferable, but they may be repurchased by the credit union. The major use of funds is in consumer lending to their own members. The low true interest rate for 12 months is usually stated as 12 percent for 12 months. In actual practice, the true annual interest rate is slightly under 10 percent.

Comparison of Dividends and Safety. Generally, credit unions pay members the highest returns on their savings when compared with the other institutions mentioned in this chapter. Because almost all loans are consumer loans returning up to 12 percent annual true interest, and because operating costs are low, some credit unions pay dividends as high as 6 percent. Those that charge less than 12 percent interest are able to pay dividends of 4 to 5 percent. A very small percentage of credit unions pay no dividends.[7]

Despite the good record of credit unions, the safety of savings may not be quite as good as in some other savings institutions. But investment in a credit union with a long history of prompt payment may be desirable for a part of one's savings.

In the first section of this chapter, you have seen how savings can achieve financial security for the family. In the opinion of experienced financial advisors this means, first, adequate insurance protection for dependents; sec-

[7] See Bureau of Federal Credit Unions' latest report on operations of federal credit unions. Department of Health, Education, and Welfare, Washington, D.C.

ond, a cash reserve in a savings account or in United States savings bonds; and, third, for some families, a mortgage-free home. Following these, there should be an educational fund for the children and a basic retirement plan through United States savings bonds, annuities, insurance, Social Security, and private pension plans, if any.

You are now in a position to consider investment in other kinds of securities in the hope of getting larger returns on savings. If you have some success in a carefully planned investment program, the time will come when you get the urge to consolidate and conserve what you possess. In that event, you will want to become informed on trust plans and estate planning in general. As your estate grows, it will become increasingly important to make adequate changes in your will. Aside from providing adequate insurance protection for your dependents, making a proper will is perhaps the next most important financial duty a person has to those dependent on him.

INVESTING IN SECURITIES

All investment entails risk. People are not infallible. Various degrees of quality determine whether one is investing, speculating, or gambling. It is difficult, of course, to draw a line separating each from the other because they are bound to overlap. A bond, for instance, is not always an investment. A stock is not necessarily a speculation. Nor can we trust all investment trusts.

Investing Entails Risk

Mark Twain's Pudd'nhead Wilson may have had something for the amateur in the security markets when he said: "April is a particularly risky month in which to speculate in the stock market. The other months are February, December, March, November, May, October, June, August, July, September, and January."

America's favorite, Will Rogers, said: "I'm not so much worried about the return *on* my money . . . what bothers me is the return *of* my money."

An internationally known banker said it this way: "After a lifetime of earning, the man who still has his savings intact, *without any interest,* is indeed a rare and fortunate person."

The following advertisement by the New York Stock Exchange represents an enlightened point of view, coming from within the professional circle.[8]

"I TRIED TO GET RICH QUICK!"

"In my own business, I base my judgment *only on facts*—all the facts I can get. Tips, rumors, and hunches are *out*.

[8] In *Chicago Sun,* February, 1946.

"I don't know why I thought the stock market would be *different.* It's *business,* too—a cross section of *all* business. But, in my dealings there, I tried to take an easy short cut on facts. . . .

"I listened to tips . . . took rumors at face value . . . relied on intuition rather than on information. *I tried to get rich quick.*

"See this headgear I'm wearing now? I put it there . . . no one else is to blame. It's to remind me—'get-rich-quick' promises are *no* substitute for *facts.*"

The man's right!

Precisely the same principles that apply to *any* successful business activity apply to dealings in securities.

There is no short cut to wealth . . . no sure, easy way to make money quickly . . . either on this Exchange or anywhere else.

Tips and rumors—promising great rewards without effort or thought—are merely traps for the unwary, the ill-informed, the heedless.

In investment, there is *always* a degree of risk, whether in stocks, bonds, or *any other* form of property.

RISK—GAIN

Experienced investors *know* this. Before they act, they *get the facts* . . . not to eliminate risk (for it can never be done away with entirely) but to avoid *needless risk.*

Facts *can* be had. Every company whose securities are listed on this Exchange has agreed to disclose essential facts needed to form reasoned investment decisions.

True, it takes seeking to get this information. Facts aren't handy as gossip, on every street corner, but they *are* available . . . in the reports of listed companies . . . on the market pages of your newspaper . . . at the offices of member firms of this Exchange.

Considerations before Investing in Securities

If you contemplate entering the securities field, it is important to discover whether you should be in the investment market at all. Ask yourself the following questions, and give yourself honest answers.

1. Do I have the emotional stability and temperament that is needed when investing in securities, particularly if the value of my securities slides downward?
2. Is the basic financial protection of my family adequately planned?
3. Is there a chance that some of the cash invested in securities may be required for current family needs?
4. Do I need the income from the securities to live on in part or in full?
5. Am I in an unfavorable position in the income tax bracket so that taking additional profits would add too much to my net income?
6. Have I paid in full for the automobile, home, furniture, and so on?
7. Will I have to pay for advice in my investing program, or can I rely on my own information and judgment?

The answers to these questions will help you to make an intelligent decision in regard to whether you should invest in conservative bonds, real estate, or carefully selected stocks, or perhaps establish a trust.

After facing the facts regarding your present status and probable future abilities to maintain the family financial responsibilities through the retirement period, the second consideration is the purpose of your investments. Do you want your investments (1) to yield high income or a steady income, (2) to be sold again to make a profit, or (3) to have a cash or liquid characteristic?

In any purposeful investment program, the aims or objectives should harmonize with individual or family needs and plans. Select securities that will best fit the family objectives.

Basic Investment Principles

The purpose or objective of the investment program can be further clarified by pointing out a few basic investment principles that wise financial counselors have successfully used. In purchasing any stock or bond, *security of principal,* or *safety,* is the most important factor for sound investing. Such a plan as setting up an educational fund for the children, for instance, demands a high degree of safety.

Next in order is *stability of income.* Usually, when security of principal prevails, you will also find little extreme variation from year to year in yield or income. After the children are through school, and when a man feels more inclined to reach for an easy chair than the lawnmower, he becomes more interested in stability than in growth.

The third principle is *growth, or appreciation, of capital.* You should not jeopardize security and stability of income for growth unless you can afford the luxury of a speculative or semispeculative program. Investment for growth of capital is generally not advised for the small investor who is dependent on the income from his securities, except perhaps as a hedge against inflationary prices.

Generally, it is desirable to have a high degree of *marketability* in an investment. This quality, however, is of less importance for personal investments than for the investments of a bank or an insurance company, which may be called on to meet large cash demands. A speculator also must have a high degree of marketability in his investments so that he can sell immediately if necessary. Bonds, as a rule, suffer from fewer marketability opportunities. Real estate may likewise be difficult to sell at the right price during certain periods in the business cycle.

In these days of high income surtax rates, *tax exemption* of securities is important. Some securities, such as state and local bonds and certain kinds of federal bonds, are tax-exempt. Consequently, a person in the higher income bracket should be more interested in tax-exempt securities. There is, however, no magic in a poor security, no matter how tax-exempt.

Freedom from care is a desirable characteristic in an investment, especially if a person is emotionally affected by personal attendance to his investments. By the time a man has accumulated retirement capital, he may want to be free from investment worries.

Diversification is an important principle in any investment program. It is the key to balancing the other investment principles. You must realize that you cannot have income, safety, and growth all at the same time. In investment planning, that old bromide, "You can't have your cake and eat it, too," is very applicable. Any plan will be a compromise in which you must weigh appreciation of capital against security, and yield today against yield tomorrow.

Diversification should be carefully planned. The best financial brains cannot accurately predict the performance of any single investment 5 or 10 years hence. Consequently, no one should place all or most of his investment resources in one or two securities. Diversification can be accomplished by thoughtful selection of industry, company, and type of security. The law of averages can be applied so that a loss or decline in one security or industry is not likely to follow in all the other securities and industries.

Some financial advisors use *geographic diversification*. The theory is that investing in securities of companies in different geographic areas, including foreign countries, serves as a hedge against possible adverse experiences of companies in certain sections. Some large corporations operate all over the world and therefore partially qualify in meeting geographic diversification.

Besides following the above principles of diversification, many financial counselors recommend *limitation of investment*—that is, that not more than 10 percent of the fund be placed in any one industry, and that the amount invested in one security be limited to 5 percent of the fund.

Another way of securing diversification is to invest in the common stock of a well-known sound *investment trust*. Such organizations are established to buy and sell securities of other companies. When purchasing common stock in an investment trust, you share in the profits of a diversified list of companies and obtain the advantage of expert and experienced management. There is a risk, as in all investments in common stock. It is important, therefore, to select the investment trust only after careful investigation. No investment trust is any better than its management.

Get the Facts, Know the Risks

After the major objectives or purposes have been decided, you are in the best position to select securities—some for safety, others for income stability, profit, and liquidity.

Few persons appreciate the difficult problems involved in selecting securities. The following advice is given by Bernard Baruch, one of the most successful stock speculators.

> If you are ready to give up everything else—to study the whole history and background of the market and all the principal companies on the board as carefully as a medical student studies anatomy—if you can do all that, and, in addition, you have the cool nerves of a gambler, the sixth sense of a kind of clairvoyant, and the courage of a lion, you have a ghost of a chance in Wall Street.

Emil Schram, former president of the New York Stock Exchange, once said for newspaper publication:

> People who are unable to judge values or have a competent adviser judge for them have no business in buying securities. Those who scorn factual information and who conduct their operations on the basis of tips, rumors, hunches, and impulses are misusing our facilities. They contribute to market instability and render an absolute disservice to our general economy.

Both these leaders in the investment field emphasize two things: *get the facts, know the risks.* The Securities and Exchange Commission (SEC), the federal body that regulates the stock exchange business, frequently receives complaints from people who, without the facts and without knowing the risks, have purchased certain securities and lost money. Their common complaint is, "Why weren't we protected?"

Facts on securities are available. Much material is on file with the SEC, and information may be obtained from other reliable sources.

A good general knowledge of the nature and performance records of securities and real estate can be obtained from professional people—bankers, brokers, trust company experts, and experienced real estate dealers. These experts, spending full time on this job, are in the best position to keep you informed about possible changes in your investment portfolio due to changes in the business cycle, changing industrial trends, price levels, and many other causes. It is necessary for you to have this information if you are to keep your money in investments.

The average person should complete a savings plan and financial independence plan before he speculates. Do not speculate with these savings. In fact, do not speculate unless you can afford to lose.

The important point is to get the facts and know the risks about the two major classes of securities: bonds and stocks.

Facts about Stocks.   When you buy stock in a company, you become a part owner of the concern. If the business succeeds, it will pay dividends. If dividends are high, you may also profit by an increase in case you sell the stock. On the other hand, if the business fails or does not pay dividends for a considerable length of time, you may lose your entire investment or a part of it.

There are two kinds of stock. The *common stock* does not carry a fixed dividend. In fact, the board of directors need not declare dividends even if a large profit is made, although that is unlikely. This fact adds to the risk. Usually, if profits are large, holders of common stock get higher dividend rates. Likewise, when profits are small, dividend rates decline or are nonexistent. If a company goes bankrupt, its common stock may plunge to zero—no value. The bondholders' claim on the company's earnings and assets come first, then the preferred stockholders' claims. The common stockholders get what is left, if anything.

On *preferred stock,* the return on investment, if one gets it, is fixed and limited. For the last 30 years, preferred stocks of high grade have yielded about

1 percent more income than high-grade bonds. Dividends on preferred stock may be cumulative or noncumulative. Cumulative dividends that are not paid when they should be paid (usually quarterly) accumulate and must be paid, if earnings permit, before dividends can be paid on the common stock. Since the stockholder has no claim for dividends on preferred noncumulative stock, cumulative stock is generally a better buy.

Generally, the return on preferred stock is definite, a stated 4 or 5 percent. In some cases, such as in *participating preferred stock,* the stock is permitted to share in the earnings in excess of the stated rate of dividend. Participating preferred stock is generally a better investment than nonparticipating preferred stock.

Sometimes preferred stock is issued with a conversion feature that permits it to be exchanged for common stock at a given ratio. These are rather popular stocks during an inflation period, when conversion into common stock is possible. *Convertible preferred stock* is generally a better investment than *nonconvertible preferred stock.* Ideally, the best preferred stock to purchase would be a cumulative, participating, convertible stock, but these stocks are rare because of the demand for this type of stock by pension funds, savings banks, and corporate investors. As a result, the price for this stock has increased to a point where the yield is too low for an individual investor. It would be better for the individual to buy "blue chip" common stock instead.

Here is a summary of bonds and stocks evaluated in terms of the three major principles of sound investing.

	SAFETY	INCOME	GROWTH
Common stock	Least	Variable	Best
Preferred stock	Good	Steady	Variable
Bonds	Best	Very steady	Generally steady

Analyzing Industries and Securities.   Industries and companies have important characteristics that make for strength or weakness for investing purposes. These qualities, as a rule, are not so important as the quality of management. Nevertheless, the characteristics of industry and of the companies within each industry should not be overlooked.[9]

Read the best and latest information available. Begin by reading reports and annual guides published by the leading financial services.[10] A weekly publication presents current statistics and market data on leading companies and their securities.[11] The financial sections of newspapers, especially the large metro-

[9] There is valuable reading in the pamphlet *The Background of Investment,* published by the American Institute for Economic Research.

[10] Moody's Investors Service, Fitch Investors Service, and Standard & Poor's Corporation Service.

[11] *Forbes.*

politan press, have articles by financial specialists, and of course, there are financial newspapers and weeklies.[12]

If you live in a large city, consult a reputable brokerage firm, which will have analytical guides for investors that present important, timely, and interpreted information on industries, companies, and securities. If your community does not support a brokerage firm, consult the officers of your bank.

Investment advisory and counseling firms are located in the larger cities. Trust companies, especially in the large cities, have experts available for investment counseling. There are also statistical organizations that analyze general business trends and recommend the purchase and sale of specific securities.

Since the final responsibility for investing your funds rests with you, no matter how much paid or unpaid advice you receive, the kind of information you get and analyze yourself is considerably important.

Some of the important questions to be answered about an industry, such as petroleum, railroads, public utilities, and so on, are these.

1. Who are its customers?
2. What basic factor determines demand for the product or service?
3. Who are its competitors?
4. What threat do they offer?
5. How is the raw material supplied?
6. What is the labor situation?
7. How is the industry likely to be affected by world events?

When you are satisfied that the industry is a good one, the job of selecting a company within that industry begins.

Selecting a Company. At least four important factors should be investigated before selecting a company for investment: its economic position, its management, its financial condition, and the price of its securities.

To analyze the *economic position,* you will need the same kind of information about a company that you would obtain when selecting a good industry. Particular attention should be given to the standing of the company within its industry and to the competition it faces from similar companies.

Management is most important, because you are relying on the managerial skill of others to run the business in which you are investing. This is a hard thing to judge. Generally, you must rely on the published financial reports of the position of the company, its earnings, and so on, to size up the reputation and imagination of the officers and directors.

Financial condition, like management, is different for each company. Once you are satisfied that the industry is sound and the company's standing within the industry is good, your next job is akin to dissection. Take the company

[12] *The Wall Street Journal* (New York, San Francisco, Chicago, and Dallas editions), *Journal of Commerce* (New York and Chicago editions), *Barron's,* and the *Commercial & Financial Chronicle* are among the best current newspapers offering information about securities.

apart and see what makes it tick, according to its financial reports. It is well to keep in mind that the earnings of a company over a period of several years are more significant than the figures for any one year. Moreover, the total figures are of little importance; it is the relationship of the figures that is important. Not total net income, but net income per share; not total current assets, but current assets in relation to current liabilities.

Usually, *price* is the crucial factor in selecting a security, especially common stock. Common stock prices not only vary with the ups and downs of general business conditions but also vary irrespective of earnings. The problem is to discover whether the current price is reasonable in terms of prospective earnings. In deciding the question of price, the answers to the following questions are considered important by financial experts.

1.   What are the prospects of the company in terms of competition and growth?
2.   How does the current price-earnings ratio compare with ratios of typical past years? With that of similar companies?

Stock Market Averages

Sometimes stockholders complain, "Why don't my stocks ever go up like the averages?" The Dow-Jones industrial average, for example, is based on the price of 30 leading stocks, such as Woolworth and Allied Chemical.

When the Dow-Jones industrial average was first compiled in 1896, it had only 12 stocks and was computed by adding the market prices of the stocks and dividing by 12. Later, there were 20 stocks, and the sum of their market prices was divided by 20. But then companies began splitting their stock or issuing stock dividends, and also more stocks were added to the Dow-Jones averages. So today, to get the Dow-Jones average as it is published every day, you divide, not by 30, but by 2.245 (called the "divisor"). The periodically adjusted "divisor" compensates for the changes mentioned above, so the averages reflect more accurately the movement of the prices.

Standard & Poor's publishes a number of averages, including a 425-stock industrial average. This stock average also adjusts to changes mentioned earlier. So does the New York Times Industrials (25 stocks). Actually, the average composed of a few stocks of large, widely owned companies in important industries seems to give about the same price movement as one composed of several hundred.[13]

There are other market averages, such as the "New York Stock Exchange Index," the "American Stock Exchange Index," "Over-the-Counter Industrial Stocks," and others.

Some critics of these averages say they measure activity among "blue chip" (high-quality) stocks of large corporations too much and neglect hundreds of smaller companies. Defenders of the Dow-Jones and Standard & Poor's aver-

[13] *Changing Times,* June, 1966.

ages say this emphasis is proper—not so much because their stocks are high-quality, but because their shares are so widely held by the public.

Is either of the averages better than the other? Actually, the results of the most popular averages run pretty close together as market measures. A criticism often directed by an individual investor is that the averages do not mirror the action of an individual stock. This may be true, but no average can possibly reflect the movement of *all* stocks. There are over 1,600 stocks on the New York Stock Exchange, another 1,000-plus on the American Exchange, more still on other exchanges, and about 14,000 traded over-the-counter and not on any exchange. Many are going up while others are going down at any given time. In fact, some stocks of small companies seem to have a market of their own.

The thing to remember is that all these averages are useful only in comparisons—today's market level with that of some period in the past, the performance of one group of stocks with that of another group. What is important is the averages' long-term upward tilt.

What to Look for in a Financial Report [14]

The average stockholder does not want to grope his way through a forest of figures. Furthermore, there are different kinds of accounting systems. We are not only going to try to find out what the company wants you to see, but what you *need* to see, in a financial report. The top 10 questions to which you want answers about a company are these:

1. What did the company earn?
2. What dividends did the company pay?
3. What does the company own, and what does it owe?
4. How big is the company?
5. How many people work for the company?
6. What are the total sales or revenues?
7. What kinds of services or goods does the company render or supply?
8. Where are the company's plants?
9. Where do the company's raw materials come from?
10. Who audited the figures?

In reading the corporation statement. you need not be an accountant to identify and figure out "current ratio," "operating margin profit," "capitalization ratio," "dilution of stock," "earnings per common share," and "price-to-earnings ratio." This is how you can get the answers from a financial report:

1. Current ratio is concerned with working capital. Does the company have enough working capital? The ratio should be at least 2 (current assets) to 1 (current

[14] One of the best sources that the author knows on this problem is the booklet *How to Read a Financial Report*, published by Merrill Lynch, Pierce, Fenner & Smith, Inc., available from the firm's New York office or its offices in over one hundred other cities.

liabilities) for industrial companies, and less for utilities because they need to carry few inventories. You get the ratio by dividing current assets by current liabilities.

2. The operating margin of profit. A good company increases sales annually and converts from 15 to 30 percent of sales into operating profits. You get the operating margin of profit by dividing net sales minus cost of sales and operating expense by net sales.

3. Capitalization ratio or equity-to-debt ratio. A good industrial firm has a ratio of about 5 to 1, but utilities and railroads may safely have a ratio as low as 1.5 to 1.

4. Diluting of the value stocks may come about by permitting key company executives too large a percentage of stock options. Ten percent would be a high percentage.

5. Earnings per share of common stock. A good company increases in sales and earnings each year. You get the answer by subtracting from earnings the dividend on preferred stock and dividing what's left by the number of common shares outstanding.

6. Price-to-earnings ratio. The Dow-Jones average ratio is about 19. The average ratio for growth stocks is from 20 to 45. A high price-to-earnings ratio might indicate that the stock is overpriced. Overpricing can be justified if earnings have been increasing steadily and the increase is likely to continue. You find the price-to-earnings ratio by dividing market price of a common share by the earnings per share.

Dilution of Earnings. Since 1967, two sets of earnings figures may appear in some companies' annual financial reports. The change stems from a ruling of the American Institute of Certified Public Accountants. Its purpose is to alert investors to potential dilution of earnings facing many corporations, especially those that have pursued aggressive acquisition programs with the use of convertible securities. Standard & Poor's notes, for example, that the potential increase in the number of common shares of aggressive Gulf and Western Industries was 61 percent, assuming full conversion of all convertible securities. Gulf and Western, with estimated earnings of $3.85 per common share, would have estimated earnings at $2.75 per share on a fully diluted basis. Also, if this company's price-to-earnings ratio based on undiluted common share earnings was about 14.5 to 1, its ratio would be about 20.4 to 1 on a fully diluted basis.[15]

If corporations, especially conglomerates (formed by aggressive acquisitions of other companies), follow the recommendation of providing two sets of earnings figures, investors will have a new tool to use in their investment decisions.

Buying and Selling Securities

If you buy securities, you must be prepared to watch them and know when to sell. It is not wise to go into the security-buying game with the intention of putting the securities in a safe-deposit box and forgetting about them. Securities must be watched and worked continuously. There are times when you should unload—sell.

The key to successful investment is keen judgment in *timing purchases and*

[15] Reported in *St. Louis Post-Dispatch*, Aug. 30, 1967.

sales. Consequently, you must either do your own research and play a lone game or find someone to advise you continuously. Admittedly, the job of individual research is almost impossible, but you can study the important sources of financial information and consult with competent, informed persons.

All kinds of people sell investment advice. The professionals range from the honest, studious, objective, and well informed to the tip-sheet operators. Before selecting an advisor, investigate him just as if you were hiring him to operate your business. The Better Business Bureau in your community will at least steer you away from the dangerous financial operators. Your banker or attorney is usually helpful.

The absolute minimum requirement for a securities advisor is that he have a clean bill of health from the Securities and Exchange Commission and from the state department of securities. A good advisor will not be embarrassed if you ask him these questions.

1. How long have you been in business?
2. What are your financial sources?
3. What outside agencies investigate your business?
4. Do you belong to any professional organizations?
5. What are your fees?
6. Have you an interest in the securities that you are advising me to buy?
7. Can you name any local business leaders as references?

Where Securities Are Bought and Sold.   There are thousands of different stocks and bonds—all are called "securities"—but the ones that are bought and sold most frequently are those that are traded on the floor of the New York Stock Exchange. The securities of more than 1,200 major companies are listed on that exchange, which means that they have been accepted for trading there. All buying and selling is usually done between the hours of 10 A.M. and 3:30 P.M., New York time, Monday through Friday. The exchange is closed on Saturday the year round.

The New York Stock Exchange is a voluntary association, established in 1792, and it functions as an open auction market in the Stock Exchange Building in New York City. Functionally, it is an organization consisting of over 1,300 members who have bought memberships (commonly called "seats") on the exchange.

Many of these members represent brokerage firms whose primary business is carrying out the orders of other people—the public generally—for the purchase or sale of securities. They are paid commissions for executing these orders for their customers. To provide service for investors throughout the country, these firms maintain many branch offices.

Buying Unlisted Securities

The New York Stock Exchange, or "Big Board," is the largest formal market for stocks and bonds, but there are thousands of security issues that are not traded on that exchange. Many are traded on 24 other exchanges, such as the

American Stock Exchange (New York City), the Chicago Stock Exchange, and the Los Angeles Stock Exchange.

Still other stocks and bonds are not listed on any exchange. These securities are called "unlisted," or "off-board," securities; they are traded in what is popularly called the "over-the-counter" market. Government and municipal bonds are mainly traded in that market. So are the stocks of most banks and insurance companies, as well as the securities of many big corporations.

By and large, however, unlisted securities are those of small companies that are likely to be better known locally than nationally. They are bought and sold not only by many brokers who are members of the New York Stock Exchange but also by thousands of local security dealers.

Suppose a man in New York owns some stock in an Ohio machinery company and he wants to sell it. He does not know what it is worth because there is no regular market for that stock, and its price is not published in the newspapers, as the New York Stock Exchange prices are in many papers.

He goes to his broker, and the broker may ask for a price quotation by phone or wire from other brokers or security dealers who trade entirely in unlisted securities. He may find that the best bid for the stock is $23, while the lowest that anybody else is willing to sell it for is $25. If the stock is traded frequently, the difference between bid-and-offer prices may be less. If it is almost unknown, the broker may have a hard time finding a market at any price.

In many over-the-counter transactions, the broker or dealer will buy the security himself, or he will sell such a security out of the supply of such stocks that he owns. In such trades, the dealer acts as a principal instead of as an agent, and the customer and the dealer agree on what is a fair *net price*, which includes a return to the dealer in place of a commission. In the end, the dealer may gain or lose on such transactions.

How to Do Business with a Broker

Here is what actually happens when a customer—let us call him Kenneth Smith —enters a broker's office to place an order for 100 shares of Typical Manufacturing Company.

Mr. Smith goes directly to the desk of the man who regularly handles his business (we shall call him John Ross). Ross is registered with the New York Stock Exchange, which means that he is qualified as a man of good character and has passed an examination on the operation of the securities business. He is an employee with the title of "account executive." He is a man who thoroughly knows his business.

Smith might ask Ross for information about Typical Manufacturing and discuss the findings with him. But in this instance, Smith has already checked on the company and knows that he wants to buy 100 shares of common stock. So he gets right down to business.

"What's Typical selling at now?" he asks.

If Typical Manufacturing were one of the major companies, Smith would not have to ask, for he could look at the big electric quotation board that automatically shows the price at which the last previous sale was made. It also shows the high and low prices for the day and the closing price on the preceding day. The quote board provides that information on 1,200 leading stocks, but Typical is not among them.

"Sorry, I don't know the quote," says Ross, "but I'll let you know in a minute." Ross knows he can get the quote by a quick phone call.

While Smith waits, he looks at the screen on which the ticker tape is projected to see if any sales of Typical are being reported then. When a stock is sold on the exchange floor, that transaction is reported on the tape. The price is shown and the number of shares involved in the sale. Because there are so many transactions, it is necessary to use a kind of shorthand, and the various stocks are referred to by initials or combinations of letters, such as C for Chrysler Corporation, CP for Canadian Pacific, and CGW for Chicago Great Western.

"Typical is quoted at 25 bid, 25¼ asked," says Ross in a minute or so. By that he means that $25 a share is the highest price that anyone is then willing to pay for it and that $25.25 is the lowest at which anyone is willing to sell it.

"Shall I place your order at the market?" he asks. A *market order* is one for immediate execution at the best price that prevails when the order reaches the floor of the exchange, regardless of how the price may have changed—up or down a fraction of a point, sometimes more—in the interval between the time the order is placed and the time it can be filled.

Smith agrees. His order is immediately phoned to one of the booths on the floor of the exchange. There one of the floor brokers goes to the trading post at which Typical is bought or sold. There are 18 such posts on the floor of the exchange, and at each of them a certain number of stocks are regularly traded.

At the trading post, the broker asks what the market is. Other brokers with orders to buy or sell Typical Manufacturing make their bids or offers in an audible voice. Secret transactions are not permitted on the exchange floor.

The broker immediately fills Smith's order at the lowest price at which the stock is offered, and Ross is advised by phone that the order has been filled.

The whole operation may have taken only two or three minutes. Smith may still be in the office. If he is, Ross will tell him that the purchase has been completed. If he is gone, Ross will telephone him.

As a matter of fact, most customers are likely to place their orders and handle all their business by telephone. Others do it wholly by mail. It is not necessary for a customer to go to a brokerage office to place an order.

A customer, if he wants, can set the price that he is willing to pay. This is called a *limit order*. Smith might tell his broker, for instance, to buy Typical only if it could be bought at 24½. Further, he might say that any such order is good for a day, a week, a month, or indefinitely. Then if Typical is offered at 24½ within the time that Smith has set, his order to buy is executed, unless there are other similar orders on file that have precedence. Of course, the price of Typical might move up to 26 or 27. In such case, Smith would have lost his chance to buy at 25 or thereabouts. That is why any decision to buy that turns exclusively on the probable gain of a fraction of a point is likely not to be a good decision for most investors.

Limit orders can also be used in reverse—in selling stock. Thus, if Smith owned Typical, he might tell his broker to sell the stock, if he can, at 26.

Round Lots, Odd Lots. One hundred shares—a *round lot*—is the usual unit of trading on the New York Stock Exchange. But that does not mean that a customer can buy or sell only 100 shares at a time. Many people want to buy only 5, 10, or 25 shares at a time. These are called *odd lots*.

Suppose Smith wanted to buy only 10 shares of Typical. When the broker gets that order, it is filled through an odd-lot dealer whose business it is to buy or sell in smaller units than 100 shares. Such odd-lot dealers do business only with other brokers on the stock exchange floor, not with the public. For rendering this service their average charge is about 2½ percent.

Apart from that extra service charge, the 10-share order does not cost any more per share than a 100-share order. On a 10-share order for Typical, Smith would pay the price that prevailed on the next round-lot sale after the broker gives Smith's order to the odd-lot dealer. Suppose the next sale was at $25. Smith would pay $25 per share, plus the service charge for the odd-lot dealer. If Smith were selling the stock, he would sell at $25, less the service charge.

When Smith gets the bill the next day, it will state exactly what he bought, the price, the commission, postage or tax, if any, and total amount due. Brokers do not make a charge for special services, such as research or information, carrying an inactive account, or safekeeping of securities.

After Smith pays his bill—probably by check—he can obtain his stock certificate, which shows that so many shares of Typical Manufacturing Company have been registered in his name.

Brokers' Commissions. The New York Stock Exchange sets minimum commission charges that brokers must use for the purchase and sale of stocks for customers. The following rates prevail for stocks selling for $1 per share and above.

MONEY VALUE OF 100-SHARE UNIT	COMMISSION CHARGE FOR 100-SHARE UNIT
If less than $100	As mutually agreed, about 6%
$100-$399.99	2% of money value + $3 (minimum fee of $6)
$400-$2,399.99	1% of money value + $7
$2,400-$4,999.99	½% of money value + $19
$5,000 and above	$\frac{1}{10}$% of money value + $39 (maximum = $75 for 100 shares)

Odd-lot purchases add ⅛ point (¼ point in shares selling at $55 or above) to the purchase price and subtract ⅛ point or ¼ point from the price when sales are made. The odd-lot differential is $2 more than the round-lot rate with a minimum of $6 for transactions of $100 or more.

Over-the-counter dealers get their fees from the spread between their "bid" and "asked" prices. If a dealer bids $20 and asks $21 for a share, his commission, for the purchase *and* a sales transaction is the one-point spread between the "bid" and "asked" quotations. If a buy *or* sell order is taken by the dealer, his commission is about half of this spread or 50 cents per share.

Monthly Investment Plans. You do not have to be rich to own stocks. If you are budget-minded, you can buy stocks for as little as $40 each quarter or as much as $1,000 a month on a monthly investment plan.

Most brokerage firms that are members of the New York Stock Exchange offer a monthly investment plan. You simply sign an agreement to invest regularly over a specified period and give your choice of stock. You may withdraw at any time. Each time you make a payment, your broker buys full or fractional shares, depending on the cost of the stock and your payment plan. You pay the regular charges for this service. The exact number of shares or fractions thereof will be credited to your account. Dividends are mailed to you or are reinvested automatically if you desire.

Dollar Averaging

One of the advantages of a monthly investment plan is that it offers the opportunity of *dollar averaging*, as illustrated below.

In dollar averaging, you invest the same fixed sum regularly into the same stock or stocks regardless of current price. Your fixed amount of money buys more shares when the stock is low, fewer shares when the stock is high. Dollar averaging over several years results in the average cost of all shares purchased being lower than the average price at which shares were bought. In other words, your cost per share will be below the average of the prices at the separate times you made your purchases.

TABLE 14-4   HOW DOLLAR AVERAGING WORKS

	FIRST QUARTER	SECOND QUARTER	THIRD QUARTER	FOURTH QUARTER
Amount invested	$100.00	$100.00	$100.00	$100.00
Price per share	$ 20.00	$ 25.00	$ 12.50	$ 20.00
Number of shares purchased	5	4	8	5
Total number of shares owned	5	9	17	22
Total invested	$100.00	$200.00	$300.00	$400.00
Average cost per share	$ 20.00	$ 22.22	$ 17.65	$ 18.18

According to the National Association of Investment Companies, over 15 million common stocks have been purchased through over 200,000 accounts since monthly investment plans were introduced in 1954. Over 55 percent of the plans in force are quarterly, and most individuals automatically reinvest dividends. The most popular issues subscribed to under these plans are "blue chips" (good-quality common stocks) like General Motors, American Telephone and Telegraph, Phillips Petroleum, and others. This is a plan for steady investors, not for those interested primarily in day-to-day fluctuations of the market.

Figuring Profits. Investing small sums regularly in good-quality common stocks has great advantages, but there is one hitch. You should know the true annual growth rate, and this is not too easy to measure. As an example, suppose you had invested $10 a month for 52 months, and your holdings are worth $650. Are you better off than if you had put $10 per month for 52 months in a savings and loan association paying 4½ percent? Figure 14-2, Progress Chart for Monthly Investment Programs, will give you the answer.

You will need to know your gross profit and the number of months you have been investing. In this example, you invested $520 for 52 months, and your stocks are presently worth $650, so the gross profit is

$$\frac{\$650 - \$520}{\$520} \text{ or } 25\%$$

Now find this figure on the left side of the chart, and pencil a horizontal line through it. Then, on the bottom line of the chart locate 52 months. Draw a vertical line through this figure. These two lines will cross on, or close to, one of the curves labeled "True annual growth rates." In this case, the lines cross above the 10 percent curve. So the true annual rate of growth is slightly over 10 percent, more than double the 4½ percent you could receive from a savings and loan association.

Commenting on the plan in his book *Wall Street: Men and Money*, Martin Mayer observes that if a small investor put $100 a month for 12 months into the Monthly Investment Plan, he would pay a broker's commission of $67.92. If he had bought the stock in one lump, he would have paid only $14.85 in broker's commissions. If the purchase had been made on the Monthly Payment Plan and the stock had increased in value 15 percent at the end of the first year, the investor would still own stock that was worth less than the cash he had put in. Even if the investor had hit on a stock that paid a dividend of 6 percent, it would take two and a half years for the dividends to catch up with the commissions. For these reasons many brokers are cautious about pushing the Monthly Investment Plan. They will often counsel their customers to save until they have enough money to buy in larger amounts. This is almost certainly sound advice.

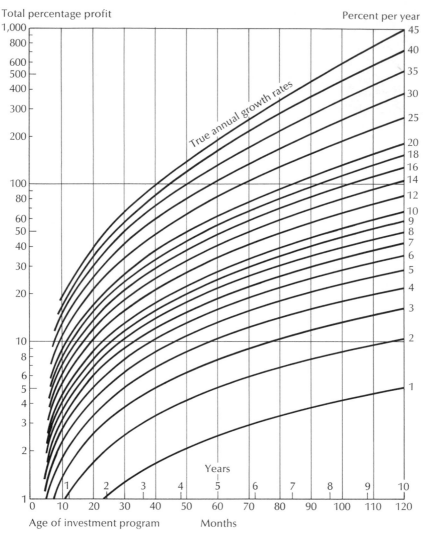

Figure 14-2   **Progress Chart for Monthly Investment Programs. Source: Prepared by Carleton Financial Computation, South Bend, Ind.**

Investment Clubs

Today there are about 50,000 investment clubs in the United States with some 600,000 members and assets over $750 million. Over 10,000 of these clubs (over 100,000 members) belong to the National Association of Investment Clubs (NAIC). According to recent statistics (1968), such clubs have been making their money grow at about 16 percent compounded annually, thus beating the stock market averages.

An investment club is a group of people (usually from 12 to 20) who band together to contribute $10 to $20 a month to a central fund that is invested in securities. Investment decisions are generally made by the members, but many clubs get such guidance from investment specialists. These groups look upon their clubs as a source of profit but, just as importantly, also as a source of education through the pooling of investment knowledge.

To give an idea of how one club works, here is a good example from the Midwest. The club is chartered to take in 25 members. All members serve on the board of directors, which annually elects officers. Each person owns one share of the 25 shares authorized. Each member puts $25 per month in a pool.

The group meets monthly, receives a monthly progress report, and listens to reports on present stocks held and proposed purchases. Discussion follows these reports. Decisions are made by a democratic vote—one vote per member. The treasurer carries out the wishes of the group. Usually, each monthly report is made by a new team of three members. An executive committee is empowered to act on emergency investment decisions that may come up between the monthly meetings.

Caution: It takes expert advice to organize a club. There are state and SEC rules to contend with. A lawyer club member and a connection with a good brokerage firm are recommended.

About 1951 a shrewd investment analyst, George A. Nicholson, Jr., put together the NAIC investment formula, which has worked well. Briefly, the formula is as follows:

1. Invest regularly each month.
2. Reinvest dividends.
3. Invest only in growth companies.
4. Diversify over several companies in different industries.
5. Try for a portfolio that doubles in overall value every 5 years.
6. Mix stocks of small, faster-growing companies with bigger, better-known growth stocks.
7. Buy into companies with good management.
8. Buy at a price that is historically low in relation to earnings.

How well are these member clubs doing? In the last 9 years performance questionnaires received monthly from some 10 percent of member clubs showed that the average compound annual growth rate was 16.04 percent. If these clubs had been putting their monthly contributions into the Standard & Poor's 425-stock Industrial Average, their true annual growth rate would have been only 5.66 percent.[16] In other words, as of 1968, these clubs were doing nearly three times as well as the S & P Average.

The experience of NAIC member clubs is rather revealing. A club is most likely to break up during its first year. The next 5 years are usually frustrating because the total value of their investment per share ($10 per month) is not growing, if at all, and members wonder if it is worthwhile. By the sixth or seventh

[16] *Changing Times,* October, 1968.

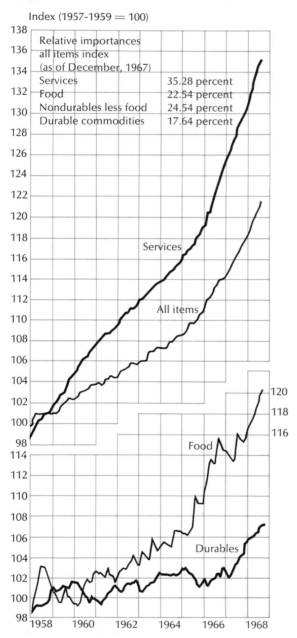

Index (1957-1959 = 100)

Relative importances
all items index
(as of December, 1967)

Services	35.28 percent
Food	22.54 percent
Nondurables less food	24.54 percent
Durable commodities	17.64 percent

Services

All items

Food

Durables

Figure 14-3 Consumer Price Index, Commodities and Services, 1958 to Date by Months. Source: Bureau of Labor Statistics.

year, a $10-a-month club should have a portfolio with $8,000 to $10,000. Almost always, a new club selects some pretty wild stocks in contrast to stocks held by older clubs. Where clubs are likely to go wrong is in trying to trade in and out of the market instead of selecting more carefully for the long pull.

Anyone interested in starting a club would be well advised to get organizational help from NAIC, Department K, 1300 Washington Boulevard Building, Detroit, Michigan 48226.

Should You Buy Common Stocks?

For a whole generation, the cost of living has been rising. Until 1967, it was rising at an annual rate of less than 2 percent a year. But during 1968, the rate had increased over 4 percent, in contrast to a 3.2 percent increase in 1967.

You are likely to have a more meaningful appreciation of the nature of the rapid increase in the cost of living since 1958 if you study Figure 14-3. Between 1958 and near the end of 1968, the cost of living increased to 121.9 (1957-1959 = 100).

Inflationary Trends. Can the inflationary trend be reversed? Most economists are of the opinion that we are likely to have to live with general inflation in the future, too. The question, then, for investors is this: What's the best way to protect my savings against inflation? The general answer is to avoid, insofar as possible, "fixed-dollar" assets such as bonds, savings accounts, and other fixed assets.

Equities, such as common stocks, real estate, art objects, gold, and silver, with their fluctuating prices, usually grow in value at least as fast as, and usually faster than, the purchasing power of the dollar declines. So it makes sense for you to consider how best to protect the worth of all the dollars you set aside for future use.

The possibilities of protection against inflation are many, and each has its own advocates. Investment advisory services, generally, recommend:

1. Buy common stocks of companies that produce labor-saving machinery on the theory that wages are rising abnormally fast and automation is increasing rapidly.
2. Buy common stocks of companies whose earnings are growing each year.
3. Invest in corporations that have large reserves in natural resources—oil, gas, timber, and the like.
4. Invest in gold- and silver-mining stocks.
5. Buy real estate or common stocks of companies that own real estate.

Certainly, you should not plunge into stock markets seeking inflation hedges without forming opinions on the following questions:

1. Is the present rate of inflation going to continue, to increase, or to decrease for a short period because of dampening action by government spending?
2. Have the prices of common stocks been pushed so high that they already reflect future values?

3. What are the chances of tighter credit and higher taxes that will not only dampen inflation but push the economy into a recession?

So, selection of the right kind of common stocks should not only help protect you against inflation, but provide you with a good profit.

Securities and Exchange Commission (SEC)

Congress passed a law in 1933, widely known as the Truth in Securities Act, and then later set up a Securities and Exchange Commission to administer that law.

The SEC requires *full disclosure* of all pertinent facts about any company before permitting it to make a public offering of new stocks or bonds. The company must also furnish a record of profits and losses for the past several years. It must describe all of its outstanding securities and their terms, and list its officers, together with their salaries, bonuses, and stock interests in the company.

If SEC finds the data honest and complete, it gives a green light to the new issue. But this does not mean that it passes judgment on the quality of the securities.

While the SEC "full disclosure" has done much to protect the investor, most investors do not examine the company's "prospectus" on file with the SEC.

Recently the SEC has come in for considerable criticism from both the public and investment firms. There are criticisms in regard to lowering of commissions on stock trading, reduced fees for investors in mutual fund shares, shorter hours for trading, curbs on trading in highly speculative stocks, and speedup in delivery of stock to investors, to mention a few. In the words of one SEC official: "This is the most turbulent era for the security industry since the 1930s." Perhaps few investors would argue with the chairman of the Securities and Exchange Commission when he said, on October 10, 1968: "We must be the voice of the investor, for . . . the investor has no real organized voice."

INVESTING IN BONDS

Facts about Bonds

When you buy bonds of a corporation, a state, or a city, you are lending money to that institution or organization. You are the creditor, and in return for the loan, the institution pledges to pay you a specified amount of interest on specified dates.

Many books have been written about bonds, and the ordinary investor can only hope to acquire a reasonable understanding of principles and various grades of bonds.

There are so-called *gilt-edge bonds,* those usually regarded as the highest grade. The organizations behind them have had a long record of paying interest and principal on time and of earning more than they spend. Such bonds have price stability and are easily marketable. There are also low-grade bonds, those usually issued by organizations that have spotty financial records. Often, the latter grade of bond is issued by comparatively new concerns.

Bonds have various maturity due dates. Those that mature within a few months or years are known as *short-term issues. Long-term issues* will mature late in this century.

Moreover, bonds have a stated rate and an effective rate of return. The *stated rate* is printed on the bond. The *effective rate* is the real return on the bond, and it depends on what is paid for the bond. If the coupon on the bond is 5 percent, and par ($1,000) is paid for the bond, the return will be 5 percent. If a person pays above par, the effective return will be less; if below par, the effective return will be above 5 percent. Thus, a 5 percent $1,000 bond, maturing in 10 years, purchased at 110, would be figured as follows.

$50 minus $10 (premium of $100 divided by 10) equals $40.

$40 divided by 1,050 (1,100 plus 1,000, divided by 2) equals 0.00381, or 3.81 percent.

Consequently, the real or effective return in the above instance would be 3.81 percent and not 5 percent. To compute the exact yield to maturity of bonds purchased below or above par, it is necessary to use a complicated formula. Security dealers use bond tables that have been worked out from the formula. Ordinary citizens should do likewise.

The fundamental principle to remember about bonds is that their income is fixed. The owner of the bond is a creditor who receives interest on his loan to the borrower. Therefore, he cannot share further if the borrower prospers. On the other hand, he does not share fully in the misfortunes of the borrower, because bonds generally have first claim on the assets of the company.

Commercial Bonds.   A commercial bond is a debt of the corporation. Just as well-selected common stocks are good investments from the long-term point of view, commercial bonds (as well as municipals) tend to be relatively assured investments from the short-term point of view; but bonds carry long-term risks because they cannot share further if the company prospers. This is especially serious over a period of years because the cost of living increases but bond yields remain the same. You can, of course, purchase a bond below par and, by holding it to maturity, receive a higher yield than the yield at issue.

In 1968 and early 1969 corporate bond yields were near the highest in a generation or more. Corporate bond yields on selected securities were the highest since early 1967 (Figure 14-4).

Yields on individual corporate bonds were, in fact, higher than the average for top-grade bonds listed in Figure 14-4. Examination of Figure 14-4, comparing yields of individual bonds—corporate, U.S. Treasury, federal agency issues, and tax-exempt—shows that some corporate bonds as of mid-1968 earned over 7 percent.

Ratio scale
of yields

*Monthly averages of daily figures.
†Monthly averages of Thursday figures.

Figure 14-4   Yields on Selected Securities. Source: Board of Governors of the Federal Reserve System and Moody's Investors Service. Latest data plotted: September.

Tax-exempt Bonds (Municipals)

Municipals are issued by states, cities, toll roads, school districts, and similar revenue-producing public bodies. These bonds are tax-exempt. They promise to repay your money at a certain time and to pay a stated rate of interest. Generally, these bonds are highly regarded—most of them are considered second in quality only to U.S. government bonds.

The important question is whether the tax-free income will help you. That depends on your income and your financial reserves. In other words, is your income high enough to take advantage of the tax-exempt feature? Also, do you have sufficient liquid resources so you do not have to cash in the bonds before they are due (generally, these bonds have a face value of $1,000 and some of them are bought and sold only in units of five bonds)?

Generally, you will find municipal bonds fall into four categories:

1. General obligation bonds are backed by the full faith and credit and, usually, the unlimited taxing power of the city, state, county, or district.
2. Limited tax bonds are only partially backed up by the jurisdiction that issued them. Examples are bonds backed by a state gasoline tax or motor vehicle fees.
3. Revenue bonds are secured by income from a specific source, such as toll roads or water, sewer, or gas departments.
4. Housing authority bonds are issued by local public housing agencies. Bonds are paid off by rents and a federal housing agency if a deficit exists.

The markup when you buy or sell municipals is not easy to ascertain. In most cases it is from ¼ to ⅜ of a point. This would be $2.50 to $3.75 per $1,000 bond, or $12.50 to $18.75 for $5,000 worth.

The big question is whether tax-exempt bonds save you anything. Table 14-5 shows you that municipals pay markedly lower interest rates than do taxable bonds. Generally, experts do not recommend tax-free bonds unless you are in the 42 percent income tax bracket or above. That would mean a taxable income, after deductions, of $32,000 for a married person filing a joint return and of $16,000 for a single person. There are exceptions, however. Check Table 14-5.

U.S. Government Savings Bonds. In early 1969, the federal government was issuing only Series E appreciation-type bonds, Series H current-income bonds, and the new Freedom Shares. Series E and H bonds yielded 4.15 percent at maturity, but both old and new E and H bonds yielded 4.25 percent as of June 1, 1968. But you must hold these bonds at least to maturity (7 years) to cash in at 4.25 percent.

Freedom Shares, or United States savings notes, as they are called, were originally issued in 1967 to yield 4.74 percent at maturity (4½ years). There were some restrictions placed on the first issue, but some of the restrictions were removed after June 1, 1968. Freedom Shares now pay 5 percent (was 4.74 percent) if kept to maturity, still a period of 4½ years. Thus, a person paying $81 for a $100 share after June 1, 1968, will at maturity receive $101.16. Previously, Freedom Shares could be purchased only by persons enrolled in a regular program of buying savings bonds. But now you may buy shares on a single-purchase basis at commercial banks, provided they purchase an E bond of the same or larger face value. Both E bonds and Freedom Shares are sold in denominations of $25, $50, $75, and $100.

INVESTING IN INVESTMENT COMPANIES (TRUSTS)

When the Investment Company Act was passed by Congress back in 1940, fewer than 300,000 Americans owned mutual fund shares. Ten years ago there were just 453 registered investment companies and their assets totaled $17 billion. By 1968, there were 967 with about $69 billion in assets. Nearly 4 million people own shares.

TABLE 14-5   WOULD TAX-EXEMPT INTEREST SAVE YOU ANYTHING?

To see whether you would gain anything by investing in municipal bonds, find your top income tax bracket and read down the column. You will find the taxable yields that will net you the same amount as the nontaxable yields on the left. If your money is now earning as much as or more than the taxable-interest figure, you would get no advantage from switching to tax-exempt bonds. The table takes only federal taxes into account. If you would also save on state taxes, you can get a rough idea of equivalent rates by adding your top state tax bracket to your top federal bracket and using the column closest to the combined total.

TOP TAX BRACKET	22%	25%	28%	32%	36%	39%	42%	45%	62%
TAX-EXEMPT YIELDS									
3.00%	3.85%	4.00%	4.17%	4.41%	4.69%	4.92%	5.17%	5.45%	7.89%
3.25	4.17	4.33	4.51	4.78	5.08	5.33	5.60	5.91	8.55
3.50	4.49	4.67	4.86	5.15	5.47	5.74	6.03	6.36	9.21
3.75	4.81	5.00	5.21	5.51	5.86	6.15	6.47	6.82	9.87
4.00	5.13	5.33	5.56	5.88	6.25	6.56	6.90	7.27	10.53

SOURCE: Changing Times, May, 1966.

Why Investment Companies?

Technology, expanding social concepts, and exploding political boundaries have brought rapid and far-reaching changes in many kinds of common stocks and in certain kinds of bonds. Some old industries have their backs to the wall and have to fight for their lives, while new industries spring up almost full-grown.

In short, the essence of life is change; the essence of investment success lies in capitalizing on change. Detecting change and then deciding what course of action to pursue requires considerable research if successful investment is to be maintained. Fortunately for a growing number of investors, such services are offered by modern investment companies.

An investment company or trust is a means of acquiring an interest in a diversified list of stocks. If, as a whole, the stocks go up, you make money. But if they go down, you suffer a paper loss, or a real loss if you sell. Buying shares in an investment company, therefore, does not remove the risk. It just transfers the job of selection to someone else—management. The advantage is that you spread a relatively few dollars over a number of different stocks and bonds and thus diversify your risks. Furthermore, if the company is well managed, these stocks and bonds are selected on the basis of careful research by professional analysts.

How do you select a good investment company or trust? There are aggressive salesmen in this field today, so beware. To select the company or trust most suitable to your needs, use this three-step process.

1. Make up your mind what you want your investment to do for you. Do you want a safe investment that will pay a low but regular return? Or would you rather take more risk in the hope of getting a larger return?
2. Study the performance records and see which trusts have shown the best management. Some of these trusts have had only average management.
3. Check the commissions (called "loading") and other charges to make sure that you are not paying too much for this service. Bear in mind, however, that good management is worth a reasonable brokerage commission and other charges.

Two Kinds of Investment Companies

There are two kinds of investment companies—open-end and closed-end. *Open-end trusts* (called "mutual funds") are those whose shares are redeemable at any time at approximate asset value. These trusts will also sell new shares at any time. Thus, the number of outstanding shares is always changing. There is generally a loading charge of 6 to 9 percent when you buy this type of share; when you sell, you usually receive the net asset value of the shares without deduction or charge. In purchasing mutual shares, the loading charge of 6 to 9 percent can wipe out earnings of 3 to 4½ percent a year for a couple of years. Therefore, never buy mutual shares unless you can afford to keep them for several years. There are a few funds, such as Scudder, Stevens and Clark and Loomis Sayles, both of Boston, the De Vegh Fund of New York, and the Haydock Fund of Cincinnati, that do not have a loading charge at all. As a result, these funds are not popular with brokerage houses.

Closed-end trusts, on the other hand, have a fixed number of shares outstanding. Since these trusts do not issue new shares or redeem old ones, you acquire shares by buying from someone who wants to sell. This is why closed-end shares are sold on stock exchanges or over the counter just as industrial stocks are traded. You pay a regular broker's commission when you buy or sell these shares.

Closed-end shares are affected by the law of supply and demand. They may sell for more than net asset value or for less, depending on demand or popularity. At times, closed-end trusts invest heavily in one company and get involved in its management. So if you want diversification, investigate before you invest.

Both kinds of investment trusts are in the business of investing money entrusted to them by their shareholders. It is difficult to say that one type is better for all investors than the other. There are differences, however, that are worth investigating.

Major Objectives of Investment Trusts

The major objectives of investment trusts are given in the latest edition of Arthur Wiesenberger's book *Investment Companies.* This comprehensive volume covers both open-end and closed-end trusts. Here are some of the major objectives of investment trusts.

1. Long-term growth of capital and income.
2. Long-term growth of capital only.
3. High current income.
4. Stability and dependable income.
5. Concentration on a particular industry, such as Chemical Fund, Inc., Atomic Development Mutual Fund, and the Axe Science and Electronics Corporation.
6. Concentration on a particular type of security, such as bonds or preferred stocks. There are very few such funds. Examples are the Bond Fund of Boston and the Franklin Custodian Funds—Preferred Stock Services.
7. Heavy investment in special situations thought to be undervalued.

So-called *common stock funds and trusts* keep most of their capital invested in common stocks. A *balanced fund* generally keeps about a quarter of its capital in cash, bonds, or preferred stocks. The balanced fund gives more protection against declining prices in return for less profit in a rising market. It is well to remember that when you buy stability or high income, you lose much of your chance for growth of capital. Also, a trust that limits itself to one industry or security sacrifices flexibility. In trusts that invest heavily in special situations, you lose diversification and accept greater risks.

Selecting an Investment Trust

It is important to select a trust with your own investment objectives in mind and one that has a good record. The largest and best known trusts are not necessarily the best. Some trusts appear to be more interested in commissions than in good management and performance. Usually those that do best are the ones in which management has its own money at stake. No one man could own a substantial interest in a trust with a half billion dollars in assets, but some trusts have substantial sums invested by the managers and their families.

An investor buying shares after a long rise in stock prices will probably be paying for past large gains. He himself, therefore, is liable to a capital gains tax without realizing capital gains. The purchase of *closed-end shares at a discount* can partially offset this tax.

If you want the best that investment companies or trusts have to offer, be prepared to study the field. Also, do not use money you will be needing soon. Plan to invest a fixed sum each month. If possible, select a company or trust that has as many of the following characteristics as possible.

1. Investment objectives that fit your own
2. Reasonable acquisition costs and management fees
3. Alert, experienced, intelligent, successful managers
4. An outstanding record in the last 15 years
5. An opportunity to reinvest capital gains and some dividends without payment of commission
6. For most investors, diversification of the investment

When you select a mutual or a closed-end fund, you expect four major benefits:

1. Convenience. You can make a single purchase of stock in a fund, rather than several investments in individual corporations.
2. Diversification. Unless you have considerable capital to invest in individual stocks of many companies, you can buy fund shares that usually have your money invested in over 50 corporations.
3. Management. Management carries the burden of selecting companies and securities for a fee. An efficient fund usually charges $\frac{1}{4}$ of 1 percent of the fund assets. Most of them charge $\frac{1}{2}$ of 1 percent, but some of them nearly 1 percent of the assets. Now there is a move toward incentive fees. If a fund beats the Dow-Jones industrial average (30 different company stocks), management fees might go up to a high of $\frac{4}{5}$ of 1 percent, and when the fund lags behind the Dow-Jones industrial average, the fee may go down to $\frac{2}{5}$ of 1 percent or less.
4. You expect the funds to outperform at least the well-known averages such as the Dow-Jones industrial average.

Do not expect, however, to bat a thousand percent on management and performance.

Management of Funds Companies.   The recent fund boom has produced management of funds companies that have their own shares on the market. For example, Keystone K-2 Growth Fund appreciated 42 percent during 1966-1967, but the stock of its management, Keystone Custodian, soared 97 percent. Putnam Growth Fund shares appreciated 33 percent, whereas the management stock gained 67 percent. So, something new has been added to the selection of funds.

"Go-Go" Funds.   Recently there has been a rather rapid growth in funds seeking maximum or fast annual growth rather than long-term steady appreciation. These are popularly known as "Go-Go" funds. These recent funds invest in volatile securities and lesser-known companies in order to achieve immediate, large capital gains. [17]

When considering a fund to purchase, keep in mind that fast growth often entails increased risk. A fund aiming at "maximum performance" does not necessarily do any better than less aggressive funds.

Performance.   Should you invest in investment trust funds? If some of them perform well, you will get a good return; if performance is mediocre or poor, you will not be happy. Most funds do not have a satisfactory performance record over 10-year periods. Then how do you select a fund from the present list of about 967 funds? It is difficult. Balanced funds, for example, did not match the Dow-Jones industrial average from 1958 to 1968. On the other hand, 39 growth stocks and 94 stock funds outperformed the Dow-Jones industrial average in the last decade. [18]

In 1968 a relative handful of funds could boast having a good performance record. Out of 967 funds in 1968, 285 funds did better than the rather low performance (4.3 percent gain) of the Dow-Jones industrial average, and 237 of these 285 funds excelled the 9.4 percent climb of the New York Stock Exchange composite common stock index in 1968. The best performance in 1968 was that of the 123 funds that bettered their own mutual fund average gain of 18.27 percent, as computed by the Arthur Lipper Corporation.

It was a good year, however, for the smaller, newer growth funds. Twelve of the top 50 gainers in 1968, such as Neuwirth and Mates Investment, were not even in existence in 1967. And some of the biggest, best-known growth funds, such as the Manhattan Fund, Investors Fund, Fidelity Capital, Channing Growth, Diversified Growth, and Massachusetts Investors Growth, were at the bottom of the 1968 performance. The newer funds, however, had a poor performance in the first half of 1969.

[17] See *Fund Scope,* a monthly magazine, and *Forbes* magazine for periodic current performance records of these funds.

[18] See Hugh A. Johnson, *Johnson's Investment Company Charts,* Hugh A. Johnson, Buffalo, N.Y.

Picking the Right Trust. It is difficult to select the right trust funds. Here are some points to keep in mind:

1. You are paying for management. If management is not good, you are in trouble.
2. Check on the size of the sales charge and the management fee.
3. Do not conclude that the oldest, biggest, and best-known funds are the best.
4. Look at the long-time performance (at least 10 years) when you select a fund. Why pay 5 to 9 percent commission for a 1-year deal?
5. In checking performance, be sure to take into account the capital gains that have been paid out.
6. Investigate new management company funds mentioned earlier.
7. Do not neglect to study the "closed-end" funds, such as Tri-Continental, U.S. & Foreign Securities, Dominick, and others. Oftentimes, you can buy these at a considerable discount.
8. The Securities and Exchange Commission has recently been critical of the funds and has made proposals for far-reaching changes which may be debated by Congress if the funds do not correct high sales commissions, outlaw "front-end load" where sales commissions absorb about 50 percent of an investor's first-year payments, and bring down too high advisory or management fees.

INVESTING IN REAL ESTATE

"They are making more people, but they are not making any more land." This remark may explain why more and more people are investing in land and buildings. To house our growing population, we have been building houses and apartments at a rapid rate. On top of housing demand, we are consuming more recreation areas, and industrial and government uses of land are increasing—including acre-devouring highways and airstrips. The result? An ever-continuing land boom. Why, then, is real estate not a sure-fire investment? Real estate "as a whole" will rise in value over the years. As a practical matter, you do not invest in real estate "as a whole." You have to make a selection of a particular piece of real estate, which involves location, price, terms, taxes, mortgage, seller, lender, agent, and so on. If you have the patience to learn, to secure facts, and to seek professional advice, you are likely to have success. But you should know that real estate investing is usually more difficult than investing in stocks. Within a short time you can get most of the information you need about a stock. To get a comparable perspective on a piece of land or a building, you may have to spend many days digging out all the facts. Real estate, as a rule, cannot be sold readily in case one needs cash. Also, a building is tied to one location. A change in the area, such as relocating of a road or highway, can result in depreciation of the value of the investment. Finally, real estate usually consumes a large amount of cash—$5,000 to $10,000 or so—and this makes it hard, for small investors in particular, to spread the risk over several situations.

To offset these disadvantages is the fact that many real estate investments make a good profit, some of which may be tax-free.

Where to Begin

Most people start with the purchase of a home for their family. Most homes purchased for family use are not likely to produce a net gain as an investment. However, if you are fortunate enough to buy for your family a home that will sell fast, if you make a small down payment, if you obtain a no-penalty mortgage in case you pay off in advance, if the house does not need much fixing-up, and if there is considerable inflation in real estate, you *might* make some profit. There are, however, many ways to make a good profit in real estate.

Real Estate Opportunities

Here are a few opportunities for alert investors in real estate:

1. Leverage.   Raw land is jumping in price on the edges of many cities, small and large. Raw land in the path of development can be purchased by the acre. With a relatively small amount of cash you can control a much larger investment by using leverage. You can usually buy raw land with about 20 to 25 percent down. That gives you "leverage," and this is what it means:

Say you buy a lot for $1,000 cash and sell it a year later for $2,000. There is not much profit in that deal. On the other hand, if you arranged a 20 percent down payment—$200—and paid $25 a month toward the purchase, at the end of the year the amount you put down ($200) plus 12 months of $25 payments ($300) adds up to a $500 total investment, plus interest cost, instead of $1,000. If you sold the lot for $2,000, you could pay off the balance owed on the land and still have a profit with only about half the investment. By using "leverage," your percentage of profit would have roughly doubled.

2. Taxes.   When raw land is sold, if it has been held over six months, the profit is generally subject only to the capital gains tax—about one-half of the ordinary rate, with a maximum tax of 25 percent, not counting the surtax.

It is also possible to further reduce the immediate tax on the sale of the land if the owner receives less than 30 percent down payment on the sales price in the year of the sale. Then he can spread his capital gain over the life of the installments and pay his tax in smaller amounts over the years.

3. Prepaid interest.   If the seller will accept prepaid interest, there will be good tax benefits. The initial down payment, consisting of prepaid interest, is deductible in the year paid, even if it is paid several years in advance. Thus, land can be purchased with money that would otherwise go for income taxes. And the higher your tax bracket, the more you benefit.

There is a danger, however, in case the land does not appreciate fast enough to cover the annual interest cost, property taxes, and other expenses.

4.   Inflation hedge.   Undeveloped land offers a growth potential that can outstrip losses in the dollar's purchasing power. Well-selected land will keep your investment well ahead of inflation.

Real Estate Investment Trusts (REIT)

Investors of modest means can share in the ownership of real estate through a real estate investment trust. A REIT is similar to a mutual fund, except that the holdings consist of real estate rather than stocks and bonds.

The first REITs were organized in the middle 1880s in Massachusetts. With the large increase in corporate profits in the 1930s, REITs (which were taxed as corporations) waned as an investment. In 1960, however, Congress passed a law which provided that justified REITs will be exempt from federal taxes on that portion of the income distributed to their shareholders if 90 percent or more of the ordinary income is so distributed. The second important requirement is that the trust must derive 75 percent of its income from real estate assets, such as apartments, shopping centers, office buildings, and nationally based business sites. Usually the annual operating costs, including trustee compensations, are limited to $1\frac{1}{2}$ percent of the net assets. Another rule is that they cannot invest more than 5 percent of the assets in undeveloped land. And no one person can own more than 10 percent of the shares.

Since the passage of the federal law in 1960, some 60 new REITs have sprung up in the country. Most of the shares were originally offered at from $5 to $10 each. In due time, the shares may be active enough to be sold over-the-counter and on the regular stock exchanges.

What's the Attraction?   If successful, REIT investments pay out a higher and more stable income (5 to 9 percent) than is offered by common stocks (averaging about $3\frac{1}{2}$ percent). There is a good possibility that some income may be tax-free. The attractive tax-free possibility centers on the "depreciation reserve." The Internal Revenue Service allows money to be put into a "depreciation reserve" tax-free. This reserve, theoretically, is built up so that eventually money will be available to replace the building.

Assume the land and building were purchased for $1 million, with cash payment of $400,000, a 6 percent mortgage on the $600,000 balance, annual payments of $45,000 on mortgage, rent income of $100,000 a year, and a total operating cost of $19,000 as shown in the table on page 488.

You can see from this example that a property that made no profit paid no income tax, but was able to return to its owners a 9 percent return on a cash investment of $400,000. If a tax loss could be established, the gain would be greater.

PROFIT AND LOSS FOR INCOME TAX PURPOSES

Rent income		$100,000
Expenses	$36,000	
Depreciation, 5%	45,000	
Operating expenses	19,000	
Total expenses		$100,000
Net profit or loss		0
Cash flow		
Rent		$100,000
Cash disbursements:		
Mortgage	$45,000	
Operating expenses	19,000	
Total expenses		$ 64,000
Balance for distribution		$ 36,000

Appraisal of REITs. In appraising these trusts it is well to keep in mind that real estate is a business built on borrowed money and wise use of depreciation and amortization, and that properly located land and buildings become more valuable as the country grows. REITs are more closely controlled by federal and state laws than ordinary real estate stocks. The true value of REITs is yet to be tested, but they have survived since the 1961 federal act mentioned earlier and are already rewarding many people who desire higher income. It is well to remember that the quality of a REIT is no better than its management.

ESTATE PLANNING: WILLS, TRUSTS, AND TAXES

To many, "estate planning" is exclusively a rich man's problem. Actually, however, anyone who owns a home, a normal amount of life insurance, and a few shares of stock can probably benefit his family by seeking professional advice. In the case of a father of minor children, an integrated financial plan, including a properly drafted will, is almost essential to prevent the hardship of unnecessary administrative expenses, forced sale of assets, and inflexible use of resources.

Since legal advice and drafting of legal documents such as wills and trusts are usually necessary to fulfill any estate plan, most of such planning is done by lawyers, although trust officers of banks, accountants, and life insurance agents are often helpful in working out solutions. And recently there have grown up firms, operating on a fee basis, devoted entirely to estate planning for those with sizable estates.

Regardless of which of these professionals is consulted first, the process of analysis is basically the same. The planner must analyze his client's existing assets and sources of income, together with his family responsibilities and goals. Then he examines the probable results if his client should suddenly die. If the results would fall short of the client's expectations, the planner will suggest one or more methods whereby estate shrinkages or other problems can be avoided.

Disposing of Your Estate

There are seven methods by which you may dispose of your estate. The first four are ways of disposing of your estate upon your death. The other three are ways of disposing of it during your life.

1. Disposing of your estate at death.
    a   You may neglect to make a will or otherwise dispose of your estate, in which case the law will dispose of your estate.
    b   You may put your property in the joint names of yourself and some other individual (your wife, husband, sister, son, etc.).
    c   You may make a will which provides for outright distribution of your estate to your beneficiaries.
    d   You may make a will which leaves all or a part of your estate in trust.
2. Disposing of your estate during your life.
    a   You may dispose of all or part of your estate *now* by placing it in a *revocable* living trust.
    b   You may dispose of all or part of your estate *now* by placing it in an *irrevocable* living trust.
    c   You may dispose of all or a part of your estate *now* by making an outright gift.

The Necessity for Making a Will.   A will is the means by which you can definitely and positively direct the economical and orderly disposal of your estate to persons of your own selection. You should make a will as soon as you are married or whenever you have dependents. Furthermore, your will should be kept up to date.

Do not be among the 70 percent of those who die in this country without a will. Modern young people should face the necessity of making a will as part of their family objectives and financial security goals. Replace any unpleasant thought of death of the testator by the happier thought of providing for those you love who will go on living.

When a person fails to make a will—that is, dies *intestate*—an administrator is appointed by the probate court to distribute the estate to the heirs of the *decedent*—the person who has died. Usually, problems of heirship arise to plague everyone. Jerome K. Jerome has said that if a person dies leaving a will, then all his property goes to whoever can get possession of the will; but if a man dies without a will, then all his property goes to the nearest villain. Jerome was exaggerating somewhat. Each state, however, has a different law of descent. If a person dies without a will, his real estate in one state will go to one set of heirs, and to another set in another state.

If a man in Illinois fails to leave a will, for instance, the law will divide his estate. If he leaves a wife and children, the wife will get only one-third of the estate; the other two-thirds will go to the children. If the children are minors, their inheritance becomes involved in guardianship proceedings. If he leaves a wife and no children, the wife gets all the personal estate, but only half of the real estate. The balance of the real estate will be divided among the wife's parents, brothers, and sisters. If he leaves no wife or children, the entire estate goes to the parents, brothers, and sisters. If no survivors exist, the estate will go to the county, nothing to charities.

Legality of Wills. Most states will give some protection to a man's wife against his creditors and the handing over of certain properties to other people. Certain kinds of property, usually the home, are exempt from creditors forever or for several years, depending on the state law.

Each state determines the qualifications of a person eligible to make a will. In the first place, each state requires that the person reach a minimum age. In some states, such as Massachusetts, the minimum age for either sex is 21. In a few states, the minimum age for the male may be 21 years and for the female only 18 years. In addition, some states prescribe a lower age for personal property and a higher age for real property.

Another requirement provided for in the laws of the various states pertains to having a sound mind and to acting on one's own volition, free from undue influence. The question is a technical one. Wills have been contested successfully and unsuccessfully on the basis of competence to make a will. The courts have usually held that a testator is of sound mind if he is capable of understanding what he has written into the will. If he fails to provide for near relatives without any rational explanation, the will may be inoperative. In cases of disinheritance, it is therefore important to name names and give reasons.

Wills made on deathbeds or when the testator is very ill are vulnerable to attack. No one should take this chance. Make a will when you are in good health.

Writing your own will. The greatest creator of litigation is the man who believes he has sufficiently mastered the technicalities of drafting a will and writes his own will. It is said that St. Ives, the patron saint of lawyers, extends to none a heartier welcome in the life beyond than to the so-called "lawyer's best friend," the Jolly Testator Who Makes His Own Will!

Contests over wills may go on for years. You remember the famous will contest of *Jarndyce v. Jarndyce*, recounted by Charles Dickens in *Bleak House.* It will bear rereading. We are told, incidentally, that Dickens himself was a little bitter over the time consumed by some necessary litigation in his own life.

Essentially, a will is a legal document. It is advisable, therefore, that a good attorney be hired to draw it. A will need not be long. Lawyers have sample forms available. Many good wills do not use the standard forms provided for such purposes. Well-known Americans have drawn wills in only one or two sentences.

Formalities of Making a Valid Will. Certain formalities are to be observed in making a valid will. In the first place, hire a good lawyer who is capable of advising you properly. He will draw up a will that will do exactly what you—the testator—intend. In most states, the following factors are necessary in making a valid will.

Signature. The will must be signed by the maker or testator. If the will covers more than one page, the testator usually signs each of the pages. It must be signed in the presence of the witnesses. The signature should be exactly as written in the body of the will. Wills have been thrown out of probate courts because the name was incorrectly spelled in the signature of the maker of the will.

Witnesses. Most states require two or three witnesses. It is wise to have younger persons, but of legal age, act as witnesses. If the wife or the beneficiary of the will or the spouse of a beneficiary acts as a witness, such persons may be disinherited. The will should state that all witnesses signed in the presence of each other. The addresses of all witnesses should be included in the document. Even if the state requires only two witnesses, it is generally wise to have three witnesses in the event that one dies before the will is probated.

Alterations. Do not take a chance on a will being voided because of alterations or erasures. It pays to have the entire will redrafted. As a rule, witnesses do not read the will. They usually are present only at the signing of the document. If called to testify later on with regard to alterations or erasures in the will, most witnesses would be unable to state whether the erasures existed at the time of the signing.

Terms. In addition to making the will legal, care should be taken so that the will distributes the properties in the way desired by the testator. This is not difficult in a simple case but becomes technical in the event of an involved will. The first step in making a will is an appraisal of the properties or the entire estate. Careful estimates of estate shrinkage from taxes, administrative costs, and immediate expenses should be made. Provision for meeting such expenses by the use of life insurance is an excellent idea. After expenses have been cared for, the disposal of the estate is next on the agenda.

Disposal of an Estate. If a will is to do exactly what the maker wants it to do, expert advice is necessary. For example, if the testator has contacts in two states, perhaps an apartment in New York, though his principal business is in another state, it is possible that both states will want inheritance taxes after his death. Such double taxation has been upheld. The heirs to the Campbell Soup fortune could tell you that Pennsylvania and New Jersey each took $15 million—just out of one little can of soup!

Also, out-of-state real property needs to be handled carefully. Usually, it is wise to get rid of such real property or place it in a revocable trust. In this way, the property will be taxable to the estate but will not be a part of it, thereby eliminating a substantial estate expense.

Some lawyers include in wills a direction to pay debts. This has little meaning, since all debts must be paid anyhow. And it may be harmful because the direction to "pay all my just debts" means all debts, moral and legal. There is no point in inviting a lawsuit.

In making gifts, use fractional parts of the estate rather then fixed amounts or particular items. If a son is willed $25,000 and the rest (say, $100,000) is willed to the wife at the time an estate is worth $200,000, and death occurs without the will being changed, the estate may have shrunk to $35,000. The son, in most states, will still get $25,000 and the wife the remainder—$10,000. Worse yet, the tax comes out of the residue.

Joint wills between spouses, as a rule, are undesirable, because they have the effect of preventing revocation without notice during the life of both parties and any revocation of the survivor.

Another important factor in drawing up the terms of a will is the determination of the portion of the estate that will bear the taxes. In some states, the taxes are paid out of the residue of the estate, which is the portion remaining after special gifts. Gifts in contemplation of death are taxable but are never a part of the estate itself. The point is to be careful so that the residue, which is so often left to the wife, is adequate. One method of accomplishing this purpose is to require the insurance beneficiaries to pay their share of the taxes and that each devisee or legatee bear his pro rata part. Exactly what should be done depends on the particular estate and the law pertaining to these matters.

If the testator, for instance, has provided $500 a month for his wife by certain insurance options, federal laws require such insurance to pay its pro rata share of the estate tax unless the will provides otherwise. The effect of this may be to reduce the widow's income to $375 a month, which is less than the husband considered adequate. Consequently, the tax apportionment clause should be drafted as a part of the estate plan so that the benefits of the legacies will be carried out as intended.

Duties of the executor. An independent executor should be designated and given as broad powers as the trustee. If the testator, for example, got a loan commitment from the bank so that ready money would be available for taxes, which must be paid in cash, then the executor should be given the power to draw on this money. It may be wise to require the beneficiaries to join in the execution of the notes, at least to the extent of the properties they will receive from the estate. This power makes borrowing much simpler.

Another requirement is early distribution of the estate. Income taxes can be saved in this way. The executor should also be under no duty to post bond— it saves expense. He should be given discretion about whether or not the estate income should be paid during the executorship. This power will mean substantial income tax savings for the family.

Whether the executor is a person or a corporation, the major qualifications are (1) ability and experience in business; (2) financial responsibility; (3) some knowledge of accounting; (4) experience in administering estates; (5) adequate facilities for safekeeping of securities, correspondence, and the like; and (6) time to do a good job.

It is customary to name a member of the family or a close friend of the family as the executor. Under certain conditions, such persons may be satisfactory. The fee of an executor or trustee is fixed by law or by court and is the same for individuals as for corporations, though the individual may waive the fee. Therefore, it is generally wise to select the best person or corporation.

The administration of an estate is a highly specialized business. An inexperienced person must hire a lawyer to do the work for him. These are some of the things that an executor must do.

1. File the will in the probate court.
2. Select and retain legal counsel. It is usually customary to name as counsel for an estate the lawyer who drew the will.
3. Aid the attorney in presenting to the court an application for letters testamentary, the oath of the executor, and proof of the legal heirs.
4. Assemble, take possession of, and safely hold all personal assets.
5. Withdraw bank deposits; locate and assemble securities; arrange for collection of interest and dividends.
6. Collect all debts due to the estate—through litigation, if necessary.
7. Take charge of real estate, if the will so provides; ascertain status of taxes and mortgages against the property; inspect the condition of the property; provide for management and collection of rents.
8. If life insurance is payable to the estate, file the necessary papers, collect on all policies, and determine what to do with the proceeds.

A Common Disaster Clause. Simultaneous deaths (such as the death of a husband and wife in one accident) are not uncommon. In the event there is no will, all the property would pass to the children, if any. If there were no children, there may be a legal battle over which person died first. If the court had evidence that the husband died first, and if the wife had a will, this property would be disposed of according to her will. In the absence of a will, any property she left would go to *her* relatives.

Many inequities result from simultaneous deaths. Therefore, a will should provide for the disposal of the property if both husband and wife die in the same accident. A common disaster clause may read: "Any person who shall have died at the same time as I, or in a common disaster with me, or under such circumstances that it is difficult to determine which died first, shall be deemed to have predeceased me." In case there is only one bequest, to the wife perhaps, and in case she does not survive the testator, the property may be left in the will to a daughter or son, or to both of them. This is a useful clause in cases of common disaster.

Letter of Last Instruction. Your executor or lawyer should have a letter of last instruction that is not a part of your will. This letter is usually opened at death and contains the following information.

1. Exact location of will.
2. Instructions about funeral and burial. Veterans should remember that they may request burial in a national cemetery and save their estate some expense.
3. Location of all documents, such as birth certificate, Social Security card, marriage certificate, discharge papers, and the like.
4. Lodge or fraternal membership certificates.
5. Location of all safe-deposit boxes.
6. List of insurance policies and where deposited.
7. Pension statements and records.

8.   List of all bank accounts, stocks and bonds, real and other property, and their locations.
9.   Instructions concerning a business, if any.
10.   Statement of reasons for disinheritances, if any.

Wills Should Be Reviewed.   Many persons hesitate to draw a will, feeling that such a document, once executed, exists for all time. Nothing is further from the truth. A will is operative and binding only at the date of the maker's death. Before death, you can make any number of wills, each of which in succession should include terms that revoke and cancel all prior wills. Or you may supplement or modify an existing will by the addition of a *codicil,* which is an amendment to a will. Whenever your family or financial conditions change, a new will should be made to meet the new conditions.

You should reread and reconsider your will each year, or oftener if necessary. A will that may be just at the time of its making may be very unjust a few years later. Take the case of a single man, the sole support of an aged and widowed mother. He marries, dies by an accident, and his wife survives. His estate consists solely of personal property of a substantial sum. When he executed his will, he was engaged to marry the woman he later did marry, but no mention was made of her in his will.

Unfortunately for the mother in such a case, the law in Illinois provides that a will executed prior to the testator's marriage is revoked by the marriage. The decedent's mother would not receive any of the estate, since it consists solely of personal property and belongs to the widow in its entirety under the law.

The moral is obvious. Review your will at least once a year in the presence of your attorney. If you are married, both husband and wife should review their wills together. There may have been changes since a year ago in the size of the family, in residence, or in tax laws. The kindest thing to do for dependents and loved ones is to be sure that your will follows your intentions.

Where to Deposit a Will.   After you have executed a will, the safest place for deposit is with the trust company you may have named as executor or in a safe-deposit box. As a safe-deposit box may be sealed for a while after death, it is preferable to place the original will with the trust company and to place the receipt for the original will and a copy of the will in the safe-deposit box. Most banks make no charge for the safekeeping of wills in which they are named as executor or trustee.

Taxation of Estates

Since the tax burden is a factor of great importance in planning the disposition of an estate, consideration of estate taxation is a desirable preliminary to estate planning. The tax burden upon an estate depends upon the value of the assets that are included in the estate for tax purposes and upon the rates of taxation. The property includable in an estate for tax purposes is the following:

1. All property in the name of the deceased.
2. Property in joint names, except to the extent that the surviving owner can show that his or her funds purchased the joint property.
3. Insurance on the decedent's life which he owns.
4. Gifts (either outright or in trust) made by the decedent during his lifetime, if such gifts were made within three years of death and in contemplation of death or if the decedent retained any interest in or control of the gift.
5. Property in respect to which the decedent had a taxable power of appointment (the right to dispose of the property by his will or by deed).

From this total may be deducted the decedent's debts, executor's fees, other costs of administering his estate, the "marital deduction" (50 percent of the net estate), and the $60,000 estate tax exemption.

Trusts

With your objectives clearly in mind, analyze your current and expected future assets, then consider how to best conserve those assets and pass them on to your family with the least amount of shrinkage. Many people rely solely on life insurance for an "instant estate," but in many cases other solutions may be available to the prudent family.

Today more families are turning to trusts, in one form or another. Even if you bequeath no more than $25,000, a trust can provide many benefits. In fact, a trust is the most flexible instrument in estate planning. Essentially, it is an arrangement whereby property is legally transferred to another person, bank, or trust company (the trustee) who handles it for you or your beneficiaries.

Life Insurance Trust.   A young couple in their 30s, for instance, can start an estate easily with a "life insurance trust." This is administered by your bank or other trustee, not an insurance company. In this elastic program, a trustee is named to manage the insurance proceeds after death for heirs inexperienced in handling large sums. They then will receive both income and principal as needed.

Funded Trust.   If the estate is set up as a "funded trust," other assets (such as securities) can be coordinated with the insurance to receive the same expert management. Such a trust does not have to be mentioned in a will or go through probate. Estate administration expenses can be reduced considerably and taxation can be averted; that is, taxes need not be paid first by the wife and then again by the children who inherit the same funds from her.

Testamentary Trust.   You can have a trust tailor-made for you. Under a will, for example, you can create a "testamentary trust" to make certain your property is managed expertly and used as you desire. The trustee—usually a bank— is given broad investment powers, with directions for paying income and principal to your heirs.

Living Trust.   If you want to control your assets during your lifetime, consider the increasingly popular "living trust." With this legal instrument, you can make the income payable to yourself while you are alive or have it reinvested for your future benefit. This type of trust will not be subject to probate.

In an emergency, you can withdraw part or all of the money from the "living trust." At your demise, the trust can be continued for other members of your family. It has all the advantages of a will with none of the shortcomings (disappointed relatives rarely will challenge it). Nevertheless, you should have a will, too.

A "living trust" can be revocable—can be altered or canceled at any time— but this type is subject to estate taxes. You can, however, make the trust irrevocable, unchangeable for a specified term. Here, taxes on income are at the lowest rates. Often, the federal estate tax can be bypassed or substantial savings made by removing assets from the estate.

When a "living trust" is handled by a bank as trustee, you also have experienced investment management at a modest cost. If you become seriously ill, the trustees can pay the bills for you. Settlement of the estate is simplified and no delays are incurred. For minor children in a family, the "living trust" can provide guardianship protection.

Budget Trusts. Lately, a number of banks have introduced what may be called "budget trusts," which permit people of modest means to build year by year for their family's future. Under one such plan, you begin with an investment of $100, then follow with monthly installments as low as $25.

Some Drawbacks. Sure, trusts have some drawbacks. An irrevocable trust ties up property you may need later. Amending a revocable trust yourself, without the guidance of professionals, can foul up the arrangement. Attorneys and bank trust officials usually recommend extreme flexibility, so that you do not run into complications.

Some Advantages. Is estate planning worth all the thought and trouble? Just look at the federal taxes. If you have a total estate, including life insurance, of $150,000 or more, $16,000 can be saved in federal estate taxes alone for the ultimate benefit of your children after the death of your surviving spouse. To do this, consult your attorney and develop an estate plan that will take full advantage of the so-called marital deduction.

Most states also have inheritance taxes. Here, again, proper planning can result in important savings. In some states, for example, life insurance payable to your spouse or any specific beneficiary (other than your estate) is exempt from state inheritance taxes.

Using Gifts to Save Estate Taxes

Let us consider a widow with one son. The mother intends to leave all of her assets to her son. Her taxable estate is $300,000. Her estate tax on $300,000 will be $62,700. Let us assume she makes a gift of one-third of the assets. Here is how the gift tax would be calculated.

Gift	$100,000
Less annual exclusive	3,000
	$ 97,000
Less lifetime exemption	30,000
Subject to tax	$ 67,000
Tax	$ 8,595

This gift has dimished her estate by $108,595 ($100,000 gift, plus $8,595 tax). The taxable estate is now $191,405. Her estate tax on $191,405 will be $30,121 (before state inheritance tax credit). Compare the tax effect on the gift:

Estate tax—no gift	$62,700
Estate tax on $191,405	$30,121
To which add gift taxes paid	8,595
Total taxes	38,716
Saved her son	$23,984

Cost of Settling an Estate

The exact sum that will be spent to settle your estate depends upon whether all or part goes to a wife or husband, whether property passes by will, trust, or joint ownership, the kind of property, and other factors. Table 14-6 gives a rough guide showing average payments for estate taxes and expenses. The estate-size figure represents the value of the property left, minus debts and the $60,000 tax-free exemption. "Other expenses" include court costs, fees to accountants, and other costs.

The total cost of settling an estate is more than many people realize. This is why estate experts strongly recommend capable legal advice when making a will. It may be that trust funds will be recommended. As we have pointed out earlier, there are important tax gains and other advantages of trusts. The fees for trustees in carrying out the instructions of the trust or trusts are not as large as some people imagine.

Fees for Trustees.   There are no standard fees for trustees. The amount depends on state law. Generally, fees are a percentage of the trust's income or capital, or both. In New York State, for example, the trustees' annual fee is limited by law to ½ of 1 percent on the first $50,000 of capital, ¼ of 1 percent on the next $450,000, and ⅒ of 1 percent on anything over $500,000. Also, there is a charge of 1 percent on any principal paid out of the trust fund. There may be other expenses incurred by the trustee that would be charged to the trust fund.

TABLE 14-6   THE COST OF SETTLING AN ESTATE

SIZE OF ESTATE	EXECUTOR'S FEES	ATTORNEYS' FEES	OTHER EXPENSES	ESTATE TAX
Up to $20,000	$1,755	$1,824	$ 446	$ 181
$20,000 to $40,000	2,227	2,244	566	1,174
$40,000 to $90,000	3,017	2,961	715	3,971
$90,000 to $140,000	4,413	4,213	1,014	11,206
$140,000 to $240,000	6,049	5,785	1,401	23,421
$240,000 to $340,000	8,732	8,175	2,106	43,036

SOURCE: *Changing Times,* January, 1968.

Summary

In choosing an executor and trustee for your estate, consider the many legal, investment, and tax questions your spouse will be facing for the first time. Many widows find it difficult to take care of even simple financial duties, such as keeping records for tax purposes. A bank with a well-staffed trust department is uniquely equipped to assist beneficiaries facing such problems, in cooperation with your lawyer, accountant, or insurance man.

In planning your estate, here are some cardinal points to keep in mind:

1.   Make sure your program is flexible—able to meet whatever contingencies may arise.
2.   Do not choose a plan solely to reduce taxes, though you should take advantage of all savings. The primary purpose is to fulfill your family's needs and objectives.
3.   This is not a do-it-yourself project. Consult a competent lawyer and choose a bank with a well-equipped trust department.
4.   Review your estate plan and your will at least once every three years.

Remember, without a well-conceived estate program, the more you are worth, the more your dependents may lose; the less you are worth, the less they can afford to lose.

QUESTIONS FOR DISCUSSION

1.   Why is it important for your investment objectives to harmonize with family needs?
2.   When selecting a company for possible investment, why is it important to examine carefully its economic position, management, and financial condition and the price of its securities?
3.   When planning an investment program, why is it important to give close attention to taxes?

4.   Why should a family complete its savings, educational, insurance, and basic retirement program before entering the security market?

5.   How do you account for the fact that so many persons die without leaving a will?

6.   Why is it important to review a will at least once annually?

ACTIVITY PROBLEMS

1.   You have $5,000 in cash to invest. Compare the advantages and disadvantages of investing this money in (a) a local savings and loan association, (b) United States savings bonds Series E, (c) a savings account in a local bank, (d) a good industrial bond, (e) common stock in a well-known and successful corporation, (f) high-grade preferred stocks, and (g) a mortgage on a new home in an urban community.

2.   Interview a judge of the probate court in your county. Find out (a) how many family heads die without leaving a will, (b) what the disadvantages are to the family when there is no will, (c) how many wills are contested and the chief reasons for contesting them, (d) what happens in your state if a husband or wife dies without leaving a will, and (e) who can make a will in your state.

3.   A large title and trust company advertised the following message: "If your will was written before April, 1948, it is probably out of date." This advertisement refers to the provision for "marital deductions," effective April, 1948. In what way does the above provision affect a will written before April, 1948?

4.   Select five stocks on the New York Stock Exchange. Keep a daily record of their performance for about two weeks. Read all the factual material that you can find about the stocks you selected. Some reliable sources of information are the security and industry surveys published by brokerage firms; analytical guides for investors; special up-to-date booklets on such industries as petroleum, utilities, steel, chain stores, airlines, and so on; *Standard & Poor's Stock Guide.* After securing all the information possible on the five stocks, would you retain all the stocks at this time? Support your decisions by facts.

5.   Comment on these wills.

   a.   "I have no available property; I owe a great deal; the rest I give to the poor."

   b.   "All my worldly goods, now or to be in store, I give them to my beloved wife, and hers forevermore. I give all freely, I no limit fix. This is my will, and she's executrix."

SUGGESTED READINGS

Barlow, R., H. E. Brazer, and James Morgan: *Economic Behavior of the Affluent,* The Brookings Institution, Washington, D.C., 1966.

"Conglomerates," *Changing Times,* April, 1968.

Engle, Louis: *How to Buy Stocks,* Bantam Books, Inc., New York, latest edition.

"Estate Planning: Why You Need It," *Changing Times,* January, 1968.

Henderson, Carter, and Albert C. Lasker: *20 Million Careless Capitalists,* Doubleday & Company, New York, 1967.

"How to Avoid Probate," *Consumer Reports,* July, 1967.

"Investing in Land," *Changing Times,* November, 1968.

"Investment Trusts," *Changing Times,* January, 1969.

"Joint Ownership Isn't Always Smart," *Changing Times,* August, 1968.

"Let's Rewrite the Probate Laws," *Changing Times,* January, 1969.

Miller, Dorothy Sherrill: *A Will of Your Own,* Cooperative Extension Service, Corvalis, Ore., January, 1963.

"Over-the-Counter Stocks," *Changing Times,* August, 1967.

"Trust Funds," *Changing Times,* November, 1965.

"What Happens to Your Will if Something Happens to You?" *Changing Times,* March, 1966.

"When Your Stock Pays Off with More Stock," *Changing Times,* February, 1968.

Wiesenberger, Arthur: *Investment Companies,* Arthur Wiesenberger & Company, New York, annual.

chapter 15

EXPENDITURES AND TAXES
FOR GOVERNMENT SERVICES

Nothing is certain but . . . and taxes.

We are all familiar with Benjamin Franklin's remark: "In this world nothing is certain but death and taxes." And the older one grows, the more certain he feels that Old Ben was so right. The tax burden on the family increases yearly despite efforts on the part of the taxpayer to take advantage of every legal deduction. It is said that one newlywed, filling out his income tax return, listed a deduction for his wife and in the section "Exemptions for children" penciled the notation, "Watch this space." He should meet the man with six "little deductions" who said, "It's got to be sort of a game with us. Every time the government raises taxes, we counter with another exemption."

Taxes in the United States are levied by three forms of government—the federal government, the states, and local governments. All three governments have been collecting more and more taxes as the years have passed.

We have proved ingenious in devising ways to tax ourselves. We levy taxes on what we earn, spend, and own. We even tax ourselves on some of the things we use, and occasionally we have taxed ourselves on the right to vote. Every American baby enters life unencumbered, but almost immediately he is tied into the tax system, if only as an exemption.

In this chapter, we choose not to teach you how to fill in a federal income tax return. The federal Internal Revenue Service furnishes various tax forms, distributes free material on how to fill in the tax forms, and even prepares an excellent teaching kit for instructors and students. With all of this information available free for the public, our emphasis will be on criteria for good taxes, federal tax reforms, local and state tax problems, and the need for revenue sharing.

TAXES AND YOU

Justice Oliver Wendell Holmes, Jr., said, "Taxes are what we pay for civilized society." As citizens, each of us has certain obligations to our society. One of these is to support the government (our society) through the payment of taxes. But more than that, as informed citizens we should know why we pay taxes, what the tax money is being spent for, and whether we can improve our tax system.

Many of us think of taxes in terms of their being too high. In reality taxes are probably higher than most college students imagine, because in addition to the federal income tax there are many other federal, state, and local taxes. Some of these are sales taxes, inheritance taxes, state and sometimes local income taxes, personal property taxes, and real estate taxes—just to mention a few.

There are other taxes that are not so obvious. The state license plate on your car, the local license permit, and your driver's permit are forms of tax. And for every cent you pay to run your car, you give a certain amount in gas tax to your federal, state, and maybe local government. But we know we receive something, too.

What Do You Get for Your Money?

Right around home you can easily see what services you get from your state and local taxes. In most places these taxes pay for streets, police and fire protection, water, sewers, parks and recreation facilities, help for the needy, public schools, and teachers' salaries.

The federal services are a little harder to see but nonetheless important. They also provide protection, but usually on a national basis. We are all familiar with the support taxes provide for our national defense. Taxes also help ensure that our foods and drugs meet safety and effectiveness standards. Taxes finance research projects that find the causes of man's diseases and continue to improve our agricultural products. They finance our relations with other nations. Through the Peace Corps and the Agency for International Development we are able to help many people to help themselves in many parts of the world. In addition, taxes help provide for most of our interstate highways, national parks, wildlife refuges, and conservation areas. Also, federal taxes provide assistance for older people, people out of work, and those who cannot afford medical care. The list is much longer, but these examples will remind you of what we get for our tax money.

Complexity of the Tax Structure

Our tax structure has grown increasingly complex, partly because the federal, state, and local governments compete for sources of tax funds. In raising revenue, certain understandings have been worked out: the federal government depends largely on the income tax, the states on the sales tax, and local units on the property tax. There are, however, enough exceptions to these guidelines to create serious problems of competition for revenue sources and problems of cooperation when functions and jurisdictions overlap. This problem is so serious that Congress set up the Advisory Commission on Intergovernmental Relations in 1959. This commission published two large volumes of recommendations in 1967 in the hope of bringing together representatives of the federal, state, and local governments for the consideration of these intergovernmental tax problems.

Citizens Expect More Services

The complexity of the tax structure, and of tax policies, is also attributable to the great growth of goods and services the present-day governments are expected to supply. Financing the tremendous demands for education, highways, welfare services, and old-age and unemployment insurance and the increasing costs of defense and foreign aid have put new pressures on our capacity to generate the necessary revenue in a fair and equitable manner.

Another factor, besides overlapping tax jurisdictions and growing demands, that has contributed to the complexity of tax policy has been the recognition that the ways in which government collects money and the timing of its tax decisions have an important impact on our economy—on the stability of its performance.

Taxes per Family

Total tax collections by federal, state, and local governments in fiscal 1968 equaled about $3,550 for each of our *families,* according to the Tax Foundation, Inc., a private organization.

The total tax was estimated at about $217 billion, up about $10 billion from fiscal 1967.

The Tax Foundation said that tax collections from each family in 1968 would be about $134 higher than 1967 and nearly double the amount for 1956.

Federal tax collections were expected to rise to $153 billion in 1968 from $149 billion in 1967.

Tax collections by state and local governments in fiscal 1968 were expected to increase to $69 billion from $64 billion in 1967.

The significance of the above information is not the $3,550 that each *family* pays out in *total* taxes, because no family is average. Some families pay very few taxes and other families pay many thousands of dollars—even millions of dollars—in total taxes. A more significant fact is that our total tax burden is increasing as we demand more and more services by government and as inflation increases. As inflation increases, individual tax rates increase (in all progressive tax systems) because taxpayers are usually transferred into higher tax brackets, or at least have a larger proportion of their dollar income in the incremental bracket. And the $600 exemption, which has remained the same since 1948 (when it was worth $856 in 1968 purchasing power), means less and less as prices advance.

Criteria for Taxes.   When exploring the impact of particular taxes, economists generally focus attention on productivity, equity, administrative efficiency, and economic effects:

1.   Productivity: How much income does the tax generate? As the economy grows, does the tax yield increase?
2.   Equity: Is the tax fair? Do people feel that it treats equals equally?
3.   Administrative efficiency: Is it easy to collect, difficult to evade, and not too expensive to collect?
4.   Economic effects: How does it affect a person's incentive to work or to invest? How does it affect the total performance of the economy?

General Acceptance.   While there is a tax revolt brewing, especially among the middle-income class (as we will note later in the chapter), the tax system as a whole in our country has enjoyed general acceptance. Many of us complain about high and unjust taxes, but public response to tax actions is characterized by cooperation. This cooperative attitude may have encouraged well-financed groups to obtain unfair tax advantages. Many of us have relaxed to the extent that we settle for the privilege of "letting off steam" about high taxes when we need to think about wisdom to use taxes constructively to promote local, state, and national objectives.

Who Collects What?

The total tax receipts of federal, state, and local governments were $189 billion in 1965—a year in which the economic impact of the Vietnam War was still mild. The $189 billion was slightly more than one-fourth of the 1965 gross national product of $681 billion. Of the $189 billion in taxes, about $2 out of every $3 was collected by the federal government.

Federal Tax Receipts. Table 15-1 indicates that federal tax receipts were largely from income taxes. In 1967 personal income taxes accounted for about 41 percent of the total. Corporation income taxes brought in about 23 percent. Interestingly, these two major sources of federal income adopted in 1909 (corporation income tax) and in 1913 (personal income tax) did not constitute a major source for federal income until after World War I.

The second largest source of federal income, employment taxes, was introduced in 1935 to finance the Social Security programs. Presently, this tax brings in about 19 percent of the total federal taxes.

The third largest federal receipts are from the excise taxes—sales taxes on tobacco and alcohol, the regulatory taxes on narcotics, and the gasoline taxes for the use of highways. The excise taxes brought in about 9 percent of federal income in 1967.

TABLE 15-1   FEDERAL BUDGET RECEIPTS—FISCAL 1967 (MILLIONS OF DOLLARS)

SOURCE	AMOUNT	PERCENT OF TOTAL RECEIPTS
Individual income taxes	$ 61,526	41
Corporation income taxes	33,971	23
Employment taxes	27,823	19
Unemployment insurance	3,652	3
Premiums for other insurance and retirement	1,853	1
Excise taxes	13,719	9
Estate and gift taxes	2,978	2
Customs	1,901	1
Other receipts	2,168	1
Total	$149,591	100

SOURCE: *Economic Report of the President,* February, 1968 (Table B-60). Also contained in *The Budget in Brief, Fiscal Year 1969,* Bureau of the Budget, Executive Office of the President, p. 68.

The other federal taxes brought in about 8 percent of the total revenue in 1967.

State and Local Tax Receipts.   State and local governments, in contrast to the federal government, are primarily dependent on sales and property taxes. States rely chiefly on the sales taxes, leaving property taxes to local governments. The U.S. Census Bureau estimated state and local tax collections in 1967 at $61.2 billion. This is considerably less than the nearly $150 billion the federal government collected in the same year. Nearly $47 billion of the $61.2 billion of tax collections by local and state governments came from property taxes and sales taxes, leaving some $14 billion from other sources.

The rising burden of state and local taxes and the trend toward revenue sharing will be discussed later in this chapter.

THE FEDERAL INCOME TAX

The individual income tax is, by far, the largest source of revenue for the federal government (41 percent in 1967). Therefore, it warrants special attention. This special attention, as indicated earlier, will center on common trouble spots, preventing errors, record keeping, cutting your tax bill, and tax reforms, to mention a few areas.

The federal Internal Revenue Service will furnish you with tax forms and directions for filling in the forms. Your instructor will, no doubt, secure from the same source excellent teaching kits.[1] All of these materials and forms are not only free from the U.S. Treasury Department but will be a better guide in teaching you how to fill in the tax forms than can be given in a few pages of a textbook.

The 1968 Tax Returns

Some of the interesting highlights of the federal tax returns in 1968 were these:

1.   Some 107.6 million tax returns were filed in fiscal 1968, and more than 51 million refunds were made. The refunds totaled $11 billion. Most were issued within 3 to 5 weeks after the returns were filed.
2.   Individual income tax collections gained $8.7 billion over fiscal 1967 and corporation tax payments dropped by $5 billion, according to the annual report of the Internal Revenue Service.
3.   Together, individual and corporate income taxes totaled $108 billion. Employment taxes added $28.2 billion, excise taxes $14.3 billion, and estate and gift taxes roughly $3.1 billion. The total was $153.6 billion (about $3 billion more than in 1967).
4.   IRS reported that nearly 27 million persons, or one in every four taxpayers, telephoned or visited IRS offices for information in helping file their returns.

[1] *Teaching Federal Income Tax,* Internal Revenue Service, U.S. Treasury Department, Washington, D.C. Free. Two inexpensive booklets, J. K. Lasser's *Your Income Tax* and *Your Federal Income Tax,* which are published annually, are informative and easy to read.

5. Computers were used nationwide for the second year to help select returns for audit examination. A total of 2.9 million returns were audited. Additional tax was assessed on 1.5 million of them, resulting in an additional $2.95 billion for the Treasury.

6. For 1.2 million returns, or more than 41 percent of those tagged for audit, no change in the tax liability was made after the audit.

7. About $178 million was credited or refunded to 150,000 taxpayers as a result of audits in which IRS found that the taxpayer had overpaid Uncle Sam.

The Importance of the Individual Income Tax

This tax is especially important because it is the biggest single source of federal revenue, affects just about everyone who earns an income, has a big impact on the level of economic activity, and raises questions of equity and administration.[2]

Furthermore, the individual income tax has been growing. This tax accounted for 20 percent of federal income in World War I, 33 percent during World War II, and an average of over 40 percent in the 1960s. During this period it has also affected an increasing proportion of the population. Before World War II only 5 percent of the people were covered, compared to about 75 percent today.

A Direct Tax

A direct tax is one that must be paid by the person on whom it is levied. Unlike an indirect tax, such as an excise tax, the individual income tax cannot be shifted readily. Policy makers, therefore, know who bears the burden of this tax, in contrast to indirect taxes. Does the business pay for the indirect tax, or does it pass the tax along to the consumer by charging higher prices for its products? Is the sales tax paid for by the purchaser, or is it absorbed in part by the seller? Such questions do not arise under the individual income tax.

A Progressive Tax

As a progressive tax, the individual income tax takes proportionally a larger share of the income of people with high earnings. Taxpayers who fill in Form 1040 know that the rate changes from 14 percent of the first $1,000 of taxable income to about 70 percent of the income in excess of $200,000 (1968 rates for married couples).

There is, of course, a difference between theoretical rates and the effective rates. Because of exemptions, deductions, exclusions, and other special provisions, Americans pay taxes on less than half of their incomes. Some income is not taxed because of special consideration to wage earners with dependents, those with high medical bills, homeowners, and those who incur expenses in connection with earning a living. But some taxpayers benefit from favorable

[2] Richard Goode, *The Individual Income Tax*, The Brookings Institution, Washington, D.C., 1963.

provisions in the tax law. These loopholes are the basis for considerable criticism, and Congress may be in the mood to plug at least some of the worst loopholes.

Exclusions.   Exclusions are payments for unemployment insurance, public assistance, veterans' benefits, and payments under the Social Security system. These are what economists call "transfer" payments that shift income from people who are better off to those who are worse off. Not all exclusions are viewed as equally justifiable. Some would argue that Social Security benefits are sufficiently different from public assistance to warrant being taxed, especially since income from private pensions is taxed.

Deductions.   Taxpayers are allowed to reduce the income subject to taxation by the amount of interest they pay on home mortgages and on installment purchases; by the amount of local and state taxes that they pay; by the amount of medical expenses and the cost of drugs and medicines that exceed a certain percentage of their income; and by the amount of their contributions to hospitals, churches, and educational institutions. Too, certain business expenses and union dues are deductible—to mention only a few.

Exemptions.   Beside exclusions and deductions, the law permits exemptions, which, at the end of 1969, were the first $600 of income for each taxpayer and each dependent. Thus, a family of four (counting the taxpayer, his wife, and two children) claims four exemptions ($2,400 of income tax-free). This is the biggest single tax break for large families at low income levels.

Capital Gains. For high-income families, the biggest concession is the treatment of capital gains. Capital gains—the difference between what an asset costs and what it is sold for, if its value has appreciated—are taxed at one-half regular rates up to a maximum of 25 percent, provided the asset has been held for at least six months. The justification for this exemption is twofold. Capital gains are usually built up over several years, and if they were taxed at regular rates in the year in which the asset is sold, the rate might be much higher than it would have been if the gain were taxed year by year as it accumulated. Then, too, the lower rate on capital gains has been defended as an incentive that encourages investors to take risks, since it rewards success by cutting the taxes in half.

Income-splitting. Middle-income families gain most from the income-splitting provision which permits husband and wife to divide their joint income for tax purposes as if each had earned half; they can do so even if the wife earned no income. A couple thus bears a lighter tax load than an individual earning the same income. For 1968, for example, a single person earning $20,000 a year was subject to a tax rate of 48 percent of the last dollar earned. A couple, however, earning $20,000 divided the income for tax purposes and paid a top rate of 32 percent. In dollars, a single taxpayer paid $6,070 and the married couple paid only $3,640. Thus the tax is much less progressive for a married couple than for a single person living alone. A separate rate schedule is provided for single persons who are the heads of households; it gives about half the benefits of income-splitting.

Collectively, these special features of our tax law help explain why the burden of the income tax is much less than one would think from a glance at the rates.

Common Trouble Spots on Income Tax Returns

All income is taxed unless it is expressly exempt by law. Deliberate hiding of income is a serious offense. Innocent failure to report income is likely to cost you a penalty. The tax law, nevertheless, permits some types of income to be tax-free. For helpful information, see *Your Federal Income Tax,* (latest) Edition for Individuals, available for 50 cents from the Superintendent of Documents, Washington, D.C. 20402.

The Internal Revenue Service reports the following list of common errors made by taxpayers when filling in the tax forms:

1.   Failure to properly sign the tax form. A joint return, for example, must be signed by both people.

2.   Using the wrong tax form. If in doubt, use Form 1040, because it is good regardless of your income.

3.   Not reporting all income—commissions, tips, fees, many kinds of fringe benefits, rewards, bonuses, and military pay (some combat service is tax-free).

4.   Interest from banks, savings and loan associations, and credit unions, some payments called "dividends" (these must be reported as interest—from mutual savings banks, cooperative banks, building and loan associations, and savings and loan associations), and corporate stock dividends ($100 exemption per person or $200 for jointly owned securities is allowed), all are taxable.

5.   Insurance, gifts, and inheritances are generally not taxed as income, but you may have to pay taxes on income they produce.

6.   Social Security benefits paid for old age, disability, or dependency are tax-exempt, as are unemployment benefits from a state or the federal government. The portion the employer contributes to retirement pay (pensions and annuities) is taxable.

7.   Generally, profit from the sale of personal property is taxable. Losses are not normally deductible.

8.   Profit from the sale of your home is generally taxable, but the taxes can be postponed. However, you cannot delay the tax if the new house costs less than the price you got for the old one. People over 65, however, have certain tax advantages.

9.   If you sell stock or other personal investments that you had for six months or less, any profit is taxed at standard rates. But if you owned them over six months, the profit is a long-term capital gain and you pay on only half of it.

10.   Income from other sources—lucky-number drawings, door prizes, gambling winnings, hobbies, recovered payments (medical expense), car-pool earnings (beyond operating expenses), and estate and trust income (same tax)—is generally counted as income for tax purposes. Major exceptions are scholarships and grants from a recognized educational institution.

Preventing Errors

In the 1968 tax Form 1040, places where errors were common in past tax returns stand out in red type. This reminder should be useful to the ordinary taxpayer making out his own tax report.

One key to the prevention of error, however, is finding a qualified person to help you. Perhaps the best source of information and service is your Internal Revenue Service (IRS). It has a taxpayer assistance service whose job it is to answer questions. Not only will they fill in your forms, but they will assist you in every other way.

One caution—there are many "fly-by-night" operators who are not certified or otherwise regulated in any way. If you use one of them and your return should be questioned, you may not be able to locate him (they usually operate between January 1 and April 15), and your errors may be his fault even though you paid him for his services. Also, beware of the income tax person who asks you to sign your forms before they have been filled in.

If your tax report is too difficult, look for accountants or certified public accountants or other such qualified people to prepare your return. Many such persons hold U.S. Treasury or enrollment cards for practice before the IRS in case of audit. Such persons can represent you with or without your presence.

If Errors Are Made

If after you have filed your return, you discover either that you made an error in your favor or that you overpaid the government, the error can be corrected. This is done by preparing Form 1040X, Amended U.S. Individual Income Tax Return, and sending it to the address shown on the instructions for that form. There are other ways of making a correction, such as by making out a new Form 1040 tax return, marking it "Amended Return," or by filing a claim for refund on Form 843.

Your amended return, however, must be filed within 3 years from the date your original form was filed, or within 2 years from the time the tax was paid, whichever is later.

A good reference for filling out your tax return this year is the copy of your last year's return.

Audits

Today the Automatic Data Processing (ADP) System computers of the IRS check millions of individual tax returns. If your return appears to be "suspicious," it will be pulled and checked. For those suspicious returns that cannot be cleared otherwise, further action may be required. An audit, for example, may be required.

In addition to suspicious returns, the computers are programmed to select tax returns at random for audit. The selection of your return for audit does not necessarily mean that you are suspected of owing more money.

"Discriminate Function." Beginning in January, 1969, the Treasury's data-processing equipment started picking tax returns representing under $10,000 gross income under its new formula system. Then, starting on January 1, 1970, this innovation, "DIF" (Discriminate Function), will be used for higher-income returns.

Under this system, each return will be scored on a mathematical formula which assigns various weights to selected "line items" on each return.

Taxpayers with the larger returns might consider these points that the tax pros cite as most likely to flag a return for some annoying questions or an audit:

1. Surprisingly, they stress the importance of neatness—it gives the agent confidence in the accuracy of your return.
2. The second concerns the occasional large item of income or deduction—a major real estate deal; a sizable sale of securities; use of income averaging; or other out-of-the-ordinary items.
3. Examining agents also seem to have an aversion for a big bunching of miscellaneous deductions and a curiosity about the value of donated property.
4. Casualty loss claims can make your return liable to audit, especially if you fail to itemize and explain how you arrived at the loss.
5. Heavy travel and entertainment deductions remain a pitfall, and the mixed business-pleasure junket gets special attention. One tip: Use Form 2106 to cover all "T & E" items—it may avoid an audit.

There is no need to panic if you are called for an audit, if your records are in order. The key to successful income tax filing is good records and accurate arithmetic.

Record Keeping [3]

You are required by law to keep records that will enable you to prepare a complete and accurate income tax return. The law does not require any special form of records.

However, all receipts, canceled checks, and other evidence to prove amounts claimed as deductions must be retained as part of your records.

If you file a claim for a refund, you must be able to prove by your records that you have overpaid your tax.

You must keep your records for as long as their contents may be material in administering any internal revenue law.

Records that support an item of income or a deduction appearing on a return must be kept until the statute of limitations for the return expires. Usually this is 3 years from the date the return was due or filed or 2 years from the date the tax was paid, whichever occurs later.

In property transactions, sometimes the basis of new or replacement property is determined by reference to the basis of the property. Records of transactions relating to the basis of property should be kept for as long as they are material in determining the basis of the original or replacement property.

Sometimes new legislation will give relief to a taxpayer if he can prove from his records of transactions in prior years that he is entitled to relief.

[3] See *Your Federal Income Tax,* (latest) Edition for Individuals, Internal Revenue Service, U.S. Treasury Department, Washington, D.C.

Copies of tax returns that you have filed can help you in preparing future income tax returns.

Cutting Your Tax Bill

The individual income tax return offers you many chances to save money—if you know where to look for them. Here are some of the frequently overlooked ways to carve out tax savings:

1. Failure to list deductions for premiums paid on medical insurance. There are some limitations, but the rule is quite liberal.
2. In adding up medical expenses, include transportation cost for trips to hospital and doctor's office; also parking or toll fees. Do not overlook buying or repairing eyeglasses, hearing aids, and dental work.
3. Deductions for sales taxes, state and local, offer opportunities. There are tables which you can use for this deduction. Unfortunately, these tables do not include sales taxes on purchase of new cars, so add that in.
4. Local income taxes are spreading now, and are often forgotten.
5. If you purchased a new home or a summer retreat, you paid part of the annual property tax on the place at settlement. This is deductible.
6. Interest rates offer some of the fattest savings of all, since nearly all interest payments are deductible.
7. Many small charitable donations can count up into many dollars, and most of this is deductible. Also, out-of-pocket expenses for unpaid work for churches, charities, hospitals, and schools are deductible, including 5 cents a mile for your car.
8. Deductions for casualty losses are hedged about with restrictions but still are worth checking. Even vandalism losses are deductible.
9. Investment losses, too, can be useful for tax savings. If your net losses were $2,000, you can deduct $1,000 against ordinary income and carry the other $1,000 forward for later use.
10. Expenses incurred in earning money are often neglected—dues to professional organizations, investment-advisory services, and safety-deposit box rent. If part of your home is used primarily for your earned income, often you can make a good thing of this, but the rules are tough.
11. Many people do not make adequate use of the rules under which exemptions for dependents are taken. A son, let us say, is a graduate student, earning $3,000 in summer work and a part-time job. He spent $600 of it on a car and banked $400. His father spent $2,000 on his support. The father can claim the $600 exemption, if his son files a separate return. Your claiming an exemption does not prevent him from taking it, too.
12. Taxpayers who work at more than one job may be paying more than the maximum amount in deductions from their wages for Social Security.
13. You can save taxes by using the rule of "income averaging" if your income shot up very sharply last year. This rule is very complex and so new many people overlook it.
14. Some of the dividends from mutual funds last year probably came from capital gains. You can report them as long-term gains even if you had held the shares only a few days.

Evaluation of the Income Tax

Congress viewed the income tax law it passed in 1913 as a constructive response to the demand for a realistic and productive system of revenue which all good citizens "will willingly and cheerfully support . . . the fairest and cheapest of taxes." Has the optimism expressed in this statement by the House Ways and Means Committee been borne out by experience? How does the tax measure up to the criteria, mentioned earlier, of productivity, equity, simplicity, and economic usefulness?

Productivity.   Certainly its productivity cannot be criticized. It has been an especially suitable tax in a growing economy because its yield has risen with the increase in gross material product.

Equity.   Equity is more difficult to assess. Even if one concedes that in principle it is as fair as any other tax, or perhaps fairer, in practice many of its features are questionable on grounds of fairness. The major questions are:

> Does the income-splitting provision unduly discriminate against single persons?
> Does the capital gains provision encourage dubious schemes for converting income into capital gains?
> Should the income from state and local securities continue to be excluded from taxable income?
> Should deductions be permitted students for costs of college education?
> Should tighter curbs be placed on deductions for entertainment and travel?

It has been suggested that in principle, since the tax is a tax on income, deductions for interest paid, casualty losses, and so on, should be permitted only for items related to the production of income.

Despite these criticisms, the tax scores high for its fairness, since it reflects the widespread agreement that ability to pay is a reasonably fair criterion. Those in the lowest income brackets pay a smaller fraction of their income in taxes than do those in higher brackets, the rate being 14 percent on the first $1,000 of taxable income, 15 percent on the next $1,000, 16 percent on the third $1,000, and so on up the ladder. Moreover, the special features introduced to take into account the additional expenses, such as those incurred in raising a family or in meeting heavy medical expenses, are in accord with public attitudes about fairness in tax treatment.

Administration.   The income tax has been reasonably easy to administer because it is largely self-reporting. Taxpayers have filed their returns and made their payments with a minimum of surveillance. Compliance has been voluntary and virtually complete. Two innovations of the past 25 years have improved the system still further. One was the introduction in 1943 of withholding—the principle that income is taxable when earned and should be deducted from the employee's pay. The tax withheld is turned over to the federal government at intervals ranging from 15 days to three months, depending on the amount. As a result, the government gets its revenue regularly and promptly, and tax-payers are prevented from building up large tax liabilities, formerly burden-some to meet each year. Taxes on dividends and interest are not withheld, but statements are made to the Internal Revenue Service listing payments to in-dividuals and organizations, as a reference in auditing individual returns. The other major change contributing to administrative efficiency has been the de-velopment of computer technology. Modern data-processing techniques have made it possible to check cheaply and efficiently on the accuracy of returns filed.

Economic Impact.   What about the economic impact of the individual in-come tax? First, recent studies have shown that this tax has served as a kind of automatic stabilizer, helping to smooth out fluctuations in the level of eco-nomic activity. It does so because its yield varies with income. In slack times, when their incomes are lower, taxpayers retain proportionately more out of their income, and in good times, when their incomes are greater, they retain proportionately less. Because changes in after-tax income were relatively smaller than changes in gross national product, owing in large part to the effects of the income tax, the duration and severity of the postwar recessions of 1948, 1953 - 1954, 1957, and 1960 were checked.

The evidence about the effect of progressive rates on individual incentives to work, and to invest, suggests that there is little discouragement to wage earn-ers in the lower and middle income brackets. At higher income brackets, incen-tives other than income have strong effects, and the effect of tax loopholes has greatly offset the nominal progressivity of the tax schedule. A frequently quoted study by the Harvard Business School[4] substantiates the view that taxes are not a significant discouragement to investors and top executives, and a more recent study[5] of the economic behavior of the affluent also bears out this belief.

A good deal of criticism of the individual income tax persists, both by those who consider it the fairest and best of our taxes, and by those who would pre-fer to place greater reliance on other forms of taxation, such as the value-added tax, which is widely used in Europe. But the place of the individual income tax in the federal revenue system seems reasonably secure. Overall, it gets good marks when tested for its consistency with the nation's total economic policy.

Similarly, the overall federal tax system has its defenders and detractors. In many areas, tax reform is overdue, and there is a continuing need to reex-amine particular taxes for their productivity, their fairness, their administra-tive simplicity, and their economic impact. To say that the American tax sys-

[4] Lynn L. Bollinger, *Effects of Taxation: Investments by Individuals,* Harvard Gradu-ate School of Business, Cambridge, Mass., 1953.

[5] Robin Barlow et al., *Economic Behavior of the Affluent,* The Brookings Institution, Washington, D.C., 1966.

tem is the best in the world—as some experts do—is not to say that it cannot be improved.

PROPOSED TAX REFORMS

Congress has been studying many kinds of improvement in federal taxes. According to U.S. Treasury Department studies, the following tax reforms are high on the agenda of Congress for the years 1969 and 1970:[6]

1. An increase in the standard deduction. The present 10 percent deduction, up to a maximum of $1,000, would be raised to 14 percent with a maximum of a possible $1,800.

2. Tax abuses of some private tax-exempt foundations would be curbed, including the small foundations used frequently to operate family businesses at lower tax cost.

3. A major tax-avoidance gimmick is the deduction of farm losses from business income. This is how it works with "city cowboys": a high-income taxpayer buys cattle. He then takes generous deductions permitted full-time farmers, writing them off against nonfarm income that otherwise would be taxed at rates up to 70 percent.

Ronald A. Buel, a *Wall Street Journal* reporter, mixed a little humor in his article on March 19, 1969, when he wrote:

I'm a rich cowhand, of the Wall Street brand
And I save on tax, to beat the band
Oh I take big deductions the law allows
And I never even have to see my cows
Yippie-i-o-ki-ay!

Well, maybe not for long.

4. Tax-exempt bonds, the basic borrowing instrument of cities, school districts, and states to finance public projects, would be discouraged. One plan provides for the U.S. Treasury to provide an "interest subsidy" to help municipalities to meet interest costs.

5. Wealthy individuals (many escape all of the federal income tax) would be required to pay a minimum tax (see Table 15-2).

6. Unlimited charitable deductions by some taxpayers—one of the techniques by which some millionaires avoid all taxes—would be discontinued over a period of years.

7. Capital gains tax rules would be tightened.

8. Depletion allowances in excess of cost of drilling for oil would be minimized or eliminated.

These are among many of the proposals for an overhaul of the federal tax system.

Middle-income Class Hurt

Table 15-2 shows clearly why the middle-income classes are likely to revolt against income taxes because certain provisions of the tax laws unfairly lighten

[6] *Tax Reform Studies and Proposals,* U.S. Treasury Department, 1968.

TABLE 15-2   PERCENTAGE DISTRIBUTION OF RETURNS BY EFFECTIVE TAX RATE
CLASSES (BY AMENDED GROSS INCOME CLASSES, 1969 LEVELS)

Amended Gross Income ($000)	EFFECTIVE TAX RATE CLASSES													
	0-5	5-10	10-15	15-20	20-25	25-30	30-35	35-40	40-45	45-50	50-55	55-60	60-65	65-70
0- 3	68.0	0.3	1.4	6.0										
3- 5	14.5	2.3	10.9	63.0	5.6									
5- 7	3.9	2.0	22.2	71.6	0.1									
7- 10	0.9	1.0	22.2	70.5	5.3									
10- 15	0.7	0.8	6.3	85.2	6.6	0.4								
15- 20	0.6	1.5	4.8	71.2	19.8	2.2								
20- 50	0.9	1.6	7.0	27.9	45.2	13.5	3.0	0.6	0.2					
50- 100	1.2	0.8	3.3	7.5	12.7	21.6	31.2	16.4	3.9	1.2	0.2			
100- 500	1.9	1.3	1.9	6.1	17.9	15.9	11.5	14.1	14.4	8.7	4.1	1.9	0.3	
500-1,000	2.1	0.7	0.8	0.7	31.9	32.8	6.3	4.3	3.0	2.4	3.1	4.6	6.7	0.4
1,000 & over	2.5	0.4	0.3	0.4	36.6	37.8	4.3	1.7	1.8	2.1	1.2	1.3	6.1	3.4

SOURCE: Office of the Secretary of the Treasury, Office of Tax Analysis.

the burden of those who can afford to pay. In other words, the federal income
tax is unfair to this income group. According to the U.S. Treasury study (Table
15-2 reveals this clearly), the "effective" rates are the basic measure of tax
bite—the tax actually paid as a percent of income. If you look at the left-hand
vertical column of Table 15-2, you will see it broken into income classes—
0 to $1,000, etc., up to incomes of over $1 million per year.

Most of us (68 percent), as the table shows, in the lowest income levels pay
from 0 to 5 percent of our income in taxes. From a level of $3,000 to $20,000,
most Americans pay from 15 to 20 percent of their incomes in taxes.

The Rich Escape

Now look at the remaining levels up to $1 million and more. From $20,000 to
$50,000, the tendency to cluster around a rate drops sharply. Then, from
$100,000 to $500,000, there is almost no cluster point. These wealthy taxpayers
are ranged widely—with 2 percent paying rates from only 0 to 5 percent. And a
similar unfair tax situation prevails with only 2.5 percent of the $1 million-and-
more class paying taxes at the 0 to 5 percent rate and only 9.5 percent of the
group paying 60 to 70 percent rates.

What has happened? The answer lies in the way income is treated for tax
purposes. It is up to Congress to deal with these unfair tax situations.

STATE AND LOCAL TAXES

In 1966, *Changing Times* magazine (October, 1967) stated that local and state
governments "spent an average of $423 per person to maintain local services."

Most of it—$170—went for education. Highways came next, with $65. The other big expenses were public welfare, $35; health and hospitals, $30; police protection, $14; and interest on debt, $14. Furthermore, taxes have been increasing each year.

A Rising Burden

The rising burden of state and local taxes can be seen in the great increase in expenditures (see Table 15-3).

All over the country, taxpayers are showing signs of revolt. More and more bond issues were being turned down in 1967-1968. School districts have reduced budgets or postponed needed buildings as voters resisted more taxes. In some cities, public schools have been closed for several weeks when money ran out.

The big question is: Where is the tax money coming from? Property taxes, the chief source of income, especially at the local level, may have reached their limit. Sales taxes, too, may be reaching a limit.

TABLE 15-3   WHY YOUR STATE AND LOCAL TAXES ARE CLIMBING

	STATE-LOCAL EXPENDITURES (BILLIONS)		
	1957	*1967*	*Increase*
Social programs:			
Education	$14.1	$38.2	Up 171%
Welfare	3.5	8.2	Up 134%
Health	3.1	6.6	Up 113%
Housing and urban renewal	0.5	1.5	Up 200%
Public services:			
Police	$ 1.5	$ 3.0	Up 100%
Fire protection	0.8	1.5	Up 88%
Sanitation	1.4	2.6	Up 86%
Recreation and natural resources	1.5	3.6	Up 140%
Transportation:			
Highways	$ 7.8	$14.0	Up 79%
Airports and water transportation	0.4	0.8	Up 100%
General administration	1.7	3.3	Up 94%
Interest on debt	1.1	3.0	Up 172%
Other programs	3.0	7.5	Up 150%
Total	$40.4	$93.8	Up 132%

SOURCE: U.S. Census Bureau.

TABLE 15-4   LOCAL AND STATE TAX COLLECTIONS, 1967

	TAX COLLECTIONS, 1957 (BILLIONS)	TAX COLLECTIONS, 1967 (BILLIONS)
Property taxes	$12.9	$26.3
Sales taxes	9.5	20.6
Personal income taxes	1.8	5.8
Corporate income taxes	1.0	2.2
Other taxes	3.6	6.3
Total	$28.8	$61.2

SOURCE: U.S. Census Bureau.

Table 15-4 shows that state and local taxes more than doubled from 1957 to 1967. It also shows that the major source of income for local and state government services is the property tax, with sales taxes a fairly close second. More than ever, citizens are asking: Where can the states get more tax money? Should the federal government share more of its tax take with state and local governments?

State and Local Tax Load Varies

The Advisory Commission on Intergovernmental Relations noted, in its study released on February 12, 1969, the "fiscal effort" that states and localities are making to use their taxing powers to solve their own problems. Table 15-5 discloses where tax burdens have been increasing most rapidly in relation to incomes.

The study reveals wide variations in the relative burdens of individual taxes. Hawaii, for example, showing state and local taxes taking $12.45 out of each $100 of personal income, tops the list. The industrial state of Ohio had the lightest tax burden in relation to income. The conclusion is quite obvious—many states and localities are not carrying their fair share of tax burdens. Fifteen states, for example, did not have an income tax, and six did not have a sales tax in early 1969.

These figures (in Table 15-5) take on increasing significance at this time when the federal government is being asked to share more of its tax income with states and localities. Should not, then, an extra helping of shared revenues, if needed, go to states with a high fiscal-effort rating?

Should the Federal Government Share Its Tax Take?

Walter W. Heller, former chairman of the Council of Economic Advisers under Presidents Kennedy and Johnson, wrote:[7] "Washington must find a way to put

[7] The Saturday Review, Mar. 22, 1969.

TABLE 15-5   WHERE STATE AND LOCAL TAX BURDENS ARE HEAVIEST

	AMOUNT*	RANKING†
Hawaii	$12.45	1
Wyoming	12.20	2
New York	12.18	3
Arizona	11.71	4
Minnesota	11.46	5
Idaho	11.42	6
California	11.31	7
Wisconsin	11.23	8
New Mexico	11.13	9
South Dakota	11.11	10
Colorado	11.06	11
Utah	11.04	12
Vermont	10.88	13
Montana	10.83	14
North Dakota	10.72	15
Nevada	10.63	16
Louisiana	10.62	17
Iowa	10.55	18
Massachusetts	10.41	19
Mississippi	10.37	20
Kansas	10.29	21
Oregon	10.25	22
Washington	10.10	23
Maine	9.96	24
Oklahoma	9.77	25
Indiana	9.64	26
Florida	9.63	27
West Virginia	9.58	28
Michigan	9.50	29
Maryland	9.50	30
Arkansas	9.47	31
Delaware	9.33	32
North Carolina	9.18	33
Rhode Island	8.91	34
South Carolina	8.90	35
Alabama	8.88	36
Tennessee	8.85	37
Georgia	8.85	38
Nebraska	8.83	39
Pennsylvania	8.79	40
Kentucky	8.78	41
Missouri	8.70	42
New Jersey	8.59	43
Virginia	8.53	44
New Hampshire	8.42	45
Connecticut	8.37	46
Texas	8.34	47
Alaska	8.26	48
Washington, D.C.	8.24	49
Illinois	7.95	50
Ohio	7.75	51

*Amount taken by all state and local taxes from each $100 of personal income.
† Ranking—highest to lowest.
NOTE: Figures are for the year 1967, the latest for which official data are available.
SOURCE: Advisory Commission on Intergovernmental Relations.

a more generous share of the huge federal fiscal dividend (the automatic increase in tax revenue associated with income growth) at the disposal of the states and cities." Almost all tax experts and tax studies share Dr. Heller's conclusion. As a matter of fact, the federal government has shared its tax income with states and localities for many years.

Federal Aid to States and Localities. Sharing federal tax income with states and local governments is not a new proposal. In fact, in the last 10 years—between 1949 and 1969—federal financial aid to states and localities has increased from nearly $2 billion to over $20 billion (Table 15-6).

Federal Government Must Share More

The renewed interest in making state and local government a vital, effective, and reasonably equal partner in a workable federalism originates as much in the realm of a changed political attitude as in the financial plight of state and local government. Yet one finds strong argument for new and expanded federal support in sharing even more tax income with state and local governments.

Argument one is that Washington collects over two-thirds of the total federal, state, and local tax take, and that nearly two-thirds of government public services (omit Social Security and defense) are provided by state and local government.

Argument two is the compelling problems of poverty and race and the related problems of disease, ignorance, squalor, and hard-core unemployment,

TABLE 15-6   FEDERAL AID TO STATE AND LOCAL GOVERNMENTS (SELECTED FISCAL YEARS 1949-1969) (IN MILLIONS OF DOLLARS)

	1949	1959	1967	1968*	1969*
Agriculture	$ 86.6	$ 322.5	$ 448.0	$ 599.4	$ 644.0
Commerce and transportation	433.6	100.6	226.3	431.7	618.6
Education	36.9	291.3	2,298.7	2,461.9	2,398.2
Health, labor, and welfare	1,231.5	2,789.7	6,438.0	8,207.1	9.135.0
Housing and community development	8.6	188.4	768.3	1,185.2	1,812.5
Highway and unemployment trust funds	. . . .	2,801.2	4,501.7	4,773.1	1,418.0
Other	5.5	319.7	1,120.2	1,239.9	1,418.0
Total	$1,802.7	$6,813.4	$15,801.2	$18,898.3	$20,823.0

*Data estimated.
SOURCE: Bureau of the Budget.

which are nationwide. Also, the efforts to overcome these causes of distress by improved education, training, health, welfare, and housing have nation-wide effects. Yet it is precisely these services that we entrust primarily to state and local units.

Clearly, then, many of these problems that states and local governments tackle are not all of their own making. And their success or failure in coping with these problems will have huge spillover effects far beyond the local and state boundary lines. In fact, only the federal government can represent the totality of benefits and strike an efficient balance between benefits and costs. Therein lies the compelling economic case for transferring funds to the states and localities.

But the interests of a healthy and balanced federalism call for a fair share of tax support from state and local governments. We learned earlier that there are untapped and underutilized tax sources in state and local finance. If all 50 states had levied income taxes as high as those of the top 10, income tax collections would have been $11 billion instead of $5 billion in 1966. The same could be said about sales taxes. It might be more difficult, however, to say as much for that sick giant of our tax system, the property tax.

Yet, in spite of taxpayer resistance, the 50 states did make 309 rate increases in their major tax sources between 1959 and 1969. Yet this effort has all the earmarks of a losing battle. The general opinion of tax experts is that the sooner Congress gets on with an intelligent system of tax sharing, the better off we shall be.

TAX REFORM ON THE WAY

Now in prospect is an overhaul of the federal tax system. Deductions, capital gains, estate and gift taxes—all these and more are under study by Congress.

Tax reform would mean higher taxes for many, especially the wealthy, but savings for others, such as the people in the middle-income brackets. High-income persons who use their losses in operating farms to offset gains from other sources would find that practice yielding far less in tax savings under a proposal expected to win favor in Congress.

Many tax authorities say money gained from closing the loopholes could be used to allow sweeping reductions in income tax rates. In fact, reduced rates may also be needed as a "sweetener" if tax reform is to have any chance at all of winning approval in Congress.

The tax reform plan of the Johnson administration—based on the most exhaustive study by tax experts in modern times—if fully enacted by the Nixon administration, would provide tax relief for 56 percent of U.S. taxpayers, raise taxes for 27 percent, and leave 17 percent with no net change.

The Nixon administration is expected to support tax reforms in general. The intensive tax hearings held by the important House Ways and Means Committee in early 1969 indicated the eventual passage of some portions of the tax reform plan of the U.S. Treasury.

The question remains: Will enough citizens in our country actively support a realistic and productive system of revenue (cooperatively managed) based upon generally accepted criteria of (1) productivity, (2) equity, (3) simplicity, and (4) economic usefulness?

QUESTIONS FOR DISCUSSION

1. What recommendations would you make to raise the money needed to provide the services Americans expect to receive from their government? Why?

2. From what sources do the federal, state, and local governments get most of their revenue?

3. Why is it necessary for the federal government to share more of its tax income with state and local governments?

4. Individuals at what income level are most likely to benefit from income tax exemptions? From allowable deductions? From capital gains provisions? From income-splitting?

5. Do you think exemptions ($600) should be the same for all taxpayers regardless of income?

ACTIVITY PROBLEM

1. The U.S. Treasury Department Internal Revenue Service prepares, each year, an excellent teaching kit on learning how to fill in tax Forms 1040A and 1040. All the forms and instructions for filling in are supplied by the Internal Revenue Service. This is a very practical exercise in learning how to prepare your own tax return.

After completing this exercise, you may be in the mood to discuss more realistically the criteria for good taxes and needed tax reforms.

SUGGESTED READINGS

"Best Bets for Cutting Your Tax Bills," *Changing Times,* February, 1969.

Bureau of the Budget: *The Budget in Brief* (annually), U.S. Government Printing Office.

Economic Report of the President (annually), U.S. Government Printing Office.

The Federal Budget, Its Impact on the Economy, Fiscal 1969, National Industrial Conference Board, New York, 1968.

Fiscal Balance in the American Federal System: A Commission Report, vols. I and II, Advisory Commission on Intergovernmental Relations, Washington, D.C., 1967.

Surrey, Stanley: *Tax Reform Studies and Proposals,* U.S. Treasury Department, 1968.

"Where State and Local Taxes Go," *Changing Times,* October, 1967.

Your Federal Income Tax (annually), U.S. Government Printing Office.

chapter 16

CONSUMER PROTECTION:
PRIVATE AIDS

Any marketing practice that renders rational choice more difficult is a subversion of the American economy.

Mildred E. Brady

Primitive man did not need standards other than his taste, his needs, and the limitations of his stomach. But as soon as he became a trader, standards for measurement (quantity and quality) came into existence. Only a few generations ago, the woman who managed a household made most of the clothes worn by the family members. She canned much of the food. She baked bread. Today these functions, as well as a host of others, for the most part are done outside the home.

The household manager and other members of the family now buy consumer goods in the market. Consequently, the homemaker's role as a purchasing agent is very important. It is not too much to say that, for many families, the intelligence with which the homemaker plans and buys is a prime factor in determining the standard of living of the family.

PROBLEMS OF INFORMING CONSUMERS: HISTORICAL BACKGROUND

Today our system of consumer protection is a four-way partnership involving the consumer's prudent management of purchases, the efforts of producers and retailers to serve the consumer, private nonprofit comparative testing of consumer products, and government regulation of marketing.

One of the major consumer challenges is the need for adequate information about the product or service for which consumers spend their money. Without adequate information on a product or a service, people cannot hope to make intelligent choices in the marketplace. Unintelligent decisions in the marketplace lead inevitably to dissatisfactions on the part of consumers and too much waste of human and natural resources. If consumers are to perform their role effectively, they must be adequately informed about products and services.

Business Discovers Consumers Want to Know

At the turn of the century and for many years—until recently—the major efforts of consumer legislation were basically primitive. Then an effort was made to enlist the cooperation of reputable businesses in providing truthful and factual information to consumers. And business discovered through consumer surveys that "consumers want to know." The result was a kind of alliance between business and consumers.

Within a 5-year period (1927 to 1931), a number of testing laboratories were established by major department stores, mail-order firms, laundries, and dry cleaners, as well as one by consumers themselves. During the decades that followed, large numbers of certification and labeling programs sponsored by trade associations were launched. Lumber, leather-glove, mirror, broom, hosiery, and other manufacturers developed such programs. In addition, citrus fruit and apple producers, soap guilds, textile fabric finishers, and manufacturers of boys' apparel all entered the act to label and certify their products for "consumer guidance."

The National Bureau of Standards, in conducting investigations for the Temporary National Economic Committee, compiled data indicating that by the late 1930s fully 700 of the 1,300 trade associations were conducting some kind of labeling or consumer standards program.

Then advertising media prepared to enter this alliance of consumers and business. Radio stations and periodicals such as *McCall's Magazine* were about to launch consumer information seals of approval when, quite abruptly, the whole movement collapsed. The long-drawn-out hearings of the Federal Trade Commission, directed against the old, established *Good Housekeeping* Seal of Approval, merely lent drama to the culmination of a movement that would inevitably have collapsed of its own weight. In having business interests provide them with information, consumers were faced with such an amazing conglomeration of symbols, seals, and labels—many of which were meaningless—that they were more bewildered and confused than ever.

Consumer Cooperation but Not Alliance with Business

It should be stressed that consumers must work with, reason with, and cooperate with business interests to some degree. Long ago the American Standards Association attempted through consumer-business negotiations to correct deceptive certification by developing a valid certification procedure. The National Retail Merchants Association developed, with consumer representation, the washability symbols that were released in 1961.

The National Institute of Drycleaning, in drawing up its Life Expectancy Table for textiles in 1961, worked under the guidance of a distinguished consumer leader. Consumers cannot fully isolate themselves from business. Nevertheless, to go to the other extreme and ally themselves with business is to establish a questionable alliance.

Alliance of Government with Consumers

The third concept underlying programs for providing information to consumers is that the federal government should ally itself with consumers to get quality and performance facts from business. A reader of the historic 1926 *New Republic* articles by Stuart Chase and Frederick Schlink, in which they pleaded for the development of a "science of buying and consuming," is struck by the fact that, from its inception, the consumer testing movement aspired for a consumer-government alliance against business.

The National Bureau of Standards conducted tests for Consumers' Research, Inc., before 1930, but this activity was short-lived, because Congress would not permit it. A bitter struggle between consumer and business groups, as a result of the innocent and routine proposal of the Office of Price Administration during World War II to require the grade labeling of canned goods during the first half of 1943, culminated in another setback for consumers.

There is already a trend toward increasing representation in state governments. California has a consumer representative in the governor's cabinet. Likewise, it appears certain that some type of consumer representation in the executive branch of the federal government is imminent. In March, 1962, President John F. Kennedy created a Consumer Advisory Committee to advise the Council of Economic Advisers, which is another advisory committee; in 1964, President Johnson appointed a consumer representative to his White House staff. (This was discussed thoroughly in Chapter 1.) This is progress on the national level—a candle lighted in consumer darkness.

Many consumer leaders are of the opinion that what is needed is a Department of the Consumer in the President's Cabinet. Such a department could then function directly for the consumer interest much like the Departments of Agriculture, Labor, and Commerce, which attempt to protect the interest of the farmer, the worker, and the businessman.

A fourth concept concerning getting information to consumers came at the behest of commercial interests. The Textile Labeling Act, for example, fits the Du Pont competitive problems more snugly than it does the consumer's need for more fabric information. The FHA Title I program is more successful as protection for the loan portfolios of commercial banks than it is as succor to the homeowner with repair and maintenance problems.

Can Consumers Do It Themselves?

This brings us to the fifth concept concerning getting information to consumers: Consumers should do it themselves. It would be trite to recite all the arguments purporting to prove that consumers are not a unified, cohesive vocal group. The fact is that consumers have failed to organize effectively in the United States.

The most successful attempt to inform consumers on goods and services must be credited to Consumers Union, and in a less degree to Consumers' Research. But most of the problems connected with securing important information about products and services cannot be solved by these two consumer testing organizations.

THE CONSUMER INTEREST AND OUR COMPETITIVE SYSTEM

The need for more objective and useful consumer information is clear to most knowledgeable people. Even in an affluent society—or perhaps more so because of the variety of choices available—consumers need to know what is available and how good the product or service is. The whole justification of our marketing system hinges upon informed consumers exercising their intelligent "dollar votes" to say what should be produced.

The burden placed upon consumer sovereignty or the "dollar vote" by the free enterprise system is a heavy one, growing heavier as products and markets reflect the mounting complexity of technology and the increasing power and ability of sellers to manipulate demand. But the priceless ingredient of effective competition remains a free and rational consumer choice. "Any marketing practice that renders rational choice more difficult is a subversion of our enterprise system." In other words, the better informed consumers are, the more competition works as it should and the less we need be concerned about truth in advertising or with detailed regulation of producers and distributors.

Our Free Enterprise System

The economists who designed our free enterprise system reasoned that there would be optimum allocation of resources if markets were competitively structured, if buyers and sellers possessed adequate information about prices and quality and the availability of consumer products, and if sales were made without artificial restrictions. If all of these conditions are present, so the economic theory goes, utilities are maximized and people secure the most benefit out of the use of our resources. In effect, a balance is struck. Producers (sellers) and consumers (buyers) are on an equal footing, and neither group will be able to take advantage of the other.

Today the essential conditions for price and quality competition, by and large, do not exist. Consequently the consumer has been placed at a disadvantage. Some producers, notably small ones, have also been placed at a disadvantage. A factor that aggravates the situation is that advertising is both the major medium of information for consumers and the major method of misinformation or omitted information. In short, buyers must depend on the seller for information they need to make a purchase decision, and in markets dominated by a few big businesses the seller uses advertising to confuse the buyers, not to properly inform them.

The problem of rational choice is further complicated by the changing nature of retailing itself. The rise of the supermarket and the discount store has meant that retailing has become impersonal. At one time the retailer was a source of information about his products, but the modern supermarket is a symbol of the impersonality of the marketplace. In such a market, advertising tries to presell via brand names, and too often the information is misleading, deceptive, or generally uninformative. In short, the consumer simply lacks the information necessary to enable him to buy rationally and, thus, wisely.

When consumers complain by many thousands of individual letters— as the Special Assistant to the President for Consumer Affairs and Consumers Union office can testify—that they cannot compare prices with quality and oftentimes quantity, and complain in regard to the safety of many products such as cars and appliances, they are not voicing a minor complaint. They are really sounding an alarm that is beginning to be heard in local, state, and national political quarters. And many of us fervently hope that this mounting concern for the well-being of the consumer may be telling business that it is time for business to leaven the traditional mass-marketing concept of the consumer with a public relations concept of the consumer. Instead of viewing the consumer solely as a sales prospect, it may be time for business to take a broader view of consumers. This will be difficult to achieve because most producers have assumed that they have conflict-of-interest problems, and are concerned primarily with getting people to buy—initiating promotional rivalry instead of price and quality competition—rather than with keeping consumers properly informed.

Apparently we cannot count on producers and distributors to supply the essential information about most of the products the consumer buys. If anyone desires scientific documentation of the kinds of problems consumers are faced with, the more than 30 years of testing and reporting on consumer goods by Consumers Union would be most enlightening. The *Consumer Reports* on testing such staple products as refrigerators, toasters, TV sets, automobiles, washing machines, and kitchen ranges, to name a few, are replete with sad, angry, critical references to the low level of quality to be found in the channels of trade. Surely the record can be better than it is. Not much progress can be expected until industry is willing to depend on the development and effective use of quality standards.

The Basic Role of Standards

There is a naïve and erroneous concept of a standard as a step toward regimentation, as a limitation on variety, as an inhibition to creativity. That standards have such effects simply is not true. Quality standards and dead sameness of end product are not synonymous. On the contrary, *meaningful* variety, as opposed to *meaningless* product differentiation, is directly dependent on the development and effective use of standards. In fact, only through the use of standards can we, as consumers, fully realize the fantastically fruitful, productive potential of modern industrial techniques. Why? Because the basic role of standards and specifications is simply to supply a common language understood and respected by producer, distributor, seller, and buyer, a language by means of which open and fair bargaining can take place and the necessary exchange of goods be facilitated. In other words, standards and specifications function as the language of careful description in the production and exchange of goods in somewhat the same way that mathematics is the language of the sciences from which our productive techniques have taken on their particular mid-twentieth-century character.

The development of a common language between buyer and seller of goods for the ultimate consumer is long overdue. To date, however, industry in general has given nothing but a negative response to effective standards and specifications. This negative attitude was pointed up by Tom M. Hopkinson, a member of a public relations firm, when he reported[1] on his independent poll of New York marketing, advertising, publicity, and product promotion executives representing 26 organizations in 17 different industries. In his personal interview, time after time, these executives told him, "It's for legal to decide," when they were asked whether there were any special ethical, moral, or public relations considerations in marketing areas heavily concerned with the "consumer interest." Only three out of 31 executives could see any such relationship.

Thus, he concludes, the philosophy of the day, in considering borderline cases involving public taste, fair dealing, and full and accurate consumer information, too often seems to be: "This is the deal—can we get away with it?"

So business managers apparently have conflict-of-interest problems and are primarily concerned with getting people to buy, not with keeping them properly informed. This is not to say that there have not been efforts on the part of business to establish standards for some consumer products, and, in a few instances, efforts made to enforce voluntary standards. But these efforts are minimal.

BUSINESS-SPONSORED CONSUMER AIDS: VOLUNTARY STANDARDS

Trade associations are conscious of consumer relations, realizing that consumers often have unsatisfactory experiences with the goods they purchase. One of the chief reasons for this dissatisfaction seems to be the lack of useful information concerning the character and performance value of merchandise. Therefore, it is easy to understand the consumer's request for some assurance of the quality of the products he buys and the manufacturer's efforts to devise some means by which to gain the consumer's confidence in his product or service.

This has led to the adoption by various trade associations of methods of certification or guarantee of commodities. Some of the trade associations' certification and labeling methods have been based on superficial inspection and testing. Others have granted approval based on scientifically conducted tests made in conformity with nationally recognized methods.

Private Testing Agencies

The *American Standards Association* is regarded as one of the top private agencies dealing with standardization and testing methods. The ASA (formerly

[1] In the *Harvard Business Review,* September-October, 1964.

known as the American Engineering Standards Committee) was organized by five leading technical societies in 1918 for the purpose of developing a plan for cooperation in standardization work. The ultimate hope was to evolve voluntary standards that would serve a relatively wide market.

The membership of the ASA is made up of many technical societies, trade associations, and governmental agencies, as well as over 2,300 industrial concerns. The association is supported by membership dues and by subscriptions. Before a standard can be approved, it must have the general acceptance of all groups concerned with the particular product. So far, several hundred standards have been approved.

Ever since 1932, the American Standards Association has had a Committee on Ultimate Consumer Goods to promote the development of standards for certain consumer commodities sold on the retail level. Much investigation has gone on, but progress has been slow, owing in a large degree to a lack of funds and disagreement about the use of quality terminology. This confusion points up the difficulty that industry continues to have when it comes to the problem of how quality identifications are to be presented to the consumer.

In 1966, the ASA was replaced by the United States of America Standards Institute; in the fall of 1969, by order of the FTC, it became the American National Standards Institute, Inc. More attention will be given to establishing a certification and labeling program.

The *American Society for Testing Materials* is regarded by some authorities as the second most important private testing agency in the United States. It is an independent association working on standardization of specifications and methods of testing. It has a membership of over 4,200, made up of individuals, companies, laboratories, universities, governmental agencies, libraries, and technical schools.

The ASTM was one of the founding societies of the ASA and is affiliated with the *International Association for Testing Materials*. It has been chiefly instrumental in developing most of the test methods for textiles that are in use today. Like the ASA, this society concentrates on standardizing aids to industry directly.

Agencies Serving Consumers More Directly

The *American Gas Association* is financed by gas companies and businesses engaged in the manufacture of gas appliances. Gas appliances carelessly made and installed could be a source of much danger. The AGA Laboratory Seal of Approval is available to a manufacturer who has met certain standards. A manufacturer may also qualify for a "Certified Performance" marker if he can prove that his gas appliance has met additional specifications in efficiency, convenience, and performance.

Today it is claimed that more than 90 percent of all gas appliances sold in the United States carry the AGA Laboratory Seal of Approval. Some cities require compliance with its standards. To ensure reasonable honesty on the part of manufacturers using its seal, the American Gas Association carries on a continuous inspection system in the factories.

Underwriters' Laboratories is a nonprofit testing organization sponsored by insurance companies. UL tests products submitted by manufacturers for safety. Its staff periodically inspects production at the factories and spot-checks items such as electric cords bought on the open market.

Valuable as the UL service is, it has serious limitations. Products are evaluated for safety rather than for the quality of the product itself. Furthermore, UL approval on a cord does not extend safety approval to the appliance. Finally, its standard for the amount of current leakage considered permissible to come into contact with the user of the product is less stringent than those of other testing organizations. Consumers Union testing, for example, often disagrees with UL standards and passes critical judgment on items bearing the UL seal.

In mid-1968, UL announced plans for reorganization that would broaden its membership base to include consumer and government groups. One year later, UL had only two "consumer" representatives (a magazine writer and a banker) out of a total of 113 members.

The National Electrical Manufacturers Association has written a number of standards for consumer items as well as for industrial equipment. NEMA is best known for finally clearing up the bad situation in room air conditioners. Units used to be sold on the basis of "tons." But one 1-ton unit may have 65 percent more cooling power than another 1-ton unit. Under pressure, especially from Consumers Union, NEMA finally adopted the recommended Btu's (British thermal units), which measure cooling output more accurately. Manufacturers willing to follow NEMA standards could apply the Certified Seal on their product.

Electrical Testing Laboratories, with the aid of the Illuminating Engineering Society, worked out standards for an IES seal on the ETL Certificate of Compliance shield. This certificate can be placed on any lamp that has met the required standards. Perhaps as many as fifty different lamp manufacturers use this certificate. ETL maintains a continuous checking service in the factories. The manufacturer pays about 3 cents a lamp for the testing service and around 10 cents a lamp to an advertising agency hired to promote the use of IES lamps.

ETL will test any product in its line for a manufacturer for a fee, but permits use of its seal only on products whose standards are printed on the label where the consumer can read them. These standards are based on performance requirements, not on construction specifications. ETL has the final word when granting its seal of approval.

Consumer Services of Individual Stores

A few large retailers have developed rather extensive programs of merchandise testing and of informative labeling. Among them are Macy's of New York, Gimbel's of Philadelphia, Marshall Field of Chicago, Lit Brothers of Philadelphia, Kaufmann's of Pittsburgh, and various mail-order houses, such as Sears, Roebuck and Company and Montgomery Ward. Moreover, certain large chain stores—notably the A & P, Safeway, and J. C. Penney—test, grade, and label some of their products.

Sears, Roebuck and Company has maintained its own laboratories and staff of technicians since 1911. This is reportedly the largest privately owned merchandise testing laboratory in the world. The company sets up minimum standards arrived at through agreement among the general merchandise office, the buyers, the merchandise comparison office, and the technical laboratories.

The primary function of the testing is to aid buyers in the selection of merchandise. The company gives special attention to its own trademarked goods. A close analysis of the descriptions in its catalogs reveals the influence of the laboratory technicians upon the advertising department.

J. C. Penney Research and Testing Laboratory in New York City was established in 1930. Most of the merchandise handled by the J. C. Penney stores is tested. The laboratory is equipped to do physical, chemical, and some types of biological testing. Besides setting up standards and testing the products, the laboratory also checks all returned goods to discover whether the article had some inherent fault that did not show up in previous tests. Staff members also spend time in the various mills and factories that produce merchandise for the J. C. Penney stores.

Macy's Bureau of Standards, established in 1927, is primarily interested in the adaptability, performance, durability, and care of merchandise sold by Macy stores. It is concerned largely with these factors from the consumer's point of view. The bureau has also established many standards for goods sold under Macy's brand names. It studies and recommends more effective garment, rug, and fur cleaning, waterproofing, mothproofing, and so on; prepares informative labels for the merchandise; assists in the training of buying and selling management personnel; and is continually working on adequate but easy-to-understand terminology for informing the buying public.

Macy's service supplements the store's guarantee policy, making it more reliable and less costly to both consumer and owner, and more enforceable than most so-called product guarantees.

Some of the large food chains, like A & P and Safeway Stores, grade certain foods according to U.S. Department of Agriculture standards—the most acceptable grades for food products. The A & P, in particular, also has developed its own grades for its store brands. As a rule, U.S. Department of Agriculture-graded goods are more reliable.

Who Should Write Industry Standards?

For American consumers, this is becoming the era of standards. The meat we eat is subject to standards for cleanliness, the cars we drive must meet certain safety requirements, and many of our clothes have to conform to fireproofing regulations.

The list of standards for consumer products and services is growing as buyers demand more safeguards in today's complex marketplace. More can be expected. And the trend raises the question: Who should set those standards?

Industry maintains that it has the know-how to do the job voluntarily. Skeptics say that only mandatory government standards can adequately protect consumers. Yet the fact is that more and more of the standards-writing chores are falling to government by default. In key areas of household safety and consumer dissatisfaction, business often has either failed to develop standards or has made them so weak as to be meaningless. Voluntary standards may well be preferable to government controls. But as William V. White, executive director of the National Commission on Product Safety, created by Congress in 1968, says regarding his realm of responsibility: "If . . . voluntary standards do not provide an adequate solution to the problem of safety in households, then I don't have to tell you that state or Federal standards . . . will be inevitable."

WILL GOVERNMENT INTERVENTION BE NECESSARY?

Many Laws Enacted

The federal involvement was broadened considerably in the 1968 Congress. Enacted were laws establishing requirements for automobile safety, meat inspection, flammable fabrics, gas pipeline safety, and disclosure of credit terms.

During the Nixon administration it appears unlikely that federal interest in consumer protection will decline. The 91st Congress and various federal agencies are expected to look into consumer problems involving auto insurance, auto and appliance warranties, job safety, mine safety, door-to-door salesmen, and radiation from color television, to mention a few.

The proliferation of government regulations naturally alarms private standard-setters. Such regulations are "valuable early warnings to standards-developing organizations of what could eventually be virtual control by government of manufacturing with licensing and pretesting requirements," warns Francis K. McCune, president of the American National Standards Institute, Inc. (ANSI), the major private standards-developing organization. Creeping federalism was a major topic at a Washington conference of the ANSI, which is made up of 800 corporate members and 150 trade associations.

ANSI officials maintain that industry is already doing an adequate job of regulating itself. There are an estimated 13,700 industrial standards in use, and most are voluntary ones. The ANSI has 3,000 standards, ranging from specifications for nuts and bolts and electrical wiring to safety requirements for power mowers and household appliances.

The private standards-setters insist that only industry has the technical experience to set standards for today's complex products. Government regulations, they say, tend to be unrealistic and too rigid, stifling innovation. "The best standard results when people who are knowledgeable in the field participate," asserts Mr. McCune. "That's better than when somebody in government goes off in a corner and writes one."

The principal complaint against voluntary standards is that what has been accomplished has not been enough. "We just want you to do more of what you are already doing," Betty Furness, who was President Johnson's consumer adviser, used to tell businessmen.

Despite the plethora of engineering standards, no national safety requirements exist for a host of consumer products. The Product Safety Commission reports that 135 of 263 items it plans to study are not covered by any ANSI criteria. And many standards that do exist were too slow in coming, complains the commission's Mr. White.

The standard for safety glazing of sliding glass doors and fixed glass panels, which became effective June 26, 1968, took more than 6 years to develop, Mr. White says. And so far, the commission frets, most homebuilders have ignored the voluntary standard, continuing instead to install the cheaper, fragile, ordinary glass doors and panels that are estimated to cause 100,000 injuries annually.

Almost every government standard typically results from similar industry inertia. The auto industry moved to install such safety items as collapsible steering columns and more padding only after federal requirements were imminent. Federal meat inspection laws stemmed from lax industry policing. And President Johnson said he asked for the gas pipeline safety law "because industry standards weren't adequate for protection."

Many voluntary standards are not enforced because they are written by the same people who are to abide by them. Before enactment of the 1966 auto-safety laws, a Senate Commerce Committee report found that autos generally were subject to standards developed by the industry-dominated Society of Automotive Engineers. "These standards are the product of a committee consensus, subject to a single manufacturer's veto, while affording no consumer or user representative. Compliance is voluntary," the report said.

Move, or Else

Officials of the 50-year-old ANSI, formerly the American Standards Association, recognize that, as a spokesman puts it, "Unless industry does a more aggressive job of setting voluntary standards, government will move in and do it for them." In the past 3 years their New York-based group has been reorganized, adding government representation on its board of directors and establishing a council to air consumers' views on proposed standards. A new goal is increased certification, including eventually a single, recognizable ANSI seal for all consumer products meeting basic standards for safety and performance.

It may be a sign that industry is ready to take on more responsibility for making voluntary standards meet the needs of consumers. If not, one thing is clear: When it comes to public health and safety, government standards are better than no standards at all.

Seals—How Reliable Are They?

Seals or certifications of approval of products as "guaranteed," "certified," "approved," or "tested" are promoted by business to put a quality ceiling on certain kinds of services for consumers and are issued to manufacturers for products that meet the requirements of a testing organization. Figure 16-1, Examples of Seals, provides information about a few of the many seals currently used.

In most cases, it is difficult to know whether consumers benefit from these seals. The American Institute of Laundering tests for colorfastness in fabrics. Its seal of approval tells consumers that the material withstands laundering. It is an aid to know that a garment can be laundered rather than requiring dry-cleaning.

The magazine seals of approval are probably more valuable to the magazines than to the public. A seal, for example, that promises "replacement or refund of money for any product advertised in the magazine whose performance proves to be defective" has little significance or meaning when selecting garments or fabrics.

This points up the fact that a healthy skepticism should prevail concerning seals that are not directly related to known tests. In short, to make intelligent use of seals, consumers must know (1) who approves the product, (2) what tests were made, (3) what the test results were, (4) what the certification includes, and (5) what the specific terms of the guarantee are and how long they are effective. Present seals of approval on consumer products fail to give answers to all these requirements.

Better Business Bureaus

The United States Supreme Court has declared that "voluntary action to end abuses and to foster fair competitive opportunities in the public interest may be more effective than legal processes." This point of view was central in the thinking of a group of businessmen who organized the National Vigilance Committee in 1911. In 1916, this group adopted the name of *National Better Business Bureau*.

The seal	Where it is found	What it means
American Gas Association	On gas appliances—ranges, refrigerators, heaters, clothes dryers.	Products have been tested by AGA, are certified for conformity to requirements of the American Standards Association and are factory tested at least annually to insure continued conformity.
American Institute of Laundering	On labels attached to fabrics and ready-made merchandise—clothing, bedding, draperies.	Products have passed ALL tests for shrinkage; color and sunfastness; fiber strength; resistance to perspiration; launderability of zippers, buttons, and snaps; and general appearance after laundering.
Canadian Standard Association	On electrical, gas, or oil equipment and plumbing brass; on general products certified to show conformity with quality and performance standards.	Products are certified by the manufacturers to conform to CSA Standards af safety and performance.
Underwriters' Laboratories, Inc.	On all appliances, equipment, and materials which could possibly be fire or accident hazards or used to stop the spread of fire.	Products have passed original and periodical factory tests and examination in accordance with standards for safety.
United States Testing Company	On products continually tested and certified by the U.S. Testing Company.	Products have been tested, meet the requirements of the U.S. Testing Company, and are qualified for materials, construction, use, and performance. They are factory reinspected to insure continued quality.
Consumer magazines *Parents Magazine* *Good Housekeeping* *Chatelaine* *McCalls*	On any article or appliance tested and approved in the laboratories of one of these magazines.	Products have been tested and have met specific requirements set up by each magazine before receiving the *guaranteed, commended, investigated and approved, laboratory use-tested, or certified* seal. Refer to the magazine for an explanation of the policy and meaning behind statements made.

Figure 16-1   **Examples of Seals. Source:** *Money Management: Your Shopping Dollar,* **Household Finance Corporation, Chicago.**

Since 1916, this central organization and some local but independent bureaus in many cities in the United States have worked hard to protect decent business and consumer interest. The local Better Business Bureaus are maintained by business itself for the purposes of (1) promoting and maintaining advertising and selling practices that are fair to business and to consumers; (2) protecting business and the consumer from frauds, misrepresentations, and chicanery in business transactions; and (3) providing certain aids for consumers in their quest for full value for their money. Millions of "facts" booklets—*Cosmetics, Health Cures, Legal Problems, Used Cars, Home Building and Buying, Investments, Color Television,* and others—are distributed free.

The annual report of the Association of Better Business Bureaus gives an impressive list of requests for information and services rendered. More than 2½ million requests for information from business and the public were recorded in 128 separate bureaus. These 128 bureaus investigated in one year more than 40,000 advertisements, and 570 trade practice conferences were held in 60 different classifications of business, resulting in the adoption of voluntary restraints against advertising abuses.

The work of the bureaus in checking advertising is especially noteworthy. Complaints come usually from business competitors and consumers. However, the major approach is the daily job of "shopping the ads." Trained persons study the local advertising, then check the advertised articles in the stores.

In the event that slight misrepresentations are found, the merchant is shown just how the advertising misrepresents the merchandise. If the merchant refuses to correct or improve the advertising, more drastic action is generally used. As a last resort, the bureau will turn the case over to the proper governmental agency, usually the Federal Trade Commission.

There are certain services that the bureaus do not give to consumers. If anyone calls the bureau by telephone and asks for the name of a reliable laundry, the answer is something like this: "I'm sorry, but we can't do that. We cannot tell people where to go or where not to go. We simply give the facts, if there are any in our records, and let people make up their own minds."

PROFESSIONAL ASSOCIATIONS AIDING CONSUMERS

Professional associations and organizations are another source of consumer protection, and they have done outstanding work in promoting consumer education. The effective programs of some of these associations will give an idea of what they are accomplishing.

American Home Economics Association

The AHEA is primarily an educational organization with over 35,000 members engaged in the fields of family economics, home management, family relations and child development, foods and nutrition, textiles and clothing, housing and household equipment, and art. The organization is active in extension service and in college clubs, with over 20,000 students majoring in home economics. Through its publication, the *Journal of Home Economics,* and joint projects with trade associations, the American National Standards Institute, and legislative activities, the AHEA has been an important information center.

The Consumer Interests Committee promotes important consumer programs and serves as a clearinghouse for all consumer activities. The textile section was a prime mover in seeking a way to set standards for consumer goods. Today, the efforts of the AHEA revolve around consumer legislation, consumer education, and promotion of standards of quality for consumer goods.

Some of the most outstanding work of the AHEA has been in the field of food facts and fallacies. This is in keeping with one of its major contributions—giving information to consumers. The AHEA has supported programs for consumer protection against misrepresentation and misleading advertising. Work in the areas of trading stamps, credit charges, fictitious pricing, good labeling, and bait advertising has received a large share of attention.

The AHEA is preparing to take even greater interest in improving the position of the consumer. To commemorate its golden anniversary (in 1959), the committee on philosophy and objectives set forth the new direction for home economics. Among the 12 objectives, three were specifically related to the consumer. This organization of over 35,000, with members in almost every county or small political unit in 50 states, could become the most effective consumer educational force in the United States.

American Medical Association

There are several medical, surgical, and dental associations that have established standards of materials and practices. These standards are of direct value to consumers.

The American Medical Association, an organization of physicians, is active in the improvement of quality and standardization of medical products. Most of the testing and education is done by five committees. Some of the findings are reported in its publication, *Journal of the American Medical Association.*

The Council on Pharmacy and Chemistry, one of the five AMA committees, judges products claimed to have therapeutic values. The accepted and unaccepted products are described in the *Journal* and published annually in a separate brochure.

The Council on Physical Therapy investigates and reports on the merits of nonmedical apparatus and devices offered for sale to consumers as well as to physicians and hospitals.

The Council on Foods and Nutrition checks the health claims made by producers for their manufactured foods. It concerns itself only with foods sold for dietary purposes. It merely "accepts" foods that offer truthful advertising and labels. The use of the seal is granted to products that are accepted. It definitely does not "approve," "recommend," or "grade" food products. Foods submitted for analysis are accepted or rejected, and the facts are so published in the *Journal*. No attempt is made to equate quality and price relationships.

The Committee on Advertising of Cosmetics and Soaps was formed to advise the manager of the *Journal* on advertisements of cosmetics and soaps that are submitted to him.

The Bureau of Investigation has for its primary purpose the investigation and dissemination of information on "patent medicines," quacks, medical fads, and other aspects of pseudo medicine.

The American College of Surgeons is actively engaged in standardization of surgical dressings on the basis of use and characteristics. The college also develops standards for hospitals with respect to services, treatments, and records.

The American Institute of Homeopathy published the first *Homeopathic Pharmacopeia* in 1897. The standards set up by this organization are for the use of the pharmacist as well as the physician. The Federal Food, Drug, and Cosmetic Act recognized these standards as well as those found in the *United States Pharmacopeia* and in the *National Formulary*. These are not government publications. They are published by scientists, doctors, and pharmaceutical manufacturers.

These standards are reviewed periodically to incorporate the latest scientific information. When new drugs are discovered, the experts study the evidence of their effectiveness, the right dosages, and the best processes for their manufacture, packaging, and labeling. This information is made available to doctors and pharmacists.

In general, a drug or standard preparation with the letters U.S.P., H.P., or N.F. on its label has been processed, packed, and labeled according to standard specifications.

American Dental Association

The American Dental Association is a professional association with a membership of a high percentage of the more than 100,000 dentists in the United States. Its Council on Dental Therapeutics evaluates dental therapeutic agents and dental cosmetic agents sold by companies directly to the public or to the profession. In the council's *Accepted Dental Remedies* are up-to-date descriptions of basic drugs used in dentistry. The council does not evaluate medicated mouthwashes sold to the public, because it feels that they are useless when used without professional supervision. Toothbrushes and cleansers for dentures are also not considered for acceptance. The council, however, continues to give consideration to dentifrices that claim to have evidence against tooth decay or any other mouth disorder.

Until 1960, the best the council had to say about dentifrices was summed up in the terse statement: "The function of a dentifrice . . . is to aid the brush in cleaning the teeth."

In 1960, there was one exception, when the official *Journal of the American Dental Association* published a report that began, "After careful consideration of the results of clinical studies conducted on Crest toothpaste, manufactured by the Procter & Gamble Company, the Council on Dental Therapeutics has recognized the usefulness of the dentifrice as a caries (decay) preventive agent. . . ."

There were resentful reactions on the part of toothpaste manufacturers because ADA allowed its name to be used. Many dentists also resented such commercialization of their professional organization.

Actually, the ADA recognition of Crest, according to a report in 1961, *The Medicine Show,* by Consumers Union, was "hedged and tentative." In view of ADA's long-standing invitation to dentifrice manufacturers to seek the kind of recognition given to Crest, it would seem to be a fair conclusion that no such evidence exists up to now. The patent on Crest formulation is held by the Indiana University Foundation, where the experiments were conducted at a cost of over $3 million financed by Procter & Gamble, who have an exclusive license to produce and market the toothpaste.

The Procter & Gamble promotion and advertising of Crest were objected to by the ADA as "gross exaggeration and a misleading distortion." Then why was nothing done about these claims? The two federal agencies that have some control over dentifrices, the Food and Drug Administration and the Federal Trade Commission, did not have enough power. Until Congress changed the law, in 1962, the FDA could only review the "safety" of the product, not its efficacy. Now that the FDA has the efficacy power, it can seize a product if its label is false or misleading. And the burden of proof is the company's headache.

The curbing of misleading advertising is the responsibility of the FTC. To prove the claims as false in regard to Crest is almost an impossibility because hearing examiners and judges (not ordinarily trained in scientific disciplines) have usually considered laboratory evidence, even if inadequate, more convincing than testimony by experts. The American Dental Association has complained about the ineffectiveness of the FTC under present rules. The remedy, said ADA, is an amendment that would shift the burden of proof to the advertiser, and until this happens, consumers must be wary of claims for dentifrices. Incidentally, the ADA does recognize the suitability of baking soda mixed with powdered salt as a cleansing agent.

The contributions of the AMA and ADA could be much greater. At the present time, the chief weakness is their inability to reach the consumer. Modern advertising reaches millions, whereas statements by medical associations may reach only a few thousand. Perhaps the greatest benefit is in the professional use of the standards set up, rather than in giving direct information to the consumer. A good consumer-education program in the schools could inform families of the importance of this kind of information and on how to get up-to-date consumer information.

Other Consumer Protection Associations

There are other consumer protection movements and associations of considerable importance in the United States on the local, state, and federal levels. They are described in Chapters 17 and 18. Some of these are centered in state colleges; others are local consumer associations. Labor, too, has set up a consumer organization with headquarters in New York City.

Such organizations as the National Young Women's Christian Association (YWCA) and the American Association of University Women have active consumer-education programs. Credit unions, cooperatives, women's clubs, parents' organizations, local labor unions, and religious groups have some consumer-protection activities.

The extension services of many universities are extending consumer education to the urban centers where 90 percent of the population lives. This particular service has tremendous possibilities because university extension services have the largest adult education programs in the United States.

CONSUMER-FINANCED NONPROFIT TESTING AND RATING AGENCIES

For any desired product, the consumer encounters a multiplicity of brands and models. Is there some rational basis for choosing one over the other? Not the wild, unsupported (and often unsupportable) advertising claims, hundreds of which impinge on the consumer's senses every day. Not the kind of judgment a consumer can make from even a careful examination at the point of sale. Not the sweet purrings of an attractive salesperson, often less informed about product differences than the customer and possibly biased by "push money" (money paid for urging a certain brand on customers). Not even your own experience, or your neighbor's, can be a rational basis for selecting many products that are bought infrequently, such as refrigerators and automobiles, which are changed radically from year to year.

Suppose a conscientious consumer decides, for some major purchase, that he is going to try to determine which of a number of products or models of products is best. In a simpler society, he might have a chance. But in countries with complicated technologies, he is stymied by the complexities and properties of new materials—plastics, synthetic fibers, urethane foams, transistors, new insecticides, and drugs—about which he is given little information and with which he has had no previous experience. He is perplexed by the various ways these materials are used in finished products—he cannot determine the virtues of one kind of weave over another, or of one construction technique over another (for example, printed versus wired circuits). No sooner did the conscientious consumer learn how to distinguish a better from a poorer carpet sweeper than the vacuum cleaner faced him. As he mastered the qualities of the upright vacuum cleaner, there came the tank and canister cleaner to consider. When he caught up with these, they sprouted revolving brushes and created a whole new set of problems requiring knowledge before decision.

With the development of still newer products—automatic clothes-washing machines; automatic moisture-sensing clothes dryers' dishwashers; floor scrubbers; air conditioners; sudsing, nonsudsing, and controlled-sudsing detergents; wash-and-wear, drip-dry, and easy-care clothing; and on and on—the poor consumer might have given up a long time ago. (Indeed, even the manufacturers find it difficult to keep up with the rapidly changing scene.)

Why Consumer Testing Is Necessary

Why should the consumer be concerned about making a rational choice? Because there are wide differences in overall quality between competing models of most products, and it follows that the individual consumer who buys an inferior product wastes his money and lowers his standard of living.

Professor Arthur R. Oxenfeldt[2] has estimated, using *Consumer Report* ratings as a basis, that the consumer could increase his standard of living by one and one-half to two times if he bought the products rated best rather than those rated average. In a broader sense, economic resources are wasted when they are used to make inferior products. The same metal, the same plastic, the same labor can be used to make a product that lasts longer and provides more satisfaction than a poorer product.

It is of interest to the individual consumer and to the country as a whole that rational choices be made. But how? If the consumer cannot have all the necessary technical disciplines himself, he can join with other consumers, and together the group can employ them. This is the essence of a consumer testing organization: the application of technical knowledge to consumer problems, particularly to the problem of product purchasing but more broadly to the problem of consumer welfare.

With such a tool, a consumer organization can concern itself more knowledgeably and therefore more effectively with general problems that have their solution in legislation or industrywide action—such as health, safety, alloca-

[2] In a study published in 1950 in the *Review of Economics and Statistics.*

tion of radio and TV frequencies, watering of ham, standards of identity and grades for foods and other products, labeling, weights and measures, and many similar matters.

The Right to Be Informed

It is, by now, commonplace to observe that purchasers of consumer goods in our half of the twentieth century are faced with almost impossible decision-making tasks if they are to choose rationally. The new technologies—from synthetics to solid-state electronics—so basic to our rising standard of living, generate complexities in the products we buy daily that affect not only how efficiently we spend our money but the very quality of our life and even its safety. No educational efforts, no matter how skillfully devised or executed, can improve the situation significantly. Not only is the subject matter too difficult, but even if it could be learned, it becomes obsolete too rapidly and is replaced by newer, more complex technologies.

Accepting this as a condition of our life, what can we do to improve this part of our lot? A number of approaches have been developed. A review of some of them will help you comprehend comparative testing.

1. Education.   Although it is futile and, even if successful, not profitable for consumers to try to understand the new technologies, it is helpful to learn something of their effects. Without understanding why, it is possible and desirable to know, for example, that synthetic detergents do better in hard-water areas than soap, that there are problems with biodegradability, that sudsing detergents are not necessarily better than nonsudsing ones, etc. The task of teaching such information is a formidable one, calling for the use of the newer, more powerful technologies which have changed the face of education itself. But the limitations of education for solving the problem we have posed should be recognized: One can teach only generalizations (the specifics are too many and change too frequently) that some detergents are better in hard water than others, some are more biodegradable, some nonsudsing detergents are poor, and so on.

2. Informative Labeling.   To be more specific, we can describe each product's significant-to-the-consumer characteristics on its label. The scheme can be mandatory—required by law. Or it can be voluntary in a variety of ways. For example, individual companies may agree to accept a set of rules drawn up by some outside agency, such as the Swedish VDN; or a group of companies may agree to accept the labeling schemes devised by their trade association; or some single company may devise a set of rules for its own products. The virtue of these schemes is obvious: They supply useful information about the product at the point of purchase. Their inadequacies are also clear: The labels are rarely complete enough to provide all the required information;

characteristics are often listed because they are easy to measure, not because of their consumer significance; they ask the consumer to evaluate the significance of the label designations, which he is often ill equipped to do because of lack of experience with the product; and the enforcement of the schemes often leaves much to be desired.

3. Standards of Identity. These define minimum requirements for a product before it may be described by a generic name. In our country, they are generally used for food products. If, for example, a product is called "butter," its minimum butterfat content, its maximum water content, the presence of color additives, salt, etc., are all prescribed. A product not conforming in any one respect may not be called "butter."

Again, the advantages and disadvantages of such a scheme are obvious. While the consumer can be assured of a minimum quality for any product he buys under the scheme, he has no way of maximizing his effectiveness in purchasing. Furthermore, at least in the United States, he has very little to say about what goes into the standard when one considers the practice and not the theory. Although he can nominally submit recommendations, his expertise as well as his time and travel funds are usually limited. The result is that the standards are largely influenced by the industries affected, to the detriment of the consumer.

4. Grade Labeling. This approach takes the minimum standards idea the rest of the way and establishes additional grades of quality. With some education on the meaning to the consumer of the different grades, it would seem that all his needs would be met by grade labeling. All products of the same grade would have the same quality level, and his purchase could then be made on the basis of style, cost, availability, and other similar factors easy to determine and to judge. The problem of a consumer-interest input into the standards-making procedure remains. And the solutions to all the problems posed in trying to set grade levels and to keep them vital are not at hand for all products and may, indeed, require formidable efforts. Yet the rewards seem so high that we ought to begin to make the effort more seriously than we have. In this country, grading is done for some food products for purposes of buying and selling. But the consumer rarely gets to see the grades of even such products. A recent law requires the government to set grades for automobile tires, an exciting development we are watching with interest.

5. Comparative Testing. This approach, conceived in the 1930s, is an obvious answer to the problems posed to the consumer by modern technology: the application of the very technology that has complicated his decision making in purchasing to the elucidation of it. The products that face the purchaser with the problem of choosing are compared as a group by subjecting them to tests by technical personnel knowledgeable in the new technologies and evaluating them in terms of the purchaser's interests and needs. The results are presented to the consumer in various ways.

In one scheme, exemplified by *Der Test*, a German consumer publication, each product is described by brand name and by the test findings applicable to it. The reader is left to do his own comparisons in detail and to make his own choice in terms of *his* evaluation of the relative importance of the factors described.

In the prototype represented by the publication *Consumer Reports,* the results are described in the form of brand ratings—"Acceptable," usually in order of overall quality, or "Not Acceptable." Some products are identified as "Best Buys" when the quality is high and the price comparatively low.

Another approach that is represented by the British *Which?* involves a discussion of each brand in terms of the test findings, dismissing those considered undesirable or less desirable purchases for reasons of performance, price, or whatever, discussing those brands considered possible purchases for specialized uses or users, and concluding with recommended Best Buys. What are the relative merits of these or other alternatives?

Merits of Comparative Testing

Although a brilliant device for developing a self-supporting, independent consumer organization, comparative testing is no panacea. Some of the questions that have been raised about it are these:

1. A prime requirement for effective comparative testing is an understanding of the criteria that should govern a consumer purchase. How can we determine these? Will one set do for all consumers? How many sets are needed?

2. How shall we test for these criteria? Where will the validated test methods come from? Should they be standardized nationally? Internationally? By what mechanism?

3. At what level of performance does a product become unsafe or unacceptable for some other reason? What level constitutes excellent performance? Should a comparative testing organization merely compare what is actually in the market, or should it also point out what could be available that the technology makes possible and even suggest how this should be done?

4. What can be done about the problem of new models that render product information developed by comparative testing obsolete, and the problem of the length of time it takes to test and get into print? What can be done about the problem of product changes without change in the name or model number?

5. Comparative testing provides more specific, particular information about the products tested than any of the other schemes tried. But it provides it without specific regard to a particular purchaser's needs, away from the point of sale, or at a time when it may not be needed. How can this deficiency be rectified?

Two Experiments

In the United States, more than in most countries, we have been plagued with a phenomenon known as the "Annual Model Change." For many products (automobiles, washing machines, refrigerators, and other large appliances), the manufacturers change models every year. Most of the time, the changes turn out, after examination and test, to be superficial—styling changes, for example.

But there is no way to tell except by examination and test. Because of costs, it has been impossible to test each product each time there is a change in model number. As a result, the ratings on many products are out of date within a year or less of the time of publication of the test results. How do you solve this problem?

Consumers Union solves this problem, in part, by storing last year's models (say, automatic washing machines) until the new models appear in the market. They buy the new models and compare their published specifications and their physical characteristics side by side with the old models. For those models that appear identical, they perform a brief check-test to confirm the conclusion. If confirmed, they use last year's test data in this year's report. If there are differences, they do complete tests.

Consumers Union has found that only about one-third of the samples have needed complete retesting. The saving in time that results from this procedure has now permitted them to publish a report on washing machines every year.

The second experiment that Consumers Union is conducting is an attempt to keep the advice current, up to date, available at the point of sale, and custom-fit for the needs of each particular purchaser. To this end, Consumers Union is trying to put the information they have learned about a room air conditioner into a computer. The computer will store the information about price, availability, and service. Access to the information will be near the point of purchase. Preliminary studies have indicated technological feasibility for several forms of information dissemination systems ranging from a vending machine for specialized reports to a coin-operated computer console tied by leased lines to a central processing unit.

If it works as hoped, a purchaser about to buy a product will consult the computer. The computer will question the purchaser to ascertain his needs (in the case of an air conditioner, for example, the size, location, and type of room to be cooled, the number of people occupying it, the cost limits, etc.) and, from its memory bank, extract the appropriate advice in the form of brand and model recommendations, shops where these may be bought, current prices, installation instructions, and other pertinent information.

This is a most exciting technological advance for consumers. If successful, in terms of service charge to consumers, people can have up-to-date information made available to them continuously by the simple method of consulting the computer in some shopping center or at home via telephone.

Consumers' Research, Inc. (CR)

In the early 1920s there was an outburst of inaccurate and misleading advertising. The prosperity following World War I brought forth a tremendous flow of consumer goods on the market, aided by mass production techniques worked out by Henry Ford and others after him. This flow of products was pushed by new methods of advertising and by what Thorstein Veblen called the "higher salesmanship." Many of the new products were shoddy and poorly designed, calling for critical examination. In a way, the testing of consumer goods at this time was an inevitable response to confused disappointment in the mass-produced outflow of products. Consumers began to ask: Is there "soapier soap," "coffee-er coffee"?

This confusion set the scene for what became a best-seller—*Your Money's Worth,* by Stuart Chase and F. J. Schlink—in 1927. The book revealed the multiple methods used by business to deceive consumers, and shortly after it appeared thousands of letters flooded the offices of the publishing company. People were concerned. Primarily, they wanted to know, "How can I select the best product?" To the authors and a small group of their friends, these letters expressed the development of a new attitude—a consumer-minded attitude—on the part of the American people. Out of Mr. Schlink's attempt to answer the queries, the Consumers' Club was organized in White Plains, New York. In 1929, the club became Consumers' Research, Inc., and in 1933 it moved to Washington, New Jersey, its present home.

This testing agency publishes twelve monthly issues of *Consumers' Research Bulletin* and its *Annual Bulletin.* The subscription cost of the former is $8 and of the latter, $2.95. Consumers' Research claims around 100,000 mail subscribers and is bought on newsstands by an additional 10,000 readers. Its financial resources are about $750,000 annually. Besides product ratings, the *Bulletin* carries ratings of motion pictures and phonograph records, short editorials, and the Consumers Observation Post. CR does not have an aggressive sales promotion department. Sales are largely dependent on recommendations by subscribers.

Most of the testing is hired out to well-known testing laboratories and to specialized consultants. Listings in the *Bulletin* are usually arranged in alphabetical order: A, recommended on the basis of quality; A-A, highest recommendation; B, intermediate with respect to quality; and C, not recommended. Price ratings, 1, 2, and 3, are given in some ratings, 1 being low and 3 high price. Quality judgments are wholly independent of price with one exception—automobiles.

Evaluation of Consumers' Research

1. The control of CR limits its potential effectiveness. Although nonprofit, the board of trustees is limited to five persons, including the president and his wife. It is a self-perpetuating organization, which excludes fresh ideas that might come from a board elected from among its subscribers. CR's full-time staff comprises approximately 80 persons, including about 15 technical experts. The board does not permit the employees to belong to any other organization without written permission. Consequently, there is no labor union in the plant.

2.   Some people question the reliability of the test reports in the *Bulletin* by arguing that large corporations pay fees to secure the highest ratings. There has never been proof of these accusations, and their reliability can be questioned for at least two reasons. First, a successful court suit on this count would be the easiest method to destroy the testing organization, and there are plenty of businessmen who would jump at this opportunity. Second, over a period of years, the products of large corporations receive about the same percentage of "not recommended" and "recommended" ratings as other producers.

3.   The financial resources of CR are limited to the sales of its publication (no advertising income is permitted). Testing of consumer products is expensive, and consequently CR is not able to test as many products as the subscribers might like. To rate more consumer goods, CR frequently borrows test samples of large, expensive items from manufacturers who sign affidavits that the goods were typical and selected at random. Typewriters, for example, were rented.[3] Consumers would feel more assured if all the products tested had been purchased in retail stores by persons unknown to the stores, rather than samples that may not have been selected at random. As a matter of policy, consumer products to be tested should be purchased in different sections of the country, to protect against the possibility of a better- or poorer-quality shipment to other sections.

4.   Branded products available in one section of the United States are not available in other sections. California and the West Coast in general have many branded products not available elsewhere. Subscribers in some sections are unhappy because their needs are not served.

5.   Consumer testing agencies restrict most of their tests to branded goods nationally distributed. This policy, a practical one to testers, excludes the testing of local unbranded products.

6.   Some subscribers would prefer to have CR test most of the products by its own staff in its own laboratories. When representatives from industry want to discuss and examine the data on the testing of their products, it is more satisfactory to talk with the scientists and experts who did the testing. When tests are farmed out to many different laboratories, adequate discussion by fellow testers and experts is usually impossible.

7.   A certain number of social-minded subscribers do not want to purchase products from businesses that have poor working conditions and low wages for their employees. CR insists that this social concern should have no place in reporting the results of testing. This decision is more reasonable today than it was when CR was established in 1929, because the federal government has set up minimum wage standards for goods sold interstate. Furthermore, unionization of plants and the nature of competition make this limitation appear less important even to social-minded people.

When the Technical, Editorial, and Office Assistants Union attempted to unionize the CR plant, and agreement seemed unlikely, a strike was called in September, 1935, which lasted four months. The National Labor Relations Board ordered CR to bargain with the employees and to reinstate three discharged employees. CR refused to comply with the order. A group of CR's subscribers, organized to aid in settling the strike, decided to set up a new consumer testing agency.[4]

[3] Sylvia Lane, "A Study of Selected Agencies That Evaluate Consumer Goods Qualitatively in the United States," unpublished doctoral dissertation, University of Southern California, Los Angeles, 1957, p. 106.

[4] Helen Sorenson, *The Consumer Movement*, Harper and Row, Publishers, Incorporated, New York, 1941, p. 47.

8. CR was criticized recently when it made an arrangement to test photographic goods for Davis Publications, Inc. The results were published in a magazine that contained advertisements exploiting the test results.

Consumers Union of U.S., Inc. (CU)

Arthur Kallet, former secretary of Consumers' Research, and 10 former CR staff workers set up the new testing agency, Consumers Union, in New York City. Mr. Kallet was director of CU until his retirement in 1957. He remained on the board of directors for a few years following retirement. In 1955, CU moved to spacious new quarters in Mount Vernon, New York.

Consumers Union is a nonprofit organization established in 1936. It is chartered under the Membership Corporations Law of the State of New York and derives its income solely from the sale of its publications (1,350,000 subscribers and 150,000 newsstand buyers). In addition, the expenses of occasional research projects of a public service nature may be met in part by nonrestrictive, noncommercial grants.

Consumers Union has no connection with any commercial interest and accepts no advertising. Its ratings and reports on products are solely for the information and use of the readers of *Consumer Reports* and may not be used in advertising or for any commercial purpose. The pocket-size *Buying Guide* is issued in December. It condenses articles in previous issues of *Consumer Reports* and includes some new material and buying advice.

The purposes of Consumers Union, as stated in its charter, are "to provide for consumer information and counsel on consumer goods and services . . . to give information and assistance on all matters relating to expenditure of family income—to initiate and cooperate with individual and group efforts seeking to create and maintain decent living standards."

Any subscriber may become a member of Consumers Union by so requesting at the time he subscribes to *Consumer Reports* or by written application at any time. Any subscriber becomes a member also by voting in the annual election of directors; ballots are mailed to all subscribers. Membership entails no financial or other obligation, except that members are expected to exercise their right to vote in the annual election of the board of directors.

The subscription rates are $6 for one year, $10 for two years, $14 for three years. A special reduced rate of $4 is available for group members, this rate applying to each order when five or more are entered together.

CU is served by its board of directors, numbering 19 in 1969, which functions through five committees. The board deals with broad policy considerations. The operation of CU, which includes testing, publishing, and servicing of the readership, is supervised by the director and a management staff of 23, including the heads of 13 departments. The total staff numbers more than three hundred persons. All except the management staff work under a contract between

CU and the American Newspaper Guild, AFL-CIO (American Federation of Labor and Congress of Industrial Organizations).

CU publishes information on more than 200 different consumer products each year. In deciding what products to test, CU polls its readers with questionnaires. If sizable numbers reply that they want reports on hi-fi equipment or clothes dryers, the staff gives full consideration to these products in preparing a list of upcoming test projects. After the staff has approved a project, a market survey is made to find out trends and pricing practices in the industry involved and to determine which brands and models—in terms of availability and consumer interest—are to be tested.

To obtain samples of products for testing, CU has a "ready reserve" of some 85 shoppers located in some 60 cities scattered throughout the United States. On orders from CU, these typical buyers go to the regular retail stores, and without revealing CU connection to the seller, buy the specified brands at the merchant's regular price. The products are picked up immediately and shipped to CU headquarters.

CU tests over 90 percent of all the products in its own laboratories. To conduct its complex testing and rating work, CU now has seven technical divisions—appliance, audio, automotive, chemistry, electronics, textiles, and special projects. In tests of boys' clothing—polo shirts, blue jeans, and shoes—CU's engineers used 96 boys, ages 6 to 12. As many as seven hundred women volunteers participated in comparison tests of 44 brands of nylon hosiery. A panel of 56 men use-tested eight widely sold brands of electric shavers.

Consumer Reports. *Consumer Reports* has a reputation among publishers second to none in being the most carefully prepared and edited magazine in the United States. Only the best professional writers are employed. The articles must not only be interesting, readable, and not too long, but must be accurate in reporting the data derived from scientific testing. The testers have the final word on the technical accuracy of the articles. The introductory paragraphs in each article tell what was tested and why, pointing out the limitations of the test, if any, and giving advice on how to use the test results for maximum satisfaction.

The reports present ratings of the brands in the order of their estimated overall quality and performance. In the range of ratings, the highest is rated by a check mark for an "Acceptable" brand that is also outstanding in quality and performance. The lowest rating, "Not Acceptable," is for a brand that was particularly poor in performance or displayed a safety hazard during the testing of the sample. If an Acceptable brand is sufficiently low in price to represent an outstanding value, it may be designated as a "Best Buy." Thus, the consumer gets comparative information that cannot be obtained from the advertising or labeling of products, no matter how truthful, or from over-the-counter inspection, no matter how careful.

A public service department investigates broad areas of public concern, among them radiation hazards, air and water pollution, and car accidents. The staff gathers information, working with scientific and technical consultants and with government agencies. Its recommendations and findings are presented for remedial action by consumers and by appropriate departments or agencies of government. By initiating investigations early—before public agencies begin investigation—the public is made aware of the dangers. Usually, the public agencies take over from that point and carry on the needed investigations.

The monthly publication also carries regular reports on health and on economics. The health reports cover such vital subjects as cancer research, new drugs, food fads, and alleged weight reducers. They also point out the real or potential dangers of certain chemical additives and pesticide residues in foods, and are widely recognized and commended by many authorities.

Regular articles on economics relate the product on the market to the broad marketing realities that consumers face. Typical subjects include the consumer's need for standard grades and labels in meats and other foods; packaging practices that mislead shoppers; pros and cons on installment buying and credit cards; the costs of price-fixing laws to consumers; and government actions affecting consumer welfare.

In addition to these services, CU rates movies, represents consumer interest in hearings of congressional committees (usually invited), and often confers with federal agencies (FDA, FTC, and National Bureau of Standards) on problems of common concern.

In another service, CU sponsors conferences at universities and colleges to help them conduct a workshop on consumer welfare problems. CU has also made modest grants to universities for special research on matters of interest to consumers.

Special Publications. CU has issued special publications on consumer problems. Examples are *The Medicine Show,* 250 pages, over 165,000 copies sold; *Health Guide for Travelers; The Consumers Union Report on Family Planning,* 146 pages, over 88,000 sold; *Passenger Car Design and Highway Safety; Silent Spring,* special edition, over 38,000 sold; *The Consumers Report on Wines & Spirits,* over 36,000 sold; an important book, *Smoking and the Public Interest;* and *Report on Life Insurance: A Guide to Planning and Buying the Protection You Need.* More books are presently being prepared.

Evaluation of Consumers Union. *Business Week* magazine for December 23, 1967, wrote: "Consumers Union puts on muscle. Its voice is carrying more weight in Washington and in industry. The rising circulation of its magazine, *Consumer Reports,* spreads its influence with the public." The *National Observer* magazine, February 26, 1968, wrote: "Consumer Reports: Read, Respected—And Feared."

Testing at Consumers Union is an effort to set standards for the "end-use" of products. The main question is always this: Do the standards and the tests for it reflect the kind of use to which the product will be put and the situation of that use? In the end, consumers will receive information on quality, quantity, durability, safety, and performance—all "end-use" standards for consumer products. By contrast, industry does not make this kind of information available, even if it possesses such information, on the "end-use" of their products. Evidence of the lack of important information not available to the consumer is quite clear when a recent public announcement was made that almost 9 million *new* cars had to be recalled to correct defects between 1959 and 1966; unsafe tires that did not meet federal government minimum standards; poor performance of many new durable goods, such as automatic washing machines; inadequate standards on textile goods, carpets and rugs, furniture, television and radio sets, toasters, and many other consumer products. Walker Sandbach, executive director of Consumers Union, feels that "if industry will not act voluntarily to give the consumer the standards and information he needs, the consumer does have a recourse—the Government."

Consumers Union does over 90 percent of testing in its own laboratories. This has an advantage for manufacturers who care to send their own testing experts to Consumers Union headquarters to review test methods and results. Many manufacturers have improved their products because of the Consumers Union rating.

While there are criticisms directed at test methods and evaluation of test results, Consumers Union has had a definite impact on sales and product quality. Westinghouse, for example, credits a favorable rating for a 20 percent jump in washing machine sales in 1966. A Norge executive said, "Consumers Union put us in the washing machine business." A West Coast hi-fi dealer said 5 to 10 percent of his customers arrive with an opinion influenced by *Consumer Reports.* [5]

Evidence of how useful Consumers Union's comparative testing and rating were in earlier years (1957 to 1963) can be judged by the following studies:

HOW USEFUL IS COMPARATIVE TESTING AND RATING?

QUESTION	ANSWER
Do brand ratings influence buying patterns of households that refer to them?	Yes. (Sargent study,[a] Lane study,[b] Dear CU letters[c])
Do households that consult consumer publications do more shopping around than nonconsulting households?	Yes. (Sargent study[a])
Do people who consult consumer publications have higher formal education than nonconsulting persons?	Yes. (Sargent study[a])
Is CU rendering a valuable social service in helping some 4 million readers to stimulate quality improvement?	Yes. (Sargent,[a] Lane,[b] Beem[c])
Do CU ratings encourage product improvement?	Yes. (Werner,[d] Dear CU letters[e])

[5] *Business Week,* Dec. 23, 1967.

HOW USEFUL IS COMPARATIVE TESTING AND RATING? (Continued)

QUESTION	ANSWER
Do CU ratings influence consumer purchases? (Asked of retailers.)	Yes. (*Home Furnishings Daily*, Oct. 7, 1959, p. 30; Dear CU letters;[e] Nelson Foote[f])
Do CU ratings save readers money?	Yes. (CU returns of 40,000 readers:[g] 32.6 per cent saved $50 to $100 a year; 37.7 per cent saved $10 to $50 a year; 29.7 per cent saved less than $10 a year.)

[a] Hugh W. Sargent, "Consumer Product Rating Publications and Buying Patterns," *University of Illinois Bulletin*, Urbana, Ill., December, 1959.
[b] Sylvia Lane, "A Study of Selected Agencies That Evaluate Consumer Goods Qualitatively in the United States," unpublished doctoral dissertation, University of Southern California, Los Angeles, 1957, pp. 491, 535.
[c] Eugene R. Beem and John S. Ewing, "Business Appraises Consumer Testing Agencies," *Harvard Business Review*, vol. 32, no. 2, pp. 113-126.
[d] M. R. Werner, "A Detective Agency for Wary Buyers," *The Reporter*, reprint, 1958.
[e] Consumers Union, Mount Vernon, N.Y., 1961.
[f] Lincoln Clark (ed.), *Consumer Behavior*.
[g] The *Wall Street Journal*, Mar. 15, 1962, p. 1.

How Useful Is Comparative Testing and Rating to the Consumer?

The best all-round answer was given by Dr. Arthur Kallet, when he was director of Consumers Union.[6]

> Suppose a buyer were in the market for an automatic washing machine and suppose that the buyer knew an intelligent housewife who had actually used in her own kitchen, each with several loads of clothes, the twelve leading washing machines on the market. Which would the buyer find more useful, the hyperbole of the advertisement and sales claims for the different washers? Or the housewife's off-the-cuff reaction as to ease of loading and unloading, ease of setting controls, ease of adding detergent, cleanness of the clothes, effectiveness of dryer, noisiness, etc.? Substitute for the housewife engineers able to examine and test all of the machines side by side under simulated home-use conditions, keeping accurate records of the behavior and operation of each machine, scoring each factor studied in terms of its effect on the utility and desirability of each machine. There is, of course, room for error, but even in the absence of standards and of a multiplicity of test samples of each model, there are enough differences in design and construction affecting performance and convenience to make purchase decisions based on such tests far more reliable than decisions based on brand names, price, advertising, or the chance recommendation of a neighbor or a salesman.

[6] Dickson Reck (ed.), *National Standards in a Modern Economy*, Harper and Row, Publishers, Incorporated, New York, 1956, p. 279.

Consumer Product Testing and Reporting—a Third Force. Walker Sand-bach, executive director of Consumers Union, told *Business Week* magazine that "industry's considerable influence in Washington often leads to the government's working hand-in-hand with industry. There's need for a third force to represent the consumer, and we want to play an important part."

Sandbach's point of view is backed by Washington observers, who detect a spreading tactic in dealing with the government. They point to auto and tire makers that publicly supported safety standards for their products, then influenced the final form of the standards in quiet negotiation.

Consumers Union does not lobby. Its effectiveness as a third force depends mostly on how good a job it does in testing, how widely it can spread its information, and how much impact its disclosures have on manufacturers, government regulatory agencies, and Congress. Consumers Union hopes to put enough pressure on both industry and government for both to become more responsible to the best interest of all consumers.

Changing Times

Changing Times was first issued in January, 1947. During the first year and a half, this monthly magazine seemed to be designed primarily for businessmen. Gradually the magazine broadened its content until today it can be described as a magazine for consumers. Most of the articles concern such subjects as budgeting, investing savings, buying insurance, borrowing money, buying or building a home, running a car, and protecting health. Some of the articles have excellent charts and tables useful to a consumer. On the whole, the articles are objective, readable, and to the point.

Occasionally an article appears that omits important information for the consumer. When this occurs, one is tempted to say that the magazine has forsaken the consumer interest; but perhaps it would be more accurate to say that the magazine was not designed to be a 100 percent consumer magazine. At $6 a year, consumer-minded citizens can get their money's worth. At least, its subscribers, mostly nonbusiness people, think it is worth the price. Like *Consumer Reports* and *Consumers' Research Bulletin*, *Changing Times* accepts no advertising.

New subscribers receive an up-to-date 96-page book, *99 New Ideas on Your Money, Job and Living*. This volume is a collection of consumer articles and ideas from recent issues of the magazine.

CONSUMER RESEARCH ORGANIZATIONS

We have selected three consumer research organizations—the Weights and Measures Research Center, the Center for Consumer Affairs, and a recent organization called the Consumer Research Foundation—to examine because these are voluntary, nonprofit organizations run by enlightened, professional, consumer-oriented personnel.

The Weights and Measures Research Center

Dr. Leland J. Gordon has been director of the Weights and Measures Research Center at Denison University (Granville, Ohio) since 1955. As an economist, he had become aware of the importance of adequate and well-enforced standards of weights and measures. As early as 1959, Gordon recommended changes in weights and measures legislation and in enforcement at the state and local levels. Since then he has made two national surveys of state weights and measures legislation, administration, and enforcement—in 1963 and in 1966. In 1968 Dr. Gordon made a study of the implementation of the Fair Packaging and Labeling Act and tells the story as it was in July, 1968. All of these studies were distributed by Consumers Union, Mount Vernon, New York.

Denison has supplied office space and equipment while Consumers Union has made modest grants for the operation of the center.

The Center for Consumer Affairs

The Center for Consumer Affairs was established in March, 1963, by the University of Wisconsin Extension Division. Dr. Gordon E. Bivens of the economics department was the first director of the center. Its objectives are:

1. To identify and analyze problems of concern to consumers
2. To develop among consumers an understanding of the economic system of the United States
3. To foster appreciation of the consumer's responsibilities and opportunities in the economy

The Center for Consumer Affairs plans the following activities.

1. Sponsoring workshops, clinics, and institutes on consumer affairs
2. Offering credit and noncredit courses on consumer financing, consumer marketing, and family finance
3. Sponsoring action-oriented research on topics like consumer credit, burial costs, trading stamps, family financial counseling, and legal protection for consumers
4. Developing the usual aids for use in consumer education
5. Conducting experimental work in family financial counseling and training of counselors

Since consumer affairs have many dimensions, the center plans to use people trained in economics, law, social work, psychology, home economics, communications, sociology, political science, and possibly others.

The Consumer Research Foundation

CRF was established in Berkeley, California, on February 6, 1967, as a nonprofit organization dedicated "to research and education for the benefit of consumers." The foundation is organized, for example, to conduct research in:

1. Consumer problems affecting low-income families, senior citizens, and young families.
2. Consumer needs involving credit, food buying, housing, medical care, transportation, money management, etc.
3. Developing consumer education and teaching materials for the schools.
4. Preparing programs tailored to individual family needs for budgeting and money management.
5. Professional presentation of technical information concerning consumer interests before public and private forums.

One of the first research jobs completed by CRF was a *Critique of the Uniform Consumer Credit Code.* This information analysis of the proposed 127-page uniform code for consumer credit law being submitted to most of the state legislatures in 1968 and 1969 will be useful to anyone interested in understanding how the code, if passed by a state legislature, may eliminate some of the protection the consumers had in the recently enacted Federal Consumer Credit Protection Act (better known as the Truth-in-Lending Bill). This research also points out how the proposed code will improve protection of the users of consumer credit in states with poor consumer credit protection.

As is the case with most nonprofit organizations, Consumer Research Foundation depends on memberships, donations, grants, and research contracts to carry on its programs. Mrs. Helen Nelson, economist and formerly consumer counsel to the Office of Consumer Counsel in California, is president of CRF.

LOCAL VOLUNTARY CONSUMER ORGANIZATIONS COMBINE NATIONALLY

There were three important voluntary consumer groups in the United States in 1969 organized on a national scale. The National Consumers League (NCL), the oldest, came into being in 1899 in response to the need for a "consumer conscience" to combat sweatshops, child labor, and inhuman working conditions. After most of these abuses were eliminated, NCL focused its attention on consumer problems. It sought legislative remedies. The Consumer Federation of America, like the NCL, seeks legislative remedies, but unlike NCL, it is a national organization of consumer-oriented organizations, working to unify and speak for all consumers and consumer groups in the country. The American Council on Consumer Interests is a national professional educational organization concerned with problems of our economy considered from the point of view of the ultimate consumer of goods and services.

The National Consumers League

The NCL, with headquarters in Washington, D.C., depends on dues and contributions from its members. It is frankly committed to legislative action in the interest of consumers. The NCL has never been a mass movement. Yet it has been in the thick of successful battles to protect and promote the welfare of all consumers. The NCL, for example, led the fight for the original Pure Food and Drug Act. Later it fought for drug safety and efficacy, truth-in-lending, truth-in-packaging, and better health insurance. An important function of the league is the publication of *Fact Sheets,* legislative alerts, and other information regarding consumer protection needs. Finally, NCL has been active in presenting the consumer point of view at hearings before congressional committees and federal agencies.

The Consumer Federation of America (CFA)

The CFA was chartered in late 1967 and opened its Washington, D.C., office on May 20, 1968, with 56 charter member organizations. It ended its first year of operation on September 30, 1968, with 126 member organizations in 37 states. The CFA employs a full-time executive director, Mrs. Erma Angevine.

Membership.   Consumer group (voting) members are city, county, regional, state, and national consumer associations that support the objectives of CFA. There were 108 such organizations on September 30, 1968.

Supporting group (nonvoting) members are state or national consumer-oriented organizations that are sympathetic to the work of CFA, such as trade unions, state organizations, and national organizations such as the National Board of the YMCA and the National Council of Jewish Women. Eighteen such nonvoting organizations were members on September 30, 1968.

Action.   The CFA is clearly an action organization. It publishes a newsletter, *Consumer Action,* to keep membership organizations informed on what is ahead. For example, it lets everyone know well in advance when Congress or a state legislature is due to consider legislation in the areas of interest rates, insurance, consumer frauds, drugs, safety, guarantees and warranties, product pricing, and many others. Through its annual consumer assembly programs, delegates from its group members gather to hear and discuss the current consumer problems in the country. The 1969 assembly registered about 500 delegates.

CFA also serves as a clearinghouse for exchanging project information among local, state, and national groups. CFA cannot hope to have funds to compete with big lobbying staffs of private business. Instead, the federation will rely on its Washington office to stir up grass-roots opinions on such issues as prices, quality, safety, food inspection, medical costs, warranties, the effectiveness of regulatory agencies, and home improvement rackets. People can then use their own influence and that of their consumer associations to prod their representatives in Congress or in their state legislature.

Will CFA ever become a sort of national "Ombudsman"—receiving complaints, taking test cases to court, following up complaints and reporting on them, etc.? Not yet, but maybe later. For the present, CFA will concentrate on fact-finding and analysis of consumer issues, alerting its member groups, testifying before congressional committees and federal agencies, and providing a responsible and articulate voice for all consumers in this country.

The American Council on Consumer Interests (ACCI) [7]

The American Council on Consumer Interests was born at a conference of 21 educators in the consumer field on the University of Minnesota campus in April, 1953. The Preamble of the Constitution of the ACCI reads: "This organization is concerned with problems of our economy considered from the point of view of the ultimate consumer of goods and services. . . . People, as consumers, need information to use the economic resources available to them in a way to secure maximum satisfaction."

The need for the council grew out of the fact that teachers and research workers interested in consumption specialize in many fields, including economics, sociology, psychology, education, natural sciences, home economics, business administration, business education, and public welfare. Publications on consumer problems come not only from educational institutions but also from business, consumer, labor, farm, and government groups. It is difficult to keep abreast of the contributions from all these sources.

Activities.   The American Council on Consumer Interests is the only national, independent, professional consumer organization in the United States. Through its quarterly *Newsletter,* its annual conference, and its official *Journal of Consumer Affairs,* the ACCI keeps its hundreds of members informed on the latest developments in the consumer field.

From 1954 to 1967, ACCI published 17 pamphlets on current, critical consumer issues. Since 1966, the organization's research and publication efforts have been centered on its professional *Journal of Consumer Affairs.*

QUESTIONS FOR DISCUSSION

1.   What is the basic difference between a "standard" and "standardization"?

2.   Why is quality information on consumer goods a necessity today?

3.   There are many private aids and services available to consumers who may be looking for information on merchandise. Recall the last time that you

[7] American Council on Consumer Interests, 15 Gwynn Hall, University of Missouri, Columbia, Mo. 65201.

made use of one or more of such private aids or services. Was the information satisfactory?

4. What help can you obtain from the American Medical Association and the American Dental Association?

5. Can you depend on the information on labels that a consumer cooperative places on its products? Why do cooperatives use the U.S. Department of Agriculture standards whenever possible?

6. How do the Better Business Bureaus serve consumers? What are the limitations of their service?

7. Can you name any private organizations whose seals of approval or guarantees are practically worthless to consumers?

8. How would you evaluate the guarantees of *Good Housekeeping* and *Parents' Magazine?*

9. Examine a recent catalog of Sears, Roebuck and Company. Can you see any evidence of the Sears testing laboratories in the descriptions of the merchandise?

10. Consult *Consumer Reports* and *Consumers' Research Bulletin* for some merchandise that you expect to purchase in the near future. Did you find the information that you need to make an intelligent selection?

11. What are some of the limitations of consumer-owned testing services?

12. What is the consumer's stake in standards?

13. Do labels include information concerning "invisible qualities" in the product?

14. What are the limitations of brand names and trademarks?

15. What right does the consumer have to be adequately informed before buying a product?

16. What are the limitations of private-store testing of consumer products?

17. Why is it important to read the introductory material in CU and CR publications before reading the ratings of the products?

ACTIVITY PROBLEMS

1. The point is raised from time to time that consumers do not want grade labeling. (See Jessie V. Coles, *Standards and Labels for Consumers' Goods,* pp. 328-330.) Why not take a poll of as many housewives as possible? Ask them whether or not they prefer grade labels. Be sure that each housewife understands the ·meaning of grade labels.

2. Make a table or chart of all the private organizations that help consumers to select goods more intelligently. Indicate for each organization: *(a)* nature of membership, *(b)* kind of products tested, *(c)* who pays for the service, *(d)* interest of agency in sales, *(e)* to whom it is of value, and *(f)* limitations.

3. Secure materials from as many private organizations that test consumer goods as possible. Arrange an exhibition of the material secured. Make a placard for each agency, and include an evaluation of the service on each placard.

4. If possible, visit a good private testing laboratory or secure detailed infor-

mation from such an agency or institution. Report all essential facts to the class. No doubt you will receive considerable material that can be displayed. Keep in mind, particularly, the reliability of the testing information that is made available to consumers.

5.   Test the buying habits of students. Select such merchandise as food brands, electrical appliances, and antiseptics. List the brands in the order of frequency of purchase. How do these purchases compare with the information given by private consumer rating agencies?

6.   Arrange a panel discussion on grade labeling. Invite a housewife who is known for her interest in consumer welfare, a national chain food store manager, a cooperative food store manager, and the owner of a privately owned food store. After the panel discussion, compare the conclusions with those offered by other sources, such as Jessie V. Coles, *Standards and Labels for Consumers' Goods,* pages 323-384.

7.   Arrange with Consumers Union, Inc., Mount Vernon, N.Y., for a showing of the new film "Consumers Want to Know." Prepare a paper on your reactions and evaluate the film.

8.   Compare *Consumer Reports* or *Consumers' Research Bulletin* with *Changing Times.*

SUGGESTED READINGS

Advertising Age: "Government and Test Data," editorial, Aug. 12, 1968, p. 14.

Boyd, Harper B., Jr., and Henry Claycamp: "Industrial Self-regulation and the Public Interest," *Michigan Law Review,* May, 1966.

Caveat Emptor: Product Testing and the Consumer's Right to Know, by Morris Kaplan, University of Missouri, American Council on Consumer Interests, Columbia, Mo., Apr. 23, 1965.

Coles, Jessie V.: *Consumers Look at Labels,* American Council on Consumer Interests, University of Missouri, Columbia, Mo., 1964.

O'Connell, Jeffrey: "Detroit's Double Talk on Safety," *Progressive Magazine,* January, 1967.

Ray, Hugh L.: "Radical Change in Voluntary Standards," *Home Furnishings Daily,* Dec. 11, 1968.

Troelstrup, Arch W.: "The Consumer Interest and Our Competitive System," in *Freedom of Information in the Market System,* booklet, School of Journalism, University of Missouri, Columbia, Mo., 1967.

"New Standards for Tires," *U.S. Consumer Newsletter,* May 3, 1967; Nov. 29, 1967; Aug. 21, 1968.

"What Is a Better Business Bureau Anyhow?" *Changing Times,* October, 1965.

chapter **17**

CONSUMER PROTECTION:
THE FEDERAL GOVERNMENT
AND THE CONSUMER

Government agencies seldom create anything that may rock the boat.

A deputy commissioner of the Food and Drug Administration, John L. Harvey, said in 1955: "It is abundantly evident that the complexities of modern civization require a greater degree of protection to the consumer than is now available. Obviously, he is largely beyond self-protection."[1] Seven years later, in 1962, the late Senator Estes Kefauver told a group of consumer leaders in Washington, D.C., that "the consumer is the forgotten man in our governmental structure." In 1969, Representative Benjamin S. Rosenthal said: "Until the consumer interest is the primary motivation of a statutory agency of government . . ., the consumer will remain a second class citizen in the marketplace."

Protection of the consumer interest, in an era of technological revolution, cold war, strontium 90, subsidies, and recessions, continues to languish as a do-it-yourself program in many respects. In our democratic society, government at all levels inevitably succumbs to powerful lobbies seeking special privileges. Consequently, if consumers are to receive any protection, they must organize and become articulate in making their demands known. Unity of consumers, however, seems unlikely in the foreseeable future.

The main reason for this lack of unity is that consumption is a function common to all and peculiar to none. We are all consumers, but we think of ourselves first as workers, teachers, retailers, farmers, manufacturers, doctors, lawyers, and so on, and only secondarily and incidentally as consumers. Psychologically, community of interest with these primary income groups far overshadows the broader interests of being consumers. The primary-group interest comprises a vertical division of our economy. All members can unite to promote the interests of the group. On the other hand, since consumption is a function rather than a group, and comprises a horizontal division across an entire population, there are no group members to promote the interests of all concerned. It becomes apparent, then, that in our democratic society, where government responds to pressure groups, inarticulate consumers are at a distinct disadvantage. And lacking organization, consumers are largely at the mercy of effectively organized groups.

REDRESSING THE BALANCE BETWEEN SELLER AND BUYER

Democratic government is powerless to act, for the most part, in the absence of expressed need. The consequence for consumers is that government action is inevitably tardy, sporadic, and ineffective.

Interest groups are organized primarily to improve the relative position of their members; they are not organized to improve the position of all members of society. The interest groups attempt to present their own special intents as being identical with the interests of the general public, but their behavior frequently indicates a pathetic ignorance of consumer welfare.

This is not entirely a criticism; freedom to organize and speak are guaranteed by the United States Constitution. Prevalence of active groups is a barometer

[1] *Food-Drug Consumption*, March, 1955.

of social action. Recognition of antisocial behavior, however, is important to an understanding of consumer problems. It is also important to recognize this aspect of the problem if the unrepresented consumer is to survive the fierce conflict of interests.

Marketplace as Regulator

As long as the marketplace was an adequate regulator and coordinator of economic activity, admittedly in the distant past, less need existed for government to act as protector of consumer interests against exploitation by producer interests. But as industrialization developed with its urbanization, consumer dependence on source of supply beyond their own control continued to increase rapidly. This increasing consumer dependence, in turn, has been responsible for partial public realization that the health of each individual is becoming inseparably bound up with the health of the entire community.

As merchandising and marketing practices grow progressively more complex, the unassisted consumer becomes progressively more defenseless. Consumer education is not even in the race with technological and marketing advancement. In fact, it appears that the consumer is becoming more confused and illiterate as a buyer in an increased ratio with modern business and marketing advancement.

What Concerns the Public

In 1968, the ORC Public Opinion Index report of the Opinion Research Corporation released a study that found seven Americans in 10 thought that present federal legislation was inadequate "to protect their health and safety." The majority also believed that "more federal laws are needed to give shoppers full value for their money."

Careful reading of current literature on major problems facing consumers indicate that drug safety, drug prices, and auto insurance rates are areas that need congressional investigation. There is also public support for more government investigation of packaging and labeling, auto safety, and car service and repair. There is strong support for federal action toward generic versus brand-name drugs. Other consumer areas that the public thinks needs federal attention are these: manufacturers' warranties and guarantees, cigarette advertising, consumer credit, and tire safety, to mention a few.

Will Consumerism Go Away?

E. B. Weiss, director of special merchandising service for Doyle Dane Bernbach, said in 1967: "Consumerism will not go away. To the contrary, it will gain momentum . . . either marketing will cooperate in providing the new standards . . . or politicians will go it alone."[2]

[2] E. B. Weiss, *A Critique of Consumerism*, Doyle Dane Bernbach, Inc., New York, 1967, p. 8.

Henry Ford II put it this way in January, 1967: "The real question for businessmen is not how to stop the growth of government. To meet our nation's growing problems and aspirations, both government and business must expand their responsibilities and activities."[3]

It would appear, then, that business may have to accept some new responsibilities—and may have to formulate a new and more socially responsible and sophisticated philosophy of marketing.

Failure of Education to Help Consumers

A traditional national respect for the "acquisitive spirit" has relegated intelligent consumption to a position of relative unimportance. In fact, there is much evidence to support the contention that extravagant spending is a badge of honor; conspicuous consumption—emulation of people of great wealth—is an indication of financial power and success. As a result, certain types of wastefulness have received social approval.

The attitude of consumers regarding intelligent consumption is, to a large extent, the product of our educational system, which, in turn, is largely a product of the traditional American pursuit for the highest material standard of living. Much of the responsibility for the retarded development of intelligent consumption must rest on our educational system, which is weighted in favor of the producer interest as against the consumer interest. In short, our system does a good job of teaching how to make money, not how to spend it intelligently.

The solutions to improving the consumption habits of people are not simple at all. The late President John F. Kennedy emphasized this in his special "consumer message" to Congress in 1962.

> The march of technology has increased the difficulties of the consumer along with his opportunities. . . . Rational choice between and among [products] would require the skills of the amateur electrician, mechanic, chemist, toxicologist, dietician, and mathematician. . . . Marketing is increasingly impersonal. Consumer choice is influenced by mass advertising utilizing highly developed arts of persuasion. The consumer typically cannot know whether drug preparations meet minimum standards of safety, quality, and efficacy. He usually does not know how much he pays for credit; whether one prepared food has more nutritional value than another; whether the performance of a product will in fact meet his needs; or whether the "large economy size" is really a bargain. Additional legislative and administrative action is required, however, if the Federal government is to meet its responsibility to consumers in the exercise of their rights. These rights include—
>
> 1.   The right to safety . . .
> 2.   The right to be informed . . .
> 3.   The right to choose . . .
> 4.   The right to be heard—to be assured that consumer interests will receive full

[3] *Ibid.,* p. 9.

and sympathetic consideration in the formulation of Government policy, and fair and expeditious treatment in administrative tribunals.[4]

Failure of Federal Regulatory Agencies to Regulate

Back in 1872, Congress evidenced its first interest in consumer problems when it enacted a law to protect consumers from frauds involving the use of the United States mails. Since then, legislation and executive action in the name of consumer protection has produced a sprawling, uncoordinated maze of laws and agencies, frequently working at cross purposes and usually cursed by a too-little-too-late timidity. Thus, consumer interests have not been served.

The regulatory agencies were set up by Congress under its power to regulate commerce in the public interest. But though many of their decisions (as, for instance, those of the Interstate Commerce Commission affecting railroad rates, the Federal Power Commission in setting gas rates, and the Federal Trade Commission in its decisions with respect to unfair business practices) are of direct concern to consumers, consumers are not regarded as an interested party. Even if consumers were allowed to appear in these cases, under existing circumstances they would not be in a position, generally speaking, to prepare and present significant data.

In actual practice, the regulatory agencies are preoccupied with settling conflicting claims among rival groups of producers. Thus, the Interstate Commerce Commission is caught in disputes between railroads and trucks, the Civil Aeronautics Board between large certificated carriers and the smaller airlines, the Federal Communications Commission between rival applicants for television and radio licenses, the Federal Power Commission between gas producers and public utility companies, and the Tariff Commission between companies that want tariff protection and those that do not.

One can go on almost indefinitely with such a roster of conflicting producer groups that are fighting to make their views prevail with the agencies of regulation. Is it surprising then that, amid this constant tug of war between contesting private interests, there is little room for the consumer to be heard? And, unlike these private pressure groups, which are well organized, highly disciplined in the art of exerting influence, and omnipresent when decisions are to be made, consumers are scattered, unorganized, and often unaware that decisions of vital import to their standard of life are being made. The initiative for action has been left increasingly to the companies that are being regulated. As the late Dr. Walton Hamilton, after a lifetime of study of these agencies, said in his last book:[5]

[4] Message from the President of the United States Relative to Consumers' Protection and Interest Program, 87th Congress, 2d Session, House of Representatives, Doc. no. 364, Washington, D.C., Mar. 15, 1962.

[5] Walton Hamilton, *The Politics of Industry*, Alfred A. Knopf, Inc., New York, 1957, p. 155.

The result is that the commission on all its levels becomes busy, in fact over-busy, but largely with detailed problems of the moment, problems which have been raised by complaining parties. It has adequate legal authority to raise questions on its own motion, but amid all the bustle of everyday activity there is very little leisure in which to do it. The larger questions of holding the regulated industry to its function, of improving its capacity to serve the public, of looking to the hazards ahead and guarding against them, and of making of it a more effective instrument of the general welfare are neglected. Matters of policy get immersed in the quagmire of detail. The agency fails to direct the activities of the industry to public objectives, and the industry is left to effect for itself such structure and practices as serve its purposes.

Public Interest versus Ultimate Consumer Interest.   Although charged to act in the public interest, regulatory commissions can fulfill that obligation only if the public interest is defined with respect to each issue. But there are few opportunities and few effective spokesmen to define the public interest, and in the heat of controversy the general welfare is all too often overlooked. The major issue, then, is how to place the public welfare in the forefront of governmental regulatory activities. Without the balance wheel of concern for the general welfare, government by regulatory agencies tends to solve only short-term, shortsighted private struggles for privilege.

In most of the issues raised before government regulatory agencies, the interests of the ultimate consumer have been those most consistent with the general welfare. In many countries, notably Great Britain and Sweden, where governmental regulatory agencies have been subject to detailed investigations (the Final Report of the Committee on Consumer Protection, 1962, and Sweden's Cartel law), the public interest is specifically defined as the interest of the ultimate consumer.

As government by regulatory agencies has expanded, the necessity for an increasing emphasis, within government, on the interests of the ultimate consumer has become urgent. The effective expression of the ultimate consumer's interest is now essential to the very functioning of government and to the economy.

Lee Loevinger, recently of the Federal Communications Commission, said it best:

> Unfortunately, the history of every regulatory agency in government is that it comes to represent industry or groups it's supposed to control. All of these agencies were fine when they were first set up, but before long, they became infiltrated by the regulatees and are now more or less run by and for them.

REPRESENTING THE CONSUMER INTEREST IN GOVERNMENT

To appreciate the inadequate and haphazard character of current consumer protection activities calls for a brief review of existing programs at the federal level.

Government Consumer Activities

The most complete tabulation of federal consumer programs was compiled in 1961 by the Committee on Government Operations in a report on "Consumer Protection Activities of Federal Departments and Agencies." The report showed that 33 of the 35 principal departments and agencies of the federal government were involved in some activity that protected or promoted consumer interests. In a total of 296 activities listed by 33 federal departments, only 103 activities dealt directly with protection of the consumer. The government spent less than $1 billion on these agencies in 1961. This cost figure is overstated because this includes compensation to many workers who devoted some of their time to other job assignments.

The great bulk of these federal programs deal with fraud and deception and with enforcement of laws banning the sale of adulterated and unsafe foods and drugs. This is an important job, but the emphasis is on a negative quality— namely, prohibition of practices. Few programs call for the affirmative disclosure of information essential to informed purchase decisions.

Some federal laws do have the effect of providing the consumer with facts useful in buying products. Food and drug labels, for example, must disclose net weight, contents, and manufacturer's identity. The 1962 Drug Act Amendments provide for disclosure of generic names as well as trade names for drugs. The labels of textiles and wool products must also specify content. Prices of new cars must be displayed on the car. In due time, practically all fresh meat, whether intrastate or interstate, will be grade-labeled and inspected. Finally, standards of identity are prescribed for some food products (minimum standards), and in due time the recent truth-in-packaging act will establish some control of size, shape, and number of different-weight packages of food and certain other products.

No Comprehensive Consumer Program

The point to be emphasized is that the specific situations that gave rise to each consumer-related activity of the federal government are random, being responsive to narrowly defined needs rather than the product of a comprehensive effort to assess the situation and develop generalized corrective programs. This aimless policy is reflected in the absence of any administrative apparatus in the federal government designed to view the consumer problem as a whole.

The establishment of consumer representatives in the National Recovery Administration, the Agricultural Adjustment Administration, and the Bituminous Coal Commission created in the 1933-1937 Great Depression period was an attempt to fill the need for assertion of the consumer interest. But this effort failed because in each of these three agencies, the programs were designed to aid producer groups by artificially raising prices that the consumer was expected to pay.

Consumer Rights

Since 1962, however, there has been renewed federal interest in the consumer's plight. Steps were taken by both President Kennedy and President Johnson to give the consumer a spokesman. In 1962 President Kennedy, declaring that consumers have a "right to be heard" and to have their interests given "full and sympathetic consideration in the formulation of Government policy," created a Consumer Advisory Council as an adjunct to the Council of Economic Advisers "to examine and provide advice to the Government on issues of broad economic policy, on government programs protecting consumer needs, and on needed improvements in the flow of consumer research material to the public." The council was given more formal status by an Executive order issued by President Johnson on January 3, 1964. In addition to the council, which was composed of 12 private citizens, President Johnson established a Committee on Consumer Interests. This committee was composed of private citizens who served on the Advisory Council and representatives of 10 federal agencies. A Special Assistant for Consumer Affairs was appointed by the President early in 1964. The holder of this White House position (Mrs. Esther Peterson; later, Betty Furness) was the principal spokesman for the consumer in the federal government and also served as chairman of the President's Committee on Consumer Interests. Following Mr. Nixon's inauguration as President of the United States, the status of these nonpermanent consumer organizations is uncertain.

The Nixon Administration and the Consumer

In December, 1968, Father Robert McEwen, president of the Consumer Federation of America, asked Mr. Nixon to "appoint somebody for the consumers." Mrs. Patricia Hitt, President Nixon's top woman in government in early 1969, assured 500 conferees at the third annual Consumer Assembly (organized by the Consumer Federation of America) on January 31, 1969, that the new administration "will develop programs . . . designed, not to weaken, but to strengthen the response to consumer needs."[6] On April 9, 1969, President Nixon appointed Mrs. Virginia Knauer, Director of the Pennsylvania Consumer Bureau, to succeed Betty Furness as a Special Assistant for Consumer affairs.

The Consumer Advisory Council (CAC), the President's Committee on Consumer Interests (PCCI), and the Special Assistant for Consumer Affairs (SACA), gave the consumer some representation in the major agencies of government. And the Special Assistant for Consumer Affairs, with offices in the White House, had direct access to the President. This was progress in the right direction. Yet there were some major weaknesses in this conglomeration of councils, committees, and special assistants.

[6] *Washington Post,* Jan. 31, 1969.

Kennedy and Johnson Institutionalized the Consumer

These organizations, CAC, PCCI, and SACA, were supposed to represent consumers at the federal government's highest policy-making levels. But there was no clear sense of purpose. The President's Committee on Consumer Interests was to consider federal policies and programs of primary importance to consumers, while the Consumer Advisory Council was directed to "advise the Government on issues of broad economic policy of immediate concern to consumers." Both groups were served by the same staff, which in turn reported to the Special Assistant, and the holder of that office was chairman of the President's Committee on Consumer Interests and an ex officio member of the Advisory Council. If this committee implemented programs developed by the council and approved by the President, its function would be understandable. The committee's job, however, was not to implement, but rather to advise, and that was also the responsibility of the Advisory Council.

The single most important weakness was the lack of authority noticeable in all three organizations. Each was charged with responsibilities of "advising," "reviewing," and "consulting," but none had the power to modify, execute, or instigate a program. All that these three organizations could do was to hope that their recommendations would induce the President, the Congress, or federal agencies to take corrective action.

The recommendations made by the Advisory Council and the President's Committee on Consumer Interests were excellent and timely and probably had some influence on departments and agencies such as the Department of Housing and Urban Affairs, the Federal Trade Commission, the Food and Drug Administration, and other federal agencies. Certainly, individual members of Congress were alerted, from time to time, and congressional hearings were held on some of these consumer issues. Finally, powerful business interests became alarmed by the "consumerism movement" generated, in part, by these three federal organizations. Business in general, the Better Business Bureaus, and the public relations officers of corporations, trade associations, and advertising companies have felt the impact of the consumer movement ever since the Kennedy administration. Whatever weaknesses the PCCI, the CAC, and the Special Assistant for Consumer Affairs may have had, the fact remains that consumerism promises to be a long-term and powerful trend.

A Look at Three Federal Agencies

Although there are about 33 federal agencies and departments having some responsibility in protecting the consumer interest, we will center attention on three federal agencies—the Federal Communications Commission (FCC), the Federal Trade Commission (FTC), and the Food and Drug Administration

(FDA). The FDA is probably the most consumer-oriented agency in the federal government today and as such deserves more of our attention.

The Federal Communications Commission (FCC).   During the last half century, producer groups have captured American radio and television. Modern communication is harnessed to sales objectives primarily. From the look of TV schedules, one would hardly guess that the broadcasting industry and its regulator, the FCC, are undergoing as far-reaching a public reexamination as any since the revelations a decade ago of rigged quiz shows, payola, and faked commercials.

Congress passed the Communications Act of 1934 establishing the Federal Communications Commission. The concept called for a nationwide system of locally based stations to ensure that broadcasting would be attentive to the specific needs and interests of each community and that local groups and leaders would be guaranteed an adequate opportunity for expression of diverse and even antagonistic viewpoints. FCC was given the sole power to issue broadcasting licenses, but Congress decreed that each license should automatically expire after 3 years. It also instructed the FCC to "prescribe the nature of the service to be rendered" by each station "as public convenience, interest or necessity requires."

As of 1965, not one of the 40 very-high-frequency television stations (channels 2 through 13) licensed in the nation's 10 largest metropolitan areas has been independently owned: 37 belong to firms with other TV-station holdings, and the other three belong to newspapers. This situation remains, as of 1969.

FCC in Trouble.   The FCC is in trouble today because of its long and implacable neglect of duty. The Senate has held hearings. A House group is proposing to legislate better programming. A blistering attack on the FCC majority has come from two of its commissioners, Cox and Johnson, while a third commissioner, Bartley, would split the FCC into three agencies. The Antitrust Division of the Justice Department is proposing that the FCC deny license renewals to any station owner who owns another station or a daily newspaper.

The view of the present majority of the FCC is expressed by a former commissioner, who said when the American people do not like what they see or hear, "they can and they do turn it off." Too often, however, it is not a choice between one program and another but a choice among a number of poor programs and none at all.

The Consumer Stake.   Consumers have a far larger financial stake in broadcasting than does any private segment of the industry. They have spent an aggregate of more than $20 billion for their radio and TV sets, plus about $3 billion for antennas. They spend more than $1.25 billion a year for maintenance and repairs. Consumers also pay for advertising that in turn pays all broadcasting costs. In 1967 close to $4 billion in radio and TV advertising revenues was built into the price of sponsors' goods and services.

The FCC's mail had grown from 8,000 expressions of public opinion in 1961 to 67,700 in 1967. It appears that about half of these letters were complaints about program content or advertising.

TV and the Radio Code. Matters of "leadership and conscience" on the publicly owned but privately occupied commercial airwaves fall under the purview of the Television and Radio Code Boards of the National Association of Broadcasters. The code loftily says, "Material which is excessively violent or would create morbid suspense, or other undesirable reactions in children, should be avoided." But *Consumer Reports* for October, 1968, quotes a report which appeared in *The Christian Science Monitor* six weeks after the murder of Senator Robert F. Kennedy which counted 372 acts of violence or threats of violence portrayed on the three television networks during a week of prime-time evening and Saturday morning shows. Some stations subscribe to the code without living by it, and others—37 percent of all television stations—find it so restrictive that they do not even subscribe to it.

A public opinion survey done for the National Association of Broadcasters reveals the stunning fact that more people find commercials annoying than amusing. Many people polled also believe the government sets rules for sex and violence and for the number of commercials permitted. The government does not, though it could. (Starting September 15, 1968, the television industry's code had authorized four commercials in a row instead of three during programs, and three instead of two during station breaks.)

License Review. The entire ritual of license review is a sham, according to FCC Commissioners Cox and Johnson. Programming deficiencies—even the most flagrant indifference to the local-service obligations imposed by the Communications Act—raise no eyebrows. In 1966 a United States Court of Appeals decision stated that: ". . . After nearly five decades of operation the broadcast industry does not seem to have grasped the simple fact that a broadcast license is a public trust subject to termination for breach of duty."

In dissenting from FCC approval of a new FM station in 1967, FCC Commissioners Cox and Johnson pointed out that the station owner frankly proposed to devote up to 33 minutes per hour to commercials. They sent questionnaires to 51 stations applying for license renewals and found that only 10 percent of the commercial TV stations devoted as much as two hours a week to local affairs. Ten percent carried between one and two hours, 60 percent devoted less than one hour, and 20 percent carried no local public affairs at all.

Intervention by Other Means. Intervention by other agencies of government or by private citizens has accomplished what the FCC should be doing on its own. The Justice Department intervened to challenge the merger, under the antitrust laws, of the American Broadcasting Company and the International Telephone and Telegraph Company. A New York lawyer obtained a ruling that stations broadcasting cigarette commercials must also accept antismoking commercials. Private citizens in Chicago stopped, temporarily at least, the FCC-approved sale of WFMT-FM Chicago to a subsidiary of the *Chicago Tribune,* which already owns other Chicago TV and radio outlets.

In 1959 Consumers Union submitted a 13-point proposal to the FCC designed to make it more responsive to the public interest. At the head of the list was the establishment of a Television and Radio Consumers Council with full power: (1) to review all Commission licensing decisions; (2) to request, if necessary, additional data on a licensee's performance; and (3) to publicize its findings. Consumers Union's proposals, if accepted, would go far in making television and radio more responsive to the public interest.

Cigarette Advertising. On February 5, 1969, the FCC said that the evidence of a link between cigarette smoking and lung cancer, as well as other diseases, was so overwhelming that it had no choice but to rule cigarette advertising off the airwaves, under its legal responsibility to regulate broadcasting "in the public interest, convenience and necessity." This was probably the most courageous act in the history of the FCC, despite the fact that the FCC rule cannot go into effect unless Congress permits a provision of the 1965 Cigarette Labeling and Advertising Act to expire as scheduled on June 30, 1969, because of the opposition of the billion-dollar radio, television, and tobacco industry. Immediately after the FCC's announcement of the proposed ban on cigarette commercials, 13 Senators and Representatives from tobacco states introduced bills to extend the 1965 provision indefinitely. So the battle lines were drawn. Whatever the outcome, the FCC *did* do what it had to do, within its area of responsibility to the public.

Federal Trade Commission (FTC). At the very top of the FTC pyramid, the Commission is composed of five members, appointed by the President and confirmed by the Senate for terms of 7 years. The President also appoints the chairman.

The official manual of the FTC assigns the responsibility for controls over false and misleading advertising to the Bureau of Deceptive Practices. The FTC's well-publicized activities in the control of false and misleading advertising have led many elements of the general public to overlook the fact that the Commission was originally created to combat concentrations of excessive economic power accumulated by trusts and monopolies before and around the turn of the twentieth century. The FTC received wide authority to investigate "unfair methods of competition in commerce."

Dual Responsibilities. Over the years the FTC has had to work out overlapping and duplication of its activities with those of other federal agencies such as the Food and Drug Administration with respect to misleading advertising of foods or proprietary drugs, the Post Office Department in the matter of lotteries and frauds via the mail, and the Federal Communications Commission in regard to obscene, profane, and fraudulent or deceptive advertising.

New Consumer Powers. New and potent powers were given the FTC. The Commission can now center its attention on the direct protection of the consumer, where formerly it could protect the consumer only indirectly through the protection of the competitor. The Wheeler-Lee amendment also gave the FTC authority to proceed against false advertising of "foods, drugs, cosmetics and devices by United States mails, or in interstate commerce by any means." Also, "criminal proceedings" may be instituted when intentional efforts to defraud or mislead are made in connection with a product which is injurious to health. Finally, in *all* cases of alleged deception or misleading advertising, an FTC order to "cease and desist" becomes final if no judicial appeal is made within 60 days.

The FTC tries to educate business with sets of "basic ground rules" aimed at seeking voluntary compliance. The FTC effort at voluntary compliance centers around its *Trade Practice Conference Industry Guides, Advisory Opinions,* and *Trade Regulation Conference Rules* for more than 160 industries, and has published 11 sets of *Advertising Guides.*

The FTC does not hesitate to use its powers when it feels the need to do so. Critics of FTC, however, are quick to say that these powers are seldom used on important cases.

Evaluation of FTC. Generally, commentary on FTC actions relating to deceptive advertising has been favorable, according to Earl Kintner, former chairman of the FTC.[7] The courts, too, have given solid support to the FTC in most advertising deception cases, according to recent annual reports of the Commission.

But this general approval does not prevail among all the critics. Some businessmen, for example, fear the recent trend to proceed against advertising which "confuses" the consumer. The case in point was an order from the federal government to tire manufacturers to produce minimum-standard tires for cars and trucks. The words "informative labeling and advertising" are increasingly heard today. What will the FTC do in this new area of control? Recently, the Commission objected to the "barrage of commercials on television, which portray smoking as a harmless and enjoyable social activity that is not habit-forming and involves no hazards to health." Even more objectionable to business interests was the recent Supreme Court ruling which directed Procter & Gamble to sell Clorox, which came about after the FTC invoked its powers relating to antitrust and advertising regulation.[8]

Ralph Nader Recommends. Early in 1969, a 185-page report by Ralph Nader and investigators recommended a thorough overhaul of the agency's policies, practices, and staff. Among the findings and recommendations are these:

1.   The Commission "fails woefully to enforce its laws properly. It relies too heavily, nearly exclusively, on voluntary non-binding enforcement tools. These cannot be expected to work at all unless backed up by stricter coercive measures, which are almost completely lacking now."

[7] "Federal Trade Commission Regulation of Advertising," *Michigan Law Review,* May, 1966, p. 1279.

[8] See *Editor & Publisher,* Apr. 15, 1967.

2. The "methods of becoming aware of consumer problems are woefully inadequate. It relies almost exclusively on letters of complaint from the public to detect possible violations of its laws, yet cannot obtain monetary satisfaction for injured individuals." This causes it to "proceed in purely random fashion."

3. There is a preoccupation with the trivial while ignoring large-scale deception by big firms, particulary the ones that advertise heavily on television.

4. There is too much secrecy about what it is doing.

5. The Chairman (Paul Rand Dixon) ought to resign because he allegedly has "institutionalized mediocrity, rationalized a theory of . . . inaction, delay and secrecy, and transformed the agency into the Government's Better Business Bureau."

6. A "limited number of engineers, doctors and product experts" should be employed, and office procedures should be modernized.

7. Congressional committees "should undertake a full-scale study" of the FTC.

Coincidentally, the FTC issued a report that illustrated some of the points brought out in the Nader report. The FTC report on supermarket games of chance, for example, has been in the works for more than 2 years. Despite ample evidence for prosecution, the FTC decided to lick the problem by only issuing trade regulation rules. One rule proposed by the FTC to clean up the practices would be to prohibit rigging of games and misrepresenting the chances of winning. Another rule was aimed at gasoline games. This rule would prohibit oil companies from pressuring retailers to participate in the games.

In short, the Nader report says that the FTC, with the most responsibility to protect consumers from unfair and deceptive selling practices, is wasting much effort on trivial matters, giving the impression that it is vigorously policing the marketplace while actually letting the biggest culprits get away with unfair and illegal activities. The American consumer, continues the Nader report, is not getting the protection he needs or thinks he is getting.

State FTCs. The FTC has also been pressured by private citizens to improve on their "cease-and-desist" orders against merchants who make misrepresentations in guarantees, advertising, sales, or credit practices, but could not sue in behalf of the complainants. A forthcoming secret report of the FTC will call for the creation of state-run trade commissions similar to FTC. It also will recommend close cooperation between these "little FTCs" and neighborhood legal aid services. This recommendation may give considerable relief to ordinary citizens if the 50 states are willing to set up their little FTCs. At best, this will be a long-term dream. Meantime, individual consumers have no effective relief for complaints of deceptive practices.

The Food and Drug Administraton. The protection of the ultimate consumer from the questionable and rapacious practices of producers is not a modern invention. In the precapitalistic feudal economy, the consumer was protected by guild regulations covering the size, weight, and quality of products.

During the era when the United States economy was largely agricultural, most consumers were fairly well protected by common law—recourse to the courts. But in the last quarter century or more, the legal protection provided by common law has been entirely inadequate. To try to meet these new conditions, due to the mass production and mass distribution revolution, a few states in the latter part of the nineteenth century attempted to protect consumers against abuses in the sale of food and drugs. In 1848, the first federal inspection action was taken on imported drugs, medicines, and related products. Later, importation of impure tea and adulterated food was stopped.

In the 1890s, attempts were made to authorize limited supervision by federal regulation of interstate sales of foods and drugs. This campaign was led by Dr. Harvey W. Wiley, of the Bureau of Chemistry in the Department of Agriculture, in 1890.

Pure Food and Drug Act of 1906. In 1906, the Pure Food and Drug Act was passed by Congress. It took Upton Sinclair's *The Jungle* (a novel about the unsanitary conditions in the Chicago meat-packing plants) and the exposé of political and economic corruption by the muckrakers in the family magazines, notably *McClure's,* to get the average citizen stirred up sufficiently to overcome the influence of business in Congress against food and drug regulations.

The Pure Food and Drug Act of 1906 had several weaknesses that began to appear as time went on. For one thing, women began to use cosmetics in the "roaring twenties." The cosmetic trade, quite untouched by moral and safety principles, had scores of cases of poisoning in the 1920s, caused by hair dyes, face bleaches, face creams, rouges, powder, and hair tonics.[9] In 1937, in *The American Chamber of Horrors,* Ruth de Forest Lamb described the cosmetic industry in detail. Thus the public was made aware of the need to have federal regulation of the cosmetic industry.

Another weakness in the original act was its failure to regulate advertising as well as labeling. The truth, even if presented on labels, could be and was misrepresented in false and misleading advertising. With the advent of radio and television, this problem became acute

Federal Food, Drug, and Cosmetic Act. A third weakness in the 1906 act was the failure to provide for the safety of drugs and medical preparations for human use before making them available to the public. In 1936, the public became aware of this weakness when 73 persons died from the use of a patent medicine, Elixir Sulfanilamide. So in 1938, the 1906 act was amended to include the federal regulation of cosmetics and to prohibit the sale of drugs and medicines until they had been proved safe for human consumption. The effort to include the regulation of false and misleading advertising under the Food and Drug Administration was defeated, but the Wheeler-Lea Act provided for regulation of untruthful advertising in another federal regulatory agency, the Federal Trade Commission.

By the early 1940s, the great increase in the use of chemical food additives led to the demand for protection from dangerous chemicals in food. The FDA did not have authority to prevent their use unless it was first demonstrated

[9] Stuart Chase and F. J. Schlink, *Your Money's Worth,* The Macmillan Company, New York, 1927, p. 22.

beyond a reasonable doubt that the chemical additives were dangerous to human beings. Finally, in 1958, this was corrected. Chemicals in the form of food additives must now be proved harmless to human beings before they can be used in food as preservatives or emulsifiers.

Drug Amendments of 1962. On October 10, 1962, the Drug Amendments of 1962, overhauling and strengthening the drug provisions of the Federal Food, Drug, and Cosmetic Act, became law. The amendments deal mainly with drugs sold only on prescription and with "new drugs." A new drug is one that is not generally recognized by qualified experts as safe and effective for the uses recommended in its labeling.

Here are some of the major changes in the law.

1. Before the new amendments, only safety clearance of new drugs was required. Now there must be substantial evidence that any new drug is effective as well as safe before it can be approved for marketing.

2. All manufacturers must now have adequate controls—test procedures and checks—with trained personnel and proper facilities, to assure the reliability of drugs. Absence of such controls will of itself violate the law, without the necessity for proving that a particular shipment of the drug was defective.

3. Previously cleared drugs may be ordered off the market immediately if new information indicates an imminent hazard to health. And any prior approval may be withdrawn, after a hearing accorded to the manufacturer, in any case where tests or experience show that the drug is not safe or will not be effective for its intended uses.

4. The FDA is given 180 days instead of 60 days to consider a request for a safety clearance of a new drug, and the new drug cannot be marketed without FDA approval.

5. Manufacturers are required to report promptly to the FDA on experience with new drugs, including any adverse effects they learn about after the new drug goes on the market. This also applies to previously cleared new drugs and antibiotics.

6. A firm legal basis is provided for regulations to prevent testing of drugs on humans unless and until specified safety conditions, including thorough animal testing, are met.

7. Manufacturers are required to get assurance that the patient's consent will be obtained if experimental drugs are to be used, unless this is not feasible or unless the investigator believes that obtaining such consent would be contrary to the patient's best interest.

8. All drug producers must register annually with the FDA, even if their output does not actually move in interstate commerce.

9. The FDA is directed to inspect each registered establishment at least once every 2 years.

10. The scope of authority for inspection of manufacturers of prescription drugs is broadened to include legal access to pertinent records, files, papers, processes, controls, and facilities.

11. Authority is provided for the federal government to establish an official name for a drug when this is desirable in the interest of usefulness and simplicity. Drug labels must bear the established name of the drug and, for prescription drugs, the quantity of each active ingredient.

12. Prescription drug advertisements must include a brief summary of side effects, contraindications, and effectiveness, as well as the established name for the drug and the quantitative formula.

13. The FDA batch testing and certification of safety and effectiveness is extended

to all antibiotic drugs for humans. This adds some thirty groups of antibiotic drugs and their derivatives to the five previously subject to this requirement. Manufacturers pay fees to cover the costs of the FDA tests.

Consumers have every reason to hail the Drug Amendments of 1962 as a major advance in the cause of safe, effective, and honestly promoted drugs.

A final set of drug control rules by the FDA included these requirements for drug manufacturers.

1. Prove to the satisfaction of the FDA that new drug products are effective as well as safe.
2. Adopt the "good manufacturing practice" guidelines of the FDA at all drug-production and drug-testing facilities.
3. Include in all advertising of branded drug products the drug's technical, or generic, name as well as brand name, and list any side effects it may have had on previous users.

The last requirement was hotly opposed by many drug firms. The FDA's purpose is to acquaint consumers with the generic term so that they can shop for drugs and get the lowest price possible.

In recognition of the protests of drug companies, the final set of rules omits an earlier proposal that would have permitted the FDA to pass on certain advertising before it is used. Another change gives drug producers the right to demand a prompt ruling on the safety and effectiveness of a new drug if the FDA fails to clear it for use within the specified 180 days.

Federal Hazardous Substances Act. This act went into effect on February 1, 1962. It is enforced by the FDA. Accidental poisoning from hazardous household substances accounted for 40 percent of fatal poisoning of children under 5 years of age, according to statistics. In one year, 1959, doctors reported over 90,000 fatal and nonfatal poisonings in this age group.[10]

This act is a lifesaving measure, aimed at alerting parents and others to the potential dangers in common articles stored and used around the home. But the law can fulfill its job only if consumers read and heed the labels on such articles.

All household products that are toxic; corrosive; irritant to skin or eye; strong sensitizers; or flammable or extremely flammable; or that generate pressure, which presents a special hazard, are required to bear warning statements on their labels. Some such products have carried warnings for years. All must now do so.

The law and regulations reserve the skull and crossbones and the word "POISON" for highly toxic substances to mark their extreme hazard. Highly toxic products must also bear the word "DANGER." Many products are extremely flammable or corrosive or have some other special hazard, such as danger of in-

[10] *FDA Memo for Consumers,* Food and Drug Administration, U.S. Department of Health, Education, and Welfare, Nov. 26, 1962.

halation. All other products that can cause illness or injury must be marked "CAUTION" or "WARNING."

Instructions for safe use and storage must also appear on the labels of all substances covered under the Federal Hazardous Substances Act. The statement "Keep out of the reach of children" must also appear on such labels.

The Child Protection Act of 1966. This act extends the coverage of the Federal Hazardous Substances Act by giving the FDA authority to ban from interstate commerce any product so dangerous that no warning can make its use safe. The new law also declares null and void any state laws that conflict with the federal standards for warning labels. This act should eliminate or minimize the sales of such items as the stuffed baby chicks contaminated with arsenic, poisonous jequirity beans, and crackerball firecrackers which exploded in the mouths of some children who bit into them thinking they were candy.

The Drug Abuse Control Amendment of 1965. There is widespread abuse and illegal traffic in depressant, stimulant, and hallucinogenic drugs. Lives are being shackled in chemical chains because the users do not recognize the potential dangers of these drugs. The users can become physically and emotionally dependent on these drugs, but the drugs do not yet have the social stigma that is usually associated with the use of narcotic drugs. The use of LSD has been openly and irresponsibly promoted for alleged mind-expanding effect. Experience has shown, however, that users of LSD may lose their capability to think clearly, to reason, and to create or otherwise use their minds productively. There may be other effects not known at this time.

These are some of the reasons why a federal amendment to the Food, Drug, and Cosmetic Act was passed in 1965. The amendment prohibits (1) the sale or disposition not covered by legal prescriptions; and (2) illegal possession for resale. The penalties are quite severe. The FDA has some 200 specially trained investigators to carry out enforcement provisions of the law.[11]

Some Current Problems. The FDA faces a critical challenge in its effort to revamp federal drug marketing requirements to more fully assure that all versions of the same drug, regardless of trade name, are equally effective. The FDA also faces problems of high cost of drugs and stricter testing of antibiotic drugs.

1.   *Efficacy of Drugs.* In the 1962 Amendments to the 1938 Food and Drug Act, the FDA was instructed to ensure that all drugs sold to the public were effective as well as safe. But there are legal and scientific difficulties posed by the large number of drugs on the market. In the past the FDA relied largely on the evidence presented by the manufacturer. Furthermore, the FDA must end the sale or curtail claims for ineffective drugs originally marketed between 1938 and 1962. The removal of hundreds of drugs from the market is based on an exhaustive scientific review by nongovernment experts at the National Academy of Sciences of the usefulness of 2,900 drugs sold in as many as 17,400 different formulations. Some FDA officials estimate that about 290 drugs, sold in 1,740 different formulations, will be kept off the market. It will be up to the drug manufacturers, however, to prove that these drugs are effective and

[11] See *Fact Sheets,* 1 through 10, from the FDA Bureau of Drug Abuse Control.

safe. An overly permissive approach by the FDA could allow ineffective products to remain on the market. In 1968, for example, the FDA conceded significant shortcomings in its certification procedures for antibiotic drugs which must be tested by the government before release to the market. The agency said it had received manufacturers' samples that were not adequately labeled or that reflected careless handling by the companies. Evidence of the shortcomings led to reassignment of three ranking members of FDA's division of antibiotics and insulin certification, which handles this activity, according to a *Wall Street Journal* story. The FDA also issued a letter to 250 makers prescribing stricter standards which must be followed in submitting antibiotic samples to FDA for testing.

2. *Drug Prices.* In Chapter 12 we presented some of the evidence of excessive prices for some drugs on the market today. According to a special HEW "task force" study of the cost of drugs, which was presented to Secretary Cohen of the Health, Education, and Welfare Department in 1968, much of the blame for high cost of drugs was due to the lack of price competition. Our patent system gives patent owners exclusive rights for 17 years to manufacture or sell licenses for the patented product. In addition, the report says that profit margins are exceptionally high. The special "task force" thinks drug prices can be substantially reduced by shortening the legal life of a patent and by compulsory licensing of other manufacturers in exchange for royalties after a specified number of years. The United States and Belgium are alone, among industrial nations, in not specifying some forms of compulsory licensing of drug patents. [12]

Strengthening the FDA. Consumer leaders generally agree that the FDA, over the years, has been the most consumer-minded agency or commission in the federal government. Consequently, the report on the Food and Drug Administration by the Citizens Advisory Committee, October, 1962, under the chairmanship of Dr. George Y. Harvey of the University of Missouri, should be studied carefully. This hard-hitting and industry-oriented committee report evoked reaction among agency officials ranging from a "wait and see" attitude to frank statements that the report was "naïve and unrealistic." [13] The committee, however, believes that the FDA will be strengthened by carrying out the following recommendations.

1. Substitute "preventive policy" in place of "after-the-fact" enforcement.
2. A change in the role of the commissioner of the FDA, with a major change toward decentralization of decision making.
3. Upgrading of the scientific program by setting up a Food and Drug Institute headed by a scientific director to attract better scientists and to result in improvement of analytical methods.
4. Improve FDA-industry relationships.
5. Establish a National Advisory Council to the commissioner, appointed by the Secretary of Health, Education, and Welfare, authorized to make annual reports to the Secretary.
6. Upgrade personnel and provide better training opportunities for the staff.
7. Provide more effective program planning.
8. Educational program should emphasize education of the consumer, of industry, and of the state food and drug agencies rather than publicize the FDA.

---

[12] *Report of the Task Force on Prescription Drugs,* U.S. Health, Education, and Welfare Department, 1968.

[13] According to the *Drug Trade News,* Nov. 12, 1962.

9.   Secure closer cooperation between the FDA and the Public Health Service and other governmental agencies.

10.   Develop FDA programs to strengthen the state laws and administrative agencies and to maximize consumer protection by coordinated harnessing of federal, state, and local regulatory programs.

More Suggestions. Other suggestions to improve the FDA have been made recently. Dr. George Nichols, Jr., a Harvard University medical professor, proposed that a central agency, jointly financed by the federal government and the pharmaceutical industry, should take over the testing of new drugs. [14] George S. Squibb, former vice-president of E. R. Squibb & Sons, a drug manufacturer, claims that drug research by drug companies is often "poor, wasteful, extravagant, unproductive, unimaginative and pointless." Furthermore, he thinks that pharmacists should be permitted to substitute lower-price drugs of identical formula when a doctor prescribes a higher-price drug. [15] An intensified inspection of drug plants has been in the plans of the FDA, but funds have limited this important activity. Vincent A. Kleinfeld told the food, drug, and cosmetic division of the American Bar Association in 1967 that drug manufacturers should appoint a top lawyer as an Ombudsman to police drug firm ads. This watchdog could prevent drug firms from making false claims or breaking the law in their advertising and promotion activities.

Keep FDA Independent. Implementation of these recommendations could lead to improvement in the effectiveness of the FDA. It is possible, however, that the drug industry, with profit motives in mind, might acquire too much influence over FDA policies. Politicians, too, might acquire unhealthy influence over the organization. Many consumer leaders are much concerned about producer-oriented and politically administered federal agencies that have been organized, theoretically, to protect the public.

There are two basic reasons for keeping the FDA independent of political and industrial pressures. (1) The FDA is basically concerned with protecting consumer health and safety. (2) To the extent that the FDA—through its declarations of standards of quality and standards for fill-of-containers, and its prohibition of mislabeling and misrepresentation—enables the consumer to become a better-informed buyer in the market, it meets one of the basic prerequisites of a free-enterprise competitive economy and thus is of basic significance to all consumer citizens.

SHOULD THE FEDERAL GOVERNMENT RELEASE ITS CONSUMER PRODUCT-TESTING INFORMATION TO THE PUBLIC?

Over a thousand consumer products which the federal government buys—automobile tires, cars, clothing, floor waxes, tape recorders, hearing aids, batteries,

[14] *Washington Post,* Jan. 18, 1968, p. A 26.

[15] *U.S. Consumer,* Dec. 17, 1967.

lamps, building products, washing machines, detergents, home freezers, and food—to mention only a few—are tested by one or another of its agencies.

Unfortunately, such information has hitherto been released only to producers and has not been made available to private nonprofit testing agencies like Consumers Union for dissemination to the general public or to any individual.

Government Testing

The Department of Agriculture collects information on the effectiveness and toxic effect of insecticides. The Food and Drug Administration tests clinical thermometers and condoms. The laboratories of the Quartermaster Corps evaluate such consumer items as clothing and textiles. Navy laboratories evaluate paints, detergents, and other products. The General Services Administration and/or the National Bureau of Standards will be testing tires, seat belts, and brake fluids. (Seat belts and brake fluids have now been transferred to the new Department of Transportation.) They have tested auto batteries and other items. It is abundantly clear that a search of governmental agencies would reveal a considerable body of information concerning the performance of available goods and services offered on the American market. Some of this is direct brand information; some relates more generally to product categories such as gas versus electric appliances, or alkyd oil paint versus water-soluble paint for interior and exterior use. Such information includes valuable data concerning care, maintenance, and safety in use. The need of today is to unlock this information.

A Test Case

In 1967, the House Government Operations Subcommittee began hearings to determine whether Congress should permit consumers to have access to the federal test results of consumer goods. To date (1969) nothing has happened. So Consumers Union, with support from some congressmen, economists, and other interested citizens, has been trying to persuade federal agencies performing tests on consumer products to make their test results public information. It tried with special determination to get from the Veterans Administration the complete results of tests it made on hearing aids purchased for VA for distribution to disabled veterans. Consumers Union told a Senate subcommittee on consumer interests that the VA bases its refusal on the Freedom of Information Act, which exempts from disclosure "privileged and confidential trade secrets."

It is difficult to see how the VA can retreat behind that act's exemptions, inasmuch as what the hearing-aid manufacturers provided to the agency were the same hearing aids and instructions for use which are available to consumers, and hence about as secret as a transistor radio.

Moreover, as Consumers Union observes, it seems strange that the VA should spend public funds on tests designed to aid hard-of-hearing veterans and at the same time withhold its test data from all other American consumers. There are about 18 million Americans with impaired hearing who could profit from this information.

So in 1968, Consumers Union was suing the Veterans Administration to release the test information on hearing aids to the public. If Consumers Union wins the case, and if such a decision is upheld in the higher courts, it may force release of test data on other consumer products. The release of such information would benefit all American consumers.

In April, 1969, the Veterans Administration, under pressure, released brand names of 20 hearing-aid devices which it purchased on the basis of the best quality. VA still refuses to release its test data.

SHOULD THERE BE A DEPARTMENT OF CONSUMER AFFAIRS?

In 1959 Senator Estes Kefauver proposed a Department of the Consumer at the Cabinet level. Since 1959, there have been other proposals to secure more effective representation of the interests of the consumer in the federal government. In 1968, one advocate of a Department of Consumer Affairs was Representative Benjamin S. Rosenthal, of New York, who got 58 congressional colleagues to cosponsor a measure to establish such a department. The bill died without action.[16] In early 1969, 95 members of Congress joined in sponsoring the same bill.

Why Cabinet Rank?

The protection of consumers today is spread in some 33 major federal departments and agencies that now administer over 260 consumer-related programs. These programs, proliferated throughout the government and administered by agencies having conflicting interests to protect, provide the consumer with weak and uneven protection. Fish standards, for example, regulated by the Department of the Interior, are geared to producer needs. Meat and egg standards of the Department of Agriculture accent the values of the packers and farmers mostly. The work of the Department of Commerce is essentially limited to producer requirements. There exists no agency that draws together consumer protective functions into a single body which will assure that consumer goods are accurately advertised, accurately and adequately labeled, and produced according to discernible consumer standards. Today, a consumer with a complaint has not the slightest idea where to write. There is no clear focus of re-

[16] H.R. 17097, A Bill To Establish a Department of Consumer Affairs, 90th Congress, 2d Session.

sponsibility. Consumer protection remains a diffuse, scattered interest backed by limited appropriations. Until the consumer interest is the primary motivation of a statutory agency of government, instead of an afterthought, as it is in so many agencies today, the consumer will remain a second-class citizen in the marketplace. Colston Warne, president of Consumers Union, said that the primary objective of a Cabinet-level department for consumers is "to place a spokesman for the consumer at the highest level of government, in so far as is possible, and to bring together under a single head all of the major relevant bureaus."[17]

Consumer Representatives in Agencies Now

During the Johnson administration most of the 33 agencies having some consumer responsibilities had a consumer representative of sorts. For example, the consumer counsel in the Justice Department would alert the agency whenever the consumer interest was likely to be adversely affected. In the Federal Trade Commission (FTC), the consumer representative of the agency would argue the consumer cause before that regulatory agency. Such a friend of the consumer would represent the consumer when the Interstate Commerce Commission (ICC) heard pleas for increase in railroad fares or curtailment of service, and he would appear at airline rate increase or license hearings of the Federal Communications Commission (FCC) and at Federal Power Commission hearings on natural gas rates.

President Johnson made a beginning. A strong consumer counsel might evolve from it. But, as it stands now, these offices owe their existence to the President alone and face possible elimination whenever there is a change of occupancy in the White House.

What Might a Department of Consumer Affairs Do?

The DCA would handle complaints on such topics as home repair frauds, unsafe cars, and contaminated foods. Its officials would represent the consumer in courts and in regulatory agencies and departments to speak for the consumer on milk marketing practices, tariffs, and many other problems. An Office of Consumer Information would gather facts on consumer products and make them available to the public. A National Consumer Information Foundation would run a voluntary consumer product-testing program, and the official test results would be printed on information tags attached to such products. The Institute for Consumer Research would do the testing. An Office of Consumer Safety would run checks on the safety of consumer products. (The present National Commission on Product Safety is a temporary group exploring safety

---

[17] "Is It Time to Re-evaluate the Consumer Activities of the Federal Government?" *The Journal of Consumer Affairs,* Summer, 1967.

problems now.) Economic surveys and special investigations would be made to uncover other important consumer problems.

The majority of the National Commission on Food Marketing thinks that "a centralized consumer agency should be established in the executive branch of the Government by statute."[18] But business and industry argue that since everyone is a consumer, the specialized agencies of government can deal best with these problems.

Government spokesmen say that the FTC already has the power to do some of the things proposed for the Department of Consumer Affairs. Congress, however, has never appropriated money for the FTC to do them.

Bureaucracy Fears Change.   Passage of the act to esablish a Department of Consumer Affairs would cause upheaval in some of the present agencies. The new department might take over the Agriculture Department's Consumer Marketing Service; home economics and nutrition research from the Research Service; price and cost-of-living reporting of the Bureau of Labor Statistics; the HEW's police work on packaging and labeling and safe food standards. Despite these possible upheavals, the National Commission on Food went on record, as we pointed out above, as favoring a centralized consumer agency —not necessarily a department with Cabinet status. Historically, other departments of the federal government have evolved in the same way suggested for a Department of Consumer Affairs.

Advocates Argue.   Advocates of the department proposal argue that consumers cannot be ignored any more than you can write off the labor movement by saying that all men and women are workers and therefore there is no need for a Department of Labor. Although some 33 agencies presently do something for the consumer, the consumer's voice is drowned out by better-organized voices of the industries being regulated by these same agencies. Both Norway and Sweden, they noted, have Ministers of the Consumer and Family Affairs at the Cabinet level.

The approach the Nixon administration takes toward consumer problems, and the mood of the new Congress, will determine the fate of the proposal in the immediate future. Even if nothing comes from the idea just yet, the fact that the bill had 95 congressmen joined in sponsoring legislation to establish a Cabinet-level Department of Consumer Affairs indicates that some politicians are growing sensitive to consumers as an interest group and to their problems as an issue.

An Independent Department of Consumer Affairs

A Department of Consumer Affairs, federally chartered and financed, but independent of the President and Congress, deserves serious attention. This department would confine itself to investigation, research, testing, information

---

[18] See the commission report, *Food from Farmer to Consumer,* June, 1966, p. 109.

dissemination, handling complaints and advocacy before agencies and courts, and presentations before Congress and its investigating committees. This department would not administer anything; it would not regulate anything.

It would be confined to finding out the truth about all the goods and services we buy, and about the environment we need to live, play, and work in. Then it would publish and circulate what it found. The operating idea here is that most people are not so dumb that they will continue to buy a prescription drug that is not effective, or a car that is not safe, if somebody they can trust tells them about it and can prove what he says.

The idea of an independent, federally chartered corporation is based on the horribly realistic understanding of the way government regulatory agencies work and on an appreciation of the current demands and rising expectations of quality in goods and services that people exhibit today.

Weakness of Regulatory Agencies. Unfortunately, the weakness of every regulatory agency of government is that it comes to represent the industry it is supposed to control. All these agencies were fine when they were first set up, but before long they became infiltrated by the regulatees and are now run more or less for them.

So there has been a public reaction to this comforting relationship between regulatory agencies and industry.

It is impossible to keep lobbyists representing business out of a regulatory agency. They have the money, the organization, the expertise, and the staying power that consumer organizations will not have for years to come, if ever.

Another reason for an independent agency is that the regulatory agencies are not set up to help consumers except when forced to by a Ralph Nader or a courageous investigating committee of Congress. These agencies help the industries they regulate. They divide markets, protect them from antitrust suits, administer prices, and generally make sure that free enterprise and real competition are confined to the small businessman. If this reasoning is sound, the suggestion for creating an independent consumer affairs agency has considerable merit.

Other Suggestions. At least four other suggestions have come forth for creating permanent representation of the consumer in the federal government.

1.   Appointment of a special assistant to the President (statutory) to handle consumer affairs.
2.   Establishment of an independent federal Office of Consumer Affairs charged with representing consumers' interests in departmental hearings, before federal regulatory hearings, before federal regulatory agencies, and in antitrust and other court proceedings.
3.   Establishment of a joint congressional committee to deal with matters affecting consumers.
4.   Establishment of an Office of Consumers in order to secure within the federal government effective representation of the economic interests of consumers; to act as a clearinghouse in government for consumer complaints; and to disseminate information to consumers.

HOW CONSUMER-CONSCIOUS WILL THE NIXON ADMINISTRATION BE?

The Johnson administration has been called the "Consumer Congress," and its record shows it. Enacted were laws dealing with truth-in-lending, truth-in-packaging, auto safety, flammable fabrics, meat and poultry inspection, mail fraud, deceptive land sales, auto liability insurance, and a number of product safety laws. And, of course, President Johnson's Special Assistant for Consumer Affairs was located in the White House.

Preelection Statements

What will President Nixon's attitude be toward the consumer? Prior to the presidential election, Nixon expressed his opinions on consumer protection in a *Business Week* interview and in a questionnaire from the Consumer Federation of America. He said he would place his emphasis on the "forces of free enterprise" to assure fair play in the marketplace. Conservative economist Milton Friedman, an advisor to Nixon, said, "In effect, Nixon will start moving in a new direction, and that direction will be toward less authority." In the opinion of some consumer advocates, this laissez-faire attitude at the highest level of government could set consumer protection back considerably. On the other hand, if Nixon believes in more free enterprise and fair play in the marketplace, it could mean giving consumers more important information on consumer products and services so that they can make more intelligent decisions before buying in the marketplace.

An unfriendly administration could be a damper on the future of some key consumer measures still pending, such as fish inspection, the deceptive sales act—which would give the FTC the right to issue certain preliminary injunctions—the entry of banks into the credit-card game, the door-to-door sales act, and other proposed consumer laws.

Still, it has been reported that Nixon's office has been flooded with mail from consumers who want the administration to maintain a firm policy of regulating business to protect shoppers. Another aspect which may make President Nixon take a second look is the number of consumer investigations which have made headlines. For example, the Hart Senate Antitrust and Monopoly Subcommittee hearings on auto repairs and on protection of privacy and local credit bureaus' ratings of consumers had not been completed when Mr. Nixon became President. Senator Nelson is continuing hearings on the prescription drug industry. And hearings by Representative John Dingle have pointed up the abuses of the gasoline and food games of chance.

Willie Mae Rogers

On February 12, 1969, the White House press secretary said that it was "quite likely" that Mr. Nixon would appoint a successor to Betty Furness. A day or two later, Willie Mae Rogers, director of Good Housekeeping Institute, was appointed as a "part-time consultant" on consumer affairs.[19] On February 15, 1969, Miss Rogers declined the appointment. Questions were raised over a possible conflict of interest because of her continued association with the Good Housekeeping Institute, which gives its seal of approval to its advertisers' products. The presidential press secretary said, on the same day Miss Rogers declined the invitation, that the President's Committee on Consumer Interests would continue, and repeated that it was "very likely" that there would be a Special Assistant on Consumer Affairs named to replace Betty Furness, who served in that post in the Johnson administration.[20] As reported earlier, President Nixon did appoint Mrs. Virginia Knauer to this important position on April 9, 1969.

Betty Furness said at the time she sent her letter of resignation to President Nixon, that "the consumer has a voice now and is using it. No administration can or should ignore it."

If consumer advocates can agree on one or several approaches to more effective consumer representation in the federal government, then their problem will be to get their plan or plans through Congress. Congress may share President Nixon's concern about the dangers of meddling with the free enterprise system. But as the public keeps on learning from bitter personal experience—and from reading—how poorly private enterprise is meeting its responsibilities on product safety, durability, and honesty, there will be a rising clamor for warranted meddling to protect the consumer. Consumer protection may then attain a popularity with politicians that it has never achieved before. When this happens, let the seller beware.

QUESTIONS FOR DISCUSSION

1. In what ways does the Federal Trade Commission protect the consumer? What have been the major weaknesses or limitations of the FTC?

2. Why do we need consumer protection laws and agencies at the federal level?

3. How would you evaluate the Consumer Advisory Council, the President's Committee on Consumer Interests, and the Special Assistant for Consumer Affairs? Did they help consumers?

4. Many industries prefer self-regulation with regard to standards for consumer products and to the kinds of information on labels and tags. How has self-regulation worked out for consumers?

5. Do you favor a Department of Consumer Affairs?

[19] *Wall Street Journal,* Feb. 12, 1969.
[20] *St. Louis Post-Dispatch,* Feb. 16, 1969.

ACTIVITY PROBLEMS

1. Collect many labels from canned goods. Analyze each label according to exactly what it tells you. Are some kinds of information legally required on the label? Do U.S. Department of Agriculture grading labels carry more accurate and important information for the consumer than private grades and descriptions?

2. Study two of the recent News Summary reports of the Federal Trade Commission. Make a report to the class on the nature of the FTC activities as seen through these reports.

3. Should consumers press for a Cabinet-level Department of Consumer Affairs? Send for H.R. 17097, A Bill to Establish a Department of Consumer Affairs. The latest version of the bill at this time was dated May 7, 1968.

4. Write to your congressman for a copy of *Consumer Information Responsibilities of the Federal Government.* This is a report on the Hearings before a Subcommittee on Government Operations, House of Representatives, June and July, 1967.

5. Read *Silent Spring,* by Rachel Carson, and report to your class.

6. Make a study of what the Nixon administration has accomplished to help the consumer. List the gains and losses to consumers as you view these changes.

7. Select one of the federal agencies (FTC, FDA, FCC, or the Antitrust Division of the Justice Department) for a detailed analysis of what it is doing or not doing to help people as consumers.

SUGGESTED READINGS

Bishop, James, Jr., and Henry W. Hubbard: *Let the Seller Beware,* The National Press, Inc., Washington, D.C., 1969.

"Cabinet Rank for Us Shoppers?" *Changing Times,* January, 1969.

"Child Protection Hazardous Substances Act," *FDA Papers,* July-August, 1967, U.S. Government Printing Office.

"Dangers of Diet Food and Diet Drinks," *U.S. Consumer Newsletter,* Dec. 25, 1968.

Dickerson, F. Reed: *Product Safety in Household Goods,* Bobbs-Merrill Co., New York, 1968.

"Drug Abuse Control Amendments of 1965," *FDA Papers,* May, 1967, U.S. Government Printing Office.

"50 Years of the Food and Drug Act," *Consumer Reports,* July, 1956.

"Flammable Carpets," *Consumer Reports,* February, 1969.

"The FTC," *U.S. Consumer Newsletter,* Jan. 8, 1969.

House of Representatives, Bill No. 17097, to Establish a Department of Consumer Affairs, May 7, 1968, Committee on Government Operations, Washington, D.C.

Nader, Ralph: An individual crusader for the consumer. See articles: "Meet Ralph Nader," *Newsweek,* Jan. 22, 1968; "Ralph Nader, Crusader or the Rise of a Self-appointed Lobbyist," *New York Times Magazine,* Oct. 29, 1967; *Business Week,* Jan. 25, 1968.

"Profits of the Drug Industry," *U.S. Consumer Newsletter,* Dec. 17, 1967.

Swankin, David A.: "The View from Washington," *The Journal of Consumer Affairs,* Summer, 1967, American Council on Consumer Interests, University of Missouri.

"Testimony of George S. Squibb on the Drug Industry," *U.S. Consumer Newsletter,* Dec. 27, 1967.

"Testing for Safety, Efficacy," *FDA Papers,* May, 1968, U.S. Government Printing Office.

Troelstrup, Arch W.: "The Consumer Interest and Our Competitive System," in *Freedom of Information in the Market Place,* University of Missouri School of Journalism, Columbia, Mo., 1967.

"TV Radiation," *Consumer Reports,* February, 1969.

Warne, Colston: "Is It Time to Re-evaluate the Consumer Activities of the Federal Government?" *The Journal of Consumer Affairs,* Summer, 1967, American Council on Consumer Interests, University of Missouri, Columbia, Mo.

"What's Happened to Truth-in-Packaging?" *Consumer Reports,* January, 1969.

chapter 18

CONSUMER PROTECTION ON THE STATE AND LOCAL LEVELS; CONSUMER JUSTICE—CONCLUSIONS

The individual consumer voice in the community "should not be only loud and authoritative, but reasonable and responsible."

British Molony Report

Every American consumer lives under at least three governmental units—federal, state, and local. When people think about government, they tend to think primarily of the federal government. While federal government services to consumers are important, as we learned in Chapter 17, they are only a part of the total pattern of government services.

As citizens of their respective states, consumers are aware that their state governments operate in a variety of areas to provide economic goods or services or to regulate certain private enterprises. There are important gaps in state government services, notably in the regulation of weights and measures, in the control of advertising, in the assurance of pure foods and drugs, and in the effective regulation of public utilities, to mention a few. Also, it has been shown that the sovereign power of state government is sometimes misused by minority pressure groups to the detriment of consumers.

The federal government must take responsibility for formulating and enforcing laws that are needed on a national or interstate scale. But to the states falls the primary job of curtailing consumer deception. The states possess the greatest potential for quickly spotting and halting the unscrupulous. After 17 months as President Johnson's Special Assistant for Consumer Affairs, Mrs. Esther Peterson was convinced, from the thousands of letters that poured into her office, that "the place where the real consumer protection is needed, and where the action is needed, is at the state and local level where the people are." She said, "One thing has become very clear—consumer representation at the federal level is not enough. The consumer must also receive representation at the state and also at the local level."[1]

CONSUMER PROTECTION IN THE STATES

At the state level, officials who attempt to protect consumers are incredibly handicapped by inadequate laws. Although some states have recently passed effective laws and set up machinery to enforce them, the picture of state consumer legislation is, on the whole, not good. A survey in 1967, for example, by the FTC showed that only 19 states could be said to have "good" or "excellent" laws prohibiting deceptive selling practices. In a few states legislation did not exist. Only 20 states outlawed bait advertising.

Absence of laws, however, is not the only problem in the states. For, as the *Columbia Law Review* noted, "The states have adopted a staggering number of statutes noteworthy for their ad hoc and piecemeal approach to the problems of advertising control and for the very slight degree to which they are enforced." Many attorneys general and county prosecutors freely admitted that they had never tried to enforce their *Printer's Ink* mode law (aimed at untrue, deceptive, or misleading advertising). It is not a secret, according to Gale P. Gotschall of the FTC, who confided to the National District Attorneys Association in 1966, that lawyers and judges usually do not feel that a businessman belongs in jail.[2]

[1] Warren G. Magnuson and Jean Carper, *The Dark Side of the Market Place,* Prentice-Hall, Inc., Englewood Cliffs, N.J., 1968, p. 63.

[2] Reported by Sidney Margolius in *The Innocent Consumer v. The Exploiters,* Trident Press, New York, 1967, p. 43.

One of the major weaknesses in consumer protection at the state and local levels is that state and local legal authorities tend to let the fraud proceed until they have accumulated enough evidence to prosecute. So said Bronson LaFollette, Wisconsin State Attorney General and a leader in fighting consumer frauds. Consumers, however, want frauds stopped *before* they themselves become the victims.[3]

The clearest examples of inadequate consumer protection at the state level are in the areas of weights and measures and in state regulation of public utilities.

The Price of Pseudo-regulation of Public Utilities

State commissions for the regulation of public utilities have long been characterized by weakness, with rare exceptions. Commissioners without the expertise of or subservient to the utilities, staffs without the required skills or manpower or currying favor with the utilities by looking to them for professional advancement, insufficient funds for operation, and inadequate salaries to attract able men have often resulted in failure to protect the consumer from exorbitant rates.

An appalling absence of hard information on these points has hitherto existed, according to reports of the Consumers Information Committee on Resources and Energy. So in 1968 the Intergovernmental Relations Subcommittee of the Senate Committee on Government Operations set about to get the facts. The state utilities commissions were polled with a questionnaire and all but two responded.

Sixteen commissions had only one rate analyst and six had none. Six had not a single engineer and nine had only one. Twenty-six commissions had no securities analyst. Thirteen had only one accountant and one had none at all. Only three commissions had an economist. Seventeen had a single attorney and four had none.

Thirty-seven state utilities commissions had no permanent research staff, and 13 reported they did not even have a research library.

Thirty-four said salaries of administrative and professional staff were inadequate to attract and retain competent persons. One hundred and three former staff members of state regulatory commissions are now in the employ of public utility companies.

The net result of all these incompetencies is that the regulated electric utilities are overall obtaining profits which the Senate subcommittee reported are substantially higher than the state regulatory commissions set as the maximum.

The extreme example is Montana Power Company, which the state utility commission allows a return of 5.33 percent, the lowest reported in the Senate survey. In 1965 the company's actual return was 11.37 percent, the highest

[3] *Ibid.*

in the nation, and for the previous three years it had been over 10 percent and rising.

These are the prices consumers pay for state regulatory commissions that do not regulate.

Inadequate Weights and Measures Laws and Enforcement

Some of the inadequacy of weights and measures laws and enforcement was pointed up in Chapter 7. In 1966 and 1967, state weights and measures personnel found considerable short weights in and misleading labels on meat products, packaged foods, gasoline pump meters, petroleum gas meters, and fuel oil in Pennsylvania, California, Virginia, Michigan, Ohio, and New York.[4] Most of the other states no doubt have similar problems with weights and measures enforcement. In fact, a study by Leland J. Gordon, director of the Weights and Measures Research Center, found a hodgepodge of weak laws, poorly enforced; weak laws strongly enforced; and strong laws feebly enforced. Effective consumer protection, according to Gordon, might cost $12,500,000 a year, or only about 25 cents a year per family.

A solution to the problem of more effective enforcement of weights and measures laws, in addition to improved enforcement at the state and local levels, is to arrange for some kind of effective cooperation of state and federal agencies.

Will Federal and State Cooperation Work?

Unfortunately, there are conflicts, cross-purposes, and some gaps in the protection offered consumers. After Congress passed the important Fair Packaging and Labeling Act (FPLA) in 1966, it was a matter of record that the FDA and the FTC were "looking to the states for the enforcement of FPLA."[5] The question, then, is this—Will federal-state cooperation work in the enforcement of FPLA? Some state officials are jealous and fearful of the federal agencies such as FTC and the FDA. As of early 1969, we have to continue to "wait and see" what kind of cooperation there will be between the federal and state agencies in enforcing the FPLA. Meantime, consumers are not receiving the protection the act anticipated.

CONSUMER REPRESENTATION IN STATE GOVERNMENTS

The problems of consumers do not result from the lack of potential legal authority. Although it is true that men cannot be made good by law, it is equal-

[4] *Changing Times,* March, 1968.
[5] Leland J. Gordon, "Fair Packaging and Labeling—When?" July 15, 1968, p. 24.

ly true that some men will not be good in the absence of law. Though nothing human is infallible, it is equally true that the fallibility of some men can be improved upon. Although consumer laws provide no automatic guarantee of protection, nevertheless consumers cannot be safe without them.

Pioneer Effort in New York State

One of the most significant achievements of the states is the statutory establishment of consumer representation at the executive level. The pioneer effort in this field was the 1955 action of Governor W. Averell Harriman of New York State in establishing a Consumer Counsel to the Governor. In the latter office, Dr. Persia Campbell showed the immense potentiality of according consumer recognition in state administration. Her work included participation in hearings with reference to basic consumer issues, such as resale price maintenance and installment credit legislation, and the issuance of publications regarding the responsibilities and actions of scattered bureaus for consumer protection.

Early in 1959, Governor Rockefeller failed to continue the office of Consumer Counsel in his executive department. Consumer interest organizations in New York have been working, without success, for its reestablishment, this time by legislative action.

Kinds of Consumer Representation in States

As of early 1969, nine states had some kind of consumer representation at the executive level. They are California, Connecticut, Florida, Kentucky (by executive order), Massachusetts, Michigan, New Hampshire, New Jersey, and Rhode Island.

To date, consumer representation at the state level has taken one of five forms:

Consumer Advisory Council (Florida, Massachusetts, Michigan, New Hampshire, and Rhode Island)

Office of Consumer Counsel (California)

Department of Consumer Protection (Connecticut)

Consumer Affairs Commission (Kentucky)

An Office of Consumer Protection in the State Department of Law and Public Safety (New Jersey)

Consumer Representation in the Executive Branch

At the present time only one state, Connecticut, has a consumer department in the executive branch of government. There the Department of Consumer Protection, established in 1959, headed by the commissioner, has units that are responsible for the administration of laws and regulations pertaining, for example, to foods and drugs and to weights and measures. The Connecticut setup has the great advantage of concentrating many different consumer-protective responsibilities and services within one department of the state government.

The California Office of Consumer Counsel

California has an Office of Consumer Counsel, established in 1959, located in the Governor's Office. Prior to Governor Reagan's administration, the consumer counsel carried on a wide range of vigorous and effective programs of consumer representation, information, and education. The consumer counsel worked closely with the governor and with his executive departments, most notably with the state attorney general's office in the fields of consumer frauds and consumer legislation. In addition, the consumer counsel presented the consumer point of view at hearings held by legislative committees and by state regulatory commissions. The consumer counsel also provided channels for the two-way flow of information and suggestions between the state government and the people of the state with reference to consumer-interest matters.

When Ronald Reagan became Governor of California, the budget as well as the activities of the Consumer Counsel were curtailed considerably. The hesitancy in continuing this office could also be seen when the governor appointed an acting consumer counsel.

Massachusetts Consumer Council

The MCC is fairly representative of the consumer activities and programs in Florida, Michigan, New Hampshire, and Rhode Island. In Massachusetts, the Consumer Council, established in 1963, is made up of an eight-man council in the Office of the Governor. The council is empowered to "conduct studies, investigations and research and advise the Executive and Legislative branches in matters affecting consumer interests." It is also to coordinate other consumer services to further consumer education. In addition the council informs the governor and the attorney general and other law enforcement agencies of such violations of laws and regulations affecting consumers as its investigations or studies may reveal.

New Jersey Office of Consumer Protection

In New Jersey the Office of Consumer Protection in the Department of Law and Public Safety was established in 1967. This consumer office receives consumer complaints and forwards them to the proper agency; communicates with the governor and the attorney general as to all matters affecting the interests of consumers; reviews state policies and programs of primary importance to consumers or the unmet needs which can be met through state action; recommends legislation to protect consumer interests; appears before governmental agencies and departments on behalf of consumers; establishes necessary liaison with voluntary consumer organizations; and assists in coordination of federal, state, and local activities relating to consumer affairs.

Kentucky Consumer Affairs Commission

The KCAC, created by executive order in 1968 (some future governor may not continue the commission), may make recommendations to the governor on consumer policies, develop legislation to implement policies, conduct research on consumer problems, appear before hearings to represent the consumer, and implement consumer education programs. Major emphasis will be on consumer education. The commission is composed of 11 appointees of the governor with the heads of the various state agencies with consumer interests serving as ex officio members. The commission meets regularly and is served by the governor's staff.

Future Models

There are likely to be other kinds of organizational models for consumer representation in state governments than those reviewed above. There might be, for example, an Interdepartmental Consumer Interest Committee chaired by a Consumer Counsel. There could be a Joint Select Consumer Interest Committee made up of the members of similarly named committees of the state legislature.

The whole area of consumer representation in state government is complex, vast, and changing from year to year. Therefore, the nature of the consumer representation in the state is likely to be modified to fit changing consumer needs. As we said earlier, only nine states had some form of consumer representation at the executive level in 1969. The need for consumer representation at the executive level in the other states is likely to be as great as in the nine states presently having such representation. When apathy is replaced with concern in the other 41 states, the legislatures are likely to do something about it.

CONSUMER FRAUD BUREAUS

As of early 1969, 30 states had some form of consumer fraud or protection agency, functioning, for the most part, in the office of the attorney general. The pioneering was done in New York under Attorney General Louis J. Lefkowitz, who set up a consumer fraud and protection bureau in 1957.[6]

[6] See "Consumer Frauds," *University of Pennsylvania Law Review,* January, 1966, p. 395.

Activities of Consumer Fraud Bureaus

The bureau provides a centralized agency through which consumers' complaints can be funneled. Illinois and New York handle about 150 complaints each day. In 1966, the state of Washington received about 5,000 complaints and California received over 10,000 complaints. The bureaus which are generally considered outstanding because of their legal authority, experience, and initiative are those in New York, California, Illinois, and Washington. In these bureaus the staff follows up nearly every consumer complaint—bait advertising (seller tries to sell you a higher-priced article than the one advertised), false advertising or labeling, misrepresentation, selling under false pretenses, fake correspondence of vocational schools, deceptive real estate offers, and many others—and sometimes arranges individual adjustments and takes full-scale court action against gypsters if necessary.

The Attorney General Must Have Strong Powers

To be effective the law must give the attorney general strong powers. The primary weapon against gypsters is the authority to obtain a court injunction, forbidding the hucksters to continue their fraudulent enterprise in the state. To avoid long, drawn-out trials, giving the swindler time to continue his fraudulent business, some states wisely empower the attorney general to ask a judge for a temporary injunction. This forbids the company to continue the alleged shady dealing pending the outcome of the injunction trial—if there is one. In many cases, the company, when confronted with the prospects of a trial, with all its ugly publicity, will agree to stop the deceptive selling or servicing by signing a consent injunction. If a state injunction is signed by the company, there is not a single case on record of a firm continuing shady operations in that state.[7]

Four states (New Jersey, New Mexico, New York, and California) can impose fines for misdeeds prior to the time the injunction is final. Several states can dissolve a corporation engaging in deceptive practices or, as in New Jersey, put the company into receivership, sharing the distributed assets with the consumers who were cheated.

Several states make vigorous efforts to see that a cheated consumer is compensated. From 1962, when the Illinois bureau was established, until June, 1967, it succeeded through the cancellation of debts and the return of money in saving Cook County (Chicago) residents over $1,158,000. New York's state bureau in 1966 obtained refunds for consumers of over $1 million.

Poor Protection in Some States

States lagging behind other states in consumer protection are caught in a deteriorating situation. For, as fraudulent operators are driven out of one state,

[7] According to the March, 1967, *Harvard Law Review.*

they migrate to another with weaker laws. Unless other states adopt strong laws, they will become the country's reservoirs for swindlers. Colonel George Mingle, chief of Ohio's Consumer Frauds and Crime Section, estimated that in 1966 Ohio consumers lost $300 million through all types of deception. This is one hundred times more than the estimated loss by consumers in the state of Washington, which has strong consumer protection laws and enforcement. Although Ohio has a consumer frauds law, the bureau had no budget in 1966 because the legislature refused to fund the law.

Some legislatures refuse to take action on establishing a consumer frauds bureau because they fear business interests will object. Experience shows that ethical businesses have been solidly behind the establishment of consumer protection bureaus, and even more so after they have seen their beneficial effects.

VOLUNTARY CONSUMER ORGANIZATIONS AT THE STATE LEVEL[8]

As of November 1, 1968, there were 44 voluntary consumer organizations existing at the national, state, and local level. Thirty-one of these were in 29 states. These are voluntary groups drawing membership, for the most part, from individuals and group organizations. They seek to promote consumer interests through consumer education and the initiation of needed legislative action.

In two states there are two voluntary consumer organizations. Colorado has Colorado Consumers Association and the Colorado Housewives Encouraging Consumer Knowledge. In Ohio there are the Consumers League of Ohio and the Ohio Consumers Association.

Activities of Typical Voluntary Consumer Associations

The purposes of state voluntary consumer associations are to ensure the protection of the consumer in the marketplace through:

1. Legislation—to promote sound consumer laws and to provide for their effective enforcement
2. Education—to make consumers aware of practices in the marketplace and to provide the knowledge necessary to buy wisely
3. Representation—to provide consumers a voice before those agencies of government which regulate or affect consumer goods and services
4. Coordination—to work for coordination of other organized groups and individuals interested in consumer protection and education
5. Information—to gather, exchange, and disseminate information of value to consumers

[8] For details, see *Consumer Protection,* published by Consumers Union, Mount Vernon, N.Y., 1966; also, the President's Committee on Consumer Interest, *Forming Consumer Organizations,* Washington, D.C., January, 1969. The latter publication gives the names and addresses of all voluntary consumer associations as of Nov. 1, 1968.

The consumer associations, typically, engage in such activities as giving testimony at hearings, speaking and enlightening members of other community or statewide organizations, preparing position papers or letters for members of the legislature or for legislative committees, pressing for consumer representation in the executive branch of state government, and working for the creation of consumer fraud or protective bureaus in state government. The Virginia Citizens Consumer Council, for example, installed a phone called "Dial-a-consumer" to spread important consumer information. Radio, newspapers, and TV are playing up "Dial-a-consumer."

Membership.   Membership in most state consumer associations is on an individual or organizational basis. Many of the national organizations, such as the AFL-CIO, American Association of University Women, American Home Economics Association, General Federation of Women's Clubs, League of Women Voters, National Congress of Parents and Teachers, NAACP, CUNA International, and Cooperative League of the U.S.A., have encouraged their state chapters to participate in state and local consumer organizations.

Membership dues in the state consumer associations usually range from $1 to $5 a year for individuals and from $10 to $25 for organizations.

Inadequate Financing.   The most effective state consumer organizations have a part-time or full-time paid executive secretary. It usually takes several years of successful growth to achieve even a part-time paid executive. The Association of California Consumers, an active association, felt that they "must have a regular lobbyist in Sacramento, for consumers cannot be represented on a hit-and-miss basis." Some of the consumer organizations have reached the stage of growth where they need a full-time executive secretary. It is extremely difficult, however, to secure sufficient income for paying even part-time leadership.

Federal Aid?   Because it is extremely difficult to become an effective consumer organization without some outside financial aid, Senator Hart of Michigan has proposed legislation which would establish independent consumer councils with local branches in each state. The consumer councils would be operated by local citizens and financed partly by federal funds; also, they could accept grants from foundations and other private sources. These consumer councils, possibly using the facilities and personnel of the American Arbitration Association, would, among other services, try to settle disputes for consumers that "are too small for legal action and too big to ignore."

Senator Jacob Javits of New York said on January 31, 1969, that he was going to reintroduce a bill called the Consumer Protection Assistance Act to provide effective consumer action at the local level. This act could provide for federal matching grants to assist states in establishing and strengthening their consumer protection programs. The federal grants would cover "up to 50 percent of the cost of the state plan, which would have to be approved by the Secretary of Commerce." The state consumer programs must include a "consumer protection office within the state to deal with dishonest practices." The act would also require states to license or otherwise regulate such businesses as those of appliance repairmen, car repairmen, home movers, and home improvement contractors. There are other requirements, all of which would identify the businesses that practice deception and intimidation.[9]

THE CONSUMERS' VOICE IN LOCAL AND COUNTY GOVERNMENT

By early 1969 there were two county government consumer associations and about a dozen city consumer organizations. Cities having voluntary consumer organizations are:

Cincinnati (Consumer Conference of Greater Cincinnati)

Detroit (Consumer Protection Association)

Kansas City, Missouri (Kansas City Consumers Association)

New York City (Metropolitan New York Consumer Council and the New York Consumer Assembly)

Palo Alto, California (Peninsula Consumers Association and the Automobile Consumers Protective Association, Inc.)

Philadelphia (Consumer Education and Protective Association)

Sacramento, California (Citizens for Consumer Action)

St. Louis, Missouri (St. Louis Consumer Federation)

And before this edition is on the market, there may be more consumer organizations established in other cities.

Consumer action is needed at the local level. Mrs. Esther Peterson, Special Assistant for Consumer Affairs, after 17 months of experience in the Johnson administration, concluded that the consumer must have protective assistance at the federal and state levels and "also at the local level."[10]

Limitations of Consumer Aid

A number of community agencies do provide at least some preventive and remedial guidance. The local Better Business Bureaus (more details on these appeared in Chapter 16) promote standards for truthful advertising and selling. The most valiant fighters in the war on such consumer problems are the legal aid societies and legal aid committees of local bar associations in over 250 communities. The legal aid societies, however, are available only to those who cannot pay regular legal fees. One of the most helpful new legal services for consumers, limited to low-income families, is that provided by local Economic Opportunity and Community Action programs as part of the war on poverty.

[9] Paper read at the annual meeting of the Consumer Federation of America, Jan. 31, 1969.

[10] Magnuson and Carper, *op. cit.*, p. 63.

Some of the labor unions also have become conscious of the need for legal advice and consumer guidance for their members. Some cities have organized special consumer agencies or departments.

City Departments of Consumer Protection

Columbus, Ohio, for example, has a five-member City Consumer Protection Commission as of January, 1969. Mayor Lindsay of New York City signed a bill in 1968 which gives that city the first major agency devoted exclusively to consumer affairs. This agency, called the Department of Consumer Affairs, will hear all consumer complaints, conduct research, develop consumer education programs, and seek recommendations from other consumer organizations. In January, 1969, for example, the Commissioner of Consumer Affairs called on the state to operate its own car inspection facilities because the annual inspection of cars by private garages was "fraught with corruption."[11]

The Commissioner of Markets. The Commissioner of Markets in New York City has organized a Consumer Protection Corps. Membership is open. Consumers join simply by volunteering. They receive a study kit reviewing consumer protection laws, bone up on this information, and telephone improper retailers' practices to the commissioner of markets. These complaints are then investigated by the commissioner's professional staff.

County Government Consumer Office

There were only two county government consumer offices in this country in 1969. The oldest county government consumer office is located in Nassau County, Long Island, New York. The most recent office, in Dade County, Florida, became effective on October 1, 1968. The county ordinance established an Office of Trade Standards and incorporates the provisions of the federal Fair Packaging and Labeling Act. The emphasis is on the enforcement and revision of the state weights and measures regulations. It is too early to know how effective this office has been in protecting consumers from frauds and in securing enforcement of the state weights and measures law.

Nassau County. The Nassau County Office of Consumer Affairs was established in June, 1967, and is the first county office of its kind in the country. Its purpose is "to develop and put into action programs for education, information and protection" of the one and a half million consumers in this Long Island county. The office is headed by a commissioner of consumer affairs with a budget of over $265,000 in 1968.

Since its inception, the Office of Consumer Affairs has:

1. Developed a gasoline mixture inspection program with the cooperation of industry to ensure that the consumer paying for premium (high-test) gasoline does, in fact,

[11] *New York Times,* Jan. 14, 1969.

receive it. Upon the complaint of the Office of Consumer Affairs, the first county prosecution of this fraudulent practice was initiated and the violators convicted.

2.   Caused the abandonment of certain deceptive meat packaging procedures in food stores.

3.   Conducted an investigation of, and issued a report on, sales tax overcharges on gasoline sold at retail service stations and misleading price-posting practices at these stations. The activities of the office contributed to the adoption of statewide regulations governing price and tax posting at gasoline stations.

4.   Received and processed hundreds of consumer complaints involving the quality and quantity of goods and services sold. Some of the areas of complaint included home improvements, appliance and auto repairs, faulty merchandise, misleading advertising, and high-pressure and misleading sales tactics.

5.   Caused the enactment of a local law governing fuel oil deliveries to consumers. These regulations protect the consumer from losses due to overheating of preheated fuel oils which artificially inflates the gallonage total.

6.   Continued a vigorous weights and measures inspection program and commodity control through constant check-weighing of various prepackaged foods and goods.

7.   Initiated a countywide program of direct meetings and educational presentations to the Nassau County consumer through the medium of civic and business organizations, the extension service, poverty groups, and high schools. A library of sound films, visual aids, and brochures on various topics of consumer interest was developed.

During the first year, the Office of Consumer Affairs recorded more than 600 complaints, plus carrying on their regular business of seeing that commercial products were properly packed, weighed, and measured. The 17 inspectors listen over the "hot line" telephone for consumer gripes. At night the office gives educational talks to senior citizens' clubs, poverty organizations, and adult education classes. [12]

The Office of Economic Opportunity (OEO)

The Office of Economic Opportunity is a creation of the federal government. At the present time OEO is financing a legal services program in about 150 communities to help limited-income families. The OEO's legal help for consumer action through local Economic Opportunity and Community Action programs is in the form of grants to consumer action agencies or directly to the administering agencies for credit unions, food-buying clubs, and consumer cooperatives of various kinds.

In 1967, over 300,000 poor people received legal advice in over 700 community groups, according to William Greenwalt, of the Office of Economic Opportunity. In Suffolk County, New York, for example, the Economic Opportunity Commission handled 100 cases in six months involving just home improvement misrepresentation cases. In a typical case, a widow living on Social Security income only had signed a note for $3,775 for work on her basement. The job was never completed but the finance company sued her for the money. In other instances, the neighborhood OEO legal services have been able to se-

[12] *Changing Times*, May, 1968.

cure lower credit terms, to get a merchant to abandon repossession of an article, or to agree to replace, or refund the purchase money on, a defective article. Sometimes nothing can be done. Yet, for thousands of poor people, especially in the large cities, the legal services program of the OEO is the most helpful consumer service they can receive at this time.

Local Voluntary Consumer Groups

In this country, the consumers' voice in local communities is only a whisper at best and practically nonexistent in most of our communities. Why is this true? No one seems to have an answer. The failure of local consumer group action programs in this country is in contrast to successful local group action in England, where they have been functioning since 1961. Today in England there are some 80 local consumer groups with about 80,000 members. An examination of how local consumer groups function in England may give us some ideas that will be useful in our own country.

Local Consumer Groups in England.   These groups are independent, nonprofit, nonpolitical party organizations of interested people in a community that aim to raise the standard of consumer goods and services, to give their members facts which will save them money, and to express the consumers' point of view publicly. The groups' local magazines (usually mimeographed) might say which shop in town sells the best at the cheapest, or which local shop is giving the biggest discount on the best washing machines, or which local garage does the best repair work at a fair price. Some groups have managed to get local swimming pools improved, public libraries made more convenient, hospital hours extended, footpaths established, and a host of other services established for their members.

Consumers' Association, publisher of *Which?*, a magazine similar to our *Consumer Reports,* budgets about $20,000 annually to support the National Federation of Consumer Groups with offices in the CA headquarters. The purpose of this national organization is primarily to help any local consumer group get started.

Local Consumer Groups in Sweden. [13]   The organizational structure and the character of local consumer groups in Sweden differ widely from those of the local consumer groups in England. In Sweden a joint committee of the Social Democratic Party and the Confederation of Trade Unions has recently suggested a pilot study which will be conducted by the central government and financed by the central government's Consumer Council.

The reason underlying the idea of local consumer organizations is the strong feeling of many consumers in Sweden that there should be more direct contact between producers, retailers, service stores, and consumers. Consumers should deliver their ideas and experiences and points of view as consumers to business organizations and to municipal or national governmental agencies so that busi-

[13] *International Consumer,* no. 2, 1968.

ness and government can cooperatively solve the consumer issues.

This cooperative effort of consumers, business, and government to improve the quality of life of consumers is in the Swedish tradition.

Ombudsman. The Swedish consumer has known this public figure since 1809. This official, appointed by the legislature, hears all consumer grievances and acts immediately. This official does not make decisions; instead he investigates the complaint and, if the grievance is real, he will take the issue directly to the proper government agency. The Ombudsman makes all valid complaints public—a feature of his office which has a desirable effect upon all public officials and civil servants.

This political concept might provide us with a practical model which we could adapt to help solve our own administrative problems. The presence of an agent for all consumers, inside the bureaucracy itself, would have a salutary effect on all state workers.

The Ombudsman idea has spread to other countries. Finland adopted it in 1919, Denmark in 1955, and Norway in 1962. Other countries—New Zealand, England, Australia, and several provinces of Canada—are considering setting up similar offices. It has also been suggested by political leaders in several states of our country.

CONSUMER JUSTICE [14]

Today, consumers in the United States are basically concerned with "consumer justice." Ideally, consumer protection in the marketplace is a three-way partnership involving consumer decision making in the marketplace (through consumer education, standards for products and warranties, informative labeling, etc.); efficient production and distribution of consumer products (through effective competition); and effective government laws and enforcement to give consumers and ethical businesses the opportunity to buy and sell informatively (through standards, safety, and fair prices based on competition).

Consumer Injustice

We have not been successful in achieving "consumer justice" via a three-way partnership. The consumer movement's relentless documentation (as pointed up in earlier chapters) reveals that consumers are being manipulated, defrauded, and injured, not just by marginal businesses or fly-by-night hucksters, but in many instances by large, blue-chip business firms whose practices are unchecked by laws or by the older regulatory agencies. Because this kind of injustice still prevails in the marketplace, seven out of 10 Americans (as pointed out earlier in the January, 1967, confidential nationwide survey by Opinion Re-

[14] Reprinted with permission from the *New York Review of Books,* Copyright, 1969, *The New York Review.*

search Corporation) think present federal legislation is inadequate to protect their health and safety and that more consumer protection is needed.

What has taken place in the last few years may be seen as an escalating series of disclosures by more and more independent Congressmen, by congressional investigations, and by individuals like Ralph Nader. As these charges get attention, the consumer movement escalates, as noted earlier, and demands increase for new legislative action at the federal, state, and local levels. This, at least, has been the case with exposure of defects of vehicles, air and water pollution, gas pipelines, overpriced or dangerous drugs, unfair credit, harmful pesticides, cigarettes, land frauds, electric power rates and reliability, household improvement rackets, exploitation in slums, auto and durable-product warranties, radiation, high-priced auto insurance, flammable fabrics, and boating hazards.

Consumer Justice Emerging

A more concrete idea of a just economy is beginning to emerge. Consumers are beginning to have a broader definition of consumer rights and interests. It appears quite clear that consumers must not only be protected in the voluntary use of a product such as a car or a flammable textile product, but also from involuntary consumption of industrial by-products such as air and water pollutant, excessive pesticide and nitrate residues in foods, and antibiotics in meat.

These demands on the part of consumers are ethical rather than ideological. Their principles and proposals for solutions are derived directly from solid documentation of common abuses whose origins are being traced directly to the policies of some of our largest corporations.

It is becoming apparent that the reform of consumer abuses and the reform of corporate power and policies are different sides of the same coin. New approaches to the enforcement of consumer rights are necessary.

New Approaches Needed

We need to strengthen present consumer protection and to try new approaches to the enforcement of the rights of consumers. The following major forces need our careful attention:

1. Rapid disclosure of the facts relating to the quality, quantity, and safety of a product is essential to a just marketplace. Buyers must be able to compare products via some kind of national standards in order to reward the superior producer. This process is the justification for a free market system.
2. The practices of refunding dollars to consumers who have been bilked and recalling defective products are finally becoming recognized as principles of deterrence and justice. Over 6 million vehicles were recalled between September, 1966 (the date of the auto safety law), and 1969. The FDA now requires drug companies to issue "corrective letters" to all physicians if their original advertisements are found to be misleading.

The threat of liability suits is causing companies to recall defective and unsafe products "voluntarily" in some cases even where no law or regulation exists. In 1968, Sears recalled about 6,000 gas heaters after public health officials warned of lethal carbon monoxide leakage. Likewise, General Electric made changes in 150,000 color TV sets which had been found to be emitting excessive radiation by Consumers Union and reported in its *Consumer Reports* magazine. The duty to refund, however, remains less well recognized than the duty to recall defective products. The usual FTC orders to "cease and desist" after it learns about the defects do not require the company to refund to the consumer. Without this sanction, a major deterrent is lost. The mere order to "go and sin no more" is easily evaded. The recent development of filing treble damage suits against violators of antitrust laws has strengthened private actions against malpractices by established corporations. In the early 1960s, for example, customers and governments collected about $550 million in out-of-court settlements after General Electric, Westinghouse, and other large companies were found guilty of carrying on a criminal antitrust price-fixing conspiracy. The second development is in the use of "class actions" in which suits are filed on behalf of large numbers of people who have been mistreated in the same way. Class actions help solve the problem when thousands of consumers have been cheated in such small amounts that it does not pay to take individual legal action. Presently, some 2,000 poverty lawyers, supported by the U.S. Office of Economic Opportunity (OEO), are beginning to use this important technique.

3.   Disputes in courts and other judicial means need to be conducted under fairer ground rules and with adequate representation for consumers. The OEO neighborhood poverty lawyers, representing the poor against landlords, finance companies, car dealers, and other sellers of goods and services, is a hopeful legal sign. For the first time, these lawyers are having success in court in exposing illegal repossession of goods, unreasonable garnishment, undisclosed credit and financing terms, and many other illegal practices. What is important is that these recent cases are documenting a general pattern of abuses and injustices in the legal system itself. This may prod law schools to more relevant teaching, as well as guide legislatures and courts toward reform of laws, court procedures, and remedies. Furthermore, this trend is resolving many consumer conflicts in neighborhood arbitration units which are open in the evenings when dependents need not be absent from their jobs in order to attend.

4.   The practice of setting government safety standards and changing them to reflect new technology and uses is spreading, although much more should be done. Many years after banking and securities markets were brought under regulation, products such as cars (with casualties of 53,000 dead and 4½ million injured annually), washing machines and power lawnmowers (with 200,000 persons injured annually), chemicals, and all pipeline systems did not have to adhere to standards of safety performance other than what companies set up themselves. But with the passage of the auto safety law in 1966, other major consumer products have been brought under federal safety regulation. To avoid more piecemeal safety legislation, Congress in 1967 passed an act establishing the National Commission on Product Safety to investigate many household hazards, from appliances to chemicals. The commission must recommend by 1970 a more detailed federal, state, and local policy toward reducing or preventing deaths and injuries from these products.

5.   To set up effective standards of safety, the government will have to conduct research—or contract for its own research—on safety of products and methods of improving unsafe industrial products. Without this additional power, the government will have to rely on what industry claims is safe, and the government's efforts will be crippled. Also, the existing safety laws do not permit government to find out quickly and accurately whether industry is complying with the law. The National Highway

Safety Bureau, for example, has little idea whether or not the 1969 cars meet all the safety standards, since no government testing facilities yet exist.

6.   In theory, business, free competition, and corporate responsibility are supposed to protect the consumer; in practice, all have long ignored him. Price-fixing, for example, is common throughout our economy. The Department of Justice does not have the manpower to cope with this problem. All of us know that price-fixing means higher prices for consumers. An even greater danger exists when the failure of large industry to compete prevents the development of new products that might save lives and the improvement of consumer products. Ideally, one of the potent forces for consumer justice would be the exercise of corporate "responsibility." The casualty insurance industry, for example, should have a strong interest in safer cars. It chose to raise premiums instead. The insurance industry has not raised its voice to demand legislation to improve the design and inspection of cars; nor has it encouraged the rating of cars according to their safety.

7.   Professional and technical societies (American Society of Safety Engineers, etc.) have up to now been little more than trade associations for the industries that employ their members. It is rather shocking, for example, that none of these societies has done much to work out public policies to deal with pollution of air and water. With few exceptions, societies of law and medicine have done little to protect the public from victimization. Engineers and scientists, however, had no procedure for undertaking these new roles. The societies may have to create special independent organizations willing to get facts and take action in the interest of the public. There are the beginnings of such societies. The Committee for Environmental Information in St. Louis and the Physicians for Automotive Safety in New Jersey have shown how people with even small resources can accomplish much in educating the public and in an action program.

8.   The courts have been making progress in rulings that give injured persons fairer chances of recovering damages. The expansion of the "implied warranty," mentioned earlier in the book, is one example of the trend toward more justice for the consumer because under this concept the injured need not prove negligence if injured through the use of a defective product. The law of torts (personal injuries) still does not protect the consumer against the pollution of the environment, which indiscriminately injures all the people exposed to it. Pollution in Los Angeles is a serious health hazard, but how many of their people sue? True, some 80 residents in Martinez, California, are suing Shell Oil's petroleum refinery for air pollution. Shell claims, perhaps justly, that it is abiding by the state's mild pollution-control regulation. It may be that justice in the courts must be paralleled by better state laws.

9.   The most promising development in recent years is the growing belief that new institutions are needed within the government whose only function is to protect consumer interests. Reference, here, is to the Office of Consumer Counsel in the Justice Department, created by the Johnson administration, and to the creation of other consumer organizations within large government departments. The Office of Consumer Services in the Health, Education, and Welfare Department is one such example. Perhaps some day we may have a Department of Consumer Affairs in the President's Cabinet. Clearly, something needs to be done to expose present regulatory agencies (FTC, ICC, FCC, and others) and challenge them to take more vigorous action. Senator Lee Metcalf introduced legislation to create an independent U.S. Office of Utility Consumer's Counsel to represent consumers before regulatory agencies and courts. Even such an independent office would, in time, have to be encouraged continuously by consumer organizations at the local, state, and national levels to avoid the dangers of bureaucratic attitude and atrophy.

10.   Finally, there is urgent need to stimulate professional people, such as lawyers,

engineers, doctors, and economists, to develop local consumer service organizations similar to the OEO neighborhood poverty lawyers, mentioned earlier, that could handle consumer complaints, give information, and work out plans for public action.

Consumer Voice Still Feeble

The voice of the consumer is being heard in the land. Legislators are listening. Alert businessmen are beginning to pay attention. And, as we have noted earlier, the consumer is beginning to organize at the local, state, and national levels.

The current consumer movement dates from a statement on March 15, 1962, by the late President Kennedy when he declared that every consumer has four basic rights—the right to be informed, the right to safety, the right to choose, and the right to be heard. Thus, the President breathed life into the consumer movement, and President Johnson continued to champion the consumer by word and by initiating legislation. Consumers' organizations sprang up, and states, too, got into the act. So did many cities.

The growth of the current consumer movement has not followed traditional patterns. In the past this type of protest originated at the grass-roots level and eventually converged on state capitals and on Washington. The current consumer crusade *started* in the nation's Capital, was fanned impressively by an independent consumer crusader, Ralph Nader (also in Washington), and is currently spreading slowly to the grass roots of America.

Whither the Consumer Movement? The progress of the consumer movement since 1962 is impressive when judged by the growing number of laws passed by Congress, by some state legislatures, and by a few local governments. Notwithstanding the progress in consumer legislation since 1962, in particular, the wide publicity the mass media have given to the single consumer crusader, Ralph Nader, and the recent alarm of industry over the publicity about auto safety, drug costs, and other scandals, the consumer movement is still a feeble force in American power politics. Almost any way you look at it, the interests of consumers are low on the list of election issues. Too, the government's expenditures to protect those interests are negligible. Some would argue that this situation will always prevail in view of the tremendous financial and political power in the hands of industry in and out of government. But new approaches to influencing corporate behavior are emerging. It is possible that more people, not merely a few articulate consumer leaders, may begin to react with greater concern to the enormity of their deprivation—the hundreds of ways in which their income is being milked. The current assault on the health and safety of the public from many industrial products, drugs, and foods has resulted in violence that even dwarfs crime in the streets. Since 1965 about 260 people died in riots in American cities; but every two days some 300 persons are killed and 20,000 injured while driving on our highways. Add to these violence records the economic loss *each* year—$500 million loss in security frauds, another $500 million in home repair frauds, and even more loss in dishonest and fraudulent repair bills, to name only three of hundreds of ways in which our income is unjustly taken from us—and we have an astronomical annual financial loss to Americans.

What the current consumer movement is beginning to say—and must say much more strongly if it is to grow—is that "consumer justice" must prevail. The rule *caveat emptor* (let the buyer beware) should not be relied upon to reward deception and fraud. The modern rule, *caveat venditor* (let the seller beware), should prevail.

QUESTIONS FOR DISCUSSION

1.   Why is consumer legislation at the federal level not enough?

2.   Can you see any difficulties in dual (federal-state) control in consumer protection laws? (Examine how the federal Fair Packaging and Labeling Act is enforced in your state).

3.   The failure of state laws to protect consumers lies in the slight degree to which they are enforced. How do you account for this tendency? You might investigate how your consumer frauds bureau (if there is one) or your public utilities commission functions in behalf of consumers.

4.   The primary weapon against gypsters is the authority to obtain a "court injunction." Does your state give this authority to your attorney general? How do court injunctions work?

5.   If your state has a voluntary consumer association, find out as much as you can about its activities, financing, and effectiveness in promoting the consumer interest.

6.   There are some people who would destroy the Office of Economic Opportunity. Do you think the OEO Economic Opportunity and Community Action programs, presently in some 150 cities, fill unmet consumer needs in these cities?

ACTIVITY PROBLEMS

1.   If you have a consumer organization in your community, invite its president and other enthusiastic members to attend a class discussion of its purposes and activities and the results of its combined efforts. Possibly the class might attend one or more of its general and committee meetings. That is where you will see the best in organized consumer education functioning on the local level.

2.   Think of all the ways in which people might learn how to develop pride in being intelligent and skilled consumers. Does this pride tend to decrease as the family income increases? If a manufacturer takes pride in his products

and an athlete takes pride in excellent performance, why should not an individual take pride in being a good consumer?

3.   The statement is made that the foundation of consumer education is to help each of us to (a) develop a sense of values, (b) determine what we most want out of life, (c) set our goals and see them in proper balance, then (d) act according to our developed principles. What are your reactions to the above point of view? Support your views in an objective manner.

4.   Prepare a paper on consumer protection legislation and enforcement in your state.

5.   Investigate the consumer protection services rendered by your local community. Does the federal government enter into any aspect of these local services?

SUGGESTED READINGS

Barber, Richard J.: "Government and the Consumer," *Michigan Law Review,* May, 1966.

Bishop, James, Jr., and Henry W. Hubbard: *Let the Seller Beware,* The National Press, Inc., Washington, D.C., 1969.

Consumer Guardian, Consumer Research Advisory Council, 242 East Warrent Street, Detroit, Mich.

Consumers' Voice, Consumers Education and Protective Association, 6048 Ogontz Avenue, Philadelphia, Pa. 19141.

Digest of Proceedings, January 13, 1968, Consumer Assembly of Greater New York, 465 Grand Street, New York, N.Y. 10002.

Metcalf, Lee, and Vic Reinemer: *Overcharge,* David McKay Co., New York, 1968.

chapter 19

THE INTERNATIONAL
CONSUMER MOVEMENT [1]

[1] The sources of information on the consumer movements in the world are many. The author's visit to countries in Western Europe and to Japan in 1962 and 1963 gave him valuable information and insight. Much information comes from unpublished sources. Notable among the unpublished sources is the material collected by Dr. Colston E. Warne, of Amherst College and president of Consumers Union of U.S., Inc. Dr. Warne has been most generous in permitting the author to use his excellent material on the consumer movements of the world. The consumer organizations in various countries have also been generous in their efforts to be informative and to discuss common problems. Jan van Veen, executive secretary of the International Organization of Consumers Unions, has given generously of his knowledge about the international consumer movement since 1965.

Intelligent American consumers should be interested in and knowledgeable about the consumer movement in the rest of the world. There is a rapidly developing European consumer movement. An unprecedented number of consumers protection organizations has emerged in Europe, some stimulated by the cooperative movement, some given governmental assistance, and some arising from independent efforts. The same forces that have brought into existence consumer organizations in Europe have spread to Canada, where the Consumers Association of Canada has embarked on a consumer testing movement. The consumer movement has likewise spread to the Near East, Iceland, Australia, New Zealand, and Japan.

Although the structures of the consumer organizations of the world vary, all have one central element in common—the aim to furnish impartial advice and recommendations concerning trademarked consumer goods. Consumers in all countries are increasingly angered at being misled as to product claims and are bewildered by competing advertising slogans. The spectacular advance of new technologies has created a vacuum in product information which has not been filled by producers. The consumer movement forms a practical answer that can improve living standards by directing consumers toward meritorious products and away from those that contain virtues which exist only in the promoter's imagination.

The heart of the modern consumer movement lies in accurate testing and more testing, and in the issuing of reports on testing that will guide consumers to a higher standard of living.

The consumer movement, however, is more than a testing organization. It is also an educational organization—a new and significant phase of adult education. It punctures false claims, it spreads knowledge of new quality products, it harnesses science for the service of the buyer. The consumer movement also helps restore the capacity of the competitive system to reward those companies that are producing better products. The central aim of the consumer movement is to help organize the economy in ways that will best serve the consumer interest.

Another purpose of the consumer movement is that of becoming a countervailing power in legislation that will afford better protection to all consumers against the more common hazards of the marketplace, such as elaborate packaging, extravagantly promoted brand names, deceptive weights, improper measurements, restraints on retail competition, fictitious prices, unknown credit terms, restrictive patenting and licensing arrangements, tariff barriers, and many other impediments to competition.

Just as the International Labor Office for more than fifty years has been championing the development of international labor standards, the international consumer movement has an obligation to insist that a parallel international organization be developed to promote international consumer standards. Just as the earlier legislation insisted that water supplies be sanitary and that food be unadulterated, so in this period of chemical revolution, new social safeguards on the social front must be developed.

TYPES OF CONSUMER MOVEMENTS

Consumer movements throughout the world are of three different types.

In the United Kingdom, Australia, the Netherlands, Belgium, and Canada, as in the United States, consumer testing is undertaken without government support. The private consumer testing agencies in these countries have been most careful to steer clear of business entanglements. They have recruited technical personnel to give impartial assessments of products bought on the open market. The most rapidly growing testing agency among these newer movements, Consumers' Association, Ltd., in the United Kingdom, had a membership of over 525,000 at the end of its eleventh year, 1968.

The second type of consumer organization undertakes consumer testing through government subsidy. The two most vigorous examples of this type are Norway and New Zealand. Both of these product-testing groups have been in a position to publish comparative product ratings as well as to handle consumer complaints. In New Zealand, the government linked the testing facilities of its Bureau of Standards and of its universities with the consumer testing movement and has developed a quasi-autonomous consumer testing movement supported by voluntary subscriptions. This effort, like the Norwegian, has as its basic objective the governmental establishment of a nonpartisan consumer movement.

The third type of consumer agency that has emerged in the international picture is the extension of the work of standards associations into the field of comparative product reporting. Notable examples in this field are in England and in Japan. In Japan, until 1963, the newly formed Japan Consumers' Association used a combination of government subsidy, subscriptions to its magazine, donations by manufacturers of products to be tested, and government testing agencies. In 1963, the JCA made a serious effort to reduce possible outside influences when it decided to purchase in the open market the products to be tested. It remains to be seen whether this association can demonstrate complete independence and objectivity and yet become self-sustaining.

Most of the organizations in the nearly two dozen countries described in this chapter deserve more attention than space permits, but the brief summaries will give a picture of the great progress made on behalf of consumers in these countries. There is ample reason to believe that other countries, notably many of the newly formed nations in Africa, will also be active in promoting the consumer interest.

INTERNATIONAL ORGANIZATION OF CONSUMERS UNIONS (IOCU)

Dr. Colston E. Warne, president of Consumers Union of U.S., Inc., was largely responsible for promoting the creation of an International Organization of Consumers Unions. After many preliminary discussions with consumer leaders in Europe and elsewhere, the Consumers Union of U.S., Inc., appropriated funds for an organizing meeting of consumer union officials at The Hague, Netherlands. On April 1, 1960, the International Organization of Consumers Unions was made a *stichting* (foundation) under Dutch law, and it functions in accordance with legal regulations. The registered office is at The Hague, Netherlands. The financial resources consist of the *Stichting* Fund, contributions from members, and the sale of its publications.

Affiliated with United Nations

IOCU is in consultative status with the Economic and Social Council of the United Nations (ECOSOC) and the United Nations Educational, Scientific and Cultural Organization (UNESCO), and in liaison status with the Food and Agriculture Organization (FAO).

The IOCU has an authorized observer at all meetings of the Bureau Européen des Unions Consommateurs. The BEUC is composed of the IOCU member organizations and other consumer groups in the European Economic Community (EEC—Common Market). The EEC authorities have agreed to give special consideration to consumer problems presented by a committee composed of authorized representatives of four groups of organizations: consumers unions, trade unions, family organizations, and consumer cooperatives.

Fifth Biennial Conference, 1968

The nature of some of the activities to receive the attention of the IOCU can be seen from the agenda of its fifth biennial conference at Bronxville, New York, in June, 1968. The conference included papers and discussion on the right to be heard; on the right to safety; on the right to be informed; on consumer rights as human rights; on the right to be protected; and on a consumer 5-year plan.

International Product Testing Standards (Codex Alimentarius Commission)

The Codex Commission of the Food and Agriculture Organization (FAO) and the World Health Organization (WHO) have jointly made considerable progress since 1963 in establishing standards for labeling, for pesticide residues in food, and for food additives that will be incorporated into national legislation of many UN member nations. By August, 1967, for example, 71 governments had accepted standards for milk and milk products.

At the fourth biennial conference of IOCU in Israel, it was suggested that consumers should take an interest in international testing of consumer products. The first international testing project of IOCU was on watches, but there were too many difficulties in 1962 to proceed with this kind of international testing cooperation. However, international surveys on consumer services could be organized more easily. The first international survey project was on telephone services; the second project, on package holiday tours, was under way in 1969.

Consumers' Declaration

When the delegates to the Brussels Conference of IOCU met in 1964, they decided that the organization should be a voice which has so far been largely silent for the consumer interest. The following declaration was drafted, expressing further the sound reasons for an international organization of consumers.

The purpose of an economy is to produce, for the maximum satisfaction of consumers, goods and services which are: good in quality; sufficient in quantity; safe; reasonable in price.

In practice, consumers frequently find goods of shoddy quality; insufficient legal control to guarantee safety; gluts or scarcities; prices having no relation to quality; confusing advertising; insufficient information; poor retail service.

Consumers should not acquiesce in this state of affairs, but are urged to act, individually and via their consumers' organizations, to get improvement.

To do so, consumers are urged to organize themselves to: fight ignorance with reports and labels based on comparative tests on consumer goods and services; with accurate, unbiased advice on buying consumer goods and services; with the information necessary to assess the validity of advertising claims and the value of the goods inside the packaging; make themselves heard in every section of the government or economy where the consumers' interest is, or may be, involved. This is particularly important where the quality and price of goods or services are involved and essential where there is any question of safety.

To achieve this, the consumer organizations are urged to enrol, wherever possible, the help of governments, educators, the press, radio and television.

They are urged to work not only for well-educated, conscientious consumers, but for those who are uninterested and hard to reach: not only for the consumers in advanced countries, but for those in the underdeveloped areas as well.

Consumers everywhere should be able, if they so choose, to buy goods and obtain services whose essential qualities they can discover without great effort on their part, and which are safe, of good quality and reasonable in price.

Objectives of IOCU

The objectives of IOCU are these:

1.   To authenticate, assist, and actively promote genuine efforts throughout the world in consumer self-organization, as well as governmental efforts to further the interests of the consumer;

2.   To promote international cooperation in the comparative testing of consumer goods and services, and to facilitate exchange of test methods and plans;

3.   To promote international cooperation in all other aspects of consumer information, education, and protection, and to collect and disseminate information relating to consumer laws and practices throughout the world;

4.   To provide a forum in which national bodies may work exclusively in the interest of the consumer problems and possible solutions to them;
5.   To act as a clearinghouse for the publications of such bodies and to regulate (subject to any regulations promulgated by or applicable to the bodies themselves) the use of such published material;
6.   To publish information on subjects connected with the interests of the consumer;
7.   To maintain effective links with United Nations agencies and other international bodies, with a view to representing the interests of the consumer on the international level;
8.   To give all practical aid and encouragement to the development of consumer educational and protective programs in the developing countries, through the United Nations agencies and in other suitable ways;
9.   And in general to take such actions as may further these objects.

Rules, Services, and Responsibilities

The IOCU is a noncommercial organization. Its members agree to refrain from any use of their membership for advertising purposes, for promoting the sale of any product, or for any commercial purpose whatsoever. The name of IOCU or references to IOCU publications and other materials may not be used for advertising or for any commercial purposes.

The following publications are for the use of members of the IOCU.

1.   *International Consumer* (English and French). Bimonthly report with news of consumer organizations, consumer test equipment, operational methods of different consumers' associations, the juridical position of the consumer, and other matters of interest about consumers. Subscription rate: Dutch florins 25 per year. No reduction allowed to agencies, etc.
2.   *Circular Letter* (English).   A monthly review with news from the headquarters office, financial reports, and other confidential items. The *Circular Letter* is sent to IOCU members only.
3.   *Yearbook.*   Information about all IOCU members and other consumers' organizations.

Structure

Originally only five consumer nonprofit, independent consumer testing organizations served in the important policy-making IOCU Council (U.S.A., England, Belgium, the Netherlands, and Australia). Later Norway and Denmark were added.

In 1968, under the revised constitution, the five original consumer testing organizations remained on the council. These were now matched by five governmentally supported consumer groups (Norway, Denmark, Sweden, Austria, and the British Consumer Council), thus reflecting the more recent trend toward efforts financially assisted by the state.

Five more members were elected from a list of Associate Members of IOCU (Canada, France, Israel, Japan, and New Zealand). This brings the council to 15 members. This arrangement allows for a balance between its various kinds of consumer organizations and for an opportunity to give representation to more countries which have hitherto had no part in control of the organization. These 15 groups elect the executive committee which guides the organization.

Membership Qualifications

As of June 26, 1968, there were 45 consumer member organizations from 27 countries in IOCU. Of these 45 consumer organizations, 21 were eligible for the council; three others were noneligible but did have voting rights; three more were noneligible with no voting rights. There were also nine corresponding members.

IOCU is not unlike other international organizations in that the constituent organizations must comply with certain qualifications before being admitted as a member. For example, national and regional bodies are eligible to be Associates of IOCU if they comply with the following qualifications:

1. That they are active exclusively on behalf of the interests of the consumer;
2. That they are totally unconcerned with the advancement of commercial or party political causes;
3. That they are nonprofit-making in character;
4. That they do not accept advertisements in their publications;
5. That they do not allow selective commercial exploitation of the information and advice they give to consumers;
6. That their independence of action and comment is in no way influenced or qualified by the receipt of subsidies;
7. That they pay such financial dues to IOCU as are laid down from time to time;
8. And that they comply with such other requirements as may be laid down by the council from time to time.

An Associate of IOCU must satisfy the council that it continues to comply with the aforementioned qualifications by providing at regular intervals such information as may be specified.

An Associate of IOCU ceases to be an Associate in either of the following circumstances:

1. If it gives not less than six months' notice in writing of its desire to resign from IOCU;
2. If its Associate status is revoked in accordance with the provisions of Article 10 (h).

Membership and Founding Dates.   Table 19-1 lists the consumer testing organizations that were members of IOCU on June 1, 1968.

Influence

The influence of IOCU is not extensive yet. This is primarily because the idea of consumers' unions has not caught the imagination of the "man in the street"

TABLE 19-1

FOUNDING DATE	COUNTRY	ORGANIZATION
1957	Belgium	Association des Consommateurs
1959	Australia	Australian Consumers' Association
1957	United Kingdom	Consumers' Association
1936	United States	Consumers' Union of U.S., Inc.
1947	Denmark	Forbrugerrådet
1953	Norway	Forbrukerrådet
1953	Netherlands	Nederlandse Consumenten Bond
1956	Sweden	Statens Konsument Råd
1963	United Kingdom	Consumer Council
1959	New Zealand	Consumers' Institute
1935	Denmark	Statens Husholdnigsrad
1947	Canada	Consumers' Association of Canada
1966	Ireland	Consumers' Association of Ireland
1964	West Germany	Stiftung Warentest
1963	United Kingdom	National Federation of Consumer Groups
1965	Malaya	Selangor Consumers' Association
1963	United Kingdom	Research Institute for Consumer Affairs
1953	United Kingdom	Council on Consumer Information
1951	France	Union Fédérale de la Consommation
1955	Israel	Israel Consumers' Association
1961	Austria	Verein fur Konsumenteninformation
1953	West Germany	Arbeitsgemeinschaft der Verbraucher-verbaende E.V.
1960	Japan	Japan Consumers' Association
1968	United States	Consumer Federation of America, Inc.

or the "woman in the supermarket." Their membership is generally confined to the upper middle-class intellectuals. Although many prime movers of the consumer movement are women, the consumer organizations have been singularly unsuccessful in interesting housewives—the major consumers—in their programs.

Nevertheless, the consumer organizations have prevailed upon governments to recognize the interests of consumers. They have done so even without agreement among themselves as to the nature of this interest. Government consumer programs, or government-financed activities, are now in operation in the United States of America, in most Western European countries, and in some Asian countries. The programs themselves reflect this ideological vacuum.

While the programs may be weak, with a few exceptions, the fact remains that the consumer movement *is* a reality, and it is growing. As of now, it appears that the consumer movement will not go away, but will slowly gain momentum.

CONSUMER ORGANIZATIONS IN AMERICA

There are only two product-testing consumer organizations in North America interested and active in promoting an international consumer movement—Consumers Union of U.S., Inc., and the Consumers' Association of Canada.

United States of America[2]

Consumers Union of U.S., Inc., Mount Vernon, New York 10550, was chartered in 1936 as a nonprofit, independent, product-testing organization. The purposes are to provide information on consumer products and services and to give information relating to expenditures of family income. CU publishes *Consumer Reports* from January through November and a *Buying Guide* that comes out in December. As of early 1969, there were 1,550,000 subscribers to *Consumer Reports,* and over 50,000 issues were sold annually on the newsstands.

Consumer Reports summarizes the results of current product testing. All test products are purchased in the open market by CU's shoppers, who do not identify their CU affiliation. Most products are rated in the order of estimated overall quality. "Best Buy" ratings are given to products of high quality and relatively low price. Poor-quality products or those having a serious safety hazard are rated "Not Acceptable."

Consumers Union initiated discussions which led to the formation of IOCU in 1960.

Canada

The Consumers' Association of Canada started as a women's organization for consumer education and consumer protection, but it included men in 1961. Observing the marked success of testing groups in other countries, the fourteenth annual meeting, held in Toronto, September 12 to 14, 1961, adopted the recommendation of a special committee to include testing of products on the Canadian market. Any person living in Canada may become a member of the association on payment of an annual fee to be prescribed from time to time by the delegate body.

In 1961, the meeting also passed resolutions dealing with the labeling of textiles, meat inspection, chemical sprays, grade standards for canned fish products, aspirin, trading stamps, labeling of soap, ground beef, a food and drug directorate, standards of flammability for fabrics, serial numbers on household equipment and appliances, and the metric system of measurement.

The first issue of a new magazine, *Canadian Consumer,* published six times

[2] See Chap. 16 for details.

a year with an annual subscription rate of $3, appeared in English and French in mid-1963.

As of 1969, CAC has not resolved the issue of testing their own Canadian products. Consumers Union of U.S., Inc., has, at times, tested Canadian products at the request of CAC. Although *Consumer Reports* (U.S.) is sold in Canada in considerable numbers, CU would much prefer that CAC establish their own testing laboratory.

Government Interest. Most of the income is from about 20,000 subscribers. The Canadian government grant to CAC was about 30 percent of their budget in 1966.

The Ministry of Consumer and Corporate Affairs was established in 1968. There are now three cabinet-level ministries of consumer affairs—Sweden and Norway preceded Canada.

Caribbean Organizations

The three consumer organizations in the Caribbean area, all of them founded since 1963, have very few members and are financially weak. Nevertheless, these groups are making some progress and hope to improve the standard of living of the people.

Consumers' Association of Jamaica. CAJ, founded in 1964, with the largest membership in the island organizations, aims (1) to investigate consumer complaints, (2) to represent the consumer in government, and (3) to improve the quality of consumer products. It is a membership organization.

Jamaica Consumers' Union. JCU, founded in 1963, aims (1) to provide information relative to wise spending of family income, and (2) to cooperate with the government to secure better protection for consumers. This group publishes *Consumer Guide,* a monthly. It also is a membership organization.

Consumers' Association of Trinidad and Tobago. The CATT, founded in 1964, attempts (1) to disseminate consumer information, and (2) to improve economic development by working for higher standards for consumer products and services. Their publication, *Value?,* is mailed to members only.

Venezuela. The National Association of Consumers, founded in 1961, is a membership organization of local consumer groups. The major objectives are (1) to improve standards for consumer products, (2) to work for truth-in-advertising, (3) to inform consumers on best ways to spend their money, and (4) how to use credit. The organization publishes a monthly, *Cartas—Circulares.*

CONSUMER ORGANIZATIONS IN ASIA

There were six consumer organizations in Asia in 1969 (in the Philippines, Japan, Malaya, India, Pakistan, and Israel). All of these consumer groups have been established since 1948 and most of them since 1965.

India

India has two active consumer organizations at the present time.

1.   The Consumers' Association of Eastern India, with headquarters in Calcutta, is a membership group founded in 1965. The organization expects to conduct and encourage testing of consumer products and to represent the consumer in the government and in consumer standards bodies. A *Quarterly Newsletter* is sent to members only.
2.   The Consumer Council of India, in New Delhi, was founded in 1968. The organization is too recent for a progress report. They intend to publish a monthly magazine called *Indian Consumer.*

Pakistan

The Pakistan Consumers' Council, in Karachi, was organized in 1968. The council will urge more consumer protection, conduct research on adulteration of food products, and assist the producers in knowing the needs of consumers.

Israel

There are three organized consumer groups in the small country of Israel. All are located in Tel Aviv.

1.   Israel Consumers' Association, organized in 1955, claims 3,000 members and publishes a quarterly, *Consumer's Tribune.* This group plans (1) to undertake testing of consumer products, (2) to protect consumers' rights, and (3) to represent the consumer in government, industrial, and other bodies.
2.   Consumers Protection Council, organized in 1964, aims (1) to eliminate false labeling and advertising; and (2) to safeguard the public from the marketing of unsafe products. They plan to publish a quarterly. This group claims 1,300 members, largely from labor unions.
3.   Israel Consumer Council, founded in 1966, will attempt to advise government on consumer problems and to coordinate the activities in the consumer field on a national level. This organization is financed by the government.

Japan

There are two legitimate consumer associations in Japan, both with headquarters in Tokyo.

1.   Japan Consumers' Association, established in 1961, has over 10,000 members. This group undertakes comparative testing of consumer goods and publishes the results in a monthly magazine, *Consumer.* It is financed by the government, corporations, and membership subscribers. JCA now claims complete independence from government and business influence.
2.   Japan Housewives' Association. The JHA, organized in 1948, is a national federation of some 443 women's local groups. Their main objectives are to inform and educate the consumer on consumer commodities and to influence government in protecting consumers. Most of the finances come from membership fees, but the government makes modest annual grants. This group, quite militant, puts considerable pressure

on manufacturers to improve their consumer products. A monthly, *Schufuren—Dayori,* presents consumer news and product-testing results.

Malaya

The Selangor Consumers' Association, located in Kuala Lumpur, was founded in 1965. The major objectives of the association of some 200 members are (1) to protect consumers from high prices and poor quality of products; (2) to encourage adoption of a nationally uniform weights and measures system; and (3) to advise consumers as to their legal rights. The organization is financed by the government of Malaya and through membership fees. A monthly newsletter, *Berita Pengguna,* is mailed to members only.

Philippines

The Consumer Federated Groups of the Philippines, Inc., founded in 1963, with headquarters in Manila, is an organization of local and provincial consumer groups. The federation promotes public understanding of consumer needs and research on the best ways to meet these needs.

CONSUMER GROUPS IN AUSTRALASIA

There are three consumer associations in Australia and one in New Zealand.

Australia

Australian Consumers' Association, in Chippendale, N.S.W., founded in 1959, is the most successful consumer organization in Australia. Its 60,000-member association publishes an excellent monthly magazine, *Choice.* This magazine, like *Consumer Reports* in the United States, rates tested consumer products and evaluates services for the association's members.

The Brisbane Consumer Group, founded in 1964, is not very active at the present time. The BCG does publish a news sheet called *Counter Balance.*

Canberra Consumers, organized in 1963, with some 1,500 members, aims to assist members and the general public in their capacity as consumers. This group publishes *Canberra Consumer,* a quarterly.

A new Consumer Council was organized in Australia in 1968. It is too early at this time to describe the nature of the organization except to report that it will be financed by the government.

New Zealand

The Consumers' Institute in Wellington, founded in 1959, has over 60,000 members. It is financed in part by government grants and partly by membership subscriptions for a bimonthly publication, *Consumer*. The results of quality testing are published in the *Consumer*.

CONSUMER ORGANIZATIONS IN EUROPE

In most of Europe, the "consumer interest" means the interest of the buyer at the point of sale, in contrast to the interest of the buyer in developing broad, national economic policy or interest in the purchase of public goods. The primary purpose of government consumer programs in Europe is to provide consumers with adequate and accurate information about products and services in the marketplace.

The tools for accomplishing this are consumer goods testing, informative labeling, and consumer education. In a few countries (Norway and Sweden, for example) government consumer programs have been broadened to include factors affecting the structure of the marketplace. In no case do consumer agencies, in or out of government, have sufficient funds or expertise to concern themselves with broader problems. European consumer leaders are apparently confident that the broader economic interests of consumers will be adequately represented in the Ministries of Economics and Commerce. Even where special Ministries of Consumer Affairs have been established (in Sweden and Norway), the primary emphasis is on consumer information and education rather than on influencing national economic policy and planning.

Austria

At the end of 1960, the Verein für Konsumenteninformation (Society for Consumer Information) was founded, with its main office in Vienna. As of the same date, two previously existing societies were disbanded, but their functions were taken over by the new society, which is sponsored by four member organizations.

> 1. Der oesterreichische Arbeiterkammertag (Austrian Chamber of Labor Diet) (with the exception of public employees and farm workers, all Austrian employees are obligatory members of the Chamber of Labor. Each of the nine Austrian federal provinces has a separate chamber)
> 2. The Austrian Trade Union Federation
> 3. The Austrian Federal Chamber of Commerce (of which any Austrian firm is an obligatory member)
> 4. Die Praesidentenkonferenz der oesterreichischen Landwirtschaftskammern (the president's conference of the Austrian Chambers of Agriculture of the nine Austrian federal provinces)

The four member organizations finance, with modest grants from the state, the new society and name representative members to the supervisory board, which decides on the budget and the general work program. Apart from these principal matters, the executive secretary (a nominee of the Vienna Chamber of Labor approved by the other members) directs the operations of the society with relatively little overseeing.

The chief emphasis of the society is on quality tests, using its own testing facilities as well as outside testing laboratories, and on publishing results periodically in the form of a list detailing the advantages and disadvantages of products deemed recommendable to the public. Products found inferior are excluded from the list. In this indirect way, manufacturers of low-quality goods are given the opportunity and incentive to improve their products. The society does not issue seals of approval. However, it may recommend seals of other organizations. For example, it has recommended the placing of orders only with those sales agents using special-seal order forms issued by a certain agents' association.

The society issues three different types of publications: *Konsument,* with 10 issues a year distributed to member organizations and to subscribers, occasional brochures devoted to lengthy studies and investigations, and press releases. No advertisements will be accepted.

Attempts to establish a consumer protective organization in Austria date back many years and were initiated by Austrian labor organizations. In 1955, the Vienna Chamber of Labor established the Society for Purchasing Counsel. In 1958, the Austrian Trade Union of Building and Wood Workers, backed by the Austrian Trade Union Federation, established a similar society. The functions of these earlier societies are now carried on by Verein für Konsumenteninformation.

Belgium

The Association des Consommateurs (formerly Union Belge des Consommateurs) was founded in 1957 as a nonprofit independent association of private consumers. Its activities cover educational work, including shopping-club meetings and general information published in *Test Achats* (both in French and in Flemish), and information on the comparative value (price quality) of products available on the market.

Tests have been carried out on ball-point pens, corned beef, pressure cookers, electric irons, new floor coverings, plastics, table syrups, yogurt, edible oils, liquid bleaches, and canned pineapple. Under agreements concluded with other consumer associations, the results of tests carried out in other countries have been published by the association.

UFIDEC. The Union Féminine pour l'Information et la Défense du Consommateur (UFIDEC) was founded in 1959 as a nonprofit association. Its associate members include Femmes Prévoyantes Socialistes (Socialist Women's Provident Association) and Ligue Nationale des Coopératrices (National Women's Cooperative League). There are also six affiliated member organizations.

UFIDEC is active in these fields.

1. Encouragement toward better household management, primarily through research, experiments, and information on domestic science
2. Protection of the consumer against all forms of abuse and fraud in the matter of quality or price
3. Representation of the consumer on all bodies dealing with questions that affect his interest, whether or not in conjunction with other economic or social bodies
4. Education of the consumer on as wide a range of consumer problems as possible, particularly through publications, courses, lectures, and seminars

The association does not automatically publish results of comparative analyses. It uses laboratory tests to determine the composition or properties of certain products, particularly food and cleaning products. The results of this research educate the consumer by showing where fraud is possible, by checking the good faith of trade classifications, by exposing practices designed to deceive the consumer, and by backing appeals to government departments when necessary.

Conseil de la Consommation. The Consumer Council, founded in 1964, is financed by the government. It aims to coordinate consumer information activities, promote consumer research, and present the consumer's point of view at the Ministry of Economic Affairs.

Denmark

Consumer activity in Denmark is channeled mainly through two organizations, the Statens Husholdningsrad (Danish Government Home Economics Council) and the Danish Consumer Council, which jointly share the same building in Copenhagen. Both these organizations are governed in such a way as to elicit the cooperation of a wide variety of participating groups, although the former is supported through governmental funds and the latter through grants from constituent organizations. While there are a number of overlapping areas between the two, the former is dedicated centrally to research and testing problems, and the latter centrally to consumer representation and consumer informational problems.

Statens Husholdningsrad devotes its central effort to the quality testing of products in a wide variety of fields, including foods, textiles, and household equipment. It employs films, exhibitions, and radio programs, and handles the complaints of consumers. The laboratories of the council are engaged in the testing of brands of equipment available on the Danish market.

The test reports, published in monthly bulletins, give comparative brand performances, together with other useful consumer information, particularly concerning the product use and product attributes. Coupled with this product research is an interest in such problems as heat conductivity of materials and construction characteristics of equipment. The agency also cooperates with a quality declaration program, sponsored by producers and consumer groups in Denmark, by checking on colorfastness and wearing characteristics.

Special studies were made in the field of nutrition to assess varying techniques of food preservation. Research of a practical character, such as the best type of covering for preserves, is undertaken at the request of household and governmental organizations.

The council has been concentrating on raising quality standards of consumer goods and propagating objective consumer information. It will continue to influence public opinion, to further the consumer's sense of quality and price, and, for this purpose, be guided by objective research of consumer's habits and needs.

The Danish Consumer Council.   The Consumer Council is made up of representatives of 12 important women's organizations in Denmark. Work of the council includes consumer education, the representation of consumers on government boards and committees, handling of complaints, work with quality marks and seals, and publicity about its work in the press, on radio and TV, and by meetings. The council also cooperates with consumer organizations in other countries.

The council has published a series of booklets on such subjects as clothes for infants and necessary layette garments, what to look for when buying bedding, the fit and construction of shoes, the urgent need for wider adoption of national standard sizes for labeling garments, the reading and use of the Dansk Varedeklarations-Naevin (DVN) Informative Label, and many other subjects of interest to the housewife and home economist. There are kits for use in schools to teach garment-size designations. The council publishes a bimonthly magazine *Taenk,* with test results and other consumer information.

An investigation resulted in the use of new weights on nearly all food packages. A committee is at work on improved legal protection for consumers in the field of packaging. The council is making excellent use of its limited income to protect consumers.

Consumers in Denmark may fill in complaint forms and send defective merchandise to the council if it is a small thing that can be easily shipped, such as a pair of shoes, a blouse, or hose. About 1,000 complaints a year are investigated, and in many cases (about 60 percent), when the consumer has a proper complaint, he is given repair without charge, money back, or a replacement. There is a special complaint board for shoes, and consumers are represented in retailing, manufacturing, and importing firms and in the shoe repair industry.

A textile engineer handles textile complaints that come to the council. These are processed either by direct reply or by referring the complaint to a laboratory for investigation. Consumers do not pay for this work. The council sends the bill to the textile industry organization, which pays without a report or a discussion. The industry is responsible and prefers to pay and assume that the charges are correct and justified and have been competently handled. The council has planned a similar arrangement with the furniture industry.

The Danish Consumer Council assists the DVN in helping consumers to understand labels and look for them when shopping. There is also a program for care labeling of garments and textiles. Small tapes sewn into a garment show with line drawings and a few numbers whether washing or dry cleaning is permissible, water and ironing temperatures, and the kind of bleach that may be used. A large X indicates any process that is not to be used.

About 150 of the more than 500 laundries have been granted a seal. These laundries do more than 50 percent of all laundry work in Denmark. All military laundering is sent to approved laundries. The council suggested this. The system of checking involves visits to laundries and examination of garments that have been through 10 to 50 washings. The checking is carried out in a thorough manner by the Technological Institute. A similar system was started in 1961 for dry-cleaning establishments.

In textile labeling (the four "F" seal), there is a special mark for imports. Standards are developed by committees that include representatives from consumers, traders, manufacturers, and research institutions. The Danish Consumer Council works with the textile testing organization in the development of standards. The manufacturers must agree to have their products checked by random sampling. Legal action can be taken by the Board for Textile Testing if there is a violation of the contract.

The Danish Standards Association. DSA is an independent, nongovernmental organization, consisting of a council of 29 members appointed by the Ministry of Commerce, representing several governmental departments, trade organizations, and technical high schools. The budget of the association is based on a yearly contribution from the government and contributions to a similar amount from private sources, such as industrial organizations, trade organizations, and larger firms outside these organizations. Smaller contributions are also received from various societies and institutions. The association has registered the mark DS to be used on products to indicate conformity with Danish standards. The use of the mark without license is not permitted. The licensee must certify that he is able and willing to manufacture the products in question according to Danish standards.

The Dansk Varedeklarations-Naevin (DVN). The Danish Institution for Informative Labeling is a private institution established in 1957 by organizations of commerce, industry, and consumers, from which it receives contributions. Firms that want their goods provided with declarations and the mark of DVN pay a yearly fee, a contribution to administrative expenses, and the expenses of approval and testing.

The institution works for voluntary use of instructive marking of consumer goods sold in the retail trade. Each declaration gives instructive facts about the goods; therefore all declarations are named "Varefakta." The purpose of declaration of consumer goods is to help consumers to judge the contents and quality of the goods in question. The institution must see that the declarations are uniform and correct, and the registered mark DVN on products indicates that the information given on the label is correct.

England

The Consumers' Association, Ltd. (CA). The CA was incorporated in March, 1957, and published the first issue of *Which?* on October 7, 1957. This monthly magazine had about 525,000 subscribers in 1968.

A council of 11 is elected annually. The members are unpaid and may not be directly engaged as principal in the manufacture, distribution, or sale of goods or commodities; in the rendering of services to the public; or as a servant or agent in promoting the sale or use of such goods, commodities, or services.

While its constitution permits the association to undertake any work on behalf of the consumer, its policy is to concentrate on comparative product and service testing and publishing of the results. About 150 test projects a year are undertaken. A cumulative index in each issue of the magazine lists reports published to date. CA is nonprofit-making and completely independent financially.

Money Which? A second publication by CA began in September, 1968, and was aptly named *Money Which?* The purpose of the magazine is to provide information on how best to invest, borrow, insure, and legally avoid taxes. Other information will be presented to help consumers make more sensible choices. Over 80,000 subscribers to *Which?* are also subscribing to *Money Which?*

CA Achievements. The consumer movement in England began when *Which?* was founded by the Consumers' Association. CA has helped to improve the climate in which all consumers' interests are given more weight and consideration by government. Other consumer organizations in England owe their existence to its stimulus and aid.

The National Federation of Consumer Groups. The NFCG, founded in London in 1963, acts as a central agency to maintain communication among some 85 local consumer organizations. Over 90 percent of the income is in the form of grants. Any local group desiring to organize can secure information from the federation.

Research Institute for Consumer Affairs (RICA). RICA, organized in 1963, aims to conduct research to determine whether goods and services—commercial, professional, and public—are adequate to the wants and needs they claim to meet. Inadequately financed at first, it now receives grants from Consumers Association, the government, and two charitable trusts.

The Consumer Council. The council is financed entirely by the government.

Organized in 1963, the council has a full-time director, Miss Elizabeth Ackroyd, and a board of other members appointed by the president of the Board of Trade. The council publishes a monthly magazine, *Focus*.

The objectives of the council are: to become more aware of the major problems of the consumers; to consider the action to take to deal with these problems; to provide advice and guidance for the consumer, in particular through the Citizen's Advice Bureaux and other appropriate organizations and by its own publications; and to publish an annual report.

Finland

The Finnish Institute for Informative Labeling, founded in 1956, consists of 23 associations and firms representing manufacturers, consumers, trade, and research. Branch committees, which prepare the labeling specifications and corresponding test and measurement standards, have been formed within the institute.

Informative labeling is voluntary, covering at first a fairly limited number of commodities and manufacturers. Public reaction toward the system has been favorable, and the Finnish government is participating in its financing. A manufacturer is free to decide which of the standardized labeling statements he wants to use concerning the characteristics of his product.

The institute examines the product concerned and is allowed to buy samples for examination from any retail outlet. If the product does not correspond with the standardized statement, the manufacturer can be refused the right to use labels approved by the institute. The labels bear a four-pointed "compass rose" sign.

The care symbols are line drawings on tape that can be sewn into garments in the factory. A line drawing of a pan of water with recommended temperature in numbers shows whether the garment can be washed in very hot water or must be washed in lukewarm water. There is a large X if not washable at all.

A line drawing of a hand iron with temperatures indicates regular ironing and the equivalent of a cool iron. For dry cleaning, there are easy-to-understand symbols, and if a garment is not suitable for dry cleaning, a large X is used. The space for bleach also uses a symbol, and if no bleach may be used, an X appears in the space. The line drawings and numbers make the message completely clear, and no language is needed.

In Finland there are detergents with the informative label and the care symbols to indicate the proper temperature of water for different kinds of fabrics.

Consumer Council. The Consumer Council, organized in 1965, is financed entirely by the government. The president of the council is the Minister of Social Affairs. There are 15 members of the council, representing consumer associations, research institutes, press, commerce, and industry.

France

The Institut National de la Consommation (The National Consumers' Institute), founded in 1967, is the most recent consumer organization, financed entirely by the government. The institute consists of 23 members, 12 of which are representatives from consumer associations, six represent business, industry, and advertising, and five are representatives from various ministries of the government.

The objective is to test consumer products and carry out a consumer education program. The de Gaulle government insisted the institute would be entirely independent of the government.

Comité National de la Consommation. The National Committee of Consumers, organized in 1960, is also financed by the government. The president of the committee is the Minister of Economic Affairs and Finances. There are 11 representatives from various ministries, and 11 from consumer organizations.

The purposes of the NCC are: to establish exchange of opinions between authorities and the consumers; to distribute consumer information; and to involve consumers in drafting consumer legislation.

Organisation Générale des Consommateurs. This organization, founded in 1959, is financed in part by the government but mostly from membership fees. The purposes are: to inform the consumer on prices, quality, and services; and to represent consumers when meeting with business organizations. The organization represents over 60,000 individual members. Members receive a bimonthly publication, *Information Consommation*.

Union Fédérale de la Consommation. The organization, founded in 1951, is partly financed by the government (50 percent) and the rest by subscribers to the quarterly magazine, *Que Choisir?* and a quarterly, *Bulletin d'Information*.

The aims of the organization are: to disseminate consumer information; to educate and protect consumers; and to represent consumers in governmental and juridical bodies.

West Germany

The Arbeitsgemeinschaft der Verbraucherverbaende E. V. (Working Group of Consumer Organizations) is located in Bonn. Founded in 1953, it consisted of seven member organizations; 10 years later there were 20, representing about 7 million persons and covering a wide variety of German consumer groups.

The statutes of the organization provide that it must be independent and have purely nonprofit and common-interest aims. Its purposes are to represent the interests of consumers in relation to legislation, administration, and business, and to provide accurate and independent information and counsel relating to consumer goods and to the expenditure of family income. The organization's income is derived from membership dues, sale of publications, and grants from the government.

Institute of Home Economics.   The institute, founded in 1952, is financed by the government. Research is concentrated in the socioeconomic fields concerned with home economics problems. A bimonthly journal is published for general distribution.

Institute of Commodity Tests.   This institute, organized by the government in 1964, is a central government product-testing organization. The test results are published in a monthly magazine, *Der Test*.

Iceland

Neytendasamtokin (The Consumers' Union) is a wholly independent association, and no other association or institution appoints any representatives to its management. It was founded in 1953 on the initiative of a number of interested persons who called a public meeting for its establishment. The management of the union consists of a chief executive board of five, but a representative council of 27 is also elected at the general meeting.

The position of the union has been strengthened since 1957, but before that it was recognized officially and received a grant. Earlier the union had been sued for publishing the findings of quality control in the form of a warning. Proceedings lasted for 5 years and the union lost before the lower court, but it was completely acquitted by the Supreme Court of Iceland in February, 1960.

This verdict recognized the Consumers' Union as a qualified party in law to safeguard consumers' interests. The acquittal meant that the union was authorized to tell the truth officially about consumer goods if this was in the interests of consumers as a whole. The Minister of Commerce agreed to appoint a committee, to include a representative of the union, that would deal with the marking of goods relating to regulations, as this was lacking in the country. The union wanted information concerning net weight and ingredients to be given on packages and fixed by law.

Since its inception, the union has granted legal aid and information to the public and runs an office for this purpose. The publication of guides continues (at one time there were 14 publications and 8 booklets). These are supplied free to members on payment of a small annual subscription, but their cost is defrayed mostly by advertising, which must be unostentatious. The union has concentrated on the publication of news items in the press, and there has been less need for the regular issue of the publications, which are first and foremost documentary. To introduce consumers' views, the union cooperates with various official institutions, including the price control authority, the electricity board, and ministries.

A committee for the assessment of dry cleaners and laundries has been reorganized on the basis of experience gained. Cleaners and laundries can now display placards on their premises and are free to participate through their trade organizations. Most of these firms near and in Reykjavik are members of the committee and pay a fee on receipt of placards.

Ireland

The Irish Housewives Association is a voluntary organization, nonpolitical and nonsectarian, its object being to unite housewives so that they may realize and win recognition of their right to take an active part in all spheres of planning for the community. The organization is the only voluntary one in Ireland concerned with the protection of the rights of the consumer. It was founded in 1942 by a group of housewives who were anxious that commodities should be evenly distributed at fair prices during World War II. Its income is derived from annual subscriptions of members, proceeds from social functions, and the sale of a yearbook published by a subcommittee.

The association's program includes the following activities.

To further cooperation between producer and consumer and manufacturer and consumer, while watching the difference between producer and consumer prices

To agitate for legislation requiring the weight and nature of contents to be clearly marked on all packaged goods

To further the work of the Institute of Irish Industrial Standards through members appointed to sit on advisory committees

To investigate any rise in consumer prices and to protest when these are excessive

To encourage sales resistance by consumers when prices are excessively high or quality below standard

To press the need for the registration of all nursing homes

To help with the care of the aged

To raise funds for world refugees

To continue work with the International Alliance of Women, with which the association is affiliated

Consumers' Organization of Ireland. This consumer group, organized in 1966, had about 300 voting members in 1968. All income is from membership fees. The purposes of the organization are to help consumers make wiser decisions in the marketplace; to improve packaging and handling of goods; and to work for honest advertising and labeling.

National Consumers' Union. The Unione Nazionale Consumatori was formed in Rome in 1955 for the representation and protection of consumers. A bimonthly magazine, *Il Consumatore,* for educating and orienting the consumer, was published for the first time in December, 1960. The union has also published several reports and studies.

The union is open to individual consumers as well as to trade unions and consumers' cooperatives, but membership is reported to be 50,000. It receives income from membership fees and the sale of publications and from government subsidies if and when obtainable. It has no facilities for comparative testing and does not publish brand names and test results.

The Istituto Qualità Italia.   The National Association for Maintaining and Controlling Quality and Awarding the Quality Seal was founded in January, 1959, as a result of numerous exchanges of views between manufacturers and traders, consumers, university teachers, market research specialists, and others, following the Journées d'Études Qualité-Europe held in Brussels. It is an independent and entirely objective association, directed by a board with up to 30 members.

The institute has adopted a set of rules that clearly define the objectives and principles that will serve as guides for future activities, for example, the objective certification of quality of products by means of a seal. Though the intention is to adapt these rules to Italy's specific requirements, the institute has based them on those already followed by similar bodies, such as Qualité-Belgique and Qualité-France. Numerous Italian firms have applied for permission to display the seal.

Luxembourg

The Consumer Council, organized in 1965, is financed by the government. The purposes are: to keep the Minister of Economic Affairs in contact with consumer groups; to suggest actions with regard to price of products; to propose quality regulations; and to promote consumer research.

Consumers Union.   Consumers Union, founded in 1961, concentrates on defending consumers' interests. It is financed mostly by government grants (90 percent) and through membership fees. A quarterly magazine, *ULC*, is distributed to member organizations and individual members.

The Netherlands

The Nederlandse Consumenten Bond (NCB) (Netherlands Consumers Union) was formed in January, 1953, and continues to register steady growth. There are 200,000 subscribers to its bulletin. Sources of income are subscription fees from private memberships, contributions received from participating organizations, and a small government grant.

The NCB was established as a consumer counterweight against the increasing number of agreements and mergers in industry and commerce. Any consumer whose interests are not dominated by any other economic interest may become a member. Participating organizations may in no way be related with trade or industry. It is a nonprofit organization that accepts no advertising, allows no commercial use of its test results, and receives no subsidies. Both brand names and test results are published. The NCB has selected dramatic items to arouse public interest. It has developed use tests and is eager to co-operate with other organizations.

CCO. The Stichting Consumenten Contact Orgaan was founded in 1957 for the general protection of consumers. Its members include NCB coopera-tives and labor unions. Members receive a monthly publication, *CCO Infor-matie Bulletin.*

NHR. The Nederlandse Huishoudraad (Household Council of the Nether-lands), formed in 1950, is a council through which 17 women's organizations, three national advisory services, and seven specialist organizations cooperate. These organizations have approximately 380,000 members, who are asked to contribute information on household problems.

The council has an interest in the home as a whole and presents the case for housewives to private organizations, such as designers, architects, and gov-ernment authorities. For tests, which are made on receipt of complaints, the NHR uses scientific institutes and laboratories. It often cooperates with the government-sponsored National Organization for Applied Scientific Research. Most of the income comes from government grants.

CCA. The Commissie Voor Consumentenaangelegen heden (Committee for Consumer Affairs). This committee, founded in 1965, is a government-financed organization. The primary purpose of the committee is to advise the govern-ment on all problems concerning consumer interests. The 21 members of the committee are selected from most of the consumer organizations, central trade unions, cooperatives, and industry and trade groups.

Norway

Consumers' Council. Forbrukerrådet is an independent institution having its own secretary. The statutes of the council were formulated by royal reso-lution of September 11, 1953. The council consists of a chairman and seven members who are appointed by the crown on the recommendation of seven cooperative and consumer organizations.

The main object of the council is the testing of consumer goods. It receives 50 percent of its income from government appropriations and the remainder from the sale of publications. A magazine, *Forbruker rapporten,* a monthly, gives results of testing and advice on purchasing. The total circulation of 10 issues in 1968 was 100,000 copies.

Forbrukerrådet handles complaints, which total more than 2,000 a year. There are consumer days in different areas, which members of the council staff at-tend on a rotating basis and where they make speeches and answer questions.

In addition to the magazine, there are special publications, including a *Family Account Book* and books on buying. Consumers are kept informed through press releases, radio, lectures, courses, conferences—in fact, in every possible way.

The council, partly financed by the state, has no further contact with the ministries other than to assure them that the work is carried out according to the statutes and that the accounts are properly kept. The Norwegian government has increased the budget of the council every year, and it is now approximately 10 times the amount set aside for the work in 1953.

Institute for Informative Labeling.   On the initiative of the council, the Central Committee for Informative Labeling and Quality Marking was founded in 1954. The committee consist of 24 members representing the consumers, industry, and research. Its purpose is the promotion and coordination of informative commodity labeling and quality marking. Informative labeling is used on the commodities of 80 producers, and the number is increasing rapidly.

Norway is unique in having a consumer cabinet post, the Royal Ministry for Consumer and Family Affairs, which is filled by a woman. She works in close cooperation with the Forbrukerrådet through its household research division and its information services.

Other active groups in Norway include the government Research Department for Home Economics, the National Standardizing Organization, and the Informative Labeling Organization.

Sweden

The Swedish consumer program is the most comprehensive of all in Europe. Consumer goods testing, informative labeling, complaint services, and consumer education programs are all part of an active program that reaches a large portion of the Swedish people. The economic interests of consumers are adequately represented in government by the cooperatives and, to a lesser extent, by labor unions. Swedish manufacturers and distributors cooperate in the program. Swedish radio and television set aside several hours each week for consumer programming. The Swedish program has served as a model for many of the consumer programs in other European countries.

Sweden and Norway are the only two countries in Europe having consumers represented at the cabinet or ministry level.

Consumer Council.   The Statens Konsument Råd, founded in 1957, consists of 15 members appointed by the state. Seven of these represent consumer groups and at least three represent business interests. The rest are specialists of various kinds.

This council allocates government grants for research and consumer information and promotes collaboration among various interests in the consumer area.

Consumer Institute.   The Statens Institut for Konsumentfragor, organized in 1957, is financed by the government. The institute undertakes comparative testing of consumer goods and reports the results in *R åd och R ön* (10 issues annually).

Institute for Informative Labeling. Informative labeling in Sweden is the work of the Varudeklarationsnamnden (VDN) (Institute for Informative Labeling). It is one of several independent organizations affiliated with the Swedish Standards Association. The activities of the VDN are financed mostly by the government, with contributions from various national organizations, and partly by the fees paid by business enterprises using the institute's design.

When a manufacturer or producer requests a label, the VDN organizes a committee to work on the test methods, the specifications, and the list of items that must be included in the label. This working group includes consumers, producers, and technical experts. When the test methods have been prepared, the specifications are worked out for the content of the label. The draft VDN sheet is circulated to all interested organizations—including the industry, retailers, importers, wholesalers, and distributors—and to consumer organizations and technical specialists. The items on the label must be accurately worded, must refer to test methods, and must give bad features as well as good features.

Each VDN sheet includes an example of a correct label for the product. The manufacturer must prepare the label, must make sure that all products labeled meet the standards, and must agree to have random samples checked. Each manufacturer must check-test his own products to determine the grade and regularly recheck to make sure standards are maintained. In Sweden some competitors are interested enough to do check testing.

The VDN is concerned with consumer education. It issues booklets and uses press releases and leaflets, radio, and TV to help people understand the meaning of the labels. The first print order for a booklet is usually about 150,000 copies, and these are supplied to schools, libraries, organizations, and other groups. The manufacturer also promotes the label. About 30 committees have been working on projects, and about 75 specifications have been completed.

Switzerland

Among six of the most important Swiss consumer organizations, four are involved in comparative testing of consumer goods. There appears to be considerable activity, if not rivalry, among some of the consumer organizations.

Federal Commission on Consumer Affairs. The Commission Fédérale de la Consommation, founded in 1965, is a government-financed consumer council representing consumer organizations, cooperatives, women's organizations, and business. The major objective is to chart the Swiss consumer program. The government generally accepts recommendations from the commission as to allocation of government grants.

Consumer Information Organization. The Forderungsfonds fur Konsumenteninformation was founded in 1965 for the purpose of establishing a "neutral organization that is exclusively active on behalf of consumers to undertake comparative testing" of products. It might be difficult to achieve neutrality in testing because the membership is made up of 72 production and commercial organizations.

Swiss Consumers Association. The Schweizerischer Consumentenbund was organized in 1964 for the purposes of making comparative testing of consumer products, undertaking informative labeling, and representing the consumer at government hearings. Most of the income is from business-dominated organizations and corporate subscribers. A free monthly, *Informatious,* is distributed.

Yugoslavia

The Federal Board of Family and Household, organized in 1957, is financed by the state. The primary purposes of the board are: to serve the interests of the consumer; to teach families how to plan their spending and get the most satisfactory returns for expenditures; and to test consumer products.

Testing Products. When a product is rated below acceptable quality, the manufacturer is notified of this deficiency. If the below-acceptable quality product is not corrected within a given period of time, the board calls a press, radio, and television conference. This threat of effective publicity is generally sufficient to force improvement in the quality of the product.

Demonstration Home. One of the unique ways to help consumers make more intelligent decisions—purchasing goods, decorating rooms, building a home, etc.—is the demonstration home in Belgrade. Everything one needs in a home, for example, is on display. The kitchens, bedrooms, living rooms, bathrooms, and utility rooms are all supplied with tested consumer goods. Experts are present—even an architect—to discuss the quality of the goods on display. The author can testify that in about one hour's stay in the demonstration home, some 50 to 60 people, most of them young couples, visited the demonstration home.

CONSUMER ORGANIZATIONS IN AFRICA

In 1968, at least five countries had established consumer organizations—Kenya, Liberia, Nigeria, South Africa, and Zambia. Most of these organizations were founded by housewives and are still operating because of the interest of housewives. They are inadequately financed—by membership dues almost entirely—and seem to be in need of outside financial help. In most of these countries the standard of living is so low, comparatively, that the consumer help needed must be given at absolute basic levels—more food, better housing, nutrition, and health care and information. Some day consumers in most or all of these countries will be confronted with all of the consumer problems the industrialized Western countries know so well.

THE INTERNATIONAL CONSUMER MOVEMENT

After some 20 years of increasing prosperity throughout the free world, nations are beginning to give official recognition to something called "consumer interest." In our own country, President Kennedy issued the well-known basic rights of consumers. President Johnson followed up by creating a mechanism within the executive offices to see that consumer rights were represented in the councils of government.

Simultaneously, in Western Europe, Japan, and Australia also, efforts to achieve representation in government were undertaken.

Government Consumer Programs

The primary purpose of government interest and activity in consumer programs is to provide consumers with adequate and accurate information about products and services available in the marketplace.

The means of accomplishing this are (1) consumer goods testing, (2) informative labeling, and (3) consumer education. In a few countries (Norway, Sweden, and Japan), government consumer programs have been broadened to include the structure of the marketplace. Yet, even when this is true, the primary purpose is consumer information and education. Most government consumer agencies are still silent about economic policy and planning—taxes, price policies, tariffs, and monetary policies. These are considered the responsibilities of other government agencies.

Even where special ministries of consumer affairs have been established (in Norway, Sweden, and Canada), the major emphasis is still on consumer information, product standards and testing, and consumer education.

Consumer Councils

In England, Netherlands, Switzerland, Belgium, Israel, India, Sweden, Norway, Luxembourg, and Australia, government consumer councils have been established which are, theoretically, free and independent of the governments. The idea is for these councils to be financed by government but to maintain an independent voice. Thus, they can, in theory, speak out against the government in power.

In practice, however, the councils are limited by three important factors: (1) With the exception of Norway and Sweden, their mandates are limited to the area of consumer information and education, which might include advertising, marketing, safety of products, and standards; (2) businessmen sit on every council, with the exception of Norway; and (3) the councils are financed by ministries (usually the ministry of commerce or economics) which could tighten the pursestrings should council statements become too objectionable. More important, perhaps, is the lack of propriety to speak out on broader issues—tariffs, monetary issues, and taxes, to mention a few.

Financing Consumer Goods Testing

In addition to government-financed consumer agencies, the governments of six of the nine Western European countries also finance consumer goods testing by private consumer organizations. The three exceptions are West Germany, Sweden, and England.

Ministry Status

Consumer affairs has achieved ministry status in three countries—Norway, Sweden, and Canada. In Sweden and Norway, consumer affairs are lumped together with family affairs. In Canada, it is combined with corporate affairs. In Norway, the major consumer program is carried out by the Consumers' Council. In Sweden, the Ministry of Commerce has operating responsibility for consumer programs. In both Norway and Sweden, the ministries introduce legislation into the national parliaments.

The French National Consumer Committee is composed of government, consumer, industry, and other organization representatives. This committee is located in the Ministry of Finance and Economic Affairs. It is not independent of the government.

Summary

Thus, European governments, and several other governments throughout the world, have endorsed, as a matter of public policy, the principle that its citizens have a right to be fully informed about the quality, price, and performance of goods and services. Most of these countries have taken the next step by establishing or planning to set up some kind of consumer agency to finance activities designed to improve consumer information, product standards, and testing of consumer goods.

A SUMMARY OF WAYS TO SAVE MONEY
FROM MARRIAGE TO RETIREMENT

The primary purpose of Appendix A is to describe briefly some of the important consumer choices (which you have read about in this textbook) your family can make, or may have to make, if you are living on a lower budget, a moderate budget, or a higher budget.

The use of three different family income budgets permits selection of choices to fit various socioeconomic backgrounds. We learned in Chapter 2, for example, that the American consumer fits no single mold. He has no one level of buying competence. But his choices or purchasing habits reflect his income, his position in the life cycle (marriage to death), his education, and his occupation, as well as his nationality and cultural background and environment. Yet the fact remains that family resources are important factors in influencing choices in the marketplace. Furthermore, a considerable amount of data is available to illustrate the relationship between resources of the family and expenditures. One such source is the recent study by the Bureau of Labor Statistics of the U.S. Department of Labor of three standards of living for an urban family of four persons in the spring of 1967. And since most families live in urban centers (small and large), we are using the cost-of-living data from this important study.

ANNUAL COSTS OF THREE STANDARDS OF LIVING FOR AN URBAN FAMILY OF FOUR PERSONS, SPRING OF 1967

This study (Table S-1) marks the first time the Bureau of Labor Statistics has developed lists of goods and services and cost estimates of three family income levels: lower, moderate, and higher. All three budgets share the basic assumption that maintenance of health and social well-being, the nurture of children, and participation in community activities are desirable social goals.

For the lower budget, the U.S. urban average cost was $5,915—35 percent less than the moderate cost. The moderate budget cost $9,076. The higher budget amounted to $13,050—44 percent above the moderate budget. These costs include all of the costs of consumption—food, housing, transportation, clothing and personal care, medical care, gifts, education, and recreation—as well as other expenses.

Consumption costs account for 82 percent of the total budget at the lower level, 79 percent at the moderate level, and 76 percent at the higher level.

The Bureau of Labor Statistics, recognizing that inflation will alter the budget requirements, plans to update the family consumption costs from time to time.[1]

[1] Write to Bureau of Labor Statistics, U.S. Department of Labor, Washington, D.C. 20210, for latest revisions.

Importance of Table S-1

For our purpose, Table S-1 is useful in that you can recognize the difference in the amount of money generally available for each expenditure. These differences in costs will help you understand the importance of making more intelligent choices in the marketplace.

CHOICES FOLLOW A PATTERN ASSOCIATED WITH AGE [2]

Many family choices in the marketplace follow a pattern associated with age. The number of children at home, for example, tends to increase, then stabilize, and finally drop off. Food expenditures, also, change as families move from the newly married couple without children to the period when they have children, on until the children are on their own economic power, and finally to the retirement age.

Recognizing these changing purchasing decisions based on age and on income, from marriage to death, we are attempting to summarize how families can improve their purchasing decisions in the marketplace.

To carry out family spending patterns associated with income and age, we have arbitrarily divided the marriage-to-death period into six cycles—under 25 (newlywed—for richer or poorer); 25 to 34 (the children are small); 35 to 44 (hitting your stride); 45 to 54 (peaking out); 55 to 64 (children gone); 65 ("golden years").

There is bound to be overlap from one family cycle to the next, and from a lower but adequate income to a moderate and higher income. We hope that you will be able to identify yourself with one or more of the age and income levels and thereby discover the secret of converting dollars into contentment.

FROM MARRIAGE TO DEATH

You are getting started in marriage. About half of you have children, and your income is apt to be quite modest. For practical purposes, use Table S-1 as a basis for living standards and for allocation of income for food, housing, and other costs. Only one out of three earns $5,000 to $7,500 under age 25, and only 12 percent earn from $7,500 to $10,000. And only 6 percent can claim $10,000 a year. So be realistic.

[2] The National Industrial Conference Board, a private nonprofit economic research organization, has recently analyzed families in terms of income, homeownership, education, and other characteristics which are helpful when relating purchasing decisions to age.

TABLE S-1 ANNUAL COSTS OF BUDGETS FOR THREE LIVING STANDARDS FOR A FOUR-PERSON FAMILY, URBAN UNITED STATES, 39 METROPOLITAN AREAS, AND FOUR NONMETROPOLITAN REGIONS, SPRING, 1967

ITEM	URBAN UNITED STATES								
	Total			Metropolitan areas			Nonmetropolitan areas		
	Lower	Moderate	Higher	Lower	Moderate	Higher	Lower	Moderate	Higher
Food	$1,644	$2,105	$2,586	$1,664	$2,135	$2,634	$1,550	$1,973	$2,375
Food at home	1,427	1,779	2,114	1,439	1,793	2,127	1,369	1,717	2,059
Food away from home	217	326	472	225	342	507	181	256	316
Housing: Total	1,303	2,230	3,340	1,331	2,302	3,464	1,179	1,909	2,789
Renter families	1,303	1,756	2,966	1,331	1,799	3,115	1,179	1,568	2,301
Homeowner families	......	2,388	3,406	......	2,470	3,525	......	2,022	2,875
Shelter	1,013	1,745	2,308	1,041	1,819	2,414	889	1,413	1,833
Rental costs	1,013	1,271	1,934	1,041	1,316	2,066	889	1,072	1,345
Homeowner costs	......	1,903	2,374	......	1,987	2,475	......	1,526	1,919
Housefurnishings	137	268	531	139	270	537	129	260	504
Household operations	153	217	404	151	213	403	161	236	412
Transportation: Total	446	872	1,127	420	856	1,124	563	941	1,139
Automobile owners	607	919	1,127	617	914	1,124	563	941	1,139
Nonowners of automobiles	107	157	......	131	192	......			
Clothing	538	767	1,139	546	777	1,151	504	718	1,088
Husband	138	177	261	139	176	259	134	181	270
Wife	118	190	315	119	194	322	111	171	286
Boy	132	171	227	134	172	230	123	167	214
Girl	102	156	215	106	161	216	88	133	208
Clothing materials and services	48	73	121	48	74	124	48	66	110
Personal care	162	218	307	168	221	311	139	203	286

Medical care: Total	474	477	497	488	491	511	412	415	432
Insurance	226	226	262	232	232	269	197	197	230
Physician's visits	92	92	92	97	97	97	70	70	70
Other medical care	285	289	292	292	295	298	257	260	263
Other family consumption	295	552	967	306	570	997	244	476	832
Reading	51	66	90	55	72	97	32	42	60
Recreation	93	258	540	98	263	557	73	235	465
Education	44	55	64	47	60	67	31	35	50
Tobacco	13	15	23	13	15	22	14	16	23
Alcoholic beverages	60	72	93	59	73	93	62	69	93
Miscellaneous expenses	34	86	157	34	87	161	32	79	141
Cost of family consumption: Total	4,862	7,221	9,963	4,923	7,352	10,192	4,591	6,635	8,941
Renter families	4,862	6,747	9,589	4,923	6,849	9,843	4,591	6,294	8,453
Homeowner families	....	7,379	10,029	....	7,520	10,253	....	6,748	9,027
Other costs	265	410	730	267	414	742	257	389	680
Gifts and contributions	145	250	490	147	254	502	137	229	440
Life insurance	120	160	240	120	160	240	120	160	240
Occupational expenses	50	80	85	50	80	85	50	80	85
Social Security and disability payments	265	303	303	269	305	305	247	293	293
Personal taxes: Total	473	1,062	1,969	485	1,092	2,043	419	925	1,641
Renter families	473	945	1,842	485	968	1,922	419	843	1,484
Homeowner families	....	1,101	1,992	....	1,134	2,064	....	953	1,669
Cost of budget: Total	5,915	9,076	13,050	5,994	9,243	13,367	5,564	8,322	11,640
Renter families	5,915	8,485	12,549	5,994	8,616	12,897	5,564	7,899	10,995
Homeowner families	....	9,273	13,139	....	9,453	13,449	....	8,463	11,754

SOURCE: Bureau of Labor Statistics, U.S. Department of Labor, Spring, 1967.

Slice the Food Bill

1. Stick to your "buying list."
2. Convenience foods are almost always considerably more expensive. Some of the extra costs are made in the name of "built-in maid service." The major objective of the food industry today, however, is to convert inexpensive ingredients into costly processed foods and to provide them in convenience form, which is often a myth. So, if you want to save $400 to $500 a year on your food bill (family of four), look the other way when tempted to purchase prebuttered vegetables, cheese slices, processed cheese, frozen dinners, stuffed baked potatoes, cheese in spray cans, presweetened ready-to-eat breakfast foods and those with fruit in them, diet margarine, meat products with filler or extenders, dehydrated mashed potatoes, frozen meat and chicken pies, frozen chow meins, chopped poultry with broth, frozen deviled crab, snack foods, flavored cottage cheese, stuffed turkey, and frozen beef patties, to mention a few.
3. Private store brands are usually considerably cheaper than and are equal in quality to manufacturers' advertised brands.
4. Vitamin products, special dietary foods, and food supplements are costly and unnecessary. Food *is* the best source for vitamins.
5. "Diet pills do more harm than good."
6. Trading stamps and games do not save money.
7. Check weights, especially of prepackaged meats, vegetables, and fruit. Short-weighting is common.
8. Highly advertised products cost more.
9. Orange "ades," "punches," and "nectar" are expensive and contain little food value.
10. Non-fat dry milk and "imitation" milk are cheaper than fresh milk and have all the nutrients except butterfat.
11. Freezer-meat contracts are an expensive convenience.
12. Shop for advertised specials—usually at weekend.
13. Buy in quantity.
14. Buy USDA grades whenever possible.
15. Purchase lean meat—by the cut, not by the cost per pound.
16. Food away from home (restaurants) is costly but nice.

These suggestions for converting food dollars into contentment and economic security are valid for almost any age bracket or income level. There are, however, a few additional suggestions for parents who are over 45. Their children are in college (food bills at home should go down if the children are away from home). A retired couple is likely to have food restrictions and may be able to eat more often in restaurants if income permits. Incomes of many people in retirement, however, are so low as to create money troubles. The general suggestions above are as important for them as for young marrieds on lower or moderate budgets. For lower-income older couples, the best suggestion is to do more home cooking (with savings up to about 25 percent).

Housing

Average housing costs in urban centers range from $1,303 to $3,340, at spring, 1967 prices (Table S-1).

1. Renting a house is usually less costly than owning.
2. Mobile homes have special appeal to young marrieds and are economical.
3. The cheapest way to buy a house is to pay cash.
4. If you borrow money to buy a house, shop around for the best deal.
5. Select a mortgage which permits prepayment without penalty.
6. When buying insurance for your home, furnishings, liability, fire, and theft, buy a package deal. If necessary, take a "floater" policy to cover special items such as art objects and valuable jewelry.
7. Renting furnished for newlyweds or young marrieds is usually less costly. The costs of setting up housekeeping in an unfurnished one-bedroom apartment, for example, are apt to cost about $1,500—add some extras, and it may jump to $2,000.
8. Retired couples needing less room and possibly all space on one floor may prefer renting an apartment or purchasing a cooperative or condominium apartment. Some prefer a nice mobile home in satisfactory surroundings and climate.
9. Older people need grab bars at several heights in the bathtub; also, they need large refrigerators because they shop less often and buy more each trip.

Transportation

Average transportation costs of three urban living standards in the spring of 1967 ranged from $446 to $1,127 annually. Car-owner costs ranged from $607 to $1,127, compared to about $107 for non-car owners (Table S-1).

1. Car ownership is very expensive—14 to 17 percent of family income.
2. In large cities, it usually pays to use local transportation and rent a car for special trips.
3. If you can afford a family car, keep a new car at least two years; if run only 10,000 miles a year, it is usually economical to keep a new car for 4 or 5 years.
4. Look for repairability and safety when buying a new car.
5. The total cost of leasing a medium-priced car for two years (30,000 miles of driving) is estimated at about $3,120.
6. If you buy a new, medium-size car, read the list price on the sticker, deduct freight charge, apply 22 percent discount, and you have the dealer's approximate cost.
7. Pay cash for a car. Next best bet is to borrow the money from the cheapest source—usually your bank or credit bureau.
8. A car warranty "giveth and it taketh away"—so read its limitations in particular—the "implied" warranty may help you recover damages due to defective product.
9. Soon, car insurance is apt to be sold at reduced rates and payable "without regard to fault" and at a lower premium.
10. With proper car design, accidents can be safe or safer. Buy safety.
11. After children are of school age, you may need two cars. This is convenient but very expensive. When children are on their own, get rid of the extra car.

Clothing and Personal Care

The cost of clothing a family of four varied from $538 to $1,139 a year in the spring of 1967 in lower, moderate, and higher budgets. Personal care costs ranged from $162 to $307 (Table S-1). Footwear, in particular, had increased in price. Clothing and shoes increased a whopping 26 percent in constant dollars between 1957-1959 and July, 1968. The point is—if you have to cut clothing costs, consider the following tips.

1. Follow basic wardrobe planning and spending.
2. Avoid credit costs.
3. Look for and understand fabric standards on the labels.
4. Take full advantage of regular and special sales.
5. Consider costs for repair and care of clothing.
6. Do not hesitate to use good discount stores, reliable mail-order companies, and variety stores.
7. Bulk dry cleaning can save many dollars.
8. A clever woman with sewing ability can create most of her own clothes at half the retail cost for comparable quality and style.
9. Make liberal use of wash-and-wear and "permanent press" clothes.
10. Size tags, expecially for women's and children's wear, are not reliable—try the garments on.
11. Neither reliable industry nor consumer standards exist for new synthetic-fiber stretch fabrics—watch out!
12. Check recent *Consumer Reports* and *Consumer Bulletin* for objective evaluation of standard brands of clothing and shoes.
13. Older women can ease the burden of dressing by purchasing dresses with zippers in the front.
14. Look for sewed-on labels giving specific information on care and cleaning (you are not apt to find sewed-on labels with reliable information as of 1969). Most trouble is with bonded fabrics, press-on linings, plastic zippers, color stains, pleats, felt, buttons, foam lining, and lace.
15. Firms are still making and selling flammable fabrics despite federal legislation.
16. Select self-help features which children can handle themselves and easy-care features.
17. Clean, hang, and store clothes properly.

Medical Care

Medical care costs are very high. Hospital bills have more than tripled and doctors' fees have increased almost as much in the last 20 years. Drug prices are much too high when compared to costs. Who can afford to be sick unless adequately protected by health insurance and disability income insurance?

1. Evaluate your health care needs and set up a plan for health care and loss-of-income protection. Change protection as children arrive, as they leave the home, and as retirement is near.
2. Probably the best health-medical protection per dollar cost today for pre-age-65 people is nonprofit, prepaid, comprehensive group health plans such as Group Health Cooperatives, Health Insurance Plan of Greater New York, and others.
3. The next best plan in terms of cost and services for pre-age-65 people is likely to be Blue Cross-Blue Shield Group Hospital-Medical plans. Many insurance companies have good plans also, but these are probably more costly.
4. A married couple, with no dependents, can purchase coverage at a lower premium than when children and other dependents are included. After children are on their

own, cut premium costs by returning to husband-wife coverage. A year before retirement, make inquiry about Medicare from the closest Social Security office.

5.   Include major medical coverage, because it is designed to handle costs of serious and long-term illness and accident cases. This plan is a supplement to your "basic plan." Some plans combine basic protection and major medical coverage. Group plans cost less.

6.   Loss of income is not included in health and medical care insurance. Do not be without it. Costs are comparatively low and oftentimes your employer will pay for it or for part of the coverage.

7.   Social Security carries important financial aid if children under 18, or to age 22 if they are in school, are left fatherless.

8.   Dental care insurance is now available—an orthodontist for 2 years may cost from $800 to $2,000! Prepayment group plans cost less than individual family plans.

9.   Join Medicare (hospital and medical insurance) early enough to have it go into effect on your sixty-fifth birthday or as soon thereafter as the law permits. This is a voluntary program, so you have to make application through the Social Security office. The coverage is not complete yet, but it is still the best protection per dollar available to most people. It is generally wise to carry a supplementary coverage, such as Blue Cross-Blue Shield, to plug the gaps in Medicare. The supplementary premiums are comparatively low.

CONSUMPTION COSTS

Consumption costs—food, housing, transportation, clothing and personal care, medical care, and other miscellaneous consumption items—for three standards of living of four family persons accounted for 82 percent, 79 percent, and 76 percent of the *total* budgets of lower-level ($5,915), moderate-level ($9,076), and higher-level ($13,050) living standards in spring of 1967.

Differences in family size affect the budget levels. A young couple without children, for example, needed less for living purposes—$2,380, $3,540, and $4,880, respectively—to maintain equivalent levels of living in the spring of 1967. On the other hand, a family with three schoolchildren needed $5,640, $8,380, and $11,550 for consumption goods and services for these three budgets.

Budgets and Rising Prices

Rising prices since spring, 1967, have increased the consumption costs of all three budgets. A rough approximation of the fall, 1968, costs of family consumption in the three budgets, using price changes in the Consumer Price Index, had increased 6 percent in the lower budget and 5.7 percent in both the moderate and higher budgets.

The Bureau of Labor Statistics plans to publish periodically, for the same areas as those included in the present study, the cost of living of the three budgets for the four-person family and for a retired couple as of the spring of each year.

FEDERAL CONSUMER AGENCIES
AND AIDS IN WASHINGTON, D.C.

Civil Aeronautics Board 20428
Department of Agriculture 20250
  Agricultural Research Service
  Consumer Advisory Panel
  Consumer and Marketing Service
  Federal Extension Service
  Information Office
Department of Commerce 20230
  National Bureau of Standards
  Environmental Science Services Administration
  Bureau of Public Roads
  Office of Weights and Measures
Department of Defense 20301
Department of Health, Education, and Welfare 20201
  Administration of Aging
  Bureau of Family Services
  Children's Bureau
  Food and Drug Administration
  Office of Education 20202
  Office of Consumer Services
  Public Health Service
  Social Security Administration, 604 Security Blvd., Baltimore, Md. 21235
  Medicare
  Bureau of Federal Credit Unions
Department of Housing and Urban Development 20410
  Federal Housing Administration
  Office of Metropolitan Development
  Office of Renewal and Housing Assistance
Department of the Interior 20240
  Bureau of Commercial Fisheries
  Bureau of Sport Fisheries and Wildlife
  Geological Survey
  National Park Service
Department of Justice 20530
  Antitrust Division
  Consumer Counsel
Department of Labor 20210
  Bureau of Labor Statistics
Department of Treasury 20220
  Comptroller of the Currency
  Customs Service
  Internal Revenue Service
Department of Transportation 20590
  Federal Aviation Administration
  Federal Highway Administration
  National Highway Safety Bureau
  National Transportation Safety Board

National Motor Vehicle Safety Advisory Council
U.S. Coast Guard
Federal Communications Commission 20554
Federal Deposit Insurance Corporation 20429
Federal Home Loan Bank Board 20552
Federal Power Commission 20426
Federal Reserve System 20551
Federal Trade Commission 20580
General Services Administration 20405
Government Printing Office 20401
Interstate Commerce Commission 20423
Office of Economic Opportunity 20506
Post Office Department 20260
President's Committee on Consumer Interests, Room 6025, Federal Office Building 7 20506
Securities and Exchange Commission 20549
Veterans Administration 20420
Address letters to your:
Congressman, to House Office Building 20510
Senator, to Senate Office Building 20515

HOUSE COMMITTEES WITH ASSIGNMENTS OF CONSUMER BILLS:

Committee on Agriculture
Subcommittee on Domestic Marketing and Consumer Relations
Committee on Banking and Currency
Subcommittee on Consumer Affairs
Committee on District of Columbia
Committee on Education and Labor
Committee on Government Operations
Committee on Interstate and Foreign Commerce
Subcommittee on Commerce and Finance
Committee on Judiciary
Committee on Merchant Marine and Fisheries
Committee on Ways and Means

SENATE COMMITTEES WITH ASSIGNMENTS OF CONSUMER BILLS:

Committee on Agriculture and Forestry
Subcommittee on Agricultural Research and General Legislation

Committee on Banking and Currency
  Subcommittee on Financial Institutions
  Subcommittee on Securities
Committee on Commerce
  Subcommittee on the Consumer
    (Has a Consumer Advisory Council.)
Committee on District of Columbia
Committee on Finance
Committee on Government Operations
  Subcommittee on Intergovernmental Relations
  Subcommittee on Executive Reorganization
Committee on the Judiciary
  Subcommittee on Antitrust and Monopoly Legislation
Committee on Labor and Public Welfare

INDEX